BAD MONEY

FINTECH AS AN INSTRUMENT IN THE BATTLE FOR GLOBAL DOMINANCE

BRAD RIGDEN

Copyright © Bradley James Rigden 2022
Published: December 2022

ISBN: 9789655180077 Paperback
ISBN: 9787889221313 Hardcover
ISBN: 9785983089921 ebook
All rights reserved.

The right of Bradley James Rigden to be identified as the author of this Work has been asserted by him in accordance with sections 77 and 78 of the Copyright, Designs and Patents Act 1988.

No part of this publication may be reproduced, stored in retrieval system, copied in any form or by any means, electronic, mechanical, photocopying, recording or otherwise transmitted without written permission from the publisher. You must not circulate this book in any format.

Copyright of all illustrations and imagery used within remains solely with their originator. No breach of copyright is implied or intended and all material is believed to be used with permission. Should you feel that your copyright has been impinged, please contact the publisher to ensure appropriate acknowledgment may be made.

Cover Design by Woodbridge Publishers.

Woodbridge Publishers, 1200 Century Away, Thorpe Park, Leeds, LS158ZA

DISCLAIMER

The author has made every effort to ensure the accuracy of the information within this book was correct at time of publication. The author does not assume and hereby disclaims any liability to any party for any loss, damage, or disruption caused by errors or omissions, whether such errors or omissions result from accident, negligence, or any other cause.

Note to reader for future reading reference, this book was written in the duration between April 2020 to December 2021.

DEDICATION

This book is dedicated to the memory of my dear friend and mentor, Gilad Shafir (1974 - 2001).

Gil lost his life while bravely defending his friends, of which I was one.

In a rare act of valour, Gilad fought off multiple attackers during a deadly home invasion, perpetrated by armed assailants.

Tragically, he succumbed to a gunshot wound, although not before prevailing against the gunmen.

He was survived by his parents, brother and sister, as well as his fiancé; all of whom he loved dearly.

Gilad was deeply respected and admired by his friends, peers, colleagues, and all that knew him. He was an inspiring and visionary technologist, entrepreneur and thought leader who lived his life honourably, with a deep sense of purpose and an unwavering dedication to excellence. He embraced the world with a profound sense of promise, optimism and wonder.

In his final moments he cared not for his own welfare, but purely for that of his friends. It would not be an embellishment to state that although a solitary bullet penetrated his chest, it pierced over a thousand hearts. A 'wound' that two-decades-later has yet to heal.

Gilad's courage reflected an indelible and rare sense of strength and fortitude. The world is poorer for his loss and I am eternally indebted to him for his sacrifice. I can only reconcile that in an act as noble as this was, a measure of immortality is derived through all of us he saved, and our achievements.

To Gilad, without reservation, my solemn hope is that your soul, rests now, in the company of history's greatest of men.

TABLE OF CONTENTS

Disclaimer ii
Dedication iii
INTRODUCTION 1
PROLOGUE 5
CHAPTER 1: FINTECH 12
Electronic Money 19
Banks 20
Global Financial Crisis 21
Disruption & Proliferation 23
Perfect Storm 24
CHAPTER 2: CAPITAL EVOLUTION 30
Competition 30
Strategy 31
Creative Destruction 31
Innovation Paradox 33
Inertia 33
Elementary Decomposition 36
Value 41
Value Proposition 42
Value Chains 45
Vertical–Integration 47
Commoditisation 49
Evolution of Computing 54

Communication Technology 57
Peace, War & Wonder 59
Ubiquity vs. Certainty 60
Standardisation 63
Componentisation 68
Co-evolution 69
Abstraction 75
Higher-order Systems 77
Commodification 78
CHAPTER 3: ECOSYSTEMS 80
Genesis of an Ecosystem 84
Technology Ecosystems 87
API Economy 88
Microservices 98
Elastic Cloud Computing 102
Co-evolution of Practice 108
Commercial Co-evolution 112
Smart Device Apps 116
Vertical to Horizontal 119
Innovate, Leverage & Commoditise 122
CHAPTER 4: SURFACING UTILITY 131
Business Model Evolution 132
Accessing Credit 135
Evolutionary Flow 136
Apex Predator Hypothesis 137

First Principles 142

Straight-Through Processing 144

Know Your Customer 145

Customer Acquisition 145

Identity Brokers 146

Know Your Data 147

Data Privacy 147

Big Data 149

Artificial Intelligence 159

Robo-Advisors 174

Algorithmic Trading 175

Open Banking 175

Harvesting Data 180

Runaway Leadership 185

CHAPTER 5: PAYMENTS 192

Anatomy of Payment Transactions 193

Interbank Payment Systems 196

Banking Business Model 199

Cross-Border Payments 202

Balance of Payments 207

Swap Lines 209

Card Payments 210

Alternative Payment Methods 224

Electronic Money Institutions 226

PayFacs 226

Digital Wallets	**233**
Disbursement Hubs	**234**
Mobile Payments	**235**
Push vs. Pull Payments	**236**
Payment Convergence & Dominance	**236**
CHAPTER 6: MONEY	**244**
Confidence	**244**
Functions of Money	**245**
Characteristics of Money	**245**
Types of Money	**246**
Formats of Money	**251**
War on Cash	**257**
CHAPTER 7: CENTRAL BANKS	**262**
Central Banking	**263**
The Bank of England	**264**
The Fed	**266**
The European Central Bank	**273**
Forward Guidance	**274**
CHAPTER 8: ECONOMIC CYCLES	**276**
Monetary Policy	**276**
Fiscal Policy	**281**
Inflation	**282**
Deflation	**284**
Gross Domestic Product	**285**
Recession	**286**

Depression 286

Velocity 288

Credit & Debt 289

Deleveraging 294

The Middle Class 295

Populism 297

Unconventional Methods 297

Deficit Spending 298

Modern Monetary Theory 302

Quantitative Destruction 304

CHAPTER 9: GOLD..**308**

What is Gold? 310

Why Gold? 312

Properties 313

Measurement 315

Assurance 316

Refinement..317

Gold Producers 320

Gold Reserves 322

Gold Specie 324

Store of Value 326

Gold Standard 328

Depositories 336

Exter's Pyramid 338

CHAPTER 10: FINANCIALISATION......................................**340**

Functions of Finance	340
The Roaring Twenties	345
The Wall Street Crash of 1929	346
Glass–Steagall	348
Bretton Woods	348
Guns & Butter	348
Dollar Confidence Crisis	350
King Dollar	351
Financial Innovation	352
Dot Com	354
Securities	356
Maturity Transformation	357
Derivatives	358
Shadow Banking	362
Securitisation Chain	363
Moral Hazard	363
Information Asymmetry	364
Adverse Selection	364
Coup de Grâce	365
Dodd–Frank	367
Deregulation	368
Arsonists & Firefighters	369
CHAPTER 11: HEGEMONIC DOMINANCE	373
Pre–Hegemony	377
Hegemonic War	379

Hegemony 383
Hegemonic Decline 385
Monetary Hegemony 386

CHAPTER 12: GLOBAL MONETARY SYSTEM 391

Bretton Woods System 392
Clash Of The Titans 392
World Trade Organisation 394
World Bank 394
International Monetary Fund 394
Special Drawing Rights 396
Global Reserve Currency 399
Triffin's Dilemma 400
Nixon Shock 400

CHAPTER 13: GLOBAL TRADE RAILS 405

Dollar Hegemony 405
Exorbitant Privilege 407
London Gold Pool 409
Aftershock 411
Dollar Jurisdiction 413
Nine-Eleven 414
Ground Zero 415
Intermediating Cross-border Remittances 416
Terrorist Finance Tracking Program 424
Extraterritorial Sanctions 426
Non-Proliferation Treaty 427

Joint Comprehensive Plan of Action 428
Dystopian Diplomacy 431
Instrument in Support of Trade Exchanges 432
System for Transfer of Financial Messages 434
Mir 435
Cross-Border Inter-Bank Payments System 435
Single Euro Payments Area 437
International Bank Account Numbers 439
New Channels 441

CHAPTER 14: TOKENISATION 443
Money is Memory 443
Distributed Ledger Technology 445
Blockchain 445
Consensus & Transparency 447
Efficiency & Performance 450
Transactions with Tokens 454
Convertible Virtual Currency 458
Central Bank Digital Currency 464
Unregulated Proliferation 484
Peer-to-Peer 491
Non-Fungible Tokens 492
Expectations & Challenges 494

CHAPTER 15: ECONOMY OF THINGS 497
Behavioural Surplus 497
Digital Exhaust 497

Surveillance Dividend 498

Surveillance Capitalism 501

Internet of Things 504

5G Radio Area Networks 508

Mobile Edge Computing 511

Touchless Experiential Environment 512

Smart Cities 513

M2M Commerce 518

InsureTech 520

Economy of Platforms 527

Embedded Finance 535

Metaverse 541

Immersive Commerce 544

CHAPTER 16: THE RISE OF CHINA 546

Special Economic Zones 547

World Trade Organisation 549

State-Dominated Banking Sector 550

Financial Inclusion 551

Chinese Tech Giants 554

COVID-19 Pandemic 558

FinTech Regulation 559

Authoritarian Capitalism 561

The Middle-Income Trap 568

One Belt, One Road 577

China's FinTech Pearls 584

CHAPTER 17: ODYSSEY 587
General-purpose Technology 588
The Future is Deflationary 590
AI Agency 592
Data Sovereignty & Privacy 596
Asymmetric Monetary System 598
New Challenger 610
Statecraft 614
De-dollarisation 616
Tectonic Shift 625
Unrestricted Warfare 627
Thucydides' Trap 631
Looking Ahead 632
Monetary Edifice 635
Final Thoughts 643
GLOSSARY OF TERMS 646
REFERENCES 665
ACKNOWLEDGEMENTS 696

INTRODUCTION

Money is arguably one of our species' longest standing and most important inventions. It influences how we are raised and what we experience. Money tests our integrity and resolve on a minute-by-minute basis. It affects every aspect of our lives as individuals, as well as a community of global citizens.

Without a monetary system which society can trust, the global economy and our societal fabric will persistently decay. Over the course of the twentieth and early twenty-first centuries, the global monetary system has experienced a number of substantial changes. Several events and economic phenomena have reshaped currencies and the financial system, as well as given rise to the present world order.

The incursion of financialisation, combined with the fundamental flaws of the global monetary system has induced money to deteriorate. This has materialised as a consequence of anachronistic practices, institutions, and policies, which have left the system evanescing. Furthermore, several events and transgressions have amplified these effects and ostensibly compromised public confidence in the institutions upon which monetary integrity is reliant.

Simultaneously, technological advancements have transformed our world over a relatively concentrated period of time. Today, our society is increasingly reliant on communicating, shopping, working, and banking digitally. These advancements have boosted our capacity for learning and enhanced our understanding of one another. Additionally, they have altered our perceptions and become an essential dimension of society.

FinTech synergises the financial and technological worlds in an unprecedented juxtaposition; forging a plethora of near-limitless possibilities. Furthermore, FinTech may fundamentally function as the technological vehicle through which financialisation reaches its apex potential. The initial relationship between FinTech and the financialisation phenomenon has been passive. This has manifested itself in the incremental digitisation and optimisation of an existing financial superstructure. As FinTech has become increasingly pervasive, the shift from passive digitisation to active disruption is in evidence. Consequently, FinTech is playing an increasingly disruptive role in the global economy, and thereby actively influencing its financial superstructure at all levels.

The significance of this shift should neither be underestimated nor dismissed, as the implications thereof have potentially grave consequences for the future of not only economic and financial stability, but prosperity as well. To an extent, this is a natural consequence of damage sustained through incremental attrition and meddling with the fundamental principles which underpin and safeguard the monetary system. In other ways, it is the result of exploiting the system's tolerances in order to prevent an immediate and catastrophic event from manifesting. However, these decisions have consequences. The residue of which has espoused a form of quantitative destruction. The latter evinces a capricious climate, the casualties of which is marred monetary stature and a weakened economic substrate. There is no doubt that the necessity to re-establish the integrity of our financial system and rehabilitate money's standing is increasingly pressing. This may transpire through repair thereof, or perhaps induce a global maelstrom through which to create something entirely new.

As our monetary integrity has perniciously degraded, the global economy has persistently sustained the fallout. This has fuelled social and income inequality, while financialisation and digital advancement have starved our society of its primordial spirit. Furthermore, vested forms of prejudice and adversarial friction among the nations of the world have been amplified in response to the economic climate which this entropy has provoked. Through the coalescence of these factors, an escalation of interstate tensions has fostered money's metamorphosis, essentially transforming it from an artefact of value and exchange into an instrument of geopolitical leverage and economic asymmetry. Collectively, this has incubated extra-systemic pressure through which co-opting FinTech innovation has given rise to crypto-currencies and alternative international payment channels. These developments existentially threaten the monetary system's primacy, and perhaps by extension, eventually may depose our world order.

The digital revolution in which the world has been engrossed is, in part, a response to financialisation, technological advancement, and commoditisation manifesting as a consequence of an intrepid evolution of capital. A further distillation of this is among the factors which have given rise to surveillance capitalism. The latter is fuelled by, and dependent upon, data-driven commerce, the staple of which is data gleaned through interacting with digital services. Large technology companies have realised substantial growth through monetising data via this vehicle and incessantly claimed a substantial stake within the financial services sphere. This success has created an insatiable appetite to harvest many forms of data in order to profit therefrom across numerous industry segments via digital channels.

Data is, furthermore, indispensable in making advances in the development, refinement and enlightenment of Artificial Intelligence. Primacy over data has thus surfaced an unenviable challenge in resolving the conundrum of privacy versus progress. Maintaining agency over our data will undoubtedly constitute a contentious and laborious endeavour as the digital century unfolds.

Whilst digital channels proliferate, the transformative effect on the economy will compel greater FinTech development and prompt a deeper entrenchment thereof in our society. As this trend persists, financial institutions will face existential pressure to evolve and compete within a technological envelope. Moreover, as the digital supervenes upon the physical, the finance sector will likely embrace entirely different business models and restructure itself in order to emulate the dimensions of digitally orientated market actors. As financial institutions adapt, reshape, and potentially reinvent themselves, FinTech will further industrialise and thereby enable non-financial businesses to stage a deeper incursion into the financial services value chain.

Ultimately, FinTech may join Artificial Intelligence among the ranks of general-purpose technologies, and in so doing, further exploit the foundations of an increasingly digitised economy. This should reciprocally complement the rise in immersive commerce in which surveillance capitalism alongside machine-driven economic activity, via the internet-of-things, may become increasingly prevalent.

Eventually, the resulting 'Economy of Things' may compel a redesign of the financial system and, with it, unveil an opportunity to reconstitute its resilience in a manner fit for the digital era.

As we gaze eastwards in awe of the rapid economic growth, technological sophistication, and imperial ambitions of China, we are witnessing general-purpose technologies and FinTech being deeply embedded within the foundations required to realise a digitally gilded neo-industrial vision.

Furthermore, FinTech and the instrumentation it engenders are likely to function as the vehicle through which either monetary rehabilitation is realised, or through which the digital century's neo-financial and geopolitical landscapes are sculpted. In either case, this will likely unfold aberrantly to any time prior to this throughout human history.

With money's integrity reflecting the vestiges of its former standing, new threats are palpable, both from the private sector, as well as from nation states. Several actors are among those eager to exploit the opportunity this represents.

There should be no doubt that a battle for dominance is underway. Money is among its principal theatres, and FinTech is a nascent yet potent instrument with which this war is being waged.

PROLOGUE

In March 1872, Yellowstone National Park was established in the United States. This was the world's first national park, designed to be conserved as a natural habitat for a variety of wildlife species. The 2.2 million acres of the park's woodlands, rivers, mountains and valleys provide unparalleled opportunities to explore an intact ecosystem preserved within a pristine wilderness.

APEX

The Grey wolf, *Canis Lupus,* by its scientific name, is a carnivorous mammal with a pack structure. They live an average of between six to eight years.

The grey wolf is known as an Apex Predator. An Apex predator, also known as an alpha predator, or top predator, is a predator at the top of a food chain, with no natural predators, which threaten its survival.

The word Apex (*noun*) means the top, or highest point of something; especially one forming a point. It is the highest level of a hierarchy, an organisation, or other power structure regarded as a triangle or pyramid.

At one point in time, the grey wolf was the most widespread mammal in the world, with large populations roaming North America, Asia and Europe. By the time of the Great Depression, the grey wolf was severely threatened in the United States. The wolf population had dimished to approximately thirty wolves in Yellowstone. In 1973, the Endangered Species Act was passed, at which point there were virtually no remaining packs in the western side of the United States.

SYSTEMS

There are fundamentally three types of natural systems that occur.

The first is a 'Chaotic System.' A chaotic system is a system that lacks any form of constraints. Hence, without any constraints imposed, there is no structure to it, everything that occurs within is random. The second type of system is that of an 'Ordered System.' An ordered system is the polar opposite of a chaotic system, as by its nature, it is constrained. It is through these constraints that the system finds order. However, if an ordered system becomes excessively constrained, actors within such a system will adapt and potentially find ways to circumvent the constraints imposed therein. Finally, there are 'Complex Systems.' Most systems are complex, whether they are ecological, political, social or financial. Complex systems also feature constraints – although, these are generally characterised as enabling constraints. However, as is evident with ordered systems, over-constraining a complex system will also typically prompt circumvention. A critical distinction between complex systems and ordered systems, is the lack of linear causality. Instead, complex systems feature disposition.

Linear causality is illustrated by the example of: if I do "*x*" then "*y*" will occur. The outcome of an action is understood, defined and predictable. Disposition by contrast, is characterised by how we expect something to transpire or evolve. Thus, disposition allows for inherent uncertainty. Interacting with complex systems reveals that there is no direct relationship between cause and effect, rather a series of dispositional states.[1]

COMPLEX ADAPTIVE SYSTEMS

Returning to Yellowstone; this ecosystem is a perfect example of a complex adaptive system. Through human interference, it was severely disrupted, via culling the grey wolves from the national park. This led to unintended consequences as elaborated below. This highlights the only absolute certainty about a complex adaptive system in that whatever we change in the system, will have unforeseen outcomes. Such unforeseen and unintended consequences may be immediately apparent or may take years to realise. We can endeavour to forecast as to what may transpire or what these consequences may be by understanding disposition. However, with the lack of linear causality, unpredictable things may occur.

Some such occurrences may be favourable, others may be detrimental. Either way, this carries with it an ethical responsibility incumbent upon those that intervene for the outcome of these effects.[2] The same is true of the world of finance. Many wish to believe that the financial sphere is an ordered system, set about with strict rules and constraints. They wish to believe that it is subject to linear causality and that if we study it assiduously, we can anticipate and prevent catastrophic outcomes from occurring.

Since the Global Financial Crisis of 2007-2008, there has been a significant increase in the number of economists questioning the validity of the efficient-market hypothesis (EMH) and related paradigms, as well as financial models. As the finance world has undergone incremental digitisation and more importantly, become more deeply connected globally; the greater credence should be given to treating such, as a complex adaptive system.

EXAPTATION

An important characteristic of complex adaptive systems to bear in mind, is that they are conducive and predisposed to failure.[3] It is through these failures however, that the system adapts, evolves, and is hopefully improved.

Unexpected consequences, as a result of a change or failure within complex systems, may take a number of forms. From an anthropological perspective, a non-linear and unexpected outcome, could be illustrated through the evolutionary phenomenon of exaptation. Whereas adaptation shapes a characteristic or trait for its current use, exaptation describes the phenomenon by which features or traits may acquire functions for which they were not originally adapted or selected, however, are later co-opted. An exaptation is common in both anatomy as well as behaviour, and usually manifests under conditions of stress.

By way of example, feathers originally evolved for thermal regulation in dinosaurs and were later co-opted for display. Arboreal dwelling dinosaurs, like Archaeopteryx, required greater thermal protection in tree-top habitats where they would be less protected from the elements, naturally accrued greater feather density and eventually *exapted* their ability to fly by co-opting this feature for a different purpose. Flight is thus an exaptation.[4] The need to fly was driven by survival and the presence of feathers made the exaptation possible in order to satisfy this need.

TROPHIC CASCADE

Trophic cascades are indirect interactions that substantially affect an ecosystem. Typically, a top-down trophic cascade will be evident, should an Apex predator be introduced into an ecosystem. In such circumstances the species should be both effective in predation, as well as in influencing the behaviour of its prey. The cascading effects thereafter should affect every level of the ecosystem.

Between January 1995 and December 1996, the incremental reintroduction of thirty-one grey wolves into Yellowstone was met with polarised opinions. Some believed this would result in wolves encroaching into residential areas and the surrounding ranches, and thus pose a threat to people, pets and livestock. However, the remarkable effect, the reintroduction of the wolves had in the wake of a seventy-year-absence, is nothing short of astonishing. As expected, the wolves culled some of the deer population in the park. However, what was notably profound, was the wolves' presence altered the deers' behavioural patterns. Consequently, the deer began avoiding areas of the park where they were more vulnerable, such as the valleys and the gorges in particular.

Almost immediately thereafter, those nether areas began to regenerate. In some instances, the height of the trees in these areas quintupled in a mere six years. Thus, the valley sides transformed into forests of Cottonwood, Aspen, and

Willow. As a result of this transformation, the forests began attracting vast numbers of migratory birds. With newly abundant trees to feed upon, the park's beaver population grew substantially. The beavers, arguably one of nature's most industrious ecosystem engineers, also known as a *keystone species*, created niches for other species to flourish. The dams that the beavers created in the rivers provided habitats for otters, muskrats, ducks, fish, amphibians, as well as reptiles.

The wolves culled mesopredators (mid-ranking predators), such as coyotes, which induced an explosion in the populations of rabbits and mice, thus; attracting hawks and increased the populations of weasels, badgers, and foxes. Bald eagles and ravens were drawn to scavenge on the carrion of the prey, which the wolves had left. This simultaneously attracted bears, the populations of which were flourishing with the abundance of berries, then bearing fruit on the regenerating shrubs. Moreover, the bears then reinforced the impact of the wolves, by culling some of the deer.

Finally, the wolves altered the behaviour of the rivers, which altered the landscape. The rivers began to meander less, due to less erosion. Thus, the channels narrowed, forming a greater number of pools and riffle sections, all of which began to teem with wildlife. The rivers responded to the wolves' reintroduction by stabilising the riverbanks, thus becoming more fixed in their course. This was possible through increased vegetation and a reduction in soil erosion, all of which brought stability to the system. This effectively restored the equilibrium in Yellowstone to its former state prior to the wolves being eliminated. Essentially, the wolves, although few in numbers, not only changed the ecosystem but also fundamentally altered its physical topography.

Much like Yellowstone National Park, the financial system is a complex adaptive system, which needs enabling constraints and requires an Apex predator to operate effectively. Removing any species from an ecosystem can seemingly have no effect in the short term. However, unintended consequences will eventually become evident as the system's natural balance gets affected. The higher up the food chain this occurs, the greater the impact will be. Thus, the removal of an Apex predator has the greatest effect, via a trophic cascade. Essentially, the greater the imbalances that accrue, the greater the extent to which the system's very existence is eventually threatened.[5]

ASYMMETRY

Asymmetry (*noun*) is defined as a lack of equality or equivalence between parts or aspects of something. Essentially, a lack of symmetry.

A trophic cascade illustrates a crucial aspect of most systems, both natural, as well as those which human beings have created, in that they are predominantly asymmetrical. In other words, whether economic, political, or financial, there is a hierarchy in which parties maintain asymmetric relationships. Examples include the asymmetric relationship an employer maintains with its employees, or a government maintains with its citizens. In the financial sphere, this may be illustrated in the relationship between a bank and its customers. The relationship between an Apex predator and its environment, is asymmetrical in nature.

CYCLES

Asymmetric relationships furthermore illustrate the basis for which a variety of cycles emerge. Consider the asymmetric relationship between the earth and sun; in which the precession of the axis of rotation of the earth alters the earth's position while orbiting the sun's gravitational field, thereby influencing the world's climatic shifts which we experience as seasons. Each season runs its course, and thereafter the cycle repeats itself.

While seasonal cycles are fairly consistent, there are many forms of cycles in which our world's systems operate. Examples of this include business cycles, debt cycles, and even cycles which govern technological advancement. Each such cycle may elapse over protracted periods of time; in some instances over centuries, while others may iterate rapidly, within the course of weeks, if not shorter intervals. The cadence of the former, may make these cyclic phenomena more challenging to identify, when compared to the latter. Regardless, recognition thereof, provides a degree of insight with which to comprehend how the future may be predisposed to unfold. Unfortunately, since the majority of our world systems are complex and not subject to linear causality, making precise predictions is a highly challenging endeavour. However, identifying cyclical predispositions and asymmetric relationships will assist in illuminating such.

RENAISSANCE

While the financial system has co-evolved in conjunction with political and economic systems over the course of human history, it has evolved steadily at a leisurely pace. However, as a complex adaptive system, it is predisposed to failure. Individuals, businesses, and state actors have played various roles in pushing the boundaries of the system, and in so doing, a number of its 'Apex predators,' and 'keystone species' have subsequently been 'culled.'

As the system has adapted to these conditions, its fundamental flaws have become increasingly apparent. Thus, it becomes increasingly probable that over the course of the 21st century, a new digitally-enabled financial system will likely emerge. The embryonic incarnation of such a system, has manifested in the form of innovations within the sphere of FinTech.

1

FINTECH

Finance serves the function of exchanging and accounting for economic value. Hence, financial systems have evolved to enable funds to be stored and moved between economic actors.

These systems enable individuals, organisations and businesses to share and exchange ownership with the associated risks and potential returns.

Finance is part of nearly every human endeavour in the contemporary world; from choosing what to study, what career to pursue, where and how to live, as well as how and where to shop. In our contemporary world, little would be possible without finance. Without it, there would be no functioning businesses, no goods, and no services.

Over the course of millennia, the global financial system has evolved to become an extraordinarily complex system. Financial systems function as the information layer which record and mediate economic discourse. This has manifested itself in a multitude of overlapping and interdependent networks, systems, and mechanisms, which have emerged to serve people and businesses in moving trillions of dollars daily, facilitating purchases, trade, and investments worldwide.

However, beneath the façade, this industrial age system is far from optimal. It represents an agglomeration of tremendous complexity, often making it slow, frictional, expensive, and lacking in transparency. It promotes speculation, lending itself to instability, and promotes a disequilibrium, creating concentrations of wealth that leave societies vulnerable and divided.

Over the course of history, the specific financial institutions through which this has been realised have manifested in a variety of forms. Over the centuries, the world has evolved from a community-based financial system to an industrial age centralised system. Although, today, we are building new forms of global financial institutions based entirely upon information technology.

Modern financial systems were distilled from the coalescence of new innovations in record keeping (in the form of double-entry accounting) combined with the formation of the new political unit of the nation state, and its single common economic systems that spanned over extensive geographic areas. Furthermore, infused with the new economic model of capitalism, which was specifically designed to create large financial accumulations, while large investments in industrial infrastructure required ever greater and more sophisticated institutions for the amassing, storing, investment and exchange of financial assets. With industrialisation, the systems of organisation evolved from the local and regional levels to the national level. In this context, small local community banks and financiers no longer sufficed as a centralised national banking system ascended to dominance. As large industrial installations require concentrations of large capital investment, centralised national banks assumed the role as enablers, which complemented the driving forces of capitalist economic expansions over the course of the past few centuries.

During the course of the twentieth century, the banking system made numerous technological advances to improve customer service and to move money faster and more efficiently. With the advent of the computer and the proliferation of telecommunications, significant improvements in financial services were made.

Combined with the confluence of trends in the late twentieth century, from financial deregulation and globalisation, to the rise of information technology, and financialisation, the financial system has remodelled substantially within a few decades. The financial system expanded to become a global system, managing the vast flows of capital, systemically interlinking the assets and liabilities that interconnect societies and organisations around the globe.

Simultaneously, within the span of a few decades, the financial system has metamorphosed. Fuelled by information technology and combined with the exploitation of financialisation, the financial system has become an all-pervasive force. Through globalisation combined with the reach of the internet, the system has expanded in scope and scale, as greater spheres of society, and the economy have become financialised through a veritable explosion of financial instruments.

Financialisation has worked to make the system increasingly abstract through the creation of ever more complex derivatives and structured products, with a growing disconnect having formed between finance and society. As this dichotomy has matured, the proportion of financial flows yielded from the largest financial institutions have contracted for investment in real economic activity. The demise of western industrialisation and the expansion of financial products has reflexively made it more lucrative to create new types of instruments and speculate, rather than to invest in the real economy. Derivative instruments such as futures, forwards, options and swaps, draw investment away from manufacturing, farming, and infrastructure development with the promise of high short-term yields by contrast to long-term sustainable growth that benefits the economy as a whole. This disconnect in displacing investment with speculation makes the system inherently unstable and prone to periodic collapse. Collapses are disruptive and costly to the economy at large.

As the financial system has grown in scope and scale, its centralised architecture has analogously made it increasingly complex internally – obscured and insulated behind a digital façade of online banking and digital apps. Behind this barrier, banks and insurance companies are immersed in paperwork and facing a deluge of challenges, while layers of intermediaries exact their own transaction fees, making it less efficient, as well as costly. Consequently, the system has been prevalent with issues to the detriment of society and the economy. Additionally, the financial system has been exclusionary, denying access to financial facilities and tools for parts of society that are increasingly underserved. Examples include rural dwelling communities, and the elderly.

Today the world is in an unparalleled technological revolution. This raises the question as to whether in a world experiencing such significant societal, economic and technological transformations, could the financial system remain structurally unchanged.

Historically, the finance sector has been reasonably diligent in integrating technologies which enable institutions to better organise themselves, as well as to service customers. However, this practice altered course dramatically in the wake of the global financial crises as, banks in particular, dealt with numerous reforms encompassing new regulations, procedures, and requirements.

Coupled with a simultaneous rise in internet use at the time, an ever-broadening chasm between what financial institutions were offering, and customer expectations, was formed. With growing adoption of e-commerce, and the emergence of the smart phone, those that recognised the evolving appetites amongst consumers, and were armed with the tools to capture the opportunities this presented, embarked on occupying the niche this shift represented. Technology companies were at the forefront in building new propositions that would erode the financial sector's monopoly. Hence, the term "FinTech" emerged, to describe the wave of emerging innovations seeking to improve the financial sector by co-opting the internet and nascent technological capabilities at the time.

FinTech is shorthand for 'Financial Technology,' however, it is deceptively named, as the 'Technology' aspect, although fundamental, is predominantly an enabler. The significant paradigm shift is in surfacing the utility of banking and financial services via a digital medium, thus creating entirely new channels in the sphere of financial services.

FinTech services differentiate themselves by prioritising consumer convenience and personalising their experiences in managing, spending, and investing their money. This has reciprocally permeated into businesses which must evolve and maintain pace, to effectively and efficiently service their customers or face displacement. The factors which have led to the successful proliferation of 'FinTechs' were formed through a 'perfect storm' of technological, social, political, and economic conditions, creating virgin territory for disruptive innovation and incumbent disintermediation. This is known as 'Creative Destruction,' which is an economic principle whereby existing business models, processes and methods are 'destroyed' and replaced with new innovative models and methods which are more efficient.

This Creative Destruction is facilitated through the synergy of utility technology services, digital tooling, nimble methodology, community driven co-operation and skilled human capital. These capabilities have symbiotically matured into a competitively priced marketplace, which can be expediently harnessed to effect significant micro and even macroeconomic change.

This combination is enabling new entrants to; innovate, embrace new business models, and rapidly exploit a vacuum within a market which is buoyant with near limitless opportunities. Furthermore, this has left the majority of incumbents amongst industries and sectors across the globe vulnerable to disruption by a digital form of industrial revolution.

In the sphere of financial services, this 'technological tsunami' has enabled the creation of a new, vibrant and dynamic plethora of digital services competitors, in the orbit of a stale financial ecosystem.

Exploiting these conditions relatively unchallenged, has been largely made possible by established financial institutions, predominantly banks and insurers, having been distracted by the fallout of the Global Financial Crisis of 2007-2008 (GFC). In the wake of the crisis, these financial institutions were compelled to prioritise investment resources towards compliance with regulatory reforms, perform rigorous overhauls in risk management, and establish increased thresholds in their liquidity.

In parallel with the increased economic and transactional velocity of digital natives, intuitive smart technology products have promoted and simplified technological literacy across the board, thereby democratising technology and bridging society's generational gaps. Furthermore, this incremental cultural transformation from emergent to digitally dominant has seen businesses adopting technology-facilitated commerce flourish in the consumer goods and services segment.

By contrast, well established financial institutions, have largely found themselves in an unenviable position. Increasing competition and the demand for contextual services presents a significant challenge in keeping pace and meeting the rapidly evolving demands of consumers and businesses.

The financial sector, regulators and governments have long been accustomed to slow and steady rates of change, leaving them ill equipped to cater to the diverse and demanding cadence of today's society. This is evident in the relentless revolution in information technology, whereby the internet is facilitating the metamorphosis into a new decentralised model into which finance and technology may emulsify in new and creative ways. This constitutes a posture reinforced through new forms of decentralised financial systems that are emerging and which are native to the internet. With the proliferation in distributed ledger technologies, and the adoption of tokenised value exchange via crypto-currencies, the potential for the evolution into a very different financial system over the course of this digital century is increasingly viable.

This results in a competitive dichotomy where incumbents are legally and culturally governed by risks and constraints in contrast to challengers who are driven by compelling propositions, and the 'art' of the possible.

For many years, traditional financial institutions have endured and benefitted from an impenetrable monopoly, perpetuated by high barriers to competitive entry, while investing myopically in their technological infrastructure and business practices.

Under these conditions, incumbents have prospered, leveraging a densely captive market of consumers, and accruing a critical mass of varying business models, processes and products.

These factors resulted in highly lucrative transactional revenues, accompanied by incrementally accrued inefficiencies through duplication of skills, technologies and processes- although marginal costs remained low in relative terms.

Potential challengers to these incumbents found themselves cocooned in a labyrinth of legal bureaucracy and unreasonable constraints, whereby they must either elect to join the echelons of the status quo, or succumb in deference to their unequivocal dominance.

On balance, these barriers are set by governments, monetary authorities and regulators for good reason. By way of example, if a bank could arbitrarily be established, policing and auditing the sheer volume of entities would rapidly become untenable.

There is also the question of protecting the economic integrity of a jurisdiction's standing, both domestically as well as internationally. Without rigorous controls and high barriers to entry, the economic impact of inexperienced, ill equipped and/or irresponsible leadership could lead to the simultaneous economic collapse and depression of a country, a global region, or potentially even the entire world.

The consequences of these factors could lead to widespread poverty, famine, or even escalate into an armed conflict. The stakes are high, therefore, so are the standards, regulations and legislation.

ELECTRONIC MONEY

During the 1990s a range of electronic purses and new payment products emerged, predominantly within the banking sector. However, a conservative number of new players emerged, such as Confinity (later known as PayPal). Banks viewed these products as an opportunity to reduce the volumes of base money (cash and coin) used in day-to-day transactions, and benefit from seigniorage by effecting electronic payments, which both reduced their risk exposure, and offered greater efficiencies through technology. Banking customers (known as depositors) were expected to embrace these products in order to benefit from convenience, speed, and reduced risks of their own. This is a trend which had begun decades earlier with the introduction of credit cards in the 1950s, and the widespread use of cheques (checks) in lieu of cash transactions. In 1994, the European Monetary Institute (the predecessor of the European Central Bank), published its report regarding the issuance of such products. The report suggested that within the European Union, such products should be confined to existing banking institutions.[6]

This prompted a series of debates among European central banks and regulators as to whether there was merit in broadening the scope of electronic money issuance, beyond that of traditional banking incumbents. This distilled into the emergence of the 'Narrow Bank' concept. This is a régime, whereby, a type of credit institution may be formed, which benefited from reduced capital requirements. Although the activities of which would be constrained solely to the issuance and redemption of electronic money (e-money) products. Such products included; pre-paid payment cards, digital tokens, as well as pre-paid online accounts. E-money was defined fairly broadly in order to enable a variety of business models and propositions to emerge without creating constraints that would otherwise inhibit innovation. The common features thereof, were that of pre-payment, use of the product or instrument to make payments to third-parties, and its existence as an electronic medium.

Legislation to support this paradigm in the form of the Electronic Money Directive came into effect in September, 2000. This enabled e-money issuers to register as electronic money institutions (EMIs), as well as benefit from recognition as a form of credit institution. However, in a comparable manner to banks, EMIs were subject to prudential regulations inclusive of capital requirements, appropriate internal controls, protection of customer funds, as well as the obligation to redeem e-money for money upon demand.

BANKS

These characteristics allowed for differentiation of EMIs from that of banks. Although there is no exhaustive definition of a bank under the common law (a legal system of the United Kingdom), there is however, a landmark precedent set by a British case from the 1960s which disambiguates the common law interpretation of what constitutes a bank. In United Dominions Trust v Kirkwood, the Court of Appeals listed the following characteristics to be that of a bank:

1. The maintenance of current accounts

2. The payment of cheques drawn on bankers

3. The collection of cheques for clients

The case held that in the course of conducting the 'business of banking,' it is imperative that a banker accepts money from customers to conduct the customer's current account from which sums of money are paid by the customer, or withdrawn by the bank. The presiding judge clarified that the characteristics (listed above) were not an equivalent to a definition. Stability, soundness and probity were in addition to the aforementioned, deemed by the judge to be the defining features of a bank. Ultimately, the notion was accepted that banks were easier to recognise than they were to define.

In a modern context, differentiating between banks and other financial institutions should be a great deal easier. The Bank of England stipulates that banks are financial institutions the duty of which, is to safeguard your money, assist you in paying for things, and provide loans. Banking activities would thus include accepting deposits from customers and subsequently using those funds to loan to others. The key distinction in the United Kingdom as to what constitutes a bank by definition, is the taking of deposits.

Definitions vary by regulator, jurisdiction, and often pivot on the performance of a specific service or the conduct of specific activities. However, banking activities traditionally command the necessity to obtain a banking license, whereas e-money activities require an e-money license. The latter commands a significantly lessor set of criteria which must be met, thus, lowering the barriers to entry substantially.

GLOBAL FINANCIAL CRISIS

Following the deregulation of the 1980s, a financial services boom in the late 1990s and the 2000s was catalysed partially through an expansion in the scope of financial firms, both in terms of product offerings, as well as greater risk exposure through financial innovation. Financial innovation, in this regard, included sub-prime mortgages and other forms of toxic loans. This introduced additional complexities, which circumvented internal controls as well as the governance functions in many financial institutions, while simultaneously rendering decision-making increasingly complex and less effective.

Nevertheless, the Global Financial Crisis of 2007-2008 (GFC) and ensuing recession, very publicly and irreparably damaged the general public's confidence in established financial institutions and regulators, disenfranchising any hope of restoring the faith therein, and establishing favourable conditions for new market entrants. The inherent closed and centralised nature to the system cultivates a lack of transparency, which in turn, incubates a lack of trust therein. This constitutes a posture compounded by the banking sector having declared ethical bankruptcy through the billions of dollars paid in fines and damages each year for misconduct.[7]

The initial events of the GFC were subsequently overshadowed by an orchestrated deleveraging through abhorrent mass bailouts, gluttonous bonuses and zero accountability, taken neither by banking leadership nor governments, regulators or monetary authorities.

The instruments of quantitative easing and austerity combined with deflation, credit evaporation and stalled transactional velocity created a protracted recession (known as 'The Great Recession').

This resulted in a set of ideal peripheral conditions to act as an accelerant in the adoption of digitally delivered alternative financial services, and catapulted the proliferation of speculative investment in FinTech entities on an unprecedented trajectory. This resulted in a proliferation of new digital channels during the decade that followed the GFC.

In 2015, the introduction of Open Banking in the United Kingdom and the broader European Union, via the EU's revised Payment Services Directive (PSD2), materially altered the regulatory landscape for FinTech innovation. Open Banking provided a means with which either EMIs could broaden their offerings to include more traditional banking like services, or furnish new market entrants exclusively focused on the latter to compete for market share.

Distracted, disenfranchised and technologically stunted, incumbent financial institutions were no longer assured in their ability to remain as the Apex predators within the financial ecosystem. As new FinTech companies have emerged along the value chain, some have grown into formidable competitors, such as Ant Financial, which displaced JP Morgan's Treasury Fund as the largest money fund worldwide in 2017 with $268 billion in assets under management by March 2018.[8] Others brought new propositions to market, focused on greater customer convenience and superior user experiences, predominantly in the payments sphere.

DISRUPTION & PROLIFERATION

Advances in technology, namely the internet, the smart phone, elastic cloud services and the rise of social media, have played a significant role in this shift. However, it is the change in consumer behaviour and mind set, regulatory posture, as well as the business response to these, which has galvanised an immutable trend of disruptive business reform.

These factors collectively account for the unstoppable momentum created in propelling the world into an era dominated by continued FinTech innovation and entrepreneurship.

FinTech is an exaptation of technology, co-opted to disrupt finance and financial services. It represents a radical repurposing of existing technology under conditions of stress to the financial ecosystem. This exaptation has manifested in the creation of a broad vista of digital 'Neobanks,' 'Challenger banks,' banking software providers, payments and remittance providers, alternative finance companies, accelerated vendor payments, InsureTechs, RegTechs, digital identity verification brokers, digital wallets, FX exchanges, Blockchain/DLT technology providers, crypto-currencies, and even robo-advisors. The ecosystem keeps growing.

In the UK as an example, Challenger banks differentiate themselves from Neobanks by being regulated under the Financial Services and Markets Act 2000 (Regulated Activities), Order 2001/544 Part 4A, in order to qualify for deposit-taking. Thus, Challenger banks are banks, while Neobanks are financial services firms which may offer a broad spectrum of traditional banking services, although may not take deposits. Both forms of institutions distinguish themselves from traditional banks by generally being branchless and offering their services exclusively online via digital channels. In recognition that these distinctions lend themselves to confusion, the UK's Financial Conduct Authority (FCA) released a communication in May 2021, implying that EMIs should refrain from using the word 'bank' in communications and promotions. The communication emphasised the differentiators between EMIs, and

Financial Services Compensation Scheme (FSCS) protected banks, which institutions must share with existing and new potential customers.[9]

PERFECT STORM

In advanced economies, since 2007, the proliferation of FinTech has been cultivated and subsequently accelerated through rapid and dominant smart phone penetration, mature and ubiquitous communication infrastructure, social networking, cloud technology, and the rise of big data and artificial intelligence in conjunction with consumer appetites for 'instant gratification' and convenience. Consumer acceptance and adoption has grown extensively in realising the value that FinTechs are able to deliver through enabling frictionless, high-velocity monetary intercourse. These enablers empowered FinTech companies to surface the utility of financial services in new and innovative ways. This is an endeavour supported by applying first principles and interdisciplinary thinking in conjunction with complexity-based approaches to create exaptive propositions.

In developing and emerging market economies, less developed and conservative coverage of 'traditional' communications infrastructure services has been prevalent, while traditional banking services have limited reach and a corresponding reduced market share. However, high-ratios of smart phone adoption, mobile networks proliferation, and alternative banking services have made tremendous strides in mitigating these deficiencies and enabling broad FinTech penetration of these underserved markets.

Consequently, there are further incremental changes in political and regulatory posture as FinTech has transitioned from 'Too small to care' to 'Too significant to ignore.' FinTech has become a battleground for competitive parity and differentiation amongst countries. A flurry among numerous jurisdictions has been evident, underscoring a sense of desperation not to be left behind in the wake of this new 'financial arms race.'

Unfortunately, with regulation and legislation in some areas lagging behind these 'digital pioneers,' combined with low barriers to entry, a number of significant casualties amongst the FinTech actors is inevitable. These failings will likely temper consumer confidence in the short term, however, represent growth opportunities for existing channels and new market entrants in the longer term.

It should be reasonable to expect a number of mergers, acquisitions and partnerships to emerge periodically to consolidate the market share and improve the competitive posture among FinTechs and legacy incumbents.

Furthermore, globalisation of digital communication and sophisticated supply chains have radically altered the reach of goods, services and financial assets across the world.

Combined with geopolitical and global economic factors, the fabric of the macroeconomic superstructure and the fundamentals that underpin global finance have become fertile arenas, which are no longer impregnable to digital disruption and disintermediation.

There are a number of these animals which will be explored in subsequent chapters to assist in shaping a view of where some of these changes might be anticipated.

These conditions are favourable for the cultivation of a series of lucrative and exciting opportunities in order to sustain the speculative cadence in new ventures and in incubating challengers. The future in this field has a well-lit runway.

While the first generation of web technologies radically changed the face of communication through email, the second generation changed the face of media. The latter essentially catapulted the world from a few centralised media channels and newspapers to a world where anyone could have their own channel surfaced via social media. In addition, it enabled people with substantial followings to become influencers. The third generation of the web, however, is anticipated to offer the vehicles and connectivity to do the same for finance. The third-generation web may well have native capabilities to accomplish what currently costs financial institutions substantial sums of money in technology investments to achieve. This leads to the conclusion that the financial industry will not necessarily be disrupted by the FinTech start-ups of today, however, it would be more prudent to assert that they will likely be disrupted by the internet itself.

As technology continues to evolve, the rise of artificial intelligence, immersive technology, the internet of things, robotics and autonomous vehicles, provide the new instrumentation and channels through which advancements to influence the development of FinTech may be exploited to enrich society's digital future.

Historically, a centralised model to finance has been created, consisting of many closed organisations that function and fulfil their roles within a national and global hierarchy. These institutions, and the rules under which they are governed, were largely organised in this fashion as this was the only way political leaders could ensure mutual trust in the system and formalise the channels that support trade and economic growth. Governments subsequently outsourced the administration thereof to the nations' institutions that it regulated, by ensuring that they complied with laws and regulations built upon the foundations of this world order.

The consequence of this approach is that all the resources in the system are compelled to flow exclusively through those limited sets of centralised institutions. A centralised model has certain advantages – however, numerous disadvantages exist, particularly when the system becomes complex. Notwithstanding these vulnerabilities, the financial system depends on centralised adjudication in order to cushion the impact of financial panic. This creates a dependence on central banks to act as the sentinels which safeguard the financial system. In extreme circumstances, these institutions additionally function as lenders of last resort to governments. Additionally, central banks issue and regulate the money supply upon which businesses and consumers depend. However, currencies do not command an equal standing in the global economy. While central banks maintain an asymmetric relationship with the financial sector, the United States maintains an asymmetric relationship with all other countries. The nature of this relationship places the US dollar at the heart of global trade and finance.

Since the fifteenth century, six countries have consecutively enjoyed the privileges associated with such a leadership position. The incumbent benefits from low borrowing costs and superior purchasing power throughout the world. Furthermore, the nature of this relationship empowers the incumbent to formulate a world order, project its influence, and if necessary, police the world.

In the past, the value of money was anchored by commodities such as gold and silver, whereas today, money is anchored by the creditworthiness of governments and the confidence therein. Since the GFC, the instruments at central banks' disposal have been exploited to shield the world's economies from bearing the full brunt of the catastrophic fallout which would otherwise have manifested. Since the US dollar plays an indispensable role in international finance, these measures have left the United States' standing in a questionable position. Repeated attempts to rehabilitate its posture have been met with limited success and thus far proven unsuccessful. Furthermore, comparable challenges in other advanced economies are in evidence. This has left the integrity of the financial system and confidence in the value of money on an unsound footing.

With the emergence of FinTech, the instrumentation has emerged, to not only offer new innovative financial services, but to create new asset classes, and perhaps, even new forms of money. Simultaneously, countries which have recognised the opportunities and potential this instrumentation presents have exploited nascent technologies in order to serve broader geopolitical ambitions. This behaviour has been further reinforced by the emergence of state-sponsored FinTech initiatives to function as alternative 'plumbing' with which to circumvent and potentially challenge the existing monetary system's primacy.

The dollar's privileged and omnipresent status reflects many dimensions, including the extent to which other countries are willing to align themselves with US foreign policy. The stability of the world order is furthermore influenced by both how powerful, and the extent of a given country's convictions in aligning with the United States' views on the global stage.

As powerful competitors have emerged and consolidated their strength, it has become increasingly complex to maintain global stability, both economically as well as politically. Russia's gold and foreign currency reserves increased substantially in the wake of its 2014 annexation of Crimea. This was broadly interpreted as a form of insurance against future US extraterritorial sanctions. Thus, earning the name 'Fortress Russia.' Furthermore, China's large holdings of US Treasury Securities were once seen as a potential source of geopolitical leverage.

'How do you deal toughly with your banker?'

- *Hillary Clinton, then-US Secretary of State, 2009.*

The weaponisation of finance, among other instruments, has profound implications for the future of international politics and economics. Thus, many of the fundamental assumptions about the post-Cold War era are being challenged, as countries engage in a new era of competition. Globalisation and free trade were once viewed as barriers to conflict, a web of dependencies that would bring former adversaries ever closer together. Instead, it has become a new battleground. The compromised posture evident in the financial system further amplifies these effects and invites challenges.

The loss of confidence in money, financial institutions, central banks, and governments is symptomatic of a system designed for a different era struggling to meet the needs of today's economic conditions and geopolitical climate. In simpler times, the system was highly effective, but as the world's needs become more complex, it induces redundancies, compartmentalisation, bottlenecks, and engenders systemic resistance that collectively render the system increasingly torpid. Furthermore, as the system loses touch with the needs of modern society, its antiquated and exclusionary nature becomes increasingly apparent. Exploitative practices, that are cultivated behind the curtain of opacity in the institutions to which the system has been outsourced, eventually breach the trust with which they have been imbued. The system becomes fragile, untrustworthy, and promotes adversarial behaviour both nationally and globally. It remains clear that the international monetary and financial system is increasingly anachronistic and due for a change. As the digital century unfolds, technology will undoubtedly play a central role in facilitating this transformation. A 'storm' is brewing.

2

CAPITAL EVOLUTION

All capital evolves over time- although within a cyclic pattern. As capital is invested in the development of innovations, these innovations begin to evolve into goods and services. Each phase of this evolution requires further capital. These evolutions have historically unfolded slowly. In some instances, over the course of centuries. In a contemporary context, the cadence thereof, is of a notably greater tempo. Thus, representing a tendency to exhibit far shorter cyclic iterations, which ultimately make this evolutionary process far more visible and apparent.

The evolution of capital is framed within the industrialisation process of commoditisation, fuelled by investment, enhanced by credit and driven by competition.

COMPETITION

Born in 544 B.C., Sun Tzu was a revered military general, philosopher and strategist in imperial China. His notable work is a book entitled, 'The Art of War.'[10] In this text, Tzu identified five material factors within the sphere of warfare. A model for competition.

1. **Purpose,** as in the moral imperative. To achieve victory, to survive invasion, or to conquer an objective

2. **Landscape**, the terrain or our surroundings. The theatre (field) of competition

3. **Climate**, the seasons, the weather; or factors and patterns that affect the landscape

4. **Doctrine**, the universally applicable principles, regardless of the context

5. **Leadership**, the ability to marshal resources towards an objective and engage in context specific gameplay

STRATEGY

The purpose of a strategy is to guide and enable a business to achieve superior economic performance, in order to yield and sustain a Return on Invested Capital (ROIC).

Economic performance is linked to value. An effective strategy, is thus, a means of harnessing value through the creation of a unique value proposition, amidst a competitive environment.

At the outset, the fundamental differentiators required to achieve superior economic performance are an effective strategy, coupled with an acute sense of situational awareness. Unfortunately, the majority of mature and in numerous instances, larger enterprises eventually fall short on either one, or more commonly, both of these fronts.

The consequences of these shortfalls is usually displacement through weak economic performance brought about by either market saturation (through competition), or an unsustainable business model, or a combination thereof.

CREATIVE DESTRUCTION

In order to navigate these challenges, recognition of the state of the prevailing business environmental conditions (Tzu's factors of 'Landscape' and 'Climate') is imperative for business survival. Optimising value chains (see below) to greatest achievable efficiency and simultaneously innovating is the required remedy in order to remain competitive. These innovations compel a necessity to be accompanied by a series of co-evolutions in order to remain relevant in the market of the imminent future. This is a principle unequivocally conveyed by Austrian economist, Joseph Alois Schumpeter (1883 - 1950), in which:

*'The fundamental impulse that sets and keeps the capitalist engine in motion comes from the **new** consumers, goods, the **new** methods of production or transportation, the **new** markets, the forms of industrial organisation that capitalist enterprise creates.'*[11]

- Joseph A. Schumpeter, 1942.

According to British economist, Christopher Freeman, an eminent researcher within the realms of Innovation Studies, modern Kondratiev Waves and Business Cycle Theory, with regards to Schumpeter:

*'The central point of his whole life's work is that capitalism can only be understood as an evolutionary process of continuous innovation and **creative destruction**.'*

- Christopher Freeman (1921 - 2010), founder and first director of the Science Policy Research Unit at the University of Sussex.

The economic concept of 'Creative Destruction,' also known as 'Schumpeter's Gale,' posits that the *'gale of creative destruction'* describes the *'process of industrial mutation that continuously revolutionises the economic structure from within, incessantly destroying the old one, incessantly creating a new one.'*[12]

In other words, it is necessary, and furthermore inevitable, to create a means of *destroying* what is making you money today by *creating* something new. Subsequently, you need to evolve in order to deliver this. Doing so is critical to ensure you are able to make money, tomorrow.

INNOVATION PARADOX

The challenge in succeeding within this *Creative Destruction* paradigm is evident in remaining operationally efficient today, while simultaneously innovating for tomorrow. This is elegantly articulated by the "Innovation Paradox" as follows:

'Paradox is at the heart of innovation. The pressing need for survival in the short term requires efficient exploration of current competencies and requires "coherence, coordination and stability"; whereas exploration/innovation requires the discovery and development of new competencies and this requires the loosening and replacement of these erstwhile virtues.'[13]

- Graeme Salaman & John Storey, Managers' theories about the process of Innovation, 2002.

Determining when to innovate, and how expediently to bring this innovation to market in order to be effective, is dependent on an acute comprehension of the market (the landscape) and the prevailing economic conditions (the climate). However, recognition thereof and the conviction to act upon such, is dependent primarily on executive competence and fortitude (leadership).

INERTIA

In physics, inertia is a property of matter, by which it continues in its existing state of rest or uniform linear motion (in a straight line), unless that state is changed by an external force.

'Any organization that designs a system (defined broadly) will produce a design whose structure is a copy of the organization's communication structure.' - Conway's Law [14]

- Melvin E. Conway.

In business, *inertia barriers* form through the maturation of communications structure (Conway's Law), business models, practices, processes and culture. These factors initially breed successful economic performance within a market amidst rising competitive conditions. However, as the market saturates through competition and inflation, downward pricing pressure and commoditisation (see below) renders these business models and practices less effective. Businesses respond by periodically initiating process optimisation programmes, leveraging methodologies such as Lean and Six Sigma. Further optimisation activities are usually accompanied by reorganisation, outsourcing, offshoring and potentially divestment. These behaviours breed a false economy of expectation, akin to Zeno's dichotomy paradox.

ZENO'S DICHOTOMY PARADOX

'That which is in locomotion must arrive at the half-way stage before it arrives at the goal.'

- Zeno's dichotomy paradox, as recounted by Aristotle.

By way of example, if an individual were to take a single step towards covering a specific distance and was constrained to reaching only half the intended distance with each step, they could walk *ad infinitum* ('to infinity,' Latin) and never reach their intended destination.

Fig 2.1 An illustration of Zeno's Dichotomy Paradox

In other words, each step covers only half of the previous step's distance, thus, incrementally expending equivalent effort to realise perpetually diminishing returns, and ultimately, never reaching the intended destination (or objective).

Overcoming inertia is a function of Tzu's factor of *doctrine*. Inertia builds as a result of success. A profitable business model tends to cultivate confidence therein, and dissuades any incentive to alter course. Industrialisation and competition, however, alters the efficacy of a business model and the commercial viability of the good or service. These are, essentially, the various phases of evolution of an innovation into a commodity or utility (see Commoditisation below). Consequently, it thus requires businesses to undergo a co-evolution in business model, practices, culture and processes to accompany the innovation itself, disruptive or otherwise (see Co-evolution below). Each transition of the evolution from one phase to another, requires a corresponding evolution of doctrine, which is then applicable. Reticence to invest in innovation may be influenced by external forces. This is particularly evident in advanced economies, whereby investors demand greater returns on their investments, thus posing challenges for enterprises to devote resources to research and development (R&D) in order to innovate. This is a common symptom of financialisation, which amplifies the challenges in overcoming the *Innovation Paradox* (see Chapter 10: Financialisation).

In some circumstances, the market responds to these challenges through consolidation via mergers and acquisitions (M&A), or forming either coalescent partnerships or joint ventures. Regardless, new challengers enter the market unimpeded by entrenched inertia barriers, thereby fuelling competition.

Alternatively and simultaneously, either prior, or in parallel with conditions reaching a saturation apex, inertia barriers are breached in order to evolve and give way, for *new* consumer appetites, *new* technologies, *new* methods, *new* practices, *new* culture and *new* business models, qualified amidst suitable economic conditions. Businesses that fail to innovate and evolve beyond inertia barriers eventually disappear through bankruptcy or acquisitions. This phenomenon illustrates the dichotomy of the *Innovation Paradox*, and substantiates, as well as, reinforces the compelling necessity for *Creative Destruction*.

ELEMENTARY DECOMPOSITION

The economic atrophy of a business model and its associated inertia usually closely precedes the emergence of an innovation (representing an *inertia-to-change*), which may take the form of higher-order systems (see Higher-order Systems below). The emergence of higher-order systems are generally chaotic and unpredictable. In other words, these are new realms to be discovered. Effectively, they emerge in an 'Uncharted' state.

Common characteristics of higher-order systems are hierarchical and elementary in nature. They are underpinned and abstracted (term of art) by the previously emergent, now either partially or fully industrialised systems.

In physics, much use is made of the concept of the 'elementary particle,' although these particles rarely remain perceived to be elementary for prolonged periods of time. Historically, atoms were considered to be elementary particles, however, to the nuclear physicist, atoms are vast and highly complex systems. In the study of biology, a cell may be considered to be an elementary subsystem. In the context of microbiological research, a protein molecule, and in yet another, an amino acid residue. All of these are perceived to be an elementary particle in one realm, however, in another context, each is a complex system or subsystem (see Prologue). Each of these subsystems represent an elementary decomposition of the previous, and each is hierarchical in nature.[15] This is a contention advocated by American economist, political scientist and cognitive psychologist, Herbert A. Simon (1916 - 2001), in his 'The Architecture of Complexity,' published in 1962.[16]

This phenomenon is particularly evident in the world of technology, however, additionally applies unequivocally, in the sphere of Financial Services. A FinTech centric example is illustrated through the emergence of Blockchain technology, hierarchically exploited to create crypto-currency, such as Bitcoin.

Technology examples include computers evolving from products into commodities; accruing an inertia-to-change, prompting *Creative Destruction,* and evolving into services and utilities known as 'Cloud Computing.' These commodities, services and utilities build up a further inertia, subsequently enabling higher-order systems such as, the 'Internet of Things' and 'Big Data' to emerge.

Higher-order systems are facilitated by decomposition and abstraction (see Componentisation below); which is a precursor, enabling these new systems to evolve into independent sources of new value and future worth.

The inertia-to-change is accrued through competition, standardisation and best practices amongst utility-computing services (Cloud), combined with the Internet of Things and Big Data, which then trigger innovation by creating new value through the re-emergence of Artificial Intelligence (AI). The emerging higher-order system of Artificial Intelligence in the form of 'Machine Learning,' leverages the decomposition of computing utilities (Cloud Computing) and Big Data, subsequently rebuilding inertia, to facilitate the next higher-order system in the form of 'Predictive Data Analytics,' which leverages Machine Learning, and so on and so forth.

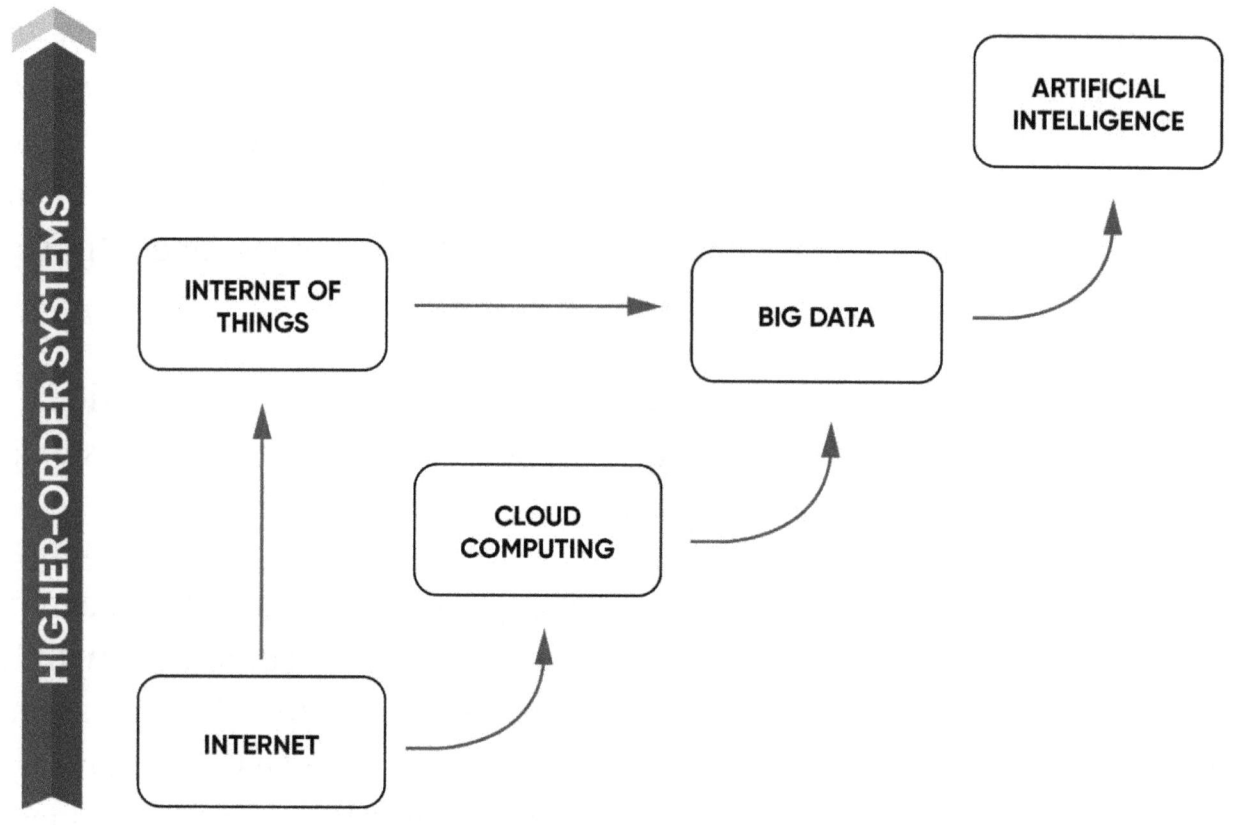

Fig 2.2 illustrates the hierarchy of Higher-Order Systems. Each enabled by the previous.

RED QUEEN HYPOTHESIS

A business differentiates itself by recognising the current state of this landscape (Tzu's factors, see Competition above), and provides a meaningful roadmap to evolve through innovation in order to drive new and future value (Tzu's factor of Leadership).

This is elegantly articulated by Evolutionary biologist, Leigh Van Valen's (1935 - 2010) Red Queen Hypothesis, a tangent to Van Valen's Law; also known as the 'Law of Extinction.'

'The need to constantly evolve in order to stand still relative to a surrounding ecosystem.'[17] *- Red Queen Hypothesis*

- *Leigh Van Valen, 1973.*[18]

The Red Queen Hypothesis surfaces the concept that there exists a constant "arms race" between co-evolving species – a metaphor for inter-enterprise competition. The observation is in reference to 'Through the Looking-Glass.' A novel by Lewis Carroll, published in 1871, in which the Red Queen's chess board is in constant motion, thus forcing the protagonist, 'Alice' (of Carroll's previous novel 'Alice's Adventures in Wonderland' published in 1865), to run, in order to remain perceptively stationary.

In other words; to remain the greatest value generator at the apex of the value chain, a constant evolution is required. In order to achieve this, businesses must continually innovate.

INNOVATION CONDITIONS

In order for such an innovation to take hold, however, a number of conditions must be favourable to complement the initial concept. These conditions comprise a *receptive consumer attitude*, appropriate *enabling technology* and *economic suitability*.

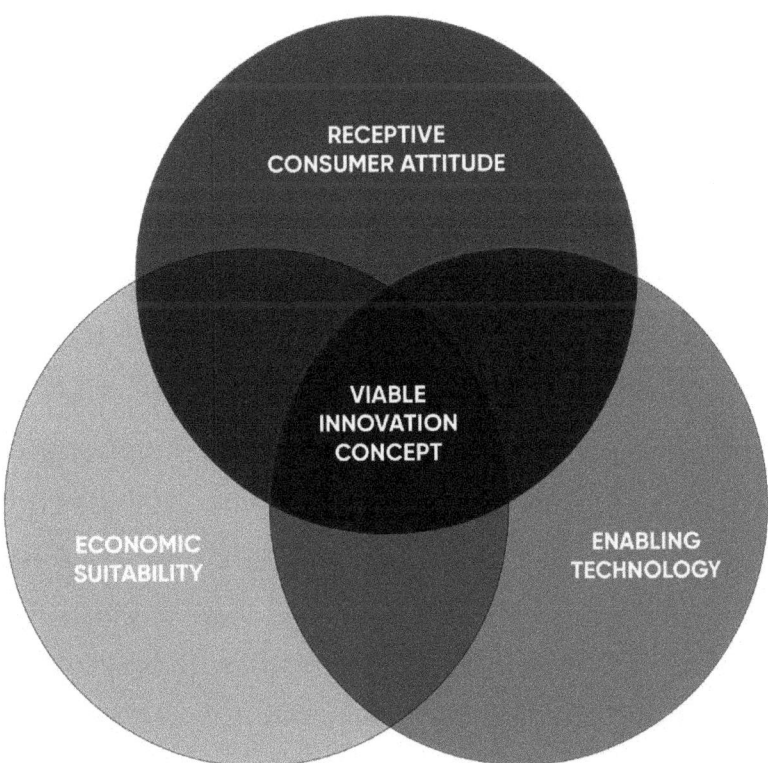

Fig 2.3 Venn diagram illustrating the conditions required to yield a viable innovation

HAWTHORNE EFFECT

Between the years 1924 to 1927, a lighting study was conducted at Hawthorne Works. Hawthorne Works was a Western Electric plant in Cicero, Illinois, USA. Hawthorne Works had commissioned the study in order to determine whether changes in the ambient lighting within its facility could influence productivity. Increasing brightness prompted a change in behaviour, however, eventually productivity returned to prior levels. Decreasing the brightness had a similar temporary effect. The 'Hawthorne Effect' has since become the emblematic means through which to describe the ephemeral surge in interest should something new emerge. Essentially, this is the 'novelty factor,' which does not represent the viability of long-term value realised from an innovation.

Determining the economic suitability of an innovation is partially, although critically, dependent on identifying the value to the intended consumer(s) at the point of market entry. Other factors which may affect macroeconomic suitability are influences such as short-term and long-term debt cycles (see Chapter 8: Economic Cycles). These are akin to Tzu's factors of *Climate* and *Doctrine* (see Competition above).

BLACK SWANS

Navigating these influences, is highly dependent on an acute level of understanding as well as awareness of the 'landscape' and the 'climate.' A conceivable exception, however, is arguably a 'Black Swan' event (a random event, beyond the realms of predictability, yet usually high in impact). These events may act as an accelerant, or conversely have a decelerating effect on the aforementioned factors. The COVID-19 outbreak in November 2019, which originated in Wuhan, China, and led to a global pandemic, may be construed as such an event which had an accelerant effect in digital commoditisation. Social distancing rules and national lockdown measures in response to the pandemic acted as a major accelerant in FinTech adoption and e-commerce penetration as consumers were either prevented or limited in accessing bricks-and-mortar banking and shopping facilities.

VALUE

In devising a successful strategy to yield an effective outcome (ROIC) in each iteration of this cyclic phenomenon, the objectives need to be clearly discerned. The objectives are distilled from Tzu's factor of *purpose*. This is the *moral imperative,* which includes qualifying the perceived value to an identified market of potential customers (representing the 'receptive consumer attitude,' see Elementary Decomposition above). Historically, there are three prevalent hypotheses which act as suppositions as to how society (and business) perceives value.

INTRINSIC VALUE THEORY

The *Intrinsic Theory of Value,* otherwise known as the *Theory of Objective Value,* was originated in 1811 by British economist, David Ricardo (1772 - 1823). The theory posits that value is determined by the sum of the costs associated with producing the good or service. In other words; the value of a good is discerned from the sum of its raw materials and the costs of transforming these materials into a finished good. Thus, advocating that the value of an item should not fall below its intrinsic (or essential) cost of production.

SURPLUS LABOUR THEORY

In 1848, Karl Marx (1818 - 1883) challenged Ricardo's *Intrinsic Value Theory* by advocating that the value of a good or service is determined by the *socially necessary labour* required to produce it. In other words; the value of economic goods is derived from the amount of labour necessary to produce them. The *Surplus Labour Theory* is also known as the *Labour Theory of Value* (LTV). The LTV is largely rejected by orthodox neoclassical economics in favour of subjectivism which superseded value-based thought during the latter 19th century, as a consequence of the Subjectivist Revolution.[19]

SUBJECTIVE VALUE THEORY

There are three prevalent schools of economic thought from which others are derived. The first is that of Classical Economics, originated by British economist, Adam Smith (1723 - 1790). The second is that of the Austrian School of Economics, founded by Viennese economist, Carl Menger (see below). The third is that of Keynesian Economics, originated by British economist, John Maynard Keynes (1883 - 1946).

In 1871, Carl Menger (1840 - 1921) advocated that the two previous value theories were flawed. Menger posited that the value of a good or service is *subjective*. Thus, its value is determined by the sum a potential customer (or the market) is willing to pay for the good or service.[20] Menger advocated that the costs associated with producing it, as well as the labour associated, are not the governing factors in determining its value. Subjectivism is the prevailing hypothesis as to how society values goods and services.[21]

In order to establish the monetisation potential of the value realised by a strategy and harnessed by an innovation (or good/service), a *value proposition* is forged.

VALUE PROPOSITION

A *value proposition* must satisfy three criteria. The *first* criterion is to identify the *specific* customers for which the value proposition is tailored to target. This is considered critical, as different types of consumers will perceive and weigh this value differently (subjectively).

By way of an example, a woman in her early 20s, earning an entry level wage, will not be enticed to purchase a revolutionary skin care product, where the stated value is, 'a guarantee to make her appear ten-years younger.' This is particularly unpalatable for her as a consumer, especially at a premium.

However, a woman in her mid-50s or above, with significant disposable income, will likely perceive the value of a youthful complexion as highly desirable and affordable; even at a significant premium.

It is vital for success to ensure that customer specificity is well defined and understood, as targeting too broad a spectrum of customers introduces exponential variance, which will have to be addressed. An aspect which may dilute the value through a reduction in operational effectiveness.

The dilution may occur through introducing complexity, unsuitable management methodology, and poor standardisation. These characteristics tend to fuel inefficiencies and ultimately diminishes the value irrevocably. Circumstances such as these result in inferior economic performance and a loss of a competitive advantage. In general, successful exceptions may be evident, albeit fairly rare. However, broad customer-targeting should never be the intent from the outset.

Historically, incumbent Financial Institutions have shared these characteristics, yet remained profitable and prevailed against this principle. However, this sector has been shielded by outside influences in the past. These 'outside' influences, include high-barriers to competitive entry through capital requirements and a highly-regulated legislative posture.

The past successes of these incumbents, creates a potential paradox of 'derivative ingenuity.' In other words, a regression to looking rearward for assurance of future success. This behaviour manifests itself, in a number of myopically uttered platitudes. Examples of which include:

'this is how we've always done things'; 'this is what the competition have done, and it worked for them'; 'we still have critical mass'; 'we're still profitable'; 'we're too big to fail'; 'look at our share price.'

Ironically, investment literature is riddled with disclaimers that 'future investment performance should not be inferred from, or predicted based on past investment performance.' This overstated warning is taken from the Securities and Exchange Commission's Rule 156, underpinned by the Securities Act 1933, in the United States. Similar legislation with comparable stipulations are evident in most advanced economies throughout the world.

Success tends to breed complacency, enabling inertia barriers to form, and poor awareness of the surrounding environment (landscape) cultivates conditions (a climate) which erodes profitability, diminishes confidence and ultimately leads to displacement. A process which is accelerated by competing to be efficient (Innovation Paradox), in lieu of competing to be relevant and unique. Unfortunately, there is no one "best" way to compete. Furthermore, one of the common downfalls in devising a strategy is to attempt to compete with rivals on parallel dimensions.

The *second* criterion provides the means to combating this behaviour by identifying the specific needs of the intended customers, which the business is attempting to satisfy. This is imperative in ensuring that the value proposition delivers a unique and relevant advantage. The business objective (Tzu's factor of Purpose) is to competitively differentiate itself from its peers.

The *third* and final criterion is to establish the price which a business will ask for this good or service. This price, is either set at a premium, a discount, or at parity.

In order to establish *how* the value proposition is supported in achieving superior economic performance, a *value chain* is either introduced (disrupted by a new market entrant), or strategically augmented (by an incumbent). The introduction or augmentation thereof, combined with the *value proposition* surrounding an innovation, is collectively synonymous with the paradigm of *Creative Destruction*.

VALUE CHAINS

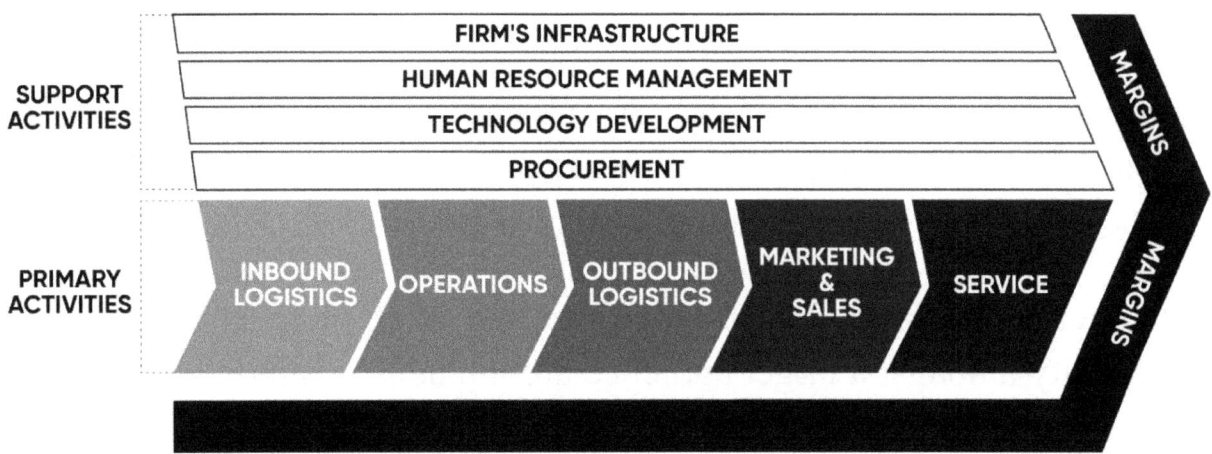

Fig 2.4 an example of Porter's Value Chain Model

A *value chain* is a set of activities working together as a vehicle to deliver value for specific goods and/or services for the market. The concept was first pioneered by acclaimed Harvard Business School Professor, Michael Eugene Porter, published in his book, 'Competitive Advantage, Free Press, New York, 1985.' Although published later, Porter first promoted and applied this concept publicly much earlier. Porter described value chains as a 'decision support tool' in his 'competitive strategies paradigm,' as early as 1979.

The intent of a value chain is to define a 'chain of needs,' to quantify the value of a monetised output.

Porter's value chains define a variety of *primary* and *support* activities. These activities are effectively stores and flows of capital, essential to quantifying the value and creating a competitive advantage for a firm's goods and services.

PRIMARY ACTIVITIES

1. Inbound Logistics - This includes the warehousing and associated inventory control of raw materials. This also includes the nature of the relationship with suppliers.

2. Operations - This encompasses any process that transforms raw materials into a finished good ready for sale, including labelling, branding and packaging.

3. Outbound Logistics - Concerns any process where the good is distributed to a customer. This includes the storage and distribution of goods and the processes involved in fulfilling customer orders.

4. Marketing & Sales - Any processes that attempt to enhance product visibility amongst a target audience are included in marketing and sales. This activity is also heavily reliant on customer relationships.

5. After-sales Service - Services include any processes that occur after a purchase has been made, including customer service, repairs, refunds, and warranty acknowledgement.

SUPPORT ACTIVITIES

1. Infrastructure - Company infrastructure entails any process that supports daily business operations. Administration, clerical, financial and line management are all value creating infrastructure processes.

2. Technological development - Technology can create a competitive advantage in Porter's value chain because it can streamline important processes. These include; payroll automation software, customer service procedures, and distribution networks.

3. Human Resources management (HRM) - HRM covers any process related to the training, acquisition, or termination of employees. HRM departments and their ability to hire talented and motivated staff are crucial to a company's competitive advantage.

4. Procurement - Procurement is simply the acquisition of necessary goods or services. The most typical example is the procurement of raw materials

and the negotiation of pricing and product purchase contracts. It may also include the purchase of equipment, offices, buildings and machinery.

A number of these activities are highly-visible to the external market, while others are less so. Ironically, Porter's Value Chain model is centred on quantifying and optimising the intrinsic value of goods and/or services (see Intrinsic Value Theory above) in order to achieve a competitively viable, if not successful position amidst market actors within a subjective value economy (see Subjective Value Theory above). The rationale for the above being that as the elements within the value chain become increasingly commoditised (see Commoditisation below), the resulting downward pricing pressure will erode the subjective price point (Premium) that the market is willing to pay through an increase in the supply, thereof (see Peace, War & Wonder as well as Ubiquity vs. Certainty below). Thus, the margin between the intrinsic and subjective value of a good and/or service is predominantly governed by its qualitative utility (see Chapter 4: Surfacing Utility). Since such is constantly evolving (see Red Queen Hypothesis above), the necessity to constantly innovate to achieve parity remains a necessity.

VERTICAL – INTEGRATION

Porter's Value Chain was conceived at a juncture when companies were embracing vertically-integrated supply chains. In examining the functions and capabilities required to produce a good or service, businesses largely cultivated the capabilities and capacity of supply, production and distribution within the sphere of control of the organisation. A vertically-integrated approach provides businesses with the means to control every aspect of the organisation's quality of output and the associated costs for doing so.

A vertically-integrated business owns (or controls) its suppliers, distributors, or retail locations in order to optimise its value (or supply) chain. Vertical-integration benefits companies by enabling them to harvest margins at each layer of the value chain through controlling processes, reducing/optimising costs via collective bargaining (demand aggregation), and driving efficiencies through consolidation and standardisation. This is a practice synonymous with the formation of conglomerates (see Hegemonic War, Chapter 11: Hegemonic Dominance).

Banks and traditional incumbent Financial Institutions have historically emulated this model. Generally, incumbents exploited vertical-integration in order to achieve scale, given that the costs associated with the coordination of activities beyond organisational boundaries were typically higher, less predictable and vulnerable to volatility driven by external influences.

In this context, these organisations have utilised technology within the sphere of value chain *support activities*. Technology, in this sense, has formed part of the 'infrastructure' and 'technological development' activities, fulfilling a role of supporting administrative functions such as 'human resource management' (HRM), 'procurement,' in addition to interbank functions and supporting the banking business model. However, the *Creative Destruction* of FinTech is evident in the departure from this paradigm, whereby technology assumes the role of value chain *primary activities*. This exaptation (see Prologue) is accomplished through technology providing the means with which to surface the utility of financial services digitally, realising a new, typically superior value proposition for the end consumer, directly.

Synonymous with this shift in paradigm (*Creative Destruction*) is a fundamental exaptation in instrumentation ('enabling technology,' see Elementary Decomposition above) to enable this revolution. Consequently, the vertically-integrated supply chains of Financial Institutions are being challenged (disrupted and disintermediated) by new competitors (FinTechs), which are exploiting a horizontally-layered (Value Clustering) approach (see Vertical to Horizontal, Chapter 3: Ecosystems). This shift is not unique to Financial Services. However, in the financial services sphere, it represents a significant and material disruption to a previously impregnable business model. Ultimately, made possible via Commoditisation. The field of commoditisation was substantially advanced by British scientist, researcher and business advisor, Simon Wardley in 2003 - 2005.

COMMODITISATION

Comprehension of the manner in which value erodes and descends through the value chain over time is a function of commoditisation (not to be confused with commodification) (see Commodification below). Commoditisation is the process that governs the transcendental states an innovation undergoes from the 'Uncharted' (Emergent) to the 'Transitional,' and finally, to the 'Industrialised' state. There are a number of forces and barriers which influence this journey, predominantly experienced in temporal increments between a series of 'waypoints of maturity,' along this evolutionary path.

The waypoints begin in the 'Emergent' (Uncharted) state with an innovation, signified by the **'Genesis'** waypoint. This artefact (innovation) evolves until it reaches the **'Custom Built'** waypoint. Custom built evolves until it reaches the **'Product'** waypoint. Product (and/or service) evolves into a **'Commodity'** (and/or utility).

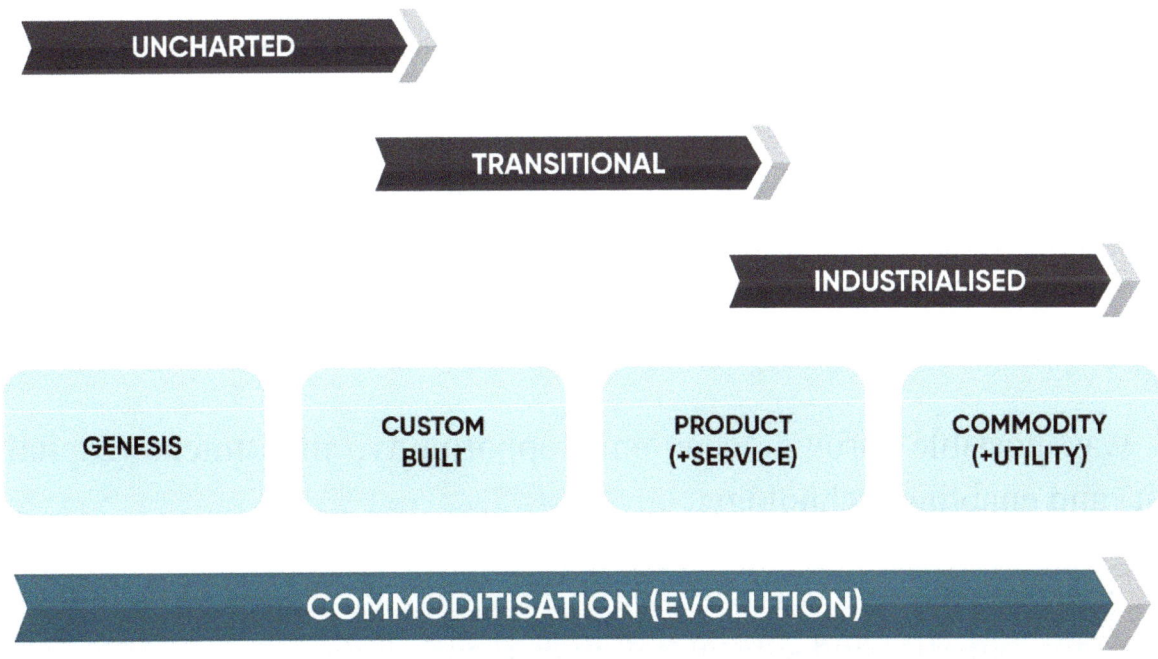

Fig 2.5 Illustrates the Phases of Commoditisation (Evolution) vs. the States of Industrialisation

In considering this phenomenon through the lens of industrialisation, there are three innovation factors which are required to trigger an industrial revolution.

1. Energy

2. Communications

3. Mobility

In the first industrial revolution (1760 - 1840), the principal invention was the steam engine driven by fossil fuels (the energy innovation) which facilitated the means to power the printing press, (the communications innovation) and later the steam engine, combined with a coach on rails (exaptation) which created the train (the mobility innovation).

At their inception, these innovations were expensive to develop, expensive to fabricate and required tremendous skill to design, build and operate.

These three capabilities combined led to other innovations in textile manufacturing, resulting in enormous factories being erected which were producing goods, while an ecosystem of other businesses emerged, such as publishers and news agents.

Progressively, information was being shared through books and newspapers, as well as a means of marketing the goods being produced, which combined with train networks and provided the logistic capability to transport people, goods and information to numerous destinations.

This was possible through economic opportunity, investment (capital and credit) and enabling technology.

These innovations were not available to everyone, they attracted a high barrier of entry for expertise and substantial investment capital.

However, this is where the impact of commoditisation is surfaced. As today's new innovation matures, it becomes tomorrow's 'old hat.' In other words, when a new innovation emerges, it is proprietary, difficult to understand and expensive to fabricate. Tomorrow, it is commoditised, thus, it is either inexpensive or affordable to purchase and likely available in abundance. Most critically, if it is worth having, everyone will have it.

This is elegantly articulated in the relationship between *ubiquity* and *certainty*. In other words, if something is *ubiquitous*, (as in it's everywhere) it provides *certainty*. If it instils *certainty* (confidence), it will proliferate everywhere, essentially becoming *ubiquitous*.

'Ubiquity acceleration is driven by consumer adoption. Certainty acceleration is driven by business competition. The mean between these two forces is commoditisation.'[22]

- Simon Wardley, 2005.

In considering this concept in the context of the second industrial revolution (1870 - 1914). As before, *energy*, *communications* and *mobility* are the three enabling factors.

In the case of *energy*, electricity was harnessed via a series of inventions. *Communications* radically advanced through the invention of telephones and radio. Finally, *mobility* advanced through roads, cars, buses, trucks, aeroplanes and airports. These factors distilled into catalysts for economic growth, consumerism and globalisation.

Note that these capabilities emerged at different junctures, however, the combination catalysed an acceleration in advancement within the economy as well as growth in productivity.

Each of these capabilities, in isolation, passed through a lifecycle of *ubiquity* versus *certainty* (commoditisation).

Electricity was essentially commoditised by Thomas Edison (1847 - 1931). Edison was a prolific inventor who held 1093 US Patents, as well as numerous Patents in other countries.

Edison pioneered numerous advancements in the fields of electric power generation, mass communication, motion pictures and sound recording. He eventually founded General Electric, which went on to become one of world's largest and most successful companies.

When electricity first emerged, it was highly proprietary, difficult, as well as expensive to generate and challenging to harness. In the 21st century, in developed countries with advanced economies, anyone can learn how to generate electric power; everyone has access to it in their place of business and in their home, and can purchase electricity as a utility (commoditised and industrialised). Furthermore, anyone can generate their own electricity, should they wish to do so. This can be done either through generators, wind turbines or solar panels (photovoltaics).

Consider this in the context of *ubiquity* versus *certainty*.[23] Electricity generation advanced through an evolution of commoditisation, emerging as a disruptive innovation, which as it gained traction, rose in ubiquity through adoption and competition, lowering its cost, as its methods of generation became safer and more efficient, as well as better understood (through further innovation and *Creative Destruction*), fortifying its certainty, displacing its predecessor (steam), and ultimately commoditising from a product to a utility (a ubiquitous low cost and abundant service).

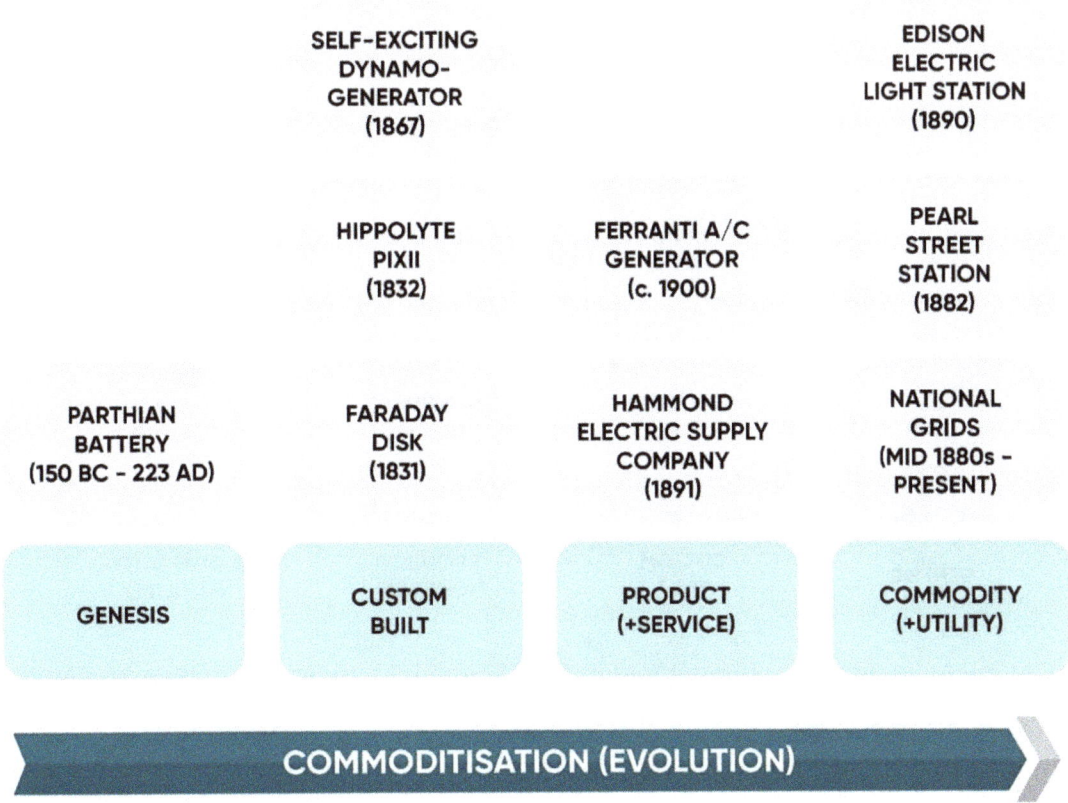

Fig 2.6 commoditisation of electricity from an innovation to a utility

Electricity, in itself, facilitated the *Creative Destruction* of numerous other industries by enabling the creation of precision and bulk manufacturing machinery, processes and automation (see The Roaring Twenties, Chapter 10: Financialisation). Thereby, displacing the previous orthodoxy. Each of these industries has undergone an independent evolution towards industrialisation, via commoditisation. Most critically, the commoditisation of electricity has enabled industries to emerge that would not have otherwise been possible to be created. A principle and pattern that is material to the emergence and proliferation of FinTech in contemporary terms.

EVOLUTION OF COMPUTING

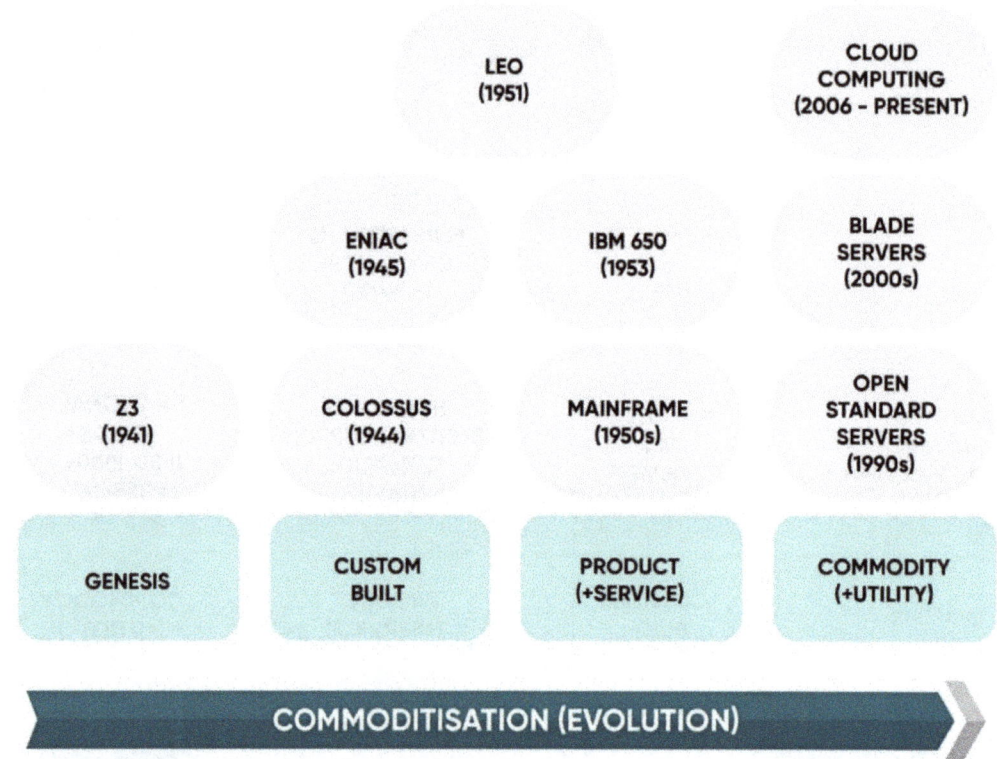

Fig 2.7 commoditisation of computing from an innovation to a utility

GENESIS (THE INNOVATION)

In 1941, the Z3, the world's first programmable computer, capable of performing floating point binary arithmetic, featuring a 22-bit word length, was built in Germany. The Z3 was invented by German engineer, Konrad Zuse (1910 - 1995). It was used in aerodynamic calculations.

CUSTOM BUILT EXAMPLES

In 1944, the first Colossus was put into operation at Bletchley Park, England. Designed by Alan Turing (1912 - 1954), a British mathematician, considered to be the father of Artificial Intelligence (see Artificial Intelligence, Chapter 4: Surfacing Utility). The Colossus was used to tackle the complex Lorenz ciphers used by Nazi Germany during World War II (1939 - 1945). Notably, Turing's invention ultimately broke the codes based on these ciphers used by the Nazi Enigma Machines.

In 1945, the Electronic Numerical Integrator And Computer (ENIAC) was completed, although officially introduced in February, 1946. An endeavour which began in 1943 to assist in winning a war (World War II) that was over by the time it was completed. It was designed primarily to calculate artillery firing tables for the US Ballistic Research Laboratory. It used 20000 vacuum tubes, 70000 resistors, 10000 capacitors, 6000 switches and 1500 relays.[24] This was reminiscent of first-generation computer processing. With varying frequency, a bug would either crawl or fly into the system and short out either a resistor or a vacuum tube. These components were connected in series, thus, the offending component had to be hunted down and replaced before the computer could function again. Hence, the origin of the terms, 'bug in the system' and 'debugging.' The ENIAC was enormous. It occupied the entire 50-by-30 foot (15-by-9 metre) basement of the Moore School of Electrical Engineering, Pennsylvania, USA. Hence in practice, debugging the ENIAC elapsed over several days, and in some instances, over the course of weeks.

The Lyons Electronic Office (LEO) computer ran its first business application in 1951. The LEO system was a transitional system, built in England. It shared the characteristics of both a 'Custom Built Example,' as well as a 'Product' (Fig 2.7).

PRODUCTS

In 1953, IBM announced the introduction of the IBM 650. A significantly smaller digital computer marketed to business, scientific as well as engineering customers. The IBM 650 was easier to program and significantly cheaper than its predecessors. This was a major stepping stone in the commoditisation of computing.

The IBM 650 could easily be accommodated in a room (as opposed to a warehouse or large basement) and provided an affordable platform suitable for purchase by businesses and universities. With the introduction of computers in learning institutions, students were afforded the opportunity to gain programming skills, and with growing skills in the work force, applications could be developed to be used by business to enhance productivity and promote a competitive advantage.

FURTHER INNOVATION

In 1958, Jack Kilby (1923 - 2005), an American engineer at Texas Instruments, invented the first hybrid integrated circuit (third-generation processing). The introduction of third-generation processing in itself represented the *Creative Destruction* of computer processing. The first customer was the US Air Force. Unfortunately, Kilby's hybrid integrated circuit featured external wire connections, making it difficult to fabricate and impossible to mass produce. In 1959, Robert Noyce (1927 - 1990), an American physicist at Fairchild Semiconductor, invented the first monolithic integrated circuit based on Silicon, an improvement over Kilby's Germanium-based circuit.

Noyce's version placed all the components on a single silicon chip, connected with copper lines. Fabricating the chip was made possible by the Planar Process, developed by Jean Hoerni (1924 - 1997), a Swiss-American engineer and colleague of his, earlier that same year.

The integrated circuit is the basis for all modern day computer processors (pre-Quantum Computing), the advancement of which, may be forecasted, via Moore's Law.

MOORE'S LAW

Moore's Law is the observation that the number of transistors in an integrated circuit will double every two years (although 2.5 years in practice). The observation is named for Gordon Moore, who co-founded Fairchild

Semiconductor, where Robert Noyce (see above) was employed. Subsequently, Moore went on to become co-founder and Chief Executive Officer (CEO) of Intel, arguably the best-known name in microprocessors since the 1990s.

Moore's Law has historically held true, whereby, as the number of transistors has doubled every two years (or 2.5 years), the commensurate price has largely remained at parity for each new iteration. Hence, the previous generations become cheaper and ubiquity rises. A principle reinforced by the Jevons Paradox.

'Technological progress that increases the efficiency with which a resource is used, tends to increase the rate of consumption of that resource.'[25] *- The Jevons Paradox*

- William Stanley Jevons, 1865.

COMMUNICATION TECHNOLOGY

In considering communication technology through a similar lens, in the 1930s, the Telex messaging network was brought online, leveraging communication between Telex machines, via the prevailing telephony network.

In 1969, the Advanced Research Projects Agency Network (ARPANET) emerged as the first wide area packet-switching network with distributed control. Additionally, it was among the first networks to implement the Transmission Control Protocol/Internet Protocol (TCP/IP). Both of these technologies became the foundation for the modern day internet.

The Advanced Research Projects Agency (ARPA) was a division within the US Department of Defense. The ARPANET project was initiated in 1966 to enable access to remote computers. These were based on the ideas of American computer scientist, Robert W. Taylor (1932 - 2017) and American psychologist as well as computer scientist, Joseph C.R. Licklider (1915 - 1990).

The first computers were connected in 1969, and a year later the Network Control Program was implemented. Further software development added capabilities such as email, remote login and file transfers.

Following a period of rapid expansion, the network was declared operational and stewardship passed to the US Defense Communications Agency.

In the 1970s research by American internet-pioneer, Vinton G. Cerf at Stanford University, partnered in collaboration with American electrical engineer, Robert E. Kahn at the Defense Advanced Research Project Agency (DARPA) led to the Transmission Control Program, which later incorporated concepts from French computer scientist, Louis Pouzin's CYCLADES project in France. CYCLADES was an early data packet communications network. This distilled into the creation of IP/TCP.

In 1983, TCP/IP version 4 (originally IP/TCP) was installed for production use in the ARPANET. This is also known as Internet Protocol version 4 (IPv4). The US Department of Defense had declared it to be standard for all military computer networking.

TCP/IP had been designed and developed to allow a network-of-networks to be formed by numerous separate networks.

The ARPANET project was formally decommissioned in 1990, following partnerships with telecommunications and computer industry conglomerates, making way for a new *World Wide Web* (www) of networks, now known as the Internet. Sir Timothy Berners-Lee, a British computer scientist, is best known as the inventor of the *World Wide Web*. In March 1989, Berners-Lee proposed a network-based information management system and subsequently implemented the first successful communication between a 'client' and 'server' via the HyperText Transfer Protocol (HTTP) in November 1989, thus establishing the '*www.*'

PEACE, WAR & WONDER

The primary force that drives commoditisation is competition. Once a new innovation gains a foothold within the market (usually in the form of, or facilitated by a higher-order system), it displaces its predecessor's position in the value chain. This displacement can manifest itself either in the form of a new good or service, or in competition with other similar goods or services.

As the new goods or services gain traction, they gain market share. This is achieved by either creating a new market, or siphoning market share from other actors, usually incumbents. Once the new business model and its differentiated value has made an impact on the market and is better understood by other actors, it is likely to advance to the next commoditisation waypoint (e.g. from "Custom Built" to "Product"). These actors either engage in peaceful competition by attempting to achieve parity independently, or through hostile tactics which may include acquisitions (M&A) and price wars. Market actors which neither innovate themselves, nor engage in either "peaceful" or "hostile" competitive practices, are eventually displaced altogether.

This is representative of an economic pattern known as *'Peace, War & Wonder.'* [26] The term features prevalently in Simon Wardley's work surrounding commoditisation and competition. The *'Peaceful'* phase of competition fuels greater understanding and promotes the proliferation of goods or services within the market. This, in turn, invites many more market entrants to begin competing with incumbents.

Increasing competition results in eroding prices and narrower margins. Narrower margins drives austerity, and the necessity to achieve greater economies of scale and efficiency.

As profit margins are abraded, this typically prompts divestments or market consolidation via strategic partnerships, mergers or acquisitions and joint ventures. This phase of industrialisation additionally introduces pressures to outsource, offshore and divest. Irresponsible market actors, begin 'taking shortcuts' and forego quality and safety controls. They regress into adopting abusive behaviours, forming cartels and engaging in predatory pricing practices. This competitive phase is frictional and adversarial, thus, synonymous with the '*War*' phase of this pattern.

Finally, there is the '*Wonder*' phase. By this phase, the original innovation is largely industrialised and is either a commodity or a utility. This evolution has accrued an *inertia-to-change* throughout its lifecycle and the industrialised commodity (or utility) is leveraged to create a new higher-order system or innovation. This disruption to the status quo, represents a re-introduction into the 'Uncharted,' through a new 'Genesis.' Ultimately, triggering the industrialisation process of commoditisation, from 'uncharted' to 'industrialised' once again.

This pattern may be observed at micro as well as macroeconomic scales. The larger scale waves, which surround the impact of a disruptive innovation or artefact whereby many value chains are affected, are known as Kondratiev Waves. Such artefacts include examples such as electricity, money and computing. The pattern of *Peace, War & Wonder* is reflected in the work of Carlotta Perez, whereby, *Wonder* is synonymous with 'eruption and frenzy,' *Peace* with 'synergy and maturity,' while *War* is reflective of the phase between these waves. In addition, this broadly correlates with Holling's Renewal Cycle Model (Fig 3.1) from an ecological perspective (see Chapter 3: Ecosystems).[27]

UBIQUITY VS. CERTAINTY

Tracking the dimensions of this phenomenon may be achieved through a contrast of two vectors; **ubiquity** against **certainty** (see above).

As consumers realise the value of these goods or services, an augmentation in broader behaviours in acceptance is evident, which in turn, drives greater adoption (see Network Effects, Chapter 3: Ecosystems). This adoption, can be measured in terms of a ubiquity vector. Ubiquity broadly correlates to consumer demand (over time), which consequently places pressure on the certainty vector (over time).[28]

Certainty is a measure of competitive actors improving and creating supply to cater to these consumers, which in turn, drives increased ubiquity. These are largely adjacent forces struggling to achieve an equilibrium.

The mean of these forces, which generally follows a linear trajectory, is commoditisation, however, the pathway of an innovation evolving into a commodity or utility is not linear in itself.

Many natural processes, such as those of complex system learning curves, exhibit a progression from small beginnings that accelerates and approaches a climax over time.

A principle reinforced by:

'One of the principal findings of structural studies of innovation is that there is a reflexive relationship between innovations and their society and economy; they influence each other. Innovations are the mechanism by which societies and economies 'modernise' or are restructured. Equally, societies and economies influence which innovations are produced and their rate and incidence of adoption.'[29]

- Gordon Clark, 1984.

Common economic patterns such as *'Peace, War & Wonder'* illustrate the phenomenon of what transpires as an innovation evolves through competition. Through an increase in the cadence thereof, further development and understanding enhances. This not only enables these to become more efficient as well as cost effective through increased supply, but additionally, enables higher-order systems to emerge, which then in turn, introduce new sources of value and future worth. This is facilitated through componentisation. Componentisation (see below) is a function of Elementary Decomposition (see

Elementary Decomposition above) and is typically accelerated via Standardisation (see Standardisation below).

Inertia is evident in the lifecycle due to past success combined with the knowledge that certain aspects within the economy are predictable. Nonetheless, it remains challenging to predict what higher-order systems will appear accurately. However, when they do appear, they will begin to commoditise through the same lifecycle of commoditisation driven by competition. It is additionally challenging to predict when specific commoditisation lifecycle transitions will occur, as these depend on the actions of individual actors. However, as an innovation evolves into a commodity, new innovations will appear and these will also evolve through competition.

There's an uncertainty principle in the economic system. This accounts for why, in some instances, the commoditisation of a particular innovation may elapse over a month, a year, a decade or even centuries (Fig 2.6). In some instances, this uncertainty may enable actors to forecast, and to an extent, predict the "what" and the "how," but not the "when." Yet in other instances, may enable actors to anticipate the "when," but not the "what."

By way of example, Douglas F. Parkhill's book, 'The Challenge of the Computer Utility,' accurately predicted the emergence of cloud computing.[30] Parkhill's book was published in 1966. This was 40 years prior to 'Cloud Computing' becoming a reality (see Chapter 3: Ecosystems). Parkhill could extrapolate and predict the "what" and posit a theory as to the "how," but not the "when." However, Parkhill could not predict that utility computing would become known as 'Cloud Computing.'

Although many companies may possess the insights and resources to navigate these changes, many are still disrupted by this phenomenon, even when it remains highly predictable (see Serverless Computing, Chapter 3: Ecosystems).

STANDARDISATION

Competition is generally characterised as a rivalry between two or more actors, which may be striving towards achieving a common objective in which one or more party's gain represents the other's loss. One or more party's success represents another's, or many other's failure. As such, competition is generally construed to be the opposite of co-operation. However, in practice, this is quite the opposite, whereby, a blend of co-operation and competition is the norm and vital to progress. In economics, philosopher Robin Collingwood advocated that:

'The presence of these two opposites together is essential to an economic system. The parties to an economic action co-operate in competing, like two chess players.'[31]

- Robin G. Collingwood, 1926.

This surfaces the notion that co-operation, to some extent, is required in order to accelerate advancement (see Genesis of an Ecosystem, Chapter 3: Ecosystems). Competitors are consequently compelled to improve in order to stay competitive (see Red Queen Hypothesis above), thus, making them more capable.

Capital evolves via commoditisation through competition, yet, may be accelerated through the use of open standards, collaboration and community co-operation; or impeded through introducing constraints such as isolationist behaviours, bureaucracy, patents, regulations or restrictive legislation. By way of an example, proprietary software may be compiled from source code (programmed code) and distributed as a binary executable program. The user may execute the program and benefit from its use, however, is unable to see how it was programmed. Open-source software, by contrast, is distributed and publicly available to allow the user to examine the underpinning source code from which a binary executable was compiled (or interpreted). Open-source, thus, promotes community-driven advancement and acts as an accelerant for commoditisation.

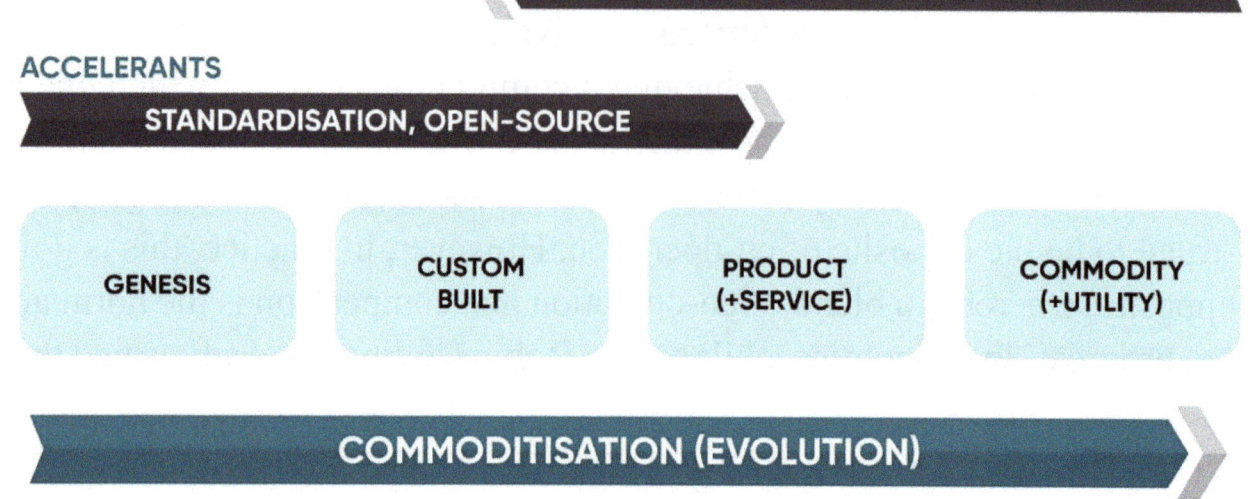

Fig 2.8 Accelerant versus decelerating effects on commoditisation

DECELERATING EFFECTS

The insurance sector is periodically accused of manipulating the commoditisation of its industry. A tactic for achieving such, has been achieved through exploiting decelerating behaviours. If an industry is enabled by technologies that are purely a commodity or utility, the barriers to entry for its competitors are very low.

By way of an example, a number of large incumbent insurers have long-suffered from *inertia barriers* and accrued inefficiencies through the aggregation of legacy technologies, process duplication and an entrenched risk-based culture. These factors collectively increase an insurer's costs, relative to Gross Written Premiums (GWP). An insurer operating at 3% - 4% total cost of ownership of its technology and operations expenditure relative to its GWP is considered lean and competitive. However, most large insurers run in excess of 7%. More than a few run in double-digit-percentages. In a multibillion-dollar enterprise, such ratios represent a substantial cost burden for technology expenditure, a tremendous risk to liquidity and an existential threat to its long-term solvency.

Thus, in an attempt to maintain competitive dominance, many larger insurers impede attempts to agree on industry standards (although a minority do exist, see InsureTech, Chapter 15: Economy of Things), and have advocated for greater regulatory scrutiny, as well as restrictive legislation in order to discourage the introduction of new nimble market competitors. These efforts collectively introduces a decelerating effect on commoditisation within the sector and may dissuade disintermediation in the near-term. Ironically, insurers heavily weigh standardisation into their risk formulae, and thus, encourage standardisation in the industries for which they underwrite the risks. Businesses which comply with industry standards tend to benefit from reduced insurance premiums, in contrast to competitors which don't.

Examples include:

- ISO 9001   - Quality Management
- ISO 27001 - Information Security
- ISO 22301 - Business Continuity
- ISO 14001 - Environmental Management
- ISO 45001 - Occupational Health & Safety

A decelerating effect may defer the inevitable, however, will not prevent it. Ultimately commoditisation may be slowed, however, not stopped.

BRITISH STANDARD WHITWORTH SYSTEM

At the outset of the first industrial revolution (1760 - 1840), in the process of building machinery and erecting structures, every nut and bolt was custom turned and fitted. Hence, every machine and structure required custom and unique manufacturing materials, leading to excessive delays and expense. The introduction of the British Standard Whitworth System in 1841, devised by Sir

Joseph Whitworth, espoused an end to this highly inefficient practice. It was through standardising the dimensions of screw threads, nuts and bolts that ultimately catalysed an acceleration in manufacturing and advancement.

CONTEMPORARY STANDARDISATION

Standardisation defines how goods, services, people, methods and processes interact with each other and their environments. It provides requirements, specifications, guidelines or characteristics that can be applied consistently in order to ensure that materials, goods, processes and services are fit for their intended purpose.

The term 'standard' may be interpreted differently in a variety of contexts, dependent on geography, demographics and industry. However, a standard is essentially an agreed way of doing something. Whether that 'something' is producing a good, rendering a service, or managing a process; standards provide a reliable basis for creating shared expectations. The development of standards typically undergo rigorous consensus gathering worldwide, involving the collaboration of experts from businesses, regulators, policy makers, consumers and any other relevant stakeholders (see Genesis of an Ecosystem, Chapter 3: Ecosystems).

Notable standardisations in a contemporary context include door sizing, electrical outlet configurations, battery voltages and numerous other artefacts which benefit from standardised form factors and characteristics. Standardisation tends to reduce costs by creating common artefacts (see Componentisation below), which may be exploited by a broader community with a lower barrier to entry. Collectively, standardisation and the cascading effects it espouses, act as commoditisation accelerants.

In the sphere of modern technology, proprietary communication protocols, codecs, closed-loop systems, proprietary binaries and unpublished Application Programming Interfaces (APIs), are all attempts to decelerate and diminish the cadence of commoditisation. Whereas, Open-source, Open APIs, Open Data,

Open Hardware and community or industry-driven standardisation, are all accelerants.

STANDARDISATION BODIES

Include:

ISO	-	The International Organisation for Standardisation
IEEE	-	The Institute of Electrical and Electronic Engineers
IETF	-	Internet Engineering Task Force
ANSI	-	American National Standards Institute
NIST	-	National Institute of Standards and Technology
ISA	-	International Society of Automation
BSI	-	The British Standards Institution
CEN	-	The European Committee for Standardization
ASME	-	The American Society of Mechanical Engineers
ASTM	-	ASTM International, formerly known as the American Society for Testing and Materials
SAE	-	SAE International, formerly known as the Society of Automotive Engineers
CSA	-	CSA Group, formerly known as the Canadian Standards Association

Additionally there are community-driven standards bodies such as:

W3C   -   World Wide Web Consortium

OAI   -   The OpenAPI Initiative

ODI   -   The Open Data Institute

COMPONENTISATION

The standardisation of screws, nuts and bolts, brought about by the introduction of the British Standard Whitworth System (see above), facilitated the phenomenon of Componentisation.

Componentisation describes the emergence of components that are espoused as a result of the commoditisation process; often triggered, or accelerated, via standardisation. These are more often than not either abstractions (term of art), reusable artefacts, methods or elements that give rise to new *doctrine* and the *co-evolution of practices,* that emerge to complement them. Componentisation is additionally the usual process through which a new innovation or higher-order system emerges.

As with the example of screw, bolt and nut standardisation, competitors that refused to exploit these new standardised components found themselves in a less competitive position. They were stalled behind inertia barriers, unable to adapt to new *doctrine* and new best practices, which ultimately resulted in their demise. Those who embraced the new standardised components were able to exploit their lower cost and their abundance (ubiquity) to become more productive and profitable.

With the complementary change in *doctrine* (see Competition above), the new standards and new components allow competitors to advance and outperform their rivals, leading ultimately, to an enviable competitive advantage. Those who embrace the new components and standards, however, do not embrace the new best practices or *doctrine* that complement them, ultimately failing to realise their value. This weakens their position through lost time-to-market and squandered resources. Resources that could otherwise be directed towards greater value endeavours.

CO – EVOLUTION

An innovation appears and evolves at the start of the lifecycle, and through competition, its characteristics begin to evolve through the process of commoditisation.

At its genesis, it emerges in the state of being 'emergent' and 'uncharted.' As it evolves it changes characteristics from the emergent (or uncharted) state – which is inherently novel and new – to a transitional state, and then further evolves to a state of becoming industrialised (Fig 2.5). In the industrialised (commoditised) state which was once uncharted and novel, it becomes well understood, standardised and mundane. This occurs over an unspecified period of time. These states are characteristically varied, and as a consequence of such, there remains no 'one size, fits all' approach in methods of management and best practice.

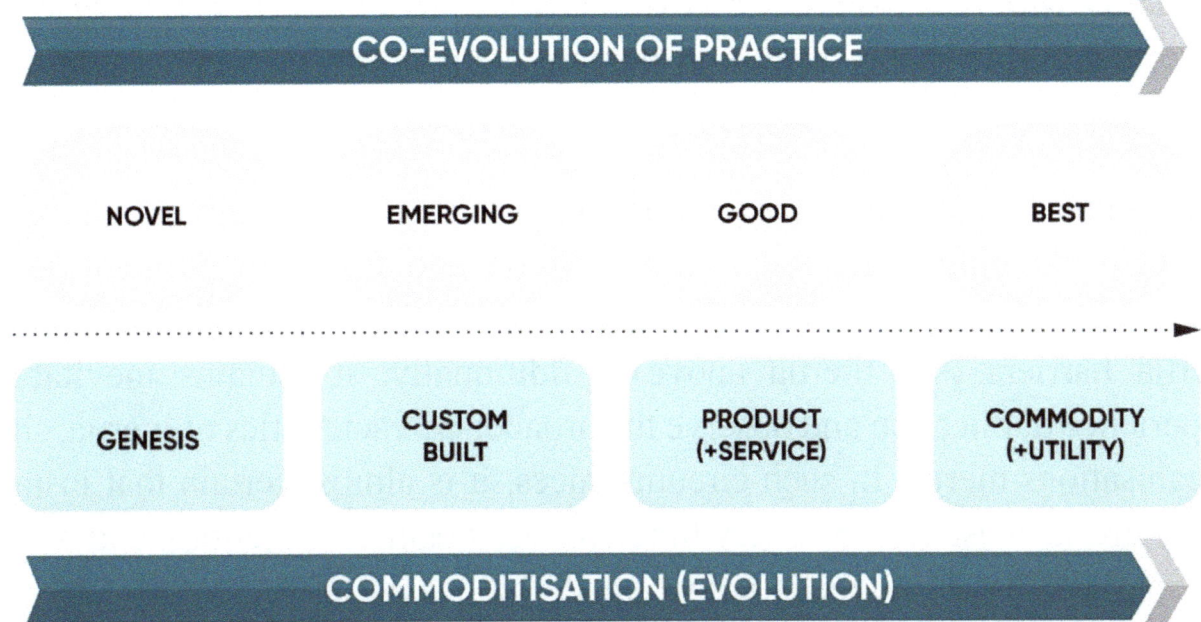

Fig 2.9 illustrates the co-evolution of practice, in tandem to the phases of commoditisation

TECHNOLOGY CONTEXT

Agile methodology and 'in house' development is excellent and highly suitable in the 'emergent' or 'uncharted' state, and very weak in the industrialised state, whereas Six Sigma, Waterfall, ITIL and outsourcing are strong in the industrialised state, yet weak in the emergent. Methods such as Lean and occasionally Scrum as well as Waterfall, are more suitable in the transitional states in between. As new technologies begin to evolve into products and propositions, focus tends to increase in reducing waste, removing duplication and improving efficiency. Thus a *co-evolution of practice* is to be expected in alignment with each phase of maturation (evolution) towards industrialisation.

In the emergent state, the characteristics of a new innovation are novel, chaotic, uncertain, unpredictable, changing, different, exciting, as well as a potential source of future worth and highly differential in nature. By contrast, in the industrialised state, the characteristics of the identical artefact will be ordered, known, measured, stable, dull, low margin and essential.

Since commoditisation is fuelled by competition, duplication will occur, both internally within a business, and externally within a market. The latter is to be expected, and is highly visible to potential customers, as well as vital to the commoditisation (evolutionary) process.

The former is less visible (see Value Chains above) and symptomatic of poor strategic planning, fractured communication and frictional political barriers within organisations (Conway's Law). These are signature characteristics of inertia barriers (see Inertia above). Additionally, it remains inevitable to experience duplication and observe the broader characteristics of inertia, should organisations merge. In such circumstances, it is almost certain that instantly, there are at least two of everything. Roles, business functions and systems (people, processes and technology) are all duplicated.

Duplication within a business is of greater prevalence with functions, processes, services and technology systems, which are in a pre-industrialised state. The greater the scale of the organisation and the greater the entrenchment of methodology, as well as differential culture, the greater the proliferation of duplication and other inefficiencies will be evident.

Businesses may combat this phenomenon by organising the company's structure in order to reflect its varying states of commoditisation, whereby, the organisation's value chains will be optimal. In doing so, the business may apply the appropriate methodology in each of its organisational units. This is achieved by three commoditisation profiles (Uncharted, Transitional & Industrialised), which are synonymous with the roles and characteristics of *Innovators*, *Optimisers* and *Curators*.

If a business were to organise its people, processes, and methodology around these three cultural profiles which are synonymous with each culture, aptitude and attitude, this should enhance productivity and ultimately drive superior outcomes for the organisation.

INNOVATORS

The *Innovators*, by their nature and the R&D in which they are engaged, will function best through exploiting methodologies such as Agile, Scrum, SAFe and eXtreme Programming (XP), whereby their work product is developed in-house.

OPTIMISERS

The *Optimisers* will engage well using a collaboration of in-house and outsourced resources, using commodity off-the-shelf (COTS) tools (or products), as well as exploiting capabilities to develop products and propositions. Additionally, they will perform some internal business functions such as finance, treasury and procurement (see Secondary Activities, Value Chains above). These functions are conducive to Lean processes, and in some instances Scrum, as well as Waterfall methodology (such as PRINCE2).

CURATORS

Finally, the *Curators*, which by nature work in the industrialised (commoditised) state. The *Curators* exploit repeatable processes and functions, predominantly abstracted by, or insulated and outsourced to third-parties, which are engaged in negligible incremental variance. In this instance, Six Sigma, outsourcing and the use of Key Performance Indicators (KPIs) and Service Level Agreements (SLAs) is optimal. The latter being signature characteristics of frameworks, such as, the Information Technology Information Library (ITIL). Collectively, these methodologies and instrumentation is optimally suited to the industrialised state, whereby, the characteristics thereof are qualitatively and quantitatively measurable.

The goal is to cultivate a culture conducive to the various phases of commoditisation and to enable work product from each group to cascade to the next, as it matures during the natural progression of its lifecycle.

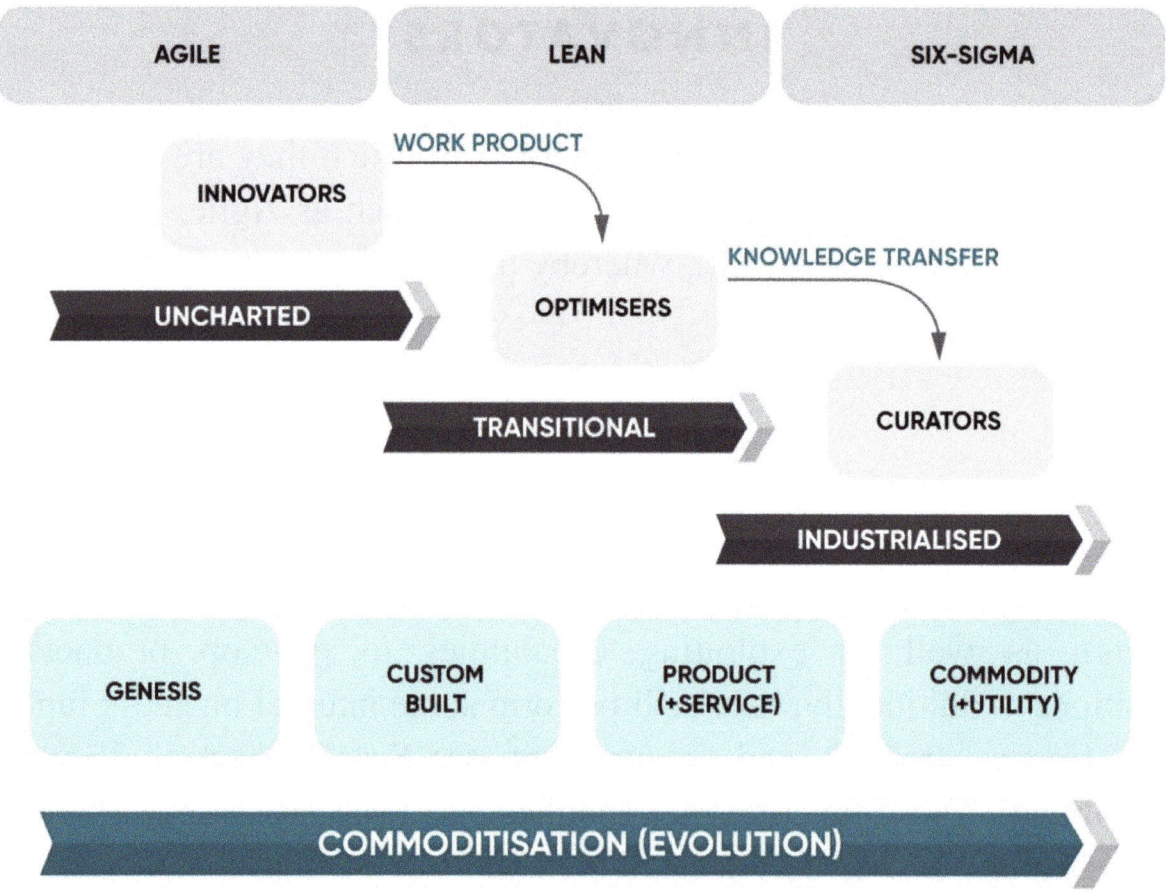

Fig 2.10 Cascading Work Product/Knowledge and methods synonymous with Commoditisation

The key to success in this regard, is to balance and to evolve through continuous learning. Recognition, that as concepts and artefacts evolve, so does the culture and practices, as well as business models that surround them, are essential. Without the accompanying co-evolution, inertia barriers form and ultimately overwhelm the entity, eventually resulting in catastrophic failure. A common short-coming in large organisations is the tendency to outsource too much, which while economically palatable and sensible for its industrialised functions and services, conversely attracts unfavourably high variances in the costs incurred to new innovations and initiatives. This is prevalent in an organisation which may outsource its technology assets and operations to systems integrators (SIs), and subsequently lack the capacity or necessary budget to build a new innovative application or service. This may be due to the associated 'change control' costs that the systems integrator will charge, in order to facilitate the change.

This imbalance tends to manifest in further duplication and inefficiency by cultivating the requirement to build parallel functionality in-house, accruing duplication and variance as well as technical debt, which in turn, undermines the value of the outsourcing arrangement. Thereby, creating a false economy. This practice is synonymous with another tendency in larger organisations, which is to standardise processes and methods across the organisation. A frame of thinking which attempts to make a business more efficient, however, cripples the entity in cultivating an environment as well as culture in which to innovate (see Innovation Paradox above). Furthermore, standardised organisational processes act as constraints to bring about an ordered system. Whereas innovation (synonymous with exaptation in this context), is more likely to occur in environments which resemble either a chaotic or complex system (see Prologue). Essentially, cultivating environments which lend themselves to interdisciplinary and first principles thinking (see First Principles, Chapter 4: Surfacing Utility). An example of such is the development of the Scaled Agile Framework (SAFe), which is an attempt to apply Agile methodology at scale while incorporating elements which are either transitional or industrialised, a state as well as context in which Agile is inherently weaker. Another such example is that of business intelligence and consultancy firm, Gartner's 'Bimodal' paradigm. An emulsion of elements of DevOps, ITIL as well as Agile and Waterfall.

In order to reduce inefficiencies such as those brought about by duplication as well as the dogmatic application of universal methodology or emulsions thereof, this is where Tzu's factor of *doctrine* (see Competition above) may be applied. *Doctrine* may take the form of an approach to guiding the suitable or appropriate methodologies being applied by the organisation. An example of which is that of 'Fast, Inexpensive, Simple & Tiny' (FIST), which was pioneered by the US Air Force.

The FIST doctrine was devised by retired US Air Force Lt. Col. Dan Ward, and promoted in his book 'F.I.R.E.: How Fast, Inexpensive, Restrained and Elegant Methods Ignite Innovation,' published in 2014. [32] Ward's military career spanned more than two decades, specialising in leading high-speed, low-cost technology development programmes. FIST is an evolution of the National Aeronautic and Space Administration (NASA), 'Faster, Better & Cheaper' (FBC) approach from the 1990s. FIST defines an approach that exploits a small team of talented individuals working within tight time and resource constraints, while adhering to a particular set of principles and practices.

Since technologies are constantly evolving through innovation, *componentisation* and *commoditisation*, the principles, practices and associated *doctrine* should be expected to co-evolve with them.

Paradigms such as FIST, thrive in environments with rapidly changing contexts (which are conducive to exaptation) and are synonymous with exploiting methodologies such as Agile.

Another by-product of *componentisation* is that of abstraction (or insulation). This is evident when illustrating the evolution towards cloud computing.

ABSTRACTION

Abstraction is a term of art, used to describe the various layers of complexity in the computational stack. From a commoditisation perspective, the genesis occurred with the arrival of the Z3 in 1941, marking the original innovation. Later, followed by custom built examples (including Prototypes), such as the Lyons Electronic Office (LEO) system in 1951, and ERMA in 1955. The introduction of the IBM 650 in 1953 emerged as a product. The products evolved into commodity computers by the 1990s and into utilities known as cloud services in the 2000s (see Chapter 3: Ecosystems).

When examining the evolution of applications through this lifecycle, a noteworthy observation is that at both the *genesis* as well as the *custom built* phases, the application was tightly-integrated with the hardware.

As these technologies evolved through the lifecycle of commoditisation, so did the abstraction of applications evolve through componentisation, evolving from monolithic architectures, which were tightly-coupled and integrated, to insulated and abstracted architectures, which became loosely-coupled (componentised).

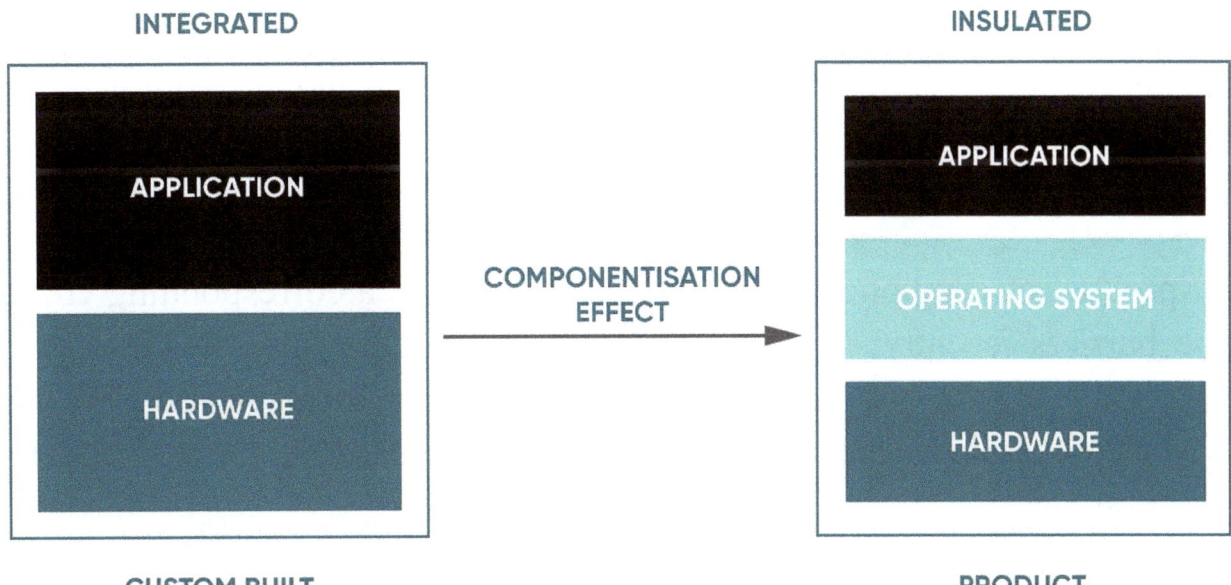

Fig 2.11 the abstraction effect of componentisation in the transition from 'Custom Built' to 'Product' (Computing)

With each iteration of componentised abstraction arrives with it a reduction in complexity. This was evident though the creation of operating systems (OS), which insulated applications from the hardware as well as the emergence of programming languages, such as Assembler (Assembly Language), which abstracted machine code. Programming languages such as ANSI C as well as C++ abstracted Assembler and subsequently facilitated the emergence of programming languages and accompanying abstraction frameworks, such as Java. With each abstraction iteration, a reduction in complexity is experienced, accompanied by further componentisation and the requirement for new architectures, new practices, new culture and new doctrine via *Creative Destruction*.

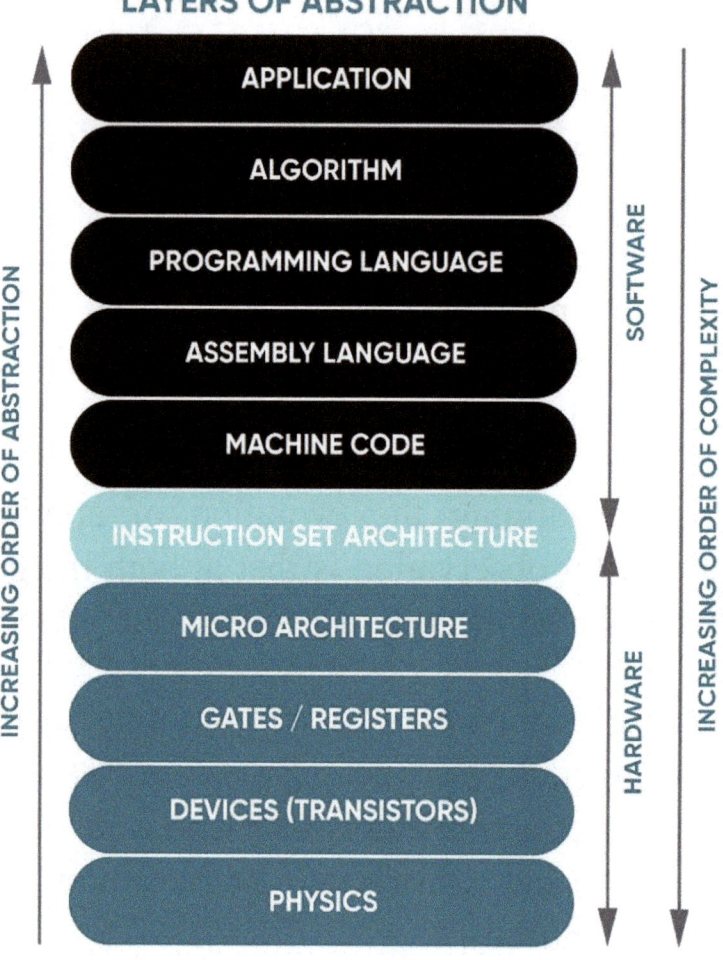

A by-product of componentisation and abstraction is a corresponding erosion in the barriers to entry. Consider the skills required if a software engineer needed soldering and wire wrap skills in order to create an application. Whether it is word processing, video editing or programming, everything benefits from abstraction.

HIGHER-ORDER SYSTEMS

The emergence of higher-order systems is symptomatic of componentisation and abstraction. A higher-order system is a system which forms a new source of value and future worth. These may emerge as the result of one or more innovations, however, are underpinned by one or more existing technologies, business models and/or processes. Higher-order systems leverage these previous advancements to displace their relative position in a value chain. This is a natural function of *Creative Destruction*, facilitated frequently by standardisation and componentisation.

Consider higher-order systems through the lens of an industrial revolution. As mentioned above, *energy, communications* and *mobility* are the three innovation factors which trigger an industrial revolution.

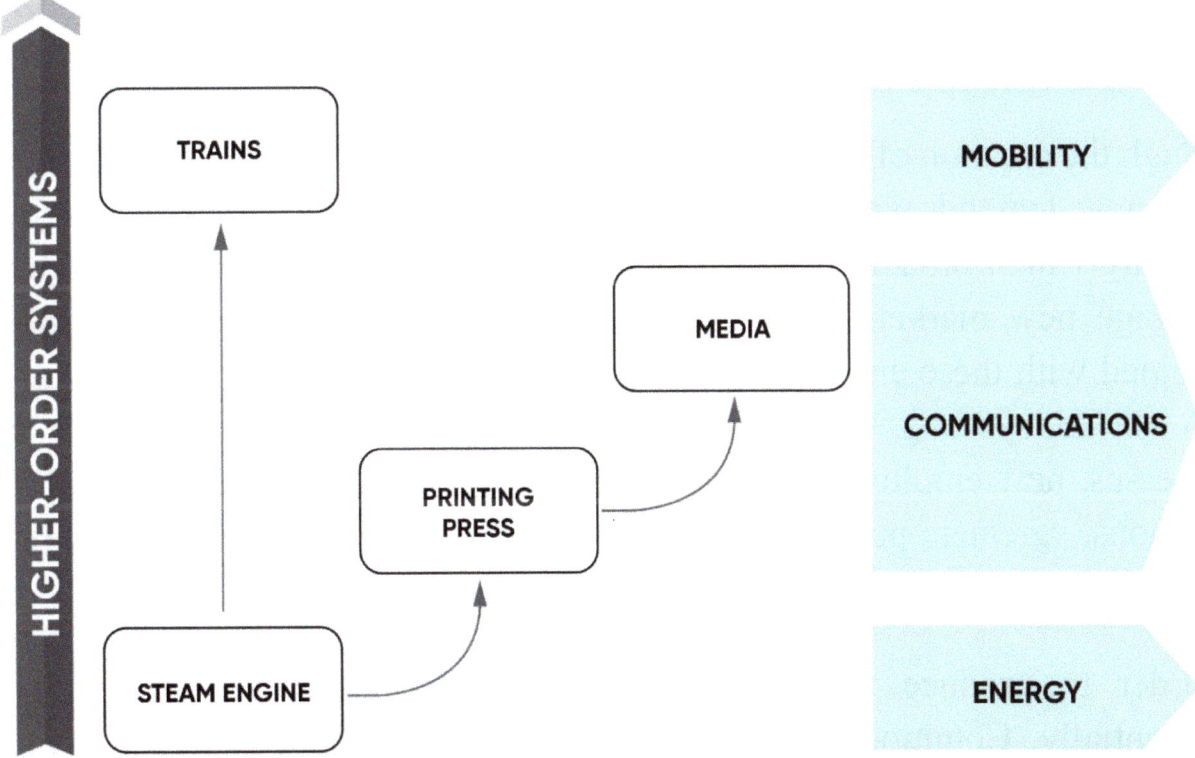

Fig 2.13 Higher-Order Systems – first industrial revolution (1760 - 1840)

These three capabilities formed an emulsion of productivity enablers, reciprocally driving standardisation and commoditisation through competition. Along this pathway, fuelled by competition and proliferation, each became better understood, increasingly standardised and cheaper to manufacture. These factors imposed downward pressure on prices, forcing greater efficiency through better practices and fuelling increasing consumerism. All the while, this enabled inertia barriers to form, cultivating an inertia-to-change, prompting new disruptors to emerge, creating further innovations and new higher-order systems, accompanied by the emergence of new business models and new practices. Each iteration disintermediating the previous incumbents and disrupting the value chain with new sources of value and future worth, via *Creative Destruction.*

These manifested in the form of emerging industries, using new building methods and materials. Factories began producing new forms of goods, while an ecosystem of other new businesses emerged, supporting new forms of media, as well as new appetites for consumerism.

COMMODIFICATION

Through the creation of new business models for marketing and producing new goods, new demands were created. Train networks emerged, creating a logistics capability which broadened the market potential for goods, people and media to engage new markets over great distances. Capital and credit expansion, combined with these enabling technologies, facilitated the emergence of these higher-order systems, following each iteration, creating new value, new businesses, new employment opportunities, improved education, better living conditions, greater productivity, greater economic velocity and greater prosperity.

In order to produce these new goods, demand for raw materials grew exponentially. Commodification describes the transformation of raw natural resources into commodities. Essentially, objects of trade.

Thus, forests are harvested for lumber, while land is transformed into real estate. In a capitalist economic system, tangible natural resources, as well as intangible resources may be commodified. The latter includes ideas, data and even people.

As new higher-order systems emerge, their underpinning foundations are progressing along a pathway of industrialisation. They are being commoditised. However, as this process unfolds, raw materials transformed in the process are commodified. As these advance along this pathway, they descend within the value chain, building an inertia-to-change, facilitating *Creative Destruction* through new innovation. This subsequently makes way for the new higher-order system(s) to emerge at the value chain apex. Thus, this facilitates the emergence of the instrumentation to create and nurture ecosystems.

3

ECOSYSTEMS

In biological terms, an ecosystem is a community of interacting organisms and their physical environment. In general terms, it is a complex network or interconnected system. The concept of a business ecosystem was promoted by James F. Moore in the 1990s.

Moore's definition of this analogy is detailed in his book, 'The Death of Competition: Leadership and Strategy in the Age of Business Ecosystems.'

Moore initially pioneered the concept in a Harvard Business Review article, in which he defined a 'business ecosystem' as:

'An economic community supported by a foundation of interacting organisations and individuals—the organisms of the business world. The economic community produces goods and services of value to customers, who are themselves members of the ecosystem. The member organisms also include suppliers, lead producers, competitors, and other stakeholders. Over time, they coevolve their capabilities and roles, and tend to align themselves with the directions set by one or more central companies. Those companies holding leadership roles may change over time, but the function of ecosystem leader is valued by the community because it enables members to move toward shared visions to align their investments, and to find mutually supportive roles.'

- James F. Moore, 'Predators and Prey: A New Ecology of Competition,' HBR, May/June 1993.

Moore's introduction and use of ecological metaphors and nomenclature represented a pivotal shift in the paradigm of how we interpret the world of business, economics and technology.

Through the lens of an ecology, a particular business may be interpreted as an organism that occupies a niche, which may be challenged by a newly arriving species. In the finance arena, this is the manner in which many interpret the sphere of FinTech. Essentially, giving rise to a new species, disrupting, infesting and/or modifying the niche occupied by incumbent financial institutions.

This thinking is complemented by the earlier reference to Van Valen's Red Queen Hypothesis.

'The need to constantly evolve in order to stand still relative to a surrounding ecosystem.'[33]

The implication, thereof, largely addresses the dimension of innovation in congruence with *Creative Destruction*.

Moore's contentions that a company is an embedded actor within a broader business environment, and therefore, there exists a need to co-evolve with other companies, establishes the paradigm of a business ecology in which symbiotic relationships exist within the business environment. A contention reinforced by Robin Collingwood's economic philosophy regarding competitors (see Standardisation, Chapter 2: Capital Evolution).

'The presence of these two opposites together is essential to an economic system. The parties to an economic action co-operate in competing, like two chess players.'[34]

- Robin G. Collingwood, 1926.

In order to remain dominant, thrive or even survive, companies, particularly incumbent financial institutions, much like any organism, need to reconcile that they are actors within a complex adaptive system. The necessity to innovate and evolve is essential, however, there is an additional necessity to be proactive in developing mutually beneficial "symbiotic" relationships. These relationships of a mutualistic nature should be established with customers, suppliers, regulators, standards bodies and even competitors.

An isolationist philosophy, or an approach whereby reciprocity is limited, even within an entity where innovation is an entrenched trait, is unlikely to maintain either a dominant or competitive position indefinitely. This is demonstrable through the formation of trade associations and consortium standards, pioneered by competitors who benefit from a common platform that benefits all players. It is imperative to recognise that isolationist behaviours are synonymous with, and reinforce inertia barriers which companies accrue as a result of past success. A posture that additionally may fall within the sphere of 'Competence-induced Failure'[35] (see Apex Predator Hypothesis, Chapter 4: Surfacing Utility).

Returning to the concept of complex systems, it is imperative to recognise the significance of FinTech as an exaptation of technological commoditisation, co-opted for financial systems disruption and adaptation thereafter. The "Ecosystem" paradigm allows us to qualify a context for the emulsion of these two complex adaptive systems (see Prologue). Historically, finance and technology have largely evolved separately, yet reciprocally enabled one another to progress. Finance has facilitated investment in technological development and the resulting technologies have enabled finance to become further reaching, faster and more efficient. However, since the GFC, finance and technology have become "genetically" intertwined. From an omnifarious perspective, these progenitors have 'given birth' to an inter-species juxtaposition of new micro and macro ecosystems of their own, effectively forming a new nimble and 'energy efficient' ecology which challenges the dominance of the finance industries' 'Apex and Meso predators.' This altered posture challenges the existential fabric and the manner in which the finance industry is structured at both domestic as well as global strata. As with any complex system which is altered, there may be unintended consequences. It remains merely a question of what these are, how they may manifest, and when.

A principal characteristic of most complex systems and ecosystems in particular, is that they are perpetually evolving though a constant state of change. Thus, virtually never in a fixed state and therefore, highly dynamic in nature regardless of scale, both spatial and temporal. This is demonstrable through Holling's Renewal Cycle Model (Fig 3.1), which identifies ecosystem phases over time. These four phases are:

1. Exploitation   - new opportunistic species colonise

2. Conservation   - stronger, more competitive species dominate

3. Release   - ecosystem is exposed to an altering (or disruptive) influence

4. Reorganisation   - ecosystem is reorganised as a consequence thereof

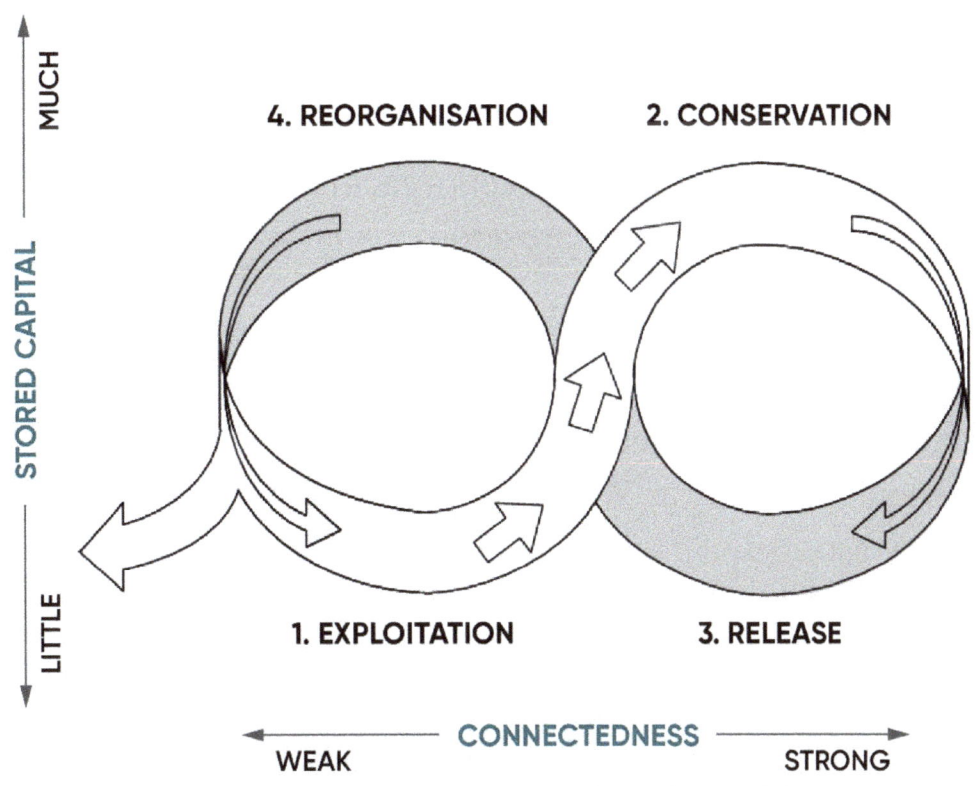

Fig 3.1 Holling's Renewal Cycle Model

In Fig 3.1 the x-axis is representative of the connectedness between 'organisms' and the y-axis represents the change in stored capital which in an ecological context represents the volume of stored biomass and nutrients, whereas in a business context, is representative of market capabilities and business potential. The arrows indicate the time spent in each phase, where one long arrow is a short period of time.[36] An ecosystem could diverge out of the cycle between the *reorganisation* phase and the *exploitation* phase, and thus, initiate a fundamentally different ecosystem cycle.[37] This is synonymous with the economic pattern of *Peace, War & Wonder* (see Chapter 2: Capital Evolution). Thus, providing an informative lens through which to examine the digital revolution and the FinTech disruption.

GENESIS OF AN ECOSYSTEM

At its core, an ecology relies on interactions between entities in order to form an ecosystem. These entities could be compared with organisms within a habitat or with business competitors in an economic marketplace. Either represents symbiotic relationships which reflexively influence one another. By way of examples, money provides a medium through which an exchange of value facilitates economic interactions within a market ecosystem. Communication is a medium through which entities interact to facilitate commerce. Both of these artefacts are componentised. They are additionally both highly standardised.

This casts a spotlight on the earlier concepts of standardisation and componentisation (see Chapter 2: Capital Evolution). In an evolutionary context, standardisation is an accelerant. In an ecological context, it plays a vital role as an interaction catalyst. With regards to componentisation, it facilitates the evolutionary ascension in value, and furthermore, provides for an ecological vehicle through which standardisation may manifest itself in the creation of entities which grow the ecosystem.

These concepts may be observed through examining an organisation that develops a valuable process or method of creating a good or service. The organisation benefits from sharing that knowledge through sponsoring industry standardisation. This may initially seem counterintuitive; however, the objective is to allow other organisations to build against and upon those standards. By doing so, the organisation is able to scale its own business by optimising its domestic outsourcing and manufacturing capabilities in the market in which it operates. With broader adoption of these standards, it enables the organisation to exploit growth opportunities in new markets by leveraging non-domestic manufacturing and distribution channels elsewhere. In adopting this approach, opportunities emerge to harness extra-organisational innovations underpinned by these standards from around the globe. By sharing their know-how through standards, competitors benefit. However, when strategically leveraged at scale, this allows the originator ('ecosystem leader,' J.F. Moore) to flourish by a superior order of magnitude.

Embracing standardisation through collective intelligence and industry co-operation is a key enabler in accelerating commoditisation, promoting competition, removing friction and creating greater consumer value. This is the fundamental means through which to build an ecosystem. An ecosystem leadership role will ultimately fall to the organisation, the standards of which, are most broadly adopted.

Consider an example of an organisation which develops a socket form-factor which both conducts electricity, as well as shares data. Should the form-factor be adopted as a national standard, the organisation will benefit from selling its products nationally, as other manufacturers develop and sell goods which use its socket. If this standard is adopted internationally, the order of magnitude for the proliferation thereof will be exponential. Thus, the associated revenues should reflect this uplift.

For the manufacturers which adopted the standard, it may be of benefit by demonstrating their credibility and competence to their stakeholders and customers. Furthermore, complying with a specific standard may be a legal obligation in some sectors. Numerous examples of this practice are evident in a broad spectrum of industries, including the automotive, aerospace, rail, vertical transport, mining and energy sectors, to name a few. Thus, should a company devise a good or service and successfully create a national, regional or global standard surrounding such an artefact, the broader adoption, thereof, will benefit the originator from the spill over and network effects across the cascading value chains. Furthermore, organisations that follow the standard set by the originator will incur a cost in designing, adapting or modifying their product or service to meet the standard. This gives the originator an additional competitive advantage.

However, new market entrants and adopters thereof, will benefit from lower barriers-to-entry and broader market potential by building upon a broadly accepted foundation. This, furthermore, benefits the originator, should a new innovation emerge, which is dependent upon the originator's standard. This is evident in the adoption of the new innovation, driving downstream demand for the originator's product upon which the innovation is dependent. This is furthermore demonstrable as higher-order systems emerge, which in turn, drives consumption of their underpinning subsystems.

Furthermore, businesses which adopt the originator's standard assists in cultivating trust in their offerings. Ultimately, this may be pursued to bolster their own credibility, rather than for the direct benefit of their customers. However, the originator benefits more broadly as adoption of their standards proliferate.

This is the unequivocal power of global standardisation in the forging of a business ecosystem.

In such a paradigm, peripheral manufacturers and competitors benefit from these symbiotic relationships by being able to fabricate fewer industry variations with better defined tolerances, resulting in higher quality and consistency. Improved communication and co-operation has encouraged better practices to emerge and mature, creating focused, rather than disparate skills and methods.

The originator and sponsors of these efforts benefit from a network effect, via leveraging the peripheral industries domestically and abroad to grow its business through global economies of scale, enabling greater penetration of new markets worldwide. This represents the manner in which the commoditisation of an industry may be influenced, and through the growth thereof, an ecosystem may emerge. The ecosystem participants may include all manner of actors within the value chain, from manufacturers to suppliers and service providers to value-added resellers, as well as distributors.

The resulting superior economic performance of the originator typically yields a significant return on investment, when contrasted with the necessary investment directed towards industry standardisation.

TECHNOLOGY ECOSYSTEMS

In an internet-centric ecosystem, the core originator ('ecosystem leader,' J.F. Moore) typically exposes its capability or service via an Application Programming Interface (API). The API allows the originator to insulate its internal systems, processes and data from the outside world, while providing a secure interface to third-parties in exchange for a fee.

The API acts much like an adaptor between a power socket and an appliance. The consumer may be unaware of how power is generated behind the socket, however, understands that power is generated and will incur a fee for its consumption on a utility basis. The power is necessary to run the appliance, which in turn, provides the consumer with a service or outcome.

APIs facilitate a 'loosely coupled' relationship between services and consumers. This form of componentisation promotes better practices such as idempotent behaviours, reducing variance, improving quality and enabling greater focus toward creating new forms of value through innovation and digitisation.

APIs provide functional interfaces and communication protocols between parties to access data and transact securely in real time. This may be exploited to facilitate frictionless coordination across internal business functions, as well as with external parties. Financial Institutions (FIs) may exploit APIs in order to structure and distribute products or services, via third-party channels. Additionally, organisations may leverage APIs in order to engage external capabilities or services, via third-party APIs, in order to execute critical operations without the necessity to engage in lengthy inter-organisational technology integrations. Consequently, development teams within all manner of organisations are moving towards an internal service-orientated architecture (*Co-evolution of practice*) in order to enable both the internal componentisation, as well as the external exposure of APIs for third-party consumption.

Through building a new innovative service surrounding one or more APIs, an increasingly complex system emerges. Such new services may emerge as higher-order systems, or end-consumer services. Through leveraging APIs, an ecology begins to emerge.

API ECONOMY

As its name suggests, an API is a computerised interface around which an application can be programmed. Building applications around APIs enables abstraction (see Abstraction, Chapter 2: Capital Evolution) of the underlying systems and simplifies the programming required by exposing pre-defined objects, resources and actions that the developer may leverage in its use.

An API defines the types of 'calls' (requests/interactions) that can be made, how to make such calls, the associated data types and the formats, as well as any programming conventions to follow.

APIs enable modularity between applications, and hence, systems, as well as between business entities (via computerised services). The conceptual introduction of an API is largely credited to British computer scientists, Sir. Maurice Vincent Wilkes (1913 - 2010) and David John Wheeler (1927 - 2004), who pioneered modular software libraries for the Electronic Delay Storage Automatic Calculator (EDSAC) in the 1940s.

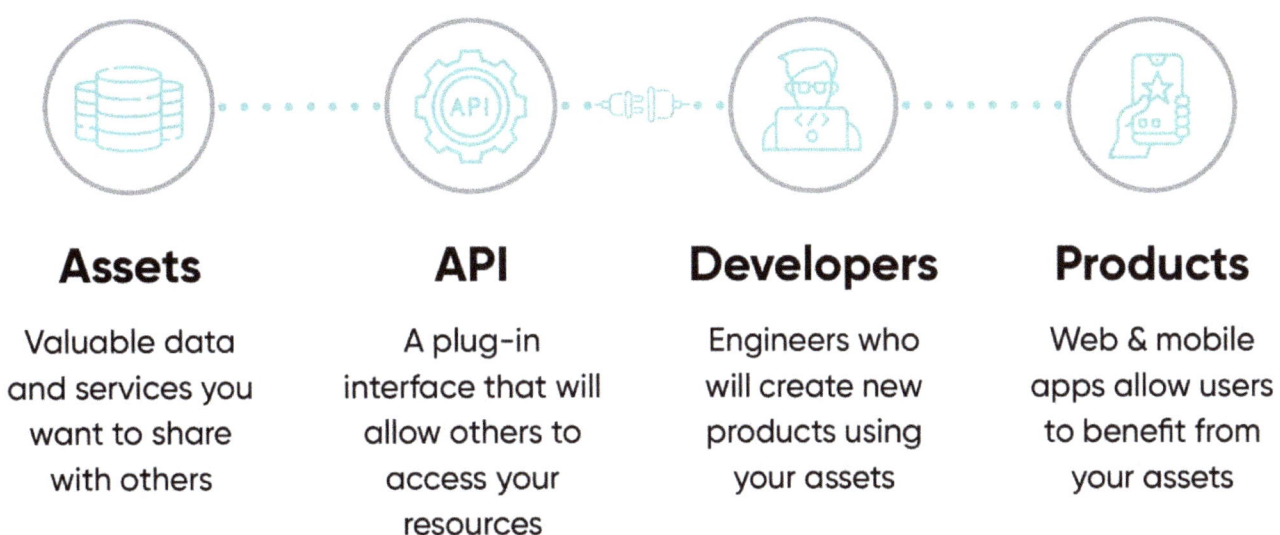

Assets
Valuable data and services you want to share with others

API
A plug-in interface that will allow others to access your resources

Developers
Engineers who will create new products using your assets

Products
Web & mobile apps allow users to benefit from your assets

Fig 3.2. APIs play a significant role in insulating assets and facilitating modularity (componentisation).

An API economy is best described as a 'loosely coupled' service centric or modular ecology of component services, which are leveraged by one another and/or a technology application, to yield an outcome. An example of this phenomenon is an e-commerce website. As e-commerce websites emerged in the 1990s, the computational power and data storage was provided by tightly coupled servers, and either internal or external data storage subsystems. Typically, the servers would run independent services, predominantly in the form of databases, applications and web services.

Although the servers themselves were largely a commodity at this juncture, each server was generally dedicated to, and specifically optimised for a unique role or series of tasks. Generally these roles would fit within the spheres of either an application, a web service or database. These single-role (uni-polar) practices were enabled through the proliferation of inexpensive rack-mountable commodity computers and the growing popularity of Microsoft's graphical processor-independent multi-user server operating system, known as New Technology (NT). Introduced in 1993, Microsoft's NT operating system (originally embarked upon as a joint development with IBM), coupled with

Microsoft's easy-to-manage database and web service applications, dramatically lowered the barrier-to-entry for training 'Microsoft Engineers' (server administrators). Microsoft Certified Systems Engineers (MCSEs) could typically be trained and certified in a matter of weeks. Inexpensive servers, coupled with an abundance of expediently available MCSE 'graduates' in the market, acted as an accelerant in amplifying the volume of servers and data centres deployed, particularly while the 'Dot Com' boom drove a frenzy of demand among new market entrants (see Dot Com, Chapter 10: Financialisation).

These uni-polar practices were further reinforced by poor-stability and performance expectations from these low-cost commodity systems. A condition which was exacerbated by limited random access memory (RAM) addressability in thirty-two-bit commodity computers. Hence, greater volumes of servers were purchased and deployed in order to spread the load (through load-balancing) and mitigate the risk (of intermittent failures). Coupled with numerous security vulnerabilities, these factors influenced the development of network-layer security capabilities such as firewalls, load-balancers and routers, which accompanied a co-evolution of development in network architectures that were designed to police and shape the network traffic between public (demilitarised zones or 'DMZs') and internal facing services. A series of architectural practices which were reinforced by the necessity for load management, business continuity planning and security segmentation.

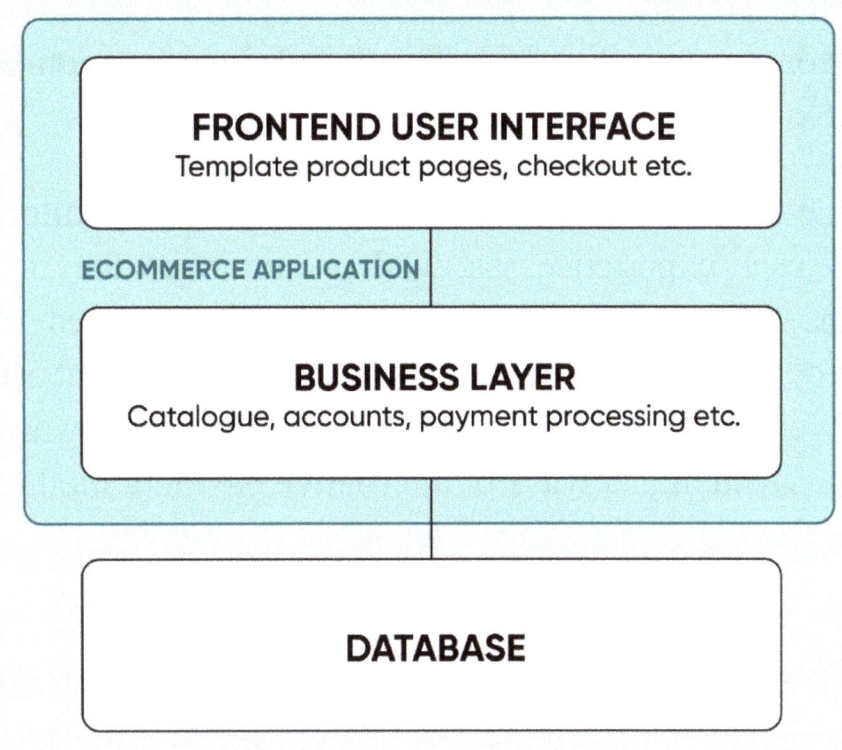

Fig 3.3 an example of a monolithic, 'tightly-coupled' e-commerce web architecture

In this era, the e-commerce website would be custom coded (programmed), the web server would then be tightly integrated with the database server using either product-specific, or in rare cases, standardised connectors. The application server would typically be tightly integrated between the two (web and database) in order to house the business logic underpinning the e-commerce website. Each implementation was different and as a novel and emerging use of technology, there were no best practices or well-defined products. This is reminiscent of, what today, is known as a layered architectural pattern (also known as an n-tier architecture). Layered architectures typically tend to reflect the communications structure within the business entities within which they may be applied. An example of Conway's Law (see Inertia, Chapter 2: Capital Evolution). Typically, components within a layered architecture pattern are arranged into horizontal layers, whereby, each layer fulfils a specific role in order to realise the desired business outcome. Most layered architectures consist of four standard layers. These are *presentation, business, persistence* and *database*. However, in some instances, it is not uncommon for the *business* and *persistence* layers to be consolidated into a single business layer. This is particularly common when the persistence logic is embedded within the business layer components (Fig 3.3). This was fairly common in many of the early e-commerce implementations.

Hence, all such e-commerce capabilities were individually tailored to enhance the customer's user experience, as well as engineer the user journey to maximise online sales conversions. This generally required further custom programming to incorporate product entries into the database in order to populate the website. Additional custom development was required for integration with payment gateways or alternative payment methods, in order to accept payment from customers (see Chapter 5: Payments).

With growing success and adoption over time, these elements were organically metamorphosed into, or supplemented with custom developed and tightly-integrated applications. Examples of such were Customer Relationship Management (CRMs) systems, accounting and treasury applications as well as inventory management systems (Business Layer, Fig 3.3).

Invariably, these environments were complex systems with significant interoperability challenges and a mesh of applications as well as technology infrastructure interdependencies. The stack of technology was heterogeneous in nature; a veritable 'fruit salad' of technologies, vendors, products and customisations. Examples included blended environments incorporating proprietary systems such as Mainframes and 'open systems' which included vendor distributed UNIX variants. These systems, although powerful and reliable, required substantial investment in hardware, software, hosting and maintenance.

The introduction of Berkley Software Distributions (BSDs), as well as Microsoft NT, and the then nascent open-source Linux processor-independent operating systems, were designed to run on low-cost commodity servers, as well as embedded hardware systems which radically increased the complexity. These latter systems, which could exploit hardware powered by Intel (and later AMD) central processing units (CPUs), were far less expensive to procure, however, less stable and mature – thus, requiring greater staffing resources and expertise. Each of these computational operating system platforms were constrained to using a specific set of third-party or natively distributed databases, applications, shell interpreters (for systems programming), application programming languages, as well as web services.

The proliferation of competing application, database, network and data storage technologies during this period, amplified the complexity incomprehensibly. The 1990s represented an exceptionally challenging and chaotic period in which to introduce, grow, manage or maintain technology within businesses. The variances would often lead to the inefficient use of resources. It was a costly period, during which companies required varied skills, data centre facilities as well as numerous staff, methods, practices and architectures. All of these factors led to poor allocation of capital and uncontrolled operational expenditures.

In the modern world of utility (cloud) computing, these capabilities are highly industrialised, hence, measurable and predictable. These capabilities are surfaced through a portfolio of loosely-coupled utility services available on a 'menu' in a marketplace of competitive providers. These utilities are componentised and commoditised (see Chapter 2: Capital Evolution).

By contrast, building an e-commerce website in the cloud era is largely frictionless and expedient. A cloud-based e-commerce site provider offers a plethora of options between themes and templates to populate corporate branding and artwork. The proposition allows the proprietor (merchant) to create a product catalogue and integrate payment capabilities and payment methods, from a variety of FinTech providers. This can be achieved without programming (no-code), as objects are pre-defined, modular and reusable. However, customised programming (typically low-code) may be added to certain aspects when and where required. Cloud-based accounting software for an entire business may be seamlessly integrated. Furthermore, cloud-based inventory and supply chain management may either populate the product catalogue or integrate fully with the website system. All of these services are available from varied Software-as-a-Service (SaaS) companies and communicate seamlessly through a loosely-coupled service-orientated architecture (SOA), via their respective APIs. All the charges for these services are metered on a consumption, transactional or subscription basis as (cloud) utilities.

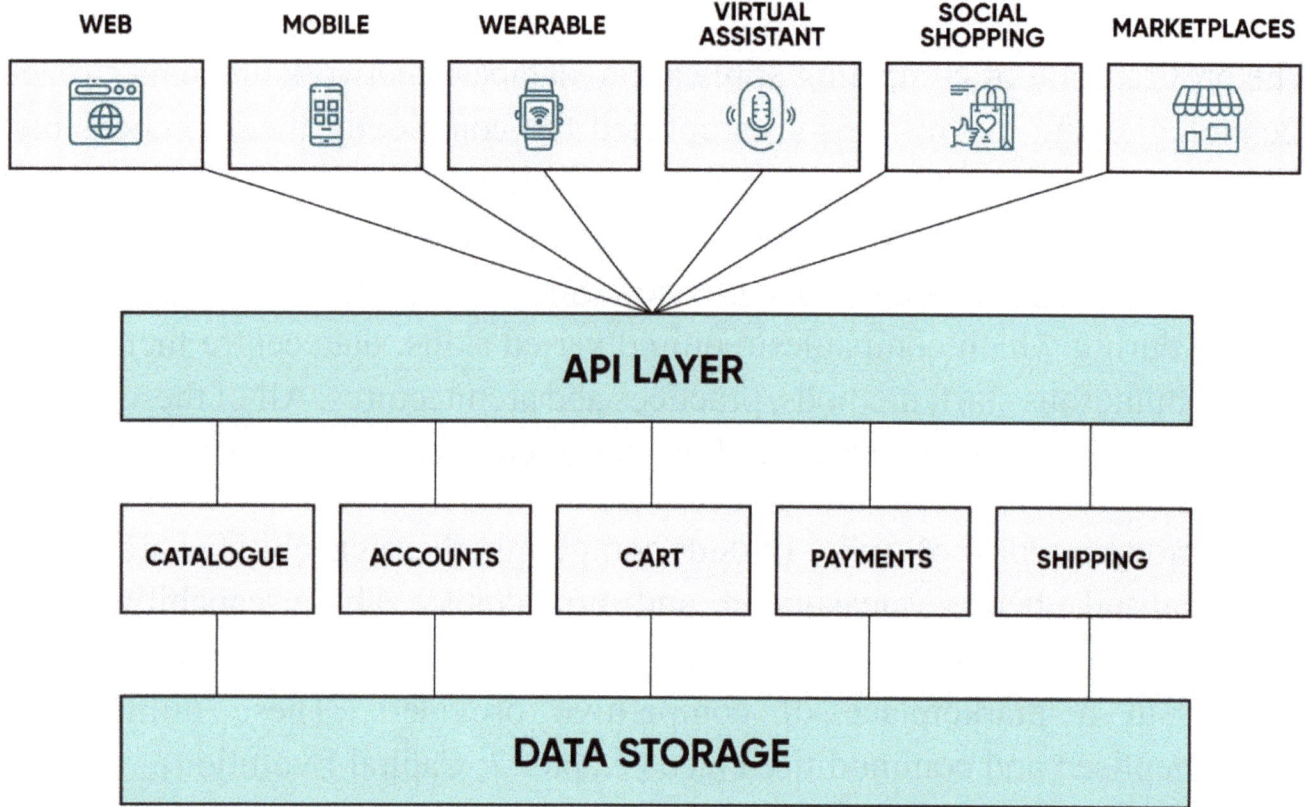

Fig 3.4 'headless' loosely-coupled and horizontally-layered 'modular' e-commerce architecture

Consequently, a merchant or B2B enterprise may create and manage an e-commerce capability within a few hours, off-balance sheet, with no IT staff and no capital investment. Furthermore, this may be instantly integrated and exposed across multiple sales channels, via the API economy (Fig 3.4). By contrast in the 1990s, a single interface web proposition required significant upfront capital investment and substantial operational expenditure to employ IT, as well as project management staff. These represented expensive human resources, combined with data centres (hosting capacity), internet service providers and extensive development and customisation. Months, if not years, would elapse to accomplish what can now be achieved in a few hours, with negligible expertise and minimal expenditure.

APIs typically use technology agnostic communication protocols, such as HyperText Transfer Protocol (HTTP) (see Communication Technology, Chapter 2: Capital Evolution). In instances such as those of interactive services which require the exchange of credentials, secure interactions with the services are required. These interactions call for the use of HTTPS, which is a secure version of the HTTP protocol and a typical necessity in the development of Financial APIs. HTTP is used to communicate with external consumers (web browsers, mobile apps), as well as other APIs. Typical commands (known as HTTP requests) which correlate to database operations 'Create, Read, Update and Delete' (CRUD) are executed via HTTP methods, such as:

- GET - retrieve a single item or a collection of items
- POST - add an item to a collection
- PUT - replace an existing collection
- PATCH - edit/modify an item that already exists in a collection
- DELETE - delete an item in a collection

This affords developers enormous versatility in the programming languages, as well as flexibility in the choices of technologies required to create the service. These factors facilitate the role in creating interfaces which provide a degree of insulation. As all such dependencies are insulated (or abstracted), via common interfaces, this affords developers significant latitude to be creative and responsive to a rapidly evolving business climate.

Although this should be expected to evolve, the most common paradigm for structuring the HTTP communications between services and consumers, via an API, is accomplished through the use of a RESTful architectural approach. RESTful is an accepted term of art, when describing the use of a Representational State Transfer architecture.

Representational State Transfer (REST), is an architectural system centred around resources and hypermedia, via HTTP protocols. CRUD is a cycle aimed at maintaining permanent records in a database setting. CRUD principles are mapped to REST commands to comply with the goals of RESTful architecture. The REST architecture defines the constraints to be used in creating web services, particularly where interactive (bi-directional) HTTP traffic is expected to be prevalent. REST constraints are as follows:

- Client-Server Mandate
- Stateless
- Cache
- Interface/Uniform contract
- Layered System
- Code-on-Demand (optional)

RESTful web services allow the requesting (client) software or application to access and manipulate text-based representations of resources by using a consistent and predefined set of stateless operations, via HTTP methods. These typically include CRUD operations, which are mapped to REST commands (HTTP methods) as follows:

- POST ⟶ CREATE
- GET ⟶ READ
- PUT ⟶ UPDATE (Replace)
- PATCH ⟶ UPDATE (Modify)
- DELETE ⟶ DELETE

The stateless characteristic is fundamental to enabling the loose-coupling of API enabled services in interacting with one another. The client-server mandate underscores the scalability of the RESTful approach through enabling it to be distributed. Each service has multiple capabilities and listens for requests, which are either accepted or rejected. Hence, clients to the service may be local or external, few or numerous, making it highly scalable. Statelessness infers that requests contain all the necessary information to prompt a response from the service, therefore, it is transactional in nature. Caching assists in partially mitigating the constraints associated with being stateless. An example of which, could be a cached response, which may avoid the necessity to resubmit an identical request. A uniform contract ensures that one interface is distributed by hypermedia connections, which in turn, prevents the use of multiple self-contained interfaces being embedded within an API. Layering ensures that multiple layers are used to grow and expand an interface, however, while preventing each layer from piercing into one another. This allows for new capabilities to be added without compromising the original commands and functions of the API interface. Code-on-demand facilitates the separation of logic between clients and servers, allowing them to be independently updated.[38]

Another architecture, although not as prevalent as it once was, is the Simple Object Access Protocol (SOAP). While SOAP and REST share similarities in leveraging the HTTP protocol, SOAP is constrained to a greater extent in its messaging patterns than REST. The constraints in a SOAP architecture make it challenging for developers to achieve any level of standardisation. REST, as an architecture, does not require processing and is more flexible by nature. Both, REST and SOAP, rely on coherent conventions and practices that developers have largely harmonised upon, in the interests of seamlessly exchanging data and facilitating compatibility. Other common architectures were that of Common Object Request Broker Architecture (CORBA) and Remote Method Invocation (RMI), a Java programming based approach to API development.

The componentisation and abstraction made possible by APIs enables the API economy to be competitive, highly versatile and economically palatable for businesses to build new services and capabilities expediently, efficiently as well as cost effectively. Furthermore, the exposure of inter-service, and more importantly, inter-company APIs, allows an ecosystem to grow, innovate and evolve organically.

MICROSERVICES

A Microservice, is as the name implies, a small collection of programmed business functions which create a form of technology enabled service. Unlike monolithic applications, a Microservice is a self-contained 'piece of functionality,' with clearly demarcated boundaries. This enables Microservices to function as separately deployable units, each of which may be easily deployed through a streamlined delivery pipeline. Microservices interface with external components or a combination of internal and external components. Microservices will generally interface with one or more external components, via one or more APIs to enable a flexible as well as modular architecture in contemporary application development.

The critical concept surrounding this architecture pattern is that each Microservice is a service component. Each service component is modular, which can vary in granularity to form either a small or large proportion of the overall business application. Furthermore, these components are intended to be capable of being part of a distributed environment. Thus, enabling this architecture pattern to benefit from superior scalability and deployment capabilities.

At a fundamental level, Microservices are business logic functions (or classes), cocooned around an interactive web service (typically an API). These serve as single-purpose modules in order to perform a specific task. Alternatively, Microservices may be accessible, via another form of remote access protocol. However, more commonly, Microservices are remotely accessed as web services.

As with all web services, content is served and formatted via mark-up languages to web clients (including web browsers) via HTTP. In 1993, the HyperText

Mark-up Language (HTML) emerged, which remains the most common of mark-up languages. HTML was derived from the Standard Generalised Mark-up Language (SGML), based on the ISO 8879 standard, which emerged in 1986. These mark-up languages were designed to format documents for consumption, via the web.

In 1996, the Extensible Mark-up Language (XML) emerged with the aim of standardising the encoding of documents, via a format that would be suitable for both human, as well as machine consumption. Although the design of XML is highly focused on document formatting, the mark-up language is conducive to representing data structures ideally suited for creating web services. Consequently, web services, APIs and Microservices have all benefitted from the use of XML to structure and deliver content.

With a greater trend having emerged in language and platform independence, particularly in facilitating the API economy, the JavaScript Object Notation (JSON) emerged in the early 2000s as an open standard for both file formats, as well as data interchange formats. JSON is capable of storing and transmitting attribute value pairs, as well as other serialised value types in both human as well as machine consumable structures. JSON was first officially standardised in 2013 as ECMA-404, and later standardised under ISO/IEC 21778 in 2017. JSON is largely considered to be a 'low-overhead' alternative to XML.

In much the same manner that SOAP (see above) and XML were paired for the creation of APIs and web services, the mid 2010s onwards has seen the Microservice revolution largely dominated by API development and inter-service communication using REST (see above), paired with JSON.

The truly noteworthy paradigm shift in the use of Microservices is that a new idea or an old service capability can be rapidly brought to market by developing a 'light weight' application. Thus, an entirely new business can be built through exploiting a new method or service offering. This may be achieved by embedding the business-logic thereof within the Microservice, and leveraging the industrialised components of the surrounding API economy to bring this service to fruition.

In the FinTech sphere, many new challengers as well as incumbents have exploited this approach to build Microservices, leveraging external third-party APIs and subsequently using their Microservice(s) to expose an API of their own. APIs provide a means through which others are then able to build their services. Using this approach, novel and innovative payment instruments and financial propositions have been brought to market. This methodology creates a form of valence, whereby new complex ecosystems may emerge, grow and adapt 'organically.'

The Microservice architectural approach is intended to be light-weight and fine-grained. In monolithic applications development, iterative changes made to the codebase affects the entire application. This prompts the necessity for full regression testing prior to redeployment, even for the most superficial alterations. By way of example, if one element of the business logic within the source code (the programming code which is later compiled or interpreted) is constantly being iterated, this forces redeployment of the entire application. Redeployment expends time, resources and increases the risk profile. However, with Microservices arranged to collectively yield an outcome, one component may be updated without the necessity to recompile, retest and redeploy the others.

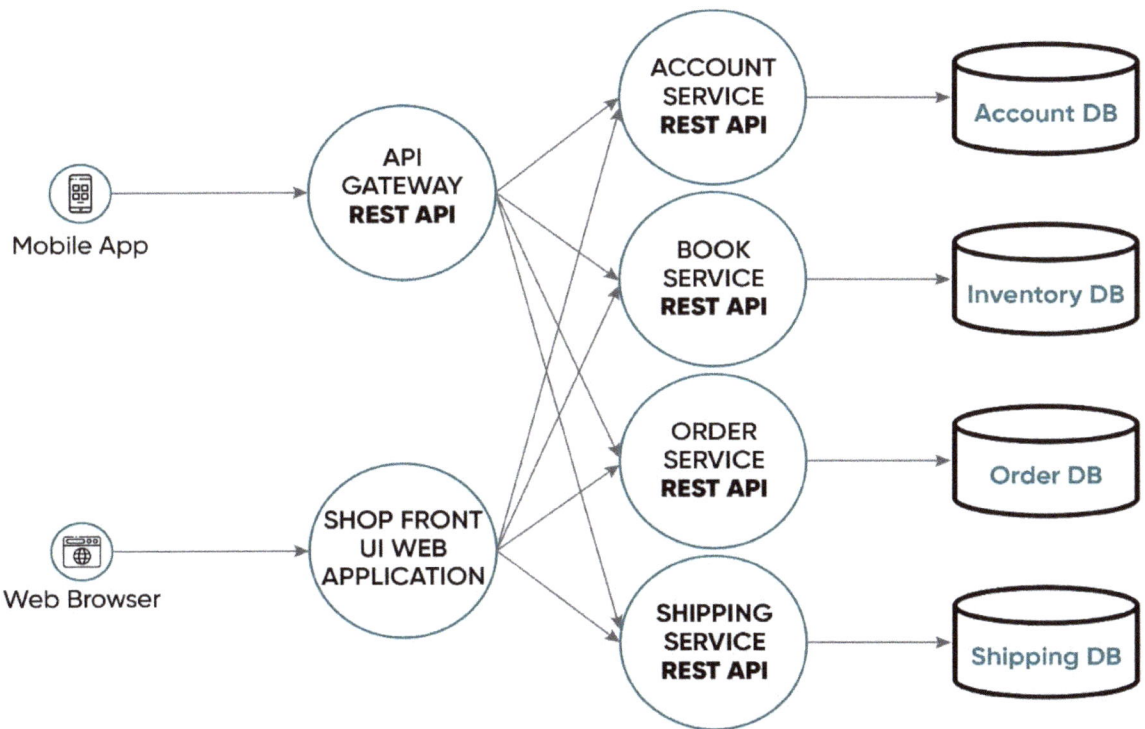

Fig 3.5 modular collection of Microservices, collectively delivering an e-commerce service

This approach additionally enables organisations of all sizes to experiment with innovation, as well as pilot and test new features, products and services with consumers. Microservices can be developed inexpensively and quickly, without investing substantial sums of capital in a concept that may or may not gain traction. Microservices are synonymous with the concept of componentisation (see Componentisation, Chapter 2: Capital Evolution), manifesting in lightweight, nimble and purpose-built applications. Since Microservices are componentised, these may be developed in numerous different programming languages and run on any platform capable of executing these programs.

The introduction and adoption of APIs, REST, XML and JSON is synonymous with the introduction and adoption of the *British Standard Whitworth System* and a co-evolution in practice, invoked in 1841 (see Standardisation, Chapter 2: Capital Evolution). These standardised components are the contemporary technological reflections of standardised screws, nuts and bolts, which accelerated development and innovation (as well as commoditisation) in the wake of the first industrial revolution.

ELASTIC CLOUD COMPUTING

SERVERLESS COMPUTING

Serverless computing represents a higher-order system, a consequence of standardisation and componentisation, with which the concept of abstraction may be reinforced (see Abstraction, Chapter 2: Capital Evolution).

The higher-order system of *serverless computing* is essentially achieved through the *commoditisation* of common objects previously embedded within applications, including those which are found in Microservices. The concept is to standardise and abstract these objects to the extent to which developers can build functions, which 'call' these objects to effect the intended outcome.

This paradigm prompts further ascension in the value chain, promoting greater granularity in componentising the creation of differentiated value. In a *serverless computing* paradigm, the cloud service provider alters its business model to assign transactional charges to the execution of the developer's functions on a usage or consumption basis. This is in contrast to hosting the application for a fee, whether it is used or not. In other words, when an application is executed, presumably the result of a customer interaction, it should conceptually be generating revenue for the organisation. It is for this usage-period and activity for which the application is exclusively charged or billed. This is measured through the use of the objects within the *serverless framework* and charged accordingly. Conceptually, this is comparable to an electrical appliance plugged into a power socket, whereby, costs are incurred exclusively for electricity consumption when the appliance is in use. If it is not used, there is no fee. Thus, synonymous with a utility.

In 2005, Fotango, a wholly-owned subsidiary of Canon Europe based in London, developed the first *serverless computing* platform under the codename "Zaphod" (named for a character in Douglas Adam's novel 'The Hitchhiker's Guide to the Galaxy,' published in 1979). The proposition was brought to market as 'Zimki' with a beta release in March 2006 and released to the general public in September 2006.[39] Zimki was a Framework-as-a-Service (FaaS) proposition which was designed to expose a JavaScript Execution Environment (front-end) and Server-Side JavaScript (back-end) to developers on a transactional utility basis. Zimki featured granular billing to the individual software 'function' level. Billing was based on storage and network resource consumption combined with JavaScript Operations (JSOPs) in the form of 'function calls.' Development, monitoring, billing and application control were all exposed through APIs. In September 2011, the National Institute of Standards and Technology (NIST) defined this category of cloud service as Platform-as-a-Service (PaaS).[40] Zimki was a multi-tenant utility-computing (cloud) platform designed to allow developers to create applications inexpensively and to scale-up seamlessly (elastically), as demand for their applications increased.

Despite Zimki's instantaneous success, subsequent growth, as well as profitability from its inception, it was soon shut down indefinitely by the parent company in 2007. Canon Europe was engaged in a major outsourcing and restructuring programme at the time. This cultivated an unreceptive climate in which to champion an innovation outside of Canon's core business comfort zone. By contrast, Amazon, which originally came to market as an online bookseller, brought its Simple Storage Service (S3) and Elastic Compute Cloud (EC2), its flagship cloud services to market in March and August 2006 respectively. These Infrastructure-as-a-Service (IaaS) propositions eventually evolved into the 'anchors' of the Amazon Web Services (AWS) portfolio.

Under the leadership of Simon Wardley,[41] Fotango's Chief Executive and James Duncan, Fotango's Chief Scientist, the small Canon subsidiary had developed the Zimki *serverless computing* service, as Wardley had recognised that a major technology organisation (Wardley presumed Google, however, it turned out to be Amazon) would imminently commoditise the 'infrastructure layer' as a publicly available computing utility. Wardley's strategy was therefore to approach commoditising computational services as a utility 'higher up the stack' (value chain), hence, at the software framework level. This was a level where Zimki could grow and thrive free of immediate competition.

Unfortunately, even though Zimki was tremendously successful in its innovative approach to cloud computing and had achieved an unchallenged first-mover advantage, Canon's leadership were intransigent towards Wardley's efforts to secure continued support for the initiative and remained unwilling to endorse further development thereof. This is a decision which draws parallels with Xerox PARC's invention of the Graphical User Interface (GUI), Ethernet Network Interface Card (NIC) and the Stanford Research Institute (SRI) Mouse. Xerox failed to fully capitalise on these innovations, which became the cornerstones to IBM's and Microsoft's meteoric success in personal computing during the 1990s.

'Xerox could have owned the entire computer industry, it could have been the IBM of the nineties, it could have been the Microsoft of the nineties.'[42]

- Steve Jobs (1955-2011), founder and former Chief Executive Officer, Apple Inc.

This is an emblematic example of competence-induced failure (see Apex Predator Hypothesis, Chapter 4: Surfacing Utility) as a result of inertia barriers and poor awareness of the surrounding ecosystem and market landscape (see Competition, Chapter 2: Capital Evolution). In the absence of an innovative competitor following Canon's directive to withdraw Zimki, Amazon dominated the cloud computing market and was largely unchallenged for several years.

In June 2007, Heroku, a Ruby based programming platform was founded in San Francisco, California, and in April 2008, Google's AppEngine proposition was released (to a limited developer base). Zimki, Heroku and AppEngine were early *serverless computing* innovations which were introduced to the market. However, it wasn't until November 2014, nine-years after Fotango's original innovation, that Amazon released "Lambda," its own *serverless computing* proposition.

The consumption and transaction economics of software, developed to make use of *serverless computing,* represents a powerful shift in cloud computing elasticity. As with previous shifts from products to services, and again to commodity enabled utilities, a co-evolution of practice and architecture is to be expected.

CLOUD COMPUTING

Cloud is arguably the best understood of the capabilities, enabling digital transformation as well as FinTech disruption. Being well understood lends credence to its state of industrialisation. It is well commoditised and is priced on a unitary basis and consumable as a utility. Its characteristics are well defined and unambiguous. There is abundant expertise in the marketplace. There is ample competition to offer choice and significant presence to offer localised service and performance ubiquitously (see Co-evolution, Chapter 2: Capital Evolution).

The adoption of utility (cloud) computing signals a significant shift in practices and architecture. This is notable when examining the characteristic of Mean-time-to-Recovery (MttR).

The transition of computing from 'Custom built' to 'Product' was accompanied by the componentisation of hardware, operating system(s) and applications (see Abstraction, Chapter 2: Capital Evolution). Prior to this, the applications were integrated or 'tightly coupled' within the system. The emergence of operating systems provided for the insulation or abstraction between different hardware products and different applications (Fig 3.5). An architectural change of this nature offered businesses and consumers a choice in selecting their technology at these various levels. The componentisation of hardware and software promoted competition and further commoditisation.

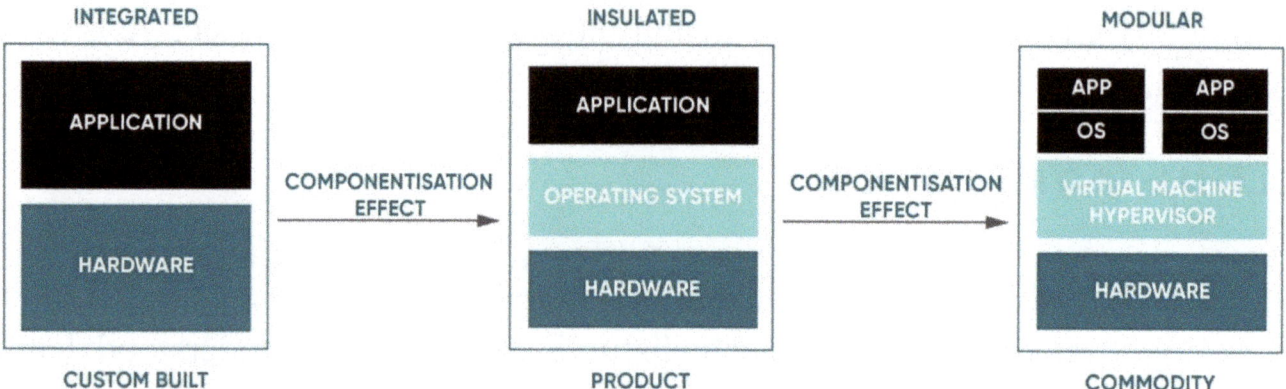

Fig 3.6 Modularity of computing componentisation in transitions from 'Custom Built' to a 'Commodity'

This evolutionary transition was accompanied by a change in characteristics in the form of MttR and prompted a change in practice, whereby, accepted 'best practice' was no longer applicable. Novel practices emerged in creating greater resilience surrounding this characteristic. Introduction of new business continuity practices in the form of carrying spare parts, then 'N+1,' resulting in the duplication of hardware and resilient clustering technology. As business reliance on technology grew, this prompted practices to mature. These manifested in the form of disaster recovery procedures with duplicate infrastructure as well as services, mirrored across regional data centres to create geographic resilience. These practices prompted changes in architecture and methodology to support further business reliance on these technologies.

As business has come to depend on technology to support productivity, so greater demand distils into increased technology procurement. Thus, in addition to MttR, there are the lead times experienced between ordering and delivery, known as Mean-time-to-Delivery (MttD), of new technology infrastructure to provide capacity, giving rise to practices such as capacity planning/management. Thereafter, there are activities and potential delays to be expected in commissioning, testing and finally deployment. This process gives rise to waterfall style project management (PRINCE2) and service frameworks, such as the Information Technology Information Library (ITIL), capacity management and architecture frameworks, such as Zachman and The Open Group Architecture Framework (TOGAF). All of which requires skilled IT staff, security specialists, risk management and project managers.

Practice evolves in parallel through commoditisation, from '**Novel**' to '**Emerging**' to '**Good**' to '**Best**' (Fig 2.9). As practice matures to 'Best,' it correlates to building inertia and is later disrupted with the emergence of innovation, componentisation (with abstraction) and higher-order systems. The disruption gives way to new novel practices, which emerge to complement the genesis of innovations. These are then accompanied by novel architecture and service practices.

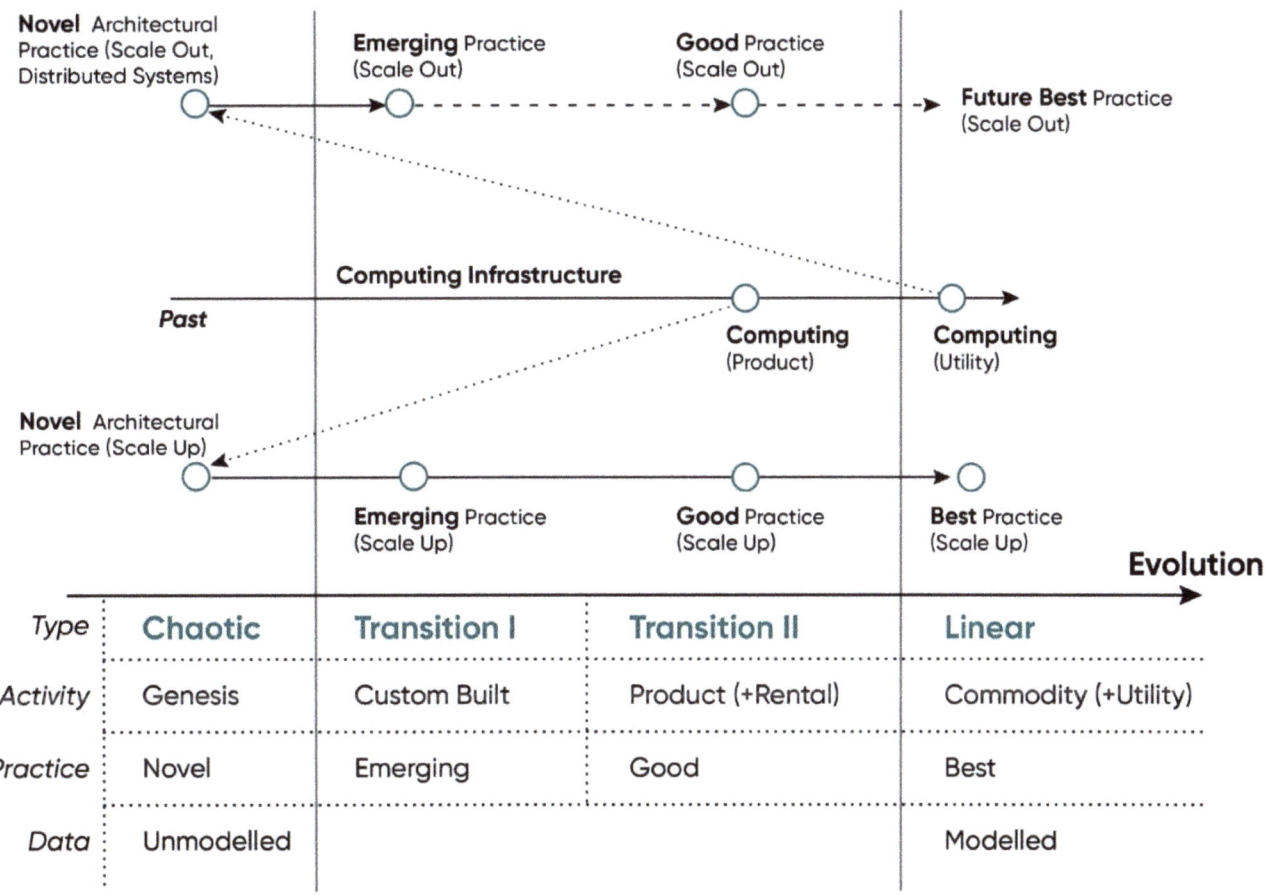

Fig 3.7 illustrates the co-evolution in architecture experienced as computing has evolved

The introduction of cloud computing represents the emergence of new business models, new architecture and new practice through *Creative Destruction*. In a cloud environment, there is no MttR. If there is a fault with the underlying technology, the cloud service provider repairs or replaces it. Businesses, thus, design their applications for failure resilience, in lieu of infrastructure fortification. This represents a shift away from designing for robustness, towards designing for resilience.

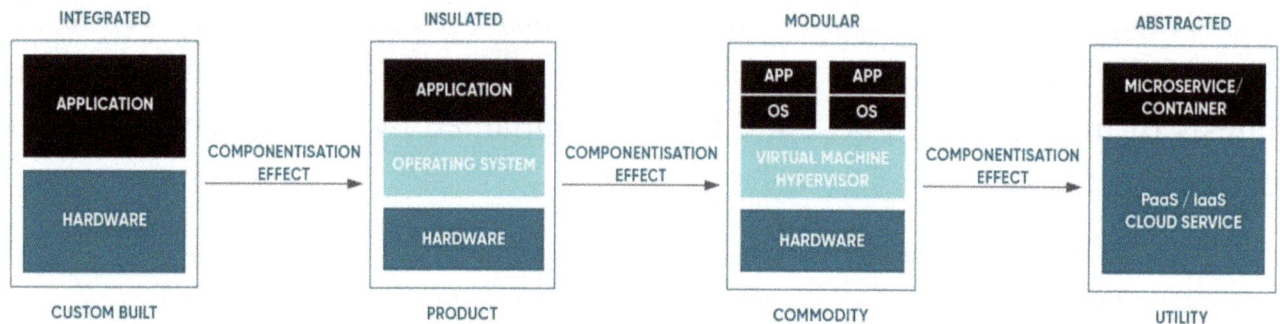

Fig 3.8 abstraction via the 'Componentisation effect' in the commoditisation of computing to a 'utility'

In a cloud ecosystem, the infrastructure is abstracted (see Abstraction, Chapter 2: Capital Evolution). Capacity management and planning is also abstracted, MttD, is thus, no longer applicable. Capacity is available on demand, eliminating delays and diminishing complexities in project management, thereby, reducing costs in project resources and delivery logistics. This radically alters the dynamics of the time-to-market in bringing new capabilities to bear, as well as increasing the capacity of resources exploited by existing services relative to growing consumer demands. The shift in these characteristics, prompted the co-evolution of practices. Thus, resulting in the creation of DevOps.

CO–EVOLUTION OF PRACTICE

DEVOPS

DevOps is a set of practices centred on greater integration, as well as collaboration between developers and operational staff. The principle is to achieve continuous iterative delivery (and improvement) through breaking down organisational silos, and is synonymous with using Agile and Scrum (an Agile software development practice based on incremental integration) methodologies. In the late 1990s, eXtreme Programming (XP) methodology, developed by Kent Beck, grew in popularity from which DevOps has largely evolved. XP represented a reflection of the changing methodology amongst developers from procedural-based programming, towards object-orientated (idempotence) programming. This was accompanied by a strong time-to-market focus, viewed as a competitive differentiator during the 'Dot Com' boom of the 1990s (see Dot Com, Chapter 10: Financialisation). XP was a methodology conducive to programming using short yet high frequency feedback loops which were required to develop applications to a high standard rapidly. Thus, a precursor to DevOps.

CI/CD

DevOps represents the manner in which an organisation's developers and operations are arranged, in order to embrace paradigms such as 'Continuous Integration/Continuous Delivery' (CI/CD).

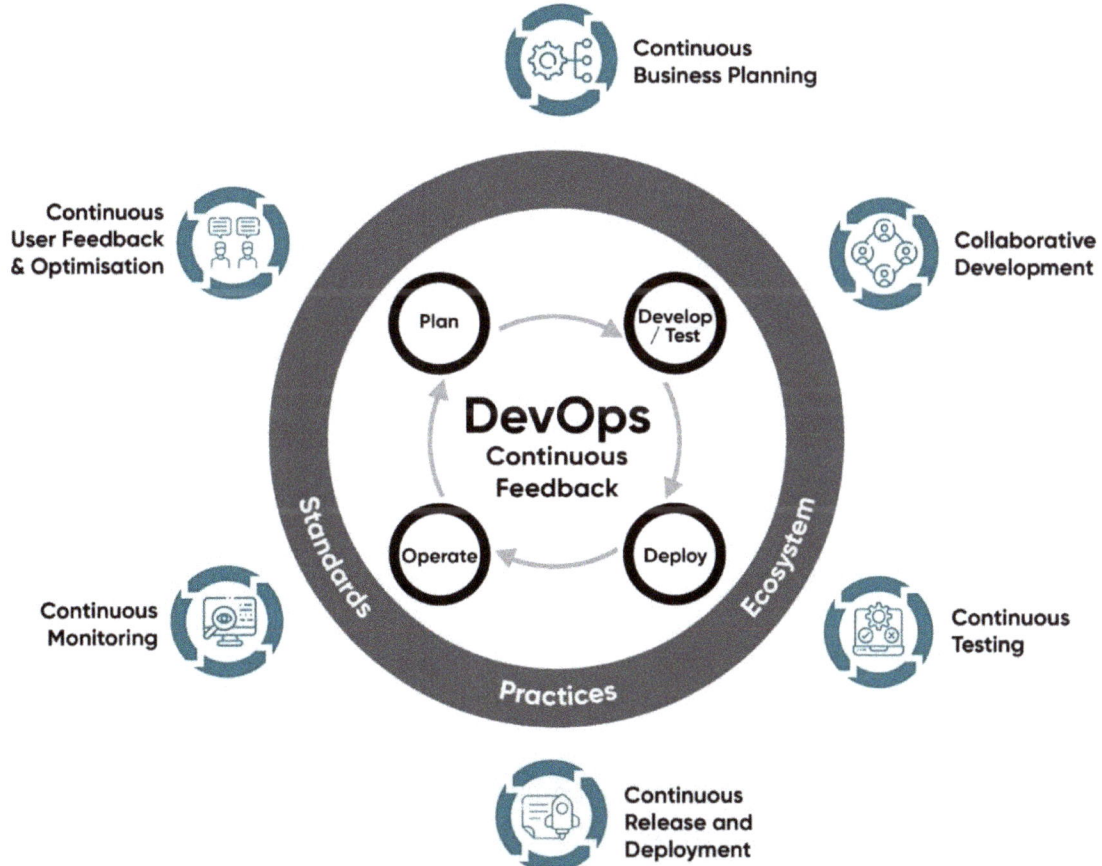

Fig 3.9 illustrates the cyclic paradigm of CI/CD methodology in conjunction with DevOps

Businesses that have adopted CI/CD and DevOps are largely embracing an ethos of 'Fail Fast, Release Often.' Hence, perpetually learning and improving. These companies heavily exploit services within cloud ecosystems and adopt this approach in order to create a differentiated cadence in bringing new capabilities and services to market in an ever increasingly competitive landscape.

DevOps is additionally conducive to creating conditions, which lend themselves to interdisciplinary thinking. This, in turn, lends itself to promoting innovation by creating 'Exaptive Moments.' DevOps additionally removes friction between business silos and as a consequence, yields outcomes with a faster release-to-market schedule. Furthermore, DevOps is a highly attractive practice in environments which aim to cultivate complexity based approaches to development. Such approaches often prove critical in aid of tackling challenging and unpredictable problems.

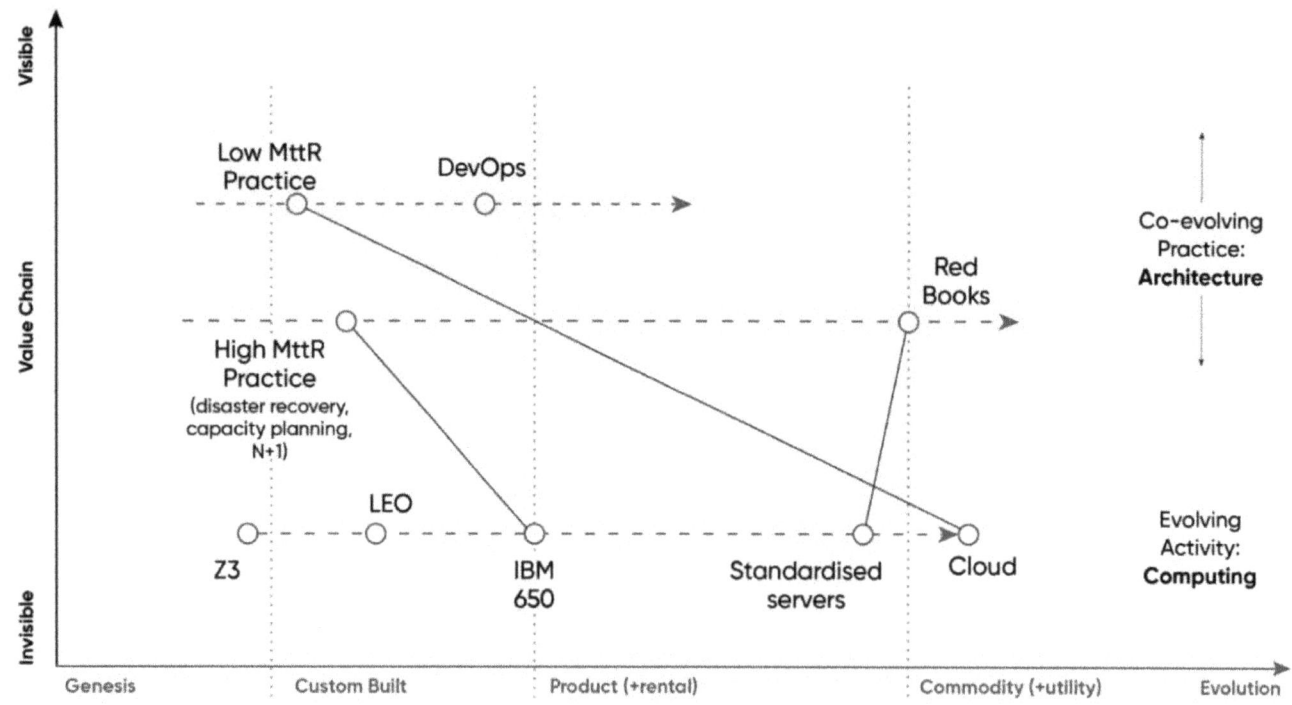

Fig 3.10 Wardley Map illustrating the co-evolution of practice accompanying the commoditisation of computing featuring MttR and DevOps

NOOPS

With the commoditisation of development frameworks, resulting in serverless computing utility services (e.g. Zimki, AppEngine, Lambda), there is a co-evolution of practice which accompanies a further componentisation and abstraction.

'Make each program do one thing well.'

- *Douglas McIlroy, the UNIX principle, 1978.*

And reiterated by:

'Every module, class, or function should have responsibility over a single part of the functionality provided by the software, and that responsibility should be entirely encapsulated by the class.'

- *Robert C Martin, Single Responsibility Principle, 2003.*

These principles give rise to an increased focus on the paradigm of idempotence. In other words; ensuring that there is a prioritised focus on creating small, well written programs, which are consistent and repeatable. This paradigm is, furthermore, synonymous with componentisation that has manifested through the iterative progression of virtualised servers (virtual machines and hypervisors), followed by containers, and eventually, to Microservices.

With the increased adoption of serverless computing, the environment is increasingly industrialised and standardised. This significantly diminishes the necessity for the 'Ops' (Operations aspect) in DevOps. As a consequence, there is a natural shift (co-evolution of practice) towards focusing on programming as the underlying infrastructure services are further abstracted by software objects. It is, therefore, reasonable to anticipate that DevOps will eventually evolve into NoOps (or an equivalent term), prompting new architectural practices and new characteristics to emerge, as a result of the elasticity and abstraction that serverless cloud computing has introduced.

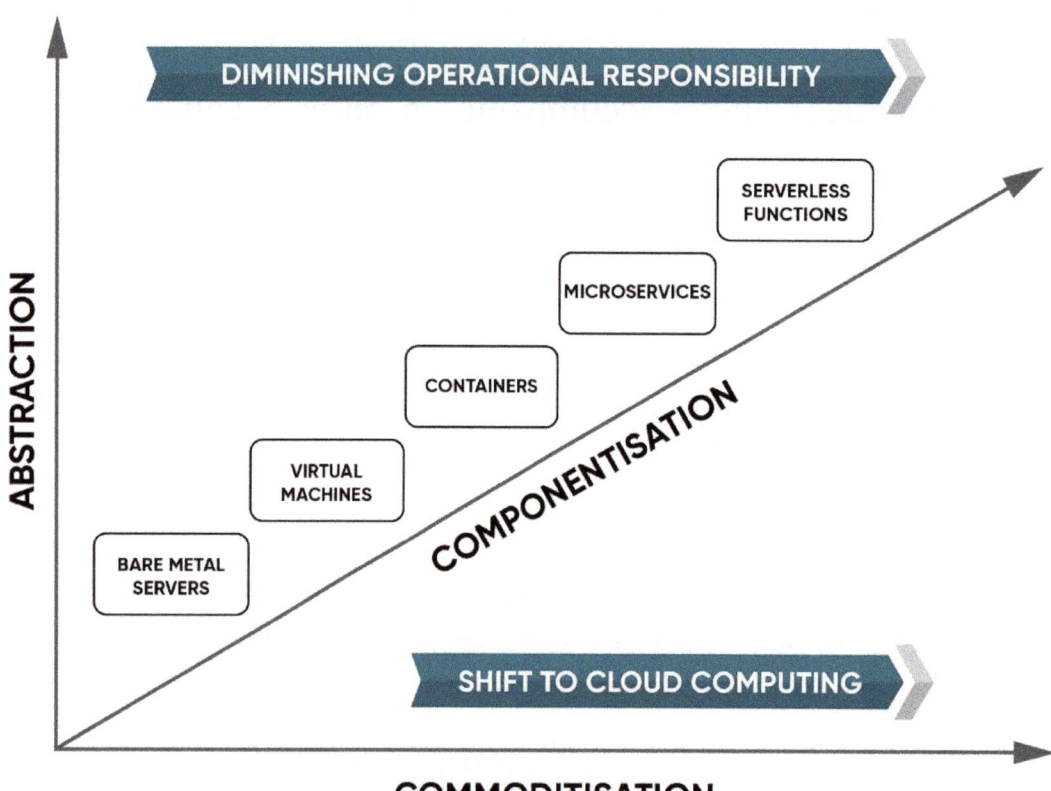

Fig 3.11 diminishing operational responsibility through iterative componentisation and abstraction via utility (cloud) computing

COMMERCIAL CO-EVOLUTION

During the 1990s, in the lead up to the 'Dot Com' bubble collapse of 2000 (see Dot Com, Chapter 10: Financialisation), it was a prevalent practice for businesses to align asset depreciation cycles with Moore's Law (see Moore's Law, Chapter 2: Capital Evolution). As a consequence, businesses would embark on technology refresh and replacement initiatives every two-to-three years. The latter years of the 1990s significantly altered this behaviour amongst businesses, due to an anticipated risk of a synchronised crash unfolding across IT systems, as a result of the millennium bug.

Y2K

The millennium bug is succinctly described as a design flaw in computer hardware and software, whereby provision for date encoding was based on two digits for day (01-31), two digits for month (01-12) and finally two digits for year (80-99). Since neither hardware nor software developed in this era made provision for four-digit-year values (e.g. 1999 transitioning to 2000), it was broadly forecasted that systems would fail as 1999 came to a close (at the strike of millennium midnight).

In order to avoid a potentially catastrophic and simultaneous failure of IT systems, innumerable businesses engaged in an early refresh of systems, to year-two-thousand (Y2K) compatible infrastructure and software. This premature and synchronised technology expenditure created commercial and accounting challenges for some businesses, predominantly experienced in an unplanned strain on capital expenditure, as well as premature write-offs for assets that had yet to fully depreciate.

This created another significant shift in paradigm, which is that of cost profiles and the financial treatments, thereof. It has since not been uncommon for companies to capitalise technology infrastructure, software and any project costs incurred as 'assets under construction.' Practices such as this lead to lengthy depreciation cycles.

These factors collectively prompt the question in a contemporary world of elastic cloud ecosystems — *why would any business maintain their own data centre(s) and infrastructure?*

This conundrum is akin to a factory building its own power plant, rather than consuming electricity from the national grid. *How could they hope to be competitive on this basis?*

The above question illustrates the phenomenon of evolutionary flow (see Evolutionary Flow, Chapter 4: Surfacing Utility), whereby, capital is more productively allocated towards developing new products and services, rather than investing in custom building capabilities which are already available as industrialised utilities.

In many instances, companies (especially financial institutions), in realisation that IT has detracted focus from their core business, do inevitably attempt to displace these expenditures. Unfortunately, entrenched legacy system constraints and lengthy asset depreciation cycles often lead to outsourcing, rather than cloud transformation.

The challenge then becomes motivating an outsourcer to transform IT systems to consume cloud utility services on the customer's behalf. This approach is usually met with immense obstacles and usually results in failure, representing a false economy. Leveraging a third-party (outsourcer) to transform a legacy technology environment and shrink its profitability simultaneously is counterintuitive. It is not in the third-party's interests to do so expediently (if at all), particularly if the outsourcer has displaced the technology assets from the organisation's balance sheet (as is commonly the case).

This predicament is further reinforced by virtue of the outsourcer's capabilities being stronger in the industrialised state, rather than in either an emergent or transition state (see Chapter 2: Capital Evolution). Outsourcers (Systems Integrators) are heavily focused on processes and practices exploiting methods such as Lean and Six Sigma. The outsourcing business model is predicated on removing variances, via standardisation and driving efficiency, through optimisation and economies of scale. These characteristics are synonymous with highly industrialised, granular and predictable services, which are managed via highly-optimised operational runbooks, as well as measurable with Key Performance Indicators (KPIs), and clearly defined Service Level Agreements (SLAs). Consequently, it tends to prove challenging, if not prohibitively expensive to execute a cloud transition, via a traditional outsourcer. In such circumstances, which are disruptive, chaotic and where practices are novel, nimble internal teams embracing methodologies which thrive amidst chaos and uncertainty such as Agile and Scrum, are likely to realise greater success.

In addition, this raises the spectre of the role technology has historically played in large organisations. Technology was originally embraced to facilitate greater efficiency and productivity of internal functions in support of the business. Examples of which included accounting, human resource management, customer relationship management etc. The contemporary role of technology is not to exclusively support these business functions, however, to be the business service itself (see Value Chains, Chapter 2: Capital Evolution). The shift prompts organisations to embark on 'digital strategies' to transform into 'digital first' enterprises, engaging the appetites of a growing digital consumer base (see Chapter 4: Surfacing Utility).

This places incumbent financial institutions at a competitive disadvantage, in contrast to nimble FinTech challengers, which can rapidly exploit cloud technology to develop high value-to-cost-ratio capabilities with negligible, if any potential waste in IT expenditure.

Another transition barrier to cloud consumption for incumbent financial institutions is the realisation that cloud technology is not less expensive than like-for-like internal IT from a total cost of ownership (TCO) perspective. It is therefore probable that a transition to cloud will simply enable their environments to be more efficient, which is exceedingly challenging to qualify into a tangible benefit. This is illustrated by The Jevons Paradox (see Chapter 2: Capital Evolution).

'Technological progress that increases the efficiency with which a resource is used, tends to increase the rate of consumption of that resource.' - The Jevons Paradox

- William Stanley Jevons, 1865.

In other words, an organisation doesn't save money by exploiting cloud computing – they simply tend to do more with it as a utility resource, thus, becoming more efficient and consequently more productive. Hence, this represents a challenging endeavour when attempting to secure funding in a mature organisation like an incumbent bank or large insurer.

CONSUMPTION & TRANSACTION ECONOMICS

However, the relative cost of performing transactions internally in lieu of externally, tends to constrain the scope of a Financial Institution's activities, ultimately limiting its growth potential. Thus, a limiting factor in remaining competitive. Although, efficiency and productivity are largely intangible when constructing a business case against capital expenditure, the allocation of capital towards duplicating industrialised capabilities, rather than exploiting those which already exist in the market, tends to starve an organisation of the resources needed to invest in research and development to generate high-value revenue streams. Thus, as the exploitation of cloud computing becomes increasingly pervasive and incrementally accrues sophistication through the commoditisation of higher-order systems, the consumption and transaction economics thereof, broadens the marginal value between internal technology capabilities and the external utility.

As a consequence of increased complexity experienced by Financial Institutions, since the GFC through greater regulation, internal transaction costs have commensurately risen. This creates an incentive to externalise transaction workloads in order to benefit from the economic flexibility of cloud computing. Those that resist exploiting these newer capabilities and practices, as well as fail to adapt their business models, usually find themselves at a competitive disadvantage, and eventually face challenges to remain financially viable.

SMART DEVICE APPS

The launch of Apple's iPhone in January 2007, and its accompanying 'App Store,' irrevocably disrupted the mobile phone industry, which had previously been dominated by companies such as Nokia, Sony Ericsson, Motorola and Samsung.[43] The shift came as incremental innovations in internet-enabled mobile phone devices using Symbian OS, Windows CE, as well as Blackberry's Personal Digital Assistant (PDA), phone propositions attempted to bridge the gap between telephony and computing. These propositions were largely fuelled by market demand to offer a number of mobile 'smart' phones suitable for corporate use. These PDA devices utilised mobile data connections, via General Packet Radio Service (GPRS) and wireless networking protocols, based on the IEEE 802.11 standards (known as Wi-Fi) to facilitate internet use for a minority of internet applications, predominantly email and instant messaging, as well as limited web browsing. This drastically limited the market potential for these devices.

The iPhone instantly differentiated itself, eliminating a fixed keypad by using a touch screen interface, which doubled as a high surface area rich display (high, relative to previous displays). Furthermore, the computational processing capability over previous handheld devices was greatly enhanced, which combined with Apple's Operating System (precursor to iOS, complete with desktop-class 'Safari' web browser), furnished the product with the ability to render a compact, yet rich web-browsing experience. Additionally, it enabled the device to run sophisticated applications, previously incapable of being supported by portable embedded technology platforms. Another factor which contributed to the iPhone's meteoric success was its aesthetic appeal, both in industrial design, as well as a rich, colourful and vibrant interface. These are characteristics which Apple internally refer to as, '*objects of material desire.*'[44] Furthermore, Apple's cult-like following for its highly successful, beautifully crafted iPod devices and Darwin UNIX-based OSX desktop, as well as laptop computers, assured immediate consumer demand.

The iPhone's screen, with touch sensitive controls and gesture interpretation capabilities in the absence of a fixed keypad, offered the flexibility for developers to devise creative and tailored user interfaces for their applications. This was a critical factor in the success of the product, as applications developed to exploit the limited device surface area was a key differentiator in assuring its viability as a desirable technology platform. Reliance on web-browsing alone would not have met this burden, as simply miniaturising a website would have perpetuated the limitations of previous mobile platforms. A number of previous platforms had attempted to overcome the limitations of miniaturisation through the use of a stylus (a pen shaped apparatus, designed to precisely engage the small controls of a miniaturised touch screen interface). The iPhone, however, a device which included capabilities for which Apple filed over one-hundred patent applications prior to its initial release, was designed to overcome the limitations associated with a miniaturised interface. Thus, the iPhone represented the *Creative Destruction* of the mobile phone industry and in so doing, usurped a substantial proportion of conventional end-user computing services simultaneously. Highly customisable applications (apps), combined with embedded finger gesturing interpretation capabilities, were instrumental in achieving this ambition. The apps act as a consumable interface (and web client) which interact with service APIs. Consequently, this drove reciprocal demand for cloud services to provide the backend data and systems functionality to support the mobile apps.

This break-through created the canvas for the development of all manner of applications, which may be exploited to surface the utility of entertainment, business, consumer, social media and financial services (see Chapter 4: Surfacing Utility). Furthermore, this increased the surface area with which consumers could engage such services on a twenty-four-hour basis with global reach, as well as while on the move. In order to support and accelerate the development of third-party applications, Apple made its own Software Development Kit (SDK), available to the general public. Providing its SDK to the public serves a dual purpose. Firstly, to lower the barrier-to-entry in order to attract revenue generating third-party use of the platform. Secondly, to stimulate innovation, which may be detected via the App Store (see Sensing Engines below).

These actions enabled Apple to consolidate its position as an ecosystem originator, by providing the platform and tooling for others to innovate and capitalise upon. Google largely replicated this paradigm through introducing the 'Google Play' App Store. Google Play complemented Google's release of its open-source Android OS in September 2008, which runs on mobile smart devices, such as those developed by itself, Samsung, Microsoft and others. By open-sourcing the platform, Google benefitted from the accelerant effects in advancement through commoditisation (see Standardisation, Chapter 2: Capital Evolution) and community-driven network effects (see Network Effects below).

Google's approach in this regard is differentiated from Apple's by providing the framework within which a broader spectrum of industries may coordinate their activities in order to participate in the value chain of the platform. This is achieved through the inclusion of handset, tablet and other smart device manufacturers within the ecosystem. Thus, encouraging these entities to participate within the ecosystem, in addition to app developers and network operators. These industries are consequently enabled to better coordinate their activities in the orbit of the platform. By contrast, Apple maintains tight control over its devices and the operating system within its ecosystem, thereby entrapping the company into a perpetual innovation cycle in order to maintain market primacy (Red Queen Hypothesis). Google's approach, by contrast, enables, and to an extent, relies on platform participants in order to innovate (see Innovate, Leverage & Commoditise below).

VERTICAL TO HORIZONTAL

The finance sector's incumbents comprising banks, insurers, investment banks, asset managers and hedge funds, were historically conceived and grown into vertically-integrated organisations. Throughout the 1990s to the 2010s, Financial Institutions (FIs) focused predominantly on creating tightly-integrated portfolios of products and services, which reflected the FIs' capabilities as a delivery channel. This strategy ran counter to structuring their services in order to cater to specific customer needs or expectations (see Value Proposition, Chapter 2: Capital Evolution). Consequently, FIs created comprehensive 'one size fits all' portfolios, which left customers starved for choice, as well as specificity.

With the emergence of FinTechs in the wake of the GFC, the 2010s were dominated by a proliferation of channels. Smaller, nimble companies emerged which could exploit the smart phone platforms and cloud ecosystems to provide niche financial services for specific customer segments, via digital channels. As the market saw new entrants, it became clear that this represented the *componentisation* of the financial services industry. A consistent pattern to the 'componentisation effect' realised through commoditisation (see Componentisation, Chapter 2: Capital Evolution) of an artefact or an industry. The net effect of this phenomenon is a metamorphosis in which vertically-integrated value chains are disrupted by horizontally-layered value clusters (see Vertical-Integration, Chapter 2: Capital Evolution). This represented an industry disruption, via an *elementary decomposition* (componentisation), of the tightly-integrated product and service portfolios, which were cultivated by incumbent financial institutions. A financial industry metamorphosis comparable to the example of a tightly-integrated e-commerce website business (Fig 3.2), transforming into an omni-channel 'headless' e-commerce ecology (Fig 3.3). Thus, creating a climate in which incumbents with generic 'one size fits all' portfolios subsequently faced competition from numerous challengers, each with a specific value proposition focused on surfacing a specialist financial utility (see Chapter 4: Surfacing Utility).

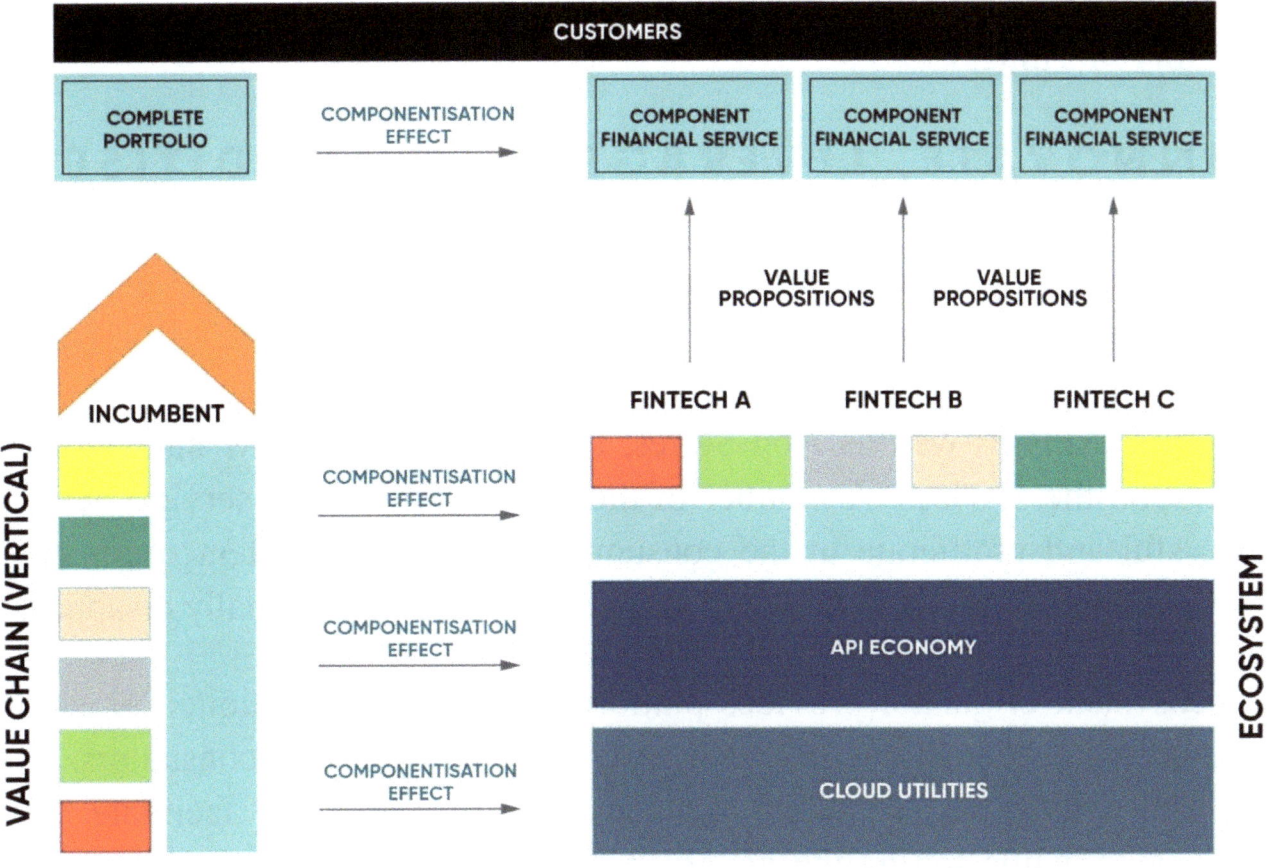

Fig 3.12 Vertically-Integrated to Horizontally-Layered 'Componentisation' of Financial Ecosystem

This draws parallels with the effect of *commoditisation* on an industry segment, whereby *inertia barriers* form, cultivating an *inertia-to-change*, prompting *Creative Destruction*, thereby resulting in a *co-evolution in practice* and business models, which incessantly begins restructuring the financial services industry much akin to an industrial revolution. As with any industry which is increasingly commoditised, market saturation drives downward pricing pressure via competition, thereby creating the necessity for further innovation to create new sources of value and future worth at the value chain apex (see Higher-order Systems, Chapter 2: Capital Evolution). Consequently, in a comparable manner to which transitions from *integrated* to *insulated* to *modular* to *abstracted* (Fig 3.8) were experienced in the commoditisation of computing via componentisation, thus, transitions towards greater modularity and abstraction in the business and organisational structure of the financial services industry should be anticipated (see Economy of Platforms, Chapter 15: Economy of Things).

INNOVATE, LEVERAGE & COMMODITISE

Innovate, Leverage and Commoditise (ILC) is an increasingly common strategy among ecosystem originators in the tech sector. The strategy relies on having successfully commoditised services and thereafter, exposing the services via platforms, APIs as well as App Stores, thereby attracting new innovators to build upon the services. A number of these new innovators' services will be successful and proliferate in the consumption of the ecosystem originator's underpinning resources. Others will stagnate, plateau or eventually disappear.

An ecosystem originator provides platforms that may be exploited to enable value-creating interactions between external producers and consumers. The platforms within the ecosystem provide an infrastructure to facilitate these interactions, while setting the governance conditions and standards to which actors must comply. Hence, actors exploiting the use of the platforms benefit from a reduction in transaction costs between participants, while the ecosystem originator maintains authority over key control points, which participants require access to. Ownership over these platform control points provides strategic leverage to the ecosystem originator.

The ecosystem originator, is thus, in a prime position to 'mine the metadata' of its service consumers, which in this case are the new innovators. Mining the metadata enables the originator to determine which of the innovators' services are growing and which are stagnating. By doing so, the originator is leveraging the innovators' success to then commoditise its own new services based on the innovators' blueprint, in direct competition with the innovator. This practice empowers the originator to grow its ecosystem by exposing new services and then repeating the process.

With each iteration, the ecosystem grows, leveraging the innovations of external actors, which the originator later displaces. The net effect of this approach is evident in the ecosystem exploiting others to innovate for itself, resulting in its apparent rate of innovation, customer focus and efficiency, growing in direct correlation to the size of the ecosystem. All the while, ensuring that the ecosystem is perpetually growing. The ILC strategy represents an elegant solution to overcoming the challenges of the *Innovation Paradox,* through remaining operationally efficient "today," while simultaneously innovating for "tomorrow." Furthermore, by relying on external *innovators*, a competitive advantage is realised through focusing resources and internal processes, as well as methods towards *optimisers* and *curators* within the organisation, thereby reducing R&D expenditure (see Co-evolution, Chapter 2: Capital Evolution).

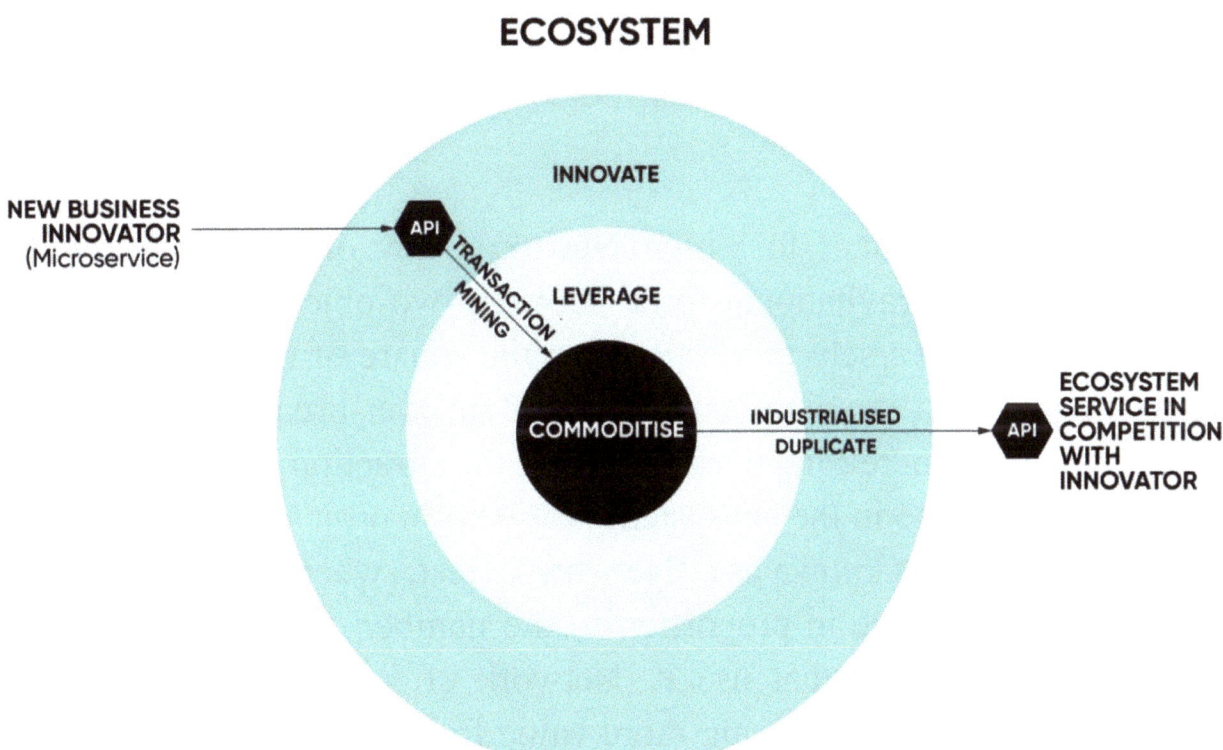

Fig 3.13 innovators "build" on platforms (ecosystem originator), thereafter exposing a duplicate service, thereby growing the ecosystem

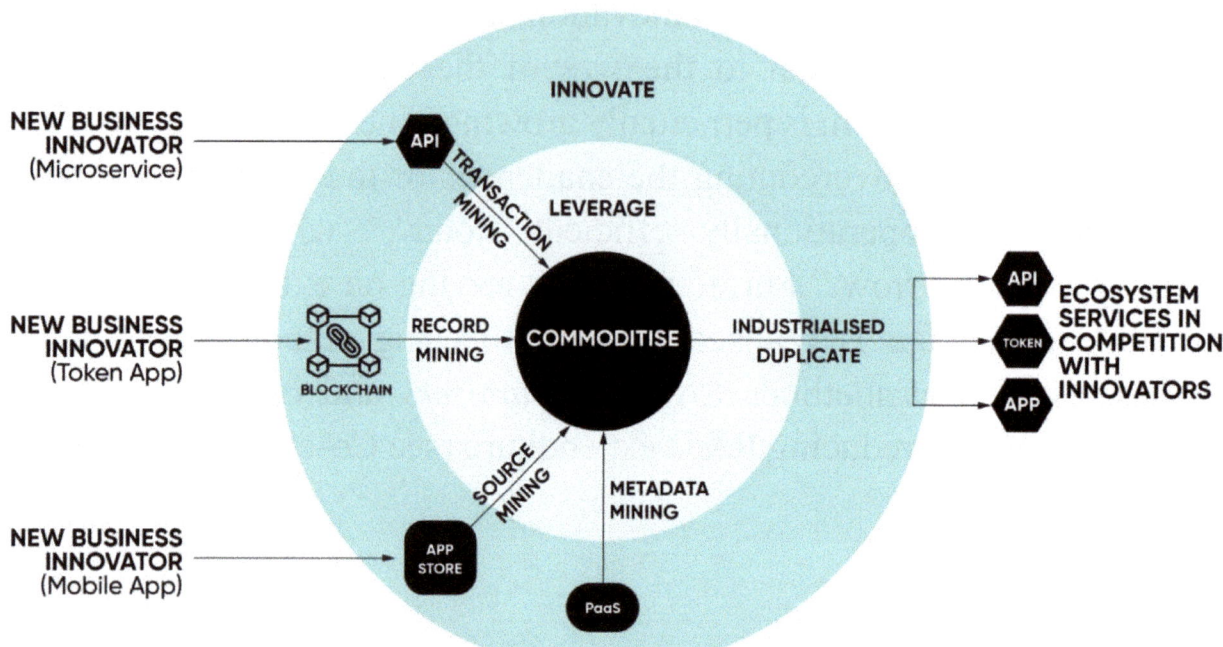

Fig 3.14 ecosystem originator exposes new platform services, increasing the surface area to absorb innovations

NETWORK EFFECTS

In a comparable manner to which Newton's law of universal gravitation advocates that the gravitational force between two objects is proportional to their masses and inversely proportional to the square of the distance between their centres; with a growing ecosystem and an ever-broadening spectrum of services akin to an increasing mass, so grows the attraction of others to use their services and innovate in the ecosystem originator's orbit. This phenomenon in terms of economics is known as a 'Network Effect,' whereby a good or service gains incremental value in proportion to the number of people or businesses (economic participants) that use it. Network effects are typically positive, resulting in a given user deriving more value from a good or service, as other users join the same network. Consider the usefulness of a social networking platform, such as Facebook. With a single participant, the network has no social value. However, with each incremental participant joining the network, the network's social value increases geometrically. Thus, reinforcing the attraction for others to join and participate therein. Consequently, this benefits the network, while simultaneously, benefitting the individual participants. This accounts for the geometric growth rate of ecosystems in the tech industry and a principal factor in the rate of innovation, which is accelerating.

LEARNING EFFECTS

This acceleration is attributed to the effects of geometric learning, known as learning effects. In a comparable manner to network effects (see above), learning effects have always existed in the pre-digital era, however, have become pervasive and essential in the digital sphere. In a classical context, learning effects are transmitted through human interaction and knowledge media, such as education, reference materials, research and development, industry standardisation, patents and practical experience. As people learn how a standard, a good, method, practice or service can become more valuable, they modify it accordingly. Human learning however, tends to be artisanal in nature. Thus, artisanal learning tends to scale at a more conservative and moderate rate.

Learning effects have the potential to generate substantial economic value, just as network effects have achieved. If businesses are able to attract customers by making their goods and services valuable, while additionally, making these products capable of learning from their consumption, this in turn enables them to cultivate superior capabilities, reflexively making them more valuable. Thereby attracting new customers while ensuring retention of existing customers, and thus, engineering and reinforcing a self-perpetuating cycle.

SENSING ENGINES

Growing an ecosystem, is thus, reliant on a means with which to attract new participants, via *network effects* and acquire new capabilities, via *learning effects*. This creates the necessity to create instrumentation and methods for weak signal detection to identify new innovations, as well as a means of attracting new participants. APIs, 'App Stores' and 'sandboxes' are among the various 'sensing engines' which function as the vehicles through which this strategy may be exploited.

Consequently, exploiting an ILC strategy appears to have become increasingly prevalent amongst cloud, e-commerce and social media tech giants, which capitalise on *sensing engines* in order to cultivate both *network*, and *learning effects*. While technology companies were the successful progenitors of this approach, the ILC strategy is growing in popularity in the finance sphere among larger FinTech organisations and some incumbents. A natural consequence of *learning effects*.

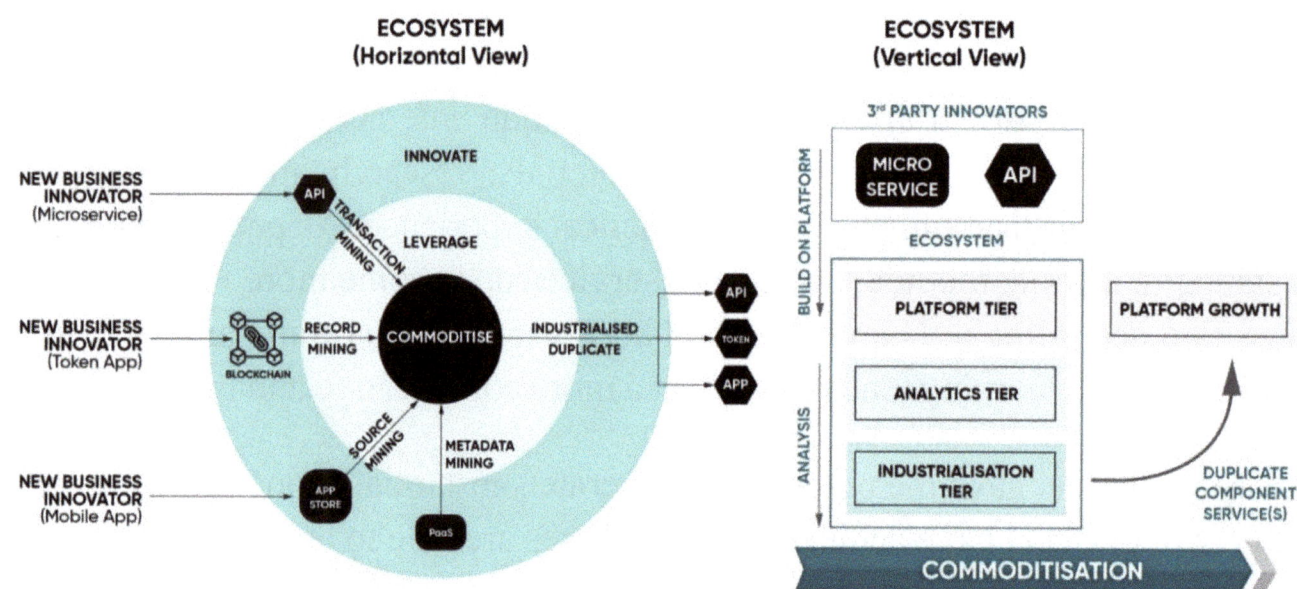

Fig 3.15 the ever-growing ecosystem platform 'horizontal' and 'vertical' views

Successfully implementing an ILC strategy provides a strategic advantage to the successful ecosystem originator. However, such success is usually dependent on being the first to commoditise a differentiated or essential capability. Additionally, being the first to release a standard upon which others may build and innovate, typically results in a similar effect. An example of which is Amazon's EC2 and S3 API blueprints, being the standards which many of its early competitors [45] emulated and supported. This further demonstrated the ecosystem leadership role that Amazon was able to assume. A consequence of the network effects, realised as a result of taking the lead in standardisation (see Genesis of an Ecosystem above).

The ILC practice simulates and sustains a first-mover advantage and may account (at least in part) for an increasingly larger proportion of the S&P 500's index being shared by a minority of companies, all of which are tech giants.[46] The Standard & Poor's 500, is a market capitalisation index (cap-weighted index) of the five-hundred largest US publicly traded companies. In 2020, one-percent of the companies represented forty-percent of the index market capitalisation. All five of which, were tech giants, also known as 'hyper-scalers.'

It should only be a matter of time before a market reconfiguration of incumbent financial institutions unfolds to replicate the disruptive business model of the tech giants (see Economy of Platforms, Chapter 15: Economy of Things). Ultimately, this will distil into the battlefield for 'FinTech innovator' absorption via ecosystem growth strategies such as Innovate, Leverage & Commoditise (ILC), also known as 'Tower & Moat.'

TOWER & MOAT

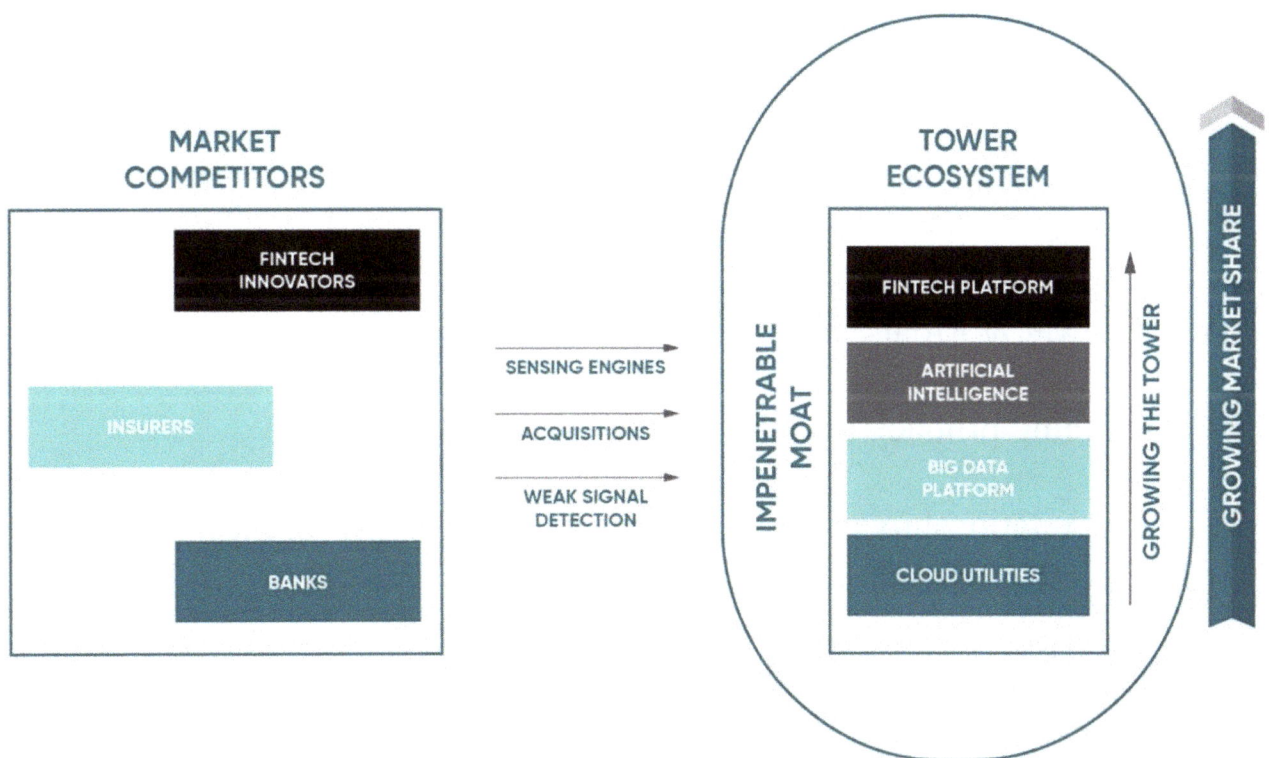

Fig 3.16 incumbent and new market competitors versus ecosystem behemoths growing via 'Tower & Moat'

'Tower & Moat' describes the protectionist practice of adding a new capability to an existing service or portfolio and subsequently raising the barrier-to-entry for either existing, or new potential competitors. The barrier-to-entry typically represents the minimum fixed costs required in order to compete with either established, or new market entrants in a specific business domain. A 'Moat' is typically formed by enhancing an aspect of the business value chain which is challenging to achieve. It should additionally provide an enduring competitive differentiator or advantage by doing so. An example would be a telecommunications company investing in a nationwide network infrastructure. A competitor would face tremendous challenges in providing comparable service coverage and struggle to achieve economies of scale or competitive pricing for its services.

Building a new technology upon the foundation of a commoditised platform, and thereafter, commoditising the new technology has a similar effect. Effectively, adding new capabilities grows or "stacks" one layer upon another akin to metaphorically building a taller 'tower' with each iteration. The act of aggregating and industrialising the new technologies raises the barrier-to-entry for potential competitors which is metaphorically creating (or extending) a moat around the tower. In the technology sphere, a 'Tower & Moat' strategy is thus typically evident in instances where an ecosystem leader (or originator) is commoditising platforms.

The ILC/'Tower & Moat' strategy is synonymous with four core practices:

1. Establishing primacy over the customer relationship.

2. Exploit relationship primacy in order to glean the highest value data generated by the customer (data primacy).

3. Exploit high value data (at scale) to create superior capabilities via learning effects, thereby displacing smaller competitors.

4. Leverage the superior capabilities (at scale) in order to attract new customers, thereby capitalising on network effects beyond the reach of smaller competitors.

At a nation state level, we observe rapidly growing economies, like that of China, applying this level of thinking in initiatives such as "Internet Plus" (see Internet Plus, Chapter 16: The Rise of China).[47] The state sponsored initiative is aimed at the digitisation of numerous services and industries, via the Internet, combined with the rapid industrialisation, (commoditisation) thereof.

This 'predator and prey' approach to growing an ecosystem has become increasingly prevalent among technology companies and enabled a number to transform into substantial organisations. While these behemoths may advocate that this approach is symbiotic in nature, through industry standardisation and co-operation, the axioms thereof, appear less than ethically motivated. Practices of this nature are alleged to undermine healthy competition, customer value and consumer wellbeing.

'From Amazon and Facebook to Google and Apple, it is clear that these unregulated tech giants have become too big to care.' [48]

- Pramila Jayapal, U.S. Representative, Washington State, June 2021.

In recognition of the ineffectiveness of prevailing US antitrust, monopoly and competition laws in limiting the predatory growth strategies and practices exploited by 'Big Tech,' a sixteen-month congressional investigation by the Antitrust Subcommittee was conducted. The investigation's report accused the tech giants of charging high fees, forcing smaller customers into unfavourable contracts and of exploiting *'killer acquisitions'* to impede their rivals.[49] Furthermore, some of these companies have engaged in litigation in defence against lawsuits alleging anti-competitive behaviour and violations of competition law.[50] Consequently, the US has introduced a number of proposed bills targeting 'Big Tech' in the form of:

- The American Choice and Innovation Online Act, a bill which prevents companies from manipulating marketplaces to promote their own products.[51]

- The Platform Competition and Opportunity Act 2021, a bill designed to impede the efforts of companies to acquire and suppress competitors.[52]

- The Ending Platform Monopolies Act, a bill prohibiting 'Big Tech' monopolies from selling products in marketplaces they control.[53]

- The Augmenting Compatibility and Competition by Enabling Service Switching (ACCESS) Act 2021, a bill making it easier for consumers to leave a social media platform and take their data to a competitor.[54]

- The Merger Filing Fee Modernization Act 2021, a bill empowering the Department of Justice and the Federal Trade Commission with the resources required to police monopoly power, without burdening taxpayers.[55]

'Big Tech's unchecked growth and dominance have led to incredible abuses of power that have hurt consumers, workers, small businesses and innovation. That unchecked power ends now.' [56]

- *Robert Weisman, president of advocacy group, Public Citizen, June 2021.*

4

SURFACING UTILITY

'We need banking, not banks.' - Bill Gates, Founder & former CEO, Microsoft Corporation.

Financial services and banking, in particular, has incrementally evolved over centuries to provide products and services to consumers and businesses in order to cater to growing demands. The core services which banks provide to their customers are:

1. Storing value

2. Making payments

3. Accessing credit

Banks have incrementally adopted technology to aid in servicing a broader customer base, while additionally, improving the efficiency of the banking business model. In doing so, banks have approached technological modernisation analogously, and often in a detrimental manner, to the utility of banking itself.

Until the introduction of the Electronic Recording Machine Accounting (ERMA) computer system, revealed in 1955 and created to automate bookkeeping and cheque (check) processing, banks kept records of their customers by name. The ERMA computer system introduced a limitation in the form of assigning numbers to customer records, in lieu of names. The limitation provoked the necessity for the creation of bank account numbers, which has prevailed ever since. This is an example of allowing the limitations of technology to reflexively influence the system which it serves, often introducing friction and inconvenience through forcing the customer to adapt to the limitation. The net effect of this practice resulted in one of numerous instances where the personalised nature of banking was eroded, in favour of impersonal 'one size fits all' products and practices. Consequently, reversing this impetus, has become the coveted competitive differentiator, through which customer retention and loyalty is now achieved. The key to success, therein, pivots on FinTech innovations through which surfacing utility and the delivery thereof is achieved in a personalised, contextualised and experiential manner.

In the 1980s, the introduction of Automated Teller Machines (ATMs) enabled customers to withdraw and deposit funds, beyond the confines of business hours. The psychology of introducing twenty-four-hour banking essentially extended the concept of bank teller services to be available around the clock. Conceptually, this illustrates how banks respond to technological changes and the approach taken in making services and products available to banking customers. The name illustrates this point, essentially automating some of the functions of a bank teller, rather than surfacing the utility of banking itself, an analogous approach.

BUSINESS MODEL EVOLUTION

'Uber, the world's largest taxi company, owns no vehicles. Facebook, the world's most popular media owner, creates no content. Alibaba, the most valuable retailer, has no inventory. And Airbnb, the world's largest accommodation provider, owns no real estate. Something interesting is happening.'

- *Tom Goodwin, Havas Media.*

Historically, companies capitalised assets in the form of equipment and premises, as well as employed labour and procured raw materials in order to produce goods and services. Taxi companies would typically purchase fleets of vehicles, as well as employ and train drivers in order to offer taxi services. Similarly, news agencies would employ journalists and purchase broadcasting and printing equipment to report news, create programs and share content. News and programs would be aired, via television and radio, at prescribed intervals each day. News and content were additionally delivered and distributed, via printed media, such as newspapers and magazine publications.

Technology enabled business models, notably those which intermediate between customers and merchants, as well as service providers, on a 'just in time' delivery basis, have disrupted the business models of the past. Consequently, these companies exact a fee for intermediating a customer with a supplier on a transactional basis, yet carry no risk, inventory or conventional liabilities. These companies create value and profit, exclusively from surfacing the utility of goods and services, rather than manufacturing or delivering the good or service themselves. These entities are brokers of value and facilitate transactions for a fee.

'Just in time' delivery models have, additionally, disrupted conventional employment patterns, giving rise to the Gig Economy and Zero-hour Contracts.

Through commoditisation, technology has simultaneously provided the tools to enable anyone to create and broadcast content, research and report news or share information ubiquitously at near zero marginal cost. Such developments, reinforced by the proliferation of social media, have created new vocations such as bloggers, vloggers (video bloggers) and influencers. Essentially, disrupting the monopolies of media broadcasters and advertising.

Conventional shopping at bricks-and-mortar merchants continues to shrink significantly in favour of an increasing trend towards growth in e-commerce and m-commerce (mobile commerce) consumption. These trends in consumer lifestyle and spending patterns are influencing significant changes in commercial activity within urban centres, giving rise to new thinking surrounding commercial real estate, town planning and transportation. Consumption and employment are incrementally becoming decentralised. Internet enabled business and communication is eroding the necessity for creating central business districts (CBDs) and diminishing the trends in urbanisation and conurbation. With diminished centralised demand, the concept of the bricks-and-mortar banking branch is incrementally becoming redundant. This is further exacerbated by the increased use of digital payment methods and instruments which erode the necessity for physical cash transactions, and thus, diminish the necessity for a banking branch model to accept deposits, or perhaps even physical cash itself.

Business models, such as Consumer Subscription Retail Services (CSRS), which from a commoditisation perspective operate much like utilities, rather than representing the sale of goods and services, offer use or access to such services on a periodic subscription basis, either monthly, annually or seasonally. Conceptually, this isn't a new business model. Its application to sectors traditionally governed by physical products, purchased face-to-face, in physical establishments, available only during prescribed business hours with virtual products, subscribed to, or purchased without cash nor human interaction, from the convenience of any location, via a smart mobile device at any time, has seen meteoric adoption.

The video rental business is a prime example, where consumers travelled to a store, selected a title to watch, then travelled home to view the content and return it "by hand" the following day. This business model evolved analogously, to a postal service model. Older millennials will remember this business model, however, to Generation Z, this is an alien concept and utterly absurd. The CSRS equivalent is digitally delivered content, consumed at the convenience of the subscriber, via smart devices, either at home or on the move. By comparison, this is simple, efficient, frictionless and experiential. In such business models, the utility has been harnessed and rather than analogously refining or optimising the process, the process has been completely recreated from first principles. Incidentally, the key technologies that underpinned the video rental business are either redundant, or in severe decline. Video Cassettes, Video Cassette Recorders (VCRs), Digital Versatile Discs (DVDs) and high-definition versions, such as HD-DVD and Blu-Ray have largely been superseded by digital streaming.

ACCESSING CREDIT

At a fundamental level, banks are in business to borrow at a low rate of interest and profit by lending at a higher rate. Banks aggregate funds from account holders (depositors) and retain a fractional reserve to accommodate customer withdrawals and payments. The bulk of depositors' funds are lent to borrowers at a premium. In contrast, an alternative means of accessing credit in the FinTech arena includes Peer-to-Peer lending.

Peer-to-peer (P2P) lending is a business model through which online services intermediate between lenders and borrowers, either businesses or individuals. P2P lenders offer borrowers credit at a lower rate of interest than institutional competitors, while lenders benefit from a higher rate of return. P2P lenders exact a fee for credit checking borrowers and intermediating between lenders and borrowers. By maintaining exceedingly low relative overhead costs to banking competitors, P2P lenders are able to facilitate credit transactions at mutually attractive rates between borrowers and lenders.

Another alternative business model to access credit is that of Crowdfunding. Crowdfunding entities, much like P2P lenders, syndicate investment from multiple lenders directed toward either a specific borrower, or a collection thereof. To the lender, this is an alternative investment instrument and to the borrower, an alternate means of raising capital.

Both P2P lending and Crowdfunding are vulnerable to poor liquidity, should lenders wish to divest themselves and attract a risk of borrowers defaulting, as loans are generally unsecured. In these circumstances, banks are better equipped to mitigate risks and insulate customers from losses (see Fractional Reserve, Chapter 5: Payments). P2P lending and Crowdfunding are business models which focus on surfacing the utility of borrowing and lending, using technology enabled services. Niche FinTech entities, however, have been able to harness this approach to underwrite tailored loans in previously underserved markets (see Peer-to-Peer Lending, Chapter 16: The Rise of China).

DELEGATED MONITORING

Both P2P Lending, as well as Crowdfunding platforms, fall within the sphere of, or are used by Microfinance Institutions (MFIs). These MFIs engage in *delegated monitoring,* whereby the MFI (delegated monitor) acts as a finance intermediary, due to its role in borrowing from depositors (investors), making use of unmonitored debt in the form of deposits. Thereafter, the MFI lends funds to borrowers, the loans to which it monitors. Monitoring is particularly critical in reducing repayment defaults of individual loans, rather than group-based loans.

EVOLUTIONARY FLOW

Process flow and process optimisation may be achieved through exploiting methodologies, such as 'Lean' or 'Six Sigma.' These methods identify and facilitate optimisation through analysis of the steps and decision points, isolating inefficiencies and employ simplification thereof. These methods are analogous in nature. Using process optimisation approaches rarely offers the opportunity to re-examine the core assumptions that form the individual waypoints within the process, hence, often leading to redundancy by not accounting for the impact of evolutionary flow.

Evolutionary flow optimisation, as a consequence, is an examination of the end-to-end process holistically to ensure the assumptions that underpin the process are valid and necessary. Evolutionary flow derives its designation from an examination of the evolutionary state of the process. By way of example, in improving the speed, efficiency and quality of video rental, optimisation was achieved by substituting low and standard definition analogue magneto optical formats, with digitally encoded laser technology. Each iteration produced better resilience in re-use, greater encoding accuracy and higher definition visuals and enhanced sound optimisations. There were numerous refinements, which were incrementally attempted, to optimise the speed, efficiency and quality of video delivery. These increments were analogous in nature, optimisations of the previous technology, delivery mechanism and business model. A holistic first principles approach to applying an evolutionary flow optimisation was ultimately to displace these technologies and their underpinning value chains, with digitally delivered streaming and the CSRS business model, which disrupted the industry and disintermediated the incumbents (Apex predators). Thus, via applying first principles (see below) and evolutionary flow facilitating *Creative Destruction.*

APEX PREDATOR HYPOTHESIS

The Apex Predator Hypothesis was developed by Welsh (British) knowledge management and complexity science researcher, David Snowden. The hypothesis is a vehicle to illustrate how organisations fail due to *inertia barriers*. Such failures are the result of past success, realised from their current operating model. The Apex Predator Hypothesis serves as a metaphor for *Creative Destruction* (see Creative Destruction, Chapter 2: Capital Evolution).

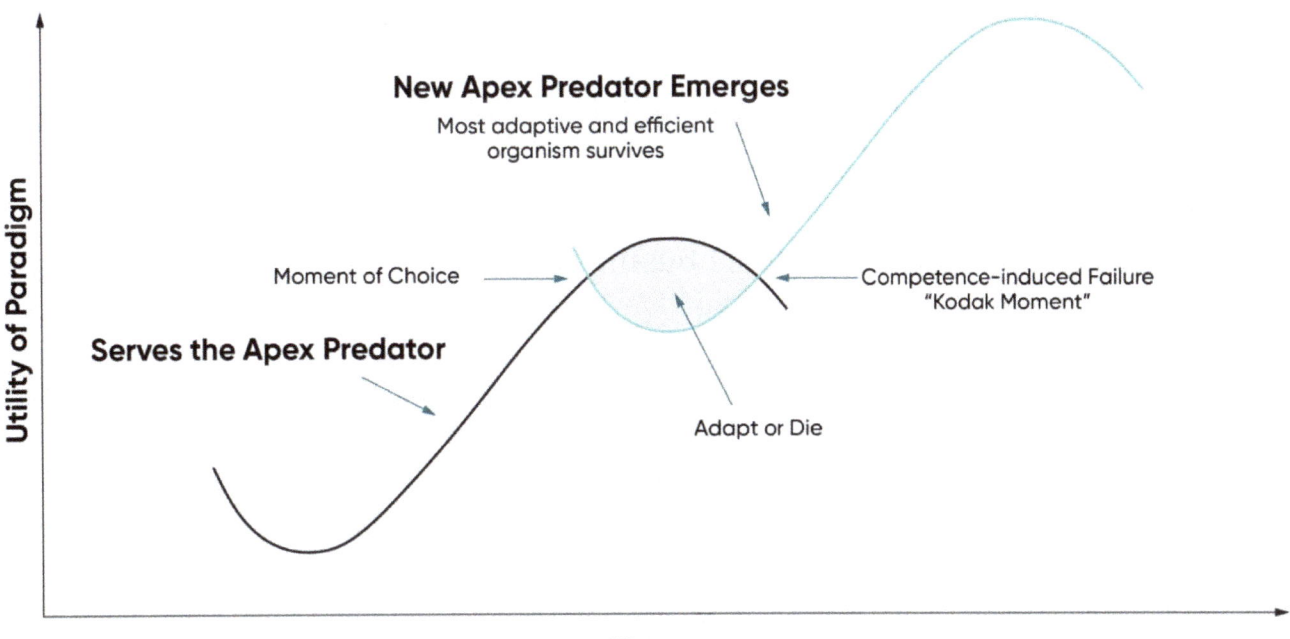

Fig 4.1 Apex Predator Hypothesis

The overlapping area of the two S-curves in Fig 4.1 contain three points of interest. The first point is the 'Moment of Choice' or 'Exaptive Moment,' where those who identify novelty and value in a new paradigm, adopt the new approach. These are the **early adopters**. At the first intersection, organisations that recognise the new shift in the business paradigm have a choice to 'adapt or die.' However, it is the third point where excessive confidence and/or competence in the current paradigm creates inertia to the change (inertia-to-change), which leads to failure as the market share descends through the **late majority** and **laggards**. A conundrum illustrated by the *Innovation Paradox* (see Innovation Paradox, Chapter 2: Capital Evolution).

This intersection is that of 'Competence-induced Failure,' a term coined by Clayton Christensen (1952 - 2020), who developed the theory of 'Disruptive Innovation,' promoted in his notable book, 'The Innovators Dilemma,' published in 1997.[57] It is additionally known as a 'Kodak Moment,' named for the failed company that patented both the digital and single-lens reflex (SLR) cameras. Once used to describe an occasion suitable for memorialising with a photograph, the term is now used to represent the moment when executives fail to realise how consumers and markets are changing (Tzu's factors of *climate* and *landscape*, see Competition, Chapter 2: Capital Evolution). Unfortunately, Kodak remained fixated on celluloid based film; a technology and associated business model which had served them profitably, until the need for film was rendered extinct and displaced by digital cameras and digital printing (the emerging Apex predator).

The hypothesis advocates that those businesses that identify and appreciate the implications at the 'Moment of Choice' and adapt accordingly will survive, while those that identify the threat at the 'Competence-induced Failure' intersection will wither (see Competition, Chapter 2: Capital Evolution). Detecting and evaluating weak signals is, thus, critical to long-term business survival, even if the organisation itself is innovating. However, in such circumstances, it is critical to distinguish between innovations which are incapable of cultivating network effects and are merely novelties (Hawthorne Effect) or by contrast are viable (Fig 2.3) and truly disruptive to the status quo.

The peak of the curve (the transition point from the **'early majority'** to the **'late majority'**) illustrates that the previous paradigm is reaching the end of its utility and from then onwards is in decline, ready for displacement by an emerging Apex predator. The polar opposite trough represents the base of the chasm. The Apex Predator Hypothesis is an overlay of Moore's Chasm and the innovation bell curve. 'Crossing the Chasm,' the title of Geoffrey Moore's book, published in 1991, identifies a chasm (gap) between **'early adopters'** and the **'early majority'** of the innovation bell curve (rendered as a Gaussian 'Normal' distribution).[58]

The 'Chasm' represents the 'Adapt or Die' vacuum of the hypothesis. A reference to Darwinism promoted by British naturalist, Charles Darwin (1809 - 1882), which encompassed his 'Theory of Evolution' in which Darwin posited that individuals most suited to their environment survive. While other species, given enough time, will gradually evolve, whereas some will perish as a consequence of natural selection.[59] The 'Adapt or Die' vacuum, may be filled by a nimble, energy efficient competitor, capable of displacing the previous incumbent (Apex predator).

Moore's work on 'Crossing the Chasm' builds on the diffusion of innovation from **innovators, early adopters** to **laggards,** based on the work of Everett Rogers, author of 'Diffusion of Innovations,' published in 1962.[60] Roger's work has, in turn, inspired other notable works such as Gordon Clark's article 'Innovation Diffusion: Contemporary Geographic Approaches,' researched at Lancaster University in England and published in 1984.[61]

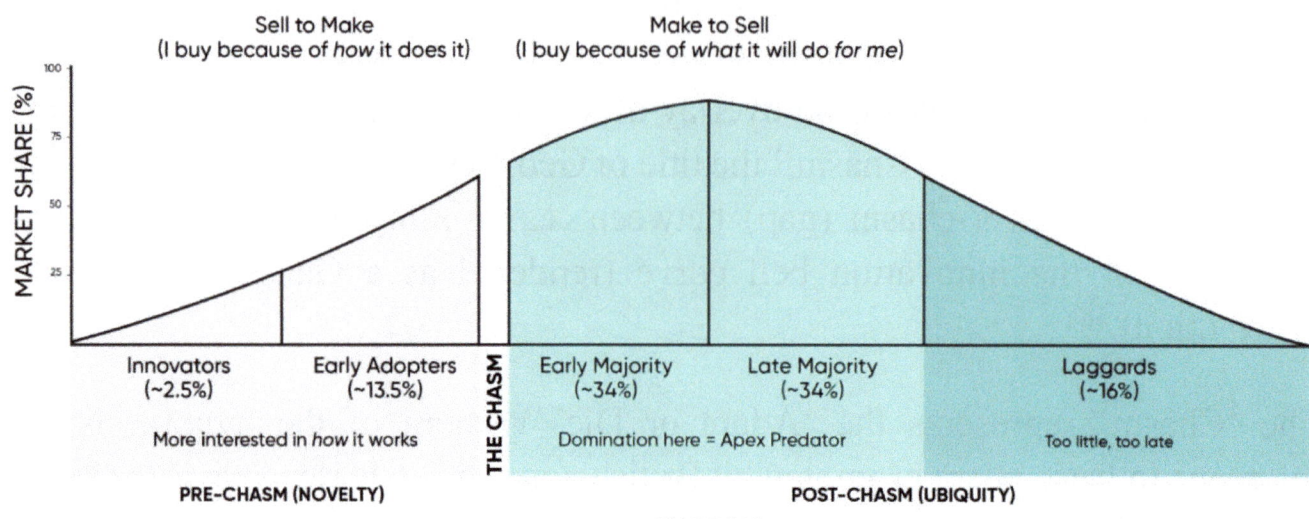

Fig 4.2 Moore's 'Crossing the Chasm' illustration of a gap between 'early adopters' and 'early majority'

Gartner, a well-established business intelligence firm, developed the 'Gartner Hype Cycle,' which describes the trough of Moore's chasm as the 'Trough of Disillusionment' within the 'Hype Cycle' instrument. Venture capital firms describe this as the 'Valley of Death.'

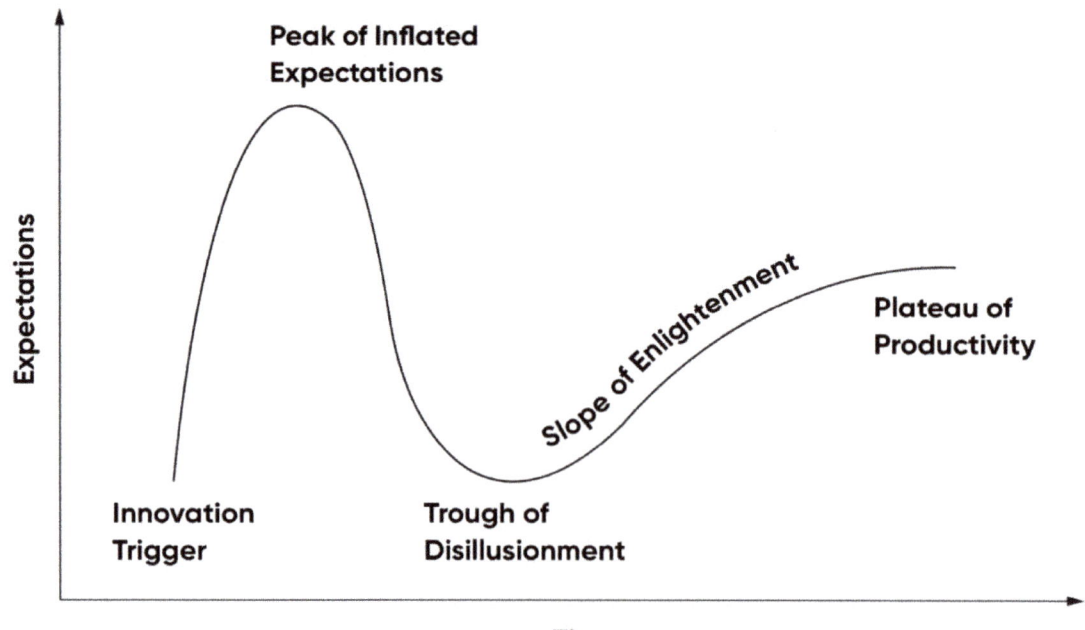

Fig 4.3 an example of the Gartner Hype Cycle Instrument

While these instruments differ slightly, at their core, they provide a consensus in conveying that the previous business models, incumbents and technologies will be disrupted by new business models, new methods, new companies and new technologies. Moore's chasm represents the *inertia-to-change,* illustrating business resistance to evolve beyond *inertia barriers,* brought about by new innovation (see Elementary Decomposition, Chapter 2: Capital Evolution). Essentially, providing a context to the *Innovation Paradox,* disruption and *Creative Destruction.* Notably, the COVID-19 pandemic acted as an accelerant in 'crossing the chasm' by proliferating the adoption of FinTech. Thereby, edging closer towards becoming the mainstream financial services orthodoxy (see Black Swans, Chapter 2: Capital Evolution).

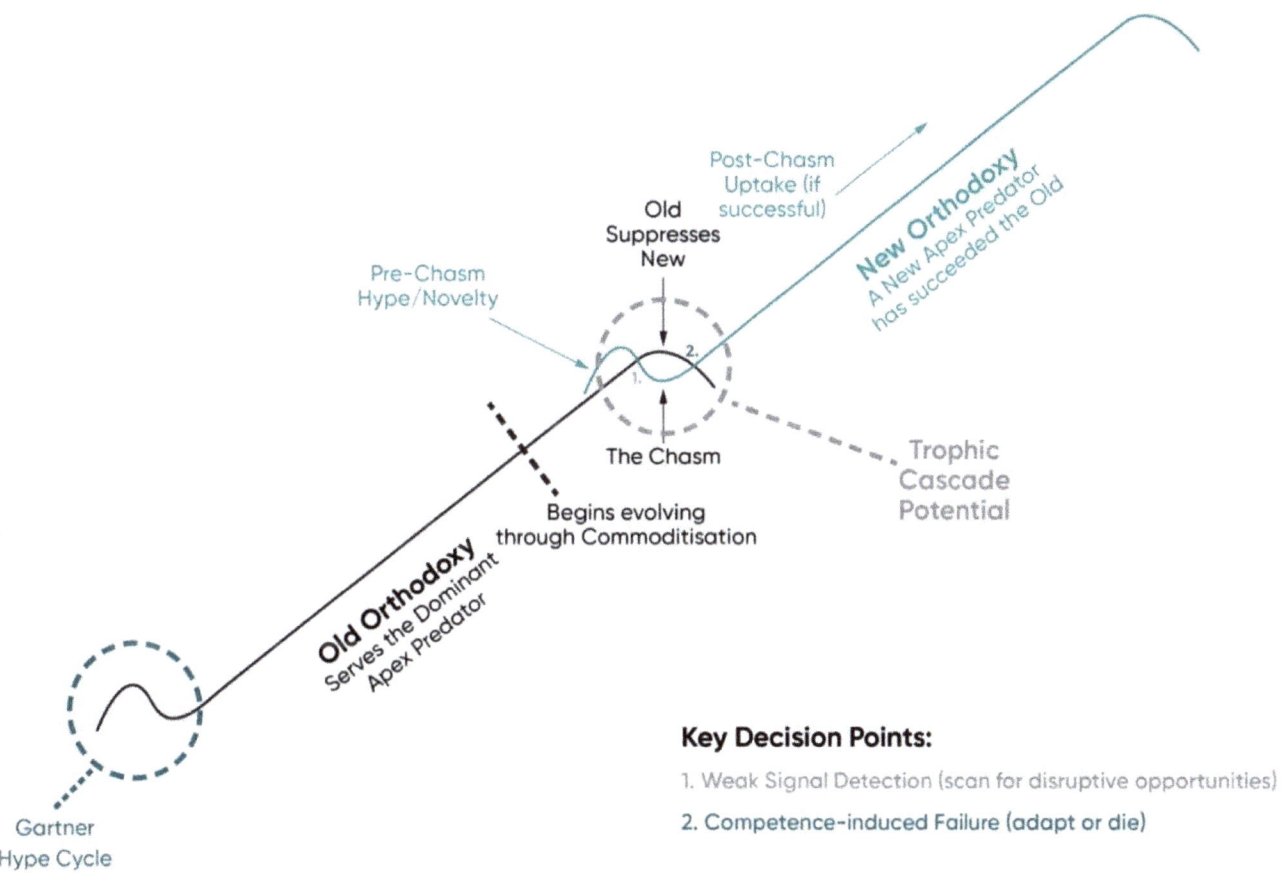

Fig 4.4 Apex Predator Hypothesis illustrating Moore's Chasm and Gartner's Hype Cycle

Displacement, via a new Apex predator, implies the close following of a trophic cascade. A trophic cascade, is thus, expected to impact the supporting industries in the value chain of the previous incumbent. In the context of video streaming, via the CSRS business model, all participants in the value chain were impacted. Manufacturers of VCRs, DVDs and their distributors were disrupted and disintermediated by the top-level change in video content delivery; an exemplary example of evolutionary flow (see Evolutionary Flow above). The fundamental success of the new paradigm hinged on surfacing the utility of video content delivery, through leveraging the technology and appropriate business model of the moment, by exploiting a *first principles* approach.

FIRST PRINCIPLES

By taking a first principles approach towards storing value, making payments and accessing credit, FinTech is assuming the role of, and has become the vehicle through which the utility of financial services may be surfaced to cater to the demands of an evolving economy. Applying first principles towards accomplishing a task involves bringing the tools and knowledge to bear which are available at a particular moment in time. As technology has evolved through commoditisation, utility-computing (cloud), data science, artificial intelligence and smart devices combined with rich platforms, highly abstracted programming interfaces and componentised constructs (e.g. Microservices/APIs), as well as standards and practices have provided a sophisticated and rich toolkit, with which to create high utility capabilities and propositions (see Chapter 3: Ecosystems).

The analogue nature of the financial system dominated by institutional monopolies, which are generic, slow, frictional, mundane and antiquated, is no longer appropriate in an economy increasingly dominated by the digitally literate. News, Broadcasting, Retail, and now financial services, have all been disrupted, and in many instances disintermediated by digital business models and digital channels. Disruptors exploit low barriers to entry, which commoditised technology enables (see Abstraction, Chapter 2: Capital Evolution), creating new value-added services, free of significant liabilities or risks.

Data-driven technology companies (DDTCs) are capable of harnessing and monetising their customers' information to create new revenue streams and create new sources of value and worth (see Chapter 15: Economy of Things). These new Apex predators, are connecting vendors and consumers using a digital framework of cloud technologies (see Vertical to Horizontal, Chapter 3: Ecosystems) and smart devices. It is the utility of financial services, free of friction and inconvenience, which creates the differentiated value for the consumer in this paradigm. Consumers' behaviours have evolved, becoming receptive to consuming services, rather than accumulating things, for example: Renting a bicycle when needed, rather than owning one, which may only be used occasionally. They value the utility of the service and the experience it provides, when and where they desire it, not the underlying asset.

Consequently, companies are evolving into successful platforms by:

1. Focusing on customers

2. Evolving their business and technology architecture around self-service, speed and enhanced experiences

3. Embracing ecosystems

4. Establishing data primacy

The most successful companies' business models have evolved into brokers of value, rather than producers of goods and services.

As companies evolve their business models, this creates dual challenges for financial institutions. The first is to adapt their services to better serve businesses, in terms of instruments, APIs and services to enable digital business. The second is to adapt to the disruption of the financial service industry itself (see Vertical to Horizontal, Chapter 3: Ecosystems). FinTechs represent the nimble innovators which threaten the incumbent institutions on both fronts simultaneously.

Essentially, banks have historically applied technology to existing business models and practices, leaving themselves vulnerable to being disrupted by new business models, which are more attractive to consumers in a digitally empowered era.

Since the Global Financial Crisis 2007-2008, banking has faced its deepest level of disruption in decades. After years of incremental change, banks must plan for a fundamental rethink of operations in order to thrive in a rapidly digitised and data-driven world. This was true long before economic and societal factors came into play. The need for better digitised customer experiences has only galvanised and accelerated, with consumers embracing e-commerce and footfall, reducing in the use of physical bricks-and-mortar shops, as well as banks.

Banking customers do not necessarily wish to visit a bank branch to withdraw funds or make a payment when they could do so remotely. Customers shouldn't be confined to visiting a bank branch to open an account or apply for a mortgage, if this could be securely and safely performed remotely, via a digitally secure medium.

STRAIGHT–THROUGH PROCESSING

Straight-through processing (STP) is a concept embraced by financial companies to accelerate processing of financial transactions. The concept is centred on automating manual processes electronically in order to improve transaction speeds. First pioneered for equities trading in London in the 1990s, STP is largely thought of as a means of augmenting slow and inefficient, predominantly paper-based processes and simplifying as well as automating these where possible to yield an accurate and expedient outcome.

Although STP is an established and well understood concept within the financial services industry, application thereof has predominantly been constrained to automating existing legacy processes, rather than creating new digital processes to achieve an optimised result.

Conceptually, STP is representative of process flow optimisation rather than evolutionary flow. Overcoming barriers imposed by regulatory constraints is a challenge, which requires collaboration and influence in concert with technological innovation. KYC represents such an area where reform is challenging.

KNOW YOUR CUSTOMER

Know Your Customer (KYC), is an essential requirement for regulated financial institutions to adhere to. There are strict requirements which have to be met, in order to assure that customer identity and risk profile is sufficiently qualified. Prior to any engagement in business activity, financial institutions are required to demonstrate 'due diligence' with regards to KYC for prospective customers. Legislation and regulations require institutions to validate the customer's identity, credit standing, nationality and legal eligibility to be serviced by the institution.

Traditionally, verifying the customer's credentials and legislative requirements for a 'wet signature' have been essential criteria, which have created a necessity for in-person customer on-boarding in the financial sector.

CUSTOMER ACQUISITION

Digital natives and a growing number among the digitally literate have demanded the capability to sign up for new services digitally and remotely, without requiring 'wet signatures,' expediently and conveniently. In the financial sector, this has created a significant challenge in new customer acquisition as the controls accepted by regulators, as well as mature internal systems and processes have been fortified to not accept anything less than a frictional, lengthy and direct face-to-face interaction.

FinTech entities have seized the opportunity to create 'low friction' mobile apps and web portals, embracing a 'digital first' approach, which enables new customers to sign up for services within minutes and requiring the minimum of manually inputted information during the on-boarding process. Evidence based on initial interest through to qualified customer concludes that should a prospective customer encounter frictional in-depth dependencies during the subscription process and should the process require greater than a few minutes to complete, the bulk of prospective customers are likely to take their business elsewhere. Comparable conclusions have been drawn, based on the conversion ratio of web site impressions to sales conversions on e-commerce platforms. There is little latitude in the way of consumer appetite for inconvenience or friction, in subscribing to modern financial services. Digital consumers expect frictionless, painless and near instant gratification when engaging digital services.

IDENTITY BROKERS

In order to cater to low friction and expedient on-boarding expectations, demands for digitally accessible identity brokers has grown exponentially. Identity brokers offer services to trusted entities such as banks and insurers, to act as the custodians of customer information. Credit rating agencies are ideally placed to offer these services, although numerous niche players have, and are expected to emerge. The Fast Identity Online (FIDO) Alliance is an initiative aimed at offering strong authentication and identity capabilities as well as standards to enable such services.[62]

In instances where customers attempt to sign up for a new service, the service provider may request the subscriber's information, to validate and authenticate their application. Since the subscriber is not inconvenienced and this process is executed automatically, largely in real time, this greatly improves the likelihood of successfully on-boarding the subscriber and meeting the rigorous requirements set out by regulators.

KNOW YOUR DATA

Customer behaviour and expectations prompts a pivotal transition from 'know your customer' (KYC) to 'know your data' (KYD), whereby, the necessity to effectively capture, process, format, manage, analyse and report, accompanied by a data-driven mind set, is the business imperative for financial institutions. Prior to, as well as since, the GFC, banks' internal technology systems had become increasingly heterogeneous and incoherent. Data, capable of profiling likely customer preferences, as well as risk models, is often highly fragmented across different systems. This raises operating costs while relegating the development of new propositions and capabilities to be increasingly onerous. Identity brokers, financial institutions and regulators are consequently challenged to collaborate in providing customers with the services they've come to expect, in an increasingly digitally enabled world. Data has transformed into a high value commodity and a mutually valuable asset to both customers, as well as financial institutions.

From a regulatory standpoint, the necessity to further validate that customers are neither unlawfully exploiting the services of the financial sector to facilitate money laundering, fraud, terrorist financing nor circumventing sanctions or enabling any other form of illegal activity, are increasingly driving the necessity to capture, analyse and demonstrate such diligence from customer data. Data primacy, has thus, become an existential imperative in the financial services sector.

DATA PRIVACY

In the United Kingdom, the Data Protection Act 1998 was superseded by the Data Protection Act 2018, to bring the United Kingdom into alignment with the European Union's General Data Protection Regulation (GDPR), which came into effect on May 25th, 2018.

The GDPR brought enhanced regulatory oversight and empowered individuals with greater protections and rights against companies' capture and use of their data. The regulation qualified the granularity of data profiles, which are associated with data subjects (people) into 'personal data' and 'sensitive personal data' categories.

Regardless of the data categorisation, companies are obliged to ensure that they capture, transmit, process and securely store only data about persons which is deemed necessary to comply with either a legal obligation applicable to their business sector, or for which they've been granted explicit informed consent by the data subject. Data subjects may demand to know what data a business entity holds about them and may demand deletion where outside legal obligations neither reasonably conflicts, nor supersedes this right.

Although regulations of this stringency level have yet to permeate throughout the world, the recognition that an individual's personal data is a high value asset is unequivocally on the rise. Corporate abuse or negligence in the control or processing of a data subject's information, attracts significant punitive measures, particularly under the GDPR, in the form of damage to reputation, via disclosure obligations and exorbitant fines.

In the United States, in the absence of legislation, several Supreme Court rulings have set precedents extending the interpretation of the US Constitution's first, third, fourth, fifth, ninth and fourteenth amendments toward protecting the privacy rights of US citizens. Notable cases include, Poe v Ullman 1961, Griswold v Connecticut 1965, Eisenstadt v Baird 1972, Roe v Wade 1973 and Lawrence v Texas 2003.

Apart from these incremental milestones in broadening constitutional protections for general privacy, the US has lagged behind the developed world in implementing clear legislation to achieve contemporary data privacy parity in congruence with an increasingly digital world.

The passage of the Consumer Data Privacy and Security Act 2020, a bill introduced for senate consideration in March 2020 as S.3456, would bring the US into alignment with the UK and the EU in terms of consumer data privacy. The US has historically maintained the 'Safe Harbor Privacy Framework' and a successive agreement known as 'Privacy Shield,' to manage inter US-EU data protection compatibility.

BIG DATA

'Big Data' describes the field of processing large data sets in order to systematically extract and analyse discernibly useful or valuable information. Large data sets are aggregated from multiple independent data sources whereby the collective data may be brought into a context. Context based analysis may be performed either statistically based on broad demographics or specific individuals and entities.

By way of an example, in order to estimate the duration of a journey, determining present location, distance to destination and velocity are all data points which could be gathered from individual data sources. When analysed in unison and contextualised, the collective data points can be used to calculate a probable journey duration as well as an estimated time of arrival. By further refining the analysis through incorporating traffic flows or factoring in peak hours into the calculations, greater accuracy may be achieved.

The principle being conveyed is that of the greater the number of data points, the greater the potential for discerning accuracy from the analysis. Some data points may be used to set parenthesis, creating boundaries for a range of possible outcomes. Other data points may be applied using statistical averages, while further data points may be applied based on real-time information or combinations thereof.

DATA WRANGLING

Data collected from multiple data sources is aggregated into a construct known as a Data Lake. A Data Lake is a system or repository of data stored in its raw format, usually object BLOBs or files. A Binary Large Object (BLOB) is a collection of binary data, stored as a single entity in a database. BLOBs are typically images, audio or other multimedia objects – though sometimes, binary executable code is stored as a BLOB. Disparate data from various systems may be formatted differently and almost certainly structured in a variety of relational ways, via database schemas. This is further complicated when siphoning unstructured data, such as files outside the ordered structure of a database. Data wrangling is the process by which data is converted from its raw format into a form suitable for analysis. Hence, a common method to describe transformation of data into a cohesive data set, is that of Extract Transform Load (ETL). Data wrangling is a critical step in data pre-processing, and includes several processes such as data cleansing, data structuring and string processing and parsing. Once data is ingested or loaded, via an ETL process, it is enriched by being pooled through correlation algorithms into a Data Warehouse and exposed through applications (known as Data Visualisation).

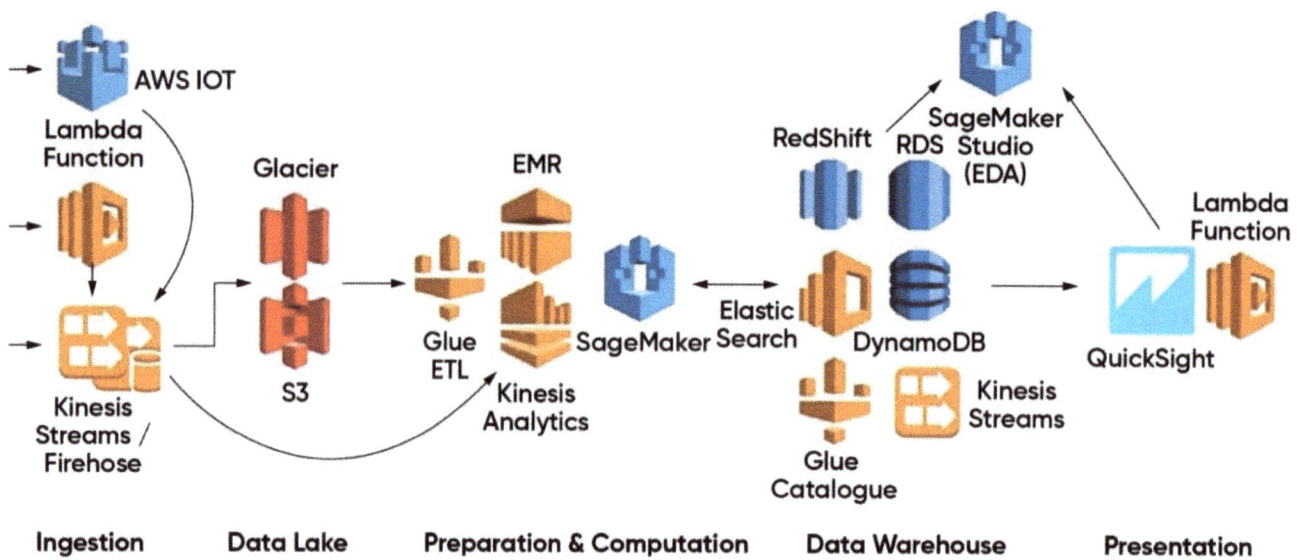

Fig 4.5 an example Data Lake & Data Warehouse architecture using Amazon's Cloud

DATA WAREHOUSE

Data Warehouses (DWs) are central repositories of integrated data, from one or more disparate sources. DWs are generally considered to be inelastic and expensive, built for performance, rather than scale. Hence, the prevalent architecture and practice of ingesting raw data into a Data Lake, heavily curating and transforming the data into the desired format and thereafter, loading into a DW via ETL where it is correlated into an enriched data set. As the elasticity of the cloud becomes increasingly pervasive, architectures and practices are co-evolving to modernise the data pipeline. In such instances, data may be ingested directly into an elastic DW, whereby, it is curated and transformed directly within. In other words, Extract Load Transform (ELT) rather than ETL, thus, a Data Lake may no longer be required. Regardless, once resident in the DW, curated and transformed, the data is ready to be harnessed via mining. Data mining is essentially 'knowledge discovery,' whereby useful information is extracted from a given data set in order to discern patterns and identify relationships.

A paradoxical conundrum exists with regards to incumbent financial institutions, whereby through decades of accrued legacy technology, data sources are increasingly fragmented and include hundreds, if not thousands of disparate sources, inclusive of varied applications and archives. These are underpinned by various databases, enterprise content management (ECM) systems, enterprise resource planning (ERP) systems, as well as customer relationship management systems (CRMs). Furthermore, this predicament is compounded by custom developed mainframe applications and innumerable unstructured content sources. These may include digital documents, as well as paper-based forms. Immense challenges exist in correlating and harnessing this data, as these various systems are likely to be incapable of negotiating the immense processing workloads required for meaningful data analysis, without impeding their normal function and attract exorbitant costs in lengthy integration projects. Incumbent financial institutions benefit from decades of pedigree in their experience and knowledge of data analysis, statistics, formulae and algorithms, to derive the greatest value from the information. Yet without adding customised ETL/ELT integrations and a form of DW, the data's value potential is exceedingly challenging to realise.

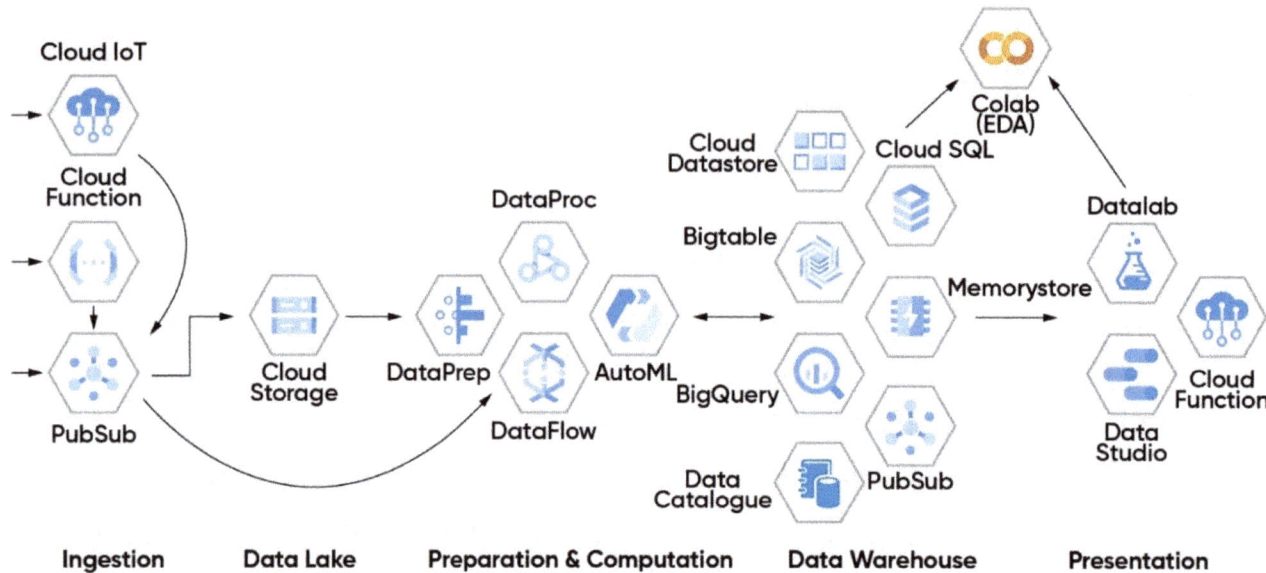

Fig 4.6 an example Data Lake & Data Warehouse architecture using Google's Cloud

By contrast, nimble FinTech entities are able to exploit a plethora of modern cloud tooling and benefit from its elasticity in performance and capacity. FinTechs are able to design their applications to collect, process and aggregate data cohesively. Such an approach enables compliance with prevailing legislation from the outset, and without the necessity to retrofit separate analytical systems, and does not require investment in costly integrations. Where integrations are required with independent or third-party systems, this is where leveraging APIs is economical and favourable. FinTech entities, however, do not benefit from the maturity in methodology, nor the pedigree of incumbents' expertise, gained through years of operation and substantial critical mass. In either case, superior contextual and experiential applications are reliant on the ability to effectively correlate and harness customer data.

CONTEXTUAL BANKING

Contextual banking is the concept of offering customers services, which are tailored to their specific needs and ambitions at the appropriate time. It is of particular importance as the trend towards increasingly well-defined markets persist. Customer appetites and priorities are increasingly diverse, resulting in diminishing tolerance for 'one size fits all' banking and financial services. Consequently, contextual banking serves, as an effective capability for customising the banking experience while cross-selling and up-selling products and services. Such services, may originate both within the banking institutions' portfolio, as well as within the broader portfolios of partners, however, combined or substituted in numerous ways to personalise the services for individual customers. This is largely achievable through the flexibility afforded by technology ecosystems and the componentisation of business services (see Vertical to Horizontal, Chapter 3: Ecosystems), via the API economy.

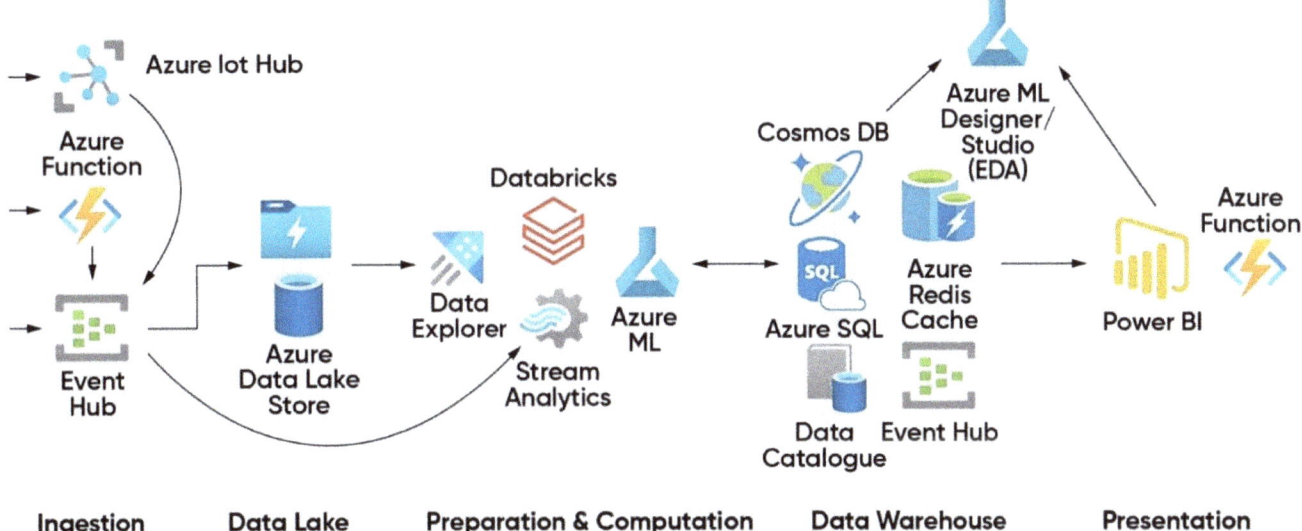

Fig 4.7 an example Data Lake & Data Warehouse architecture using Microsoft's Cloud

More importantly, a contextual approach additionally acts as a means through which banks and their partners can evolve to better serve their customers' future needs, while acting as a vehicle through which to secure customer retention. A FinTech typically exploits a high utility service, such as an easy-to-use and convenient payment app to attract a customer. This facilitates the establishment of primacy over the customer relationship. Thereafter, the customer relationship is leveraged to harvest data (see Harvesting Data below), in order to cultivate insights (see Harnessing & Monetising Data below). Through exploiting Data Science and AI (see Artificial Intelligence below), the FinTech exploits the customer's data and the associated insights to understand and anticipate the customer's needs, via inferences. Through a partner ecosystem engaged, via the API economy, the FinTech exploits these inferences to provide a comprehensive and contextual service for the customer (see Self-perpetuating Cycle below). Thereby, delivering differentiated value and assuring retention. This methodology draws parallels with the ILC/'Tower & Moat' strategy exploited by tech giants to grow ecosystems (see Innovate, Leverage & Commoditise, Chapter 3: Ecosystems).

Providing a contextual service, hinges on the volume and quality of data curated, as well as the effectiveness of the analysis, thereof. The data functions as a vehicle through which to realise customer specificity, in order to tailor the service value proposition to each and every customer individually (see Value Proposition, Chapter 2: Capital Evolution). In the absence of legislation to limit or require customer consent for such use, organisations are able to siphon data from any number of potential sources at their discretion. DDTCs additionally embed consent waivers within the terms and conditions of use for their apps and services. Subscribers are, thus, provided access to services upon granting collection and use of their data unconditionally (see Surveillance Capitalism, Chapter 15: Economy of Things).

By way of example, a bank may serve customers who are health conscious, likely to prioritise fitness, outdoor activities and activity-centric or experiential travel opportunities. By analysing spending patterns, the bank should be able to determine that these customers would be receptive to offers from institutional partners, which cater to these needs. Further data may be gathered from other sources, such as wearable (as well as ingestible) technologies, customer surveys, smart device apps, social media, and loyalty schemes.

Through analysis and frictionless automated integrations, the bank should be able to profit from intermediating customer adoption of these integrated services, while delivering greater value to the customer through preferential and collective bargaining. Further opportunities may exist to broker competitive life coverage with an insurer, leveraging a health-conscious customer's data as evidence in substantiating a lower risk profile (see Behavioural Underwriting, Chapter 15: Economy of Things). Conversely, the same data could be exploited by an insurer to highlight a potentially bad risk, resulting in higher premiums, or refusal to underwrite the risk altogether (see Adverse Selection, Chapter 10: Financialisation). Opportunities for value creation, via enhanced data-driven synergies, are extensive.

EXPERIENTIAL BANKING

Contextual banking enables customers to realise value from banks' analysis of their behaviour and priorities. In turn, customer satisfaction and a sense of personalised service cultivates loyalty, positive sentiment and raises the institution's profile in good standing.

FinTech banks have an advantage in developing these capabilities rapidly without the need for broad integration of legacy systems, however, they are challenged to attract and retain customers, in order to achieve critical mass and longevity. In order to differentiate their proposition, FinTechs are compelled to enhance their innovation efforts to reach ahead of incumbents. A mechanism for doing so is to harness data and artificial intelligence, to surface the utility of banking in experiential forms.

In an increasingly fast-paced world, the tolerance for visiting a banking branch to apply for a loan to purchase a home or a vehicle is antiquated. A creditworthy customer expects to be able to select an item for purchase and the utility of financing should be insulated from their view or direct participation. The expectation is this should be expedient, efficient and convenient. Most importantly, it should be invisible. The identical sentiment is valid in the context of communities, which find themselves either underbanked or unbanked altogether. In developing and emerging market economies, rural communities may have access to smart phones and cellular networks, providing them with the instrumentation for conducting digital banking, however, low or zero access to bricks-and-mortar banks confined to urban centres. The ability to conduct banking, via a smart phone app from a rural location, is an example in which the utility of banking has been surfaced through a convenient medium in an experiential manner.

Another experiential example would be a customer entering a supermarket to purchase their weekly groceries, unaware that they may have insufficient funds in their account. Through analysis of the customer's spending behaviour on groceries, as well as knowledge of their creditworthiness, the bank proactively offers the customer a line of credit. This is sufficient to complete their usual shopping and is catalysed by their entry to the store. An intuitive understanding of the customer and their needs is anticipated and met instantly. The bank's technology exploited the use of data and AI, focused on surfacing the utility that the customer required, in the context it was required and at the appropriate time, all in an experiential manner. Consequently, the customer's banking experience becomes discreet, convenient, intuitive and invisible. Equipped with a smart phone or smart wearable technology, the customer's location could be discerned by the bank's mobile app installed on the device. By entering the store, the app signals a Microservice hosted in the cloud as to the customer's location, using the smart device integrated Global Positioning System (GPS) receiver. The Microservice queries the AI for insights as to the customer's past behaviour and spending patterns with the merchant at this location. Through analysis of transactions, the AI determines the customer shops weekly at this merchant and spends on average $100 per week. Examining the customer's present balance, there are insufficient funds to complete a routine purchase. The AI determines that the customer is creditworthy and triggers a push notification to the smart device to offer a sufficient line of credit in the form of an overdraft to the customer. The customer accepts and uses the smart device as a payment instrument to complete the transaction at check out. Although the customer may possess an alternate means of payment in the form of credit cards or cash, facilities such as this would aid a bank in attracting business away from competitors. Thereby, retaining primacy over the customer relationship.

HARNESSING & MONETISING DATA

Through **descriptive analytics**, the bank traverses a history of records to determine what a customer has earned, borrowed and spent in the past. A descriptive analysis may additionally reveal what the customer spent their money on, what instruments and products were used, as well as how frequently. This methodology of profiling, is mature and well understood by banks, insurance companies and numerous spheres of industry. Descriptive data analysis allows us to determine what has transpired as a matter of **hindsight**.

Using **diagnostic analytics,** the objective is to determine and understand why what has previously transpired, has occurred. The value of such an analysis is to provide an **insight** into a customer's needs and behaviours. Descriptive and diagnostic analytics are common functions of the field of data science.

Anticipating customers' needs, however, is more challenging. This is an area where data analytics definitively transcends into the realms of linear regression and multiple regression analysis. A sphere where empiricism is juxtaposed with disposition, by exploiting statistical probabilistic modelling, such as Bayesian models and inference. Essentially a paradigm, whereby after data is correlated, is used to predict the value of variables (dependent variables), based on the value of other known variables within a broader field (pattern) of data points. This is the field of **predictive analytics**, where the anticipation of what will occur, or most likely shall occur (or what the value of a variable is likely to be), offers an advantage through **foresight**.

Artificial Intelligence (AI) algorithms exploit these analytical and probabilistic capabilities, combined with high quality enriched data sources. The objective is to iteratively learn through analysis, simulation and observation in order to engineer intelligence, which may be later applied to problems based on what has been learned.

Finally, **prescriptive analytics** is the means through which entities may **influence,** either an individual, or a group through behavioural engineering. The meteoric rise of Ant Financial's 'Yu'e Bao' ('Leftover Treasure,' Mandarin) was a testament as to how a FinTech smart phone app could grow a savings proposition exponentially. This is an achievement through the use of AI powered behavioural engineering (see Chapter 15: Economy of Things). The technology encourages and persuades its customers to save money into a finance construct, similar in nature, to a money market fund. 'Yu'e Bao' captured the world's attention after dwarfing the J.P. Morgan Chase Treasury Fund – at the time, the world's largest money market fund.[63]

Prescriptive analytics leverages predictive analytics (through Data Science and AI) to assist in deciding a course of action, based on near-term predictions in order to yield a desired outcome. In this sphere, constant learning through historic and real time data are essential. Prescriptive algorithms are often infused with capabilities, which are intuitively designed to elicit a specified set of cognitive activations within human psychology. Examples include, common sales methods such as assumptive, as well as incentive centric closure techniques. Peer pressure, exploiting vanity, greed and fear of shame, are among other psychological levers, which may be harnessed for this purpose (see Chapter 15: Economy of Things).

AI used to study customer behaviour and anticipating customer needs is a function of gathering and analysing data. Monetising data may be achieved through utilising data to create revenue generating opportunities or mitigating risks.

By studying past behaviour through the examination of transaction records on a customer's bank statement, an examination thereof may easily be exploited to harness value from the data in order to create new revenue opportunities.

Such an examination using deterministic techniques, may reveal the customer's income, whether derived exclusively from employment, portfolio, passive sources or combinations thereof. The customer's ability to service debt should be easily discernible from monthly earnings versus expenditures. The customer's disposable income versus fixed living expenses in contrast to their earnings should indicate their creditworthiness, and analysis of non-essential spending should provide insights into their recreational priorities, such as hobbies and/or travel habits.

The customer's interests, priorities, vocation, marital status, dependents, investments, assets and liabilities are data points of material value in training AI models, which enable institutions to monetise opportunities and create customer value.

ARTIFICIAL INTELLIGENCE

Artificial Intelligence (AI) is a higher-order system, enabled by the explosion of data and advances in suitable computer processing technology, however, it is far from a new field. A paper published by Alan Turing (1912 - 1954), *Computing Machinery and Intelligence,* arguably established the field of Artificial Intelligence in 1950.[64] In honour of Turing's contribution to Science, Technology and his instrumental work deciphering the Nazi Enigma machines during World War II, as well as to Artificial Intelligence, on his birthday, June 23rd 2021, Britain introduced its new £50 (fifty-pound) banknote, featuring Turing's portrait, as well as several technical nuances relating to him.

'Placing Alan Turing on this new banknote is a recognition of his contributions to our society, and a celebration of his remarkable life.'

- Andrew Bailey, Governor of the Bank of England, June 23rd 2021 (Speaking at Bletchley Park Trust).

EXPERT SYSTEMS

Expert systems were among the first successful implementations of Artificial Intelligence software. Introduced by researchers in the Stanford Heuristic Programming Project, including Edward Feigenbaum, considered to be the "father" of expert systems. Expert systems are intended to house the knowledge of one or more human experts, accessible within a computerised knowledge base. The systems are designed to apply specific knowledge to problems in contrast to applying specific techniques. This is built on the principle that experts do not process their knowledge differently, although they do possess different aspects of knowledge from one another. Practical use of an expert system is intended to assist a non-Subject Matter Expert (SME) in resolving a real-world problem, by applying or simulating the codified knowledge within.

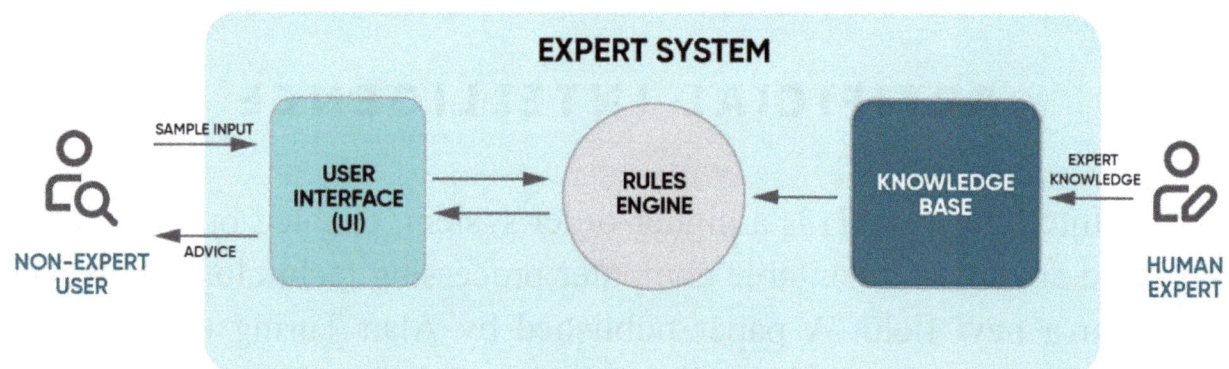

Fig 4.8 an example of the typical architecture of an Expert System

FUZZY LOGIC

A pivotal stepping stone on the journey to developing AI is that of fuzzy logic. Fuzzy logic has been studied since the 1920s, known then as 'infinite-valued logic.' The term 'Fuzzy Logic' was introduced in the proposal of Fuzzy Set Theory, published in 1965, by Lotfi Zadeh. Unlike Boolean logic, where values are expressed as integers of either "1" or "0" (true and false), fuzzy logic allows for the expression of values inclusive of "0" and "1," along with the values in between. Fuzzy Logic is employed to surface the concept of partial truths whereby the 'truth value' may range between completely true (1) and completely false (0).

Unlike probabilistic mathematics which ranges between "0" and "1," Fuzzy Logic uses vagueness, expressed as degrees of truth (or dispositions, see Prologue). A simplistic example would be expressing the value of 'warm' in between the parenthesis of 'hot' and 'cold.'

Numerous early successes in the application of Fuzzy Logic were in Japan, where noteworthy improvements to the economy, precision and comfort of the Sendai subway train, were realised through its use. Other early noteworthy examples were that of image recognition of hand-written symbols with Sony pocket computers and flight stabilising aids for helicopters. Another example is the image stabilisation technology applied in digital cameras and smart phones.

BAYESIAN STATISTICS

Significant advances in AI development, particularly predictive analytics, have been accomplished through the use of Bayesian statistics. Bayesian statistics is named after Reverend Thomas Bayes, who wrote an essay forming the basis thereof, in a paper published by Richard Price, in 1763.[65] The paper focused on 'inverse probability,' essentially determining the probability of future events through examining past events. Subsequent papers published by Pierre-Simon Laplace (1749 - 1827), developed the Bayesian interpretation of probability, articulating what is now known as Bayes' Theorem.

Bayesian statistical methods are an approach to data analysis and parameter estimation, based on Bayes' Theorem to compute and update probabilities after receiving new data. Bayesian methods require substantial computation to complete and prior to appropriate computational power being developed were unfavourable among statisticians.

A unique characteristic of Bayesian statistics is that all observed and unobserved parameters in a statistical model are given a joint probability distribution. These are known as the 'prior' and 'data' distributions. Typical Bayesian workflows capture available knowledge about a given parameter in a statistical model via the prior distribution, before gathering any data. A 'likelihood function' is then determined using the information about the parameters found within the data, which is subsequently gathered and observed.

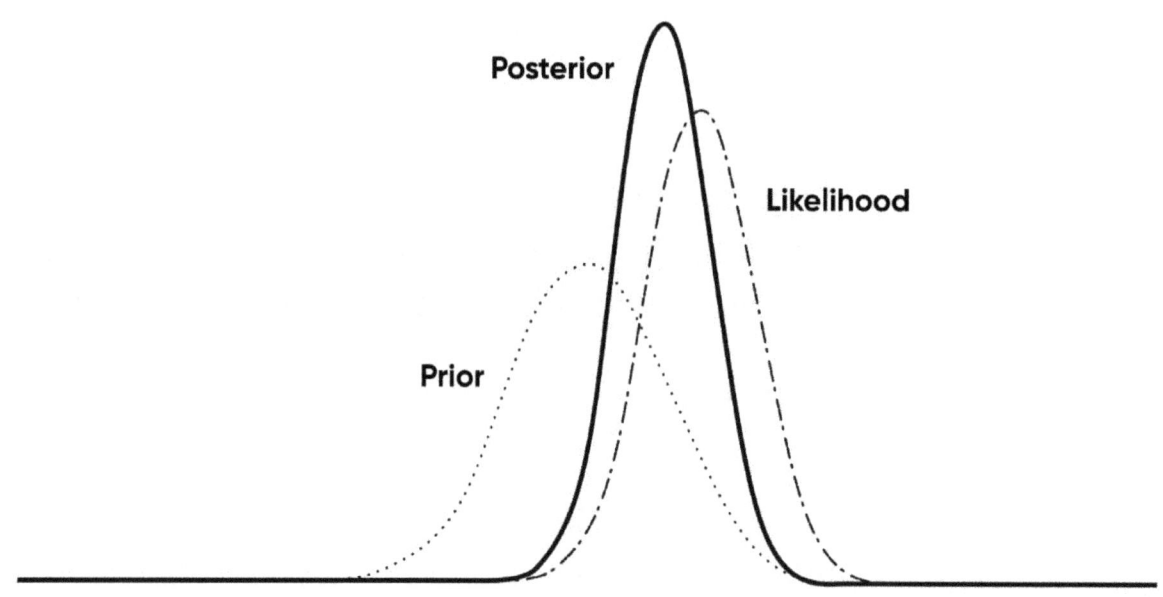

Fig 4.9 an example set of distributions including a 'Posterior' (result) using Bayes' Theorem

Combining the *prior distribution* with the *likelihood function* using Bayes' Theorem produces a *posterior distribution*. The *posterior distribution* reflects the updated knowledge gained through balancing prior knowledge with observed data. The *posterior distribution* (the results) may then be used to conduct inferences.

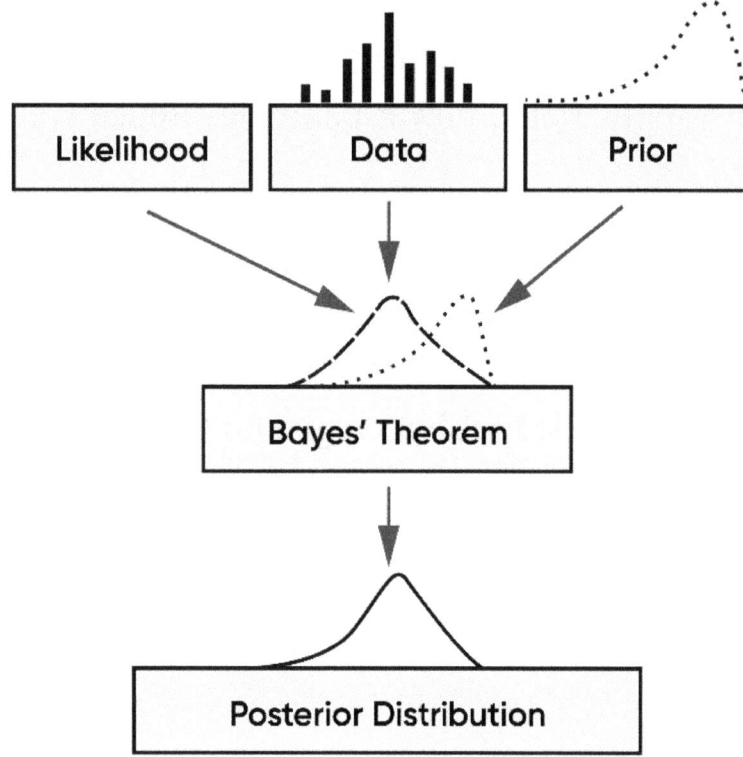

Inferences are conclusions or steps toward discerning such, based on evidence and reasoning. Consequently, the greatest advances towards producing the highest quality Bayesian inferences, hinge on the volume and quality of observed data.

Much of modern AI has seen significant advances, having been built on the foundations of Bayesian inference,

Bayesian statistics, as well as Expert Systems and Fuzzy Logic. Advancement in the field has relied on harnessing sophisticated methods to process and interpret data, calculate probabilities, and to learn from doing so.

'Exploratory data analysis seeks to reveal structure, or simple descriptions in data. We look at numbers or graphs and try to find patterns. We pursue leads suggested by background information, imagination, patterns perceived, and experience with other data analyses.'

- Persi Warren Diaconis (Mathematician known for the Freedman-Diaconis rule; Professor of mathematics and statistics, Stanford University).

CONTEMPORARY THINKING

AI development offers promising opportunities to create 'Exaptive Moments,' whereby the technology may be co-opted to surface utility in novel and innovative ways. AI should broadly be considered to fit into three levels of intelligence. Narrow, General and Super.

Artificial Super Intelligence (ASI) is a theoretical aspiration, whereby it is anticipated that at some point in the future, an Artificial General Intelligence (AGI) advances to a level that exceeds that of human intelligence potential. There is a great deal of debate as to whether achieving an AGI is possible and even more so, in achieving ASI. AGI would essentially be synonymous with human-level intelligence. Achieving parity with human intelligence, is additionally referred to as 'Human-level AI' or 'Strong AI' and would be capable of passing the 'Turing Test.' Alan Turing established the criteria for passing such a test as an AI conducting a conversation in a manner indistinguishable of that with a human being.

The level of Artificial Intelligence achieved thus far falls within the sphere of Artificial Narrow Intelligence (ANI). An ANI capability refers to the ability of a computer system to perform either a single task or a number of specific tasks extremely well. The nature of intelligence in this context is derived from the ability to learn and then apply what has been learned to these tasks.

ANI is capable of radically augmenting all manner of economic and human activities. Much of how an ANI is developed is accomplished through programming algorithms, which combine business rules and logic with mathematical equations, theorems, statistical formulae and models. These are infused with a number of programmed constructs in order to facilitate learning.

Human beings may learn how to apply a mathematical formula or statistical model to a variety of problems using data inputs, however, the value derived in calculating a result, hinges on the sample of data, the person's skill and proficiency in applying the formula and the time required to do so.

An ANI, can process numerous and vastly broader data sets with consistent proficiency and impeccable precision. It is capable of doing so, in the order of millions of iterations per second, with minimal computational resources. This distinction enables AI to drive productivity in areas for which it is suitable.

DUNBAR'S NUMBER

Dunbar's number illustrates this point. It is the number suggested to be the cognitive limit with which a human being may maintain stable and meaningful social relationships. The number is derived based on a hypothesis posited in the 1990s by British anthropologist, Robin Dunbar. Dunbar's hypothesis is derived through an observation as to a correlation between the size of a primate's brain and the size of its typical social group. In humans, Dunbar suggests the number with which an individual may maintain meaningful social relationships is limited from 100 - 250. Thus, typically considered to be 150.

'This limit is a direct function of relative neocortex size, and that this, in turn, limits group size...

...the limit imposed by neocortical processing capacity is simply on the number of individuals with whom a stable inter-personal relationship can be maintained.'

- *Robin Dunbar, 1990s.*

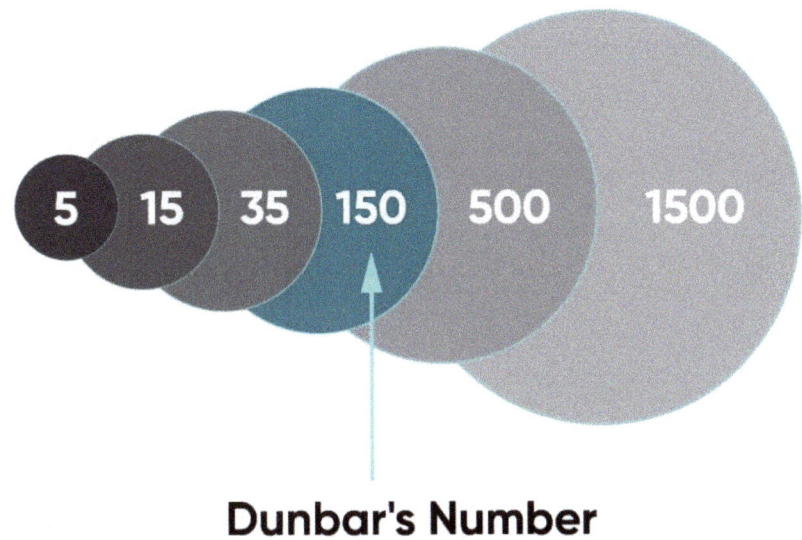

Fig 4.10 Dunbar's number illustrating correlation between brain size and social group potential

By contrast, a computer system with access to a network, is capable of interacting with innumerable others, with consistency. Furthermore, ANIs excel at performing tasks, which are time consuming for humans and at which humans may be less proficient. Such tasks may be construed as mundane and repetitive. The key to doing so effectively is learning.

MACHINE LEARNING

Machine Learning is a subset of artificial intelligence, through which algorithms are improved automatically, via incremental experience (analysis and simulation). Such experience is gained through processing and analysing vast quantities of data, whereby through repetition and noting the variances, the algorithms and models are trained to recognise and effectively learn from patterns.

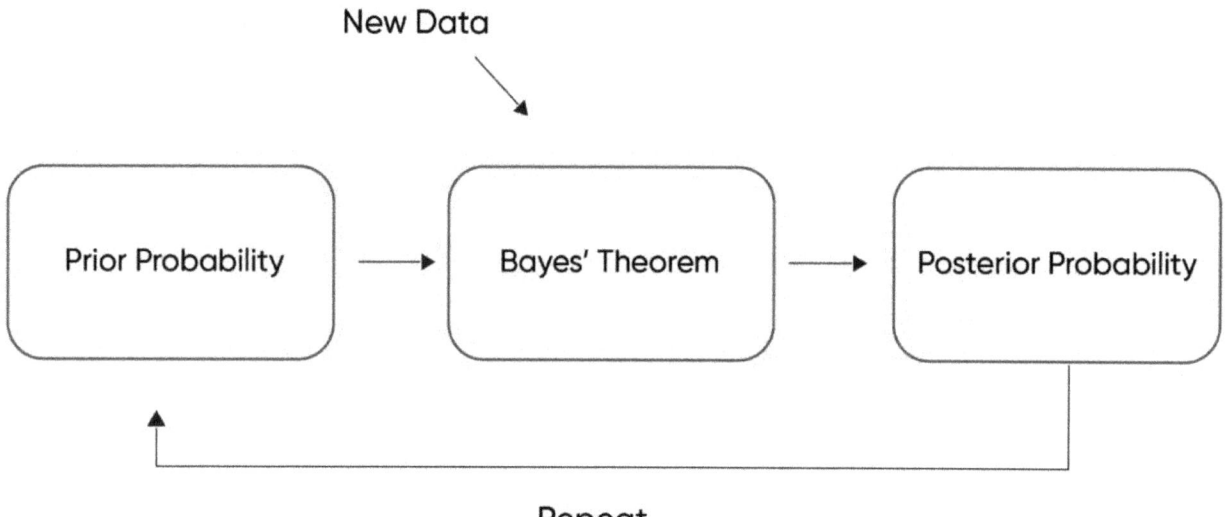

Fig 4.11 continuously adding and processing new data refines the 'Posterior Probability' re-engineering the algorithm.

In traditional programming, programs are engineered using conditions and rules (see Expert Systems above), through which data is later processed to yield outputs. Machine Learning differentiates itself by using learning algorithms to leverage outputs combined with new data in order to re-engineer the program.

The algorithms identify natural patterns in data that generate insight and may assist people in making better informed decisions or predictions.

Descriptive, diagnostic and predictive analytics using Machine Learning and Deep Learning (see below) have proven highly effective in the payments, banking and investment sectors. Identifying and intercepting fraudulent transactions, money laundering activity and terrorist financing have all significantly improved in institutions exploiting these AI capabilities (see Terrorist Finance Tracking Program, Chapter 13: Global Trade Rails). The insurance industry has exploited this technology in several areas, including assessing claims and quantifying risk, in underwriting and pricing. Further advances in the insurance sector's efforts to harness AI in conjunction with Actuarial Science and digital telemetry (see Behavioural Underwriting, Chapter 15: Economy of Things), have shown tremendous promise for the future of insurance and broader fields of risk management (see Insuretech, Chapter 15: Economy of Things). In the banking sphere, this technology additionally enables the improvement of loan book profitability. This is achieved through algorithmically contrasting revenue and margins against customer credit profiles. This enables banks to identify, as well as differentiate between profitable customers and those which are likely to default. Consequently, this capability furnishes the institution with a means to anticipate default risks, thus, enabling prior mitigation or management thereof, in advance of a default coming to fruition. Banks may additionally exploit these AI capabilities in the profiling of customers in order to prioritise and route customer enquiries or feedback. Furthermore, banks may be able to refine customer credit profiling through the use of AI to analyse collection performance of their debt recovery endeavours across varied customer profiles and business segments.

DEEP LEARNING

Deep Learning is a subset of Machine Learning that emulates the human brain in processing data for detecting objects, speech recognition, translating languages and decision making. Deep Learning bases its learning methods on artificial neural networks (see below) with representational learning. Learning can be supervised, reinforced (semi-supervised) or unsupervised.

Advances in computing hardware, particularly Graphics Processing Units (GPUs) and Application-Specific Integrated Circuits (ASICs), has unlocked the potential to exploit Deep Learning on an exponential scale, provoking significant development in the field. GPUs were designed to handle rich graphics rendering workloads. GPUs are required by games and broader graphics intensive applications, however, they have proven to be an instrumental catalyst by being co-opted to process Deep Learning workloads.

With the appropriate type and capacity of computational power required to process large data sets, leveraging Deep Learning to advance AI capabilities is proportionate to the volume of data to which it is exposed. Deep Learning derives its name from using deep (multi-layered) artificial neural networks (see Artificial Neural Networks below).

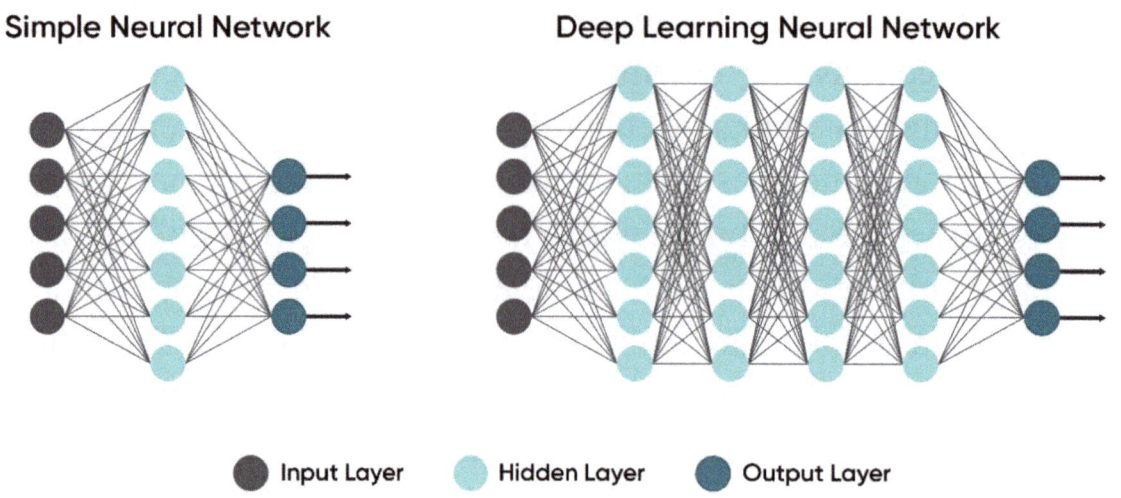

Fig 4.12 illustrates the depth of hidden layers differentiating Deep Learning Neural Nets

HOW AI LEARNS

To a human being, identifying a "chair" in a photograph is fairly simple. To a computer algorithm identifying a chair requires analysis of thousands, if not millions of examples and permutations. Once programmed to identify the properties of a "chair" through modelling, the algorithm is trained by analysing all the variances of "chairs" in a series of photographs, which are populated in the model. The more examples, the better trained the algorithm will be. An algorithm designed to identify "chairs" can either be trained in a supervised, reinforced (semi-supervised) or unsupervised manner.

In supervised learning, training is achieved by feeding the AI with data in the form of photographs of, or which include "chairs." These images would be tagged in advance as 'CHAIR.' Additionally, the AI could be fed images which don't contain "chairs" and tagged as 'NO CHAIR.'

Learning in this manner produces results which can be astoundingly accurate. Once trained, the AI may be fed with new images and discern whether or not they contain a rendering of a "chair," or provide a probability as to whether the image contains zero, one or more chairs.

Reinforced learning is achieved through practice. The AI is trained on a trial-and-error basis and reinforced when a desirable result is realised. Reinforced learning is particularly useful in building AI algorithms, which are used to play games and scenario-based simulations. With each iteration of game play, the AI learns how to better improve its skill to win the game.

Using unsupervised learning, the AI is trained in much the same way that humans learn. The AI is fed with unstructured and untagged data, while programmed to learn on an observation basis.

Being trained, via supervised learning is fastest, although, a fully trained AI may assess and return a probability of a pattern match, in lieu of an absolute result. Accuracy of the result will pivot on the quality of the algorithm, the model and the volume as well as quality of data with which it was trained.

SELF–PERPETUATING CYCLE

The business impact of Artificial Intelligence is demonstrable in the form of learning effects (see Learning Effects, Chapter 3: Ecosystems), enabling a product to learn from customer interactions and rich data sources. Thereby, providing the data to become more valuable.

Machine Learning enables digital products to benefit from learning, via data sources gleaned from their use automatically (see Data Harvesting below). Software can conceivably learn independently (unsupervised learning) with exposure to new data and simultaneously increase in value, via consumer responses (reinforced learning) in the process thereof.

In this context, *learning effects* have the potential to generate substantial economic value, in a comparable manner to *network effects* (see Network Effects, Chapter 3: Ecosystems). Should a business entity succeed in making it self-reinforcing, the products should be able to learn from experience, improve, and subsequently increase in value as a consequence, thereof.

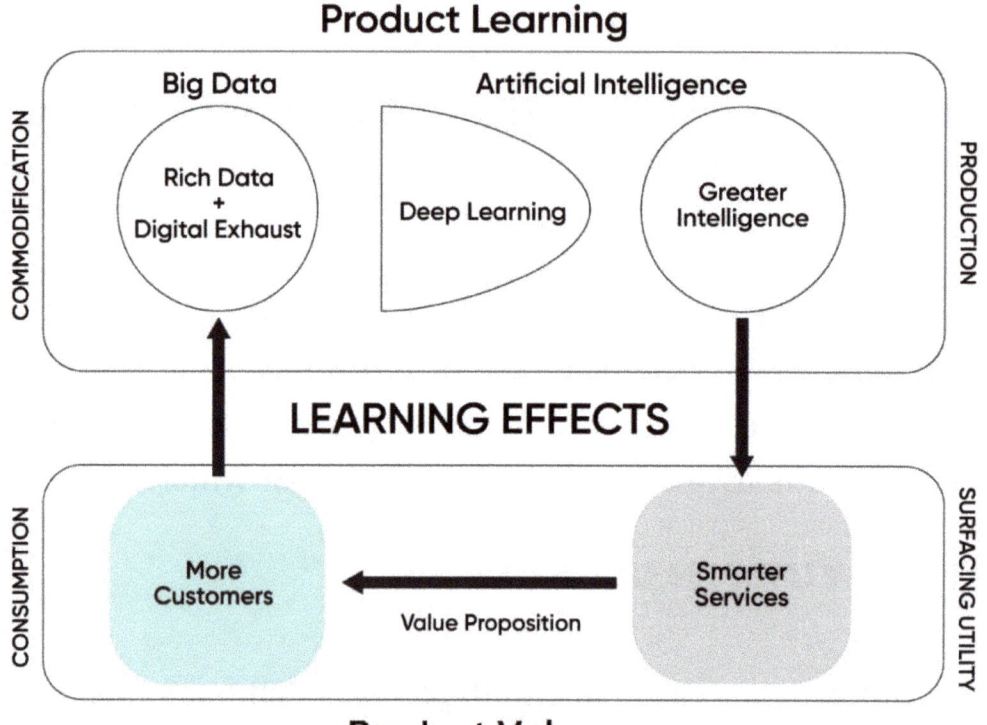

Fig 4.13 self-perpetuating cycle of value creation via self-reinforcing 'Learning' and 'Network' effects

Through perpetual improvement and value creation *(contextual, experiential, surfacing utility)*, the products should attract new customers (network effect), while assuring retention of existing ones. New customers provide new varied and richer data, which enables the products to self-refine (learning effect), thus, increasing in value. Thereby, creating a perpetual value creation cycle, via *learning effects* and growing in correlation to self-reinforcing *network effects*. The net result, thereof, is a self-perpetuating cycle. Above all else, this should highlight the relationship between the data primacy imperative and primacy over the relationship with customers.

ARTIFICIAL NEURAL NETWORKS

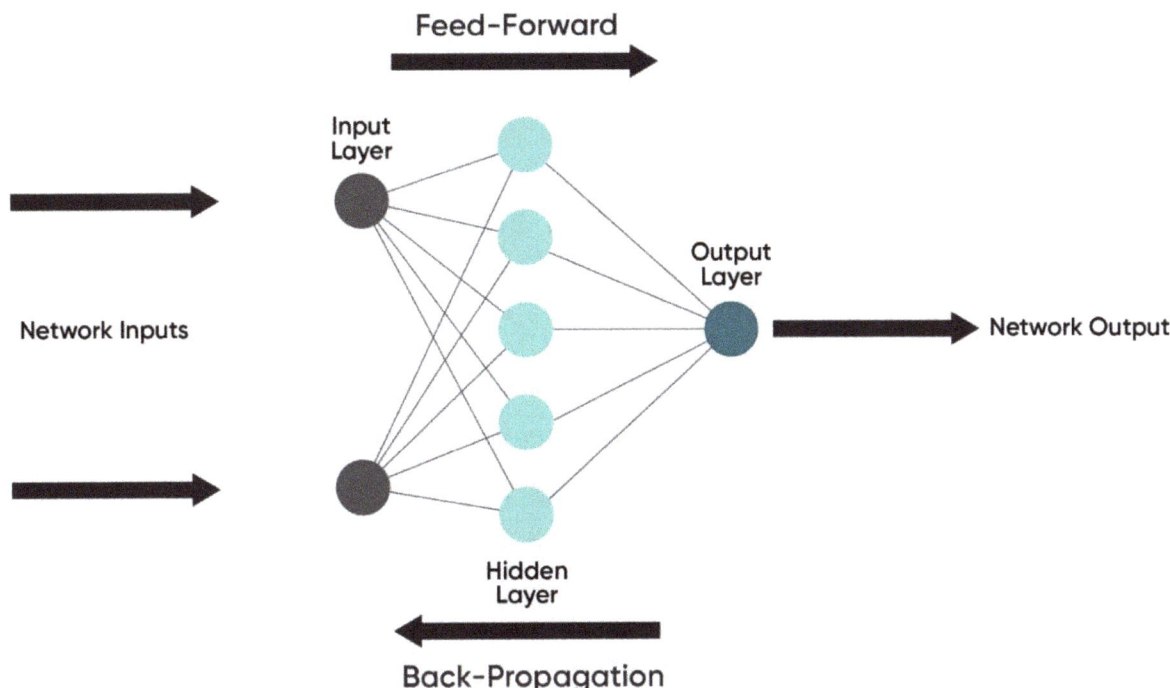

Fig 4.14 illustrates 'Back-Propagation' in a 'Feed-Forward' Artificial Neural Network

An Artificial Neural Network (ANN) is software designed to closely emulate the manner in which neurones behave in the human brain.

In an ANN, a mathematical technique known as 'gradient descent,' is used to reduce errors within a 'Backprop' (Back-Propagation) algorithm. Using the Backprop algorithm, information propagates back through the layers of neurones within the ANN. During propagation, this prompts a recalibration of weights (settings) in each of the neurones. As the ANN is incrementally trained (term of art), the entire network systematically homes in on discerning the correct answer.

Backprop is a Learning algorithm for training Feed-Forward neural networks and is prevalent in Deep learning. The concept was popularised by a highly cited paper, *Learning representations by back-propagating errors*, co-authored by Geoffrey Hinton, David Rumelhart and Ronald Williams, published in 1986.[66]

Among the architectures which describe the configurations of neural nets are that of *Recurrent, Boltzmann Machines* and *Convolutional*. These predominantly differ through the manner in which the neurones are connected to one another. Consequently, these architectures are better suited for different purposes from one another.

Convolutional Neural Networks (CNNs) are predominantly used for image processing, classification, segmentation and for auto-correlation of data. Particularly relevant to the earlier "chair" example. Boltzmann Machines (BMs) are a network of symmetrically connected neurone units, designed to make stochastic decisions as to whether to be on or off. A BM uses a simple learning algorithm, designed to surface anomalous features in data sets composed of binary vectors. BMs are known for originally making use of Markov Chain Monte Carlo (MCMC) methods. MCMC is used extensively for obtaining information about distributions, particularly for estimating posterior distributions in Bayesian inference.

Co-invented by Geoffrey Hinton, Boltzmann Machines were originally designed for use in cognitive science, although the applications thereof are extensive.

NATURAL LANGUAGE PROCESSING

A Recurrent Neural Network (RNN) is a type of ANN commonly used in speech recognition and natural language processing (NLP). RNNs are designed to recognise data's sequential characteristics and exploit patterns to predict and anticipate the next probable scenario.

NLP is an instrumental advancement in surfacing utility in all manner of circumstances and has significant potential. In the sphere of FinTech, NLP is increasingly being exploited to provide a natural language user interface (NLUI) to reduce the load in bank's call centres. Common, standardised and frequent requests for which customers phone banks and other financial institutions are increasingly being fielded by AI powered systems using NLUIs.

If a service or issue is beyond resolution, the call is qualified as such by the AI and forwarded to a small pool of human call centre staff. The objective is, no doubt, to eventually advance to the level where institutions use AI to eliminate the need for human interaction in the call centre, completely.

Using NLP to complete transactions and purchase goods or services is an example of surfacing the utility of banking that NLP can enable. Performing tasks, such as purchasing tickets to a concert or paying a utility bill, are likely to become frictionless interactions facilitated, via NLP enabled AI virtual assistants. Examples include, Apple's Siri, Amazon's Alexa, IBM's Watson and the Google Assistant.

An example of such could be, *'Order me two tickets for Friday's show of Phantom of the Opera.'* The virtual assistant would process the request, prompting a series of background tasks searching for a ticket vendor service, determine availability for two tickets seated together at each of the performances on the day, at the most proximate venue to the requestor. Once established, the assistant would respond with a statement akin to, *'There's a showing on Friday at 7pm where two tickets are available in the gallery for $50 each, or a private box available for $120 each. There are no seats available together for the 9pm show. Would you prefer the gallery or a private box?'* Assuming this is acceptable, based on the response, the virtual assistant will execute payment from the requester's account, or an alternate payment instrument to the ticket vending service, via various Microservices interacting between businesses within the API economy.

The virtual assistant will update the requestor's online calendar with the theatre venue and performance details, while additionally downloading the digital tickets to their digital wallet.

The net effect is a convenient, frictionless experience for the customer, which would otherwise have required numerous interactions searching for appropriate order criteria, and then interactively transacting to complete the purchase. In this example, all such activity is insulated from the customer. Scepticism as to whether such interactions could be securely executed, and risks of fraud and identity theft could be adequately mitigated, should be addressed through significant advances in AI technology. This is known as 'Passive Authentication,' whereby examples include voice signature recognition, facial recognition and broader biometric authentication technology. These passive authentication (AI-enabled) capabilities are increasingly prevalent in edge technologies, such as smart phones, wearables, tablets and most modern end user computers, such as laptops (see Mobile Edge Computing, Chapter 15: Economy of Things).

ROBO – ADVISORS

AI and NLP are used to surface the utility of financial and investment management advice, via Robo-advisors. Robo-advisors are essentially expert systems (see Expert Systems above). Armed with contextualised data about the customer and data surrounding the broader trends and analysis of various markets and indices, customers may exploit the services of Robo-advisors in financial planning and investment through structured products suitable to the customer's circumstances, needs, risk appetite and level of wealth.

MODERN PORTFOLIO THEORY

Such interactions are based on mathematical rules embedded within algorithms, which may be supplemented by moderate human interaction. An example of which may include, mean-variance optimisation, a subset of Modern Portfolio Theory (MPT), developed by American economist, Harry Markowitz in 1952. MPT is underpinned by a mathematical framework for assembling and optimising a portfolio of assets based on a given target return, which is offset against a specified level of risk.

Independent Robo-advisor services could be accessed on a subscription or ad-hoc basis, or embedded as either a value-added service within, or in partnership with Financial Institutions. Robo-advisors are an increasingly common manifestation of prescriptive and predictive analytics capabilities.

ALGORITHMIC TRADING

AI is additionally pervasive in applications, such as algorithmic trading, whereby executing buy or sell orders may be performed using pre-programmed trading or verbal (via NLP) instructions. The algorithms are capable of outperforming human traders by leveraging the speed of computers in accounting for variables such as price and volume. It should be noted that several high-profile algorithmic trading crimes (using high frequency algorithmic trading) have attracted negative sentiment toward the widespread use of this technology. Use of the technology to manipulate prices through placing and subsequently cancelling sell orders nearly instantly in order to short the price of a specific equity or commodity, is one of the methods used to abuse the technology.

However, in all probability, the technology will continue to be used and developed, albeit through a lens of greater regulatory scrutiny, to reduce potential abuse.

OPEN BANKING

Conceptually, Open Banking is linked to the shift in attitude towards data ownership, surfaced through the introduction of regulations like the European Union's GDPR. The principle is broadly considered a subset of the open innovation concept, whereby an information age mind-set towards innovation runs counter to the traditional corporate mind-set of secrecy and intellectual property protectionism.

Open Banking promotes the rights of data subjects to determine whom may access, and how their data may be used within the spheres of banking. Furthermore, banks are compelled to expose digital services through APIs that enable third-party developers to build financial applications around the banking institution. This effectively transforms banks into financial service platforms, much like cloud service providers (see Economy of Platforms, Chapter 15:

Economy of Things), exposing their services to the ecosystems of the API economy.

The revised version of the Payment Services Directive, known as PSD2 was enacted by the EU's European Parliament in October 2015. PSD2 brought in Open Banking rules to stimulate innovation and promote competition in internet-enabled payments technologies and services.

While the United Kingdom led the charge with over two hundred FinTech start-ups exploiting Open Banking to create new innovations and services by early 2020, other EU countries, saw marginal uptake by comparison. A vacuum created by the UK's departure from the European Union (Brexit), is no doubt a stimulant toward a latent surge of Open Banking start-ups within the bloc.

On the global stage, Australia launched an Open Banking initiative in July 2019, as part of the Consumer Data Rights Project. The Open Banking Nigeria initiative was launched in June 2017 by FinTech and Banking representatives to explore the use of common standards and APIs. Rwanda has subsequently modelled its Open Banking approach on the EU's PSD2. Towards the close of 2016, the South African National Treasury, South African Reserve Bank (Central Bank), the then Financial Services Board and Financial Intelligence Centre, established the Intergovernmental FinTech Working Group (IFWG). The IFWG provides a platform for future regular engagements with industry stakeholders to focus on areas such as crowdfunding, Open Banking and their regulation. This collectively signals that the paradigm is incrementally gaining traction. Thus, cultivating a network effect in influencing regulatory posture amongst nation states.

Open Banking represents a significant enabler towards surfacing the utility of financial services, providing FinTech incubators with a mechanism to create innovative financial instrumentation and services free of the stringent constraints and capital requirements of traditional financial institutions. Modernisation of incumbent's infrastructure and digital transformation towards enabling equivalent services requires greater investment and time, creating a window of opportunity for nimble FinTechs to exploit Open Banking interfaces to either partner with, or compete with incumbents.

A third-party FinTech, in compliance with the relevant financial services regulator may register as either an:

1. AISP - Account Information Service Provider

2. PISP - Payment Initiation Service Provider

3. A combined AISP and PISP

An authorised AISP may, with an account holder's permission, connect to a bank (via an Open Banking API) and access the account holder's bank account information, in order to provide them with a service. An authorised PISP may subject to permission, connect to an account holder's bank and initiate payments on their behalf.

An example of where a nimble FinTech may offer a customer value-added service, could be by developing an app (smart device application) which aggregates the customer's accounts across multiple banks into a single dashboard. Further value could be added by offering contextual insights or advice as to how the customer could better structure their finances to achieve greater yields or improving their credit posture.

Furthermore, the FinTech app provider could assume the role of the bank altogether, by offering the customer a series of virtual accounts, payment instruments and access to financial products through a rich user interface and experience, while using one or more bank's infrastructure to house the accounts behind the insulation of a virtual façade. In this instance, the primacy of the customer relationship is established by the FinTech, although the FinTech is intermediating between the customer and the bank(s).

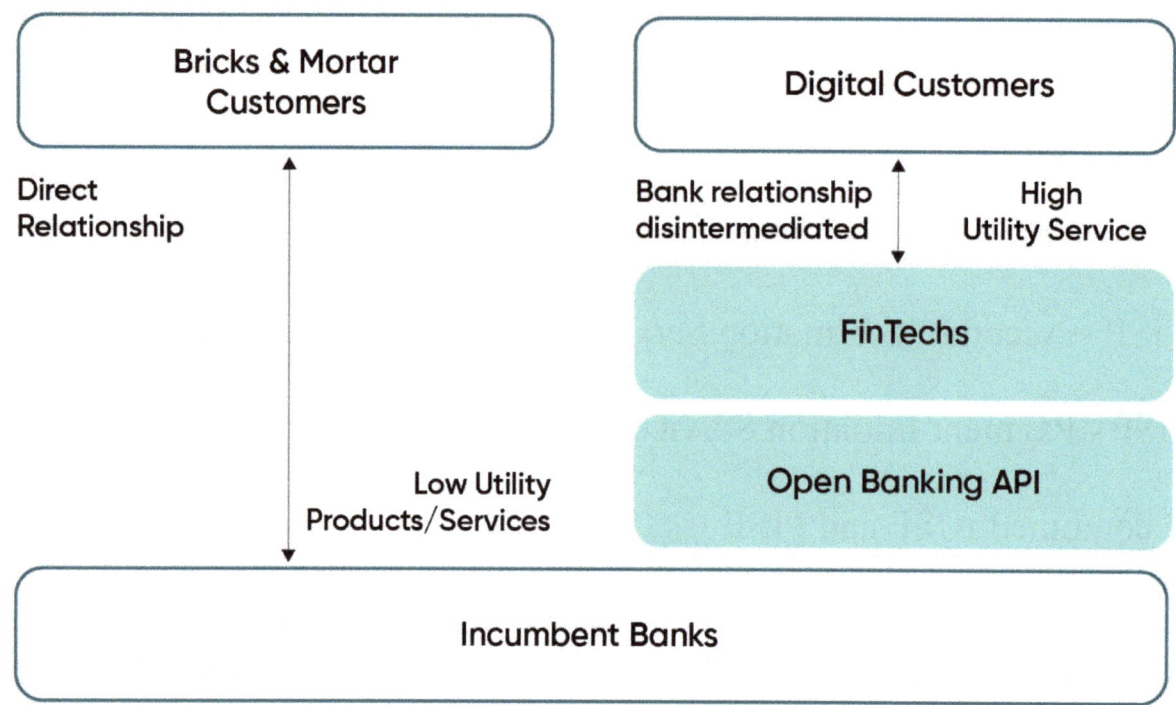

Fig 4.15 illustrates the 'componentisation effect' introduced via Open Banking, enabling FinTechs to surface utility via a digital channel

Through exploiting cloud technologies, data science and artificial intelligence, FinTechs are empowered to aggregate customer data and provide banking capabilities to surface the utility of financial services through experiential and contextualised applications. Open Banking provides a framework to offer customers greater value and integration in this utility with broader business services.

Examples include lifestyle banking services, whereby health-tech and FinTech could be combined (see Embedded Finance, Chapter 15: Economy of Things). Such entities may offer fitness and nutrition services, whereby customers' wearable technologies such as smart watches offer health telemetry data to a FinTech bank. The FinTech in turn analyses banking and health data through AI, in order to broker an adjustment in the customer's life insurance premiums with an underwriting partner (Insurer), via the API economy (see Economy of Platforms, Chapter 15: Economy of Things). Essentially, offering a contextualised experience in which the FinTech bank adds value by reducing service friction and consolidates its primacy over the customer relationship, while rewarding customers for leading a healthier lifestyle. Broader examples may include the integration between financial services, social media and instant messaging services, whereby payments may be executed between individuals, via instant chat applications or social media channels.

Another such example could be a FinTech app, designed to split the bill (check) at a restaurant, facilitating the payment to the restauranteur from one member of the group, although automatically and instantly compensating the payer from all other members of the group's individual bank accounts, hence reducing friction and reducing fees collectively.

Conversely, the restauranteur could offer a similar service, using an Open Banking API integration themselves, via a cloud-hosted Microservice of its own. Such a service may offer customers a seamless ordering and payment experience, ordering from the menu to either be consumed on premises or to be delivered. Furthermore, such an app could offer a customer loyalty scheme with special offers and redeemable vouchers.

In summary, Open Banking functions as a vehicle through which banks expose their services to the API economy of entities which can create incalculable permutations of experiential and contextual digital services. Modest barriers to entry in creating such services exist, with the pervasive and rich proliferations of cloud services. Merchants and nimble FinTech entities can create smart device applications and cloud-based Microservices, exploiting data analytics and AI to surface the utility of financial services in new and imaginative ways.

Open Banking represents a poignant example in which standardisation and open ideology are innovation and commoditisation accelerants (see Standardisation, Chapter 2: Capital Evolution). Essentially, enabling componentisation (see Componentisation, Chapter 2: Capital Evolution). Thus, promoting the creation of higher-order systems and the cultivation of new value and future worth, while benefitting consumers through surfacing utility.

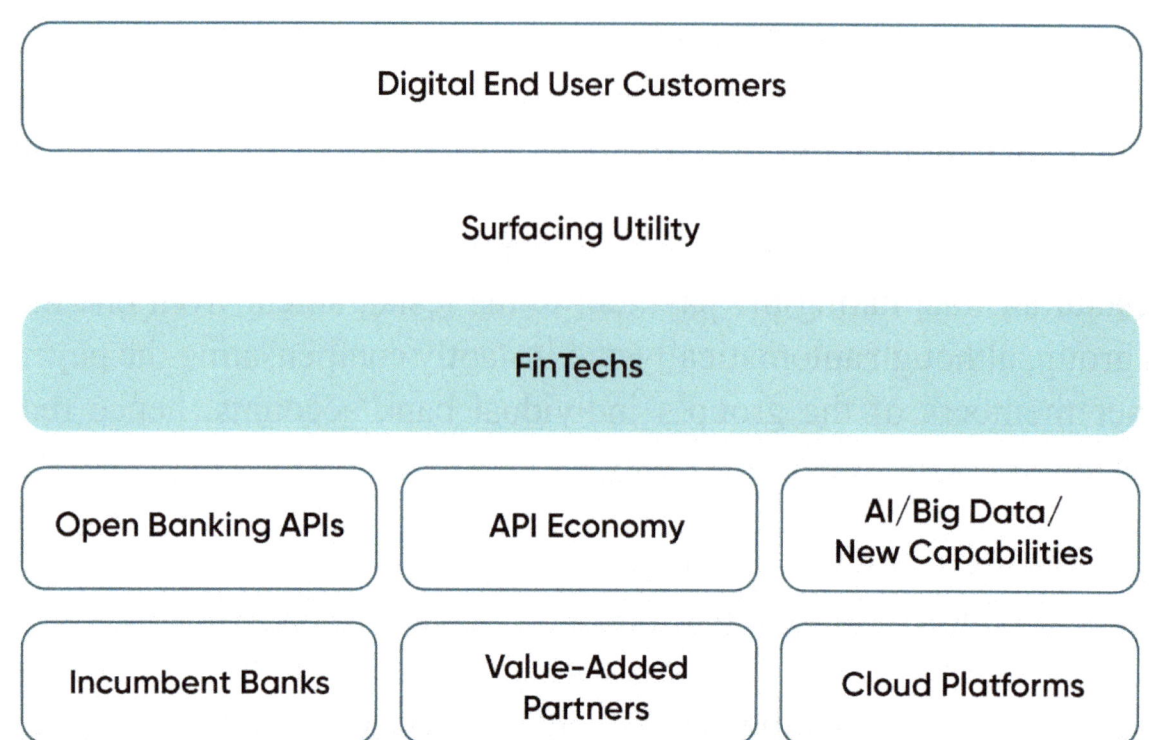

Fig 4.16 surfacing utility of Financial Services, co-opting nascent technologies and partner services

While Open Banking regulations have been pioneered within the European Union, the extensive adoption, as well as success thereof in the United Kingdom and the incremental diffusion among other nation states, indicates the direction of travel for regulators globally. As with all forms of competitive behaviour, once a new innovation, business model or philosophy is proven to offer an advantage, others follow suit in its adoption, or risk being less competitive and ultimately redundant (see Red Queen Hypothesis, Chapter 2: Capital Evolution).

HARVESTING DATA

While data mining is the process through which patterns are discovered in data sets using capabilities such as Machine Learning, data harvesting describes the practices through which data is acquired. Data harvesting is synonymous with known techniques, such as web-scraping and web crawling. These techniques involve extracting data from websites, collating it into a different format to be imported for use by another system, namely a DW. This is achieved using tools designed to download publicly visible web pages, via the HTTP protocol.

All businesses, with whom a customer has a direct relationship or interaction, are in a prime position to harvest the richest and highest value customer data. Since data is the vehicle through which the greatest innovation and value creation is expected to be realised, it is for this reason that establishing and retaining primacy over the customer relationship is a business imperative and considered crucial to data primacy (see Self-perpetuating Cycle above). Banks, Insurers, FinTechs and merchants are all engaged in business strategies to acquire or retain direct relationships with customers and pursue digital strategies to evolve into DDTCs.

Harvesting transactional data through customer accounts is achieved through logging and analysis of records in backend systems. However, harvesting non-transactional data is achieved through the use of alternative instruments.

COOKIES

One such instrument is a Cookie. HTTP Cookies are stored as text files, via web browsers and web apps on user devices. These text files house session information regarding interactions with web services. Cookies are used to compensate for the stateless nature of web service interactions (see API Economy, Chapter 3: Ecosystems). Cookies are useful to the user by storing previously captured information, which aid in subsequent interactions for the user's convenience. However, Cookies may be exploited to harvest data, which aids DDTCs in user behavioural analysis (see Chapter 15: Economy of Things).

Ad-tech businesses (including social media), in particular, exploit third-party Cookies to engage in cross-site cookie tracking, whereby user activity is tracked across multiple websites. Data collection businesses known as 'Trackers' additionally make use of this mechanism to harvest data in order to create and mine user profiles. By way of example, a business may track a user across all webpages where it has placed advertising images. Harnessing the knowledge of which webpages were visited by a user allows the business to contextualise advertisements to the user's discerned preferences.

A number of initiatives, one of which is Google's Federated Learning of Cohorts (FLoC), are expected to ultimately displace the role of Cookies in the Ad-Tech sphere, addressing growing concerns that Cookies are far too open to abuse. The challenge faced by such initiatives is to balance functionality with privacy.

DEVICE IDENTIFIERS

Identifier for Advertising (IDFA) and the Android Advertising Identifier (AAID) are unique device identifiers prevalent in smart phones, tablets, smart television devices and consoles, within the Apple and Android device ecosystems respectively. Amazon devices use an Amazon Advertising ID and other smart device manufacturers use equivalents. These identifiers are designed to allow developers and third-parties to track activity for advertising purposes. Examples of which include personalised ads (formerly known as interest-based-ads). The identifiers act in a number of comparable ways to Cookies, although tied to devices in lieu of web browsers. An identifier may be used by advertisers to run re-marketing campaigns and record purchases or application downloads.

These identifiers may additionally be exploited to correlate and profile user behaviours without revealing personal information. The identifiers may be used to discover information, such as which in-app events or features a user has triggered. The identifiers additionally signal the profile of platforms being used to engage a service or application. Such information may influence bias in development towards platforms where greater traction and profitability has been gained. Device identifiers are, however, constrained to narrower fields of data than those of Cookies.

LOYALTY SCHEMES

Store Cards and Loyalty Schemes are another such data harvesting instrument.

A loyalty scheme is a marketing strategy designed to encourage customer retention through offering an incentive, in exchange for repeat business with one or more businesses associated with the scheme. By presenting a card, using an app or web site, customers typically receive either a discount on a current purchase, or an allotment of points, tokens or similar rewards that may be redeemed for use in a future purchase transaction. Such schemes, while rewarding customer loyalty, are increasingly exploited to harvest customer data which would otherwise be anonymous.

Affiliate Programmes are another such mechanism used to exploit broader sales channels, cultivate customer loyalty and harvest data.

SENTIMENT ANALYSIS

Opinion Mining, also known as Sentiment Analysis, refers to the mining of reviews, surveys, social media, customer service and chat bot interactions using text analysis, digital web intercepts, computational linguistics and NLP to derive subjective information, with regards to customer opinions, experiential feedback and sentiment.

By integrating inferred data (CRM, clickstream and Google analytics) with feedback data, an enriched contextualised layer may be created to yield deeply informed and personalised interactions with customers.

BOTS

Bots, otherwise known as internet bots or web robots, may be designed to emulate human subscribers and are a prevalent tool used to influence social media subscribers. Bots may be used to intrude into forums to espouse synthetic comments and sway sentiments. Such programs are designed to behave and respond reflexively to commentary posted by human subscribers. Bots may be programmed to engage in sophistry in order to steer opinions and bias toward a specific agenda or toward a specific product. Bots deployed in this manner are an example of prescriptive analytics, although introduce another avenue through which to harvest contextualised information from prospective customers or gauge opinions. Essentially, a form of polling engine.

Chat bots are additionally prevalent among financial institutions, as well as merchant web sites and apps. These may be leveraged to aggregate feedback and commentary between web visitors and live agents to drive deeper intelligence and gain insights regarding customer experiences.

WEB CHAT

Similarly, capture and analysis of live chat transcriptions has proven invaluable in empowering agents to resolve challenging customer interactions. Analysis initiatives thereof have resulted in improved customer satisfaction and retention. Such insights can additionally be instrumental in identifying barriers to customer acquisition and leveraged to eliminate missed sales conversion opportunities with both prospective as well as existing customers.

CALL CENTRE NLP

Call centre (contact centre) NLP is capable of serving a dual purpose by assisting many financial institutions, including FinTechs and banks facing a deluge of customer service calls. These entities are relying more than ever on technology to boost call centre operations. In particular, using conversational AI agents that can engage directly with customers for rapid and real-time banking transactions and customer service resolutions. Financial institutions may additionally use conversational AI to relieve the pressure on high-volume call centres, as well as exploit this technology in their future plans for digital banking through mining data, harvested from customer interactions. Data mining in this manner may be harnessed to derive comparable benefits to those realised through live chat transcription analysis, as well as exploited for passive authentication to further surface the utility of services without compromising the integrity and security thereof. An example of such would be voice print authentication.

Data harvested as a byproduct of service interaction via these mechanisms is known as 'digital exhaust' (see Digital Exhaust, Chapter 15: Economy of Things).

RUNAWAY LEADERSHIP

Consumers benefit from FinTechs and incumbents surfacing the utility of banking and broader financial services. In so doing, these institutions benefit from surfacing the utility brought about by the commoditisation of technology. This, however, may very well be a short-term proposition. As with all technology innovations that emerge as higher-order systems in the form of utility, rather than a tangible good, FinTech is vulnerable to being absorbed by tech giants through their expanding ecosystems and data surveillance ingenuity (see Innovate, Leverage & Commoditise, Chapter 3: Ecosystems). A model which is supported by a value-creation advantage (see Self-perpetuating Cycle above), enabling these business titans to maintain their stature as 'Runaway Leaders.' This is likely to be replicated by Financial Institutions to prevent being displaced by emerging Apex predators (see Apex Predator Hypothesis above).

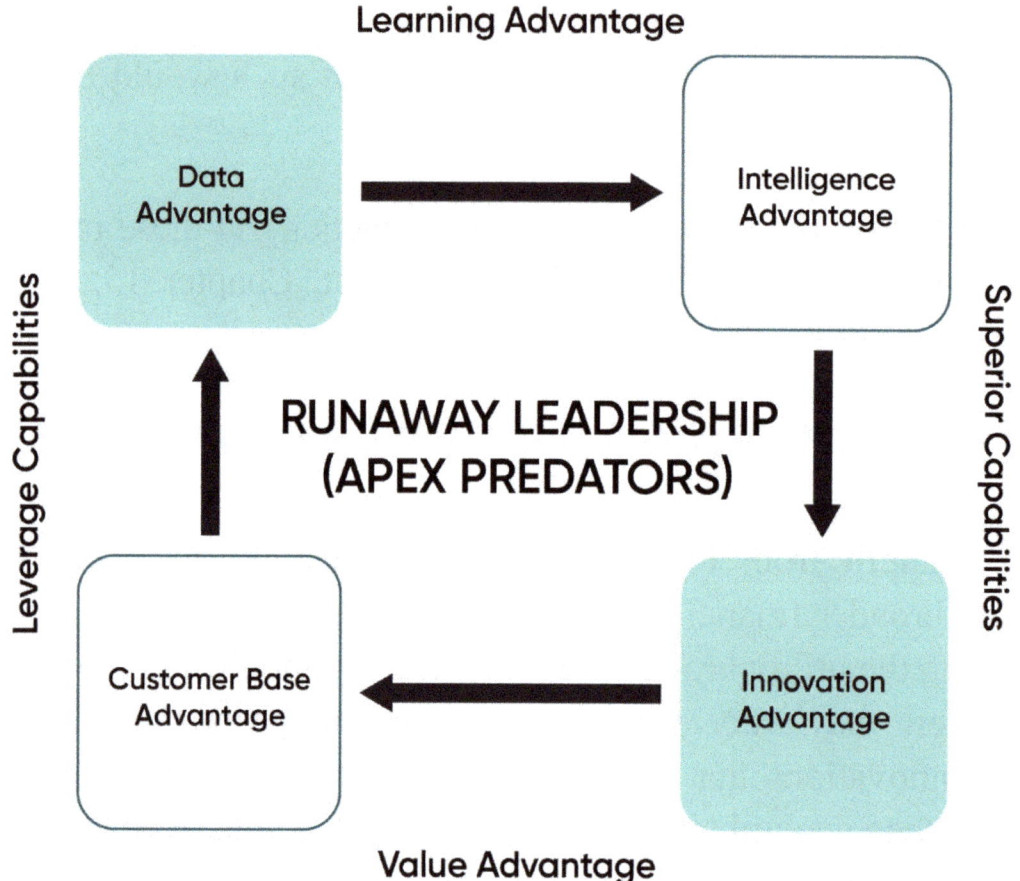

Fig 4.17 'Runaway Leadership' in value creation through AI advancement (Fig 4.13)

Such vulnerability is impossible to avoid; creating a paradoxical challenge in order to compete in a modern business landscape. Both FinTechs and incumbents are either incepted as, or transforming into DDTCs, establishing data primacy and embracing 'digital first' business models. A fundamental and inescapable criterion of realising such ambitions hinges on exploiting the competitive consumption and transaction economics of utility computing, via elastic cloud providers (see Consumption and Transaction Economics, Chapter 3: Ecosystems). Business decisions, such as attempting to custom build a technology capability which has already been industrialised (through commoditisation), would be representative of failure to account for evolutionary flow and devoid of first principles thinking. Strategies of this nature serve the previous orthodoxy and demonstrates the manner in which incumbents are displaced by a new Apex predator (see Apex Predator Hypothesis above).

To approach or continue operating its business in anything contrary to a utility computing centric business model places any such entity at a significant competitive disadvantage from both a financial, as well as an agility perspective (see Elastic Cloud Computing, Chapter 3: Ecosystems). Such cloud utilities are provided by tech giants, fortified by substantial economies of scale and scope of impenetrable magnitude. Tech giants, while calibrating the cost profile and dimensions upon which FinTechs and incumbents are forced to compete, act as a singularity, via network effects (see Innovate, Leverage & Commoditise, Chapter 3: Ecosystems), funnelling data harvested from customers into a nexus from which it can be mined (see Big Data above). Once harvested and enriched, tech giants may mine the data holistically, cultivating learning effects at a broader scale than any one of its customers could do so.

Advancements in AI are expected to continue driving the greatest competitive advantages in most business spheres and especially in financial services (see Self-Perpetuating Cycle above). AI development relies on contemporary approaches, such as Deep Learning, coupled with substantial computational processing (GPUs/ASICs) power. Significant innovations and advancements in the pre-quantum computing era, however, will be far greater weighted by access to large volumes of the richest data (Fig 4.13 & Fig 4.18).

While intuitively, Financial incumbents should be the ultimate beneficiaries of dominance in the FinTech arena, it is likely that the tech giants capable of absorbing FinTech services through their ecosystems and vast data assets accrued from aggregated customer data ('digital exhaust,' see Chapter 15: Economy of Things), will likely be able to make greater advances in AI development. Tech giants, leveraging AI innovations through processing substantial magnitudes of diverse data and surfacing the utility of FinTech, are likely to place large incumbent financial institutions and smaller FinTechs at a severe competitive disadvantage over the longer-term by capitalising on both *learning*, as well as *network effects* (see Innovate, Leverage & Commoditise, Chapter 3: Ecosystems). Thus, relegating FinTechs and incumbents to greater vulnerability in being disintermediated, acquired, or facing bankruptcy. A weakness further compounded by poor economies of scale and inefficiencies in contrast to the highly commoditised and industrialised environments of the tech giants.

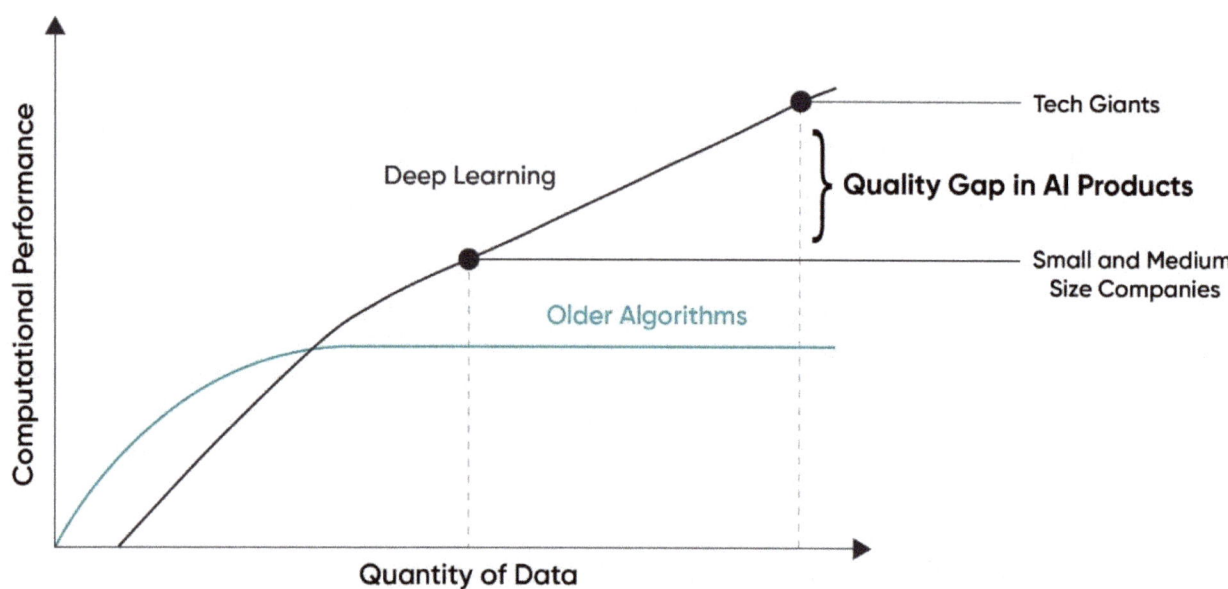

Fig 4.18 illustrates the 'quality gap' in AI advancement between Tech Giants (Runaway Leaders, see Fig 4.17 and Fig 4.13 above) and others

Once the utility of storing value, making payments and accessing credit are fully surfaced through DDTCs exploiting parallel, as well as subsequent innovations, traditional banks, unable to compete, will themselves likely engage in market consolidation through mergers and acquisitions. Some such institutions may face bankruptcy. This process may be slowed through regulations, legislation and political intervention (see Decelerating Effects, Chapter 2: Capital Evolution). The process should be further delayed by the critical mass these large financial institutions hold in substantial portfolios of liquidity reserves and asset rich balance sheets. Those that survive, however, will likely evolve by (to an extent) emulating the business models of 'Big Tech.' Yet, it is the diminishing ability to acquire new business and new customers catalysed by technology-enabled business models and personalised experiential services which will set the majority of these competitors apart. In some instances, incumbents which possess a differentiated or specialised capability may be able to harness such, via a componentised service offered to the financial ecosystem (likely via the API Economy). However, the era of 'one size fits all' banking and financial services are likely nearing their end. A cogent argument could be made that some financial institutions, namely insurers, payment acquirers, payment schemes, investment banks, asset managers, clearing houses and hedge funds will inevitably suffer similar challenges.

Weak signals, to this end, have been evident in the traction gained by tech giants through the minor disruption to payments, via the introduction of Apple Pay and Google Pay. Amazon Pay, introduced in 2007, is a payment system which allows Amazon users to pay external merchants using their Amazon accounts. Amazon have since offered credit facilities and a broader range of financial service integrations, both with partnerships and independently.

A further set of signals were evident in Google's announcements in late 2019 and early 2020, to introduce checking accounts and debit cards. Although, in October 2021, Google announced that it would not be pursuing its 'Plex' consumer bank account proposition.[67] A likely response to a regulatory charged political climate in the US (see Chapter 3: Ecosystems). Yet, another signal was Google's announcement in May 2020, accompanied by marketing materials stating:

'Google Cloud is offering the PPP AI Lending Solution, which enables lenders to integrate underwriting components into their existing lending systems to allow them to accelerate and automate the process of handling the massive volume increase in loan applications.'

Google's Pay-check Protection Program (PPP) AI Lending Solution is a cloud-based platform, designed to serve large financial institutions. However, the solution is a compelling means of making significant advances in FinTech centric AI development for Google itself. The solution may further be exploited as a 'sensing engine' towards Google's future ambitions in broader penetration of the finance sector. Platforms on this nature, enable 'Big Tech' to cultivate the specialist skills, which differentiate financial institutions from technology organisations.

In the interim, 'Big Tech' firms have largely permeated financial services to an extent, falling short of the requirement to apply for traditional licensing as financial institutions, such as Banks. Tech giants are naturally reticent to subject themselves to intense regulatory scrutiny, congruent with that of traditional financial institutions. Tech giants have consequently partnered with regulated financial institutions, content to utilise the regulated partner's infrastructure and standing. Such relationships have been made less onerous through initiatives, such as Open Banking and e-money licensing (see Electronic Money, Chapter 1: FinTech). Many of these partnerships are parasitic in nature, as tech giants provide the underpinning technology to these institutions, while simultaneously penetrating and disintermediating the relationships these financial institutions hold with customers. Thereby, establishing primacy over customer relationships and over the technology platforms upon which market actors are compelled to build and run their services. Essentially, this practice is starving these financial incumbents and challengers from the top and the bottom.

Standard Chartered, a bank which is active in over sixty markets worldwide, announced a commitment to become a fully cloud-based bank by 2025. In order to accomplish this objective, partnering with a tech giant is an inevitability. Standard Chartered openly expressed an intention to exploit the cloud platform's AI and data analytics capabilities, in order to streamline its processes and personalise (see Contextual Banking above) its client products and services.

Goldman Sachs, arguably the largest financial institution in the US, announced a partnership with Amazon to provide lending and underwriting services to Small and Medium-sized Businesses (SMBs) operating within Amazon's marketplace. Goldman Sachs' proprietary digital underwriting platform would be interfaced with Amazon and infused with rich data sets, generated from Amazon's third-party merchants, in order to offer inventory and operational financing services. Amazon, has since additionally, offered select SMBs credit facilities of up to $1 million.[68] This further illustrates the incremental incursion 'Big Tech' is making into the financial services sphere, while remaining just beyond the reach of regulators.

A compelling signal towards the potential for longer-term monopolisation of finance by tech giants was evident through Facebook's attempt to launch its Libra proposition, announced in 2019 (see Synthetic Hegemonic Currency, Chapter 14: Tokenisation).

Exploiting its primacy over the relationship with billions of customers (representing approximately 40% of the global population at the time), the sheer magnitude of anticipated systemic disruption to the finance sector and incalculable impact to the Fed, US government, IMF and the global financial system was met with significant resistance by the US Treasury, resulting in a barrage of subsequent senate hearings, which ultimately distilled into the Libra proposition being shelved. Such initiatives may be postponed or decelerated through resistance and bureaucracy in the short-to-medium term (see Decelerating Effects, Chapter 2: Capital Evolution). However, the 'Libra Scare' is a clear indicator that without government intervention, the convergence of trajectories between finance and 'Big Tech' remain inevitable.

5

PAYMENTS

The payments sphere has arguably experienced the greatest visible disruption through FinTech development, since the GFC. Payments has represented the primary ingress point for digital disruptors, predominantly due to being less capital-intensive than other financial services. The majority of FinTech innovation in payments has been focused on driving towards real-time exchanges of value and improving convenience through removing friction, reducing cost and improving speed, while surfacing the utility of payments using novel approaches with technology.

Furthermore, payments are foundational for economic activity.[69] Thus, making it an attractive area through which to exploit the data generated therefrom to cultivate greater opportunities to penetrate broader spheres within the financial services spectrum.

Electronic payments have their roots in the 1870s, when Western Union pioneered the Telegraph-based wire transfer in 1871. Ever since, the concept of sending money to pay for goods and services without necessarily having to be physically present at the point-of-sale has enamoured society and stimulated innovation in the payments sphere.

The majority of payment centric FinTechs have accomplished remarkable success in achieving these ambitions through insulating or abstracting much of the complexity and friction of domestic and international payment systems away from customers, or in some cases by disintermediating the underlying payment systems altogether.

Many of the established payment systems have evolved analogously and represent fertile areas for disruption by FinTechs, fuelled by a growing receptive consumer base. However, much of the structure of financial and payment systems is architected around regulated practices. These regulations exist for a variety of good reasons, including the ability to intercept fraudulent transactions, as well as to afford financial institutions the ability to manage liquidity and broader risks.

Most importantly, the regulations and structure governing financial institutions and practices surrounding payments are vehicles to enforce governance, via regulators, governments and monetary authorities. This is essential to ensure that the financial system is monitored, protected and moderated in an orderly fashion. Consequently, payment systems are organised around these imperatives.

Conceptually, payment describes the 'exchange of value' through the use of either money, credit or payment-in-kind (bartering). Without robust mechanisms of payment, the domestic and global economies would grind to a halt. Payment systems and methods are of vital strategic importance and are considered critical infrastructure to both nation states and the world as a whole.

Beneath the fabric of the global payments ecosystem are the contracts, schemes and regulatory frameworks which govern the processing, clearing and settling of payments. Such schemes set out the business and operational rules and agreed technical standards, to which member institutions are required to adhere.

ANATOMY OF PAYMENT TRANSACTIONS

Payment transactions fundamentally facilitate an exchange of value between a payer (sender) and a payee (recipient/beneficiary), however, involve intermediaries, hence, prescribing an anatomical structure. The anatomy of transactions is structured around three discreet concepts:

1. Messaging (Instruction or Authorisation) known as the Commitment

2. Clearing (Assessing the obligation)

3. Settlement (Settling accounts payable)

MESSAGING

Messaging is the initiation of a transaction (see Chapter 13: Global Trade Rails), whereby an instruction message (message type or MT) on behalf of the payer is transmitted, furnishing the details surrounding the exchange, to the participating intermediaries. In transaction terms, this is known as the commitment. The intermediaries parse the message to discern the value and legitimacy of the transaction, which is thereafter fulfilled, via clearing and settlement mechanisms in favour of the payee.

CLEARING & SETTLEMENT

Clearing and Settlement Mechanisms (CSMs) play an essential role in an interbank exchange of payments. Although generally mentioned synonymously, the activities of clearing and settlement are quite different functions.

CLEARING

The Bank for International Settlements (BIS) defines the term 'clearing' as the process of transmitting, reconciling and, in some cases, confirming transactions prior to settlement, including the netting of transactions and the establishment of final positions for settlement.

'Netting' refers to the offsetting of obligations between or among participants in the netting arrangement, thereby reducing the overall number and collective value of payments or deliveries required to settle a set of transactions.

At least two actors are required for the establishment of a clearing mechanism. Clearing confined solely to two participating institutions is known as bilateral clearing. Clearing among three or more participants is known as multilateral clearing. Two banks or a group of banks may elect to establish clearing among one another, without an interbank payment system (see below).

In the clearing phase of a transaction, the key task is in assessing the obligation. Assessing the obligation, refers to determining the net aggregated value, which is needed to be transferred between bilateral or multilateral participants to satisfy settlement to payees. This is usually taken at a point in time during the business day. Any transactions that occur after the prescribed time will be aggregated with transactions the following business day.

A bilateral netting example, is that of ten payment transactions of $100 each, initiated by ten different customers of Bank A, being sent to ten customers of Bank B. During the same clearing window, nine different customers of Bank B, initiate nine payment transactions to customers of Bank A, also for $100 each. Prior to netting, Bank A needs to send a collective sum of $1000 to Bank B, however, Bank B needs to send a collective sum of $900 to Bank A. After netting, Bank A owes $100 to Bank B as a net position, which is the only exchange required to settle.

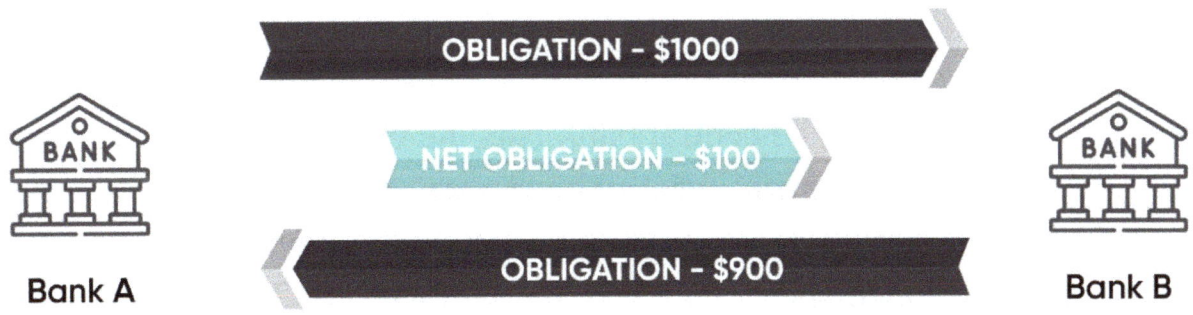

Fig 5.1 Bilateral Netting of an obligation prior to Post/Settlement

SETTLEMENT

Once bilateral or multilateral obligations have been netted, the transaction is ready for post or settlement. The period between initiation and post is known as the float. The float may extend over a number of days, dependent on the interbank system used. Once the transaction is posted, it is available as cleared effects within the payees' account.

INTERBANK PAYMENT SYSTEMS

Conceptually, interbank payment systems facilitate the clearing and settlement of payment transactions between institutions. However, in practice banks rarely exchange anything tangible.

Consider an inter-account payment transaction between an individual and a merchant, both of which hold accounts with the same bank. At the messaging (initiation/commitment) phase, the bank is able to instantly discern that it holds both the payer's and payees' account balances as liabilities on its balance sheet. In such circumstances, it's expedient to exchange liabilities between the two accounts to reflect the new balances and the net position of the bank's liabilities is unaffected. There is no need in this instance to engage an interbank payment system to manage clearing and settlement. Therefore, it is unnecessary for either party to expect anything less than an instant transfer of cleared effects.

REAL-TIME GROSS SETTLEMENT

A comparable process unfolds when two domestic banks transact with one another. Each bank holds an account with the central bank, which acts as the clearing house for banks. The central bank lists the banks' accounts as separate liability entries on its balance sheet. The central bank settles the interbank transaction by exchanging assets between each of the banks' entries (reserve accounts) on its balance sheet, which remains balanced. To the banks, these reserve accounts are assets on their respective balance sheets, however, to the central bank, these accounts are liabilities.

Unlike the internal transfer between the customer's accounts, banks initiate such interbank transactions, via a real-time gross settlement system (RTGS), provided by, or affiliated with the central bank. These systems fulfil transactions either instantly or intraday, settled in central bank funds and attract a high transaction fee for use of the service. The term 'Gross Settlement' infers that transactions are settled individually and are not netted between institutions.

Each monetary zone manages its own RTGS. In the United States, the Fedwire system was introduced in 1970, although the US is expected to replace Fedwire with FedNow in the 2023-2024 timeframe. The United Kingdom, use the Clearing House Automated Payment System (CHAPS), which along with the French SAGITTAIRE system were both introduced in 1984. SAGITTAIRE has since been superseded in the European Union, by the Trans-European Automated Real-time Gross Settlement Express Transfer System (TARGET2), which caters to the bloc. The People's Republic of China has used the China National Advanced Payments System (CNAPS) since 2005, and its successor CNAPS2, since 2014. CNAPS has several subsystems, one of which is its RTGS, the High-Value Payments System (HPVS), which has been in service since June 2005.

Real-time gross settlement reduces settlement risk (also known as delivery risk), as interbank settlement occurs on an individual real-time transactional basis, which is less prone to error than net settlement CSMs. Transactions, via an RTGS, are additionally considered irrevocable.

NET SETTLEMENT

Net settlement systems are CSMs managed by payment schemes, which act as intermediaries, to facilitate clearing and settlement for interbank payments. The majority of interbank payments settled through an RTGS are transactions which reflect the net position of obligations (Fig 5.1), accrued by banks on a multilateral basis throughout the business day.

Net settlement CSMs act as a clearing house, whereby the system receives a batch of transaction messages from each bank, parses the information holistically and assesses the net obligations of each bank to one another. Once the net obligations are established, the settlement may be initiated, via RTGS, for a minimal number of high-value transactions. This practice keeps fees economical by reducing the volume of transactions and keeps any exchanges settled in central bank liabilities between banks to a minimum.

Consequently, payments performed on this basis are not settled in real-time and may require between one or more business days to settle with payees.

CLEARING & SETTLEMENT MECHANISMS

In the United States, the Clearing House Interbank Payment System (CHIPS) and the Automated Clearing House (ACH) system are net settlement CSMs. Unlike Fedwire, which is owned and managed by the Fed, CHIPS is owned privately by the banks that use it. The term 'wire transfer' includes reference to using either the CHIPS system or Fedwire and both systems are used for high-value dollar denominated payments, both domestically and internationally. Due to CHIPS being a netting system, it is consequently less expensive to use than Fedwire, however, remains more expensive to use than ACH.

ACH evolved from the automated clearing house and was introduced and managed by the Federal Reserve Bank of San Francisco (one of the twelve Fed Reserve Banks; see Chapter: 7 Central Banks), in 1972. ACH is owned and managed by the National Automated Clearing House Association (NACHA). ACH is predominantly used for batched and netted, high-volume (bulk), yet low-value domestic interbank payments.

Using ACH, Originating Financial Depository Institutions (OFDIs) transmit batch files of accrued multilateral transactions gathered during a seven-hour window to the Fed. The Fed processes all 'batch files' and sends 'result files' to the Recipient Financial Depository Institutions (RFDIs) by a prescribed time the following morning. The RFDIs have twenty-four-hours, thereafter, to process the results and send a request to the Fed and on to the OFDI to update their respective accounts. If no errors occur during this process, it generally requires a three-day float to complete settlement successfully. If errors do occur, it requires the full three days to verify the error, and will consequently require several more days to resolve. Errors may occur using the ACH system as formatting of financial messages are neither checked nor enforced prior to transmission. This practice creates a reticence to modernise systems, as once banking institutions achieve a level of stability, modifying software or infrastructure carries substantial risks in potential payment disruptions. The ACH system has long been considered antiquated, frictional and inefficient.

In the United Kingdom, the Bankers Automated Clearing Services (BACS), established in 1968, is the bulk payment system which clears, as well as settles payments on a multilateral net basis and requires submission two days prior to the value (posting) date.

The Pan European Automated Clearing House (PE-ACH) is known as STEP2. STEP2 is a highly-resilient CSM, designed to serve multiple European banking institutions within the Single Euro Payments Area (SEPA) (see Interlinking below)

Since 2006, China's Bulk Electronic Payment System (BEPS), is one of the CNAPS subsystems, which functions as China's principal interbank CSM.

BANKING BUSINESS MODEL

Commercial banks rely on the float period facilitated by net settlement CSMs to support the banking business model. Banks rely on borrowing money from central banks, account holders (depositors) and other banks at a low rate of interest (London Inter-Bank Offered Rate or LIBOR rate and the US Federal Funds Rate) and profit by lending to borrowers at a higher rate of interest (see Credit & Debt, Chapter 8: Economic Cycles). As a consequence, bank's account holders (depositors) are bank creditors and their funds are bank liabilities, the majority of which, correspond to assets financed through lending. Banks maintain a fractional reserve on deposit with the central bank, however, the majority of customer funds are not liquid. Net settlement CSMs facilitate the exchange of these liabilities between banks, free of the necessity to liquidate bank assets. The balances paid, represent a negligible difference and, therefore, can be settled within the margin of fractional reserves. The fractional reserve is governed by the reserve ratio, set by the central bank (see Chapter 7: Central Banks). The ratio stipulates the liquidity banks must maintain relative to moneys lent in order to shield against withdrawals and meet interbank settlement obligations (see Monetary Policy, Chapter 8: Economic Cycles).

Net settlement CSMs additionally facilitate interest relief for banks, as a result of neither the OFDI nor the RFDI being liable to either the payer or the payee during the clearing window (float). While this may seem arbitrary when considering an isolated transaction, in practice, banks move billions, if not trillions of dollars (in liabilities), via these mechanisms daily. Such magnitudes are significant in terms of interest relief, whereby neither the payer nor the payee are entitled to interest on funds during the float. Furthermore, this illustrates an incentive for banks not to move funds, via an RTGS system, where transactions are instant, irrevocable and settled in central bank reserve account funds. If every payment transaction was settled, via RTGS, banks would be required to hold all depositors' funds within their central bank reserve accounts, thus, making no funds available for lending. This would essentially threaten the traditional banking business model.

FRACTIONAL RESERVE

The fractional reserve, usually a nominal percentage of a bank's total assets, is held in the bank's reserve account at the governing central bank. Banks hold a percentage of deposits and loan out the remainder. The fractional reserve held, represents the funds available to perform RTGS payments, as well as cash withdrawals. However, therein lies one of the key areas in which banks are vulnerable. During periods of financial stress, a simultaneous 'run on the banks' through mass withdrawals by a large proportion of a bank's depositors, could exhaust the bank's reserves, thereby creating a liquidity crisis (see Chapter 8: Economic Cycles) and consequently threaten the bank's solvency. Thus, banks continually explore means with which to manage long-term risks (see Maturity Transformation, Chapter 10: Financialisation).

SUSPICIOUS TRANSACTIONS

Banks in a number of monetary zones are compelled to advise authorities of potentially suspicious transactions. By way of example, in the US, banks are compelled to notify the Inland Revenue Service (IRS) of transactions exceeding $10000, allowing the early notification of potential fraud, money laundering or tax evasion, which may or may not be investigated, thereafter. Net settlement CSMs offer the authorities a window during which they may intercede in order to freeze a funds transfer or delay settlement, pending further investigation.

FINTECH NICHE

The delay and friction associated with established clearing and settlement mechanisms has provided significant opportunities for FinTechs to create frictionless, high-speed payments apps, which surface the utility of payments in novel, contextual and experiential forms. E-money licensing (see PayFacs below) and Open Banking frameworks (see Open Banking, Chapter 4: Surfacing Utility) have provided the mechanisms with which FinTechs have developed and offered these propositions by disintermediating the direct relationships banks have historically maintained with their customers. These arrangements and practices have essentially added another layer to the multi-tier banking system (Fig 5.15), whereby banks remain heavily regulated in contrast to the FinTechs that have been established in their orbit and that leverage the banks' infrastructure. In such circumstances, banks carry the burdens and costs associated with adhering to a highly-regulated posture, yet, are starved of the value associated with primacy over customer relationships, particularly access to customer data.

FinTechs are, however, vulnerable to carrying the risk when facilitating instant payments outside of their own customers' accounts. Such risks exist due to the latency of the float when using interbank net settlement clearing systems.

CROSS–BORDER PAYMENTS

It remains a generally accepted perception that cross-border payments have lagged in advancement behind that of domestic payments technology. The broadening divide between domestic and the cross-border payment spheres is highly visible across the measures of cost, transparency, speed and access. This is due to payment systems being implemented as national capabilities, in lieu of being a part of a truly international system. Thus, there is scope for numerous mechanisms to create a perceptively seamless means through which to transact between national payment systems, or even directly between parties.

As a consequence, international/cross-border payments have largely evolved into four discreet models.

1. Correspondent Banking

2. Interlinking

3. Single-Platform

4. Peer-to-Peer

In some instances, FinTechs and incumbent Financial Institutions may engage a combination of these models in order to apply an STP approach towards improving efficiency or reducing costs and friction (see Straight-Through Processing, Chapter 4: Surfacing Utility). An example of which would be, a bank engaged in the regular use of correspondent banking, electing to make use of an interlinked payment system (see below) where available.

The payment schemes and financial institutions acting as intermediaries to provide payment services for the payer and payee in cross-border payments are typically required to meet a variety of legal and regulatory criteria of multiple jurisdictions in areas such as:

- Licensing and authorisation régimes

- Prudential supervision (including risk management)

- Financial integrity (anti-money laundering and counter-terrorism financing)

- Cyber security

- Transparency, traceability and disclosure

- Consumer safeguards and protection

- Foreign exchange regulations and controls

- Data collection, harvesting, protection and transfer

DIRECT & INDIRECT PARTICIPANTS

Apart from the above-mentioned areas, national regulatory frameworks may, additionally, differ in areas such as transaction limits, as well as the types of entities authorised to operate within the payments spectrum. Furthermore, these entities may face greater scrutiny, with regards to compliance with capital controls and sanctions régimes (see Extraterritorial Sanctions, Chapter 13: Global Trade Rails). As a result of the costs arising from variance within multiple jurisdictions' regulations and the risks associated with non-compliance, payment intermediaries may incur higher costs than those engaged exclusively in domestic payments.

A national CSM interconnects banks within the boundaries of a nation state (country). Thus, banks which are external to the country may not be direct participants of that particular CSM. Examples of national CSMs include that of KIR in Poland and Iberpay in Spain. The banks within these countries execute interbank payments by exchanging liabilities amongst themselves primarily through the national CSM. A number of national CSMs may have excess capacity with which to offer their services outside the confines of their jurisdiction and offer payment clearing services to foreign banking entities.

However, proximity, language barriers and specificities within national payments markets create impediments which foreign banks may consider unpalatable. By way of example, it is challenging to conceive that a French bank may be enticed to become a direct participant of the Spanish CSM Iberpay or a British bank joining as a direct participant to KIR. Additionally, as with both of these examples, the converse is likely true. Consequently, banks are required to intermediate payments on behalf of indirect participants in national CSMs. Furthermore, some jurisdictions, such as that of the US, may impose regulations which prevent foreign banks from directly participating in US banking schemes. Thus, cultivating the necessity for Correspondent Banking.

CORRESPONDENT BANKING

In the case of international payments facilitated through correspondent banking, the Fed (see The Fed, Chapter 7: Central Banks) acts as a global clearing house for the vast majority of international transactions. In much the same manner that the Fed holds reserve accounts for domestic banks in the United States, the Fed additionally holds accounts for many foreign banks, which have a domestic presence. In practice, US dollars (USD) rarely leave the United States. An international payment denominated in USD (at least half of global trade invoicing, 2019) is transferred by exchanging Fed liabilities in favour of the reserve account held by the domestic instance (direct participant) of the foreign bank (indirect participant). The foreign bank then deducts its foreign currency assets, in favour of increasing its foreign currency liabilities held as an account by the payee.

Accounts held in this manner are correspondent accounts. These correspondent accounts are additionally known as Nostro accounts (meaning 'ours,' Latin), which are liabilities to these banks, known as correspondent banks. From the correspondent bank's perspective, the account held on behalf of a bank or entity (respondent bank) for which it offers correspondent services, is known as a Vostro account (meaning 'yours,' Latin).

Not all foreign banks hold accounts with the Fed. Consequently, many banks rely on Correspondent Banks, which intermediate between the Fed and foreign correspondent banks or respondent banks that do not hold accounts with the Fed. In instances where a bank remits its foreign currency account to a foreign bank in favour of a third bank is known as a Loro account (meaning 'theirs,' Latin).

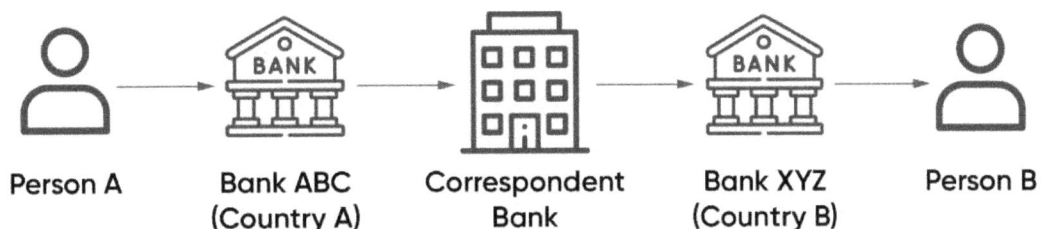

Fig 5.2 intermediating payments, via Correspondent Banks (CSM Direct Participants)

In practice, correspondent banks credit the Vostro account held by a foreign (respondent) bank and the foreign bank subsequently credits the Loro account of the payee's bank in local currency at the prevailing commercial exchange rate (less a foreign exchange fee). The local currency credited to the payee originates from the domestic reserves in central bank funds, held with the domestic central bank. To effect payment, the payer's bank may use either a net settlement CSM or an RTGS to transfer funds to the correspondent bank. The correspondent bank will use an RTGS to exchange central bank liabilities with the respondent bank. The respondent bank may either use an RTGS or a net settlement CSM to exchange liabilities with the payee's bank.

Correspondent banking historically has accounted for the vast majority of international payments and the highest value transactions outside of payments and settlements between nations/governments. The Fed plays a vital role in both US domestic payments and in international payments, due to the US dollar's role as the principal global reserve currency (see Global Reserve Currency, Chapter 12: Global Monetary System). As a result, the US dollar is the global *unit of account* (see Functions of Money, Chapter 6: Money) and thus, the common denominator in which most commodities and resources are priced internationally (see Dollar Hegemony, Chapter 13: Global Trade Rails). Hence, the US dollar is the dominant currency for transactions between countries (nation states).

INTERLINKING

Interlinking describes the bridging of national payment systems between multiple countries. An example includes the interlinking of the Mexican FedGlobal service with the US ACH interbank system. This allows certain US institutions to send funds to certain institutions in Mexico, via ACH, while allowing a number of Mexican institutions to send funds to a minority of US institutions via FedGlobal. A further example of interlinking was prevalent within the European Union, whereby countries within the bloc integrated with STEP2 (PE-ACH) and with the TARGET2 RTGS system. This infrastructure underpins the Single Euro Payments Area (SEPA) initiative (see Single Euro Payments Area, Chapter 13: Global Trade Rails), the objective of which is to integrate and harmonise euro denominated interbank payments across the Eurozone.

SINGLE-PLATFORM

The single-platform model is synonymous with in-house or intra-group payment transfers. This model is prevalent among FinTechs, which offer payment facilities and/or accounts to their customers both domestically and internationally. In instances where these entities offer these services in multiple international jurisdictions, an opportunity is created to intermediate international payments within the confines of the FinTech's own platform, without the necessity to use correspondent banks or interlinked payment systems. This business model has a long-standing pedigree among traditional money transfer operators, several multinational banks and some international card payment schemes.

PEER-TO-PEER

The peer-to-peer (P2P) payments model serves as the greatest vehicle for significant disruption to the other payment models. If P2P payments were to ascend to become the dominant payment mechanism both domestically and internationally, the hierarchical banking system would likely face significant long-term solvency and viability challenges. P2P payment mechanisms enable the payer to remit funds directly to the payee electronically, without engaging intermediaries. In such circumstances, the necessity for holding funds on deposit with banks is conceptually at risk of facing obsolescence. Without depositors' funds, banks would have limited (if any) means, with which to offer credit in the form of loans from which to generate the bulk of the traditional banking revenue stream (see Banking Business Model above). Furthermore, banks would lose the revenue generated from making payments, primacy over the customer relationship as well as access to customer data. P2P payment mechanisms are largely based on Distributed Ledger Technologies (see Distributed Ledger Technology, Chapter 14: Tokenisation), the initial instances of which, disintermediate conventional payment systems, banks and central banks in their entirety.

BALANCE OF PAYMENTS

At a macroeconomic level, the *balance of payments* of a nation state, is the difference in total value between payments into and out of a country over a period (usually annually). It represents the balance between all money flowing into a country, as a result of exports and loans over a period of time, versus money flowing outwards, as a result of imports and servicing foreign debt. The balance of payments consists of two accounts, known as a *current account* and a *capital account*. A current account reflects a nation state's net income position, whereas the capital account reflects a net position in ownership of national assets. Capital accounts record the net flow of investment into a country, while the current account records the net value of imports and exports of goods and services, as well as capital flows. These accounts (current and capital) should balance at a net zero position.

Central banks around the world hold accounts with the Federal Reserve in the United States, where the central bank may hold a variety of deposit and custody accounts and engage in the use of several services. The Fed offers custodial services through the Depository Trust and Clearing Corporation (DTCC) for USD denominated and some non-USD denominated securities. Transfers of securities are facilitated, via the Fedwire RTGS system. Custodial services include holding foreign Gold Reserves at the New York Fed, within its bullion vaults (see Federal Reserve Bank of New York, Chapter 9: Gold).

Deposit accounts are made available to foreign central banks for payments received by, or paid between central banks, denominated in US dollars. In some instances, the Fed will additionally facilitate non-USD denominated payments for foreign central banks and some international institutions, via the Fedwire Funds Service. The Fed additionally offers a set of investment services to foreign entities to aid with their funds and liquidity management. This is managed, via a pooled foreign overnight reverse repurchase agreement {foreign repurchasing (repo) pool}, and a facility to either purchase or liquidate US dollar denominated treasury securities (bonds issued by the US Treasury, also known as 'Treasuries').

Foreign reserve assets are predominantly (approximately sixty-percent of all global reserves, 2020) held in the form of dollar denominated treasuries. The Fed established another repo facility in early 2020 for temporary repo for foreign and international monetary authorities (FIMA Repo). As a consequence of the majority of the *balance of payments* settlements being made in US treasuries, the Fed's RTGS, custodial and depository services are the payments systems both equipped, as well as relied upon to settle the majority of balances between nations.

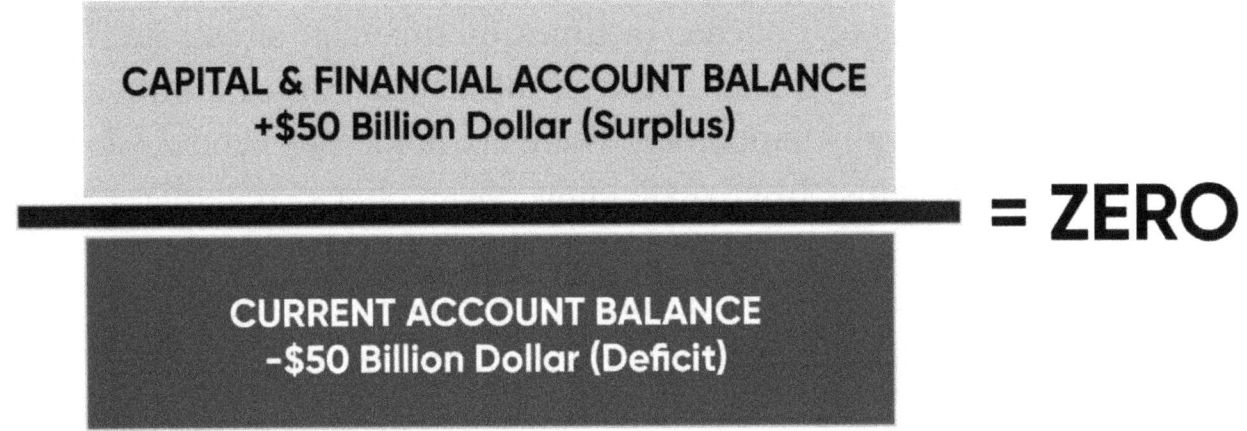

Fig 5.3 Balance of Payments (Nation State)

SWAP LINES

In order to satisfy global demand for dollars, the US is largely forced into a position, whereby trade deficits (current account deficits, see Balance of Payments above) have to be run with other nation states to supply the world's dollar requirements. A natural consequence of the *asymmetric relationship* (see Exorbitant Privilege, Chapter 13: Global Trade Rails) that the US maintains with the world, due to its principal global reserve currency status.

Swap lines (currency swap agreements) are an alternative mechanism through which the Fed can supply dollars (in the form of US Treasury Securities) to other central banks. These are bilateral agreements between the Fed and these central banks to exchange dollars for their currency at the prevailing exchange rate for a specified period of time, usually not exceeding three months at a time.

The foreign central banks are consequently able to provide US dollar liquidity for their domestic (commercial) banks when dollars are in short supply. As and when the swap period matures, the foreign central bank exchanges dollars in return for their domestic currency at the original exchange rate of the swap transaction.

This arrangement functions as a form of short-term credit between the Fed and a minority of central banks (predominantly those of advanced economies).

Permanent swap arrangements are in place with the Bank of England, the Bank of Japan and the Bank of Canada. In times of financial stress, the Fed has extended swap lines to a broader spectrum of central banks. However, these arrangements are generally temporary. There are numerous central banks with which the Fed refrains from extending swap lines regardless of the circumstances. To do so unilaterally would undermine the natural flow within the global financial system, hence, this is a privilege reserved for advanced economies, global financial centres and robust economic allies in good standing with the United States.

CARD PAYMENTS

In the sphere of card payments, debit, charge and credit cards are payment instruments, which proxy for payments between customers and merchants, as well as Business-to-Business (B2B) payments. Debit cards are a substitute for interbank payments, while credit and charge cards supplement this mechanism through short-term credit facilities.

In the payment card paradigm, the anatomy of a transaction is established by:

1. Authorisation (the Commitment)

2. Clearing (Payment Scheme Clearing)

3. Settlement

Card payments are differentiated from interbank payments by conceptually substituting *Messaging* for *Authorisation*. The principle of authorisation is centred on ensuring the payer is authorised to make the *commitment* to the payee, which will subsequently be fulfilled (settled) by the card issuer (typically a bank). In an interbank payment, the ability to commit is verified by the OFDI, prior to transmission of the initiation message, however, when a card is used, the payee needs immediate assurance that the payment amount will be settled, in order to release the goods or render the services being purchased.

Authorisation facilitates this commitment and assurance by surfacing the utility of an instant payment, while value is exchanged latently, via clearing and settlement, in favour of the payee.

In order to facilitate the use of a card payment instrument as a proxy for other forms of payment, such as cash or cheques, merchants are outfitted with Point-of-Sale (POS) terminals, which may engage one or more of the features within the card anatomy.

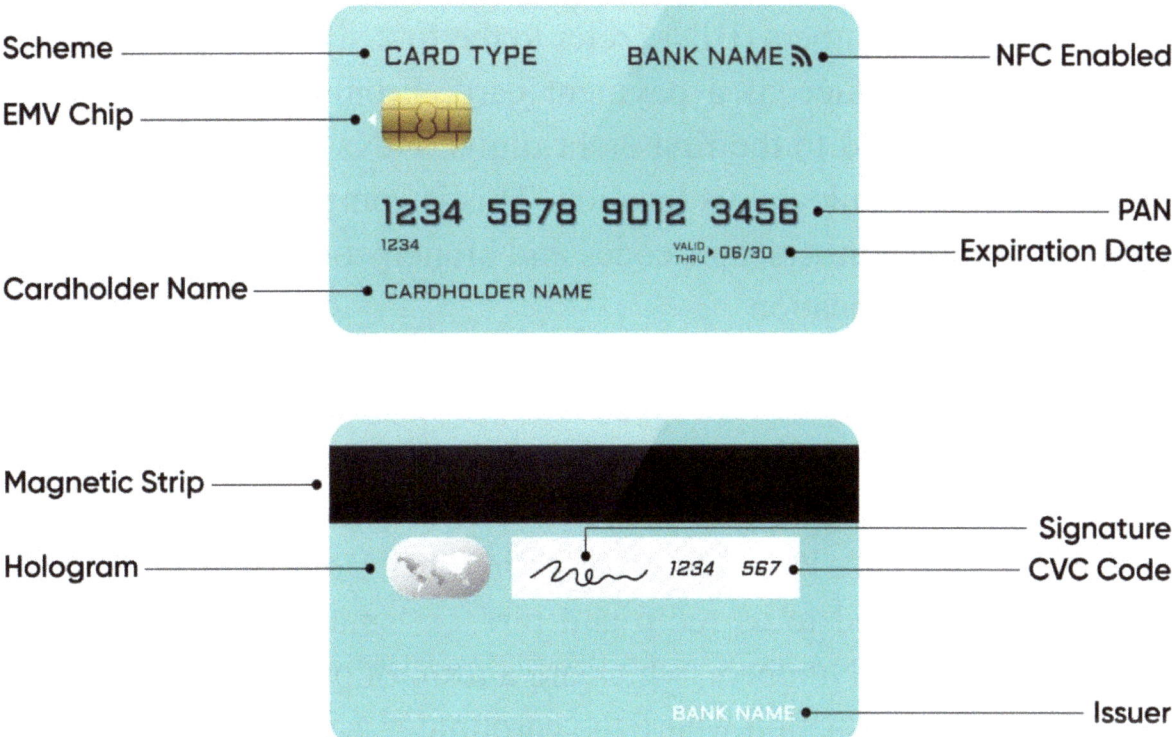

Fig 5.4 illustrates the typical characteristics of a Payment Card Instrument

Payment cards anatomically feature the logo (or corporate identity) of the card issuing bank (the Issuer), an embossed sixteen-digit Primary Account Number (PAN), an **E**uropay, **M**asterCard and **V**isa (EMV) chip, a "valid thru" or expiration date, and the cardholder's name (PAN, expiration date and the cardholder's name are embossed). The reverse side of the card features a magnetic strip, holder's signature strip, a three-digit authorisation code, based on either the card verification code (CVC), Card Verification Value (CVV) or CVV version 2 (CVV2) standards. These codes are required to verify 'cardholder not present' transactions.

The magnetic strip was invented at IBM in 1960 for use by the Central Intelligence Agency (CIA), for an access control system, however, IBM refrained from patenting the technology in order to promote its use in the banking sector. IBM were able to penetrate the banking market with extensive deployment of IBM 360 model 30 computers for use with magnetic strip cards. The technology was easily adopted thereafter, for storage of banking customer information, which could be used with card payment networks and eventually ATM machines.

Bank Identification Numbers (BINs) refer to the first six-digits of the embossed PAN number on the face of a payment card. From 2022 onwards, this is expected to be extended to the first eight-digits. BINs are used to identify the cardholder's issuing bank and its location. This is comparable to the manner in which bank routing numbers, sort codes and branch codes, are used to identify a bank and its branch location.

EMV cards are 'smart' cards, featuring an integrated circuit (chip) (see Evolution of Computing, Chapter 2: Capital Evolution), which stores the card data in addition to a magnetic strip on the card. The EMV chip facilitates use with a type of merchant's POS, known as a Pin Entry Device (PED). EMV cards are colloquially referred to as 'chip and pin' or 'smart' cards. PIN refers to Personal Identification Numbers, which are a form of passcode to use the EMV cards securely in a transaction where the cardholder is present.

Modern "smart" cards additionally include an embedded Near-Field Communication (NFC) chip for low-value contactless payments. Regardless of the card type, it usually features one or more hologram features associated with the Payment Network (Payment Scheme) branding. The Issuer is a member of the scheme depicted on the card, such as Visa or MasterCard.

The number of features illustrates the versatility and numerous mechanisms that card payment instruments are able to engage, in order to initiate a transaction at the point of sale, and to facilitate authorisation.

Features such as holograms and corporate identities, although aesthetically pleasing, are primarily intended to instil confidence that the card is genuine when presented physically to a merchant. However, other features of the card are functionally critical in authorising a transaction.

The first payment cards were charge cards, pioneered by Diners Club in 1950, and American Express in 1958. Bank of America released the first bank issued card, 'BankAmericard' too, in 1958. BankAmericard were rebranded to Visa in 1976.

While the first payment cards were fabricated from card stock, requiring substantial manual recording of information at the point-of-sale, the introduction of plastic cards by American Express in 1959 with embossed details of the cardholder's name, the PAN and the expiration date, revolutionised the expedience, with which payers and merchants could transact. This was facilitated through the invention of the credit card imprinter. This early POS device, simultaneously introduced in 1959, allowed the merchant to capture an impression of the embossed information on a plastic payment card using a carbon-copy paper form, in a matter of seconds (*Co-evolution of practice*).

An unfortunate limitation of this technology made it incumbent upon the merchant to validate the cardholder's signature, inscribed on the form by the cardholder, then comparing it to the signature on the reverse side of the card, which is highly subjective. A further limitation was the merchant remained uncertain as to whether the payer was creditworthy to make good on the obligation of the payment.

These limitations, compounded by the necessity to reduce fraud, prompted the modernisation of the payment card industry (PCI) using technology to facilitate authorisation. In 1970, the magnetic strip was added to plastic payment cards in order to use electronic POS terminals. The first electronic authorisation system was introduced in 1973, linking merchants to the Visa payment network, terminated at its data centre in California, USA. Electronic authorisation facilitated verifying the creditworthiness of the payer, however, unless reported as either lost or stolen, it failed to address as to whether the card was genuinely the property of the authorised cardholder or not.

PROCESS DATA QUICKLY

Sophisticated POS devices, known as Process Data Quickly(s) (PDQs) were introduced in 1979 and Electronic Funds Transfer Point of Sale (EFTPOS) devices were introduced in 1981. In 2006, POS machines, known as Pin-Entry Devices (PEDs), were introduced in the United Kingdom which read the EMV chips on the payment card (to substitute for the magnetic strip and signature), combined with a keypad, whereby the device reads the chip and authenticates with a personal identification number (PIN) entered by the cardholder.

This model introduced two-factor authentication (2FA), whereby an authorisation is initiated by the cardholder through producing something they have (the card) and something they know (the PIN).

Payment Networks, such as Visa and MasterCard, originated as 'Payment Schemes,' of which banks (issuers) were originally scheme members. Although these entities are independent financial institutions in contemporary terms, they remain referred to colloquially as 'schemes.' In the United States, however, these are colloquially referred to as 'associations.'

Given that payment cards can additionally be used with ATM machines, schemes and Issuers ensure that cards support a single-message system for ATMs (and card-present transactions), as well as a dual-message system for card payments (with signature confirmation, as well as card-not-present transactions). Both single-messaging, as well as dual-messaging, is governed by the ISO 8583 financial transaction card originated interchange messaging standard. In the United Kingdom, some messaging systems additionally support the antiquated Association for Payment Clearing Services 30 and 40 (APACS 30/40) messaging standards and increments, thereof. Messaging across the finance industry is incrementally converging towards the adoption of the ISO

20022 standard. A universal standard designed to accommodate all manner of financial messaging requirements (see ISO 20022, Chapter 13: Global Trade Rails).

OPEN VS. CLOSED MODEL

Payment Networks may operate within either, a 'three-corner' (three-party), also known as a 'closed' model, or a 'four-corner' (four-party), also known as an 'open' model.

In a three-corner model, transactions are captured for authorisation by an issuing bank (Issuer), with which the merchant has a relationship. Authorisation is requested by the merchant to the Acquiring/Issuing bank, via the Scheme's (franchisor) network.

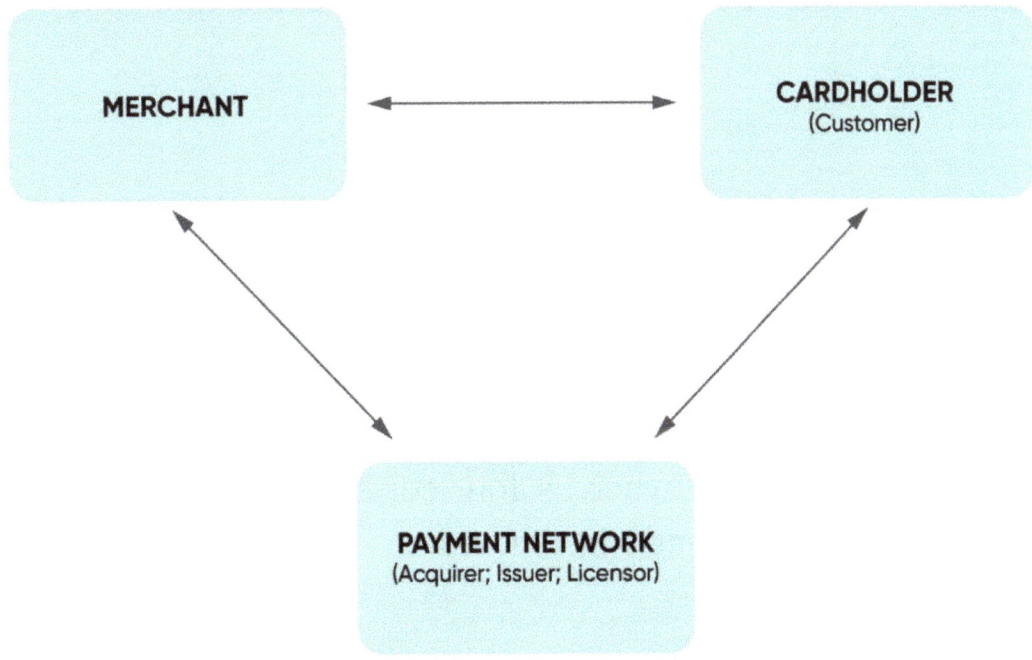

Fig 5.5 illustrates the relationships in a Three-corner 'Closed' Model

In a four-corner (open) model, the merchant's authorisation request is captured by an Acquirer, which solicits authorisation from the cardholder's Issuer, via the Scheme's payment network. Merchants (also known as Acceptors) have a business relationship with Acquirers (Merchant Acquirers or Acquiring Banks), whereas Cardholders maintain a relationship with Issuers (Card Issuers, typically Banks). Both Acquirers and Issuers maintain a relationship with Card Payment Networks (known as Schemes).

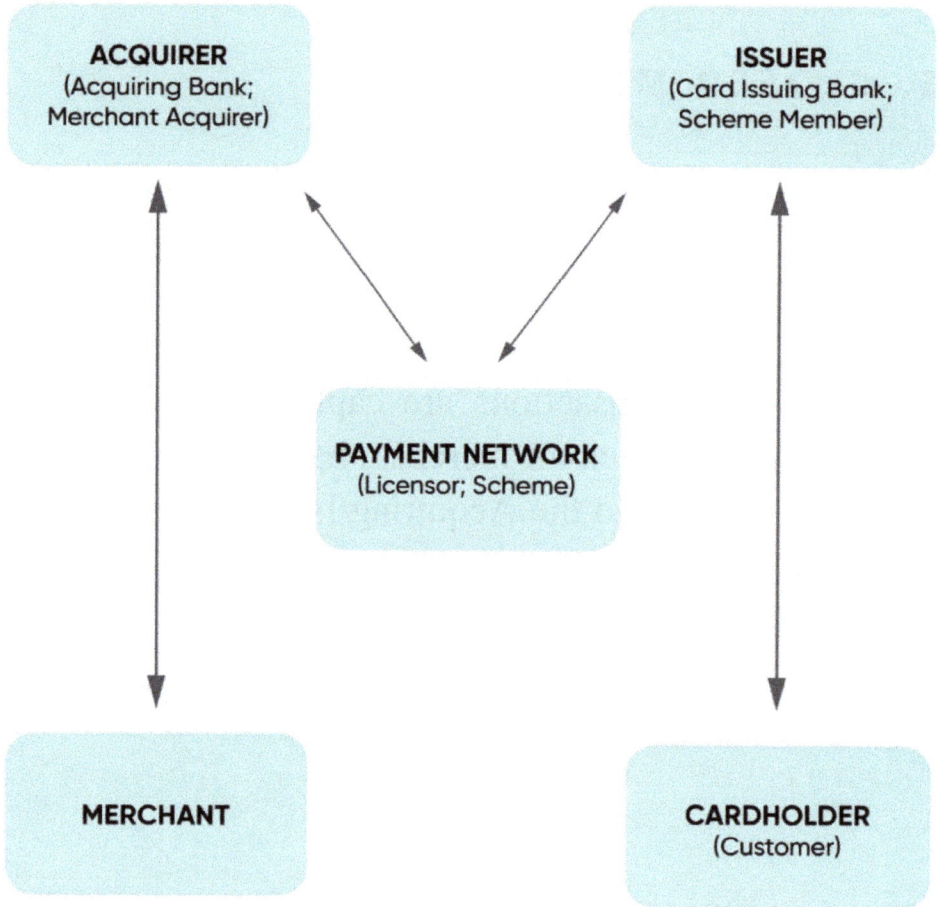

Fig 5.6 illustrates the relationships in a Four-corner 'Open' Model

Three-corner models are prevalent with charge card companies, such as Diners Club and American Express, whereas four-corner models are prevalent with Card Schemes, such as Visa and MasterCard.

INTERCHANGE

Apart from the participant architecture of either model, each scheme governs the nature of rules among participants in a card payment transaction. By way of example, in a four-corner model, **Interchange++** describes the fees charged by the Issuer which is the **interchange**, the first "+" is the processing fee levied by the scheme and the second "+," represents the fee levied by the Merchant Acquirer, known as the discount rate. Interchange fees predominantly represent a percentage of the payment transaction value for credit or charge cards and a fixed transaction fee for debit cards, regardless of the transaction value. The Issuing bank charges the interchange fee which represents the bulk of the total transaction processing fee (Interchange++).

The Issuer carries the greatest risk in recouping funds from the cardholder, once the merchant has received settlement for credit to the merchant. The rationale for this is substantiated by virtue of the fact that neither the scheme nor the Merchant Acquirer are providing credit, which the cardholder may be exploiting to make the purchase. The Scheme exacts a processing fee for facilitating authorisation, clearing and settlement processing, as well as providing the participants with network access. The Merchant Acquirer's fee (the discount rate) is charged for providing merchant services, capturing authorisation requests and facilitating processing, via the Scheme. Issuers (banks) bear the greatest risks, and thus, benefit from the highest proportion of fees.

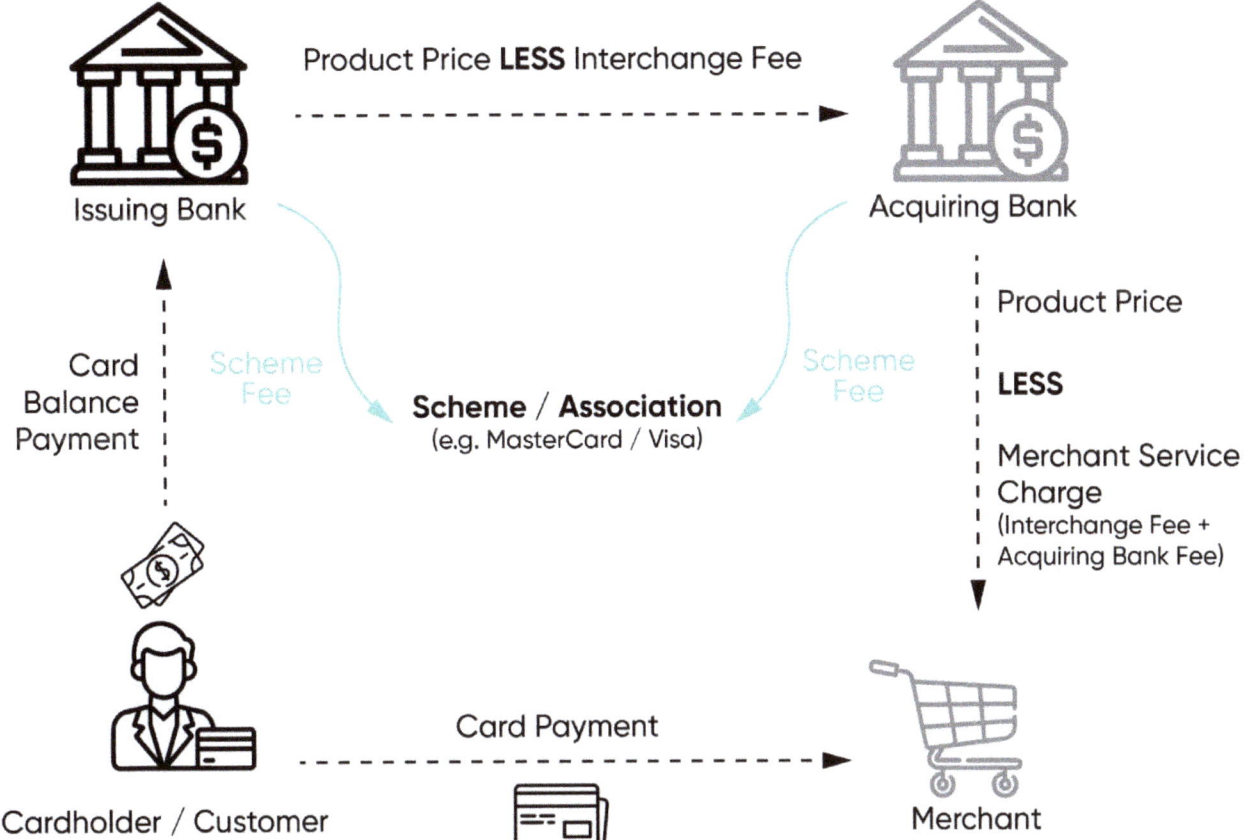

Fig 5.7 flow of payment and interchange fees in typical card payment transactions

AUTHORISATION

An authorisation request is initiated from the merchant's PDQ and transmitted to the Merchant Acquirer. The Acquirer forwards the request to the Card Issuer, via the Scheme's payment network. The Issuer provides a response to the Acquirer and the Merchant.

Authorisation request responses, result in either:

1. Approve   - transaction authorised for processing
2. Decline   - transaction is declined, although the card should be returned to holder
3. Refer to card issuer - merchant should contact the card issuing bank
4. Capture card   - merchant should confiscate the card

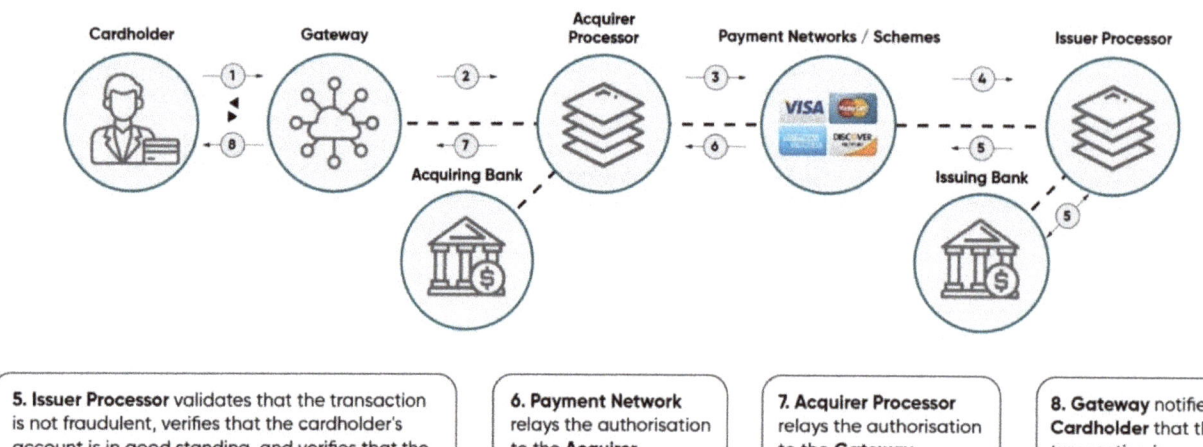

Fig 5.8 end-to-end Payment card authorisation

PAYMENT SCHEME CLEARING

Once authorisation has been rendered, the process of payment scheme clearing is followed, whereby, depending on the specific contractual arrangements the merchant maintains with the Acquirer, a float period (usually two days) follows for clearing and settlement. During this float period known as "T+2," potential payment 'disputes' and 'chargeback' processes which are available to cardholders and merchants may be followed. Disputes are usually the result of either erroneous duplicate charges, or in instances where card credentials may have been stolen and subsequently used fraudulently.

Clearing in the context of card payments is the process of transmitting final transaction (authorisations) information from the Merchant Acquirer to the issuers for settlement with the merchants. Acquirers have no control over which issuers the cardholders are with, nor which scheme the issuers are members of. The first stage of clearing, therefore, requires that the Acquirer compile and aggregate the authorisations by scheme into a batch, formatted in accordance with the standards and specifications, governed by the scheme. Each batch compilation is transmitted to the appropriate scheme, where it is processed, filtered and sub-divided by issuer into smaller batches. Once the smaller batches are received by the issuers, the transactions are posted (term of art) to the cardholder's statements. Each scheme assesses the obligations (by issuer) and calculates the net settlement positions in favour of the Acquirer. Thereafter, the scheme submits a funds transfer order to the issuing banks. The Issuers disburse funds (less interchange fees) to settle with the Acquirer and the Acquirer settles (less the discount rate and Scheme processing fee) with the merchants, by crediting the merchant's account. Settlements between Issuers and Acquirers are facilitated, via interbank net settlement CSMs.

ACQUIRERS

Acquirers (Merchant Acquirers/Acquiring Banks) grow their market share by attracting and on-boarding merchants, incentivising these businesses to broaden the channels through which they may achieve sales conversions by accepting card payments. Acquirers are responsible for courting new merchant customers, reviewing and underwriting their credit applications, as well as conducting compliance checks, such as KYC, Anti-Money Laundering (AML) and sanctions screening. This is a rigorous process, often requiring extensive paperwork, interviews, and could potentially extend over weeks or even months to discern a decision.

Once a merchant is approved, the Acquirer arranges the necessary connectivity for processing payments and creates a merchant account. The merchant account is used to receive funds from settlement. The Acquirer, additionally, issues the merchant with a unique Merchant Identifier (MID) and provides the necessary PDQ devices, each of which is usually assigned a unique Terminal Identifier (TID).

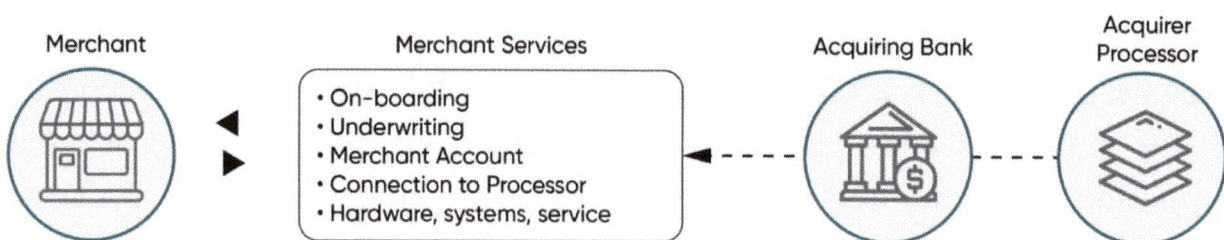

Fig 5.9 Merchants receive services from Acquirers with which they maintain a direct relationship

In some instances, Acquirers maintain the relationship with merchants, however, elect not to process card payment transactions themselves. In such models, the Acquirer outsources payment processing to a third-party, known as an Acquirer Processor, also known as a 'Front-end processor,' which provides processing services to multiple Acquirers on either a dedicated or multi-tenancy basis.

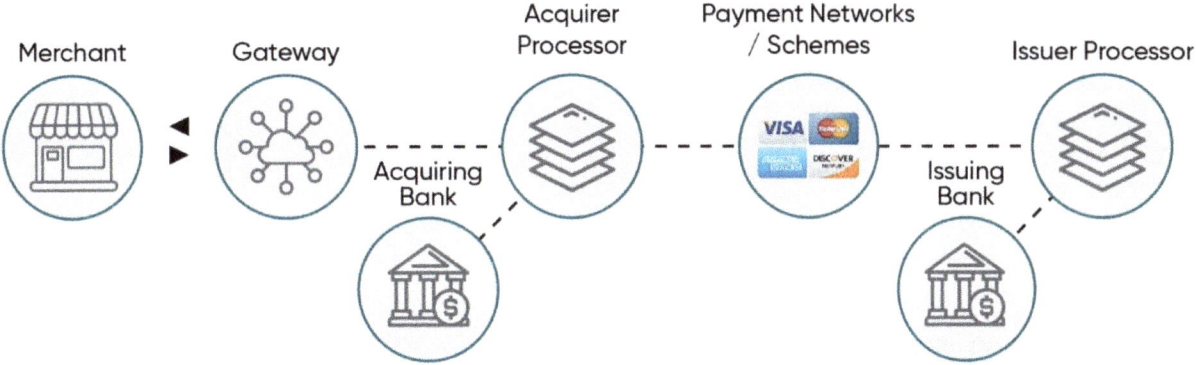

Fig 5.10 Acquirers may outsource processing to an Acquirer Processor; Issuers may outsource processing to Issuer Processors

In some instances, issuers outsource processing to entities, known as Issuer Processors (Back-end processors), which provide several services to issuing banks, including card approval authorisations and funds settlement.

INDEPENDENT SALES ORGANISATIONS

By the early 1990s, growth in the Small-Medium Business/Enterprise (SMB/SME) market had boosted demand for accepting card payments. Due to the rigorous controls and high barriers to entry, Acquirers struggled to scale up. In order to accommodate the deluge in demands for 'smaller' merchant accounts, Independent Sales Organisations (ISOs) emerged to assist in accommodating this shortfall.

ISOs initially emerged as resellers, effectively displacing the sales functions of Acquirers, and thereafter, evolved to perform broader roles of maintaining customer service relationships, as well as systems and hardware contracts with the merchants, post-on-boarding. Acquirers continued to manage the underwriting as well as the provisioning of merchant accounts and MIDs.

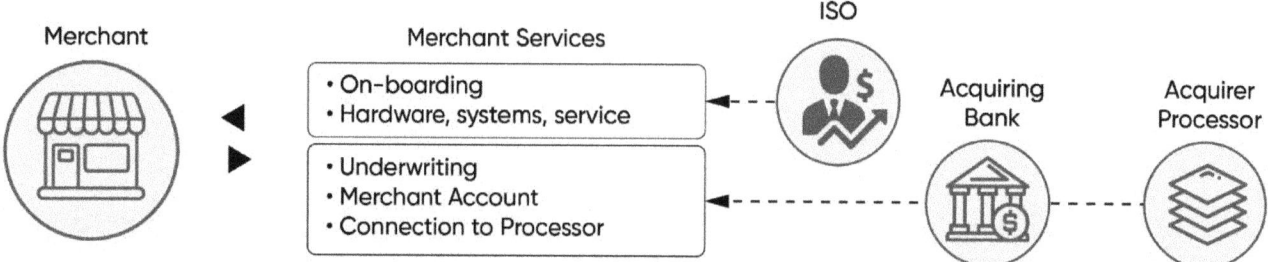

Fig 5.11 illustrates the services which an Independent Sales Organisation typically displaces from Acquirers

PAYMENT GATEWAYS

By the late 1990s, e-commerce pioneers, such as Amazon and eBay, had emerged, requiring the capability to process card payments online. Payment gateways such as Bibit, Datacash and Cybersource emerged, which enabled merchants to engage customers and take payments for goods and services online, in addition to their existing capability to accept card payments in-store. Unfortunately, this led to fragmentation in the payments ecosystem as Acquirers were slow to adapt to these demands. Payment gateways essentially maintained independent relationships with merchants, which led to merchants managing multiple relationships with payment providers.

Payment gateways provide APIs, software plugins and/or 'hosted payment pages' as web-facing facilities, which enable merchants to accept card payments to enable e-commerce and m-commerce through the merchant's website. The incremental evolution thereof, t-commerce (television-enabled commerce) using smart TV apps and payment gateway APIs, is another such facility anticipated to leverage payment gateways.

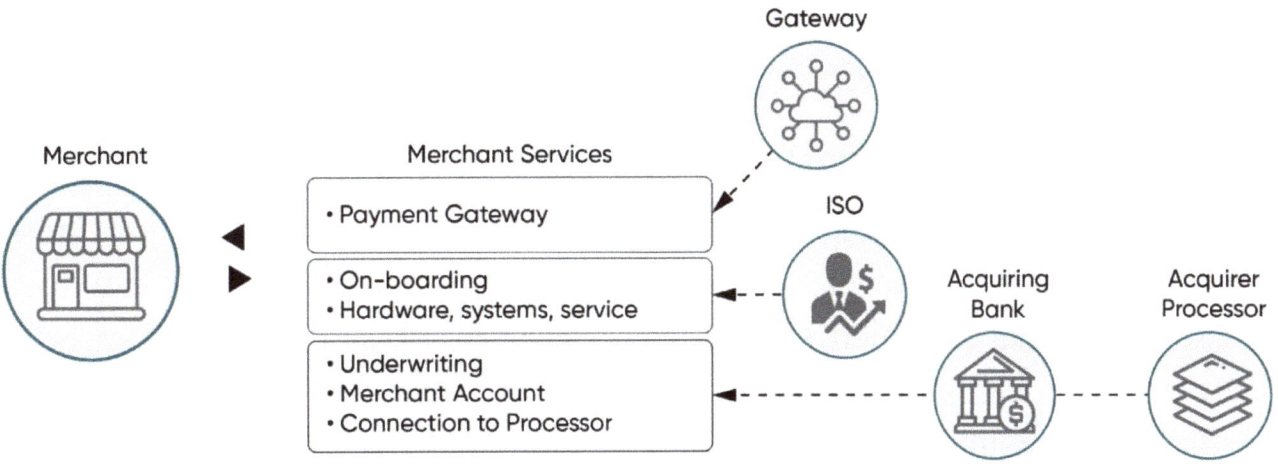

Fig 5.12 illustrates the fragmentation (Componentisation effect) initially experienced with the emergence of Payment Gateways

APIs, plugins and hosted payment pages fulfil the role of the POS device (PDQ) and the payment gateway fulfils the role of securely capturing the transaction, ordinarily fulfilled by the Acquirer, in a traditional card payment transaction. In practice, the payment gateway, intermediates between the merchant's website and an Acquirer's payment switch (apparatus/system designed to capture the authorisation request). The 'hosted payment pages' and APIs, as well as plugins are designed to compartmentalise and securely transmit the card details when transacting with the merchant's web service, in order to ensure the cardholder's credentials are neither shared with the merchant nor any other unauthorised party.

Access to card details exposes an entity to scrutiny against the Payment Card Industry Data Security Standard (PCI-DSS). By using 'hosted payment pages,' APIs or plugins, the merchant is isolated from the cardholder's details, and thus, not subject to independent PCI-DSS certification or scrutiny. This vulnerability did not exist in the PDQ model, as the terminal facilitated end-to-end encryption to provide secure intercourse between the merchant and the Acquirer.

PLATFORM PAYMENT PROCESSING

Platform payment processing, additionally known as marketplace payment processing, describes a subset of payment processing, in which in lieu of a merchant selling directly to a consumer, a customer is matched with a seller, via a platform marketplace.

Fundraising companies are typical examples of businesses that make use of platform payment processing. Platforms such as Wepay, a subsidiary of Chase, since 2017, were used to process payments for GoFundMe. Other examples include marketplaces which sell goods or services on behalf of one or more third-party merchants. An example of which is a marketplace, such as Etsy. These platforms either integrate with a third-party payment gateway or act as the payment gateway itself.

ALTERNATIVE PAYMENT METHODS

Alternative payment methods (APMs) cover a spectrum of payment methods, which neither make use of card payments, nor directly use interbank payment transfers. An early and well known APM is that of PayPal. PayPal was co-founded by Elon Musk in 1998 as Confinity. The APM introduced an alternative means of making payments, predominantly aimed at enabling an expedient means of payment for e-commerce merchants. PayPal's initial proposition offered an alternative to using a traditional payment gateway.

PayPal achieved this by offering a means of creating a customer account online, through a low-friction on-boarding process. The customer's PayPal account could be funded for purchases and receiving payments. In addition, a PayPal customer account could be linked to the customer's bank account. PayPal offered an intuitive web-driven means of conducting online transfers between customers at no charge. Merchants by contrast, are charged a transaction fee for accepting PayPal payments, although the integration itself, for e-commerce websites was intuitive and secure. Most critically, the PayPal integration enabled expedient, frictionless check-outs for customers. The latter, being a competitive differentiator, which statistically improves sales conversion rates. PayPal is one of the early success stories in the sphere of FinTech, without which, banking and finance would likely have taken a great deal longer to modernise and for e-commerce to gain the level of traction it has experienced, since the late 1990s.

Another noteworthy APM was that of M-Pesa, the name of which is derived from Mobile (M) and money (Pesa, Swahili for money). First pioneered in Kenya in 2007, the APM allowed mobile phone users to deposit funds into an account on the user's mobile phone and transfer funds, via text messages (also known as a Short Message Service or SMS).

M-Pesa was launched by Vodafone and Safaricom, the largest mobile phone operators in Kenya at the time. The APM saw meteoric adoption in the country as a result of poor traditional banking, telecommunications and payment infrastructure, which left the majority of rural inhabitants unbanked.

The business model capitalised on an existing mature practice of pre-purchasing airtime minutes, via 'top up' cards, each with a unique code, keyed into the phone. 'Top up' cards could be purchased at various kiosks and supermarkets in exchange for cash. In essence, instead of using the 'top up' credit solely for making phone calls and sending text messages, the credit could be used to make payments for a nominal transaction fee. While Kenya had little in the way of traditional infrastructure, it did have excellent mobile phone coverage. The APM exploited this position to surface the utility of payments and instantly converted the mobile phone into the dominant payment instrument in the country. The lack of an established payment infrastructure created a vacuum that could be filled by a new service based on first principles (see First Principles, Chapter 4: Surfacing Utility), rather than building analogously on an existing foundation.

Following the success of M-Pesa in Kenya, the APM was exported to a number of other nations in Africa, where conditions were comparable.

ELECTRONIC MONEY INSTITUTIONS

Electronic Money Institutions (EMIs) are representative of a relatively novel FinTech participant in the financial market, amidst the growing trend of digitisation within the financial services sphere. EMIs are most commonly characterised by the issuance of e-money (electronic money / tokens) and payment intermediation (see E-Money, Chapter 6: Money).

In the EU, EMIs were brought into regulation by the Electronic Money Directive (EMD). The EMD enabled non-banking entities to compete with banks. The EMD was repealed in 2011 and superseded by the EMD2, which broadened the scope of services that could be undertaken by EMIs. In the United Kingdom, EMD2 was implemented at a national level, via the Electronic Money Regulations 2011 (EMR). The latter legislation is complementary to the Payment Services Regulations 2017 (PSR) that since combined, have created a framework for the operation of EMIs within the United Kingdom. By contrast, British banks are regulated under the Financial Service and Markets Act 2000 (see Electronic Money, Chapter 1: FinTech).

Consequently, for an everyday consumer of financial services, the variance between FinTechs with an electronic money license in the UK and a British bank may be challenging to differentiate.

PAYFACS

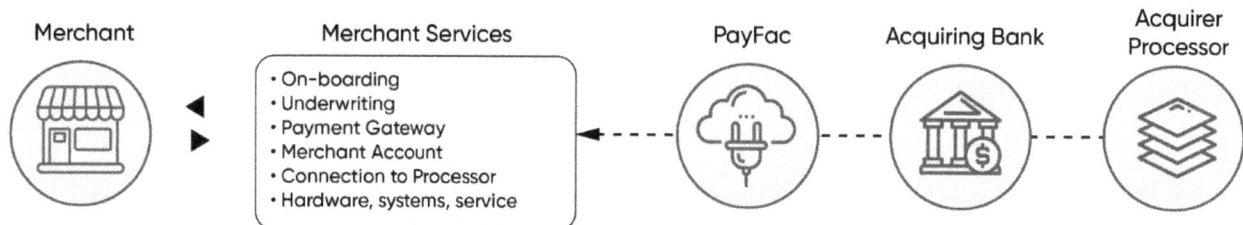

Fig 5.13 the introduction of PayFacs/PSPs intermediating between (disintermediating) Merchants and Acquirers

Payment Facilitators/Payment Service Providers (PayFacs in MasterCard terms and PSPs in Visa terms) are FinTech entities which build on the foundations established by FinTech pioneers to intermediate between merchants (sub-merchants) and Merchant Acquirers. Notable PayFacs that emerged in 2009, were that of Square and Stripe. The following year (2010), MasterCard established its official PayFac programme, with Visa following suit a year thereafter (2011).

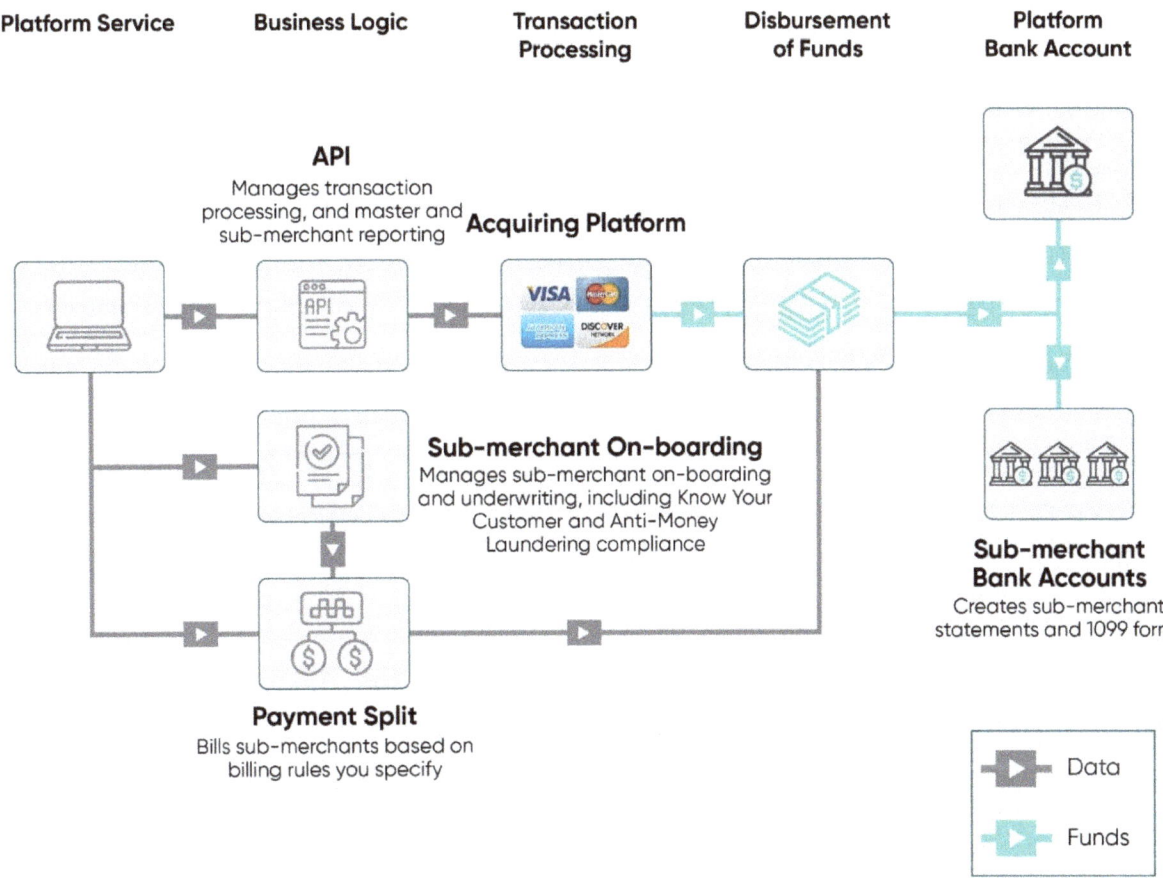

Fig 5.14 Overview of the PayFac/PSP business and technology architecture

PayFacs (PSPs) are Electronic Money Institutions (EMIs) governed by financial conduct and service regulators, such as the Financial Conduct Authority (FCA) in the United Kingdom.

By way of example, Square embarked on offering a small (dongle) device that could be attached to a smart phone to enable the acceptance of payment card transactions. The dongle enabled smaller merchants that provide off-location services, such as home delivery or portable kiosks, to accept payments, via card instruments, by co-opting the smart phone in lieu of a dedicated PDQ. Square subsequently expanded its portfolio to launch a POS terminal targeting larger merchants in the retail sector. Square's virtual terminal enables merchants to accept online payments and its reader software development kit (SDK) enables offline merchants to integrate its payments capabilities into a variety of different workflows and exploit varied third-party devices. The SDK acts as an enabler to promote a network effect.

These payments services constitute the enabler through which Square built its larger portfolio and platform. Subsequently, the PayFac launched its 'Square Card' offering. A debit card that enables a merchant to access funds in its Square account and effects payments, therefrom. Square Capital lends money to small merchants, based on sales data gleaned from the POS terminals. Thereby, exploiting learning effects (see Innovate, Leverage & Commoditise, Chapter 3: Ecosystems).

PayFacs aggregate platforms such as payment gateways, Acquirers and alternative payment methods in order to intermediate on behalf of its customers (sub-merchants). Typically, a PayFac will register as a merchant (merchant account and MID) with an Acquirer, facilitating payments from sub-merchants. PayFacs seek to enable merchants to embrace an Omni-channel suite of avenues, with which to broaden sales conversion opportunities with potential customers. The principle being, the more potential payment avenues and the better integrated with the various sales channels, the greater the opportunity and likelihood for conversion. PayFacs differentiate themselves through the mastery of payments orchestration, aggregation and unified billing.

Payments orchestration refers to the choreography in coordinating different payment methods and services, insulated behind the veneer of a seamless proposition and/or interface. PayFacs offer merchants (sub-merchants) a single entity, with which to maintain a relationship and point of contact, underpinned by a broad spectrum of payment channels and methods.

Through contemporary frameworks and practices, such as Open Banking and the maturing API economy, multiple competing entities are able to take up positions that were previously occupied by a minority of financial services organisations. Consequently, this drives down margins and expands choice amongst merchants (sub-merchants).

Hence, PayFacs are increasing in prevalence, as the robustness of backend integration is becoming increasingly frictionless. PayFacs are primed to offer value through aggregating established, as well as nascent technologies within their portfolios, offering merchants (sub-merchants) access to the newest technologies and payment methods shortly after they emerge.

PayFacs are additionally able to court merchants through attractive customer acquisition strategies, such as flat-rate transaction charging models, which are favourable to merchants that process high-value transactions, for which interchange fees are ordinarily substantial. This model is less attractive, however, for merchants which process high volumes of low value transactions. Regardless, PayFacs are increasingly popular among start-ups since sub-merchants are subject to lower barriers to entry than those which apply directly to Acquirers for traditional merchant accounts. In the PayFacs business model, the PayFac is responsible for compliance checks, KYC, AML and sanctions screening, when on-boarding sub-merchants, ordinarily facilitated by Acquirers.

CONTACTLESS PAYMENTS

Early Near-Field Communications (NFC) cards were reusable stored value instruments, such as the Octopus card, pioneered in Hong Kong in 1997. Octopus cards were introduced to replace travel tickets for use on Hong Kong's public transit system. The card, which may only be 'charged up' with cash (denominated in HKD), allows the holder to pay by proximity and where relevant, unlocks barriers when passed near to an NFC receiver at the beginning and end of a journey. Octopus cards may also be used to make contactless payments (outside of public transport) among participating merchants. Although the second card system used for this purpose after South Korea's Upass, it was the first instance in which NFC technology was used for a payment instrument.

The success of NFC stored value cards for public transit systems saw extensive adoption in other countries. Notable examples were the Oyster card used by Transport for London (TFL), the Navigo Card in Paris, Opal Card in New South Wales and EZ-Link in Singapore. Another example is that of the SmarTrip Card, which may be charged with either cash (USD) or a credit card for use in transit systems within the Washington D.C./Baltimore area. The SmarTrip system is managed by the Washington Metropolitan Area Transit Authority (WMATA).

The integration of NFC technology into Debit and Credit Cards facilitated the introduction of 'contactless payments' to a broader merchant ecosystem outside of public transit systems. Barclaycard partnered with mobile phone company Orange, which introduced the first NFC enabled credit cards in the UK in 2010.

NFC enabled credit and debit cards were introduced with low-value authorisation limits, an example of micropayments (low value payments), to mitigate exposure of fraud. The contactless facility balances convenience with risk. High value card payments require authentication, via 'chip and pin' or magnetic strip and signature, whereas contactless payments could be used for public transit systems and low-cost purchases where turnaround improves productivity and the flow of foot fall. Examples include, purchases at kiosks, coffee shops and purveyors of fast-moving consumer goods.

The World Health Organisation (WHO), encouraged merchants and the payments industry to embrace contactless payments shortly after the outbreak of COVID-19. The WHO recognised the significance of a technology which aids in reducing viral transmission by avoiding common contact surfaces during the payment process. The WHO additionally discouraged the use of cash where avoidable, acting as an accelerant for advancements in contactless FinTech solutions. The WHO noted that in most instances, plastic cards were a higher viral transmission medium than cash. However, a contactless transaction using either a plastic card or smart device was superior in reducing viral transmissions than cash.

QUICK RESPONSE CODES

Quick Response (QR) codes were originally developed for the Japanese automotive industry in 1994, as a matrix barcode system. QR codes are designed to impart a large volume of data, relative to a low surface area two-dimensional infographic. The pattern is square shaped, composed of a matrix of small squares, with three distinct larger squares occupying three corners. The area can accommodate a number of smaller squares per side, either 33x33 or 177x177. The square density correlates to the volume of data the QR code can hold within a maximum of up to 4296 characters or 23648 bits in the larger higher density variant.

QR codes are capable of housing encrypted data and can be scanned from screens, billboards, signs, posters, stickers, engravings and from paper using the native camera applications, prevalent in Apple as well as Android smart devices (phones, tablets and camera enabled devices). This is a significant differentiator from barcodes, which require a dedicated laser scanner, although many such scanners are also capable of reading QR codes.

QR codes gained significant traction in offering information and promotion of events, points of interest, as well as in the marketing of goods and services in print media and other forms of 'below-the-line' advertising. In the travel industry, numerous airlines and transit services have embraced the use of QR codes for printable and downloadable boarding passes, as well as travel tickets. Numerous entertainment and sports event ticketing services have additionally followed suit. QR codes have also gained prevalence in the development of loyalty scheme applications.

In the payments sphere, many businesses (merchants, banks or utilities) have embraced enclosing QR codes on bills, as well as statements, posted to customers in order to offer an expedient means of settling an outstanding account. The principle, being that the customer scans the bill with their smart device and a payment is initiated from a mobile payment app, to which the customer authenticates and approves payment. This practice surfaces the utility of making a payment against an outstanding account notice. Enclosing a QR code, assists in removing friction and saving the payer time in initiating an online payment, setting up a direct debit or posting a cheque (check).

QR codes can be used to facilitate payments in a variety of ways. Merchants for instance, may scan a QR code housing a customer's payment details, displayed via an app on a customer's smart phone at the point of sale. Conversely, a customer could scan a merchant generated QR code for a specific good or service through an app designed to make payments, via QR codes. Additionally, QR codes may be used in app-to-app payments between smart device users. It's a fairly common practice to combine the use of embedded biometric authentication facilitated by fingerprint scanning or facial recognition, via the smart device, with the use of a QR code payment application to provide the necessary security in limiting the potential for fraudulent use, thereof.

QR codes are used extensively in conjunction with digital wallets and are increasingly attractive in facilitating contactless payments, particularly in the light of the COVID-19 pandemic, driving the necessity for social distancing in face-to-face payment interactions. The technology is additionally pervasive among social media apps, seeking greater penetration within the payments market. The technology is highly versatile and relatively effortless to co-opt for a variety of different uses, particularly within the payments landscape.

While the European Union and the United Kingdom invested heavily in contactless payment technologies, such as Host Card Emulation and NFC, at significant expense, companies in other jurisdictions have benefitted from using QR codes to develop inexpensive contactless payment apps and methods at a fraction of the cost. These entities have capitalised on the low total cost of ownership (TCO) and simplicity, thereof.

DIGITAL WALLETS

By all accounts, a digital wallet conceptually plays the role of storing digital tokens of value and payment instruments, whereas a physical wallet stores physical cash, tickets and physical payment instruments, such as cards and cheques. This paradigm differs from a bank account where an institution stores value on the customer's behalf, although some digital wallets (those connected to the internet, known as 'hot wallets') are hosted by a third-party on the user's behalf and accessible, via the internet, in order to access value within the wallet.

Another form of digital wallet is one where the wallet takes the form of an app on a smart device or stored within a computer web browser or dedicated app. In such instances, if the device were to be lost without a backup of the data housed therein, the contents of the digital wallet is lost with it.

The Octopus card (see above), being broadened for use outside of the Hong Kong transit system as an analogue for cash, is an early example of the Digital Wallet paradigm. The Octopus card could only be charged up with cash and used for purchases traditionally made with cash. If the instrument were lost, the value was lost with it.

The catalyst for contemporary digital wallets began with an evolution of this paradigm with Sony in 2004, introducing the Osaifu-Keitai system, translated as 'Wallet Phone.' Essentially signalling a break-through by co-opting the mobile phone to create a digital store of value. Later innovations, such as the introduction of the smart phone in the form of Apple's iPhone in 2007 (see Chapter 3: Ecosystems), have subsequently leveraged NFC capability in later models in order to offer a native digital wallet app and the ability to clone payment card instruments through Host Card Emulation (HCE).

HCE describes the practice of reading a payment card into a smart phone's memory, known as a Secure Enclave (see Smart Cities, Chapter 15: Economy of Things), in order to emulate the card and use the phone's embedded NFC technology to make payments, as if the smart phone were the card. This capability formed the foundations for the introduction of Apple's payment proposition, known as Apple Pay. HCE has since additionally been incorporated into other smart devices, such as wearable technologies, including watches and smart glasses (spectacles).

Apple Pay is an example of a 'Cold Wallet' (not connected to the internet) and similar cold wallet technologies (Google Pay, LG Pay, Samsung Pay, Fitbit Pay and Garmin Pay) have further been broadened to make payments, via web interfaces in addition to NFC. Successful web integrations of this nature rely on standardisation. Electronic Commerce Modelling Language (ECML) is a protocol (based on RFC 4112) designed to facilitate a standardised integration of cold digital wallets for web-based checkout forms and payments. W3C's Secure Payment Confirmation (SPC) is another such standard targeted at elevating the web-browser's capabilities in this regard, while ensuring a secure means of doing so.[70] This functionality, essentially allows these cold wallets to be used for online payments, as if they were hot wallets.

Digital Wallets may additionally be designed to accommodate crypto-currencies. A digital wallet of this nature, is designed to use cryptographic keys, public and private, for receiving and spending respectively (see Chapter 14: Tokenisation). Crypto-currency wallets could either be "hot" or "cold," whereby the wallet may be stored online or offline. Offline (cold storage) wallets may be stored using storage devices, such as thumb drives or hard drives.

DISBURSEMENT HUBS

Disbursement is the act of paying a beneficiary from a fund or account. Examples of funds may include trusts, escrow accounts or deceased estate accounts. Accounts may include that of a business bank account used to conduct day-to-day business transactions.

A common disbursement practice is that of a business which disburses funds on behalf of a client, for which the client later reimburses the business. The distinction between payments and disbursements is evident when considering the implications of taxation. For example, payments may be subjected to Value Added Tax (VAT), whereas disbursements are generally exempt.

A prime example of disbursement would be that of a solicitor paying the stamp duty land tax (SDLT) on behalf of a client in a real estate purchase. This is the client's expense and responsibility, not the solicitor's. Disbursement generally refers to the distribution of funds to third-parties on behalf of clients, via an intermediary, such as a financial institution.

Disbursement hubs are FinTech centric propositions, designed to offer businesses engaged in disbursements on a routine basis a seamless integrated facility to do so. Disbursement hubs may additionally be used to manage payroll disbursements and recurring business-to-business disbursements. These functions are additionally facilitated, via business treasury management systems.

MOBILE PAYMENTS

Mobile payments refer to payments made via mobile devices, most commonly and particularly via smart phones. Smart phones and wearables, such as smart watches, may be used to make card payments, via HCE as well as NFC. Alternative payment methods, such as M-Pesa, additionally leverage carrier billing, via SMS. In the United Kingdom, schemes such as PayM, provide the framework for mobile payment services, such as Barclays' Pingit.

The majority of mobile payments that differentiate themselves from these aforementioned mechanisms are natively developed smart phone apps designed to engage Open Banking APIs and partnerships with larger financial institutions. These have manifested in single-platform payment propositions, Neo-banking, 'buy now, pay later' (BNPL) offerings, cross-border Forex (foreign exchange) direct transfers and alternative payment methods.

These apps and propositions seek to surface the utility of payments in novel, contextual and experiential forms, doing so through co-opting technologies, such as web APIs, QR codes, NFC and SMS. In addition, there are apps such as those provided by social media networks which are increasingly being augmented, to include payments capabilities.

PUSH VS. PULL PAYMENTS

Push payments, also known as *buyer-initiated payments,* are payments whereby the payer approves and submits a payment in a comparable manner to a *pull payment*. However, in a *push payment* the transaction is processed automatically, thus, pushed directly to the payee. Wire transfers, ACH and direct deposits are examples of such. By contrast, *pull payments* enable the payee to withdraw, or effectively 'pull' funds from the payer (provided there is a pre-existing agreement to do so). Direct debit is an example of a *pull payment* mechanism. *Pull payments* are particularly prevalent with companies which offer services on a subscription (or recurring) basis. Consequently, *pull payments* tend to offer the merchant or service provider greater cash flow predictability. This supports subscription commerce based business models such as CSRS (see Business Model Evolution, Chapter 4: Surfacing Utility).

PAYMENT CONVERGENCE & DOMINANCE

Convergence between PayFacs/PSPs, platform payment processors, alternative payment methods and digital wallets is increasingly prevalent. PayPal, which initially came to market as an APM, evolved into a PayFac, partnering with various regional Merchant Acquirers to process card payments and subsequently offered credit facilities. In 2020, PayPal announced that the platform would offer the ability to purchase and spend crypto-currency, such as

Bitcoin in 2021 (initially in the US), hence broadening its role as a hot wallet capability to complement its other services.

Payment Schemes (Payment Networks), such as Visa and MasterCard, which have traditionally maintained relationships exclusively with Banks (Issuers) and Acquiring Banks (Merchant Acquirers), have launched partner programmes and initiatives in order to remain relevant in the rapidly evolving FinTech landscape.

MasterCard launched its 'MasterCard FinTech Express,' whereas Visa launched its 'FinTech Fast Track Programme,' which has enabled FinTech entities to access the payment networks in order to enhance the provision of digital wallets, digital banking, 'Buy Now, Pay Later' propositions, B2B payments, cross-border remittance, bill payments, payments infrastructure, and person-to-person payments. In addition to access to the MasterCard and Visa Payment Networks, these programmes furnish partners with tools to enable innovation and broaden competition in the FinTech payments sphere.

Notable partners engaged in the Visa Fast Track Programme were initially Bankable (UK), Conotoxia (Poland), Enfuce (Finland), Ininal (Turkey), Modulr (UK), PayPal (US), Railsbank (UK) and Vivid Money (Germany).

Under the programme, Visa make a Fast Track Toolkit available to FinTech partners, which provides knowledge, resources and facilities to enable among other services the ability for a partner to rapidly design and bring a new payment card to market. This is a privilege historically reserved only for Card Issuer Banks.

Visa further offered a 'Visa Ready Certification' which enables a certification system for an ecosystem of expert partners in the capabilities FinTechs may require to securely and effectively engage and use the Visa Payments Network. MasterCard offer a similar framework for services and certification.

The launching of these initiatives signals recognition that the historic roles of Payments Schemes (Payment Networks) in the traditional four-corner business model are threatened by new FinTech business models and the growing popularity in digital FinTech payments, outside of the ecosystem of traditional card payments, banks (issuers) and Acquirers.

By 'opening' the card payment schemes to FinTech incubators, the payment networks, while promoting payment diversity, are essentially attempting to secure a niche for themselves in an evolving and fluid payments landscape. Failure to adapt by holding the line on the previous business models (competence-induced failure, see Chapter 4: Surfacing Utility) would undoubtedly result in diminishing returns, as the traditional banking issuers and Acquirers surrender their market share to nimble FinTech challengers and tech giants through disintermediation.

The longer-term challenge for card payment networks lies with the utility of card payment instruments. HCE is an analogous technological advancement, providing a means of digitising a physical card instrument. However, through apps and digital wallets, the necessity for cards will likely reduce significantly and eventually fall away completely (see Chapter 15: Economy of Things). In a post-card era, the role of card payment networks will likely face uncertainty, particularly once the utility of credit facilities and digital payment technologies are fully surfaced and ubiquitously available through frictionless digital alternatives.

In the medium term, card payment networks are able to differentiate themselves and retain relevance through the ability to offer merchants an instantaneous commitment, via payment authorisations, while clearing and settlement occurs latently. This is a critical feature for merchants in order to be assured that they will be paid, albeit later, in order to release goods or render services to customers immediately. A further advantage that payment networks provide to the merchant ecosystem is that of the speed and volume that authorisations may be processed. High volume events (HVEs), such as Christmas, Black Friday, Cyber Monday and Chinese Single's day, tend to attract high volumes of retail transactions for which the payment networks are substantially fortified to handle (see Chapter 14: Tokenisation).

Payment networks aspire towards sub-millisecond latency in order to render a decision for authorisation, while HVEs place substantial demands in the orders of magnitude of thousands of transactions per second (tps). Such demands may be sustained contiguously for several hours during an HVE period. In order to accommodate the combination of these performance demands, payment networks utilise specialised systems to underpin payment switches and dedicated, as well as highly-resilient, low latency networks.

In addition, the Payment Card Industry (PCI) ecosystem provides assurance over the integrity of transactions, whereby 'Dispute Management and Chargebacks' provide a means for recourse, should a party fail to meet their obligations while transacting. An example of which would be in circumstances where goods are ordered, yet fail to be delivered. In such an instance, the customer has recourse to challenge the transaction. This aspect of card payments has fostered confidence in online shopping.

Once the internet and FinTech propositions are capable of adequately substituting for the assurance, volume and latency demands the payment networks are being leveraged to deliver, the necessity and value of such payment networks will likely deteriorate. This process has already seen investment with greater focus in semiconductor telecommunications, protocols and cloud development, as well as proliferation of Content Delivery Networks (CDNs) using reverse-proxy systems at the edge (close to the user). All of which, reduce latency and enhance end-user experiences (see Chapter 15: Economy of Things).

The interbank payment systems are additionally vulnerable to disruption and disintermediation, via internet-based payment systems, cultivated by new FinTech entrants, as well as financial incumbents and non-US central banks.

Single-platform propositions, such as those cultivated by social media, which facilitate intra-platform payments both domestically and across borders represent highly disruptive influences to conventional payment models, such as correspondent banking and interlinking.

The growing traction in tokenised payments, leveraging distributed ledger technologies and effecting payments on a peer-to-peer basis (see Chapter 14: Tokenisation), which continue to attract substantial interest, investment and development, may yet prove highly instrumental in reshaping the payments landscape and as a result, potentially have a profound effect on the geopolitical superstructure.

Competition between entities within the payment stack to harvest the richest sources of data and to achieve the greatest critical mass at the heart of the payments ecosystem makes for an interesting dynamic (see Chapter 4: Surfacing Utility). PayFacs are well positioned to harvest the richest sources of data across an Omni-channel spectrum, albeit among a narrow book of business, thus lending itself to constraints within economies of scale. By contrast, payment networks (schemes) may harvest a broader spectrum of data across Acquirers and Issuers, albeit of an arguably lower-enrichment level or value, essentially challenged by economies of scope, rather than scale. This offers varied prospects for monetising data to these various entities. Hence, it should be expected that these business vehicles will attempt to increase their surface area to higher value data sources and open their ecosystems to as broad a base of consumers as possible as they continue to evolve.

A traditional institutional lender exploits an upper-limit of approximately eight-hundred data points to render a decision as to whether to approve or decline a loan. Such decisions require human intervention and an average of sixty-to-ninety days to render. Exploiting data-driven decision making, using Artificial Intelligence (see Chapter 4: Surfacing Utility), nimble FinTechs, such as Square (see PayFacs above), leverage approximately three-hundred thousand data points and render a decision in an average of seven minutes.

DDTC organisations of this nature are highly competitive in contrast with their established counterparts. The average cost of customer acquisition for a bricks-and-mortar incumbent is $950[71] per customer, requiring several years to break-even, via value-added services and fees. By contrast, the average cost of customer acquisition of a Digital Wallet proposition is $20, with a projected payback period in a matter of a few months.[72] With interest rates persistently near the zero-bound since the GFC, interest return incentives for depositors to hold funds in conventional bank accounts are at a severe low-point. A predicament which places strain on the banking business model, in raising capital from the general public. As a consequence, banks rely to a greater extent on payment facilities to attract and retain customers. A set of circumstances, which is increasingly threatened by disruptions presented by single-platform and peer-to-peer payment propositions. The latter payment models enable propositions which are inexpensive, frictionless and managed conveniently, via a smart device or web browser twenty-four-hours per day.

Amidst an antiquated set of models and payment mechanisms, attracting high transaction costs and exhibiting friction, as well as delays, it is reasonable to expect that the payments sphere will continue to see tremendous investment and competition. Dominance in this area, would be a major competitive advantage as an instrument for economic and political influence, for those who may gain a leadership position. Such a leadership position would command dominance through exporting these systems to other countries, jurisdictions or clients.

As the consumer appetite and business demand for real-time, frictionless, low cost payments continues to grow, the antiquated RTGS and net settlement CSM systems, as well as banking models governed by the Fed and central banks around the globe will continue to endure attrition. Diminishing traction among correspondent banking and interlinking models, in favour of nimble, high-speed and low-cost, frictionless payment propositions should be expected to grow exponentially. These developments by single-platform and peer-to-peer innovators are a natural consequence of commoditisation and *Creative Destruction* (see Chapter 2: Capital Evolution).

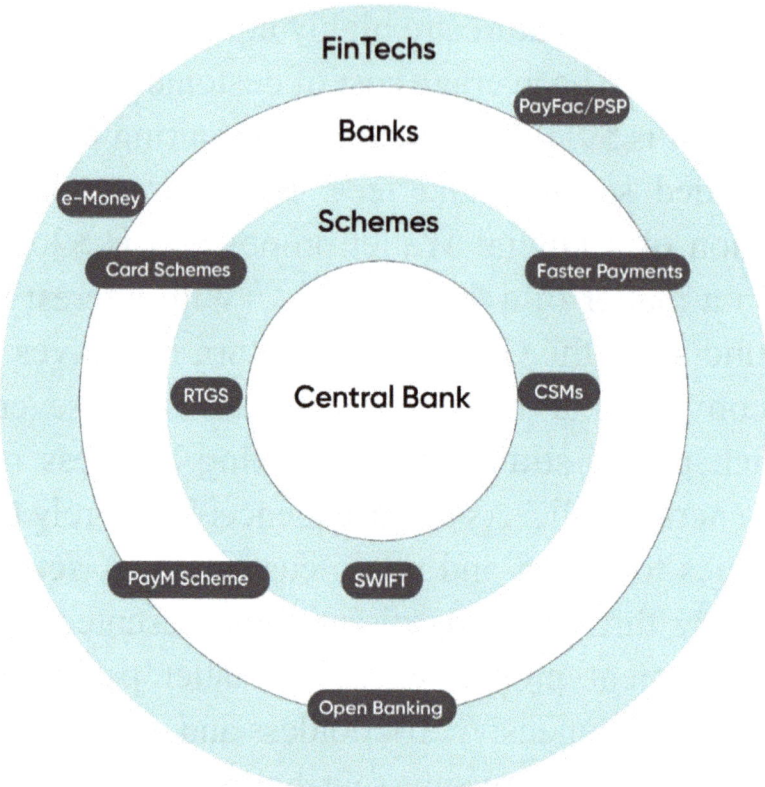

Fig 5.15 Hierarchical Banking System with an overlay of payments enablers

The European Union and the United Kingdom have created frameworks, such as Open Banking, as well as the United Kingdom's 'PayM' and 'Faster Payments' Schemes to stimulate FinTech innovation. However, they have done so in a manner conducive to keeping such innovations in the orbit of the hierarchical banking system (see Chapter 4: Surfacing Utility). By contrast, the United States has lagged behind in these areas, cultivating a climate synonymous with an overly constrained system (see Prologue). Thus, leaving its banking system and the Fed vulnerable to disintermediation.[73] From the United States' perspective this could substantially weaken its economic posture through diminished global market share of payment transactions (see Dollar Hegemony, Chapter 13: Global Trade Rails)[74]. Such a reduction could detrimentally impact fees, seigniorage and further weaken demand for US dollar denominated treasuries, the medium in which the bulk of global transactions are executed (~72% of global reserves, 1999; ~60% in 2020)[75]. With diminishing global demand for US Treasuries[76], the domestic debt-to-GDP ratio will likely climb (Fig 8.6), creating a self-reinforcing cycle of foreign divestment in USD liquidity.[77] Such a climate threatens the ability of the US to enforce a global unit of account among nation states. A predicament of this nature may, in effect, threaten its principal reserve currency status.[78] Contracting market share in payments intermediation alone wouldn't eliminate the United States' reserve currency status. However, further FinTech innovation, as well as other market forces, may cultivate the level of *Creative Destruction* required to enable such an outcome.

6

MONEY

'A perpetual non-interest bearing liability of a central bank' - James Rickards, 2018.

Everyone uses money. Money is earned, spent, saved, invested and occasionally stolen. Most importantly money in the modern era is not an object. It is the manifestation of a psychological construct. It is the representation of confidence.

CONFIDENCE

In order for an artefact to be considered money, it needs to be backed by **confidence**. If two or more parties have confidence that a particular artefact is money, it is effectively money. Such confidence is derived from trust that the money could be traded for goods and services. If such confidence exists among multiple parties, each willing to accept the money from one another on this basis, confidence therein is established. Confidence is difficult to cultivate, fragile to maintain and once lost, is nearly impossible to regain. However, once society has confidence that the money may legitimately be accepted for goods and services, it is money.

FUNCTIONS OF MONEY

Money has four functions:

1. **Medium of Exchange** - able to be traded for goods and services without the need for a barter system. This is an intermediary instrument facilitating the exchange of value between parties. Typically this is currency.

2. **Store of Value** - it needs to hold a value which can be retrieved at a later date.

3. **Unit of Account** - its value is expressed in an understandable way and allows the value of items to be compared against it.

4. **Standard of Deferred Payment** - expressing the value of a debt to be repaid in the future through a medium acceptable to the creditor.

In order to facilitate these functions, modern economies use fiat money as a means of *legal tender* to facilitate the *exchange of value* for either goods or services.[79] The means with which to exchange value between employers and employees, as well as between merchants or service providers and customers, either individuals or business entities like companies is crucial to an economy.

CHARACTERISTICS OF MONEY

Money features the following key characteristics:

1. **Valuable** - generally holds value over time

2. **Durable** - it needs to be resistant to reasonable wear over time

3. **Divisible** - it needs to be capable of being broken down into small denominations

4. **Portable** - needs to be easy to carry and use conveniently

5. **Recognisable** - easy to determine that it is genuine and difficult to counterfeit

6. **Scarce** - the supply thereof needs to be controlled

TYPES OF MONEY

FIAT MONEY – GOVERNMENT MONEY

'Fiat,' a Latin word, translated as a *determination by authority*. Fiat is defined as *'a command or act of will that creates something without or as if without further effort.'* In other words, a decree or an authoritative order.

Fiat money refers to any currency which lacks intrinsic value, apart from that which a government has bestowed upon it as legal tender. In other words, it retains value as the government has decreed it so. This, in turn, drives its acceptance as people have confidence that the money is worth something and it will be accepted by others. Fiat money is wholly 'man-made.' It is artificial and essentially works because everyone accepts it, based on the confidence that the government is a trusted entity.

Societies use fiat currencies, examples of which are the US Dollar, British Pound Sterling and the Euro, to purchase and sell goods and services.

FIDUCIARY MONEY – INSTITUTION'S MONEY

Fiduciary money derives its value based on the confidence that it will be accepted as a medium of exchange. It differs from Fiat money by virtue that it is not declared legal tender by a government, and therefore, not required by law to be accepted as a means of payment. A fiduciary money issuer, like a bank, promises to exchange it back for either a commodity or fiat currency on demand by the bearer. The confidence that governs whether it will be accepted as a means of payment is relative to the credibility of the issuer, whether it can be established as genuine and occasionally by the bearer's standing.

A prominent example of Fiduciary money is Pound Sterling notes, issued by retail (commercial) banks in Scotland and Northern Ireland, which are used exclusively as cash within these locales of the United Kingdom. British Pound Sterling notes issued by the Bank of England, are Fiat currency and are accepted throughout the United Kingdom, which includes Scotland and Northern Ireland.

In Scotland and Northern Ireland, these notes are issued by the various retail banks, rather than by the Central Bank. Each note is effectively a cheque (check) issued by the bank, which promises to pay the bearer the face value of the note in GBP fiat currency, upon demand.

As a consequence, the notes are neither legal tender, nor fiat money, as its value is underpinned by the credibility or solvency of the issuing bank. The notes themselves are liabilities to the issuing bank, which are offset against fiat currency reserves held with the Bank of England (Central Bank). Should the issuing bank file for bankruptcy (without intervention), the notes may be rendered worthless instantly (see Public vs. Private Money below).

Shoppers generally experience difficulty spending these fiduciary notes in England or Wales, where sterling denominated fiat money is in mainstream circulation. Furthermore, holders of these notes may be rejected when attempting to exchange fiduciary notes at a bank in England or Wales without being deposited into an account therewith.

In the United States however, the issue of all US dollars in circulation is a liability of the Federal Reserve. In the US, coins are produced by the Mint, all paper money by the Bureau of Printing and Engraving, and digital currency is electronically authorised by the Federal Reserve System. The US dollar currency is collectively managed by the US Treasury. All US dollars in issue are standardised and accepted universally throughout the United States.

In some instances, the bearer's standing or credibility is called into question with a form of fiduciary money. The use of cheques (checks) being such an example. Merchants which have long-standing relationships with regular customers may be more inclined to accept cheques in exchange for goods and services, with a degree of confidence that it could be redeemed for the amount specified.

This illustrates the importance of perception, reputation and relationships, which are often critical factors in financial transactions. Essentially, this returns to the concept of confidence being of paramount importance.

COMMERCIAL MONEY – BANK'S MONEY

Commercial Money is essentially bank 'book' money in the form of debt generated by commercial banks. Commercial money is not legal tender. However, it is used to represent base money in transactions, predominantly between banks. Commercial bank money currently makes up a significant proportion of most currencies. Commercial money is created when banks make use of fractional reserve banking (see Banking Business Model, Chapter 5: Payments) in the creation of account balances and in making loans worth many times the value of the actual base currency they may hold (typically up to ten times more).[80]

When a bank creates account balances or lends out money which it does not actually have, that money is generated as book money, also known as scriptural money, which equates to debt claims against the bank by account holders (depositors) and debt claims by the bank against borrowers. By way of example, if a depositor has an account balance of $1000, based on a reserve ratio of 10%, the bank loans out 90% of the funds to another party. Since the bank holds an asset of $900 in the form of a loan and a debt to the depositor for $1000, against which it holds $100 in cash reserves, the bank has essentially created $900 in the form of commercial money. Since all commercial banks engage in this practice, when payments are made between banks, net settlement CSMs facilitate the exchange of banks' liabilities to depositors, which is predominantly denominated in commercial money (see Clearing & Settlement Mechanisms, Chapter 5: Payments).

COMMODITY MONEY

Commodity money differentiates itself through intrinsic value, based directly on a commodity from which it is struck. An example of such is that of 'specie' (Gold and Silver coins).

By way of example, the largest denominations of British currency were known as 'White Notes,' which (in large denominations) were used to pass large sums of money between banks in a pre-digital era.[81] For a time, banks in Scotland issued fiduciary notes in £100 denominations. Today, the largest denomination of British currency is a Gold coin known as a 'Britannia,' containing one troy ounce of fine Gold with a face value of £100.[82] This is money that has value in itself (intrinsic commodity value), as well as monetary face value, in being able to purchase goods or services as part of legal tender. In this example, however, the face value greatly undervalues the worth of the coin. The gold content, therein, is of far greater value as a commodity than the face value as currency. Historically, the opposite is true, whereby the face value exceeds the value of the commodity from which a unit of commodity money is struck. This phenomenon is articulated through Gresham's Law.

GRESHAM'S LAW

In economics, Gresham's law is a monetary principle stating that **'bad money drives out good money.'**[83] The principle is named for Sir Thomas Gresham (1519 - 1579), a Tudor dynasty era English financier, who worked in the Netherlands as a royal agent of Queen Elizabeth. Gresham was credited with formulating the principle by Scottish economist Henry Dunning Macleod in 1860. By way of example, if there are two forms of commodity money in circulation, which are accepted by law as having a similar face value, the higher value commodity will gradually disappear from circulation.

The original purpose for the creation of the first central bank was to combat this very phenomenon (see Central Banking, Chapter 7: Central Banks). Historical examples include the diminishing silver content of the Roman Denarius which eroded from 85g in 64 A.D. to virtually zero by 270 A.D. A period of 206 years over which the face value of the money remained consistent. As the commodity of intrinsic value increases in cost or reduces in supply, so the coinage content thereof diminishes. Contemporary examples include the diminishing silver content in US coinage, for which new minting was eliminated completely by 1964.[84]

Gresham's Law surfaces a context for the manner in which money has evolved from being commodity based, to representative based, and subsequently, fiat based over time. The contemporary iterations are representative of monetary digitisation, card payments, alternative payment methods (see Alternative Payment Methods, Chapter 5: Payments) and the emergence of extra-systemic digital currencies[85] (see People's Money below).

PEOPLE'S MONEY

This is essentially money which is neither regulated through Central Banks, nor backed directly or indirectly by any commodity. Its value is derived from confidence that it will be redeemable for value in another form of money or will be accepted directly for goods or services. However, it is neither legal tender nor underpinned by any asset or commodity. It is essentially underpinned exclusively by confidence. In this context, its value is entirely subjective (see Subjective Value Theory, Chapter 2: Capital Evolution). A key example is that of crypto-currencies such as Bitcoin, Ether and Litecoin (see Convertible Virtual Currency, Chapter 14: Tokenisation). These tokens may be purchased, stored, sold or spent. They exist outside the global financial system, hence, categorised as 'people's money.'

There are numerous crypto-currencies and crypto-assets (Convertible Virtual Currencies) in existence and there are new initial coin offerings (ICOs) which appear periodically. While others have been introduced and since disappeared,

Bitcoin was the first to emerge (2009) as a pioneering example of a fully digital extra-systemic currency.

FORMATS OF MONEY

Over the centuries, the formats that money has taken have been varied. Early formats of money included feathers and cowry shells. In some instances, livestock has been used as money. However, since the emergence of specie, as new formats have emerged, they have not necessarily been displaced. Instead, new 'formats of money' emerge and are subsequently embraced, while older formats tend to remain. This is an aspect of FinTech that is not often considered, whereby as technology advances, so the influence thereof on the format of money is evident.

SPECIE

Since 520 - 550 B.C. in the Achaemenid Persian Empire, coins (specie) emerged, and have since remained as a fundamental monetary format. The emergence of specie enabled social mobility and had a profound effect by expanding trade networks with a newfound ease.[86] While the types of coins, the substances from which they are minted and the utility they fulfil have evolved, the format of coinage has remained. Although some forms of specie fall within the realms of commodity money (see above), the vast majority are legal tender forming part of the fiat monetary base (see Money Supply, Chapter 8: Economic Cycles).

PAPER MONEY

The origins of paper money stem from China, during the Tang Dynasty in the seventh century. The inconvenience experienced with coins (specie) created a compelling need to improve portability and was enabled through the invention of paper, ink and woodblock printing, dating back to 220 A.D. Paper money enabled the means with which to vary denominations of money across a broader range of values than that of coinage. This was achieved by being representative of a physical, tactile and tangible form of money, such as specie.

The introduction of paper money brought with it the ability to conduct trade over greater distances through a technological advancement (paper and printing). Thus, acting as a catalyst for economic growth and prosperity through a convenient and desirable *medium of exchange* (see Functions of Money above). This was made possible by substituting vast quantities of heavy coins with a lightweight portable medium. In turn, this enabled merchants and traders to travel greater distances without the burden of logistically moving large sums of money in the form of coins. However, the consequence of this innovation was evident in compromising money's durability (see Characteristics of Money above), as paper would suffer greater wear than coinage. Further weaknesses included the ability for rulers in China to print vast quantities of money, thus, compromising its scarcity (see Characteristics of Money above) which often led to substantial inflation (see Inflation, Chapter 8: Economic Cycles).

Despite its weaknesses, paper money ultimately permeated throughout the entire world, although this required over a millennium to do so. While paper money and other forms of cash (such as specie) may attract a high risk of theft, in addition to potentially higher handling costs, these token-based forms of money differentiate themselves by being both self-clearing, as well as self-settling forms of payment.[87] By contrast, some forms of token-based money such as cheques are not. Thus, cash remains highly desirable to both consumers and businesses, regardless of any of its apparent weaknesses as a *medium of exchange*.

PUBLIC VS. PRIVATE MONEY

A critical distinction in the sphere of money is whether it is public or private. This has been a source of acrimony between governments and the private sector for a substantial proportion of contemporary monetary history. While the majority of economic actors are unaware of this distinction, it remains a persistently critical differentiator in both advanced, as well as developing economies.

Public money is a direct liability of a central bank (see Chapter 7: Central Banks). In other words it is a direct claim against the central bank. Examples include, denominations of fiat money in the form of base money, such as banknotes (cash/paper money/coins). Bonds/Securities, issued by a national treasury, such as the US Treasury or H.M. Treasury (UK), are direct liabilities thereof, and would, thus, constitute public money. Private money, by contrast, is a liability of a private (nongovernmental) institution, such as a commercial bank. Fiduciary money, as well as commercial money (see Types of Money above), are common examples of such. Since private money represents a claim against the issuing institution (also known as a demand liability), it is possible to be rendered worthless, should the institution become insolvent.

Interbank payments are predominantly conducted through an exchange in private money liabilities between banking institutions, keeping any exchange of central bank liabilities to a minimum. The rationale being that the greater the value of private moneys being exchanged on this basis, the greater the opportunity for revenues realised through fees. Whereas, an exchange of public money between institutions represents a costly (both directly as well as indirectly) and consequently, a far less profitable means of doing so. Thus, net settlement CSMs are typically the interbank exchange vehicles for private money, whereas RTGS systems are exclusively exploited for the exchange of public money (see Interbank Payment Systems, Chapter 5: Payments). This is complementary to supporting the banking business model in which the majority of private money (such as Commercial and Fiduciary Money) is illiquid (see Banking Business Model, Chapter 5: Payments).

It is for this rationale, that during periods of financial stress, actors within the economy tend to divest themselves of private money, in favour of public money. Seeking out money that is both liquid and represents a claim against a counterparty that won't default (see Exter's Pyramid, Chapter 9: Gold). The term 'Counterparty' rose in prevalence, following the Basel I Accord of 1988, referring to legal entities on opposite sides of a transaction.

Money-market mutual funds are a compelling example of this phenomenon. First introduced in the 1970s, money-market mutual funds were centred on the concept of offering a safe investment vehicle into which investors could be assured of low risk, yet high liquidity, comparable to a bank account. Money-market mutual funds made extensive use of mean-variance optimisation among other techniques (see Modern Portfolio Theory, Chapter 4: Surfacing Utility). Although, the returns derived therefrom take the form of interest which would be greater than interest paid to a depositor using a conventional bank's savings account.

'The purpose of the money fund is to bore the investor into a sound night's sleep.'

- *Bruce Bent, 1970.*

As stated by its inventor, Bruce Bent, the principal tenets upon which the money-market mutual fund was conceived were safety, liquidity and a reasonable rate of return. Comparable to a conventional bank account, money-market mutual funds invest customer capital in order to generate a yield (see Banking Business Model, Chapter 5: Payments).

In September 2008, when the investment bank Lehman Brothers collapsed (see Coup de Grâce, Chapter 10: Financialisation), the revelation that a major money-market fund had lent $785 million to Lehman Brothers, prompted investors to withdraw funds *en masse*. Consequently, the fund in question (the Reserve Primary Fund) was unable to satisfy all the withdrawal requests, as its net asset value (NAV) had fallen to $0.97 per share. This is known as 'breaking the buck' whereby, investors could no longer withdraw a dollar for each dollar they had initially committed to the fund.

As a consequence of these circumstances, confidence in money-market mutual funds was severely shaken thereafter. This brings into acute focus, the status of depositors' funds held in conventional bank (current and savings) accounts. Deposits, therein, are private money, not public. Thus, depositors are vulnerable to claims defaults against commercial banks, should they become insolvent unless central banks intervene. In most advanced economies, depositors' funds are underwritten by public institutions, via legislation (see The Wall Street Crash of 1929, Chapter 10: Financialisation). However, such legislation often imposes limits as to the extent of such guarantees. Depositors which hold funds with commercial banks in excess of these limits do so at risk for sums beyond the threshold.

E – MONEY

Electronic Money (E-money) is money which is stored in an electronic form. Commercial banks typically record and manage depositors' funds electronically, albeit denominated in fiat currency. However, e-money is considered to cover a broader definition by including value which is held electronically (or magnetically) on a payment instrument, either locally or remotely. Thus, e-money may include pre-payment characteristics, such as pre-paid payment cards and pre-paid accounts, delivered via alternative payment methods (such as M-Pesa and PayPal). E-money additionally includes entirely digital forms of money, examples of which may take the form of digital tokens, such as crypto-currencies and central bank digital currency (see Convertible Virtual Currency, Chapter 14: Tokenisation).

As with physical formats of money (such as specie and paper money), e-money is stored monetary value as represented by a claim on an electronic money issuer (see Electronic Money Institutions, Chapter 5: Payments). The electronic money issuer may either be a private money issuer or a public money issuer. PayPal would be an example of the former, whereas a central bank or a government treasury would be examples of the latter (see Public vs. Private Money above).

In order to be considered e-money, the money must be accepted as a means of payment by a party other than the electronic money issuer. Using PayPal as an example, both individuals as well as businesses may open an account to which funds may be received or transmitted to numerous third-parties. In addition, funds may be stored electronically in the PayPal account, without the necessity to transfer the funds to a traditional bank account. The premise, thereof, is based on the expectation that e-money is issued on receipt of funds for the purpose of initiating either imminent, or future payment transactions. Thus, the element of pre-payment and the ability to store e-money is a critical differentiator. It therefore distinguishes e-money from other payment services, which act exclusively as intermediaries for transactional payments between parties (see Electronic Money, Chapter 1: FinTech).

CONVERGENCE

The confluence of finance and technology with the emergence of e-money, virtual currencies and digital payment channels has prompted a trend in the convergence of both money and payment instruments which are required to facilitate the storage and exchange, thereof. Fig 6.1 illustrates the evolution of monetary formats, all of which remain in use. However, it additionally illustrates the bias towards greater portability and the reduction in the reliance on artefacts which depend on a tangible means of fulfilling money's function as a *store of value* in favour of its utility as a *medium of exchange*. These factors enable the prospect of a future in which the necessity to maintain tangible media of exchange, such as cash and coin may no longer be required. Thus, servicing an agenda amongst policy makers and governments to which base money (in the form of cash) is considered an inhibitor (see War on Cash below).

Fig 6.1 Convergence of money and payment instruments

WAR ON CASH

FinTech is in increasing danger of being exploited to facilitate the demise of cash. FinTech has enabled greater focus in developing digital payment instruments and frictionless payment mechanisms, as well as fuelling a trend towards greater digitisation of monetary artefacts, such as those realised through the development of crypto-currencies and crypto-assets. In contemporary terms, a realistic and palpable risk exists that cash itself could be extricated from circulation altogether. Such risks draw parallels with observing the effects of Gresham's Law (see above) towards the erosion of physical monetary artefacts, although in a modern context, it is largely manifesting through digitisation rather than commodity dilution.

In exploring the consequences of the deteriorating presence of cash in society, it is critical to recognise that many of the proponents and advocates for the elimination of cash are immune to the effects, thereof. Effects which others will endure, as a result of its loss.

Much of society, particularly those who may either be digitally illiterate or simply lack access to a technologically advanced infrastructure, rely on cash in order to sustain economic activity. Examples include those in developing economies, where infrastructure limitations inhibit the adoption of technology enabled services or are simply unbanked.

Advocates for the elimination of cash predominantly rationalise such views through referencing the exploitation of cash to circumvent taxation and to support illicit, as well as illegal enterprises, such as prostitution, terrorist financing, human trafficking and the trade in narcotics and illegal weapons. Legislators additionally cite the ease with which counterfeiters are able to exploit modern digital printing technology to wash genuine low denomination bills, and transform them into fraudulent larger denomination bills.[88] Another common argument is that large denomination currency in circulation is desirable for money laundering.[89] While cash may and has been verifiably used to facilitate such activities, illicit commerce constitutes a small fraction of commerce as a whole. Much of the real economy is reliant on cash transactions, the liquidity of which, is challenging to displace at a grass roots level. Furthermore, the elimination of cash alone, is insufficient to deal a meaningful blow to illicit commerce.

KIMBERLY PROCESS

Evidence to this effect is demonstrable through the widespread practice of conducting illicit transactions in alternative media, a noteworthy example of which is that of the trade in conflict diamonds. Also known as 'blood diamonds,' these stones rose in prevalence as an illicit cash alternative in West Africa, during the 1990s. Arms were sold to insurgents in exchange for raw uncut diamonds, which financed and fuelled the civil conflicts in the region. The illicit trade in raw diamonds and bloody conflicts which the stones were leveraged to fund, permeated through countries such as Liberia, Sierra Leone, Angola, Democratic Republic of Congo (formerly République du Zaïre 1971 - 1997) and Ivory Coast (Côte d'Ivoire). The raw stones were then smuggled into and laundered through the international diamond trade, where they were cut and sold as if they were legitimate gems. This ultimately resulted in the establishment of the Kimberly Process for identifying and marking diamonds in 2003, a multilateral trade régime aimed at eradicating the trade in conflict diamonds.[90]

The premise that the elimination of cash will realise a commensurate reduction in illicit activity is fundamentally flawed. In practice the displacement of one *medium of exchange* simply increases flows into another, comparable to the market behaviours observed in a liquidity crisis, whereby pressure cascades from one medium to the next until liquidity is realised.

NIRP

As a consequence, it is imperative to challenge the true motives behind the advocacy for cash elimination from the perspective of those championing such initiatives. The principle motive is increasingly leaning towards a means of eliminating the 'firewall' or 'shielding' society may exploit to safeguard itself against policy makers applying Negative-interest Rate Policies (NiRP). In other words, in lieu of receiving interest for balances held in bank accounts, depositors are charged interest, thereby eroding their funds. It is imperative to note an important distinction with regards to NiRP, whereby inflation functions as an implicit 'tax' on holding (non-interest-bearing) cash balances. As a contrast, however, negative interest rates would theoretically directly 'tax' money in order to encourage banks to loan out excess reserves and stimulate demand for goods and services.[91]

Policies such as NiRP, once believed to be unthinkable and absurd, are increasingly being considered by Central Banks in response to mounting sovereign debt burdens accrued since the GFC. Some Central Banks have already embraced NiRP, a notable example of which was that of the Bank of Japan, which announced its intention to implement NiRP in January 2016.[92] By June 2016, Japan's largest private bank (Bank of Tokyo-Mitsubishi UFJ Ltd.) announced its intention to divest itself of dealership in Japan's bond market, due to the instability the Bank of Japan's NiRP policy had introduced.[93]

Other notable NiRP examples include that of the Central Banks of Switzerland, Sweden, Denmark and the European Central Bank.[94] According to research published by the World Bank, by July 2016, NiRP had yielded no measurable improvement in economic performance within jurisdictions in which it had been applied.[95]

A book published in 2016, by a former IMF Chief economist, Kenneth Rogoff entitled 'The Curse of Cash: How Large-Denomination Bills Aid Crime and Tax Evasion and Constrain Monetary Policy' advocated the case for the abolition of large cash denominations in order to facilitate the monetary policy ambitions centred on negative interest rates. Following Rogoff's tenure at the IMF, he went on to lecture as a professor at Harvard University. Rogoff's publication received laudatory remarks from former Federal Reserve Board of Governors Chairman, Ben Bernanke, exalting it as:

'a fascinating and important book.'

- Ben Bernanke, Federal Reserve Board Chairman (2006 - 2014).

The notable momentum and traction that NiRP has gained is of an increasing concern to savers, investors and indeed the banking sector.[96] The basis of the banking business model is to borrow at a low rate of interest and profit, through lending at a higher rate. NiRP is fundamentally at odds with this business model. Depositors in effect would see their balances shrink, while paying those who borrow money. Furthermore, without cash and an increasing focus towards digital monetary development and payment instruments, there is little in the way of insulation to provide any form of shielding against liquid wealth confiscation in this manner.[97] In February 2021, the Bank of England advised the UK's commercial banking sector to alter their Treasury Systems, and to ensure that they would be capable of seamlessly managing a shift towards a negative base rate within six months.[98]

ATTRITION

The incremental attrition of cash has already manifested itself. This is evident in behaviours exhibited by Central Banks and governments around the globe. This is a pernicious process, albeit consistent. Examples include the incremental removal of bills available in denominations greater than $100 [99] in the US, since 1969.[100] In 2014, Singapore discontinued its ten-thousand-dollar bill. In November 2016, India withdrew the 500 and 1000 denominations of rupee banknotes from general circulation. This accounted for 86% of India's cash supply in circulation at the time.[101] These bills became worthless, virtually overnight. The European Union deprecated the €500 Euro denominated banknote in January 2019.[102]

In addition to India's aspirations towards creating a cashless society,[103] numerous emerging African and Asian markets are prolifically developing FinTech apps, targeting even the lowest-value payments (micropayments).[104] Australia, Canada and a number of other countries are additionally considering eliminating coinage less than five cents in value.[105] Such a move, although a cost reduction initiative, would force cash transactions to be rounded to the nearest five cents, a practice known as Swedish Rounding. Australia,[106] and a number of Scandinavian countries,[107] are increasingly encouraging cashless transactions by making them easier and more convenient. These initiatives, enabled by FinTech and digital infrastructure are constantly broadening the instrumentation to facilitate greater transactional surveillance and scrutiny. All of which symptomatically result in diminishing privacy, and by extension, may compromise individual autonomy.[108]

In June 2021, a British charity aimed at supporting senior citizens, Age UK[109] called for guarantees from the British government to ensure that access to cash would continue. The charity cited the difficulties that many would face by being excluded from society if they could no longer use banknotes and coins. While the majority of consumers were able to embrace digital channels and FinTech during the COVID-19 pandemic, the elderly, in particular, had struggled to do their banking digitally.[110]

By 2025, some seventy-five percent of the workforce in advanced economies is expected to be digitally literate, predominantly comprising millennials (those born between 1981 and 1996).[111] With an increased weighting towards digital economic discourse, maintaining a substantial investment in cash production and maintenance is unlikely to persist beyond the 2030s, at which juncture digital natives are expected to be the principal economic participants. A reality which does not augur well for the prospects of non-digital monetary media in the longer term, for which FinTech is a major catalyst.

7

CENTRAL BANKS

Central Banks (also known as Reserve Banks) are financial institutions which function as the monetary authority which retain privileged control over the production of money and credit for either, a nation state or a monetary union (monetary zone), thereof.

This additionally furnishes central banks with a legal monopoly status over the issue of banknotes and coinage (see Public vs. Private Money, Chapter 6: Money). Central banks are non-market-based, and generally function as anti-competitive institutions. While some central banks are nationalised, typically central banks retain their neutrality from government interference and are generally considered to be politically independent entities. Consequently, central banks are not governmental entities, however, are considered to be public institutions and their privileges are protected and underpinned by law.

The US Federal Reserve System, colloquially referred to as 'The Fed' is the central bank of the United States of America.

The Bank of England is the central bank of the United Kingdom.

The European Central Bank is the central bank for all member countries of the European Union, which have standardised to 'The Euro' as their currency. Not all member states have standardised to the Euro, leaving them with their own central banks as monetary authorities.

Central banks typically determine and periodically adjust monetary policy for their jurisdiction. Central Banks, additionally, control the money supply, settle payments between banks and intermediate the *balance of payments* between nation states (see Chapter 5: Payments). A Central Bank (in most instances) oversees the commercial banking system in its jurisdiction.

The objectives of central banks are to ensure financial stability and to promote growth and employment. These institutions endeavour to do so by determining and setting aims for macroeconomic targets. The central bank engages in economic analysis to set inflation targets, interest rates and increasing the monetary base (money supply) by issuing banknotes, coins and through engaging in Open Market Operations (see Open Market Operations, Chapter 8: Economic Cycles).

Central banks act as a lender of last resort to banks to provide liquidity during periods of financial stress and ultimately act as a lender of last resort to governments. Since in principle, central banks are considered to be institutionally independent from political interference, it is incumbent upon central banks to act as a neutral entity and act in the best interests of the economy.

It is the role of the Federal Reserve…

'To take away the punch bowl just as the party gets going'[112]

- *William McChesney Martin Jr. (1906 - 1998), Federal Reserve Board Chairman 1951 – 1970.*

CENTRAL BANKING

The origins of central banking began with the formation of the Amsterdamsche Wisselbank in January, 1609. Translated as the 'Exchange Bank of Amsterdam,' the bank was formed to defend the coinage standard which made attempts to debase the value of coins less profitable (see Gresham's Law, Chapter 6: Money). The bank was the very first to offer accounts which were not directly convertible to coin. Unlike its contemporary counterparts, the bank neither managed the national currency, nor acted as a lending institution at its inception. It was initially established purely to defend the coinage standard by maintaining fully specie-backed (gold and silver coins) deposit reserves. In other words, the bank's liabilities were fully backed by equivalent value assets in the form of specie. Thus, an early instance of the specie standard rule.

The Bank issued deposits and settled payments, via transfers across deposit accounts, essentially creating a representational monetary payment system between depositors.

As Amsterdam transformed into a buoyant financial centre, the bank co-evolved, into an agent for managing disparate values in exchange and a broker of domestic and international payments. Eventually, the bank offered loans leveraged against the capital reserves that it held in specie. For a substantial period during the seventeenth and eighteenth centuries, the Dutch Guilder acted in the role of global reserve currency, as Amsterdam's role in international commerce flourished.

Unfortunately, the bank ultimately failed due to the economic disruptions brought about by the fourth Anglo-Dutch War in the 1780s. This was largely due to significant exposure as a result of lending to among others, the Vereenigde Nederlandsche Oost Indische Compagnie (VOC), also known as the Dutch East India Company and the economic hardship experienced during the war period.

THE BANK OF ENGLAND

The Bank of England was established in 1694, by an act of the British parliament. Its immediate imperative was to raise funds to enable the government to engage in war against France. Britain had suffered a series of crushing defeats against France's dominant naval power. This culminated in the defeat at the Battle of Beachy Head in 1690. William III wished to build a naval fleet that would rival that of France. However, his government lacked the funds, as well as the necessary credit to raise the £1.2 million required to do so. With the creation of the Bank of England, the funds were raised within 12 days.[113]

The Bank was granted the rare privilege of acting as a joint-stock bank with limited liability. A joint-stock bank combines the attributes of a general partnership in which owners evenly share profits, as well as liabilities with the attributes of a publicly-traded company, which issues shares that are freely tradable. Another critical distinction is that joint-stock banks are not owned by governments. Hence, the Bank of England was created as a private institution.

The special joint-stock bank status and its role as the government's banker imbued the bank with considerable competitive advantages. By the 1730s, its banknotes were widely circulated and the bank had embraced its role as banker to other banks. The Bank of England effectively managed a hierarchical banking system, whereby the bank would maintain reserve accounts for commercial banks and facilitate settlement of debts between these banks (Gross Settlement).

The bank played a pivotal role in raising capital to support Britain's involvement in the Napoleonic Wars. After the outbreak of the French Revolution in 1789, Britain had remained neutral. However, in 1793, when French troops occupied Belgian lands, threatening the Dutch as well as British overland trade, via the River Scheldt, war was instigated.[114]

In 1833, the Bank of England undertook the role of lender of last resort and broadened its responsibilities in 'printing money.' With the passage of the Bank Charter Act 1844, the act imbued the Bank of England with a range of new powers and formalised the issuance of banknotes in the United Kingdom. The act additionally placed restrictions on any banks that issued its own banknotes in England and Wales, as well as prevented any new banks from issuing notes.[115] To the extent that the Bank of England maintained a monopoly over banknote production from 1844, the gold held at the bank as backing for the banknotes were essentially the UK's Gold Reserves. In 1932, after the UK left the Gold Standard in September 1931, the Exchange Equalisation Account (EEA) was created. The EEA is a Treasury owned account that is held at and managed by the Bank of England. This account holds the UK's Gold Reserves.[116]

The Bank of England remained privately owned until 1946, after which it was nationalised. As is the case with most central banks, the bank plays an essential role in public borrowing (to enable deficit spending), providing RTGS payments as well as clearing services between institutions and/or foreign central banks and governments (see Chapter 5: Payments). It is responsible for implementing policy in the bond and foreign exchange markets, as well as advising in, and setting monetary policy (see Monetary Policy, Chapter 8: Economic Cycles).

THE FED

The Bank of North America, which opened in Philadelphia in 1782, was the first chartered bank in the United States, which essentially acted as the central bank. Eventually, the Pennsylvania government reincorporated the bank under state law, ending its role as a national bank. Thereafter, the US Congress chartered a new bank, the 'First Bank of the United States,' in 1791. Both of these banks had been established as a result of the advocacy of US founding father, Alexander Hamilton. Hamilton additionally served as the first US Treasury Secretary from 1789 till 1795.[117] The bank was liquidated in 1811, following the expiration of its twenty-year charter.

Once the United States had won its independence following the Revolutionary War (1775 - 1783), there was a degree of reticence among its founding fathers to emulate the centralised governance, instruments and practices of their former masters, England.[118] Hence, the US resisted creating a central bank equivalent to the Bank of England.

Consequently, the banking system in the United States was vulnerable to financial panics, which had a detrimental effect on the solvency of US banks. Intermittent panics would result in 'runs on the banks,' where mass withdrawals would bankrupt the banks, which would have otherwise been able to remain solvent. Notable financial panics were that of:

1857 - Decline in the international economy; over-expansion of the domestic US economy

1873 - Resulted in a depression in Europe and North America, which lasted until 1877

1884 - Occurred as the US was nearing the end of a depression from 1882 till 1885

1890 - The Baring Crisis, a panic as a result of an acute recession

1893 - A panic that resulted in an economic depression that lasted until 1897

1896 - A panic resulting from a drop in Silver reserves, triggering an acute depression

In 1906, an earthquake devastated San Francisco, California, resulting in approximately three-thousand deaths and significant damage to the majority of its infrastructure. This event triggered the panic of 1907. A few months prior, Paul M. Warburg, a prominent investment banker, had described the US banking system's maturity as comparable to that of Babylon (~2000 B.C.) and 15th century Italy, during the time of the Medicis. Warburg later served as a member of the Federal Reserve Board through 1914 – 1916, and as its Vice-Governor (now Vice-chair) from 1916 - 1918.[119]

'The United States' financial system was at about the same point that had been reached by Europe at the time of the Medicis, and by Asia, in all likelihood, at the time of Hammurabi.'[120]

- Paul M. Warburg, New York Times: Annual Financial Review, January 1907.

In the wake of the panic of 1907, the Aldrich-Vreeland Act was passed by congress to augment the US banking laws. It was also known as the National Bank Circulation Act, 1908. The passage of this legislation was considered to be an emergency measure to gain centralised control of the monetary system. It was clear that control was needed to repel the effect of panics on the banking system. This change in sentiment ultimately paved the way for the passing of the Federal Reserve Act, 1913. The act effectively created the Federal Reserve System. The interim period prior to the passing of the Federal Reserve Act was subject to lengthy negotiations, the majority of which were held in Jekyll Island, Georgia.

American financier, John Pierpont Morgan (J.P. Morgan) famously played a pivotal role in the lead up to the creation of the Federal Reserve, before passing away in March 1913, nine-months prior to the passing of the Federal Reserve Act, 1913. A key vote required in passing of the act was that of James A. Reed, a member of the Senate Banking Committee, who ultimately broke the deadlock in negotiations, paving the way for its passage. It is for this reason that the State of Missouri (Reed's State), is the only US State which is home to two Federal Reserve Banks (St. Louis and Kansas City).

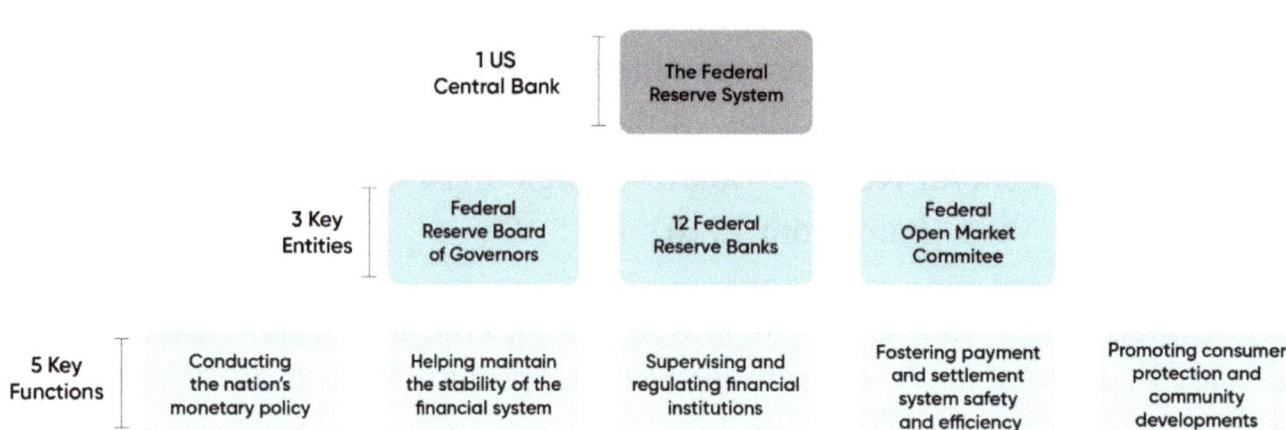

Fig 7.1 the structural entities and functions of the Federal Reserve System

KEY STRUCTURAL ENTITIES

There are twelve Federal Reserve Banks spread out across the continental United States and the Federal Reserve Board, headquartered in Washington D.C.

The twelve district boundaries were based on the prevailing economic conditions and trade regions that existed in 1913. Each district bank (Federal Reserve Bank) is an individually incorporated reserve bank, which operates independently, however, under the supervision of the Federal Reserve Board of Governors.

Fig 7.2 Key Structural Entities of the Federal Reserve

FEDERAL RESERVE BOARD

The board of governors of the Federal Reserve System is comprised of seven governors, based in Washington D.C., which are appointed by the US President and confirmed by the US Senate. US Presidents may nominate one governor every two years to serve up to a fourteen-year term. The governors oversee the Federal Reserve System in compliance with the Federal Reserve Act. The board oversees the operations of the twelve district Federal Reserve Banks and jointly shares the responsibility for supervising and regulating financial institutions and activities.

FEDERAL OPEN MARKETS COMMITTEE

The Federal Reserve Act 1913 imbues the Federal Reserve with the responsibility of setting monetary policy. While the board of governors are responsible for setting the discount rate (base rate) and (fractional) reserve requirements, the third aspect of monetary policy is governed by the Federal Open Markets Committee (FOMC). The FOMC is responsible for conducting Open Market Operations (see Open Market Operations, Chapter 8: Economic Cycles).

The FOMC is comprised of twelve voting members, seven are those of the Federal Reserve Board Governors, one is the bank president of the Federal Reserve in New York, with four remaining members nominated by the remaining district banks to serve one-year terms on a rotational basis.

Of the seven presiding governors appointed to serve on the Federal Reserve Board, the US President may nominate one to serve as Chairman. To serve as Vice-Chair, the President may appoint a district bank president to occupy one of the five remaining voting seats. The Vice Chair is also the president of the New York Fed Reserve Bank. The Chair and Vice-Chair serve four-year terms. The president may, and at his discretion reappoint, either the Chairman and/or Vice-Chair for an additional four-year-term, although, within the overall fourteen-year governorship term. A notable exception was that of Dr Alan Greenspan, who served as Chairman for an unprecedented five consecutive terms (1987 - 2006). These appointees serving as Chairman and Vice-Chair are, additionally, required to be confirmed by the US Senate. The remaining four members of the FOMC are appointed to the one-year rotation cycle by the Fed district banks. The rotating seats are filled from the following four groups of district banks, one bank president from each group. The groups are as follows:

1. Boston, Philadelphia and Richmond

2. Cleveland and Chicago

3. Atlanta, St. Louis and Dallas

4. Minneapolis, Kansas City and San Francisco

Fed district bank presidents, outside of the rotation cycle, may attend the meetings of the FOMC, participate in the discussions and may contribute to the committee's assessment of the economy and policy options. Although, outside of the rotation, the district presidents may not vote on policy decisions.

The FOMC holds eight scheduled meetings per annum, during which, the committee reviews economic and financial conditions. The FOMC determines the appropriate monetary policy posture, while assessing the risks to its objectives surrounding price stability and sustainable economic growth.

The policy makers and advisors which favour higher interest rates are known as 'Hawks.' The opposite of a 'hawk' is a 'dove,' describing policy makers who prefer an interest rate policy that is more accommodating, meaning it is lower and intended to stimulate spending in an economy.

FEDERAL RESERVE BANKS

Every commercial bank in the United States is required to keep six-percent (6%) of its reserve capital on deposit with its regional federal reserve bank. In exchange, the private bank receives an equivalent number of shares in the regional reserve bank, valued at $100 each. The price of the shares is fixed and cannot be freely traded. The shares grant voting rights to two thirds of the board of directors for the associated regional/district reserve bank. The shares attract a fixed six-percent (6%) dividend per year on the paid-in capital stock, remitted to the member banks.[121] After dividends and operating expenses, any profits realised by the Federal Reserve are remitted to the US Treasury.

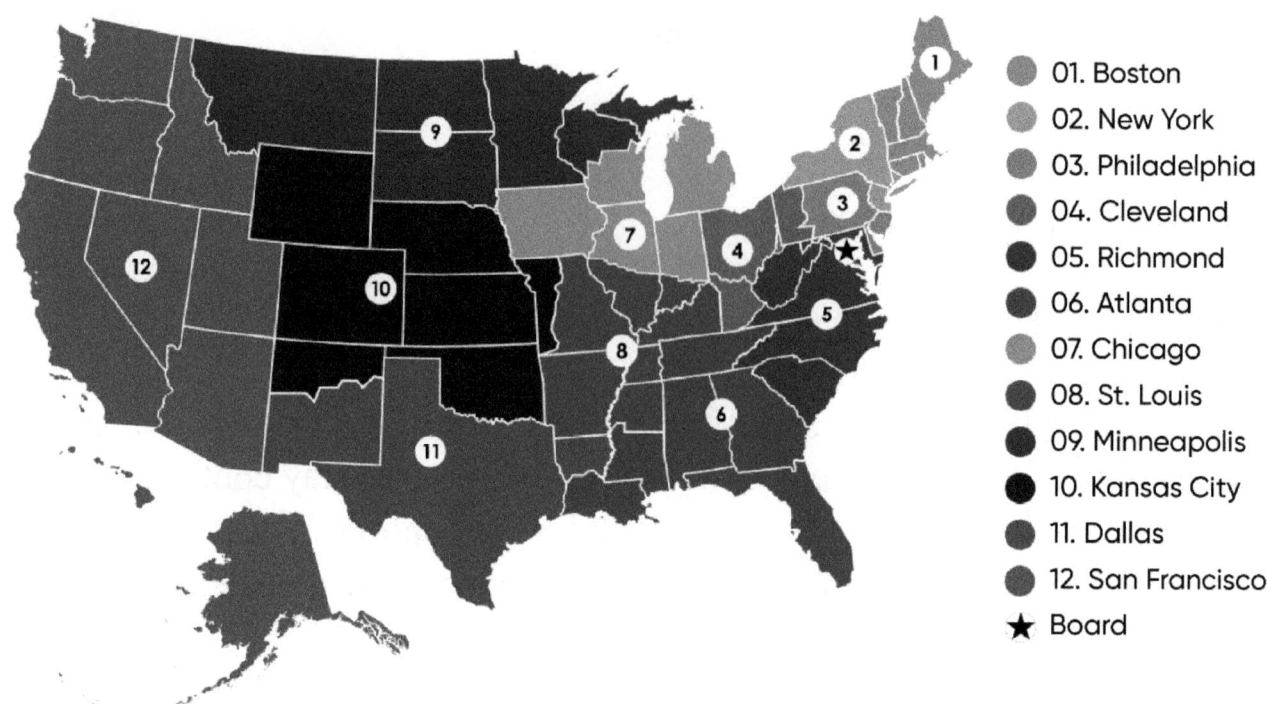

Fig 7.3 Federal Reserve Banks and Board Locations (Source: US Federal Reserve)[122]

DUAL MANDATE

The Federal Reserve operates under a mandate from the US Congress to *'promote effectively the goals of maximum employment, stable prices, and moderate long term interest rates.'* This is commonly referred to as the Fed's 'dual mandate.' Conceptually, the simultaneous pursuit of multiple objectives can be traced back to at least the 1940s, although the dual mandate has formally been in effect since 1977. However, with shifting (if not conflicting) priorities as to which objectives are of the greatest importance, it has long been recognised that such a mandate may, at times, create irreconcilable challenges for policy makers.[123]

GLOBAL ROLE

The Federal Reserve is arguably the world's most important central bank since the United States became the world's largest and most influential economy towards the end of World War II (see Chapter 12: Global Monetary System). The Fed functions as a central bank of central banks in addition to serving the domestic US banking sector. The Fed acts as the clearing house and intermediary for the majority of international transactions between countries (see Chapter 5: Payments). While the majority of other central banks are unitary institutions (such as the Bank of England) with no districts, the Fed has inspired the creation of the European Central Bank, which was modelled in its image.

THE EUROPEAN CENTRAL BANK

The European Central Bank (ECB), was created by the Maastricht Treaty 1992, which came into effect in November 1993, as the central bank of the Euro area. Seventeen member countries elected to adopt the Euro currency, introduced in January 1999, as their unit of account.

The ECB is part of the larger European System of Central Banks (ESCB), which includes a number of countries which are not members of the Economic and Monetary Union (EMU). A minority of these countries are member states of the European Union, which elected to peg their currencies to the Euro, to preserve stability. However, not all members elected to do so. Apart from Denmark which negotiated an 'opt-out' clause, all EU member states are expected to adopt the Euro and eventually join the EMU.

The 'Eurosystem' of central banking was consciously modelled on that of the Fed, hence, they are structurally similar. Each country maintains its own national central bank (NCB), which act comparably to a Fed district bank (Federal Reserve Bank). The ECB's Executive Board, headquartered in Frankfurt, Germany acts in a comparable fashion to that of the Fed's Board of Governors. The Executive Board, much like the FOMC, makes monetary policy decisions. Unlike the Fed however, the ECB does not regulate financial institutions, nor does it control the budgets of the NCBs. These functions are performed domestically by the NCBs in their respective jurisdictions.

While structurally similar to the Fed, the ECB fundamentally differs, as it is a central bank for a monetary union of independent countries. Countries within the EU that have elected not to join the EMU by adopting the Euro have typically avoided doing so in order to spare their economies from the sudden either inflationary or deflationary effects experienced historically by member states with a substantially different currency value. Examples include Italy which joined the EMU in January 1999 and Greece, which much like Italy, experienced these effects, after joining the EMU in 2001. All EU member states which are not a part of the EMU are vulnerable to this risk, should they join in the future.

In October 2021, Croatia's conservative and Eurosceptic party, Hrvatski Suverenisti (Croatian Sovereignists), collected signatures from its electorate in a bid to force a referendum on whether to join the EMU, and thereby, adopt the Euro as the nation state's currency. Prime Minister Andrej Plenkovic advocated that Croatia adopting the Euro would remove currency risk, reduce interest rates, improve the country's credit rating and open the pathway for greater investment and diversification of an economy dominated by tourism. Whereas, Eurosceptics argued that the economy was too weak and uncompetitive to adopt the Euro, and doing so would be detrimental to domestic price stability.[124]

An additional consequence of joining the EMU, would be realised through the NCB's loss of control over domestic monetary policy and the introduction of domestic governmental fiscal policy limitations in their respective countries. The Maastricht Treaty, 1992, imposes limits on government deficits to 3% of GDP and public debt to 60% of GDP.[125] Countries which are structurally and fiscally too weak to meet this burden are likely to default against their obligations. Such was the case with Greece in 2015, at which time the country failed to make a payment of €1.6 billion to the IMF – the first time in history where a developed nation had defaulted on such an obligation.[126]

FORWARD GUIDANCE

As the role that central banks play in the global economy has become increasingly visible, so the shift in communications strategy from central banks regarding the state of the economy and likely future course of monetary policy has been increasingly prevalent. This is a practice known as forward guidance, whereby policy makers attempt to prevent disruptions that might impact markets or cause volatility in asset prices. Thus, forward guidance is an attempt to provide a roadmap as to how policy makers see their policy decisions unfolding in the near term. This is largely communicated in the hope that businesses and households will make financial decisions and plans accordingly. The Federal Reserve, the Bank of England and the European Central Bank are all practitioners of forward guidance.

8

ECONOMIC CYCLES

'Credit is exactly like morphine. Either credit or morphine used habitually leads inevitably to the gutter.'

- The Dallas Fed, 1932.

MONETARY POLICY

Monetary policy is set by the central bank in each country (or monetary zone) to control inflation and to instil trust (confidence) in the value and stability (purchasing power and exchange rate volatility) of a national currency.

The bank rate, also known as the base rate (discount rate in the US), is the rate of interest charged by a central bank for its loans or advances to a commercial bank.

The reserve requirement establishes the minimum reserves that must be held by a commercial bank. The minimum reserve is generally determined to be no less than a specified percentage of the total deposit liabilities the commercial bank owes to its customers. This forms the basis for the concept of fractional reserve banking. Fractional reserve banking is a system in which only a fraction of bank deposits are backed by actual cash on hand and available for withdrawal (see Fractional Reserve, Chapter 5: Payments). This makes capital available for lending through leverage with which the economy may theoretically be expanded.

Monetary policy sets the reserve requirement and bank rate, which influences interest rates for short-term borrowing and controls the money supply in circulation, through either 'printing money' or removing excess reserves and currency. The latter is controlled via Open Market Operations (see below).

MONEY SUPPLY

The money supply is categorised hierarchically as follows:

M0 - represents the total of all physical currency in issue (Cash - banknotes and coinage) and includes (commercial) bank reserves held on deposit with the Central Bank. It is additionally known as the 'Monetary Base.' Occasionally, this is referred to as high-powered money (HPM), as it is capable of being multiplied through the use of fractional reserve banking (see Fractional Reserve, Chapter 5: Payments).

M1 - includes all elements of M0 as well as demand deposits, checkable deposits and traveller's cheques. Paper banknotes and coin, is typically fabricated by the mint on behalf of the Central Bank.

M2 - includes all elements of M1 and 'near money' in the form of savings, money market securities, mutual funds and fixed deposits (time deposits).

M3 - includes M2, as well as elements of the money supply that are less liquid, the assets of large financial institutions, such as long-term deposits, institutional money market funds, short-term repo (repurchase) agreements.

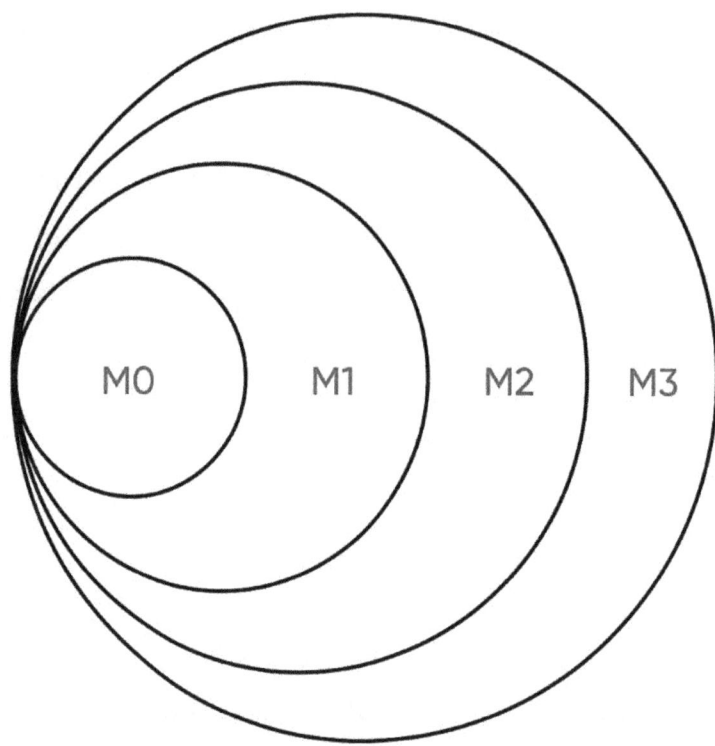

Fig 8.1 Hierarchy of the money supply

OPEN MARKET OPERATIONS

'Printing money,' or increasing the monetary base (apart from physical cash and coin) in practice, is achieved through conducting open market operations (OMOs). The majority of a currency in circulation, is account-based. An OMO, refers to the purchase and sale of bonds known as Treasury Securities (Treasuries) by the central bank on the open market. In conducting open market operations, the central bank adds to its holdings of domestic securities by purchasing them from a bank. In return, the central bank credits an equal sum of money reflective of the purchase to the bank's reserve account held with the central bank. The net result is an increase in the bank's reserves and in the monetary base.

Alternatively, the central bank may purchase securities from non-banking entities, such as dealers, institutions or from members of the public, namely investors. OMOs are used to regulate the money supply (**M0**) that banks hold on reserve with the central bank. The purchase of securities increases the money supply, whereas the sale thereof decreases it. This system additionally allows the central bank to manipulate the base rate (interest rate), by either injecting or removing liquidity from banks. The net outcome of these operations is to adjust the short-term interest rate.

Injecting liquidity into the banks (known as an expansionary monetary policy) essentially places downward pressure on interest rates, by forcing banks to compete to lend money as a result of the capital injection. The converse is true of removing liquidity (known as a contractionary monetary policy), thereby tightening capital and which drives the price higher, thus, raising interest rates.

The consequences of increasing or reducing the money supply and adjusting interest rates are 'levers,' which influence the rate of inflation, deflation and theoretically, the velocity (of circulation) at which transactions occur. These levers, additionally, influence the ease with which access to credit may be attained.

THE TAYLOR RULE

The Taylor rule, developed by American economist John Taylor in 1992, proposes a mechanism to stabilise economic activity through manipulating interest rates. The Taylor rule advocates that monetary policy has a stabilising effect by raising the nominal interest rate by a greater magnitude than the 'increased' rate of inflation. Advanced economies, such as the UK and the US, conducted monetary policy which was broadly consistent with the Taylor rule during the period known as the 'Great Moderation' (1986 - 2007). The Great Moderation was largely characterised as a period of limited inflation and general price stability. It should be noted that the Taylor rule is not as influential in monetary policy making since the GFC. Policy makers use a variety of theoretical models in order to make policy decisions which affect the economy. One such theory is that of Monetarism.

MONETARISM

Monetarism is a macroeconomic school of thought which advocates that the supply of money in an economy is the primary facilitator for economic growth. Monetarism is synonymous with American economist and statistician, Milton Friedman (1912 - 2006), who formulated the theory of monetarism. Friedman asserted that monetary policy should be conducted by targeting the growth rate of the money supply to maintain economic and price stability.[127] This combined with the Keynesian Theory of Money (see below) forms the basis for how policy makers devise such policies to influence an economy, via Open Market Operations.

MONETARIST THEORY

Central to monetarism is the monetarist theory, illustrating the primary variables which policy makers influence to stimulate economic growth within a business cycle. Former Federal Reserve Chairman Dr Alan Greenspan was a proponent of monetarist theory[128], the formula for which is:

MV = PQ

M = Money Supply

V = Velocity (of circulation); the rate at which money 'changes hands'

P = the price of goods and services

Q = the quantity of goods and services

In practice however, velocity ("V") is arguably the primary variable, as if velocity were to reduce to zero, the magnitude of the money supply becomes irrelevant. Without velocity, there is essentially no economy. Since velocity is a variable which policy makers are unable to influence directly, policy is set to manipulate the money supply. Expanding the money supply, essentially makes it cheaper (see Open Market Operations above). By contrast, reducing it, makes it more expensive. Through this manipulation, actors within the economy are incentivised to borrow and spend, hence driving velocity ("V"). However, excessive borrowing and spending is detrimental, hence, there is a necessity to expand and contract, in order to drive consumer and business velocity within a parenthesis (see short-term and long-term debt cycles below).

FISCAL POLICY

Fiscal policy is set by the government, which is a public institution, in order to influence changes in the country's economy.

Fiscal policy (core to Keynesian macroeconomists) sets levels of taxation and government spending, as well as government borrowing which are used to influence macroeconomic variables, such as aggregate demand, income distribution, savings and investment, as well as the allocation of resources.

British economist, John Maynard Keynes (1883 - 1946), father of Keynesian Economics (see Subjective Value Theory, Chapter 2: Capital Evolution), hypothesised that the key to both a healthy economy and correcting recessions and depressions entails doing whatever is required to entice consumers to continue spending. Consequently, Keynesian economists advocate (Keynesian Theory of Money) that governments should increase spending to compensate for any notable contractions in aggregate demand. Government spending would assist in boosting demand, and thus, protect jobs, which in turn will help to drive greater consumption (spending) by consumers.

Ideally, Monetary Policy and Fiscal Policy should be set to complement one another and function symbiotically to achieve sustainable prosperity.

An example of such, would be to mutually set both policies in synchronicity, in order to increase credit and lower interest rates, as well as reduce property taxes to collectively drive greater velocity in residential real estate transactions, hence tackling a decline in nation-wide home ownership. The corresponding velocity, in turn, would support asset prices, promote greater employment and drive growth in GDP.

INFLATION

The term 'Inflation,' literally means an 'increase in volume.' However, the consequence of this increase is poorly understood. The majority of economists believe that very high rates of inflation (hyperinflation) are harmful and are usually attributed to excessive expansions of the money supply (see Quantity Theory of Money, Chapter 14: Tokenisation).[129] Policy makers aspire towards realising a moderate inflation rate (typically ~2%) as this supports growth in incomes, which consequently supports growth in tax revenues. A moderate rate of inflation tends to reduce the real value of debt. When an economy is not running at a fully-subscribed capacity, inflation aids in increasing production in order to exploit the unused or excess capacity. A moderate inflation rate theoretically stimulates more spending which equates to greater aggregate demand. Greater demand consequently stimulates production to meet that demand.[130]

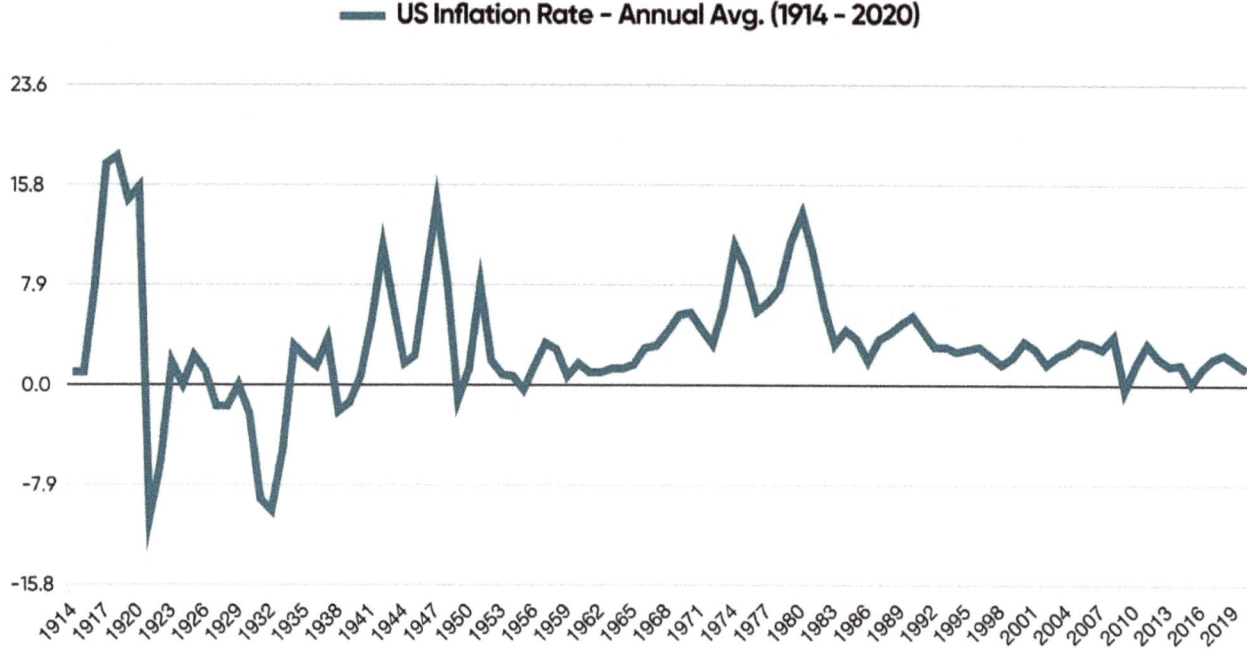

Fig 8.2 Annual US Inflation Rate (1914 - 2020) (Source data: US Federal Reserve)

Central banks generally influence the rate of inflation through increasing and reducing the money supply, as well as interest rates. When central banks increase the money supply, the value of all money in circulation over which it has purview, is expected to devalue (debase). There is a greater supply, therefore, a lower demand, in which case it is perceived to be less valuable than if there were less money in circulation.[131] In instances where hyperinflation occurs, this effect is magnified, whereby, money loses any notion of value stability.

A central bank, through monetary policy, can counter this effect by raising interest rates (through OMO), which makes that money supply more expensive. The net effect of which is raising the cost associated with borrowing money and creates a reciprocal yield for lending it, as a consequence of higher interest rates.

One of the key stated objectives of central banks is to regulate the rate of inflation at a slow and steady rate (see above), which is critical to fulfilling one of the key functions of money as a *store of value*. Controlling the supply, influences money's 'scarcity,' which is a key characteristic of money, which then in turn influences its effectiveness in storing value (see Characteristics of Money, Chapter 6: Money). This requires scrutiny over indicators as to the health of the economy and to adjust policy to suit the prevailing conditions. By contrast, Milton Friedman documented his k-percent rule, which promoted the notion that the money supply should be increased by a nominal percentage annually, in ambivalence to the state of the economy or the business cycle. This is both linked and complementary to the assumption that velocity ("V") is an exogenous variable, which is essentially constant. A supposition which is known, and has been proven to be incorrect (Fig 8.7). Policy makers have largely dismissed and refrained from applying the k-percent rule.

Most people generally experience the effects of inflation through increases in their cost of living and the price of finished goods and services they wish to purchase. Inflation, coupled with an increase in money supply, tends to devalue a country's currency, which is useful in stimulating exports. Such an advantage is usually short lived, as other countries tend to follow suit and restore parity.

Inflation is experienced as a general rise in price level, relative to available goods and services, resulting in a substantial and continuing reduction in purchasing power in an economy over time.

It should, thus, be expected that the purchasing power of money should diminish over time as a natural consequence of inflation. The rate of inflation is the measurement, thereof, and is reflected in the changes in the *Consumer Price Index*, as well as through changes in the *Retail Price Index*. By way of example, should a 2% inflation rate be successfully and consistently maintained in a particular monetary zone over the course of a thirty-five-year period, the currency, therein, should have halved in (purchasing power) value by the end of the period.

Since money's purchasing power diminishes over time as a natural consequence of monetary policy, this in turn drives investment behaviours to seek out higher returns than simply hoarding it (see Financial Innovation, Chapter 10: Financialisation). This effect additionally incentivises governments and the finance sector to accommodate investor demand, and thereby profit through the associated seigniorage, thereof.

In monetarist theory terms, inflation and deflation are expressed as "**P**."

DEFLATION

Deflation is essentially the opposite of Inflation, not to be confused with disinflation, which would still be inflation, however, at a positive, yet at a lower and slower rate.

In an economic climate, where supply is high and demand is low, deflation is likely to occur. The goods and services face greater competition, which places downward pressure on prices, providing greater purchasing power for the consumer.

A negative effect of deflation, especially when it is unexpected, is it can raise the real value of debt. Deflation may also aggravate recessions, slowing economic recovery.

Historically, when the global monetary system operated in representative money (metallism), rather than fiat money (chartalism), constant inflationary and deflationary cycles would occur to restore balance, relative to the supply of the underpinning commodity or precious metal (primarily Gold, and in some cases, Silver). The system was challenged by two key weaknesses.

Firstly, the rate at which new precious metal was discovered, mined, refined and made available, which was fairly slow and limited. Secondly, the periodic hoarding of precious metal already in circulation, which would cause a radical and sudden deflationary effect.

GROSS DOMESTIC PRODUCT

Gross domestic product (GDP) is a market value measure of all the finished goods and services produced over a specific period of time.

Nominal GDP is expressed without taking into account the cost of living or inflation, which is useful in comparing national economies in the international market, whereas GDP Purchasing Power Parity (PPP) is more useful when comparing living standards and buying power between nations.

The Monetarist theory expresses real GDP (GDP PPP) as "**Q**," whereas nominal GDP is expressed as **"PQ."**

In circumstances where an economy is expanding, the GDP growth rate is positive. A growing economy benefits businesses, promotes employment and supports an increase in incomes.

RECESSION

An economic contraction is evident when businesses experience less demand for goods and services across an economy. In order to qualify as a technical recession, the contraction persists for two or more successive quarters, evidenced through a measurable decline in GDP growth.

Businesses tend to react in response to recessions by embracing austerity measures wherever possible. Businesses tend to additionally focus in preserving cash position and cash flow, while narrowing investment exclusively towards initiatives, which reduce operational costs or improve productivity. Depending on the severity of the recession, employers may seek to reduce their workforce in line with diminishing consumer demand.

Consequently, unemployment levels rise within the economy, placing greater pressure on fiscal and monetary policy makers to make adjustments to compensate.

DEPRESSION

A depression is characterised by poor or depressed growth. A recession may end swiftly through a rise in GDP. However, an economy may remain in a depression, through depressed growth, relative to GDP levels prior to the initial recession. Depressions are characterised by, and result in, persistently poor transactional velocity, high-unemployment levels and widespread poverty.

In a depression, interest rates are either at, or rapidly descend to, very near the zero bound (near 0%). Lowering interest rates to stimulate borrowing and drive economic velocity, is the primary lever which central banks manipulate in response to recessions. Interest rates at, or near the zero bound for protracted periods, are strong indicators of depressed growth and poor economic velocity, hence a depression. Keeping interest rates near the zero bound, in a depression, is additionally critical to ensure that servicing debt is as achievable as possible, particularly while incomes are low and unemployment is rising, both of which make servicing debt increasingly challenging. If policy makers were to raise interest rates prematurely, it could manifest in a form of 'debt trap,' from which actors within the economy are unable to escape. A debt trap amplifies economic damage and severely impedes recovery.

The circumstances in which conventional monetary policy is rendered ineffective is known as a 'liquidity trap.' First described by John Maynard Keynes, in a liquidity trap bonds are avoided and funds are kept as liquid as possible, due to the prevailing belief that interest rates will imminently rise which reflexively pushes bond prices down. In circumstances such as depressions, policy makers will employ what are referred to as 'unconventional methods' as there is no appetite to spend or invest amongst consumers.

In a deflationary depression, the bulk of debt is typically denominated in a country's domestic currency, whereas in an inflationary depression, the bulk of debt is typically denominated in one or more foreign currencies. As the velocity of circulation declines ("V"), deflation sets in (see below). However, for countries the debts of which are denominated in foreign currencies, declining velocity prompts a devaluation of the country's domestic currency in order to service the debt. This typically results in an inflationary effect.

The inflationary effect, in such circumstances, typically prompts the reallocation of scarce resources towards unproductive activities, which will likely distort economic activity. By extension, this may impede domestic efficiency, and thus, affect output growth.[132] Consequently, this promotes what is known as inflation-output volatility. This is particularly prevalent amidst periods of financial stress.

Policy makers are afforded greater flexibility in responding to depressions of a deflationary nature, whereas typically limited to a greater extent in inflationary depressions. Aside from keeping interest rates at or near the zero bound, the levers (see Unconventional Methods below) which policy makers may exploit to stimulate an economy, are as follows[133]:

1. Austerity (spending less)

2. Restructuring debt (and defaults)

3. Providing guarantees (underwriting or nationalising debts and injecting liquidity, via Quantitative Easing)

4. Wealth redistribution (higher taxation and narrower tax deductions)

In a depression, there is a significant behavioural shift amongst consumers. Instinctively, people avoid non-essential spending, channelling their income towards living expenses and any surplus towards servicing existing debts and settling debts in their entirety, where possible. Any disposable income is directed towards highly-liquid savings, rather than consumer-driven spending. This is despite interest rates being near or at the zero bound, which would ordinarily have a stimulating effect on consumer borrowing and spending. The net effect of these behaviours essentially causes velocity ("V") to decline or stall, which seizes the economy. These shocks to aggregate demand are known as demand shocks.

In a depression, people whom are unable to service their debts, attempt to liquidate their assets in order to relieve their debt burdens. This behaviour tends to saturate the market with high-value assets, for which there is ample supply and little demand. The net effect, thereof, depresses prices, resulting in a deflationary effect. In other words, there are more goods, services or assets available for less money and fewer buyers, hence, resulting in deflation.

VELOCITY

TRANSACTIONS

A transaction occurs when people or businesses exchange money or credit for goods, services or financial assets. Each transaction has a buyer and a seller. The sum of the money combined with credit spent represents the spending total.

Total spending divided by the total quantity of either goods or services purchased establishes the price.

MARKETS

There are numerous markets for goods and services within an economy. A market for a specific commodity, good or service is no different. To establish the price for a commodity, good or service, the total spending divided by the total sum sold establishes the market price.

AN ECONOMY

An economy represents the total transactions between buyers and sellers across all markets within. With low-demand and high-supply, prices fall. Conversely, with high-demand and limited supply, prices rise. In either case, the buoyancy of an economy largely pivots on the rate of monetary velocity ("V" in the monetarist theory). The number and rate of transactions, (essentially the rate at which money changes hands) establishes velocity of the circulation over a specified period of time (Fig 8.7).

CREDIT & DEBT

Credit is an essential instrument in an economy and arguably the most important for promoting short-term growth. In much the same way, buyers and sellers engage in transactions within the markets, so do lenders and borrowers. Lenders are in business to grow their capital through generating a return on investments (ROIC). Borrowers seek to purchase goods, services or financial assets which they cannot afford, via an outright purchase.

Borrowers generally wish to purchase an asset, such as a residence. Alternatively, they may wish to purchase a vehicle or invest in starting a new business. Credit facilitates both parties in achieving their desired outcome. Borrowers enter into a contract with lenders to repay the principal (amount borrowed) with interest, either at or more commonly over a pre-agreed period of time. When policy makers set interest rates at a higher rate, borrowing is expensive and there is consequently less borrowing regardless of demand. When interest rates are low, borrowing increases as a consequence of it being cheaper. Credit is created when lenders and borrowers engage in a transaction built on a foundation of trust, in that the terms of a loan will be honoured.

With the creation of credit, a corresponding debt is automatically created. The credit represents an asset to the lender, which in turn is a debt in the form of a liability to the borrower. The borrower is essentially borrowing from their future earnings in order to settle the transaction, which will occur once the principal (amount borrowed) and the interest has been settled (paid in full). In the interim, the borrower is able to increase their spending, driving velocity, which in turn drives the economy.

The increase in spending by the borrower drives velocity and growth in income for whomever the borrower spent the credit. The increase in liquidity is perceived as creditworthiness, which in turn makes lenders more willing to furnish borrowers with credit. A creditworthy borrower is capable of repaying or servicing the debt and has sufficient collateral, should they find themselves incapable of doing so. Income is the key factor in the former, whereas the value of the borrower's assets are the key factor for the latter.

Therefore, increased income facilitates increased borrowing which enables increased spending. Consequently, since the buyer's increased spending drives the seller's increased income, which then in turn leads to more borrowing, a self-reinforcing pattern emerges, for which credit and debt are the fuel.

SHORT-TERM DEBT CYCLES

The compounding nature of this credit/debit fuelled pattern leads to greater and greater economic growth which is the basis for which cycles emerge. In an economy free of credit or debt, growth is sustained exclusively by productivity. Productivity is the product of two variables. These are the number of people employed and how productive these people are. Inventive, motivated individuals and businesses creating new technologies, services, goods and business models drive greater productivity.

As a contrast, those businesses which find themselves trapped behind *inertia barriers* or are complacent, tend to remain inefficient and consequently less productive realising little, if any growth. While productivity within an economy matters greatly in the longer term, it is the presence of credit which matters most in the short-term, particularly in the context of realising growth. Productivity alone tends to grow at a fairly linear rate and fluctuates very little, hence, it isn't usually a cause of economic swings.

In a credit fuelled economy, growth created by credit today will naturally result in a contraction anchored by the corresponding debt in the future. As a result, an economy infused with credit, allows for greater spending and enables incomes to rise faster than in an economy, which grows solely based on productivity, in the short-term, however, not over the longer term.

The debt created by credit can either have a positive effect by being used to purchase an asset, which creates an income or be used to purchase goods and services which produce no income. The former assists the borrower in servicing the debt and promoting productivity, whereas the latter constrains the borrower, making them vulnerable to default.

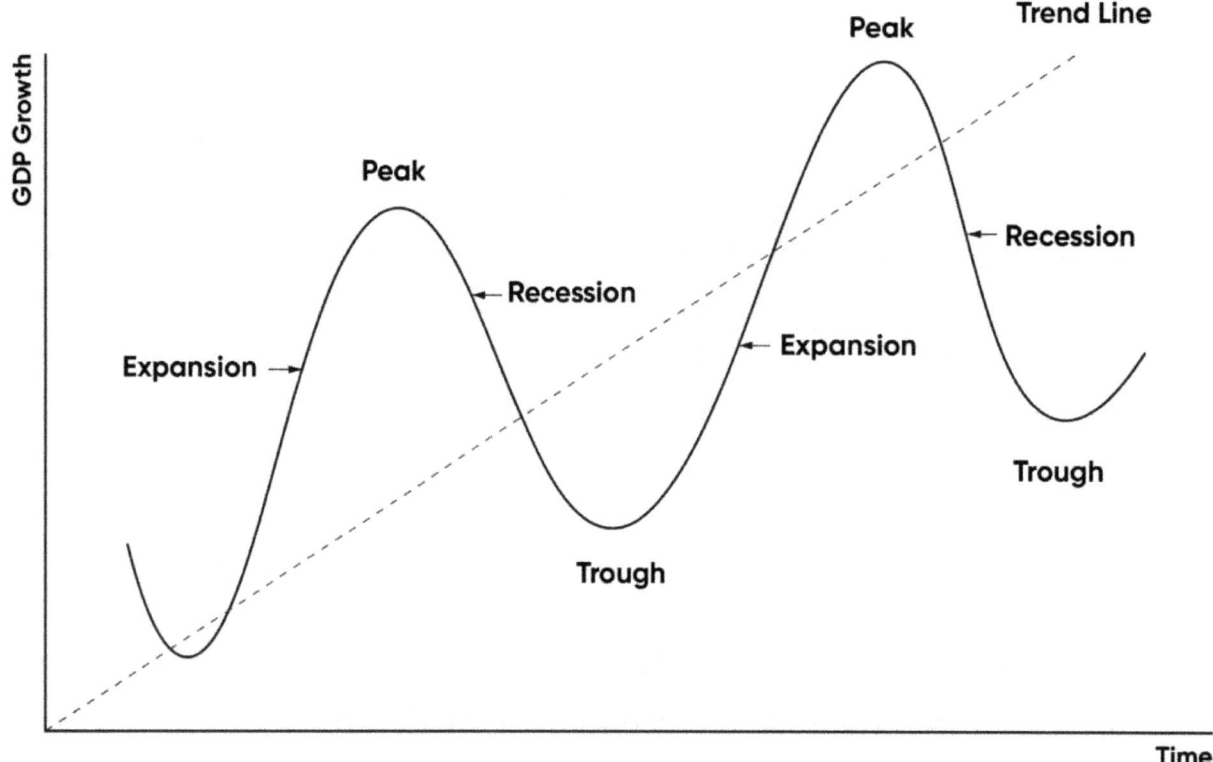

Fig 8.3 illustrates Short-Term Debt Cycles

The first phase of the debt cycle (also known as a credit cycle) is known as the expansion, largely due to the increase in spending, fuelled by credit. When the total spending and rise in incomes grows faster than the production of goods, prices begin to rise. The rise in prices is experienced as inflation. The central bank and the government welcome some inflation as rising prices and rising incomes results in greater taxation revenues. However, too high a rate of inflation can easily become problematic (see above), hence, central bank (monetary) policy makers, raise interest rates in response. A rise in interest rates, raises the cost of borrowing, hence slowing and reducing the rate, thereof. However, higher interest rates, raises the cost of servicing the existing debts already created. With incomes constrained servicing higher costs of debt and reduced borrowing results in reduced spending, reduced monetary velocity and reducing prices. This is experienced as deflation. Inevitably, persistent deflation and reduced velocity results in an economic contraction through reduced economic activity. The contraction experienced, is a recession. If the recession is perceived to be severe and the inflation level has sufficiently tapered, the central bank policy makers will again lower interest rates. These lower interest rates reduce the costs of servicing debt and broaden the availability of credit, simultaneously reducing the costs of new borrowing. This prompts a new short-term debt cycle to emerge. A typical short-term debt cycle elapses over a period of between eight and twelve years.

LONG-TERM DEBT CYCLES

Over time, debt burdens accrue incrementally with each short-term cycle in greater magnitude. Debts accrue as past burdens are rarely settled in full, thus, each short-term cycle usually peaks and troughs at a higher economic level than the previous.

The phenomenon fuels an expansion phase of a long-term debt cycle, also known as an economic bubble. For so long as incomes grow in tandem with debt burdens (the ratio of income to debt), which enables debt to remain serviceable, the bubble will continue to grow. Rising asset prices underpins creditworthiness despite rising debt, supplementing short-term poor income growth relative to the rising cost of servicing debt. Inevitably debt burdens peak, forcing a decrease in spending and by extension incomes.

Decreasing incomes make debts unserviceable, forcing creditors to demand payment, which triggers defaults and a mass liquidation of assets. Due to high-supply and low-demand, asset prices fall which in turn, represents a contraction of collateral and amplifies the effect of deflation. A protracted reinforcing cyclic fall (a crash or bubble burst) ensues. This was the case in the United States in 1929, and Japan in 1989. This is known as a deleveraging. Each long-term debt cycle persists over a period of between eighty-years to a century.[134]

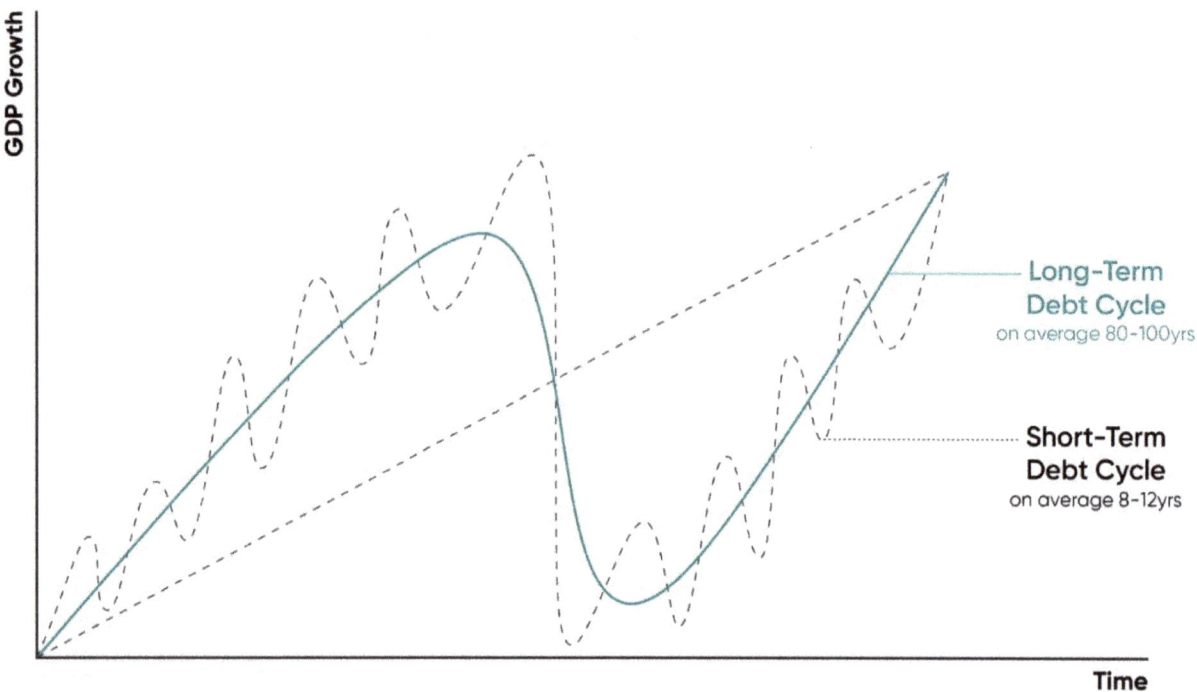

Fig 8.4 illustrates Short-Term Debt Cycles within a Long-Term Debt Cycle

DELEVERAGING

In a deleveraging, incomes fall, unemployment rises exponentially, asset prices plunge, credit availability evaporates. General consumption driven behaviour grinds to a halt. Households budget and spend conservatively, channelling spending exclusively towards necessities. Monetary velocity stalls, which geometrically reinforces further economic contractions, businesses collapse, leading to further unemployment. Seeking liquidity, financial assets are liquidated in a frenzy. With plummeting asset prices and liquidity evanescing, panic ensues.

Cyclically and rapidly, without an intervention, bank accounts are drained, portfolios are divested and the stock market crashes, while many banking and other financial institutions become insolvent and ultimately bankrupt. The economy loses creditworthiness and confidence in the financial system, its institutions and instruments is decimated.

With the banks' reserves drained from mass withdrawals and balance sheets carrying assets deemed worthless through market saturation and debtor defaults, the financial system faces a crisis of confidence and may even face collapse.[135]

A deleveraging will undoubtedly trigger a depression, as was the case in the US, following the Wall Street crash of 1929 (see Chapter 10: Financialisation), followed by the Great Depression. In Japan, the deleveraging spawned in 1989, was followed by Japan's 'Lost Decade.'

THE MIDDLE CLASS

There are three categories of income:

1. **Earned** - Remuneration in the form of wages paid by an employer to an employee.

2. **Portfolio** - Dividends, interest and capital gains derived from equities, bonds, derivatives and other marketable financial assets. Essentially, income in the form of returns realised through investment and speculation using the financial markets and associated instruments.

3. **Passive** - Income in the form of positive cash flow derived from tangible financial assets. An example of which is real estate.

Although there are exceptions, from a wealth and income perspective, contemporary societies are categorised into three generalised tranches.

1. **The Working Class** - Derive income exclusively from employment. Rarely tertiary educated. Generally characterised as unskilled labour. Modest, if any financial resources or means. Low taxation, relative to income. Weak financial literacy. Superficial knowledge of politics, taxation, economics or finance.

2. **The Middle Class** - Portfolio income and professional income earners. Tertiary educated, either self-employed or employed in academic professions within broader business enterprises. E.g., Solicitors (Lawyers), Accountants, Doctors, Educators and Engineers.

The middle class additionally comprises entrepreneurs engaged in small and medium-sized merchant businesses, such as non-conglomerate shops and non-franchised restaurants, as well as niche businesses, such as consultancies or service-centric merchants. Moderate financial literacy and varied knowledge regarding finance, taxation, politics and economics. Limited financial resources. Taxed between moderately to highly, relative to income.

3. **The Wealthy** - Passive income earners, business owners and income generating asset holders. Broad portfolio investors and high net-worth individuals. Diverse sources of wealth and liquidity. Either themselves possess extensive financial literacy and are highly knowledgeable in matters of finance, taxation, politics and economics, or retain the services of those with these levels of expertise. Typically taxed proportionately little, relative to their net worth.

In a depression, the deleveraging bores a divide through the middle class. A very small percentage thereof, become wealthier. The vast majority however, become poorer as their businesses crumble, asset values dwindle, portfolios shrink in value and debts fall due.

POPULISM

As income inequality broadens between the wealthy and the 'former' middle class, social inequality deepens, placing a strain on civility and social order. With economic conditions deteriorating, the risk of social disorder and unrest becomes prevalent. Order, civility and tolerance regress, giving rise to a range of divisive political sentiments and stances that provoke the polarisation of 'the people' versus 'the elite,' 'the have nots' versus 'the haves.'

Unchecked, these divisive forces are harnessed and exploited by charismatic leaders, whom are able to garner support for extreme social change. These sentiments are often geared towards either nationalism or socialism. A historical example includes the rise of Hitler and Nazi Germany's single party totalitarian state, with the collapse of civil liberties and constitutional governance in 1933. A symptomatic consequence, of the recall of US loans, following the Wall Street crash of 1929, which resulted in Germany's economic collapse.[136]

UNCONVENTIONAL METHODS

AUSTERITY

Households and businesses reduce spending and focus their expenditure towards reducing inefficiencies and reducing or paying down debts. With reduced economic activity, incomes dwindle, reducing taxation revenues collected by the government. Collecting less tax revenues, the government imposes austerity measures by cutting public spending in infrastructure development and modernisation. Public sector employees experience zero to very minor wage increases.

DEBT DEFAULTS & RESTRUCTURING

While the public struggles to service existing debts, banks and financial institutions may find themselves unable to repay depositors. Particularly prevalent, should depositors lose confidence in these institutions and attempt to withdraw funds *en masse*, known as 'a run on the banks.' Banks are perpetually vulnerable to panic withdrawals as liquidity is maintained as a fractional reserve of deposits held (see Monetary Policy, above). Hence, the attraction to perpetuate the use of Net Settlement CSMs, in lieu of RTGS payments (see Chapter 5: Payments).

Banks that default on their own debts reinforce the effects of an economic depression. Lenders tend to agree to restructuring debt, allowing borrowers to pay back less, rather than default by paying nothing at all. As debts are written off and restructured, asset values and incomes plummet at a faster rate, leaving further debt burdens to be serviced.

WEALTH REDISTRIBUTION

While collecting less tax revenues, the government is required to devise economic stimulus plans, as well as manage the burdens experienced by greater demand for unemployment benefits and support. Fiscal policy is adjusted to engineer greater taxation on the wealthy minority and the middle-class, usually by targeting sources of income prevalent among them. Examples include raising capital gains taxes (CGT) and raising property taxes against high-value real estate holdings. Another means of raising net taxation revenues, is reducing or eliminating tax deductible allowances, as well as rebates.

DEFICIT SPENDING

In circumstances where governments are required to spend more than they collect through taxation, the treasury issues bonds known as treasury securities (treasury bills, or gilt-edged securities) to fund the deficit. Bonds are sold to all manner of private and institutional investors, as well as foreign governments. Governments use bonds to raise the necessary capital to supplement the domestic spending budget and provide guarantees that the returns associated with the bond purchases will be settled in full to creditors upon maturity. These bonds are carried as a liability in the form of debt on the treasury's balance sheet. This debt is either settled through future tax revenues or through funds raised by issuing new bonds.

The need for deficit spending (via fiscal policy) in a protracted recession or a depression is amplified, as public spending is necessary to stimulate the economy and combat unemployment. This is crucial amidst poor economic activity and while deflationary pressures impose a materially detrimental effect on tax revenues. A climate which cultivates a liquidity crisis.

QUANTITATIVE EASING

In a liquidity crisis brought about by a deleveraging or 'black swan' event, there are limited, if any, investors with the resources to provide a meaningful capital injection through purchasing bonds. Such purchases during an economic depression are less palatable, due to interest rates being at or near the zero bound. The circumstances lend themselves to a climate of low confidence. Neither attribute encourages those with liquidity to invest in fixed-term investments for protracted periods of time, nor in exchange for perceptively low returns.

In the 1930s, during the Great Depression, public spending was highly constrained under these conditions. Debt defaults, high unemployment and bankruptcies were prevalent. Following the GFC, central banks embarked on a liquidity strategy known as Quantitative Easing in order to attempt to deleverage gracefully. A 'graceful' deleveraging would restore confidence and allow the economy to recover in an attempt to avoid a repeat of the events of the 1930s. Events that ultimately led to the outbreak of a Second World War.

Quantitative Easing (QE) is achieved by the treasury issuing bonds and the central bank purchasing them, via an intermediary through OMOs. The central bank 'prints money' and uses these funds to purchase the bonds, which are subsequently held as assets on the central bank's balance sheet. The newly 'printed money' (as is normally the case), is entered as a liability on the central bank's balance sheet. With the treasury's debt monetised, the government is able to direct spending toward stimulating the economy where required. QE is, additionally, a means through which liquidity is cascaded to banks and financial institutions to counter a liquidity crisis. Institutional debt may be monetised to avoid bankruptcies and ensure new credit is available to businesses and household borrowers.

QE is fundamentally designed to inject liquidity into the financial system to restore confidence and either prevent, or halt panic-fuelled behaviour. Furthermore, it is intended to provide the financial support to stimulate monetary velocity, which is intended to accelerate an economic recovery.

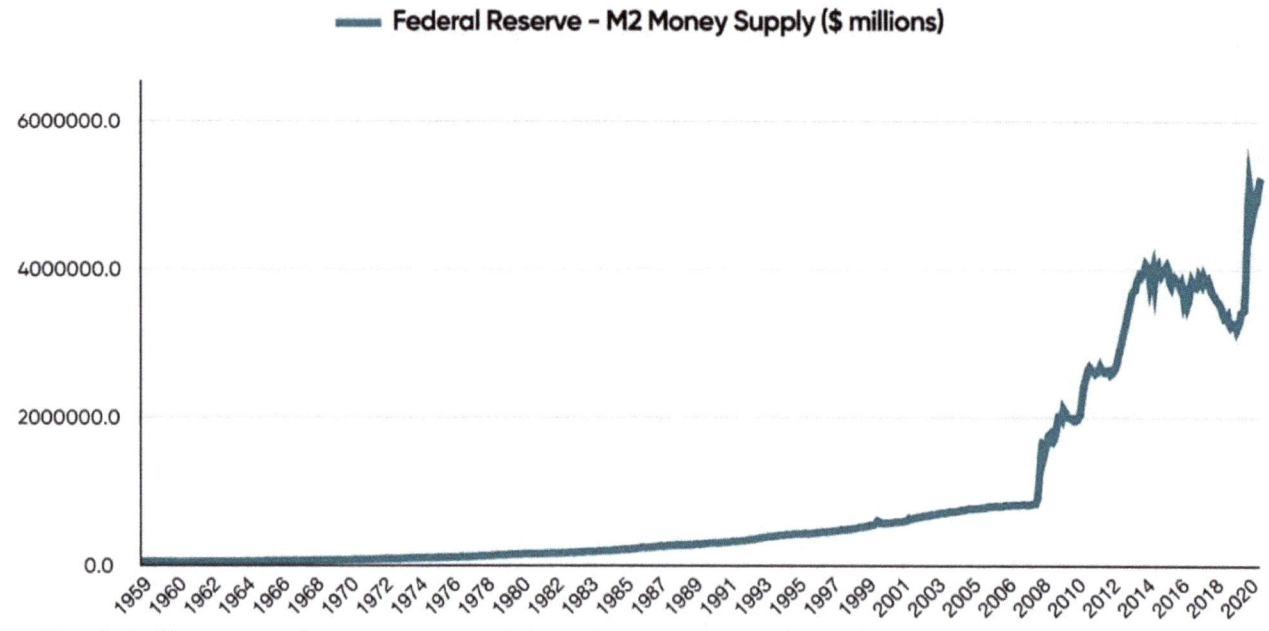

Fig 8.5 illustrates the expansion of the US Money Supply incl. GFC (QE1, QE2, QE3) and COVID-19 (1959 - 2020) (Source data: US Federal Reserve)

QUANTITATIVE TIGHTENING

Once the economy has recovered sufficiently from a deleveraging event and capable of self-sustaining growth, the central bank should be able to begin quantitative tightening (QT) by divesting itself of bond holdings and reduce the money supply. This process should incrementally return the central bank's balance sheet to pre-QE levels.

Central banks will resist raising interest rates through monetary policy adjustments in order to keep the sovereign debt being carried serviceable. Raising interest rates prematurely, could sabotage any progress made in recovery and trigger a further liquidity crisis.

An unintended consequence of excessive QE is that it tends to mask vulnerable businesses, which would otherwise become insolvent and disappear. Through monetising the debt of such entities, QE keeps excess capacity in the market, contributing to systemic instability. If QT is applied in a steady and timely fashion, such entities, largely impeded by inertia barriers, should disappear as a consequence. These insolvencies, create a vacuum for *Creative Destruction* and new challengers, new ideas and innovators to enter the market.

Should excessive magnitudes of QE be accrued and carried for prolonged periods, without corresponding QT to divest the debt which has been monetised, the system may accrue a sufficient critical mass of otherwise insolvent capacity, which may make it vulnerable to a systemic collapse. In addition, a central bank, in essence, monetises debt to underpin the newly printed money, hence potentially undermining its own credibility and by extension the money over which it is the authority. In turn, this may result in a loss of confidence in both the value of money in circulation, the central bank and the monetary system as a whole. Such was the case in Germany (Weimar Republic 1921 - 1922) and in Zimbabwe since 2007.

Zimbabwe (formerly Rhodesia 1965 - 1979) suspended issuing its own currency in 2009 and has since used other currencies, in lieu of its own, predominantly the US dollar and more recently the Chinese Yuan (Renminbi).

This perception is reinforced by virtue of the money issued, constituting the central bank's liabilities, being backed by illiquid (and potentially toxic) debt, carried as central bank assets. In essence, transforming money into a share of the debt, fundamentally a debt token. A posture, which if maintained for too long or against too great a debt, could easily undermine confidence in the money itself.

MODERN MONETARY THEORY

The act of 'printing money' is achieved by the Treasury issuing a Treasury Security and auctioning it to potential investors (seeking a return). The Treasury Security is purchased by an investor, usually a financial institution, such as a bank. When engaging in QE, the Central Bank purchases the Treasury Security from the investor, and in the process creates money to fulfil the purchase by updating its database. The central bank reflects the increase in money as a balance sheet liability. The Treasury Security purchase is, thereafter, reflected as an asset on the Central Bank's balance sheet (see above).

Through this process, the Treasury effectively issues debt and the Central Bank purchases that debt. The net effect of this activity, is the central bank 'printing money' and the Treasury receiving it.

NEOCLASSICAL PERSPECTIVE

The neoclassical perspective is that the Central Bank is an independent entity that governs monetary policy and that a separation exists between the creation of reserves (printing money) and treasury debt. Primarily the Central Bank is considered to be an institution, the role of which is to regulate inflation.

Theoretically, when the Treasury issues debt into the economy, it is withdrawing purchasing power from someone (such as a bank). It is withdrawing reserves from a bank, which temporarily removes currency from circulation prior to re-injecting it. This enables the Central Bank to regulate the quantity of the Treasury's money which is 'printed' versus the quantity which is 'recycled' through the existing money supply within the economy. By operating in this fashion, theoretically, the Central Bank can regulate inflation through Open Market Operations.

MMT PERSPECTIVE

The modern monetary theory (MMT) perspective, however, advocates that it is beneficial to treat the Central Bank and the Treasury as if these separate institutions were a single entity. Hence, potentially jeopardising the role banks play in Open Market Operations which has broader implications in sustaining a buoyant bond market. The MMT view contends that the Central Bank's and Treasury's respective balance sheets should be treated as a consolidated balance sheet.

In an MMT paradigm, as a consolidated balance sheet the Central Bank's asset and the Treasury's liability would cancel (net zero) one another out. The Treasury could then embark on spending the money "raised" from the sale of the Treasury Security, to influence aggregate demand in the economy. In practice, this is comparable to what has transpired with each wave of QE, albeit intermediated, via the open market. Conceptually, under the auspices of this theory the Treasury perpetually maintains a zero balance, by spending newly 'printed' money into existence. MMT advocates that this practice is not problematic in a country that issues its own currency. The theory posits that the practice of issuing debt on demand is sustainable, so long as the associated deficit spending remains within the confines of the domestic industrial and employment capacity within the country.[137] This limitation is theoretically established in order to safeguard the economy from severe inflationary pressures. In an MMT paradigm, deficit spending should exploit the excess productive and employment capacity in the domestic economy to invest in developing the infrastructure to support future productivity and tax revenues. In other words, supporting future growth to presumably offset the deficit.

MMT views monetary policy predominantly with an exclusively domestic lens. This surfaces concerns that the consequences to external actors that utilise the currency may not be factored into consideration should MMT be embraced. In the case of the US, this should be of significant concern among the international community of central banks, due to the US dollar's role as principal global reserve currency (see Chapter 12: Global Monetary System).

QUANTITATIVE DESTRUCTION

Regardless of the perspective, the practices of Zero-interest Rate Policy (ZiRP), QE and 'printing' large quantities of money lend themselves to undermining the credibility of the monetary system and diminishes faith in fiat money as a long-term store of value. Neoclassical economists largely accept that deficit spending is necessary to run a private sector surplus (see Sectoral Balances, Chapter 17: Odyssey) and is, therefore, required to sustain a 'healthy' economy. However, the tolerances for deficit spending and the corresponding issuance of debt is subject to limits governed by the Keynesian multiplier.[138] In simplistic terms, the Keynesian multiplier infers that so long as the level of debt remains at or below a ratio of ninety-percent of GDP (debt-to-GDP ratio), every unit of currency spent represents a yield of ten-percent. In other words, spend a dollar to derive a return of one-dollar-ten. The European Union's Maastricht Treaty advocates a more conservative view by setting this limit at sixty-percent, a threshold at which EU member states are expected to take appropriate action in order to return the debt-to-GDP ratio to a credible and serviceable level (see The European Central Bank, Chapter 7: Central Banks).

Should the ninety-percent threshold in the debt-to-GDP ratio be breached, however, every dollar spent returns a negative yield. In other words, spend a dollar to realise a return of only ninety cents. These metrics illustrate the tolerances upon which confidence in the currency may be sustained. This is largely due to confidence that the debt will be serviced from future growth, which in turn, is supported by GDP. The United States breached this 90% threshold in 2010 and has persistently weakened since, reaching a level of 138% debt-to-GDP in 2020 (Fig 8.6).[139] Additionally, since much of this debt is exploited to support consumption in lieu of investing in infrastructure or business growth, the prospects for realising meaningful returns are bleak. This thus constitutes a negative-sum game, whereby the credit created will likely transform into unserviceable debt. This is no different to borrowing money to purchase goods and services, in lieu of investing in a new business or purchasing an income generating asset. Furthermore, there are legitimate concerns that once debt-to-GDP reaches a level beyond which confidence in the ability to repay the debt is lost, a systemic collapse is likely to follow, thereafter. Thus, constituting a form of *Quantitative Destruction*, whereby excessive debt financing via Quantitative Easing has undermined the credibility of monetary and fiscal institutions. Furthermore, by extension this taints the money issued, sponsored, and governed by these institutions. It is in the interest of avoiding such an outcome that Central Banks are increasingly exploring Negative-interest Rate Policy (NiRP) and largely reticent to embrace MMT (see War on Cash, Chapter 6: Money).

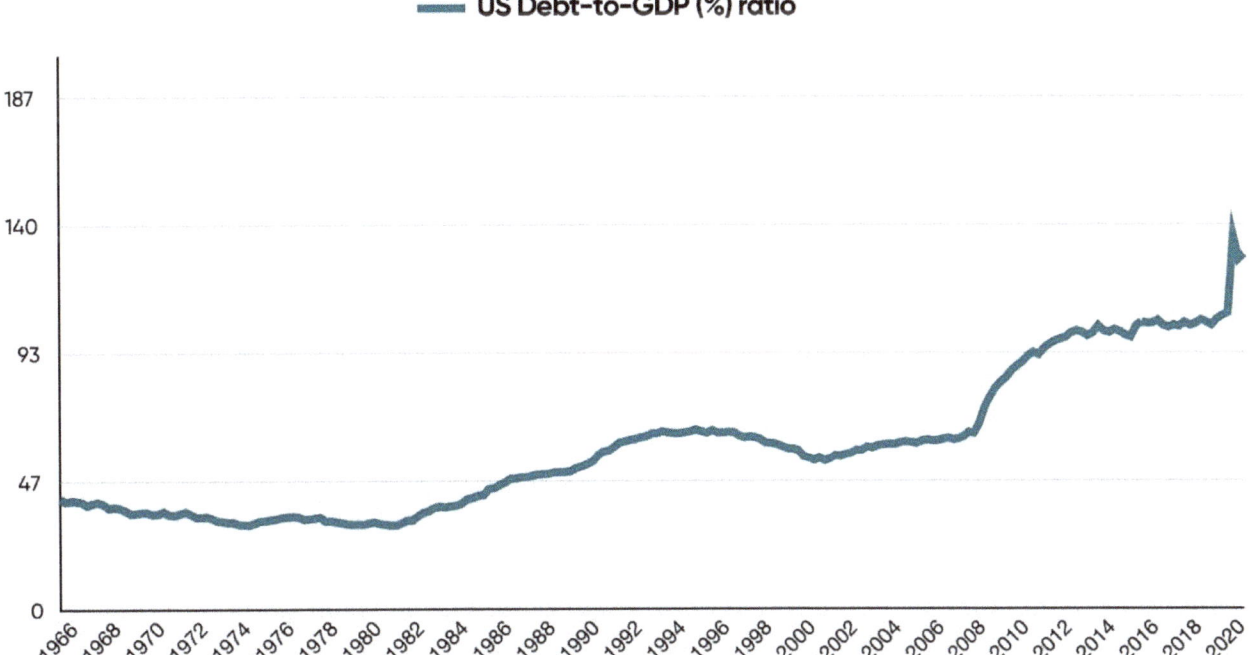

Fig 8.6 illustrates the US Debt-to-GDP Ratio (%) (1966 - 2020) (Source data: US Federal Reserve)

The rationale for the expected inflationary effects of QE blended with high debt-to-GDP ratios having not been realised is largely due to deflationary pressures experienced since the GFC 2007-2008. This phenomenon is accounted for by a persistent decline in velocity since the mid-1990s (Fig 8.7).

In reference to the monetarist theory, **MV = PQ** (see Monetarist Theory above), if velocity ("V") were constant while the money supply ("M") continued to expand, nominal GDP ("PQ") would grow, supported in the form of inflation (an expansion of "P"). However, since velocity ("V") is declining while the money supply ("M") is expanding, "P" as a consequence has been in decline, hence resulting in deflation.

This phenomenon illustrates the link between **confidence** and **velocity**. If actors within an economy have confidence, money is invested, borrowed and spent, all of which drives velocity. If confidence is low, velocity reflexively suffers. This relationship additionally surfaces the notion of stimulus. Policy makers contend that mechanisms, such as QE have a stimulating effect on the economy. However, in practice since confidence is poor, velocity declines, which results in a counter-stimulus effect. To illustrate the point through an extreme example, anything multiplied by zero is zero.[140]

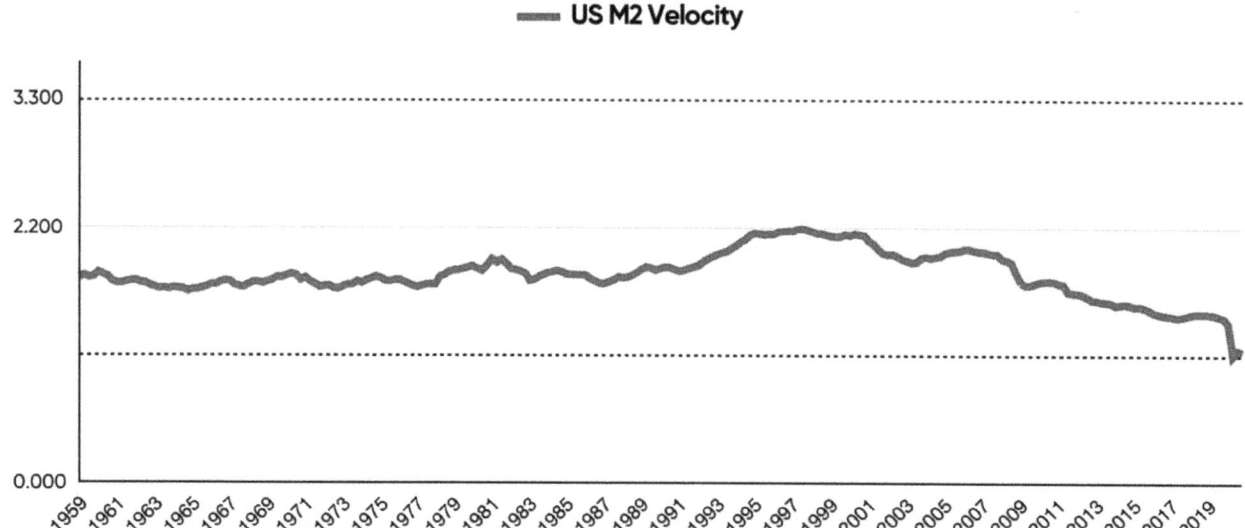

Fig 8.7 Illustrates the Velocity of the US (M2) Money Supply (1959 - 2020) (Source data: US Federal Reserve)

Therefore, if velocity ("V") were to crash to zero, regardless of the size of the money supply, there would simply be no economy ("PQ"). The money supply ("M") of any magnitude multiplied by zero, would simply be equal to zero, hence policy makers grow the money supply in a race against deflation (known as reflation). Since velocity is in persistent decline, compensation attempts by policy makers (to achieve inflation targets) through the manipulation of the broader policy variables (ZiRP, NiRP, QE, MMT etc.) cogently lends itself to a greater risk of undermining confidence in the system, potentially resulting in a crisis of confidence.

By contrast, if velocity were to increase against a substantial money supply, the stimulus effect would rapidly breach inflation targets, risking hyperinflation. Policy makers would normally respond to such circumstances by raising interest rates. However, with excess debt being carried by central banks as a consequence of QE, raising interest rates in turn raises the cost of servicing such debt. Thus, relegating any strategy pursued by policy makers to be less effective than in conventional circumstances, much akin to a Zeno's dichotomy paradox (see Zeno's Dichotomy Paradox, Chapter 2: Capital Evolution). Any options pursued may cultivate a systemic crisis, either through hyperinflation or unserviceable sovereign debt. In either case, confidence in the creditworthiness of public money is compromised (see Public vs. Private Money, Chapter 6: Money).

A systemic crisis brought about by *Quantitative Destruction* may compel policy makers to turn to a tangible means of restoring confidence. A possible, if not likely, predicament, which requires confidence to be restored through the use of an alternative anchor. A likely candidate to be considered, would be gold.

Since 2011, at least twelve states in the US have passed laws in recognition of gold and silver as legal tender.[141] In its 2012 and 2016 campaign platforms, the Republican Party called for a commission to investigate the viability of returning the US to a form of Gold Standard (see Gold Standard, Chapter 9: Gold).[142][143]

9

GOLD

"Money is Gold, and nothing else." - J.P. Morgan, 1912.

It is imperative to understand the role of Gold, when exploring finance, money and value. Gold is a paradoxical substance; it is an element, a mineral, a metal and a commodity. It is also the **universal medium of exchange.**

Gold is a monetary 'keystone,' which can be traded anywhere and with anyone in the world. Some consider it to be 'money of last resort.' Others are uncertain as to how to perceive or qualify it. Gold is money, however, it is not a currency. A critical distinction, as it is money which exists outside of the authority of central banks and governments, hence, not a currency.

The British Special Air Service (SAS), *along with the Special Boat Service (SBS)* are the elite special forces of the United Kingdom. When deployed into operational theatres abroad, operators are known to have been issued with twenty gold sovereigns.[144] The ability to trade these coins is a formidable advantage, which may be vital to the success of their missions and critical to their survival in hostile territories. A particularly useful tactic, whereby resources, shelter and allies may be procured, rather than coerced. Empowering operators with a unique capability to adapt and improvise in circumstances where discretion is essential. It illustrates a compelling phenomenon, whereby gold concentrates great value per volume and amidst systemic chaos where conventional instruments and institutions are in disarray or have collapsed, gold reprises its role as money of last resort. In such circumstances, gold may be spent **anywhere** for **anything** and with **anyone**.

'Sovereigns provided by the Ministry of Defence and carried by servicemen who, it was thought, might find themselves isolated and in need of bargaining power if confronted by unfriendly forces. Several sovereigns were used during the war, mainly by RAF crews shot down over enemy territory, SAS soldiers also carried sovereigns, as part of their kit, for use whilst on patrol.'[145]

- *Tony Blair, Prime Minister of the United Kingdom, 1997 – 2007.*

When all modes of finance stall and its institutions default, society turns to gold to restore confidence. Gold is not an asset in the traditional sense. It neither generates revenue, nor does it depreciate; it simply and unequivocally stores value. Most importantly, it carries **no counterparty risk**. It is, thus, neither legal tender nor dependent on any party or government to maintain its value and is impervious to inflation and deflation. Without exception, all forms of money, financial instruments and financial assets carry a counterparty risk apart from gold and a minority of other precious metals. As such, the necessity to cultivate trust in gold's authenticity and purity is imperative in sustaining its stature (see Assurance below). It is **universal**, **immutable** and **absolute**. Unlike other forms of money, which rely on confidence or a guarantee from a third-party such as central banks or governments (see Chapter 6: Money). It is mined from the earth, panned from the rivers, gathered and refined, however, mankind did not create it. It is highly sought-after and it is where financial institutions and markets seek out refuge from instability and uncertainty. Among precious metals and money, gold is at the apex. It is tangible and **indestructible**. Gold represents the pinnacle of financial **confidence.**

WHAT IS GOLD?

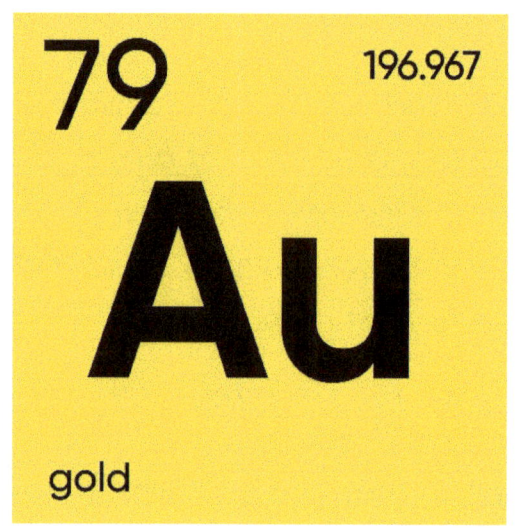

As an element and a mineral, gold is a transition metal with the chemical symbol '**Au**,' derived from the Latin name "Aurum" (shining dawn) and an atomic number of "79." On the periodic chart of elements, the atomic number is the number of protons found in the nucleus of every atom. Gold is among the highest atomic-numbered of naturally occurring elements. Its origins are extra-terrestrial, having jettisoned from star explosions, and thereafter, journeyed across the galaxy, ultimately finding its way to earth, via asteroid bombardments approximately four-billion years ago.

Over time, gold has been concentrated within the earth's crust forming ore deposits through a spectrum of geological, biological, physical and chemical processes.

Primary ore deposits are predominantly found in rock, such as quartz veins, whereas secondary ore deposits are largely found in the form of fragments within sand, such as riverbeds. The latter is largely due to gold in primary deposits being exposed to the elements such as wind and rain, known as Eluvial Gold. Gold's resilience, frees it from rock, eroded through such exposure and weathering. Over millennia, gravity and water movement allows it to eventually collect and concentrate in river basins as a result of run off. This forms Alluvial Gold.

Primary ore deposit (Eluvia) types include:

- Porphyry Copper Gold

- Epithermal Gold-Silver+

- Skarn Gold+

- Iron-oxide-Copper-Gold

- Intrusion related Gold

- Orogenic lode Gold

- Carlin-type Gold

- Volcanic-hosted massive Sulphide

- Conglomerate-hosted Gold-Uranium

Gold in its purist form has a distinct, bright and slightly reddish yellow colour. When of a high purity, well-formed and polished, it has an alluring and intoxicating shine.

The shine is the result of the metal's surface absorbing all wavelengths of incident light, which 'excite' the electrons within. This 'excitement,' causes these electrons to 'jump' (elevate) to a higher unoccupied energy level within the metal's structure. This phenomenon results in the majority of the incident light being re-emitted at the metal's surface. The combination of light re-emittance combined with its distinctive colour, bequeaths gold with a unique and warming lustre.

People are accustomed to handling metallic objects of various sizes, whether it be tools or other everyday objects. When handling gold, people are conditioned to expect it to be of similar mass to a metallic object of comparable size.

However, in handling gold, the tactile nature of its mass, relative to physical size, will surprise an infrequent handler. This is due to gold's high density, resulting in a perceptively heavier metal. A cubic centimetre (cc) of fine gold has a mass of 19.3 grams. By comparison, it is almost identical in density and mass to Tungsten (Wolfram) at 19.25g per cc, however, significantly heavier than Iron (Fe) at 7.87g per cc.

Metal	Mass (grams per cc)
Iron	7.87
Tungsten	19.25
Gold	19.30

It is an instinctive human reaction to perceive an object as valuable, as a result of being heavy relative to its size. Its mass aids significantly in determining whether a gold item is genuine, as there are few materials comparable in mass and no materials which are identical. Furthermore, relative to volume, gold is distinct in visual appearance. Mass alone is insufficient in establishing credibility. Hence, a means of verifying density is required (see Assurance below).

WHY GOLD?

From the outset, in examining how and why it is of value, anyone who has seen or handled gold should be able to convey that instinctively it aesthetically appears and feels valuable.

Gold has been the foundation of monetary value for millennia. Societies and our economies have placed value on gold, as we as people are physically and emotionally drawn to it. We perceive it as a natural and sustainable store of intrinsic value.

PROPERTIES

Although a dense metal, gold is soft, ductile and malleable (2 on the Mohs scale); Gold is the most malleable of all known metals, with a relatively low melting temperature at 1064 degrees Celsius when compared with Iron, which melts at 1538 degrees Celsius.

Metal	Melting Temperature		Boiling Temperature	
	Celsius/Centigrade	Farenheit	Celsius/Centigrade	Farenheit
Gold	1064	1947.2	2700	4892
Iron	1538	2800.4	2862	5183.6
Tungsten (Wolfram)	3422	6191.6	5555	10031

These properties make it an extraordinarily versatile material, easy to smelt, strike and fashion into all manner of objects including bars, jewellery, coins, wire and even foil.

A single gram, can be beaten into a one metre squared sheet. Gold can also be drawn into a wire of single-atom width and stretched to considerable lengths before it is broken.

As one of the transition metals, gold is highly conductive of heat and electricity, which has given rise to a plethora of industrial applications. Some notable examples include Nano wires, super-conductive circuitry and visor shielding in modern space suits.

INDESTRUCTIBLE

These characteristics contribute to gold's desirability in one form or another, however, in order to be a sustainable and durable store of value, that which differentiates gold, is its near indestructibility.

As an element, it is incredibly resistant to reactions with other chemical elements. Impervious to oxidation, gold does not rust, and although it may appear tarnished, it is easily cleaned, restoring it to its original state.

Although extremely resilient, there's a minority of exceptions against which gold is vulnerable. Gold is soluble in 'Aqua Regia' (Latin for 'Royal Water,' a solution of 1:3 parts Nitric and Hydrochloric acids). Gold is additionally soluble in Mercury, as well as alkaline solutions of Cyanide.

ACID TEST

Apart from obscure exceptions, gold's non-reactive nature, led to Nitric acid being widely adopted in the refinement process and furthermore, in testing for the presence, thereof. Thus, the origin of the term, 'the acid test.' Gold is insoluble in Nitric acid, which effortlessly dissolves base metals, however, leaves gold unaffected. Additionally, gold is insoluble in acids, such as Sulphuric, Hydrofluoric, Hydrochloric and Hydrobromic, making it fairly unique, in terms of resilience amongst all known metals and elements as a whole.

ALLOYS

Another property of gold is its ability to be blended with other metals to form alloys. This is essential in jewellery making and coin striking, in order to 'harden' gold. Gold alloys improve scratch-resistance and prevent bending or breaking. Gold itself is not susceptible to damage, however, its malleable (soft/pliable) yet brittle nature, lacks the protection of aesthetic and numismatic resilience afforded to 'harder' metals.

MEASUREMENT

Purity (%)	Carat (no. of 24 parts)	Hallmark
25	6	250
33.3	8	333
37.5	9	375
41.7	10	417
50	12	500
58.3	14	583
62.5	15	625
75	18	750
83.3	20	833
87.5	21	875
91.6	22	916
99.6	24	999

Gold has its own unique measurement system. Purity is assessed based on the 'carat system,' in which each carat is equal to 4.167% gold content out of a total of twenty-four parts. 'Fineness' however, refers to parts per thousand of gold in an alloy. By way of an example, "three-nines fine" (.999) would correspond to 99.9% purity. In the US, 'carats' are used as a weight measurement for gemstones, therefore in the context of gold, 'carat' becomes 'karats' to avoid confusion. Twenty-four carat gold for all intents and purposes is considered to be of the highest purity, where 24/24 parts are gold. In practice however, all gold objects are alloyed to increase their hardness, dependent on the application, and occasionally in order to alter the colour or to dilute the cost of the material, or combinations thereof.

Gold is often used to envelope less expensive items altogether. A process known as gilding, usually achieved through electroplating. This follows the same principle as mentioned previously. By way of example, to gild less expensive items, or to fashion jewellery.

24 carat (karat), abbreviated to 24ct. (24k), is of .999 fineness (99.9% pure) or above. There is always an allowance for a minute proportion of impurity. This is also known as 'Fine Gold' and accepted as pure.

ASSURANCE

Hallmarks display the purity assessment of precious metals, which is verified by an Assay Office. Assays discharge their function under the authority and requirements of the International Convention of Hallmarks.[146] This functions as a means of preventing fraud in the sale of precious metals by providing an independent assessment of the precious metal before it is sold to jewellers or other wholesale consumers. Assaying is the determination of whether the precious metal content meets the stated purity stipulated by the Hallmark. This provides a vital means of independent assurance, in order to cultivate trust in the precious metal's authenticity. Assay Offices apply their own markings to demonstrate their approval.

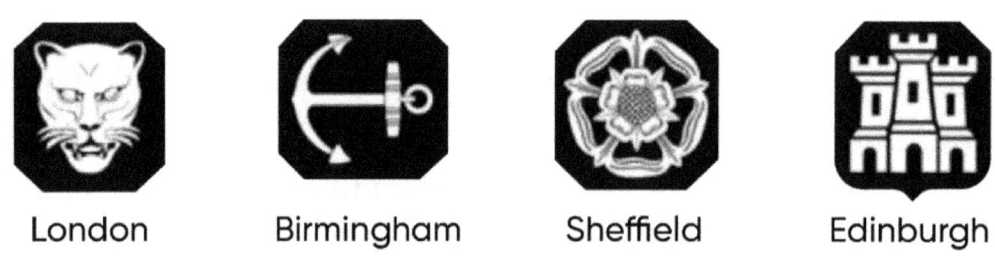

London   Birmingham   Sheffield   Edinburgh

Fig 9.1 above are British Assay Office marks as examples.

Assay Offices use X-Ray Fluorescence Spectrometers to assess purity. This method is non-intrusive and highly accurate. X-Ray Fluorescence Spectrometry is a trusted means of identifying elements and their associated density. The previous method of Fire Assay was largely deprecated in the 1980s. Fire Assay is a highly accurate method for discerning the content of gold, silver and other precious metals in ores or alloys. The process requires melting the sample being tested in conjunction with fluxes and reducing agents in an induction furnace. After cooling, the other materials are separated from the gold by dissolving them in reagents and/or oxidising them. The mass of the pure gold may then be determined.[147]

REFINEMENT

Refineries predominantly use the Miller Process, invented by Francis Bowyer Miller (1828 - 1887), patented in Britain in 1867. During the (Miller) refinement process, gold is melted in an induction furnace typically in lots of up to 400 kilograms. Refineries use Chlorine, which is blown through the melt, converting base metals and silver into chlorides. These chlorides either rise to the surface after which they are skimmed off, or due to being volatile, are removed with the off-gas. The process typically elapses over a period of 60 - 90 minutes, yielding a purity of at least 99.5%.

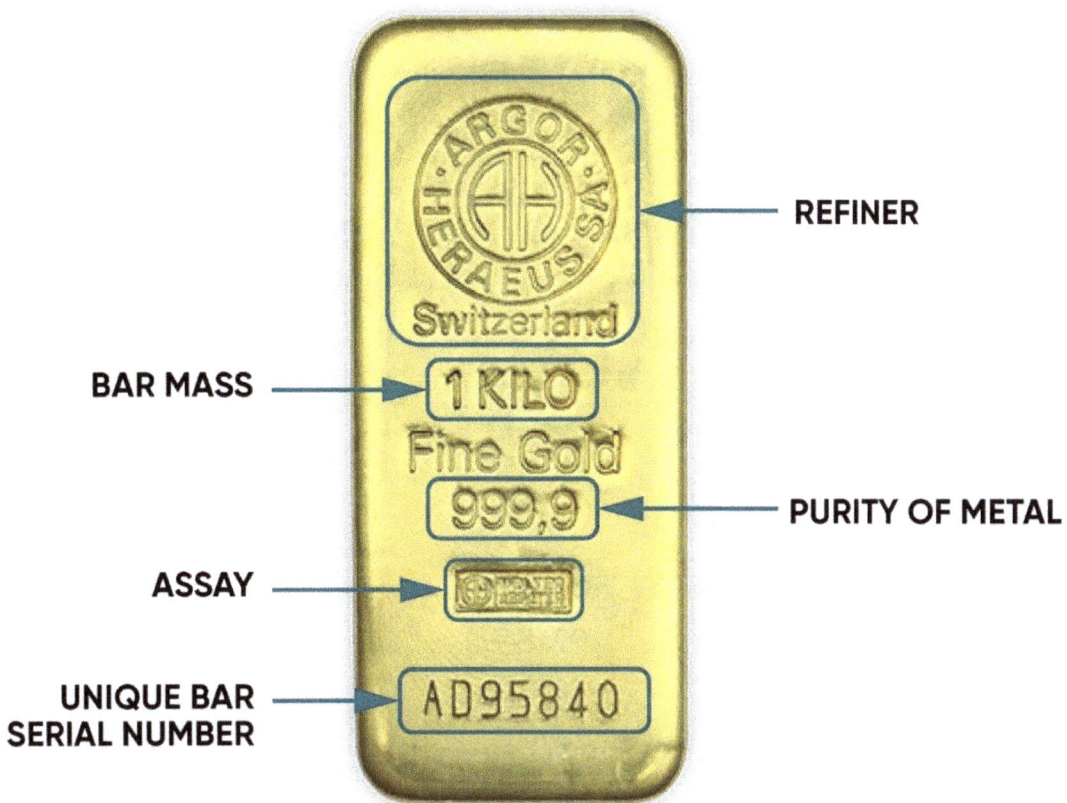

The gold is sampled at each stage of the process and is, thereafter, cast into bars weighing 400 ounces (12.5 kilograms), which are stamped (serial numbered), weighed and packed. Every bar is marked with a unique serial number. Other markings typically include that of the refinery (maker's mark), the hallmark (or purity/fineness notation), the mass and an assay office mark.[148] It is not uncommon for the year the bar was cast to be marked on bars, although this is not always the case.

FINENESS (PURITY)

Producing bullion of greater purity than 99.5% relies on exploiting an electrolytic process. Gold refined to a purity of 99.5% is not always of a sufficient purity for certain industrial and technical applications. Desirability for the production of small investment bars is another such driver for greater purity demand. To obtain greater purity levels, the gold is further refined electrolytically.[149] This method of electrolytic refinement is known as the Wohlwill Process, introduced by Wolf Emil Wohlwill (1835 - 1912) in Hamburg, Germany in 1878.

There are a number of refineries that have consistently produced purities closer to 100%, such as the Royal Mint in the United Kingdom, which has produced Gold bullion as pure as 99.99% (four-nines-fine). The Canadian Royal Mint has produced purer bullion of 99.999% (five-nines-fine) and the Perth Mint in Australia producing the purest thus far, of 99.9999% (six-nines-fine).

Refinery	Purity (%)	Country
Royal Mint	99.99	United Kingdom
Canadian Royal Mint	99.999	Canada
Perth Mint	99.9999	Australia

Once purity has been established, gold is measured in mass. While bars are commonly available in a broad variety of metric denominations from 1g to 12.5kg, the latter is equivalent to 400 ounces of 24ct (.999) fine gold and is known as a 'London Good Delivery Bar.'

The 'Good Delivery' specification are the rules set out by the London Bullion Market Association (LBMA) in order to set the standards describing and governing the physical characteristics of Gold and Silver bars for settlement, in the London wholesale bullion market. It additionally furnishes the criteria that refineries must meet, for listing on the LBMA Good Delivery List.[150]

The term 'Bullion' refers to Gold, Silver or other precious metals in the form of bars, ingots or coins, which are centred on the 'store of value' concept (see Chapter 6: Money). Unrefined precious metals or precious metals fashioned into a format for industrial purposes, are not considered to be bullion.

MASS MEASUREMENTS

Outside of metric denominations, there are three prominent mass measurements for Gold.

Unit	Metric Mass (grams)	Imperial Mass (ounces)
Tola	10 g	0.35274 oz
Tael	37.7994 g	1.3333 oz
Troy Ounce	31.1035 g	1.0971 oz

The first is a 'Tola,' also spelled 'Tolah' or 'Tole,' derived from the Sanskrit word 'Tol' and dating back to the Vedic age (1500 - 1100 B.C.), meaning 'weight' or 'weighing.' Tola was introduced by ancient India and some Asians countries to measure the mass of gold.

The mass of one Tola today, is equivalent to 10g, however, there are variations where a Tola is equivalent to 180 troy grains, which is equivalent to 3 eighths of a Troy ounce or 11.663808g. Furthermore, during the British rule of India, Tola was used as a base measurement for commodities such as grain. At the time, one Tola was an equivalent to 175.9 troy grains or 11.33980925g.

The second noteworthy measurement, prevalent in the Asian markets is the 'Tael.' A Tael is equivalent to 37.8g. The 'five-tael biscuit' is a common gold bar denomination traded in Hong Kong and mainland China.

The third and arguably the most prevalent mass measurement for gold, is the Troy Ounce, equivalent to 31.1035g. A Troy ounce is equivalent to 1.09714 ounces. It is the unit against which the US dollar price of Gold is measured, which in turn establishes the price of gold in all currencies and countries throughout the world. This is due to the US dollar's status as the principal global reserve currency (see Chapter 12: Global Monetary System). Although once uniquely synonymous with gold, troy ounces are now used as the dollar-pricing-unit against all precious metals globally. Other examples include that of Silver and Platinum.

GOLD PRODUCERS

As of 2020, out of an estimated 185000 - 190000 metric tonnes of gold in circulation, approximately 150000 tonnes is in private holdings across the globe. New metal enters the market at a rate of approximately 1.4% - 1.6% per annum. This broadly aligns with annual global population growth.

Until 2006, the South African mining industry produced the highest volumes of gold annually. In 1970 annual output peaked at approximately 1000 metric tonnes. Thereafter, output had declined gradually, due to diminishing investment and poor industry confidence in the long-term prospects of South African mining. This was due to an unsustainable political posture during the apartheid era weighing increasingly in the mining industry's investment decisions. Annual mining output consequently declined to 620 metric tonnes in

1993.[151] Since the transition to a democracy at the end of the apartheid era in 1994 (see below), mining companies have been plagued by greater uncertainty over mineral rights, widespread political corruption and government interference. Furthermore, the mining industry has experienced political resistance to exploiting efficient mining technologies. The latter increases reliance on high-numbers of domestic labourers (miners) and reduces safety through the use of antiquated technologies and methods. The mining industry has consequently underinvested in South African gold mining operations and seen production diminish by a commensurate proportion. This brings into acute focus the importance of the *rule of law* and the ability to enforce such, in cultivating confidence in a business environment.

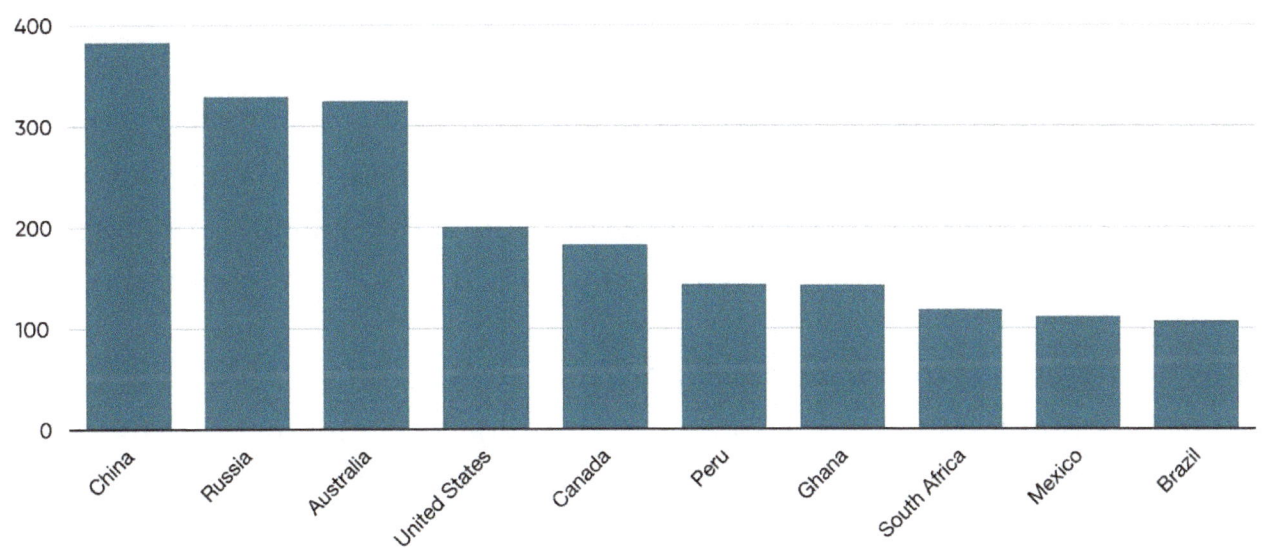

Fig 9.2 Top 10 Gold Mining Countries 2019 (Metric tonnes per annum)

Gold is abundant enough on a global scale so that all countries and their citizens could own a portion of it, however sufficiently scarce, that it can't be found everywhere, nor in unlimited quantities.

China, Russia and Australia have led global output volumes, producing in excess of the annual average of 204 tonnes, among top output countries. Labour costs are substantially higher in Australia than in China, Russia or South Africa. However, in the face of uncertainty surrounding mineral rights, government interference and political corruption, mining companies tend to commit their larger-scale investments toward environments in which they can expect these investments to be secure. Hence, investment in Australia has been prevalent, where although costs are higher, conditions are more certain and the business climate is both stable, as well as predictable.

GOLD RESERVES

Gold has fulfilled an integral role in the various monetary systems for centuries. It has functioned as a unit of account, a medium of exchange and a monetary anchor (store of value). While gold's official role has evolved under the existing system of floating exchange rates, it has retained most of the characteristics of money (see Chapter 6: Money).

With regards to fiat currencies however, central banks may expand their money supply and balance sheets elastically, using discretionary monetary policy in order to effect adjustments (see Monetary Policy, Chapter 8: Economic Cycles). Although the value of fiat currencies is linked to whether people have confidence that governments are willing and able to discharge their obligations.

Gold is different, as the available supply of the metal changes little over time, growing incrementally by less than two-percent per annum through mining production. Gold's geological scarcity and its role as a hard currency enable it to function as a natural hedge to fiat money as global GDP growth of 3% - 4% drives a commensurate nominal growth in the fiat money supply. Thus, over the course of the 20th century, gold vastly outperformed all major currencies as a store of value.

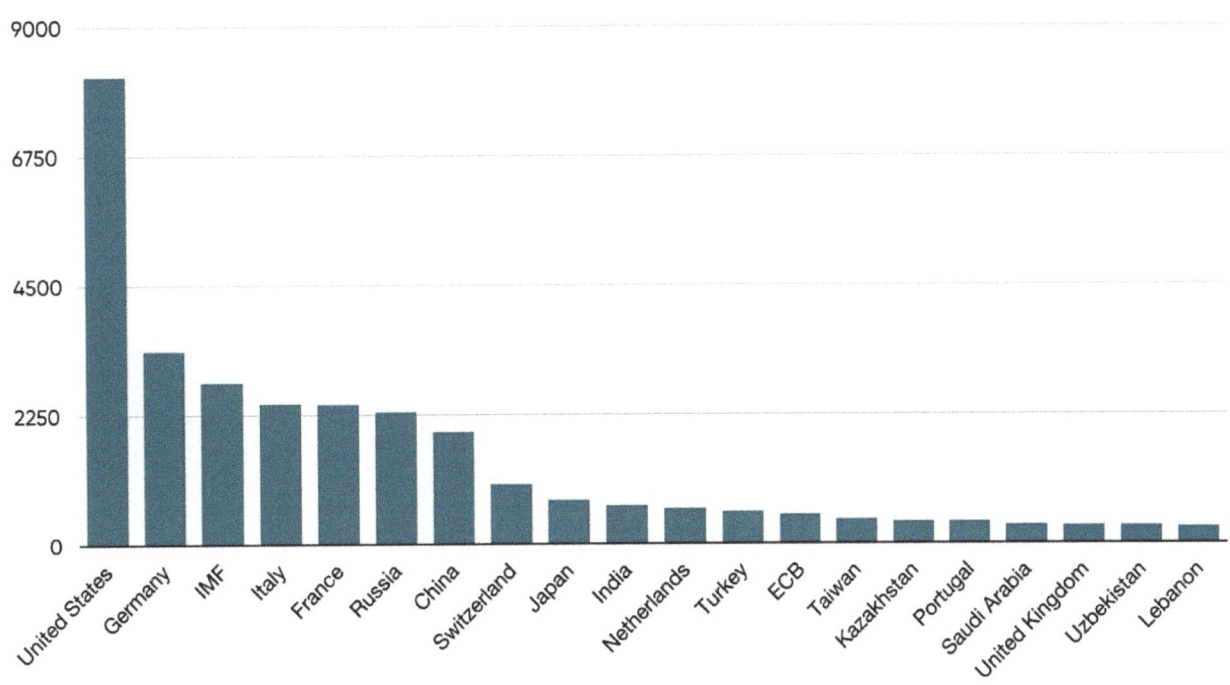

Fig 9.3 Top 20 Gold Reserves holdings as of 2020 (Metric Tonnes)

As such, gold is sought-after for its safety as a supply-constrained hard asset, particularly as governments and central banks implement confidence-erosive (discretionary) fiscal and monetary policies. Central banks use gold in the same way. It is viewed as an integral part of a country's foreign reserves, providing diversification and insulation against geopolitical and sovereign risks affecting the reserves held in treasuries.

Should a nation state default on its debts and exhaust its reserves, the asset of greatest appeal on the central bank's balance sheet will be its gold reserves. These reserves may be used to effect a settlement or placate creditors while alternative assets are liquidated. While this may seem to be descriptive of an extremely unlikely scenario, central banks ostensibly view their gold holdings as a form of insurance against such a possibility coming to fruition. Thus, to some extent a country's solvency is equated with the extent of its holdings in gold reserves.

Central banks and the International Monetary Fund (IMF), collectively hold approximately 35000 - 40000 tonnes in their vaults and on their balance sheets. Prior to the GFC, central banks were either net holders or net sellers of gold. Since the GFC, many of these institutions have altered course and become net buyers.[152] This behaviour signals a recognition that the monetary system is increasingly unstable and the vast quantities of debt accrued since the GFC may provoke a future systemic collapse (see Exter's Pyramid below).

Fig 9.4 London Good Delivery (400 ounce / 12.5kg) fine gold bars (Source: LBMA[153])

GOLD SPECIE

Gold features all six of the characteristics of money - valuable, durable, divisible, portable, recognisable and scarce (see Chapter 6: Money). However, arguably in larger quantities it is less portable due to its mass. *Portability* has long been gold's greatest weakness as a *medium of exchange*. This is far outweighed by its natural appeal and unequalled durability (see Indestructible above) which has contributed to a persistent demand for gold specie (coins). Hence, specie have historically persisted as gold's most successful monetary format. Ultimately, paper banknotes and currencies emerged in a further attempt to address this deficit.

Arguably the most famous of gold bullion coins is the South African Kruger Rand. The Kruger Rand was first minted in 1967 in order to better market South African gold around the world.

On the obverse side of the coin is a side-profile depiction of Stephanus Johannes Paulus "Paul" Kruger, president of the South African Republic from 1883 - 1900. It derives its designation from a combination of the president's name and 'Rand,' the name of South Africa's fiat currency. 'Rand,' (Dutch for 'ridge'), is derived from 'Witwatersrand.' The Witwatersrand ('White Water Ridge', in Afrikaans), where the largest gold find in history was discovered in 1886, is the ridge upon which the city of Johannesburg was built. Johannesburg, now South Africa's financial hub, is the area where the majority of South African primary (Eluvial) gold ore deposits were discovered, which produced an estimated 25% of the world's gold by 1899 and approximately 40% by 1985.[154] The reverse side of the coin depicts a Springbok antelope, South Africa's national animal.

Under South African law, there is a requirement that all newly mined gold must be offered to the South African Reserve Bank (Central Bank) within thirty days of production.

Kruger Rand are considered to be part of South African legal tender, since the passing of the South African Reserve Bank Act 1989. The coin is struck from an alloy, to increase its hardness. An alloy is used, in an effort to improve the coin's durability to handling and wear, while assigning its value against the most common denomination of gold, the Troy ounce. By design, this facilitates convenience in establishing its price, regardless of where in the world it is being traded.

The coin's empirical mass is 1.09 Troy ounces equivalent to 33.93g. The composition is one Troy ounce of 24ct (fine or 99.9% pure) gold, making up 91.67% alloyed with 8.33% copper. The net result is a 22 carat coin.

The seigniorage (numismatic value) of the coin is zero, meaning that the cost of the copper, minting the coin, and its aesthetic appearance are not reflected in the coin's price. The Kruger Rand's price, like all gold bullion, is fixed based on its mass and purity in US dollars.

Following in the footsteps of the South African Kruger Rand, a number of Troy ounce denominated, fine gold coins have emerged. These are minted by refineries across the globe. The United States, the United Kingdom, Australia, Canada, China and several others, all produce comparable bullion coins (and fractional coins), to solicit a portion of the global market share. Historically, South Africa dominated this market almost exclusively for several decades. Extraterritorial sanctions in the 1980s during the Apartheid era (1948 - 1994) however, greatly impacted South Africa's market for Kruger Rand, internationally (see Extraterritorial Sanctions, Chapter 13: Global Trade Rails). Much like South Africa, a number of gold specie producing countries now recognise their gold coins as *legal tender*. Since legal tender is free of GST, VAT and CGT, this raises their appeal as a *tax-free* store of value.

STORE OF VALUE

Gold is often referred to as a 'hedge against inflation' or a 'safe haven' for investors, during periods of turbulent economic instability or financial stress. Instability diminishes confidence. In such circumstances of uncertainty and increased risk, investment is driven away from conventional instruments such as bonds, equities and derivatives. This behaviour causes markets to become volatile, drastically reducing their appeal, until such time as perceived stability has been restored. In essence, gold isn't isolated to providing a safe-haven exclusively during periods of uncertainty. Gold regardless of the circumstances, is a definitive *store of value*.

Investors channel capital into revenue generating assets or portfolios in order to yield a return. This return could take the form of interest, dividends, capital gains or combinations thereof, however, gold offers no such returns. Gold effectively stores purchasing power.

By way of example, purchasing a good or service for an ounce of gold, today, should enable a comparable purchase for the same value good or service for an ounce of gold a decade later, or even a century later (within a reasonably small margin of variance). Essentially, gold acts as an immutable store of value, which is shielded from inflationary and deflationary influences generally experienced by fiat currencies. To illustrate this phenomenon, during the most deflationary 'peacetime' period in the 20th century, 1927 - 1934, that of the period leading up to and including the early years of the Great Depression (see The Great Depression below) the price of gold increased by almost 70%, whereas in the most inflationary period of the latter half of the 20th century 1965 - 1982 (Fig 8.1) known as 'The Great Inflation,' gold increased in price from $35 to a peak of $850 per Troy ounce (see Dollar Confidence Crisis, Chapter 10: Financialisation). Hence, regardless of inflationary or deflationary conditions, gold prevails as a *store of value*. Gold, thus, acts as a 'barometer' for the value of fiat currencies. Should the price of Gold rise, this indicates that the currency is devaluing. Should the price reduce, the converse is true.

There are, however, broader factors to consider, such as supply and demand. Gold is, in addition to its broader roles, a commodity. Should the market supply increase by a significant order of magnitude, the dollar price for gold will likely reduce. The converse is true if either demand increases, or if supply were to suddenly reduce. These influences create short-term volatility in the dollar price of gold, however, price fluctuations ultimately correct themselves and stabilise. The corrected price level, relative to value, ultimately prevails.

Many economists will argue that gold and other precious metals are perpetually volatile and the price is rarely stable, however, the volatility observed, reflects that of the US dollar's purchasing power, governed by confidence, supply, liquidity and interest rates. Consequently, it is the value of the US dollar that fluctuates, rather than the value of gold.

Other fiat currencies are subject to varying exchange rates against the US dollar, each with varying magnitudes of volatility, which ultimately reflects each currency's global purchasing power. The fluctuations in the dollar price of gold, observed on a short-interval-basis, which oscillates within varying levels of volatility is largely resultant of the decoupling of gold as backing for the US dollar (see Nixon Shock, Chapter 12: Global Monetary System).

Historically, when currency was directly underpinned by Gold (specie standard rule), through the periods described as being under 'The Classical Gold Standard,' 'The Gold Exchange Standard' and 'The Dollar-Gold Standard,' this monetary paradigm was that of 'Metallism' (see below). Historically, this shielded the US dollar and other currencies from the levels of inflation, observed during the 1970s (see Dollar Confidence Crisis, Chapter: 10 Financialisation).

Investors typically hold a percentage of their wealth in gold, as a hedge against inflation, deflation or mitigation against financial collapse. In periods of uncertainty brought about by either financial stress or conflict, the market demands for gold rises until confidence is restored.

'A currency, to be perfect, should be absolutely invariable in value.'

- David Ricardo (1772 - 1823), Principles of Political Economy and Taxation, 1817.

GOLD STANDARD

Since around the year 1500 onwards, gold has been recognised as a standard *medium of exchange* for international trade.

Historically, gold has long played a critical role in the international monetary system. Gold coins were originally struck in 550 B.C. by order of King Croesus of Lydia (now a region within Turkey).[155] Although in practice, many of the early gold coins were minted from electrum (an alloy predominantly consisting of gold and silver) due to poor refinement capabilities at the time. These coins then circulated through numerous countries prior to the introduction of paper money in these regions.

Following the widespread adoption of paper money in the 17th century, promissory notes gave way to banknotes, which maintained an explicit link to gold and importantly were freely redeemable for gold upon demand.

The 'Gold Standard' and other specie standard variations thereof, refers to this historical underpinning of currency with gold.

As domestic and international trade grew, so did the necessity for greater exchange of money to facilitate such transactions. This evolved into a practice of issuing currencies which were either specie, as well as eventually issuing banknotes (varying denominations), which were redeemable for gold or silver. In some instances a 'bimetallic standard' (combination of Gold and Silver) was embraced, at fixed ratios to a nation's currency. An early example of this was the Aureus. The Aureus was a gold coin of ancient Rome, valued at a ratio of 25:1 in silver Denarii. A contemporary example was that of the US in 1792, where a silver-to-gold ratio of 15:1 was adopted.[156] As silver declined in value, this continually created pressure to displace gold from circulation. An example of Gresham's Law (see Gresham's Law, Chapter 6: Money).

Countries which could not fulfil an exchange of currency-to-gold themselves, fixed their currency to other currencies that could do so. This led to fixed-exchange-rates between currencies and a climate where domestic currencies were freely convertible to gold with no restrictions on the imports or exports of the precious metal between countries.

As the oldest currency still in existence, British Pound Sterling, derives its designation from originally being redeemable for a pound (1 lb) of sterling silver, at the outset of its creation. Like all modern currencies, which are fiat based, this association has long been decoupled from precious metals, yet the name has remained.

The paradigm of pegging money to a precious metal is known as 'Metallism.' The opposing paradigm is known as 'Chartalism,' a concept introduced in German economist, Georg Friedrich Knapp's 'State Theory of Money,' published in 1905 (translated from German to English in 1924).[157] Fiat money is a product of the 'Chartalism' era. In the Chartalism paradigm, central banks are able to engage in *discretionary policy making*, which affords central banks significant flexibility in effecting monetary policy (see Monetary Policy, Chapter 8: Economic Cycles).

From the 1870s - 1914 is known as the period of the 'Classical Gold Standard,' although the rise of a Gold Standard began in 1660.

During this era, central banks were constrained to a strict rules-based system known as a *commitment policy* paradigm, in which unlike a *discretionary policy* paradigm they were constrained in performing three key monetary policy functions.

1. Maintaining convertibility of representative currency to gold at a fixed price

2. Defending the exchange rate

3. Expediting the adjustment process to rebalance any payment imbalances that may have occurred

Referring to the first and second of these monetary policy functions, the prevalent constraint of this monetary system is evident in that the supply of money in circulation must at all times correlate directly to, or to a multiple of, the equivalent quantity of gold held by central banks. This is the concept from which, central bank Gold Reserves originates (see above), which persists to the present day. Prior to this, banks issued banknotes and held gold to back the notes which they had issued.

PRICE–SPECIE FLOW MECHANISM

The third monetary policy function, when correctly fulfilled, theoretically determined that the global monetary system under the classical gold standard was self-correcting as the *balance of payments* between countries were periodically settled in bullion. Under this mechanism, countries with a trade or balance surplus would experience gold inflows as a result of settlement, while countries with a trade or balance deficit would experience gold outflows. The latter would reduce the domestic money supply, place pressure on domestic price levels, drive greater competition and therefore impose a correction in the balance of payments deficit.

The converse would be true for a country that had experienced an inflow, hence, creating an economic cycle of peaks and troughs between countries trading with one another. This is known as the 'price-specie flow mechanism' as set out in 'On the Balance of Trade' by 18th century economist and philosopher, David Hume, in 1752.[158]

THE GREAT WAR

Prior to the outbreak of the Great War (1914 - 1918), Great Britain, the United States and most of the world, including every country in Europe, maintained the Gold Standard.

Internationally, this resulted in gold standard countries being committed to maintain a fixed-exchange-rate with each other (see above), while facilitating the flow of goods and capital among one another (as per the price-specie flow mechanism). This posture committed these countries to domestically limiting the expansion of money and credit, which in turn restrained inflationary pressures.

Although this 'monetary discipline' (commitment policy) provided for nominal stability in the long run, the global economy suffered in the short-term from periodic depressions due to fluctuations in the world's supply of, and demand for gold. A further symptom of this credit constraint was a hindrance in the ability to effect rapid economic growth (see Credit & Debt, Chapter 8: Economic Cycles). Growth although possible, however, was limited to the volume of gold that facilitated the expansion of the money supply to make credit available.

At the time, British Pound Sterling's status as the principal global reserve currency, instilled trust and confidence in the currency's stability. This helped preserve the durability of the international Gold Standard almost symbiotically (see Monetary Hegemony, Chapter 11: Hegemonic Dominance).

In order to preserve this confidence during the war, Britain relied on keeping the Pound above the gold export point of the US dollar, which at the time was the principal 'neutral' currency. In order to accomplish this, Britain, and other warring nations, shipped large quantities of gold to the US in exchange for desperately needed commodity imports to sustain their economies.

These gold exports aided in keeping exchange rates near parity during the period of US neutrality from August 1914 to April 1917. Over this short period, the US gold stockpile substantially increased, nearly doubling in volume. While Britain needed to support the Pound, and yet still needed to import war supplies, the realisation became apparent that continued gold exports could not sustain these dual objectives without undermining global confidence in the Pound.[159]

This led to Great Britain and its allies resorting to mass international borrowing, particularly from the US, in order to maintain the frail exchange rate parities. As the war lingered on, this period of borrowing led to the emergence of a sophisticated network of international lending, which created a comprehensive web of global debt structure.[160]

Maintaining good standing in currency values and credit was critical to Britain and Europe in order to rebuild and recover after the war. By 1919, almost every country still regarded the Gold Standard as an essential institution, however, of the world powers only the US could be considered a Gold Standard country.

The US had embargoed the export of gold, which partially suspended the Gold Standard from September 1917 until June 1919.[161] Hence, the US had largely maintained its accrued gold stock after joining the war.

In 1924, the US Federal Reserve and J.P. Morgan & Co. assisted Britain in preparation to return to the Gold Standard through cutting the discount rate (base rate), as well as providing loans. In April 1925, Winston Churchill, then Chancellor of the Exchequer, signalled Britain's return to the Gold Standard with the announcement that the Gold and Silver Export Control Act 1920 would not be renewed. The act was due to expire at the end of 1925. In May 1925, Britain passed the Gold Standard Act 1925, which temporarily restored the Gold Standard, known since as 'The Gold Exchange Standard.'[162]

In September 1931, Britain abandoned the Gold Standard (Gold Exchange Standard) permanently, leaving the US as the only world power remaining with a gold-pegged currency. This followed the crash of the New York Stock Exchange in October 1929 and occurred while the US was battling the Great Depression. The Gold Exchange Standard failed predominantly due to Churchill's attempt to restore parity with pre-war levels. In other words, Britain had substantially increased its money supply during the war while it was off the Gold Standard.[163] Churchill had subsequently attempted to restore the Gold Standard at the original pre-war peg, which was consistent with past precedent in a return to the 'specie standard rule' once the circumstances (such as a war) which prompted the deviation had subsided.[164] However, in lieu of repricing gold to reflect the prevailing ratio of money-to-gold, this attempt to restore parity caused Britain to experience extreme deflation, deepening the effects of the depression, and ultimately seeing the Gold Exchange Standard crumble.[165]

THE GREAT DEPRESSION

[166] In March 1933, then newly elected US President, Franklin D. Roosevelt (1882 - 1945) suspended gold convertibility and exports. In addition, Roosevelt instituted a four-day banking holiday, which shutdown the banking system, including the Federal Reserve, under the authority granted by the Emergency Banking Act 1933. In April 1933, Roosevelt signed Executive Order 6102, which compelled US citizens and entities to surrender their gold coins, bullion and gold certificates within three weeks, to the Federal Reserve by May 1st 1933. Those that didn't comply would face fines of up to ten-thousand-dollars and/or up to five-to-ten year's imprisonment.[167] Roosevelt had unilaterally made it illegal for US citizens to own gold by fiat. A mandate that persisted until President Gerald R. Ford Jr. (1913 - 2006) signed a bill legalising gold ownership (S. 2665 Pub.L 93-373)[168], which ended the ban on December 31st 1974, over forty-years later.[169]

The 'surrendered' gold was 'purchased' from the US public at the prevailing official price of $20.67 per Troy ounce. The 'forcibly purchased' bullion and coins were smelted, cast into bars and sent to the US Federal Reserve's Bullion Depository. Over half of this bullion is stored in Fort Knox, Kentucky (see Depositories below). In January 1934, Congress passed the Gold Reserve Act 1934, which empowered Roosevelt to revalue gold to $35 per Troy ounce, effectively inflating the money supply by almost 70% and devaluing the US dollar by over 40%. A consequence of Roosevelt's action was to provide the welfare statists (those who support policies intended to bring about a welfare state)[170] with the money to unshackle controls on fiscal and deficit spending at the expense of the dollar's value. This is an emblematic example of resorting to the use of 'Wealth Redistribution' as a means of escaping a 'Liquidity Trap' (see Unconventional Methods, Chapter 8: Economic Cycles). The financial ingenuity of these acts, engineered the liquidity to fund the 'New Deal.' This was an effective strategy to overcome the dire (deflationary) climate of the depression, while simultaneously stimulating aggregate demand, albeit at the expense of American wealth preservation.

'The financial policy of the welfare state requires that there be no way for the owners of wealth to protect themselves. This is the shabby secret of the welfare statists' tirades against Gold. Deficit spending is simply a scheme for the confiscation of wealth. Gold stands in the way of this insidious process. It stands as a protector of property rights. If one grasps this, one has no difficulty in understanding the statists' antagonism toward the Gold standard.'[171]

- Dr. Alan Greenspan, 1966.

The Gold Reserve Act, 1934, greatly diminished the influence of the Gold Standard, ultimately fixing the price at a new level and restricting dollar redemptions exclusively to international settlements. However, this enabled the US to keep the dollar in alignment with the 'specie standard rule,' retaining both the dollar's as well as the Federal Reserve's international credibility.

As a result of this new 'higher' price, or competitive devaluation of the dollar, the US Gold supply soared, pouring into the Federal Reserve from London,

Paris and other bullion markets. This forced other gold-pegged countries to abandon the Gold Standard and devalue their currencies or face the economic peril of further deflation (see The Great War above).

On balance, Roosevelt's ingenuity, in this regard, is often condemned as ruthless, draconian and unthinkable. However, the strategy was quite ingenious. Unlike Churchill's attempt to restore the Gold Standard at parity, which instigated a devastating deflationary effect, Roosevelt realised that the pathway out of the Great Depression was through inflation. The 'repatriation' (forced public sale) of gold enabled the Federal Reserve to increase the money supply and Roosevelt's devaluation of the dollar against gold facilitated the raising of prices across all indices. Hence, creating the inflation as well as the necessary liquidity to offer the economy the quickening it desperately required.

DEPOSITORIES

FORT KNOX

In 1935, the US Treasury announced its intention to build a gold depository on the grounds of Fort Knox, Kentucky. In 1936, the United States Bullion Depository was built on the land, transferred to it from the military. The location was selected for its strategic position, considered inaccessible by a potential hostile invading force. With vast quantities of gold bullion pouring into the Federal Reserve, the necessity to create secure storage capacity prompted the decision to build a highly secure, high-volume gold storage facility.

The Fort Knox Bullion Depository holds 4583 tonnes of gold bullion. This accounts for 56.35% of the United States' Gold Reserves (8133.5 tonnes).

FEDERAL RESERVE BANK OF NEW YORK

The New York Fed is by far the most important of the twelve regional Fed Reserve Banks (see Chapter 7: Central Banks) since, apart from its responsibility for the Fed's international operations (see Chapter 5: Payments) and proximity, as well as relationships with Wall Street, it is also the custodian of the largest known gold inventory in the world.

The New York Fed claims to store more than 5800 tonnes of gold on behalf of 36 foreign central banks, foreign governments and international financial organisations, as well as a percentage of the US Gold Reserves. The storage arrangements for the gold in official custody makes use of two vaults beneath the New York Fed's headquarters at 33 Liberty Street, in lower Manhattan. The main vault has been in use since 1924. The second vault, known as the auxiliary vault, has been in use since 1963.[172]

THE BANK OF ENGLAND

The Bank of England has one of the largest gold vaults in the world. After the New York Fed, the Bank of England is the largest custodian of gold. Since 2014, the bank claims to hold approximately four-hundred-thousand bars (equivalent to 5134 tonnes).[173] In much the same manner as the New York Fed offers custodial services on behalf of foreign entities, the Bank of England offers comparable services to 72 central banks as well as housing the UK Gold Reserves in the Treasury's EEA account (see Chapter 7: Central Banks). In addition, it offers gold accounts to approximately 28 LBMA members, the IMF and the Bank of International Settlements (BIS).

The Bank of England's gold vaults are housed within the basement levels of its headquarters, located in the City of London on a site bordered by Threadneedle Street, Princes Street, Lothbury and Bartholomew Lane.[174] Built between 1924 and 1933, the Bank of England's basement levels accommodate several gold vaults.[175]

The New York Fed and the Bank of England represent two of the four designated depositories for the IMF's Gold Reserves. The remaining two custodians are the gold depositories of the central banks of France and India.[176]

EXTER'S PYRAMID

Exter's Inverse Pyramid is a construct developed by John Exter (1910 - 2006), economist, central banker, banker and monetary expert.

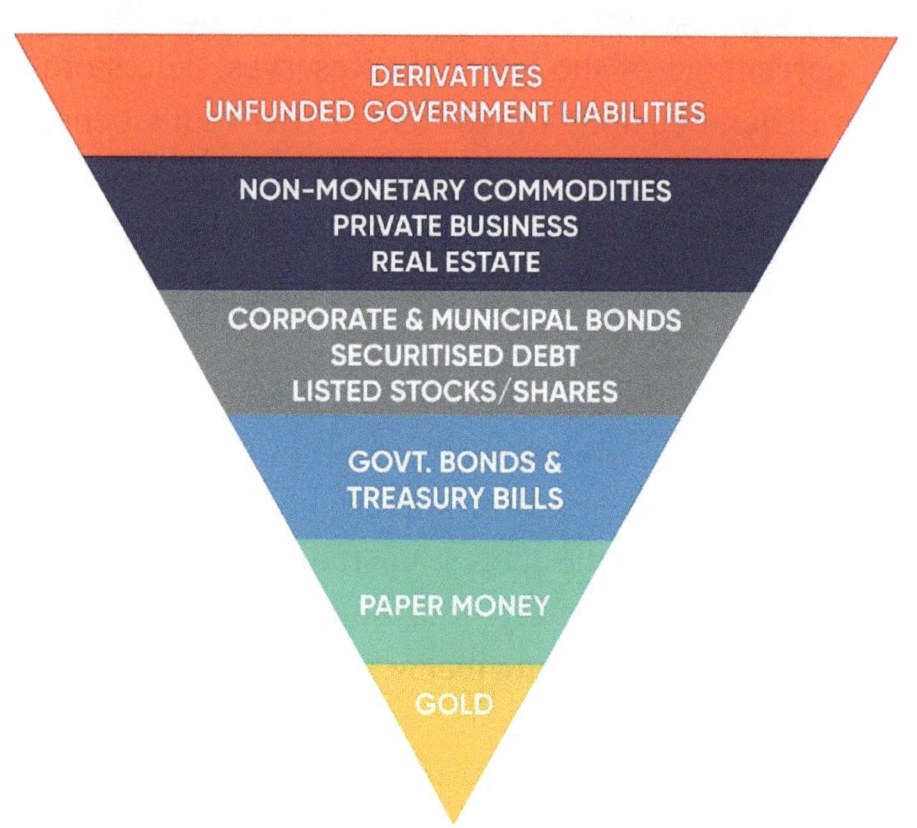

Exter concluded, in the 1950s - 1960s, during his time at the Fed, that the economy had evolved into a debt-based and credit-driven monetary system (see Credit & Debt, Chapter 8: Economic Cycles). To demonstrate the structure thereof, Exter rendered an inverted pyramid as a model to illustrate this epiphany. The US debt pyramid drew attention to the realisation that foreign economies also had debt pyramids. The structure, underpinned and balanced upon its apex. A metaphor for the unstable nature, which Exter advocated was true of the financial system. In his original inverted pyramid model, he included junk bonds, illiquid debtors, commercial paper, bankers' acceptances, developing economies' debts, certificates of deposit (CDs), Federal government debt, corporate and municipal bond debt and paper currencies.

The greatest risk categories occupied the broadest cross sections of the pyramid. Descending the pyramid were lessor risk categories. The risk declined throughout the descent, until distilling into treasuries and penultimate cash (Federal Reserve Notes), and finally gold, at the apex of the inverted pyramid.

Exter's original inverted pyramid balanced on the world's existing known quantity of gold, which at that time was a quantity representing approximately 140000 tonnes. Exter elected to illustrate gold outside of the bounds of the pyramid, as in his view, it represented the solitary 'real' money in the world. It was free of liability and the only asset class that would not default or be likely to devalue in the midst of an economic crisis.

In the Exter paradigm, at some future juncture, people would presumably lose confidence in the financial system and cascade the pyramid, seeking liquidity, penultimately to cash, and then ultimately veer outside the pyramid entirely and into gold. In such circumstances, Exter envisioned the price of gold would inevitably rise against all currencies as the value of debt and securities declined.[177]

In practice, private gold ownership, since the GFC has seen meteoric growth. Undoubtedly this was a reflexive response to the instability cultivated through debt accumulation, via unfettered deficit spending, coupled with the 'printing' of vast quantities of fiat money and the proliferation of high-risk illiquid derivatives (see Derivatives, Chapter 10: Financialisation). The consequence, thereof, is evident through the incremental withdrawals of gold from the traditional banking institutions and some central banks, where the precious metal may be leveraged at high ratios to maintain confidence on a fractional reserve basis. Such confidence is required to anchor and underpin the riskier elements of Exter's pyramid. The net condition observed however, is that while the gold volume at the pyramid apex shrinks, the ascending financial asset layers inflate, hence illustrating the amplification of potential instability which the system is capable of accruing through financialisation.

10

FINANCIALISATION

Financialisation is a term used to describe the economic process by which financial capitalism evolves from a source of financing growth in productivity to creating profit, purely through financial instruments for speculation and the intermediation, thereof.

Financialisation is evident through the manipulation of capital in order to extract greater value from an economy than the investment of capital adds to it.

'Financialization means the increasing role of financial motives, financial markets, financial actors and financial institutions in the operation of the domestic and international economies.'

- Gerald Epstein, Professor of Economics and founding Co-director of the Political Economy Research Institute (PERI).

FUNCTIONS OF FINANCE

Finance has four key functions:

1. Payments

2. Wealth Management

3. Risk Management

4. Allocation of Capital

PAYMENTS

In considering the four core functions of finance, 'Payments' which is a major area of development enabled by FinTech (see Chapter 5: Payments), represents a critical capability to the successful infrastructure of an economy. Without the ability to make payments, the economy of the world and the means to effectively conduct business, would grind to a halt.

WEALTH MANAGEMENT

Wealth management represents another key function of finance, aimed at facilitating the saving and investment of earnings of individuals and businesses to provide for the future. Investment in pension schemes and other long-term savings instruments, to provide for retirement and to cultivate value in an estate being passed on to heirs is the subject and focus of this area of finance.

RISK MANAGEMENT

Risk management deals with the area of risk mutualisation (the sharing of risk), which creates the necessity for insurance. This area of finance is designed to create a means through which companies and individuals can mitigate financial devastation in response to unforeseen events and circumstances.

ALLOCATION OF CAPITAL

Finally, the allocation of capital is the function intended to facilitate the creation of wealth and prosperity through investing in the development of productive capacity, via employment, the purchase of raw materials and the creation of goods and services; using the combination of all three. In other words, the creation of growth through investment in the 'real' economy.

Another vehicle for supporting productivity through the allocation of capital, is that of investment in infrastructure development. The development of cities, commercial and residential real estate fits within this category. The building of roads, railways and shipping ports enables the movement of raw materials, commodities and the distribution of goods, which support the productive industrial economy.

FUNCTIONS OF FINANCIAL SERVICES

When examining the functions of financial services, three core functions are evident.

1. The transfer or storage of value in space

2. The transfer or storage of value in time

3. Managing the entropy of value

Thus, financial services such as payments and banking fulfil the functions within the sphere of space, while investment (see Wealth Management & Allocation of Capital above) and financing fulfil the functions within the sphere of time. By contrast, financial services, such as insurance (see Risk Management above), fulfil the management of entropic value.[178]

FINANCE SECTOR SHARE OF GDP

The graph depicted in Fig 10.1 below, is a highly cited representation which illustrates the growth in share of GDP of the US finance sector over time, leading up to the GFC 2007-2008. The graph illustrates the rise prior to the stock market crash in October 1929, the decline experienced during the Great Depression and reaching a low point at the end of World War II. Since 1945, the sector has grown steadily until peaking in 2008 when the GFC struck. In the years immediately following the GFC, the US Finance sector, represented approximately 4% of jobs, 7% of the economy (GDP) and generated 25% of corporate profits.[179]

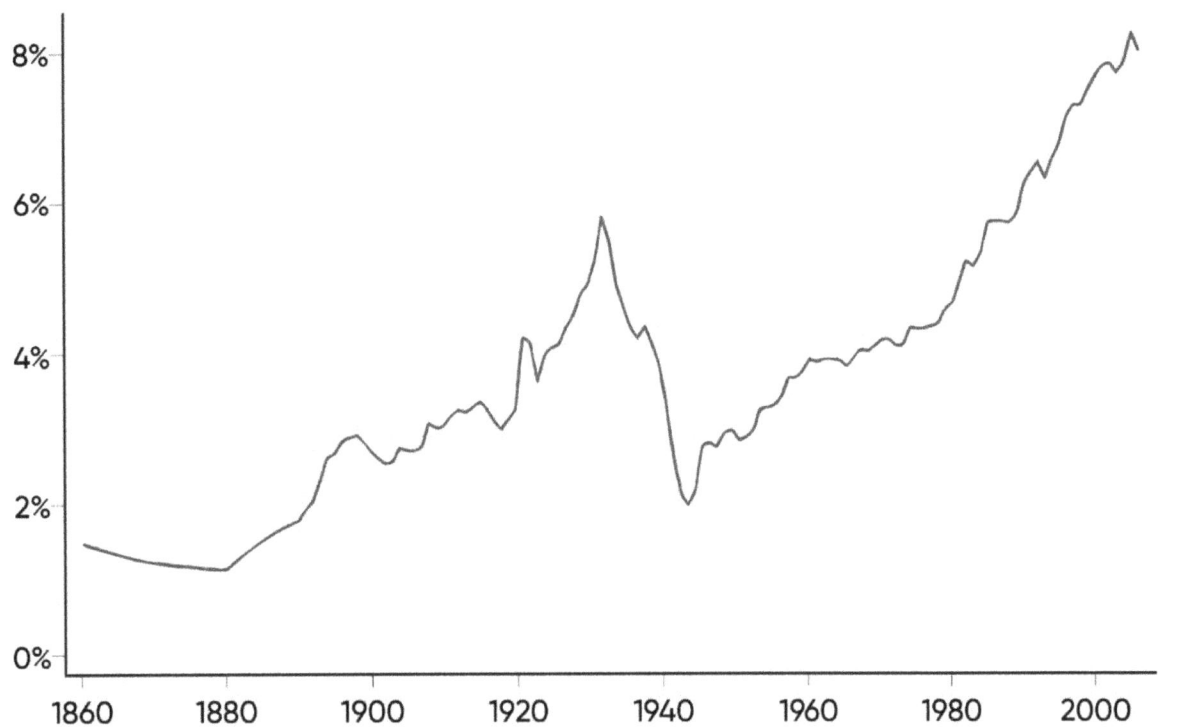

Fig 10.1 US Finance Sector share of GDP 1860 - 2008 (Source data: Philippon, 2008[180])

'Productive allocation of capital represents 15% investment in business and the "real" economy.'[181]

- Rana Foroohar, 2016.

The above statement highlights a key characteristic of financialisation, whereby capital is no longer channelled productively into businesses in order to fuel long-term growth, however, rather as a means of investing in speculative instruments for short-term gains.

'A healthy scepticism should be applied when exploring any mechanism or system which realises profits without producing anything [of value]. Such a system, economically speaking, must be exploitative in some way.'

- Paul Rigden, Physicist, Economist and Capital Markets specialist, 1994.[182]

This phenomenon raises the spectre of capital evolution, whereby as an economy matures beyond the spheres of industrialisation and the commercialisation thereof, actors within the system seek out new forms of value and worth (see Chapter 2: Capital Evolution). This begins a phase of financialisation, whereby returns on capital increases, while the return on labour and industrial productivity decreases.

This financialisation is the result of financial engineering, whereby instruments are developed accompanied by a co-evolution in practices, to extract value from an economy rather than build and reinforce it. The practice is synonymous with a culture of short-term gains in favour of long-term sustainable growth. It draws parallels with the creation of short-term and long-term debt cycles, whereby credit and debt are manipulated to sustain short-term profits, while accruing unserviceable debt burdens (see Chapter 8: Economic Cycles).

The origins of financialisation are regularly attributed to the rise in speculative practices and financial instruments created in the 20th century, however, less sophisticated financialisation is evident when examining the cycles of evolving capital over protracted periods prior to this. Earlier examples include speculative practices, which originated among the wealthy merchants who frequented Lloyds Coffee House in London during the 18th century.

The business of producing goods with capital investments and economic growth experienced as a result of the industrial revolution, prompted the growth in maritime shipping, which responded reflexively to accommodate the demand for distribution of the raw materials and goods, which in turn, fuelled the commercialisation, thereof.

The wealthy merchants who engaged in the shipping of these goods were accustomed to frequenting the Lloyd's Coffee House where they would often engage in the speculation of among many subjects, the state of the King's health, upon which they would wager. Over time, the merchants' wagering, evolved to speculate on the risks associated with their maritime shipping operations. A practice which evolved into the creation of insurance underwriting and Lloyd's of London.[183]

This suggests that financialisation is a cyclic phenomenon (see Hegemony, Chapter 11: Hegemonic Dominance). A process that's incepted by industrialisation, followed by commercialisation which later evolves to cultivate practices synonymous with the manipulation of financial instruments. The most recent cycle of which, has proliferated under the global leadership of the US economy since the 1920s.

THE ROARING TWENTIES

The Roaring Twenties (1921 - 1929) as it was known in the US and western society, also known as the 'Goldene Zwanziger Jahre' (Golden Years 1923 - 1928) in Germany and 'Les Années folles' (The Crazy Years) in France, was a period of post-war prosperity fuelled by economic growth and cultural liberalism. A period where art, music and business boomed.

The period had immediately followed the Great War, which had devastated Britain and Europe, prompting people to desire a renaissance of sorts, to cherish the "peace" that had come at far too great a cost.

The 1920s catapulted the United States from an emerging industrial nation into an economic powerhouse, a process that had been amplified through acting as a supplier and creditor to Britain and France during the Great War (see The Great War, Chapter 9: Gold). As a beneficiary of the war and fuelled by technological advancement, US industry made extensive and substantial gains in productivity. Through US electrification and new machinery (see Commoditisation, Chapter 2: Capital Evolution) which didn't require highly skilled operators, it created employment opportunities for unskilled workers. Coupled with mass production techniques, such as the conveyor belt and assembly lines pioneered by Henry Ford, the US economy transformed into a booming productivity phenomenon. New techniques in mass marketing and the creation of numerous competitively priced goods endowed the US with the creation of a mass consumer market. Much of this growth was supported by an abundance of capital and consumerism, reinforced by access to inexpensive credit.

As the economy grew, the finance sector inflated with it, giving rise to financial speculation shrouded in an assumption that the stock market would grow perpetually. Speculative practices such as 'buying on margin' whereby a commitment to purchase equities is made at an offer price, yet paid for latently (credit provided by stock brokers, usually requiring only 10% down against the order value). In such circumstances, speculators were confident equity prices would rise, between commitment and settlement, hence many would place purchase orders and sell prior to settlement falling due, enabling them to profit from the marginal yield. A practice that worked so long as prices continued to rise. Numerous practitioners of 'buying (or selling) on margin,' however, lacked the capital to make good on the full commitment.

Growth in finance sector wages grew commensurately, peaking at approximately fifteen fold over the course of the period 1920 - 1929.[184]

Speculation in the stock market (Wall Street) *'irrational exuberance'* culminated in a collapse of share prices (equities) which began on October 24, 1929 known as 'Black Thursday' and by October 29th (Black Tuesday), the Dow Jones Industrial Average (DJIA) had seen the index value culled by almost 25%. A slide that persisted until November 13th, 1929. An event which ultimately triggered a deleveraging (see Deleveraging, Chapter: 8 Economic Cycles) and resulted in the Great Depression.

THE WALL STREET CRASH OF 1929

In the lead up to the Wall Street crash of 1929 there were a few early warning signals. A brief slide in the DJIA in March 1929, prompting concerns which were quickly allayed by bankers reassuring investors. Thereafter, on August 8th, the Fed raised the discount rate to 6%. By September 3rd, the DJIA peaked at 381.17, an early indicator that the market was overvalued, being a 27% increase over the 1928 high. On September 26th, the Bank of England raised its bank rate to defend the Gold Standard and price stability. Three days later, on September 29th, the British markets descended into panic, catalysed by The Hatry Case.[185]

On October 3rd, Phillip Snowden, then Britain's Chancellor of the Exchequer, announced that he believed the US Stock Market was merely a *'speculative orgy.'*[186] Both the New York Times and The Wall Street Journal published articles agreeing with Snowden's assessment the following day.[187] Less than three weeks later, the three major trading days in which the DJIA plummeting ensued were October 24th, 28th and 29th known as Black Thursday, Monday and Tuesday respectively.

As expected, the crash prompted creditors to demand payment, which the majority of actors were unable to pay, primarily due to the widespread use of unsecured debt facilities. The resulting defaults deepened the impact of the deleveraging, as actors sought liquidity in the system while facing the effects of cascading and compounding defaults (see Chapter 8: Economic Cycles).

The crash marked a deep descent into a depression (The Great Depression) following the deleveraging, which saw unemployment rise to 25% (one in four Americans out-of-work) as businesses crumbled. Wages fell by 42%, global trade reduced by 65% and US economic growth contracted by almost 55%, which sustained 10% year-on-year deflation from 1929 till 1934.[188]

Banks, in particular, were challenged to honour their debt obligations to depositors, limited in most cases to an average of ten cents on the dollar. A predicament brought about by appropriating depositors' funds (without consent) to speculate on the stock market rather than lending to businesses or providing mortgages to prospective homeowners. A practice which is commonplace in contemporary financialisation, via shadow banking (see below). This prompted President Roosevelt to create the Federal Deposit Insurance Corporation (FDIC) in 1933, to insure depositors' funds. It wasn't until November 23rd, 1954 (a quarter of a century later) that the DJIA finally recovered to match and then surpass the September 3rd 1929 high, reaching 382.54.[189]

GLASS–STEAGALL

In 1933, the Glass-Steagall Act was passed by the US Congress, to enforce a clear separation between commercial and investment banking. The lack of separation of finance functions having been identified as a major stability shortcoming as a result of exposing bank depositors' funds to the stock market in the lead up to the Wall Street Crash of 1929. The Glass-Steagall Act marked the first meaningful US regulation of modern finance to limit potential abuse of *laissez-faire*[190] economic behaviour, first described by the father of classical economics, Adam Smith (see Value, Chapter 2: Capital Evolution).[191]

BRETTON WOODS

As World War II (1939 - 1945) drew to a close, the new international monetary system was negotiated in Bretton Woods, New Hampshire, USA in 1944 (see Chapter 12: Global Monetary System). The Bretton Woods System brought about a period of growth and financial stability, whereby nation states organised themselves, finance and the global economy in the orbit of the United States and the US dollar. The system pegged the US dollar to Gold (dollar-gold standard) and remained at the price-point ($35) set by President Roosevelt in 1934 (see The Great Depression, Chapter 9: Gold).

GUNS & BUTTER

In the midst of the Vietnam War (1955 - 1975), during President Lyndon B. Johnson's State of the Union address in January 1965, Johnson announced what would later become known as the 'Guns & Butter Policy[192].' Johnson's policies advocated for:

1. "**Guns**" - A foreign policy, promoting a rapid escalation of the US military presence in Vietnam

2. **"Butter"** - A domestic policy to create a number of social, welfare and benefit programmes under the title of 'The Great Society.'

Johnson advocated that the US was a wealthy country, which could afford both policies. Unfortunately, the US could afford one or the other, however, not both simultaneously. The policies created 'twin deficits' through running exorbitant budget and trade deficits simultaneously. This marked the beginning of a macroeconomic period from 1965 - 1982, known as the 'The Great Inflation.'[193] A period described by prominent economist, Jeremy J. Siegel as:

'the greatest failure of American macroeconomic policy in the postwar period.'

- Jeremy James Siegel, Professor of economics, Wharton School of Business, 1994.

In such circumstances, the US was forced to 'print money,' effectively expanding the money supply disproportionately to the Gold to currency ratio, which supported the US dollar. A dilution of the dollar's value brought about by essentially over-leveraging it to support the excessive expenditures, which the Guns & Butter policy demanded.

As a consequence of the US dollar's reserve currency status, other nation states were running a trade surplus with the US. Many nations concerned by the ability of the US to maintain the gold peg ratio, while printing dollars to support the 'Guns & Butter' policy, embarked on redeeming their trade surplus dollars for gold from the Federal Reserve. This, in turn placed, pressure on the US Gold Reserves, which reinforced further dilution of the dollar under the Bretton Woods monetary system.[194] By 1967, it was clear that the Bretton Woods system would eventually break down (see London Gold Pool, Chapter 13: Global Trade Rails).[195] The system was ultimately ended in the wake of unilateral action taken by President Richard Nixon in August 1971 (see Nixon Shock, Chapter 12: Global Monetary System).

DOLLAR CONFIDENCE CRISIS

Following the demise of the Bretton Woods system, the US experienced three recessions 'back-to-back,' in 1974, 1979 and 1980. During 1974 in particular, interest rates doubled.[196] Greater regulations were introduced, which heavily restricted lending and energy prices soared.[197] As the recession took hold, the US stock market plunged, halving in value,[198] while the unemployment rate doubled.[199]

Over the period 1977 - 1981, the US experienced a fifty-percent rise in inflation, effectively diminishing the value of the US dollar proportionately. Free of the constraints of the Bretton Woods system, the dollar's value plummeted. The Gold price rose (dollar devalued) from $35 in 1971 to a peak of $850 in 1980. A consequence of severe inflation, amplified by high oil prices, the Soviet intervention in Afghanistan and the impact of the Iranian revolution.

Through the credibility lost by ending the Bretton Woods system, amplified by extensive deficit spending, increased regulation and exacerbated by poor economic performance, the dollar very nearly collapsed in 1978. US dollars had become undesirable internationally, in tandem with the US becoming increasingly unpalatable and unaccommodating in attracting international business. These conditions prompted the creation of the 'Carter Bonds.' With the US dollar's diminished standing, the US resorted to borrowing money in Swiss Francs and German Deutschmarks, since demand for the dollar had eroded substantially. The 'Carter Bonds' issued during President Jimmy Carter's presidency (1977 - 1981) were US Treasuries denominated in Swiss Francs and West German Deutschmarks, a key low-point for economic confidence in the United States. The $850 Gold price peak in 1980, yet a further barometer for diminished confidence in the US dollar.

KING DOLLAR

In August 1979, Paul A. Volcker Jr. (1927 - 2019) began his first of two terms as Fed chairman (1979 - 1987), appointed by President Jimmy Carter. When President Ronald Reagan began his first term in January 1981, Reagan and Volcker together, embarked on a strategy to rehabilitate the US dollar and enabled the US to become a formidable and attractive business-friendly environment once again.

Paul Volcker raised interest rates to 20% in June 1981, effectively transforming the dollar into a sound investment platform globally, through providing strong and stable returns.[200] Simultaneously, President Reagan cut taxation and embarked on deregulating the financial sector. These actions spawned the era of the 'King Dollar' and initiated the economic period known as the 'The Great Moderation' (see Chapter 8: Economic Cycles). A strong indicator for the success, thereof, is the dollar's strength against gold, recovering to $308 by mid-June 1982. While 'The Great Moderation' ended in the early 2000s, with gold meandering between $250 and $270, the 'King Dollar' strategy survived the numerous Republican and Democrat presidential administrations, as well as Fed FOMC chairs for nearly thirty years.

President Barrack H. Obama ended the King Dollar (or Sound-Dollar Policy) in 2010, following the GFC 2007-2008. President Obama's National Export Initiative 2010 aimed to double US exports within a five-year window.[201] Since the US is a net importer due to its reserve currency status, the only mechanism available to policy makers in order to stimulate exports was to devalue the US dollar. A process which was complemented, by lowering interest rates to the zero bound and expanding the money supply through Quantitative Easing (see Chapter 8: Economic Cycles).

FINANCIAL INNOVATION

The deregulation of the 1980s under Reagan's campaign banner of "Make America Great Again" (mimicked by President Donald J. Trump, during his 2016 presidential campaign), ushered in an era of financial innovation, ultimately resulting in the repeal of the Glass-Steagall Act in 1999.[202] The repeal contributed to cultivating the ideal conditions to incubate the systemic risks, which resulted in the GFC 2007-2008. Between the years 1980 - 2008, the US financial sector's share of GDP grew at an accelerated rate, ultimately doubling from 4% to 8% over the period.[203]

SARBANES–OXLEY

In 1985, a merger between Houston's Natural Gas Company and Internorth Incorporation was completed to form the Enron Corporation. Post-merger, the company grew rapidly and was broadly regarded as a highly innovative and promising business.[204] Despite inflated expectations, the company engaged in unethical accounting practices such as mark-to-market accounting (fair value accounting)[205] and off-balance-sheet financing.

Mark-to-market accounting is an excellent accounting method in the pricing and evaluation of securities, however, had disastrous consequences when applied to a business such as Enron. The off-balance-sheet financing was accomplished through the creation of Special Purpose Vehicles (SPVs), additionally known as Special Purpose Entities (SPEs) or Special Economic Vehicles (SEVs). Enron exploited the SPVs to conceal its debt from its external stakeholders, such as creditors and investors.

Enron accomplished this by transferring a portion of its assets (those which had rising marketable value) to an SPV in exchange for cash (or notes). The SPV then hedged the stock it held against an asset held on Enron's balance sheet. The net effect, thereof, reduced the asset's counterparty[206] risk, via the SPV, while simultaneously using it to conceal losses. Combining this arrangement with mark-to-market accounting, Enron appeared profitable, due to the cash injection, however, only so long as the stock prices held or continued to rise.[207]

Without the stock price to underpin the 'fragile' arrangement, the SPVs wouldn't be able to hedge the deteriorating market price of the stock. Although the existence of the SPVs was disclosed to the public and to investors by Enron, the deliberately complex debt structure masked the transactions and the true nature of the company's finances. In 2000, Enron's shares traded at near $90.56, a price level which deteriorated to $0.26[208] (by December 2nd, 2001) at which point Enron filed for bankruptcy.[209]

In the wake of the 'Enron Scandal,' the US Congress passed the Sarbanes-Oxley Act 2002, also known as the 'Public Company Accounting Reform and Investor Protection Act,' as well as the 'Corporate and Auditing Accountability, Responsibility, and Transparency Act.'

Colloquially referred to as 'SOX,' the Sarbanes-Oxley Act was devised to fortify corporate governance and prevent the level of malfeasance by executives and accountants, which led to the elaborate fraud that Enron and its co-conspirators had managed to perpetrate. While Sarbanes-Oxley addressed governance and accounting shortfalls, ensuring executives would be held accountable for these practices in the future, the legislation failed to address restricting the instrumentation or mechanisms used. Enron has since largely become viewed as the emblematic example of corporate financialisation gone awry.

SYSTEMIC RISK

In 1998, Long Term Capital Management L.P. (LTCM), a Connecticut based hedge fund founded in 1994, lost $4.6 billion over a four-month period. The losses were brought about by highly-leveraged positions, which were exposed to emerging markets and triggered by both the Asian Financial Crisis of 1997, and the Russian Financial Crisis of 1998.

Prior to the loss, LTCM established an equity position of $4.7 billion and had borrowed over $124.5 billion, with assets of approximately $129 billion in total. Hence, LTCM had a debt-to-equity ratio of over 25 to 1.[210] LTCM held derivative positions off-balance sheet, with an estimated notional value of $1.25 trillion, predominantly comprised of interest rate derivatives and swaps. The sheer magnitude of LTCM's leverage combined with its far-reaching penetration and exposure to global markets created a *systemic risk*. An exposure, which threatened a chain reaction series of losses and defaults, likely to result in a cascading collapse of markets around the globe. Wall Street's largest investment institutions feared that LTCM's collapse wouldn't exclusively result in catastrophic losses for their own investors, however, expose the finance sector to the risks of greater regulation and scrutiny.

After LTCM failed to raise capital on its own, Goldman Sachs, Berkshire Hathaway and American Insurance Group (AIG), offered a bailout, which LTCM ultimately refused. With alternatives exhausted, on September 23rd 1998, the New York Fed brokered a bailout of $3.6 billion from capital syndicated across sixteen major Wall Street investment institutions. Effectively resulting in Wall Street bailing itself out, as the Fed merely functioned as a facilitator.

DOT COM

The 1990s was a period of rapid technological advancement (see Chapter 3: Ecosystems). In 1993, the release of the proprietary Mosaic web browser enabled many people to access the internet for the very first time. Over time, personal computers began to transition from being perceived as a high-end luxury, to a more commonplace household essential item (see Commoditisation, Chapter 2: Capital Evolution). With the rapid adoption of personal computers and modulator demodulators (modems) to access the world-wide web (www), the market experienced numerous new entrants from internet-based technology companies. The 'tech' entrepreneurs intended in capitalising on the opportunity the internet presented as an untapped medium for a new disruptive age of businesses and services. An almost perfect template for the Cloud and FinTech revolutions, experienced since 2006 and 2008, respectively.

Now referred to as the 'Dot Com' bubble, the 1990s represented the expansion phase of a short-term debt cycle (see Chapter 8: Economic Cycles), where investors flocked to participate in the growth opportunities that the 'Dot-Com' boom represented. On August 9th 1995, Netscape, a later entrant than Mosaic which offered a faster and more sophisticated web browser listed its stock, via an Initial Public Offering (IPO), on the National Association of Securities Dealers Automated Quotations (NASDAQ). Netscape's opening share price of $28 soared to $75 in its first day of trading. A notable peculiarity of Netscape's IPO was that of taking a company public that had yet to turn a profit. A trend that continued amidst a buoyant deregulated environment, as investor demand grew substantially for stakes in newly formed internet-based companies.

'Irrational exuberance' was the phrase used by the then-Fed Reserve Chairman, Dr Alan Greenspan, in a speech given in 1996 at the American Enterprise Institute[211] in the midst of the 'Dot-Com' bubble expansion. The phrase was largely interpreted as a warning that the stock market might be overvalued. A symptom of 'wishful thinking' combined with 'herd behaviour' on the part of investors, blinding them from the reality.[212] Much like Netscape, the vast majority of new tech start-ups were surfing a wave of investor capital, rather than realising any profitable revenue. A situation which incubated a foreseeable melt down, however, while stocks continued to soar in value and perceptions remained inflated, capital investment continued. Investors were led to believe that the profits were just beyond the horizon. Shortly after the turn of the year 2000, the 'Dot Com' bubble 'burst' and shares crashed.

In the wake of the crash, which as expected, triggered a recession (short-term debt cycle), the Fed's FOMC, under Dr Alan Greenspan's leadership, responded by lowering interest rates to ~1%. Although consistent with expectations in such circumstances, the Fed persisted in keeping interest rates depressed for a prolonged period. With poor returns on conventional instruments as a consequence, thereof, investors sought out new sources of high-yielding returns. Simultaneously, artificially-low interest rates and an abundance of capital led to a housing boom, the next expansion of which, created the housing (mortgage) bubble of the 2000s. The mortgage boom coupled with a deregulated environment and the instruments cultivated in a climate of financial innovation created an unparalleled market appetite for high-yield securities and derivatives.

SECURITIES

Securities are tradable and fungible financial instruments, which are used to raise capital in both private and public markets. There are primarily three types of securities: *equity*, *debt* and *hybrids*. *Equity* essentially provides ownership rights to holders; *debt* are essentially loans repaid with periodic payments; and *hybrids* which combine aspects of both *debt* and *equity*.

ASSET BACKED SECURITIES

Asset-backed Securities (ABS) are debt-based securities, the income and value of which are derived from and collateralised by a "pool" of underlying assets. The "pool" is typically an aggregate formed from a collection of illiquid assets which are challenging to sell individually. A typical example of an ABS includes the securitisation of a loan, such as real estate mortgages and auto/vehicle loans. The process of securitisation typically converts the receivables (income from the borrowers) against the loans into bonds, which are then sold to investors. The net effect of which releases capital by liquidating a pool of ordinarily illiquid assets.

MORTGAGE BACKED SECURITIES

A Mortgage-backed Security (MBS) is an Asset-backed Security derived through the securitisation of a pool of either commercial or residential mortgages. Like most financial innovations, the purpose of an MBS is to increase returns and diversify risk for the investor. For mortgage lenders, however, its purpose is to release capital.

MATURITY TRANSFORMATION

Mortgage lenders such as commercial banks and building societies, raise capital from depositors and other banks at a low rate of interest and lend it to borrowers at a higher rate of interest in order to profit from the difference. A typical residential mortgage can span two or three decades, hence the asset, although generating an income for the lender (typically a bank) represents a long-term illiquid commitment, whereas depositors' funds and loans from other institutions are short-term liabilities to the lender. This key capability is known as maturity transformation, whereby banks transform short-term liabilities into long-term assets. Since the short-term liabilities are highly liquid and long-term assets are not, banks rely on guarantees provided by central banks and governments should their liquid (fractional) reserves be exhausted (see The Wall Street Crash of 1929 above). A particularly common predicament during periods of financial stress. With persistently low interest rates being prevalent (see Dot Com above), the associated yields were marginal in contrast to the risks being carried. Furthermore, such yields were likely to shrink further over the term of mortgages as interest rates would be expected to rise during the course of the loan period. MBSs offered banks and investors a mutually beneficial means of circumventing the risks associated with maturity transformation[213], whereby, the bank may liquefy long-term assets for principal and a return, while investors may benefit from an income generating security at a higher return. Any profitable vehicle which facilitates the liquefying of long-term illiquid assets is desirable to banks, without which banks remain challenged to eliminate highly-latent payment paradigms such as net settlement CSMs (see Chapter: 5 Payments).

DERIVATIVES

A **derivative,** is fundamentally a **contract** between two or more parties, the value of which is based on an underlying financial asset (predominantly securities) or a collection of financial assets (such as an index). Typically, there are two classes of derivatives, either 'lock' or 'options.' In the case of 'lock' derivatives, such as 'swaps,' 'futures' or 'forwards,' the respective parties are bound from the outset to a specific set of agreed-upon terms for the duration of the contract. In the case of 'options,' however, the instrument entitles the holder to *'the right, but not the obligation'* to *'exercise the option.'* Exercising an option empowers the holder to either buy (or sell) the underlying asset, commodity or security at a specified price on or prior to the option's expiration date.

Some derivatives are intermediated (brokered and cleared), via exchanges and clearing houses. These are known as 'listed derivatives,' examples of which are 'futures' and 'options' and are subject to greater regulation, as well as traded, via exchanges.

OTC DERIVATIVES

Over-the-counter (OTC) derivatives, however, may be contracted and thereafter, traded between parties on a bilateral or multilateral basis without being intermediated through either a clearing house or an exchange. These instruments therefore carry a greater counterparty risk, as well as carry a greater risk of a potential default. There is little distinction between an OTC derivative and a conventional contract and as such, it is within the domain of contract law rather than finance. With less scrutiny, the contractual terms may be crafted to suit the risk appetite and returns of the counterparties. However, this lends itself to being open to potential abuse. Collateralised Debt Obligations and Credit Default Swaps fall within the sphere of OTC derivatives (see below).

COLLATERALISED DEBT OBLIGATIONS

Collateralised Debt Obligations (CDOs) are derivatives underpinned by a pool of loans and other assets, typically Mortgage-backed Securities. A CDO derives its name from the mortgages, loans and bonds acting as collateral for the pool from which it is constructed. Essentially, a form of structured asset-backed security (ABS). Much like MBSs, CDOs are created by Investment Banks. CDOs are then sold to institutional investors, such as hedge funds, sovereign funds, insurance companies and pension funds. Since the GFC 2007-2008, CDOs have largely been 'rebranded' to Bespoke Tranche Opportunities, (BTOs) in an attempt to distance the instrument from the perceptions that CDOs attracted, as a result of the role they played in the lead up to the GFC.

The typical CDO prior to the GFC 2007-2008 was engineered to aggregate Mortgage-backed Securities sold to Investment Banks and then repackaged in some instances, via SPVs (off-balance-sheet financing), into a new form of derivative comprised of three risk-based tranches of MBS. Thereafter, the Investment Bank (or SPV) sells the CDOs to institutional investors.

Tranches are as follows:
1. Superior
2. Mezzanine
3. Equity

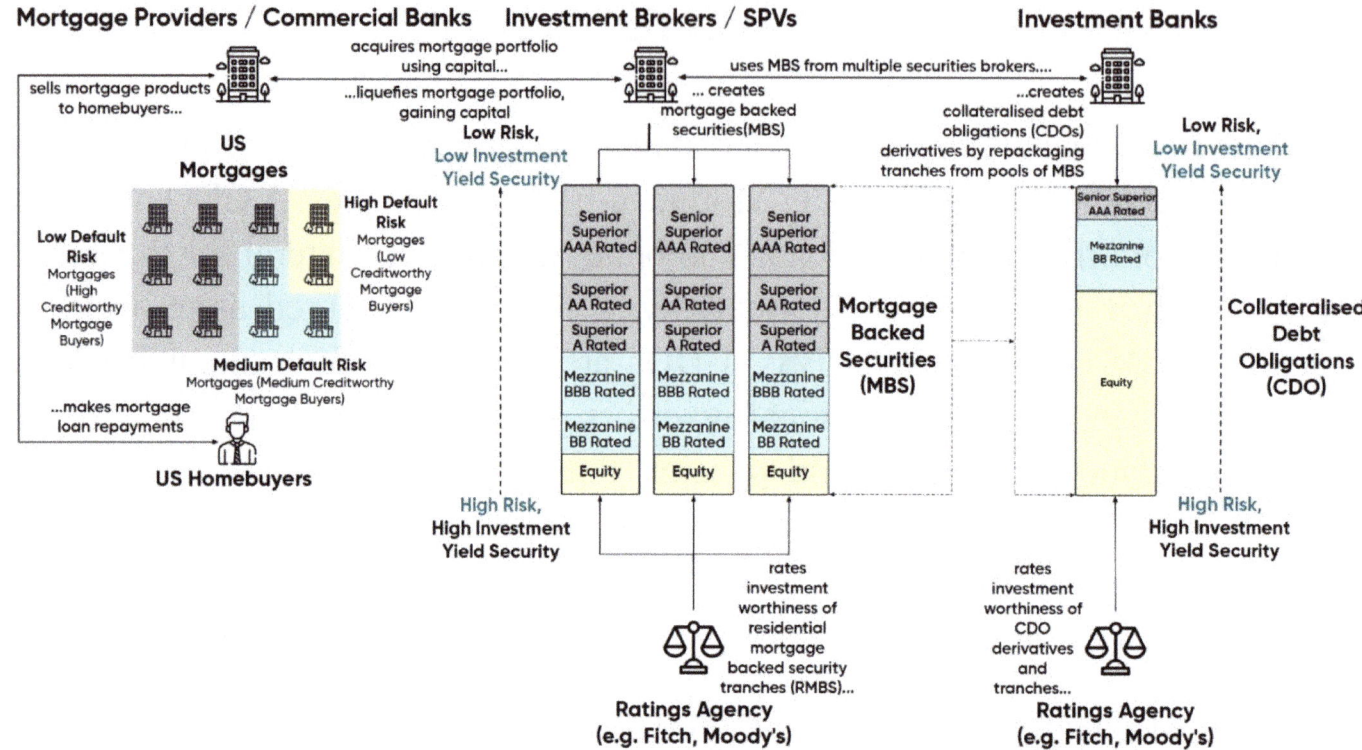

Fig 10.2 Collateralised Debt Obligations aggregated from tranches of Mortgage Backed Securities

The nomenclature is intentionally deceptive, as 'Superior' represents low-risk MBSs where the underlying mortgages are low yield loans backed by (prime) mortgages to high-income, yet low risk borrowers. 'Mezzanine' represents MBSs underpinned by mortgages to middle-income borrowers representing a mid-range risk and a corresponding higher return. Finally, 'Equity' represents MBSs pooled from mortgages to low-income, yet high-risk borrowers, also known as 'subprime' borrowers, although represents the highest yield to offset the risk.

CREDIT DEFAULT SWAPS

Credit Default Swaps (CDSs) are financial derivatives that allows an investor to 'swap' their risk with another party. A CDS effectively acts as a form of insurance against a default.

The first CDSs created were (in London) based on loans to Exxon Mobil in the 1990s. The rationale for coming into being was to exploit the difference in regulation between loans to companies versus the regulation of insurance instruments. If an insurance company insured or underwrote a risk, it was required to make regulatory provision against the amount of expected loss, whereas if a bank made the provision, it was to base it on the size of the loan. Thus if making a very large loan with a very low risk of loss, it was far cheaper to treat it as an insurance policy, rather than as a loan. This was the purpose of the CDS. Its creation was a response to the complexity of regulation in the finance sphere.[214]

The Credit Default Swap's role in the lead up to the GFC was to insure CDOs against potential defaults. Since insurers perceived the CDOs to be safe by virtue of rising real estate prices, any defaults seemed unlikely to realise losses. CDSs were extraordinarily profitable for insurers that perceived them as a 'safe bet' and enormously profitable. Unlike conventional forms of insurance, whereby one policy may be contracted to underwrite the risks of an asset, an example of which would be home insurance for a single family home, CDSs could be issued multiple times over against the same CDO. As Wall Street's debt market created high volumes of CDOs, London's dominant insurance market provided CDSs to insure them. Following the passing of the Commodity Futures Modernisation Act 2000, the US was able to offer CDSs domestically, the majority of which were underwritten by AIG.

CREDIT RATING AGENCIES

The role that credit rating agencies, such as Moody's, Fitch as well as Standard & Poors played in the GFC was to certify the superior tranche of the CDOs with "AAA" ratings, the mezzanine with "BBB" ratings, (while not rating the equity tranche) in aid of allaying any concerns investors may have raised as to the quality of the underlying MBSs. Typically a bond is considered to be of an Investment Grade (IG) if it is rated as "BBB" or higher. The "AAA" rating is the identical grade awarded to US Treasuries, perceived to be the safest of all investment instruments. The CDOs proved to be both profitable and very low risk, as the bulk of the income generated by the CDO was fed by creditworthy mortgage borrowers. The occasional default would have a negligible impact to the instrument. The property to which the underlying mortgage would relate, acted as collateral for any such default and was easily resold for a profit. A perfect mitigation, since real estate prices were perpetually rising.

Since the CDOs included a proportion of subprime mortgages (in the equity tranche), the risks associated grew as greater demand for CDOs drove greater weighting toward higher subprime backed ratios. A consequence of growing investor demand for the highly profitable instruments, yet underpinned by a diminishing number of eligible prime and mid-range mortgage borrowers.

SHADOW BANKING

Shadow banking is a term synonymous with bank-like activities (predominantly lending) that takes place outside the traditional banking system. It is now commonly referred to internationally as 'non-bank financial intermediation' or 'market-based finance.' Shadow bank lending has a similar function to that of traditional bank lending.[215] The term 'shadow bank' was originated by economist Paul McCulley in 2007. Shadow banks engage in similar activities to banks comparable to maturity transformation (see Maturity Transformation above). Shadow Banks borrow short-term funds, via money markets and exploit those funds to purchase assets with longer-term maturities. Other forms of intermediation in which they may be engaged include liquidity transformation, which entails exploiting cash-like liabilities to purchase harder-to-sell assets, such as loans. Furthermore, employing techniques, such as leverage, whereby money is borrowed to purchase fixed assets in order to magnify the potential for gains (or losses) on an investment. In addition, engaging in credit risk transfer, whereby the risk of a borrower's default may be transferred from the loan originator to another party (see Credit Default Swaps above). However, since they are neither subject to traditional banking regulations nor licensed to engage in such activities, they are incapable from benefitting from the support of central banks nor from government underwritten insurance to protect the funds of depositors. Essentially, they operate exclusively from the 'shadows.'

Prior to the GFC 2007-2008, the use of SPVs (and off-balance-sheet financing), to intermediate between banks and investment banks, as well as institutional investors such as hedge funds, pension funds and insurers became a common and prolific practice of shadow banking.[216]

SECURITISATION CHAIN

The shadow banking network is a mesh of complexity designed to elude regulatory scrutiny through opaque practices and the use of numerous intermediaries. Intermediaries exploited a series of securitisation and transformation techniques in order to monetise banks' mortgages using MBSs providing short-term highly liquid returns by selling to Investment banks through the use of SPVs. Investment banks created CDOs from MBSs and intermediated these to institutional investors. CDSs were purchased to offset the CDO risks prior to the sale, which credit rating agencies imbued with "AAA" ratings in order to allay any concerns raised by potential investors (see Credit Rating Agencies above). This became known as the securitisation chain, in which the complexity of the instruments, intermediaries and institutions involved as well as the internationalisation thereof, cultivated the conditions for malign systemic risks permeating the global markets.

MORAL HAZARD

With each derivative instrument, more complex and toxic than the previous changing hands, between each bank, SPV, insurer and investment bank, each intermediary in the securitisation chain was profiting, re-liquefying, and then repeating the process. A process, which deployed capital and attracted gains on a short-term basis, the essence of financialisation. With access to inexpensive credit (Fed's persistent low interest rates, see above), substantial sums were borrowed from the Fed to leverage and scale this endeavour, amplifying the exposure. However, this cultivated a climate, whereby none of the parties in the 'production line' (securitisation chain), thereof, were compelled to take accountability for the risks which the derivatives were carrying. In economics, this is known as the 'Principal-agent Problem.' The Principal-agent Problem, describes the dilemma which arises from circumstances in which an agent is motivated to act in its own best interests, which is contrary to those of its principal (another party).

In each transaction, between each actor within the (securitisation) chain between borrowers and investors, one acts as the agent and the next, the principal. With little regard for the consequences to the next party in the chain, each party exhibited this trait. A practice, more commonly known as 'Moral Hazard.'

INFORMATION ASYMMETRY

Information Asymmetry is a prevalent concept in contract theory which deals with the study of transaction decisions in which one party is in possession of either a greater volume of, or better quality information than the other. The consequences of this asymmetry creates an imbalance of power between the counterparties to a transaction, which may lead to inefficiencies or in extreme instances can result in market failure. While Moral Hazard is one such potential by-product of information asymmetry, another typical by-product that may result therefrom, is that of 'Adverse Selection.'

ADVERSE SELECTION

Adverse Selection (also known as 'Anti-selection') describes the situation that may arise in which counterparties to a transaction have different information, particularly surrounding the risk factors that may be associated therewith. Thus, lending itself to a set of circumstances in which one party may participate selectively in transactions or trades, at the expense of a counterparty who is not privy to the same information. Thus, Adverse Selection is most likely to occur in transactions in which there is an asymmetry of information (see Information Asymmetry above). Consequently, Adverse Selection may in some instances be a contributing factor to the manifestation of Moral Hazard.

Furthermore, Adverse Selection is prevalent in the insurance industry, whereby it is typical of people who elect to purchase insurance policies to file claims that will, over the life of the policy, exceed the total value of the premiums that they have paid. A consequence of people who knowingly have greater risk factors being more likely to purchase insurance. Paradoxically, if insurers raise premiums to cover the increased claims risks associated with this behaviour, they tend to dissuade low risk customers from purchasing insurance, thereby increasing the number of people who remain insured who will inevitably file claims.

COUP DE GRÂCE

Growing demand for CDOs backed by mortgages created a capricious climate, whereby mortgage lenders offered short-term fixed rate mortgage deals to subprime borrowers. The mortgage deals were constructed in a manner which were initially affordable. However, once the initial fixed-rate term expired, the costs of servicing the mortgage would increase, well beyond the means of the borrowers. Since each actor from mortgage brokers to derivatives traders were passing on the risks to the next principal (see Moral Hazard above), this practice metaphorically transformed the CDOs into financial 'time-bombs' being passed from one entity to the next. An emblematic example of Moral Hazard was the revelation that a number of large investment banks had purchased CDSs for their own account against the toxic CDOs which they were selling on (see Adverse Selection above). In other words, knowingly selling derivatives which were of poor quality (see Information Asymmetry above) and betting on their failure in order to profit from both the sale as well as its impending default.

A further contributing factor to the impending financial implosion, was that of insurers which had underwritten risks in the form of CDSs against the CDOs which they were then purchasing themselves. Essentially purchasing risky instruments, for which they themselves were the underwriters, all in an attempt to boost profits and maximise shareholder value. It remains unclear as to whether the insurers were knowingly complicit in these transactions or victims of the complexity and dilution of derivatives, via shadow banking.

Ultimately borrowers defaulted *en masse* (approximately ten-million), triggering a cataclysmic financial crisis in September and October 2008 which metastasised globally through uncontainable systemic malignance. The first tangible signals manifested in 2007, as severe pressure began to build in the subprime securities market. In March 2008, Bear Sterns, a well-known investment bank and brokerage collapsed. In early September 2008, the US government announced that it was assuming control of prominent mortgage lenders, Fannie Mae and Freddie Mac. September 15th 2008 marked the collapse of Lehman Brothers, one of Wall Street's most prominent investment banks. Merrill Lynch, faced with a similar fate, narrowly avoided bankruptcy (simultaneously to Lehman) by selling itself to Bank of America. Across the Atlantic, Northern Rock, a British bank which had substantial exposure to the housing market and had made extensive use of funds borrowed in the international money markets suffered a liquidity crisis as US markets dried up. When the news broke on September 13th 2007 that the bank required support from the Bank of England, queues began to form outside Northern Rock's branches, prompting the first run on a British bank in over 150 years. With the support of the Bank of England, Northern Rock was nationalised in February 2008.[217] On September 29th 2008, the DJIA fell 777 points, the most substantial fall recorded in a single day. The largest US insurer, AIG, nearly collapsed due to exposure to insuring derivatives through issuing CDSs.[218]

In October 2008, banks faced significant liquidity stress, which impeded their ability to lend. This was evident in the Libor-Overnight Index Swap (Libor-OIS) spreads, which aids as a measure of interbank liquidity stress and confidence among banks. Research published by the IMF estimated that the financial crisis destroyed asset values equal to approximately fifty-trillion dollars, equivalent to a year of global GDP at the time.[219] As the deleveraging ensued (see Deleveraging, Chapter 8: Economic Cycles), several institutions declared bankruptcy, representing a cascade of failures and panic. Central banks, as well as governments, mobilised to prevent a systemic financial meltdown, while real estate asset prices crumbled exacerbating the toxicity of the derivatives which they underpinned. The principal beneficiaries were private equity firms, which acquired substantial portfolios of mortgages in forbearance and default at fire-sale prices. Private equity firms as a consequence, represented the largest landlords in the United States, thereafter.

In a global market suffering from a near total liquidity freeze, often referred to as 'the credit crunch,' central banks under the leadership of the Fed intervened. Without central banks' intervention, the deleveraging would have undoubtedly resulted in a deep and protracted depression, the magnitude of which would have dwarfed that of the 1930s (Great Depression). Central banks essentially monetised the debt through Quantitative Easing in order to restore confidence through injecting liquidity in pursuit of a graceful deleveraging. Unlike in 1998, when Wall Street bailed itself out through the rescue of LTCM (see above), ten-years-later Wall Street came to rely on the Fed to be bailed out.

DODD–FRANK

In the wake of the GFC 2007-2008, the Dodd-Frank Wall Street Reform and Consumer Protection Act 2010, was passed having been championed by President Obama's administration. Dodd-Frank represented the most significant financial legislative reform in the US since the 1930s. The act included numerous reforms intended to be implemented incrementally over several years.[220] Dodd-Frank established a number of new government agencies, charged with the oversight of the various provisions of the act and by extension, various aspects of the financial system.

In an effort to assure future financial stability by monitoring and overseeing systemically significant organisations, deemed 'too big to fail,' the act created the Financial Stability Oversight Council (FSOC). In recognition that some of these entities may inevitably fail, the act established the Orderly Liquidation Authority (OLA). The OLA is tasked with assisting in the orderly dismantling of insolvent firms, as well as restructuring these where possible. The Orderly Liquidation Fund was established to assist in such circumstances, while assuring that public funds are not used to unduly rescue defunct organisations.

Dodd-Frank additionally imbued the FSOC with the authority to break apart institutions deemed 'too large,' particularly in instances where such organisations pose a potential systemic risk. In addition, discretionary authority is granted to FSOC to mandate institutions to increase reserve requirements.

The act, additionally, facilitated the creation of the Federal Insurance Office in order to monitor and regulate Insurers, as well as the Consumer Financial Protection Bureau to curb predatory mortgage lending practices. In response to the role credit rating agencies (see above) played in the lead up to the GFC, the Securities and Exchange Commission (SEC) established the Office of Credit Ratings (OCR). The OCR is focused on ensuring credit rating agencies provide credible ratings over the products and organisations which they evaluate.[221] Dodd-Frank additionally expanded and reinforced the Whistleblower provisions, established by the Sarbanes-Oxley Act 2002 (see above).[222]

THE VOLCKER RULE

A key component of the Dodd-Frank Act, is the Volcker Rule (named for former Fed Chairman, Paul Volcker), which restricts the avenues with which banks may invest, particularly by imposing limits surrounding speculative trading and eliminating proprietary trading altogether. Banks are prohibited from being involved with hedge funds or private equity firms, which are considered to be too great a risk. In an effort to minimise possible conflicts of interest, financial firms are prohibited from trading proprietarily without a sufficient stake. The Volcker Rule clearly represents a resurrection of the controls which were implemented by the Glass-Steagall Act, 1933 (see above), which first recognised the inherent dangers of financial entities extending commercial and investment banking services simultaneously.

DEREGULATION

Under the leadership of the Trump administration (2017 - 2021), the US Congress passed the Economic Growth, Regulatory Relief, and Consumer Protection Act 2018.[223] The act eased a number of restrictions implemented under Dodd-Frank. Notable examples included creating exceptions for increasing asset thresholds, under which prudential standards, stress testing and the mandates of risk committees would be less restrictive. Reserve requirements for institutions that do not act as lenders, yet maintain custodianship of customers' assets were reduced. The law additionally created exemptions for escrow requirements imposed upon residential mortgage loans in certain instances. It established a ten-billion-dollar asset threshold for implementation of the Volcker Rule amongst lenders and less stringent reporting requirements among those below the threshold.

Advocates of Dodd-Frank believed the regulations would reconstitute the controls to prevent a reoccurrence of the circumstances which led to the GFC. Detractors, however, vehemently opposed the regulations under the auspices of preventing the US from deteriorating as a palatable and competitive free market environment, in which to cultivate and nurture business and innovation. This draws historical parallels with the regulatory stance taken in the 1930s in response to the unfettered *laissez-faire* practices, which led to the crash of 1929 and the deregulation of the 1980s which was desperately required to reanimate the US economy. These represent cyclic tightening and loosening responses to prevent financial systems from failing by constraining the environment with rules and controls. However, attempting to seek a balance between a market free to either prosper or fail while preventing abuse.

It is the contention of a number of detractors [224] that the higher reserve requirements imposed by Dodd-Frank starve the market of liquidity. Consequently, this may destabilise the bond market, where not all securities are mark-to-market and whereby there aren't necessarily sufficient volumes of buyers and sellers to adequately support the market as a result.

ARSONISTS & FIREFIGHTERS

The asymmetric influence investors, political lobbyists and Wall Street institutions hold over the financial system, regulators and politicians is a testament to how financialisation has evolved and matured. Practices have emerged which are governed by short-term decision-making. Decisions focused in realising higher-returns for investors through dividends and an obsession with quarterly profits, rather than investing in long-term value, productivity and growth. Since the 1980s, non-financial firms have become obsessed with their share price. Firms are increasingly dedicating greater resources and focus to elevating and maintaining share prices than their core business area. Firms outsource services, optimise staffing, divest less profitable divisions and purchase their own shares (through buy backs). All such measures are taken in an attempt to maximise shareholder value. Accountants, rather than engineers, now govern the allocation of capital in the modern enterprise. This trend has unfolded over the course of several decades and is a reflective characteristic of financialisation.

This is reinforced by the notable contraction in average Research and Development (R&D) investment as a percentage of revenue exhibited across the economy. Furthermore, evident in the diminishing entrepreneurial spirit with fewer start-ups emerging in the immediate aftermath of the GFC.

These behaviours are synonymous with cultivating inertia barriers (see Chapter 2: Capital Evolution) as a result of placating shareholders, rather than through poor strategic planning or competence-induced failure (see Chapter 4: Surfacing Utility). While overwhelmingly representative of the norm, it is worth noting that some investor appetites have prioritised corporate commitments towards R&D in order to placate shareholder concerns surrounding the long-term viability of corporations.

A further consequence of financialisation is the metamorphosis of non-financial firms in emulating the practices of financial institutions (see Embedded Finance, Chapter 15: Economy of Things). Since the 1980s, non-financial firms have come to rely to a greater extent on income generated by financial assets (bonds, derivatives and real estate), whereas revenue generated by non-financial assets (such as production machinery) has been in decline. This behaviour has paved the way for non-financial firms to evolve through co-opting services in the finance sphere. Examples include supermarket chains offering banking and insurance services, as well as technology companies evolving into financial services firms through the use of FinTech, Data Science and Artificial Intelligence.

This conceptually raises the spectre of the role these nascent technologies will likely be co-opted to assume in augmenting financial engineering. A further concern may be realised through the potential societal impact of AI Agency, which raises questions over whether Moral Hazard will re-emerge under the auspices of an increasingly AI centric business environment. Exploiting these technologies in conjunction with financial principles, derivatives, in particular, will likely face an overhaul in pricing and risk methodology. Examples include leveraging data-driven insights in lieu of purely stochastic and quantitative methods for pricing, cash flow sculpting and the structuring of securities, as well as derivatives such as futures, forwards, options and swaps.

A comparable transformation should be anticipated in the context of risk management, whereby Data Science and AI may be exploited to continually engage in real-time risk assessments, and thus, reflexively influence the patterns of behaviour exhibited by those people and entities the risks of which, are being underwritten. This surfaces questions regarding the ethics surrounding paradigms such as 'behavioural underwriting' (see InsureTech, Chapter 15: Economy of Things) through the surveillance and manipulation of people, via prescriptive analytics (see Harnessing & Monetising Data, Chapter 4: Surfacing Utility), and surveillance capitalism (see Surveillance Capitalism, Chapter 15: Economy of Things).

While commoditisation (see Commoditisation, Chapter 2: Capital Evolution) may have provided the tools to create FinTech, Financialisation created the inspiration and motivated the climate for FinTech to emerge, grow and prosper. FinTech provides the instrumentation to create new vehicles for extra-systemic unregulated financialisation, by providing technological constructs to perpetuate esoteric shadow banking practices traversing the data-driven economy of an internet-enabled economic highway. A natural consequence of shadow banking following the path of least regulation. Thus, a means of enabling tech-giants and organisations which exploit shadow banking, nascent technologies, as well as neo-financial engineering to capitalise on innovation outpacing regulation. This may be achieved by providing a means of digitising financial products, services and practices. Products, services and practices that would otherwise be regulated and constrained within the spheres of post GFC financial institutions that are subject to regulatory constraints of greater stringency.

Furthermore, FinTech has evolved into the sphere in which investors have embraced speculative interest, which in itself represents a symptom of financialisation seeking out high profitability without creating goods or services which serve the real economy.[225] Collectively, these behaviours gradually weaken the economic posture, and by extension the political and military strength of western advanced economies, particularly that of the United States. A predicament, which may inevitably accelerate its decline in hegemonic dominance.

11

HEGEMONIC DOMINANCE

'If we have to use force, it is because we are America. We are the indispensable nation. We stand tall. We see further into the future.'

- Madeleine Albright, US Secretary of State, 1997 - 2001.

The concept of hegemony is centred on the dominance of one entity over another, or many others. It is critical to distinguish the concept of hegemony from that of colonisation, the latter of which implies direct or official control.

Thus, hegemonic dominance excludes forms of dominance, such as the annexing, occupation or the acquisition of foreign territories.[226] Hegemony by contrast is synonymous with a disequilibrium of power and influence in the international system, whereby one state may exercise its leadership or dominance over the others.[227] This may be achieved initially through coercion, however, eventually those whom are dominated, capitulate to being so by consensus. It, thus, becomes incumbent upon a hegemonic power to organise and lead the other nation states in the world to ensure the system which they establish is accepted and runs seamlessly. This is accomplished by the hegemon exploiting its strength to establish the institutions and rules that will govern the interstate system.[228] Historically, hegemonic powers have asserted their values upon other nation states within the spheres of political, territorial and especially economic relations. They largely do so, in respect of their own security and economic interests.

This is initially reminiscent of a relatively stable period, whereby the dominant state organises other subordinate states in its orbit. Establishing the rules that govern the interstate system results in an emulation of the hegemonic state, which in turn, facilitates a systemic expansion. Eventually, one or more subordinate states ascend in power disproportionately to its peers within the system, creating a pluralistic imbalance. This is comparable to wolf pups coming of age to challenge the alpha for pack leadership. The relations between an ascending subordinate state and the dominant becomes increasingly frictional and eventually adversarial.

As tensions build, each of these respective adversaries may solicit support from their allies, resulting in a form of polarisation of the interstate system.[229] Some states remain aligned with the hegemon and others align with the challenger. A few states usually remain neutral and ambivalent. The polarisation of the system eventually distils into a systemic crisis, and ultimately into an altercation. Finally, there is a resolution in favour of one or the other. The outcome may result in an alternate challenger being the beneficiary of a hegemonic vacuum. Neither contender may be fit to remain or ascend to dominance, in which case, a third state succeeds to hegemonic dominance in their stead. The new hegemon establishes its supremacy over the subordinate states, creating a new order, systems and hierarchy. In so doing, the cycle repeats itself.

In emerging from World War II, wealthier as well as economically and militarily superior to all other nations, the United States had ascended to become the dominant nation on the planet. Effectively, the Apex predator among nation states.

Consensus to this effect among the nations of the world was evident in the relative ease, with which the United States asserted its influence over the other nations in attendance at the Bretton Woods Conference in 1944. The US hegemonic rise prompted systemic reorganisation, which empowered the US to architect and enforce the terms upon which the modern financial system has been built (see Chapter 12: Global Monetary System). Other nation states subsequently organised themselves in the orbit of this system, in deference. The systemic reorganisation additionally included the formation of the United Nations (UN) headquartered in New York, USA. Established in June 1945, the UN is an international organisation aimed at promoting peace and security by harmonising actions among nation states through mutually motivated co-operation and diplomatic discourse. A further example includes the establishment of the North Atlantic Treaty Organisation (NATO) in April 1949, built upon the foundations established by the Atlantic Charter between the United States and Britain in August 1941. All forming the basis for the new world order, under the leadership of US hegemony.

Combined with the United States' industrial prowess, military strength and economic success (see Chapter 10: Financialisation), an instrumental factor in establishing an international consensus as to the United States' hegemonic ascent, was the sheer magnitude of the US Gold inventory, which superseded the holdings of all other nations (see Chapter 9: Gold). An attribute that reinforced confidence in America's status as the heir apparent, to be the next hegemon. The United States were in possession and command of the greatest concentration of tangible wealth in the world.

'Remember the golden rule; Whoever has the Gold, makes the rules!'

- Brant Parker & Johnny Hart, The Wizard of Id (newspaper comic strip), 1964.

The nations of the world were desperate for the re-establishment of order, stability, confidence and certainty. The United States' *economic and military might*, combined with its overwhelming *wealth* in Gold Reserves and its establishment of a *credible central banking* system, no longer vulnerable to minor economic shocks, combined with governance by the *rule of law*, furnished all of these needs.

'The United States has successfully established the Federal Reserve System, and has used her rapidly growing wealth to convert herself from a debtor to a creditor nation and to accumulate at the same time a large proportion of the world's stock of gold.'[230]

- John Maynard Keynes, 1930.

Hegemonic dominance passes periodically between nations. Historically, the hegemonic reign of a nation state is sustained between 80 - 110 years. During this period, the nation's currency typically functions as the principal global reserve currency.

Hegemon	Period	Duration (years)	Global Reserve Currency
Portugal	1450 - 1530	80	Real Branco / Real
Spain	1530 - 1640	110	Spanish-American Silver Dollar
Netherlands	1640 - 1720	80	Guilder (Florin)
France	1720 - 1815	95	Livre / Franc
Great Britain	1815 - ~1920	105	Pound Sterling

Fig 11.1 five previous hegemonies - 15th to 20th Centuries

The United States is largely considered to have been the hegemonic successor of Great Britain, since as early as 1920. The Great War decimated Britain economically, forcing Britain off the Gold Standard (see The Great War, Chapter 9: Gold).[231] As Britain attempted to restore the Gold Standard and rebuild from the war, the United States continued to boom economically (see The Roaring Twenties, Chapter 10: Financialisation). The US dollar was considered to be a 'neutral' currency and assumed a *de facto* role as a reserve currency, even prior to the end of the Great War (1914 - 1918). The dollar's *credibility* as a central bank gold-pegged *safe-haven* reserve asset, had *internationalised* the currency.

PRE-HEGEMONY

Over the course of the 15th and 16th centuries, at the outset of the period known as the 'Age of Discovery,' both Portugal and Spain had pioneered European exploration of the globe. During the course of doing so, both nations had established overseas colonial empires. As the Portuguese and Spanish empires expanded, their wealth compounded, motivating the Dutch, French and the English to emulate their success through establishing overseas colonies and trade networks throughout Asia and the Americas.[232]

A number of candidates may emerge simultaneously with the potential to ascend to dominance. The viability to ascend is usually the result of an advantage over other nation states in its capabilities surrounding production.[233] This is an advantage usually gained through technological advancement, thereby creating an epistemic inequality.

For the Portuguese and Spanish, this epistemic advantage was gained through ship building and the use of the compass for navigation. The Portuguese invented the Caravel in the 15th century. A ship design incorporating either one or two lateen sail rigs and a head sail combined with a hull that was stronger, yet lighter than previous designs. The lateen sails made the vessels fast, while additionally creating the capacity to sail windward (known as 'beating'). Consequently, the Caravel was manoeuvrable, yet able to undertake lengthy exploratory ocean voyages and subsequently return from them.

For the British, this epistemic advantage commenced with the industrial revolution in 1760, while France was the reigning hegemonic power of the day. With the decline of the Dutch system, both Britain and France had simultaneously assumed the role of challengers in the interstate system. Both candidates were worthy contenders to succeed the Netherlands as the new hegemon. While France had a greater foothold in continental Europe, Britain commanded superiority over the high seas.[234] Innovations in manufacturing automation and techniques, combined with the rapid adoption thereof, gave Britain its distinct epistemic advantage in its ascent (see Chapter 2: Capital

Evolution). A position compounded by Britain's naval superiority and its control over access to Asia and America. Eventually, the industrial revolution diffused from Britain to the European continent. Under Napoleon's nationalist mantra, the political structures of Europe had become frictional and adversarial. Social upheaval and radical movements emerged, while rapid economic shifts became prevalent, amidst a backdrop of the industrial revolution's modernisation of weapons and warfare.

'The growth of the British economy and the relative decline of French power caused an increasing disequilibrium between France's dominant position and her capacity to maintain it.'

- Robert Gilpin, U.S. Power and the Multinational Corporation, 1975

Social conflicts and interstate rivalries are signature characteristics of *hegemonic crisis*. In the case of France, this was amplified by Napoleon's banner of nationalism (see Populism, Chapter 8: Economic Cycles).

The advantages yielded through technological advancement in production capacity and throughput, gives rise to an increase in commerce and wealth generation. The resulting commercial advantage (*commercialisation*) (see Chapter 10: Financialisation) endures in parallel and largely benefits from, as well as reinforces, the *production advantage* in reciprocity, until it reaches the end of its utility.

The combination of *production* and *commercial* advantages, elevates a nation states' wealth and disrupts its posture in the existing system. This newly acquired wealth and prosperity facilitates its growth and resistance towards the dominance of the current hegemon (see Chapter 16: The Rise of China). With greater commercial and technological capabilities, comes growth, economic expansion and greater military sophistication. They, and a number of others, become potential challengers.

By the turn of the 20th century, both Germany and the United States had begun to challenge Britain's economic leadership, although it was escalating military and economic tensions between Britain and Germany that were ultimately among the major factors in causing the Great War (1914 - 1918).

HEGEMONIC WAR

Hegemonic wars have persisted for centuries. One of the earliest recorded instances, is notably the Peloponnesian war, fought between the Athenians and Spartans of ancient Greece. Articulated in Thucydides' 'History of the Peloponnesian War' (431 B.C.) is a key observation in that *it was the rise of Athens and the consequential fear that this instilled in Sparta, that ultimately made war inevitable.*[235] In Thucydides' account thereof (considered to be the first history book ever written), he inferred that:

'Those inquirers who desire an exact knowledge of the past as aid to the interpretation of the future, which in the course of human things must resemble if it does not reflect it. ...In fine, I have written my work, not as an essay which is to win the applause of the moment, but as a possession for all time.'

- John H. Finley, Jr., The Peloponnesian War, 1951 (translated from History of the Peloponnesian War)

The concepts of hegemony have a long-standing pedigree in the study of international relations. Two foundations for much theorising in this area, are that of 'Thucydides' The Peloponnesian War' published in 1961 (translated by Rex Warner), which deals with the Athenian hegemony and its implications for the Greek city-state system, and 'The Prince' by Nicolo Machiavelli, published in 1905. The latter of which deals with the issue of the hegemon and its control of the state.

FEAR, HONOUR & INTERESTS

The current international systems surrounding political and economic organisation have largely been transformed by each of three modern hegemonic wars. While these conflicts represented a contest for supremacy involving two or more great powers, they engulfed and affected numerous other states within the prevailing global system at the time. An imperative insight from Thucydides' 'History of the Peloponnesian War,' is that hegemonic wars are instigated by either *fear, honour* or *interests*. These wars have a significant structural impact on both domestic societies and the nature of international relations thereafter.

THIRTY YEARS' WAR

The first of these *modern* hegemonic conflicts was the 'Thirty Years' War' (1618 - 1648). In October 1648, the 'Peace of Westphalia,' a collective of two peace treaties was signed, ending the Thirty Years' War and resulted in a radical shift in the balance of power within Europe.

The Thirty Years' War was a series of wars fought by European nations, ignited in 1618 over an attempt by the King of Bohemia (the future Holy Roman Emperor, Ferdinand II) to impose Catholicism throughout his domains. Protestant nobles rebelled vehemently and by the 1630s most of continental Europe was at war.

As a result of the Peace of Westphalia, the Netherlands gained its independence from Spain. The power and influence of the Holy Roman Emperor (see above) crumbled and nation states were again able to determine the religion of their subjects.

The principle of 'state sovereignty' emerged from the Peace of Westphalia and serves as the basis for the modern system of nation states.[236] The Westphalian system is a doctrine upon which this is based. A global system underpinned by the principle of international law, in which each state maintains sovereignty over its own territory and domestic affairs. It established that regardless of size, all states were equal under international law to the exclusion of all external powers, on the principle of non-interference in another country's domestic affairs.[237] The Netherlands assumed its role as monetary hegemonic successor from 1640, in congruence with the Amsterdamsche Wisselbank's ascent and its economic growth and prosperity during the Dutch Golden Age (see Central Banking, Chapter 7: Central Banks).

Dutch economic prosperity was bolstered by a favourable agricultural base, as well as success in the fishing industry, carrying trade during the fifteenth and sixteenth centuries, ultimately establishing a maritime empire in the seventeenth century. The Dutch Golden Age (1580 - 1670) spanned a period during which the Dutch had proved themselves successful in their fight with the Spanish and had boomed economically through a vast global expansion, until ultimately the Dutch economy experienced a downturn (see Chapter 7: Central Banks).

In March 1602, the Vereenigde Nederlandsche Oost Indische Compagnie (VOC), known as the Dutch East India Company, was established, and formed from a consolidation of several rival Dutch trading companies. This government-led directive created what is believed to be largest corporation that ever existed. Although the VOC is referred to as a trading company, the corporation was diverse and was engaged in multiple commercial and industrial activities. These included conglomerate-style activities, such as international trade, ship building and maritime shipping. The VOC is studied extensively as a template, in an attempt to understand the modern vertically-integrated, as well as global supply chains (see Vertical-Integration, Chapter 2: Capital Evolution) that have been prevalent since the rise of modern globalisation in the latter half of the 20th century. In many ways, the VOC is viewed as a corporate pioneer, being the first instance of a publicly traded company to have existed, in which shares, as well as bonds could be purchased. Chartered corporations such as the VOC had issued debt instruments (bonds) prior to issuing shares (equities).

In the VOC's search for spices, textiles and silks, via its growing maritime empire, the corporation became a vehicle for foreign investment, whereby capital was poured into developing seaports and urban centres as it anchored itself along the spice routes. Dutch investment, via the VOC, was responsible for the initial development of Tainan City in Taiwan and Cape Town in South Africa, as examples. The company finally faltered and ceased to exist in

December 1799. During the 17th and 18th centuries, the Dutch Guilder served as a reserve currency between Europe and the Dutch colonial empire. Through the Amsterdamsche Wisselbank (see Central Banking, Chapter 7: Central Banks), the Dutch were able to use stabilising practices comparable to those performed by central banks using monetary policy (see Monetary Policy, Chapter 8: Economic Cycles). The Dutch effectively created the template for reserve currencies and bank stabilisation, via central banks, as well as formalised the issuance of bonds and equities, thereby creating capital markets.

Economic growth accelerated until about 1620 when it slowed, however, continued to grow steadily until the end of the Golden Age. The final decades of the seventeenth century were marred by declining production and the loss of market dominance overseas.[238] In May 1672, the outbreak of the Franco-Dutch War saw France nearly overrun the Dutch Republic completely.

SECOND HUNDRED YEARS' WAR

The second *modern* hegemonic conflict is that of the 'Second Hundred Years' War' (1688 - 1815) which culminated in the French Revolutionary and Napoleonic Wars (1792 - 1815). The Second Hundred Years' War was a series of Anglo-French wars from 1688 - 1815. Britain's defeat of France's naval forces and army, galvanised Britain's impenetrable dominance and brought the Napoleonic Wars to an end with Napoleon's defeat at the Battle of Waterloo in June 1815. The Congress of Vienna (1814 - 1815) was a diplomatic conference aimed at restoring the European political order in the wake of the conflict. From 1815, Britain assumed its role as the hegemonic successor from France as it consolidated its power gained, via the industrial revolution (1760 - 1840). Britain exploited the opportunity to engage in an economic expansion which enabled it to surpass all potential rivals in productive, financial and military superiority. Britain maintained a superior economic posture over all potential competitors, the main engine of which was its production sector and its exports to global markets.[239] Not only did the post-Vienna Congress order mark the rise in British hegemony, it additionally ushered in:

'a phenomenon unheard in the annals of Western Civilization, namely, a hundred years' peace-1815-1914.'[240]

- Karl Polanyi, 1957.

The period of relative peace and stability from 1815 - 1914 under the British Empire's hegemonic stewardship became known as 'Pax Britannica' ('British Peace,' Latin), also known as Britain's 'Imperial Century.' In addition to the British Empire's direct and formal control over its colonies, Britain's hegemonic dominance over global trade imbued it with the power to assert its control over the economies of many regions, particularly those in Asia and Latin America. As Britain granted autonomy to its overseas colonies, many of which became known as dominions (Canada, Australia & New Zealand), its hegemonic dominance and much of its influence remained intact.

'...people were offered a Pax Britannica instead of endless strife, and a rule by law instead of arbitrary despotism.'[241]

SECOND THIRTY YEARS' WAR

The third *modern* hegemonic conflict is that of the 20th century's 'Second Thirty Years' War' (1914 - 1945). The Second Thirty Years' War is representative of the Great War (1914 - 1918), the Great Depression during the inter-war period (1919 - 1938), and World War II (1939 - 1945).

The altercation that precedes the transfer of hegemony, typically assists in ensuring the new dominant nation state, remains unchallenged by its defeated predecessor, or by new potential rivals in the immediate aftermath that follows the conflict.

HEGEMONY

Typically, the new hegemon initiates a systemic reorganisation among nation states. This is comparable to a trophic cascade. The cascade in this context, functions comparably to the introduction of constraints, in order to establish an ordered system. The systemic reorganisation results in various nation states emulating the dominant state, which facilitates systemic expansion.

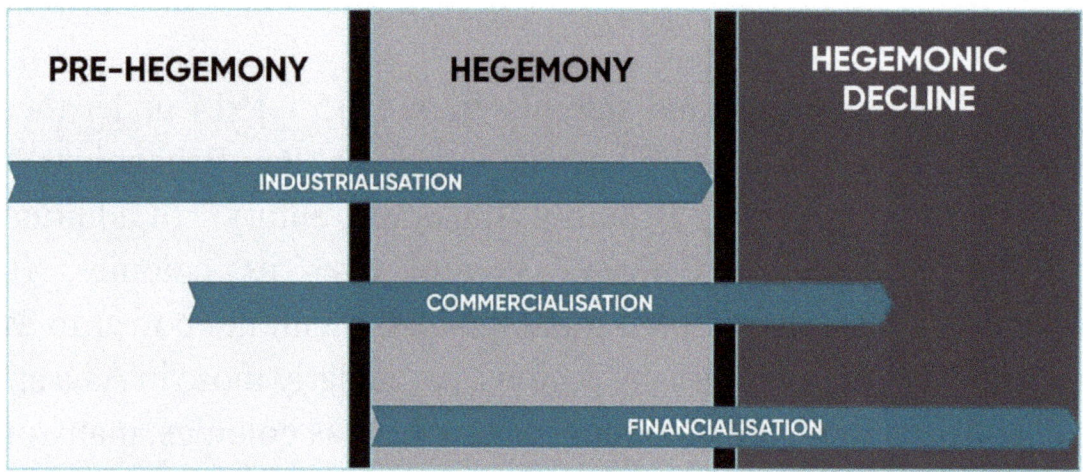

Fig 11.2 illustrates the relationship between Industrialisation, Commercialisation and Financialisation with the rise, reign and decline in a modern Hegemony

The expansion amplifies and sustains the production advantages gained by the newly empowered state, prior to its rise to dominance. In the pre-hegemonic phase, the production advantage is later complemented by a commercial advantage, typically the result of success gained through production or technological advancement. This commercial advantage endures from prior to ascension to dominance, sustains during the phase of hegemonic reign and is eventually fully diminished during the phase of decline. Prior to the decline, there is a phase synonymous with a financial advantage (see Chapter 10: Financialisation). During this phase, the hegemony embraces financialisation.[242] These phases broadly correlate to the cyclic patterns of commoditisation (see Commoditisation, Chapter 2: Capital Evolution) and are reflexively reinforced through oscillations in market forces and capital flows, governed by short and long-term debt cycles (see Credit & Debt, Chapter 8: Economic Cycles).

The industrialisation of the United States and Germany resulted in pre-hegemonic commercialisation, which facilitated their ascension as challengers to Britain's financialised hegemony. An altercation ensued, followed by a brief peace and an economic surge, which culminated in a catastrophic deleveraging during the inter-war period. This manifested in a globally protracted depression.

The depression deepened the descent into a second world-wide conflict, ultimately resulting in a transfer of hegemonic power.

HEGEMONIC DECLINE

The phase of decline is additionally one of transition and includes two distinct sub-phases.

1. **Hegemonic Crisis** (characterised by):

- Interstate rivalries

- Inter-enterprise competition (see Peace, War & Wonder; Chapter 2)

- Social conflicts (see Populism, Chapter 8)

- The emergence of new configurations of power (see Chapter 15 & 16)

2. **Hegemonic Breakdown** (characterised by):

- Systemic Chaos - which aids the new hegemonic state in systemic reorganisation

- Centralisation of systemic capabilities - which results in the emulation of the new hegemony, as well as aiding in its systemic reorganisation

This transition occurs prior to the transfer of hegemonic dominance to the next successor. With each hegemony, however, the world system becomes increasingly sophisticated, more deeply connected, yielding greater interdependence. Hence, the implications, thereof, are farther reaching and pivot to a greater extent on the levels of economic strength, military prowess, political sway and technological sophistication. Consequently, the factors that govern a hegemonic transition should be expected to reflect these attributes in the context of the era. It is, however, inescapable to consider that hegemonic wars are not inevitable. In the five previous hegemonic transitions (Fig 11.1),

Spain's succession from Portugal was not preceded by an armed conflict. In addition, as evidenced by the circumstances that catalysed the Thirty Years' War (see Thirty Years' War above), hegemonic wars are not necessarily instigated by economic conditions or influences (see Fear, Honour & Interests above).

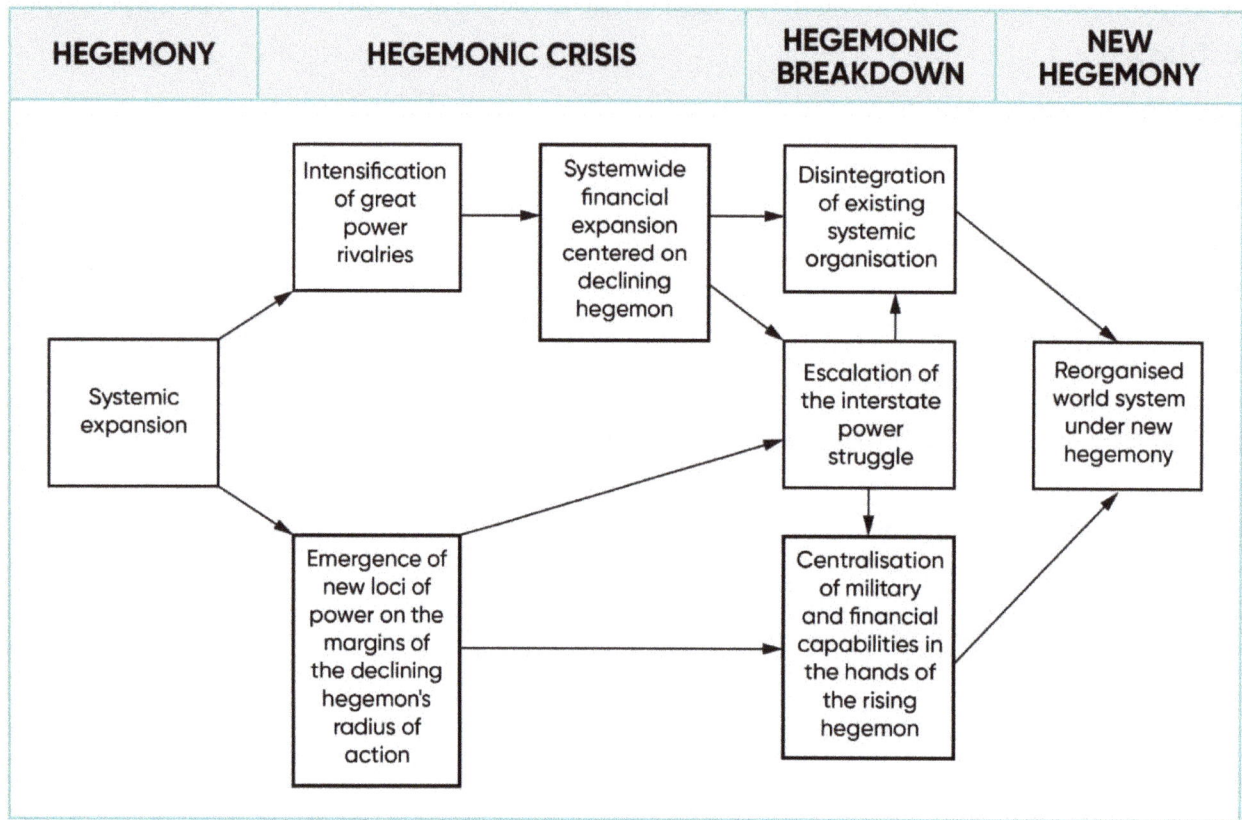

Fig 11.3 Hegemonic Transitions (source: Arrighi et al, 1999)[243]

MONETARY HEGEMONY

Monetary hegemony is the concept whereby the hegemonic dominant state asserts decisive influence over the international monetary system, which forms part of its systemic reorganisation (see Chapter 12: Global Monetary System).

The dominant state asserts its hegemonic power through its access to international credits and foreign exchange markets. This is accompanied by an unequivocal authority to enforce a unit of account in which economic calculations in the world economy are made (see Chapter 13: Global Trade

Rails). The dominant state operates under no *balance of payments* constraints and retains the mandate to resolve *balance of payments* challenges experienced by other states within the system (see Balance of Payments, Chapter 5: Payments).

Great Britain's monetary hegemony had largely reached its peak by 1871, reinforced by widespread systemic adoption (*systemic expansion*) of the Gold Standard (see Gold Standard, Chapter 9: Gold). During the course of the late nineteenth century, Britain became the greatest exporter of financial capital. London became the nexus of global financial markets. Essentially, the river through which the world's money flowed.[244]

In order to attract capital from London, financial centres, such as Berlin and Paris needed to emulate Britain's Gold Standard. Adoption, thereof (*emulation of the hegemon*), reduced transaction costs, represented creditworthiness, and promoted sound financial policy from government.[245] London was the leading source of both short and long-term credit, which was predominantly channelled abroad. Its extensive financial facilities provided access to inexpensive credit, which reciprocally enhanced the strength of Pound Sterling and reinforced its use for international transactions as a global reserve currency. During the period 1870 - 1913, Sterling-denominated banknotes and short-term credits financed approximately sixty-percent of global trade.[246]

'*In the latter half of the 19th Century, the influence of London on credit conditions throughout the world was so predominant that the Bank of England could almost have claimed to be the conductor of the international orchestra.*'[247]

- *John Maynard Keynes, 1930.*

Britain's foreign investments cultivated foreign economies for the use of Pound Sterling. Between the years 1850 - 1913, Britain's overseas assets more than quadrupled as a share of net national wealth. Never before had any one nation committed so much of its national income and savings to foreign investment.[248]

'Thus the art of the Management of Money consists partly in devising technical methods by which the central authority can be put in a position to exercise a sensitive control over the rate of investment, which will operate effectively and quickly, and partly in possessing enough knowledge and prognosticating power to enable the technical methods to be applied at the right time and in the right degree to produce the effects on prices and earnings which are desirable in the interests of whatever may be the prescribed ultimate objective of the monetary system which is being managed.'[249]

- John Maynard Keynes, 1930.

Britain's foreign lending practices possessed two technical aspects that gave materially greater prominence to Pound Sterling's reserve currency status as a universal *medium of exchange* and as the global *unit of account*. The first, is that all loans to foreign nations were issued in sterling, which enabled the borrowing country to service the debt more *conveniently* with its sterling reserves. This aspect reflexively broadened Pound Sterling's acceptance in exchange for goods and services throughout the world. The second, was that of written instructions to settle exchanges were drawn in London to finance international trade. This was facilitated by merchant banks in London lending to merchants to finance imports and exports.[250] Thereby, acting as a vehicle for international investment and ensuring Britain's role as an essential intermediary. Britain were, thus, able to command primacy over the relationship with each party, while reinforcing Pound Sterling as the accepted price measurement (unit of account) for goods, services and raw materials.

The Gold Standard, however, reinforced Pound Sterling's stature as a *store of value*. The combination, thereof, cultivated the ideal functional specificity for a *global reserve currency;* Shrouded and safe-guarding the *confidence* therein, by Pax Britannica's *rule of law*.

Britain's unparalleled ability to run current account deficits through the issuance of Pound Sterling and its bank (discount) rate (see Chapter 8: Economic Cycles), imbued the Bank of England with unshakeable controlling influence over Britain's *balance of payments*, regardless of what other central banks were doing abroad.[251]

When other central banks engaged in a '*tug of war*' over international capital flows,

'*the Bank of England could tug the hardest.*'[252]

- *Barry Julian Eichengreen, 1985.*

In this regard, British monetary hegemony was seldom threatened by crises of convertibility as Britain's Gold Reserves were insulated by the base (discount) rate and all foreign rates followed the British rate.

'*...through its [Britain's] hegemonic position in world commodity, money and capital markets enforced 'the rules of the system' upon the world's economies. The integration of national monetary systems with the London financial market endowed Great Britain with the ability to control to a considerable degree the world's money supply.*'[253]

- *Robert Gilpin, 1987.*

SOFT POWER

'*Pax Britannica held its sway sometimes by the ominous poise of heavy ship's cannon, but more frequently it prevailed by the timely pull of a thread in the international monetary network.*'[254]

- *Karl Polanyi, 1944.*

This observation highlights the differential and materially substantial advantage of waging political and economic warfare (soft power), in contrast to the short-term benefits of military superiority. A privilege held by a hegemonic power (see Extraterritorial Sanctions, Chapter 13: Global Trade Rails).

SUCCESSION

Britain's decline through the phase of hegemonic transition was fuelled by interstate competition and rivalry, insufficient domestic investment, and entered hegemonic breakdown following the outbreak of the Great War.[255] Despite its economic devastation, Britain's political influence persisted for a time after the war. However, its hegemonic posture was irreparable and throughout the interwar period (1919 - 1938), through numerous attempts, was ultimately incapable of restoring global confidence (see The Great War, Chapter 9: Gold).

'In the decline period, the hegemonic power is still a major core power, but it has lost its overwhelmingly predominant economic and military advantage. During 'declining hegemony' the hegemonic power (while still the most militarily powerful state in the core) experiences a steady erosion of its economic and military position and faces increasing challenges to its power from other states.'[256]

- Thomas R. Shannon, An Introduction to the World-System Perspective, 1989.

Following the Great Depression and ultimately the outbreak of World War II, it was clear that Britain's loss of hegemony was definitive and permanent. A posture which left a clear power vacuum for a new hegemon to occupy, the United States of America.

12

GLOBAL MONETARY SYSTEM

'...the international economic and monetary system needs leadership, a country which is prepared, consciously or unconsciously, under some system of rules that it has internalized, to set standards of conduct for other countries; and to seek to get others to follow them, to take on an undue share of the burdens of the system, and in particular to take on its support in adversity by accepting its redundant commodities, maintaining a flow of investment capital and discounting its paper.'

- Charles Kindleberger, 1973. [257]

The international monetary and financial system (IMFS) is reflective of the systemic reorganisation, which followed the emergence of the US as the new hegemon. As with previous hegemonic wars, in the wake, thereof, a conference is held to facilitate the creation of a new system and to restore confidence as well as stability.

The Peace of Westphalia and the Congress of Vienna served this purpose in the aftermath of the Thirty Years' War and The Second Hundred Years' War respectively (see Chapter 11: Hegemonic Dominance). For the Second Thirty Years' War, it was the Bretton Woods Conference.

BRETTON WOODS SYSTEM

By 1944, the US Federal Reserve Gold inventory accounted for the majority of the official Gold reserves of the world, combined (see Chapter 9: Gold). With World War II nearing its end, on July 1st 1944, the representatives of 44 countries, comprising 730 delegates assembled in Bretton Woods, New Hampshire, USA, to negotiate a new global monetary system (see Chapter 10: Financialisation). The Bretton Woods Conference was officially known as the United Nations Monetary and Financial Conference.

Following the chaos, destruction and financial instability of two world wars and the most severe depression the modern world had experienced, Britain, virtually bankrupt, was no longer the custodian of global confidence, to underpin world finance (see Chapter 11: Hegemonic Dominance).

The United States had emerged from the Great Depression and both world wars economically and militarily superior to all other countries, and was referred to for the first time as a superpower.[258] This stature placed the US in an ideal position to command the greatest influence over the negotiations and assert itself in its role, as the new hegemon.

CLASH OF THE TITANS

Although attended by the representatives of 44 nations, the conference was dominated by discussions surrounding two competing plans. John Maynard Keynes (father of Keynesian Economics) had devised a plan which he had drafted and submitted to the British Treasury, and subsequently attended the conference as Britain's principal representative. Harry Dexter White, Chief International Economist at the US Treasury 1942 - 1944 and then Under Secretary to the US Treasury had devised his blueprint, which competed with Keynes's plan.

White's plan advocated for creating incentives intended to promote price stability in the world economy, whereas Keynes's plan favoured a system that promoted economic growth.

The delegates negotiated and deliberated the terms of the new global monetary system, ultimately signing the Bretton Woods Agreement on July 22nd 1944 the final day of the conference. The attendees were cognisant that free trade was dependent on the principle of freely convertible currencies and were reticent to perpetuate the floating exchange rates experienced in the 1930s. This was an imperative among the delegates, particularly given that major fluctuations could impede the free flow of trade. This factor made exchange rate stability a common goal among the participants. Furthermore, with the Great Depression in recent memory and World War II (1939 - 1945) nearing its end, prioritising measures which would ensure peace and stability in the post-war era weighed on the negotiations. This was a view echoed by Cordell Hull, US Secretary of State. Hull vehemently believed that economic discrimination and trade warfare were the underlying causes of the two world wars.

'Unhampered trade dovetailed with peace; high tariffs, trade barriers, and unfair economic competition, with war ... if we could get a freer flow of trade…freer in the sense of fewer discriminations and obstructions…so that one country would not be deadly jealous of another and the living standards of all countries might rise, thereby eliminating the economic dissatisfaction that breeds war, we might have a reasonable chance of lasting peace.'[259]

- *Cordell Hull, US Secretary of State (1933 - 1944).*

Ultimately, White's plan although tempered to address a number of Keynes's concerns was embraced by consensus among the majority of the conference participants. Although Britain had the experience, the US had the power. This was particularly salient since the US was perceived as likely to assume the role as a major creditor to the world, thereafter.[260]

To this end, the Bretton Woods Agreement included a commitment to create a number of institutions to promote growth and stability in the global economy.

WORLD TRADE ORGANISATION

The original Bretton Woods agreement included plans for an International Trade Organisation (ITO). However, these plans lay dormant until the World Trade Organisation (WTO) was established in 1995.

WORLD BANK

At Bretton Woods, it was agreed that a new global institution would be established to provide loans to low-income countries, primarily to invest in infrastructure projects, such as seaports, roads or other critical infrastructure, which in turn would facilitate the repayment of these loans through the associated economic stimulus these projects would yield. The institution created was the International Bank for Reconstruction and Development (IBRD). Ultimately the IBRD became part of the World Bank Group.

The IBRD's objective was to leverage the wealth of the world, to tackle poverty and other inequities in under-developed countries and to create a world less vulnerable to descending into a state of conflict.

The World Bank, into which the IBRD was absorbed, would work closely with the IMF, both to be headquartered in Washington D.C.

INTERNATIONAL MONETARY FUND

Based primarily on the ideas of Harry Dexter White and John Maynard Keynes, the IMF was created to promote international monetary co-operation, international trade, high employment, exchange-rate stability, sustainable economic growth and making resources available to member countries in financial difficulty; predominantly *balance of payments* difficulties (see Balance of Payments, Chapter 5: Payments).

The IMF's initial challenge was to reconstitute an international payment system, in the wake of two world wars.

At its inception, the IMF had three stated functions:

1. To monitor the fixed exchange-rate arrangements between countries, agreed at Bretton Woods.

2. Help governments of member countries manage these exchange-rates to enable them to prioritise economic growth.

3. Provide short-term capital loans to aid countries in the balance of payments.

The IMF derives its funding from quotas and loans. The quotas are funds pooled together from member nations, with varying contributions being made relative to a country's economic and financial standing in the world. The wealthiest developed nations of greater economic importance are naturally the highest contributors within the quota pool.

In terms of the IMF's Articles of Agreement, originally accepted by 29 countries and which have subsequently been accepted by 190 member countries, altering the proportion of quotas is a decision based on weighted voting rights requiring an eighty-five percent majority vote among members.[261] An eighty-five percent majority vote is required for the majority of decisions, however, in some instances a seventy-percent majority vote is required for certain aspects defined within the IMF's Articles of Agreement. Thus, the US with its seventeen-percent weighted vote is able to unilaterally veto any decision which it views as unfavourable, apart from those which form part of the latter spectrum.

The quotas provide the IMF with the resources to aid countries in the form of Special Drawing Rights (SDRs).

SPECIAL DRAWING RIGHTS

During the Bretton Woods Conference, John Maynard Keynes had proposed the creation of a supranational currency named 'Bancor' to replace Pound Sterling as the global reserve currency under the Bretton Woods System. Keynes's proposal was for Bancor to be managed by an International Clearing Union. A distillation of his vision became the inspiration for creating the Special Drawing Rights (SDR) basket, also known by ISO code, 'XDR,' which are issued by the IMF to member countries to hold as part of their reserves. As a reserve asset, the SDRs are comprised of reserve currencies, intended to be used to settle international *balance of payments* between member nations. SDRs were created in 1969, with an initial issue from 1970 – 1972, in the amount of 9.3 billion SDRs. The second issue 1979 - 1981 was in the amount of 12.1 billion and a third issue in 2009 of 182.7 billion (equivalent to $250 billion), in response to the GFC as a measure to assist in managing the impact thereof.[262]

SDR BASKET

The SDR basket is reviewed on a quinquennial basis (once every five years), where the makeup of the basket of currencies and their ratios can be adjusted. For a currency to be included in the basket it needed to be considered stable and freely transferable between countries, as well as subject to significant demand (hard currency), being the currency of a major exporter or financial centre. Hence, a reserve currency. Prior to the formation of the Euro currency in 1999 (see Chapter 7: Central Banks), the basket was comprised of US dollars, German Marks, French Francs, Japanese Yen and British Pound Sterling.

German Marks and French Francs were consolidated within the Euro, which until October 2016, narrowed the basket to the Dollar, Euro, Yen and Pound.

As of October 2016, the SDR basket consisted of 41.73% US dollars, 30.93% Euros, 10.92% Renminbi (Chinese Yuan), 8.33% Japanese Yen and 8.09% British Pounds.

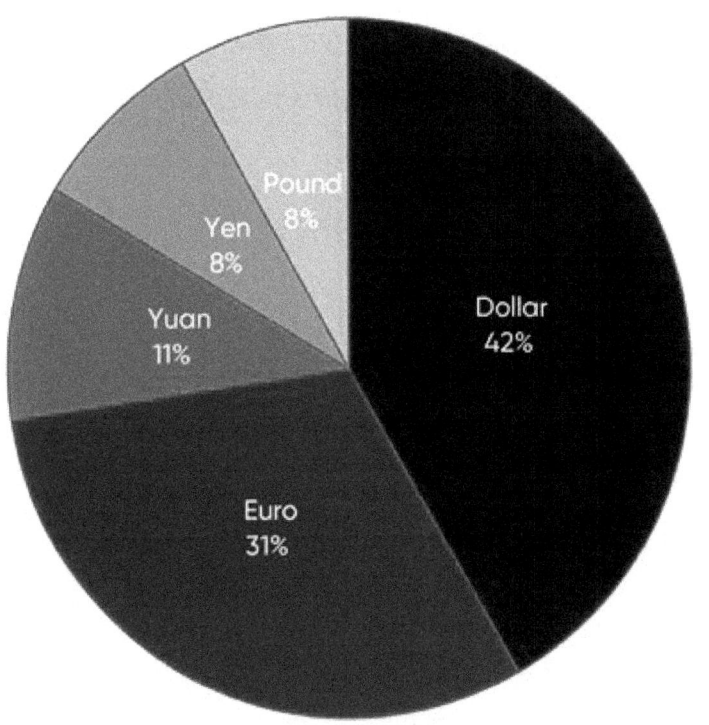

Fig 12.1 SDR Reserve Currency Basket 2016-2021

The IMF's decision in November 2015, to introduce the RMB (Yuan) into the SDR basket in 2016, officially elevated the Yuan to a supplementary global reserve asset, which could be construed as a weak signal of *pre-hegemonic commercial advantage*. A consequence of China's ascent through continued reform and at the time, recognition of its stature as one of the world's major, as well as fastest growing exporters.[263]

In March 2021, the IMF's Executive Board elected to defer the SDR basket review until July 2022, essentially resetting the five-year cycle from August 1st 2022, when it's anticipated to enter effect. A move which reflected the necessity for stability amidst the economic stress brought about by the outbreak of COVID-19.

SDR ALLOCATIONS

In August 2021, the IMF approved and issued 456.5 billion SDRs (equivalent to $650 billion) to assist countries in need of support, as a consequence of the economic impact experienced during the COVID-19 pandemic.[264]

'This is a historic decision – the largest SDR allocation in the history of the IMF and a shot in the arm for the global economy at a time of unprecedented crisis. The SDR allocation will benefit all members, address the long-term global need for reserves, build confidence, and foster the resilience and stability of the global economy. It will particularly help our most vulnerable countries struggling to cope with the impact of the COVID-19 crisis.'

- Kristalina Georgieva, IMF Managing Director, August 2021.

The GFC resulted in the IMF's issuance and allocation of 182.7 billion SDRs in worldwide support. The allocations countered the systemic liquidity crisis in order to facilitate a graceful deleveraging worldwide. This use of the global financial safety net that the IMF provides was dwarfed by the impact of the COVID-19 pandemic, which prompted an unprecedented allocation (Fig 12.2).

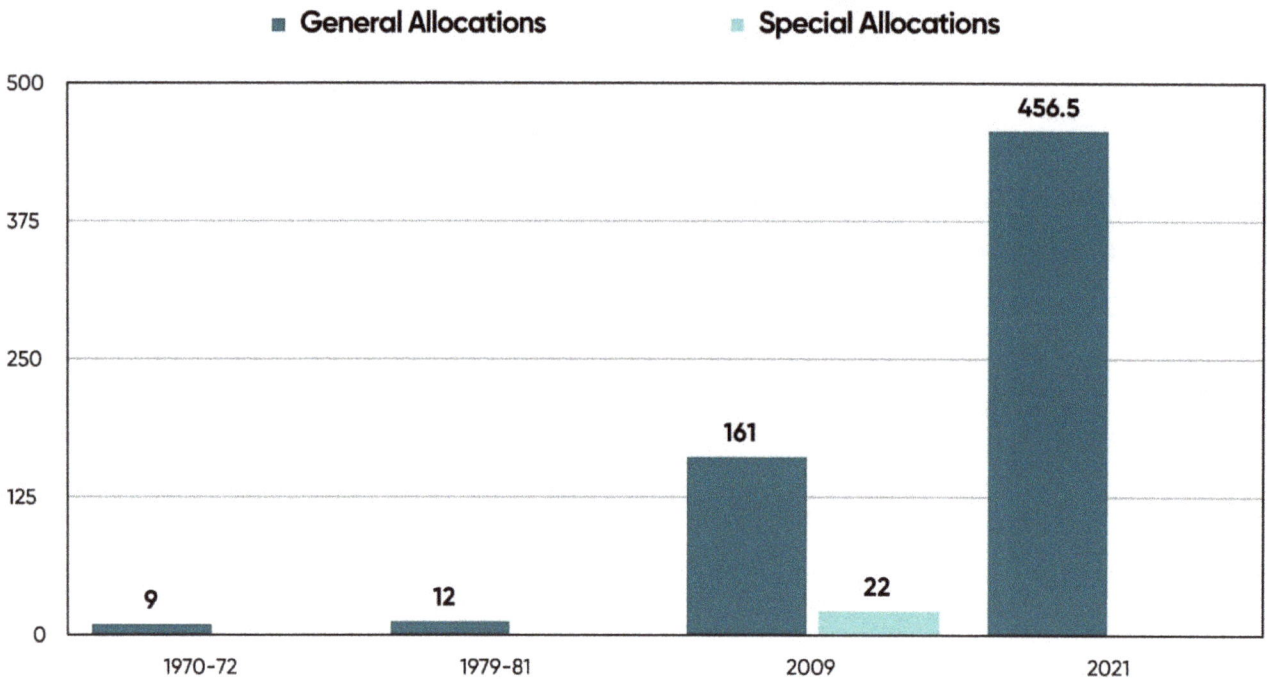

Fig 12.2 General and Special SDR Allocations (in billions) 1970 - 2021. (Source data: IMF, 2021)

GLOBAL RESERVE CURRENCY

At Bretton Woods, the US dollar transitioned in status, from 'apparent' or 'neutral' reserve currency to official principal global reserve currency. The dollar, pegged to gold, and convertible to bullion, upon demand (by foreign Central Banks) to the US Federal Reserve, would act as the world's stable monetary anchor. As a result, all other currencies (including reserve currencies) would be pegged to the US dollar at fixed-exchange-rates, creating a new Gold Standard 'by proxy' arrangement (dollar-gold-standard). The British Pound would no longer maintain its status as the principal global reserve currency, although this role had largely been undermined by Britain's post-war economic posture. Over the course of the 1920s and 1930s, use of the dollar in the reserve currency role had largely equalled that of Pound Sterling.[265] Effectively, internationalising the dollar as a *safe, stable* and *valuable* global reserve asset.

By design, the Bretton Woods System was established in order that nations could only enforce convertibility to gold for the anchor currency. Dollar conversion to gold was hence permitted, however, not required (nor encouraged). The rationale was to encourage nations to forgo converting dollars to gold, and instead, hold and transact in dollars internationally.

By establishing the US dollar as the principal global reserve currency, a system of payments based on the dollar for trade could then be created. The US dollar effectively assumed its role as the 'World's Currency,' enabling the US not only to enforce a global *unit of account*, however, additionally enforce a *medium of exchange* (see Balance of Payments, Chapter 5: Payments). Essentially, the standard to which every other currency was pegged. As a consequence, the vast majority of international transactions, thereafter, have been denominated and conducted in US dollars. This posture represented a substantial departure from Britain's monetary hegemony, whereby both Britain as well as other nations maintained a Gold Standard (see Monetary Hegemony, Chapter 11: Hegemonic Dominance). This technical differentiator, effectively established a 'Dollar Standard.'

TRIFFIN'S DILEMMA

In 1960, Robert Triffin, a Belgian-American economist (1911 - 1993), noted that holding US dollars was more valuable than holding gold, as the persistent behaviour by the US to run current account deficits reflexively made the system more liquid. The corresponding liquidity, in turn, reinforced and fuelled economic growth. The economic growth realised as a result thereof, reflexively made the dollar desirable and more valuable.

However, Triffin later noted that if the US were to cease running current account deficits, the system would lose its liquidity, and thus, reflexively impede global economic growth. The latter, would ultimately bring the system to a halt. Unfortunately, continually running current account deficits wasn't a solution either, as over time the accrued debt burdens would ultimately erode confidence in the dollar and consequently result in systemic instability (see Quantitative Destruction, Chapter 8: Economic Cycles). This paradox is known as Triffin's Dilemma.

NIXON SHOCK

By 1950, the US Federal Reserve had accumulated more than twenty-thousand metric tonnes of Gold. With more Gold reserves, this meant more dollars could be issued, for which the global demand was perpetually growing. Simultaneously, 1950 was the first year in which the US experienced a negative balance of payments position, marking a turning point from bullion inflows to net outflows.

Two decades later, US Gold Reserves had eroded by almost sixty-percent. A result of foreign gold redemptions from the US Federal Reserve. The period from 1967 - 1973, saw the US heavily extend itself, with the war in Vietnam and domestic fiscal spending within President Johnson's 'The Great Society' initiatives (see Guns & Butter, Chapter 10: Financialisation). This resulted in the period known as The Great Inflation (1965 - 1982)[266], marking a significant juncture in US hegemony (see Chapter 11: Hegemonic Dominance) and a pivotal period in global financial history.

GOLD DEMONETISATION

The fiscal policies of the Eisenhower and Kennedy administrations had placed downward pressure on the dollar, leaving it highly overvalued under the Bretton Woods System. Measures taken by both administrations to correct this imbalance, such as import quotas imposed on crude oil and restrictions on trade outflows, as well as tax cuts for domestic productivity and export initiatives, had been unsuccessful.[267] Further attempts at government-led cartel-style 'price fixing' via the London Gold Pool (see London Gold Pool, Chapter 13: Global Trade Rails), ultimately failed to insulate the dollar from a barrage of speculative attacks. France in particular, condemned this posture, as it viewed the world as having to 'foot the bill' for the United States' lack of fiscal discipline. This was a position, which in France's view, had been abused intolerably (see Exorbitant Privilege, Chapter 13: Global Trade Rails). Johnson's administration had delivered the 'Coup de Grâce,' accelerating the effects of Triffin's Dilemma (see above) with 'twin deficits' (Guns & Butter). The remedy for which, was either a dollar devaluation or a 'run on US Gold Reserves.' A practice known as 'Gold Demonetisation.' In terms of monetary power defined by reserves, the US share of reserves had fallen from fifty-percent in 1950 to eleven-percent by August 1971.[268]

On August 15th 1971 (see Guns & Butter, Chapter 10: Financialisation), President Richard Nixon, unilaterally suspended the US dollar's convertibility to gold bullion, known as 'Closing the Gold Window,' essentially reneging on the bedrock principle upon which the Bretton Woods System was built. This event has become infamously referred to as the 'Nixon Shock,' which sent shudders through the echelons of the global financial community, central banks and governments around the world. A result of President Nixon taking this action unilaterally, neither consulting the international monetary or financial community, nor the US State Department. The US has retained its remaining

8133.5 tonnes of gold stockpile since fulfilling its final redemption, in 1980 (see Gold Reserves, Chapter 9: Gold).

COLD WAR

Although this event ultimately brought an end to the Bretton Woods System, in the interests of continuity and stability, the US dollar retained its 'Principal Reserve Currency' status. A posture, which at the time, remained unthreatened by a viable alternative challenger. The Soviet Union (USSR), the only other superpower at the time, with which the US was locked in a state of Cold War in a détente doctrine of military strategy known as Mutually Assured Destruction (MAD)[269], was in no position economically or politically to disrupt or offer an alternative to the Uni-polar monetary system over which the US was dominant.

The Cold War era (1946 - 1991) additionally represented an ideological war between the US and the Soviet Union, where the former had embraced democracy and free-market capitalism, while the latter had embraced communism, totalitarian dictatorship and monetary socialism. The Soviet Union, although having attended and participated in the Bretton Woods Conference, had refused to join the IMF. In December 1945, Soviet Foreign Minister Vyacheslave Molotov notified the US that the Soviet Union would not subscribe to the articles.[270] Collectively, these factors combined with the lack of a financial infrastructure or the appropriate tooling (e.g. FinTech), eliminated the appeal of exploring an alternative to US leadership and dollar-based continuity. In addition, much of the United States' expenditure was directed towards shielding western nation states from the perceived Soviet military threat. This was a posture with which there was no appetite to interfere.

IRREDEEMABLE MONEY

From 1934 - 1971, gold had continued to remain at the official price of $35 per Troy ounce, as set by President Franklin D. Roosevelt in 1934 (see The Great Depression, Chapter 9: Gold). The Nixon Shock decoupled gold from the dollar. The official price of gold ceased shortly thereafter, leaving only a free floating open and unrestricted global bullion market.

The Nixon Shock brought an end to the reliance on gold to back global currencies (known as Metallism) and for the first time in global financial history, marked the beginning of a purely 'Fiat Money' or Chartalism era (see Gold Standard, Chapter 9: Gold).

'We are in an era of irredeemable paper money - a state of affairs unprecedented in history.'

- John Exter (1910 - 2006) US Economist, Central Banker, Banker and Monetary Expert. Creator of Exter's Pyramid.

For so long as all nation states collectively maintained the *pretence* that fiat money had worth (see Exter's Pyramid, Chapter 9: Gold), backed solely by confidence in governments (the creditworthiness of the US government in particular), the system could persist unimpeded.[271] Additionally, this event eventually unravelled the fixed-exchange-rates between the US dollar and other currencies, which float freely in a global foreign exchange (Forex) market (see Aftershock, Chapter 13: Global Trade Rails). The Nixon Shock may arguably be construed as a manifestation of Gresham's Law (see Gresham's Law, Chapter 6: Money), whereby paper money has driven out gold backed money, by fiat.

'Bad money drives out good money, but good money cannot drive out bad money.'[272]

- William Stanley Jevons, Money and the Mechanism of Exchange, 1875 (Gresham's Law).

With the dollar's *store of value* function compromised, the decade that followed the Nixon Shock (1972 - 1982), the most turbulent of the period known as 'The Great Inflation' (see above), saw the US plagued by back-to-back recessions, poor economic growth, the stock market halving in value over a twenty-month period, high unemployment and the highest inflation recorded since the 1940s, and the Great War (see Inflation, Chapter 8: Economic Cycles). A period during which the dollar very nearly collapsed (see Dollar Confidence Crisis, Chapter 10: Financialisation).

CONNALLY'S DICTUM

In spite of the immediate consequences that ensued over the course of the decade that followed it, the Nixon Shock demonstrated the extent of the United States' hegemonic power. Essentially, when the rules of the global monetary system which the US had created no longer served US interests, without consultation and free of accountability to the international community, the US unilaterally altered the rules.[273] While addressing European finance ministers in 1971, then US Treasury Secretary John Connally disdainfully remarked:

'The dollar is our currency, but it is your problem.'

- *John B. Connally Jr., US Treasury Secretary (1971 - 1972).*

13

GLOBAL TRADE RAILS

DOLLAR HEGEMONY

As the principal global reserve currency, the US dollar dominates the majority of global trading. In 2019, global trade invoices reflected that at least half of international trade was conducted in US dollars.[274]

This trade invoicing figure is approximately five times greater than the US share of global goods imports and three times greater than its share of global goods exports.[275] Consequently, the principal reserve currency posture furnishes the United States with extraordinary power over nearly any entity which imports or exports anything anywhere.[276] Furthermore, it ensures that the US is able to keep its borrowing costs low, which in turn amplifies the effects of both US economic as well as foreign policy,[277] while safe-guarding the US economy.[278] Since the Fed issues and the US Treasury maintains the dollar's liquidity through monetary and fiscal policy respectively, this reflexively reinforces the US monopoly in providing payments infrastructure and systems to trade in dollars as a *medium of exchange*. A condition which consolidates the US Federal Reserve's posture as an essential intermediary at the heart of global trade and commerce (see Chapter 5: Payments).

This empowers the US to enforce a global *unit of account* (the US dollar) and to operate under no *balance of payments* constraints (see Monetary Hegemony, Chapter 11: Hegemonic Dominance). Thus, commodities such as crude oil, coffee, grains, timber and numerous raw materials, as well as precious metals (including Gold & Silver) are all priced in US dollars, regardless of where in the world they may originate. As a global unit of account, this dominant currency paradigm (DCP) ensures that non-US entities, such as manufacturers, merchants and service providers, need to account for variances in the exchange-rate of their own domestic currency against the US dollar – a concept known as exchange rate pass-through. In instances where a nation state's, or monetary union's currency is subject to capital account (typically foreign exchange) controls, known as a 'soft currency,' this may inhibit businesses in their ability to import raw materials, goods or consume foreign services where pricing and settlement, thereof, is in US dollars. Capital controls of this nature constitute a common predicament among emerging market economies (EMEs), many of which fail to run a sufficient trade surplus with the United States. In such instances, EME central banks may face significant challenges in order to maintain a dollar liquidity position. For countries the central banks of which the Fed maintains currency swap arrangements (predominantly those of advanced economies), liquidity challenges are typically overcome (see Swap Lines, Chapter 5: Payments). However, for others this may present an insurmountable obstacle. A situation which has long frustrated rivals of the United States. Rivals include nation states such as Russia, Cuba, Venezuela, North Korea and Iran. These circumstances leave these nation state rivals susceptible to domestic destabilisation, via US foreign policy inclusive of instruments, such as extraterritorial sanctions (see below).

The US dollar came to dominate global trade, following the Bretton Woods Conference in 1944. The US had grown into the largest economy in the world, while other countries were trying to rebuild, having suffered devastation from World War II. The US dollar was stable and plentiful. By 1954, the US economy was buoyant and had largely recovered economically from the Great Depression and World War II.

As global trade grew, so did the use of the dollar to conduct the world's business. The dollar, in the role as the principal global reserve currency, is the global *unit of account* and the dominant *medium of exchange*, which prior to the 'Nixon Shock' had been pegged to gold, anchoring it as a *store of value* (see Nixon Shock, Chapter 12: Global Monetary System). This provided a stable common denominator to facilitate international trade, thus, trade proliferated in US dollars, regardless of who was trading with whom.

EXORBITANT PRIVILEGE

The phrase *'Exorbitant Privilege'* originated with French Finance Minister, Valéry Giscard d'Estaing in the 1960s. The phrase is often misconstrued as having been coined by President Charles de Gaulle, who evidently held congruent views.[279]

It describes the *asymmetric imbalance* within the financial system, which becomes apparent through one nation state holding the principal global reserve currency status. Foreigners to the United States, thus, perceive themselves to be supporting American living standards and furthermore subsidising American multi-national businesses. This concept was articulated by American economist, Barry Eichengreen as follows:

'It costs only a few cents for the Bureau of Engraving & Printing to produce a $100 bill, but other countries had to pony up $100 of actual goods in order to obtain one.'[280]

- *Barry Julian Eichengreen, 2011.*

The mid-1960s saw a parallel increase in the per-capita income of Japan and the European Economic Community (the precursor to the European Union), which narrowed the gap with that of US GDP. Economic strength in these markets had soared, fuelled by higher growth and global trade penetration, resulting in an accumulation of reserves exceeding that of the US. Essentially, the US balance sheet was weakening, while the balance sheets of Europe and Japan were strengthening. Consequently, the dollar was overvalued while European currencies and the Japanese Yen were undervalued. Under the Bretton Woods System, whereby fixed-exchange-rates against the dollar prevented a *laissez-faire* (market determined) correction, the only buffer available to compensate for the imbalance were the US Gold Reserves.

The resulting disequilibrium in Europe's and Japan's ascent, which was commensurate with the United States' decline, led to a pluralistic distribution of economic power, which antagonised the sentiments towards, and ultimately bred further contempt for, the privileged role the US dollar played in the international monetary and financial system.

The French in particular were vocal critics of the Bretton Woods System's asymmetry, since the system's inception. They believed it represented a significant disequilibrium in the financial system and a posture that was unsustainable over the longer-term. A view articulated by Triffin's Dilemma (see Triffin's Dilemma, Chapter 12: Global Monetary System). International liquidity was directly controlled through the US current account deficit, thus, US policy determined economic conditions which could limit growth in the European, as well as Japanese economies (see Convertible Virtual Currency, Chapter 14: Tokenisation).[281] However, running greater current account deficits empowered the US to engage in substantial expenditures (liability/debt financing) without a balance of payments constraint. A privilege enjoyed by the US at all other nation state's expense. A *quid pro quo* unacceptable to France. At the first sign of excessive abuse thereof, the French were poised to lead the charge in defecting from a position of compliance therewith.

In February 1965, President Charles de Gaulle, announced France's intention to redeem its US dollar reserves for gold at the official price of $35 per Troy ounce. This action was prompted by President Johnson's 'Guns & Butter' Policy, announced a month earlier.[282] Johnson's policy deepened the United States' 'twin deficits,' which undermined global confidence in the dollar's gold peg ratio under the Bretton Woods System (see Guns & Butter, Chapter 10: Financialisation). A position which left the dollar vulnerable to speculative attacks. Hence, divesting itself of dollar liquidity in favour of gold, became a national imperative for France in anticipation of the dollar's collapse. An outcome which under the rules of the system, was inevitable.

President de Gaulle steamed the French navy across the Atlantic to securely transport their gold bullion back to France. In 1965 alone, the French navy had hauled approximately 133 metric tonnes of bullion from New York to France. Soon, thereafter, several other countries followed suit. This accelerated the erosion of US Gold Reserve inventories rapidly (see Nixon Shock, Chapter 12: Global Monetary System).

French resistance towards dollar hegemony had actually begun years earlier. In 1958, de Gaulle, then Prime Minister of France, had ordered the Banque de France (France's Central Bank) to increase the rate at which it redeemed newly acquired dollar reserves for bullion from the Fed (Gold Demonetisation). By 1967, the ratio of France's national reserves held in gold had risen from just over seventy-percent in 1958 to over ninety-percent in 1967. By contrast, the European average rested a little under eighty-percent at the time.[283]

'Betting against Gold is the same as betting on governments. He who bets on governments and government money, bets against 6000 years of recorded human history.'

- *Charles de Gaulle, 1965 (President of France 1959 - 1969).*

LONDON GOLD POOL

An oversight of the Bretton Woods System is that it did not regulate the price of gold as a commodity. Thus, the price of gold was able to fluctuate due to variations in private industrial and financial demand. In instances where the free market price rose above $35, central banks had the incentive to redeem US dollars for gold and subsequently sell the gold for a higher price in other markets. In 1960, when the open market gold price breached $40, the Federal Reserve and the Bank of England bilaterally agreed that a substantial quantity of gold stored at the Bank of England would be sold to reduce the demand for US Gold Reserves.

Eight countries agreed to establish the London Gold Pool in November 1961 for the purpose of defending the official $35 gold price. The objective was to avoid allowing the London gold price to rise too far above the official price, thereby safe-guarding the stability of the Bretton Woods System. A total of 240 tonnes were contributed to this Pool. The US allocated 120 tonnes, fifty-percent of the total. Germany supplied 27 tonnes. The United Kingdom, France, and Italy each contributed 22 tonnes. Belgium, the Netherlands, and Switzerland each contributed 9 tonnes. At the time, the collective value was equivalent to $270 million.

Initially, the London Gold Pool was a highly clandestine arrangement. Operations, quotas, as well as any profits or losses remained confidential throughout its duration. Its existence was leaked to the press and first revealed by Le Courrier de Genève, in March 1962.[284]

France withdrew from the London Gold Pool in 1967, while aggressively redeeming bullion for dollars from the US (see Exorbitant Privilege above). The Netherlands was engaged in comparable gold redemptions from the US, although on a conservative scale in contrast to that of France. In November 1967, Britain devalued the Pound by almost 15% which triggered an acceleration in depleting physical gold reserves in the London Gold Pool.[285] On March 14th 1968, the US asked the British government to close the London gold markets.[286] In deference to this unusual request, Queen Elizabeth II petitioned the House of Commons to declare March 15th a bank holiday. On March 18th, the US Congress passed legislation repealing the obligation for the US Treasury to maintain its prevailing gold-to-dollar reserve ratio as backing for the US dollar.[287] This followed a meeting of the Fed's FOMC (see Chapter 7: Central Banks) in which the dire circumstances were discussed.

'The international financial system was moving toward a crisis more dangerous than any since 1931. The hurricane of speculation that had occurred on the gold market was likely to be succeeded by a similar hurricane on the exchange markets.'[288] - *Fed FOMC Meeting, March 14th 1968.*

- *Charles A. Coombs (1918 - 1981), Senior Manager, System Open Market Account, US Federal Reserve.*

The London gold market remained closed for a fortnight thereafter, which brought about an end to the London Gold Pool. During the hiatus, other bullion markets had traded gold at higher prices, further depleting US Gold Reserves. Zürich ascended into a major gold trading centre, forming the Zürich Gold Pool, via the largest Swiss banks.

At prices above $35.20, countries were able to engage in zero risk arbitrage transactions with the gold price disparity between private bullion markets and the official US price of $35 per Troy ounce. Dollars were redeemed for gold at a cost of $35.20 from the Fed and sold for a profit. A practice which accelerated the depletion of US bullion reserves. This price disparity between the official price and the open market was known as the 'Gold Window.'

With rapidly depleting Gold Reserves and diminishing confidence in the US economic posture, President Nixon 'Closed the Gold Window' with Executive Order 11615, pursuant to the Economic Stablilisation Act, 1970 (see Nixon Shock, Chapter 12: Global Monetary System). Nixon's Executive Order, additionally imposed a ninety-day wage freeze and a ten-percent duty on all imported goods. Closure of the 'Gold Window' was intended or at least communicated as a temporary measure. However, in October 1976, the United States officially altered the definition of the US dollar in all of its statutes. This action permanently purged any reference to the redemption of US dollars for gold.[289] The same year, the end of the Bretton Woods System was officially ratified by the Jamaica Agreement.[290]

AFTERSHOCK

In December 1971, the Smithsonian Agreement was signed by the 'Group of Ten' (G10), in an attempt to reform the global monetary system. The Group of Ten comprised the United States, the United Kingdom, the Netherlands, Canada, Belgium, Sweden, Germany, France, Switzerland and Japan. A move which demonstrated the international importance of anchoring the dollar with a stable reserve asset in keeping with past precedent via a return to a 'specie standard rule'[291] (see The Great War, Chapter 9: Gold), as well as reinforcing the necessity for fiscal integrity. Under the terms of the agreement, the US would reconstitute the dollar-gold-peg at $38 per Troy ounce, while other countries agreed to appreciate (increase the value of) their currencies against the dollar. Any monetary imbalances experienced, were to be equalised exclusively through the issue and use of SDRs (see Special Drawing Rights, Chapter 12: Global Monetary System).

In pursuit of the domestic policy objective of full national employment (see Dual Mandate, Chapter 7: Central Banks), the Fed lowered interest rates. A reflexive response to the impact that the dollar devaluation ($38 gold peg) was expected to have on domestic employment. The reduction in interest returns prompted an outflow of dollars into foreign central banks, placing downward pressure on the dollar, leaving it overvalued. Thus, ultimately undermining the purpose of the Smithsonian Agreement. Consequently, the dollar price of gold continued to experience pressure on its official rate, effectively creating a new 'Gold Window.' In February 1973, in an attempt to 'narrow the window,' the US devalued the dollar by ten-percent, prompting Japan and the European Economic Community to float their currencies.[292] This proved to be the 'coup de grâce' for the Bretton Woods System and fixed-exchange-rates between currencies. US dollars remained unconvertible to Gold by the Fed and limited exclusively to purchases from foreign private bullion markets until December 31st 1974 (see The Great Depression, Chapter 9: Gold). By the early 1980s, all industrialised nations were using 'floating' fiat currencies. The Fed's actions further demonstrated the paradox of Triffin's Dilemma.

'The conflict that arises between short-term domestic and long-term international objectives for countries whose currencies serve as global reserve currencies.' - Triffin's Dilemma

- *Robert Triffin, 1960s.*

DOLLAR JURISDICTION

With an already stable dollar-based trade system in place, continuity was maintained in the wake of the 'Nixon Shock' (see Nixon Shock, Chapter 12: Global Monetary System) and the demise of the Bretton Woods System. The world had become accustomed to conducting its business in US dollars, although suffering a crisis of confidence until 1982 (see Dollar Confidence Crisis, Chapter 10: Financialisation). Since the 1980s, the US dollar has been perceived to be stable and liquid (see King Dollar, Chapter 10: Financialisation). Combined with the US banking system, which is mature and highly efficient, this created the ideal conditions to make it convenient and predictable for businesses to buy and sell in US dollars internationally.

A typical international transaction in US dollars is conducted as follows:

A Canadian lumber company sells Timber to a French building company. The buyer's bank is in France and the seller's bank is in Canada. Although the former deals in Euros and the latter in Canadian dollars, they settle the payment in US dollars, via correspondent banks (Fig 13.2). Correspondent banks hold accounts with the Fed. Money is transferred seamlessly between these bank's Fed accounts as their status as correspondent banks perceives them to be either safe counterparties or intermediaries (see Correspondent Banking, Chapter 5: Payments).

Since the use of these correspondent banks is intermediated, via their Fed accounts, and settlement is in US dollars, technically, each global transaction of this nature touches US soil. In turn, this furnishes the United States with legal jurisdiction. It, thus, compels foreign countries to abide by US legislation. This is particularly enforced regarding counter-terrorism, money laundering and corruption. However, this policy may be augmented at any time, at the sole discretion of the United States. Further demonstrating the nature of the *asymmetric relationship* and the *exorbitant privilege*, the US hegemonic posture bestows.

NINE-ELEVEN

On the morning of September 11th 2001 (known as Nine-eleven), four domestic commercial flights were hijacked by terrorists in the United States. American Airlines Flight 11 and United Airlines Flight 175 were deliberately crashed into the North and South towers of the World Trade Centre in Manhattan, New York, respectively. In a coordinated strike, American Airlines Flight 77 was deliberately crashed into the US Military's headquarters (The Pentagon) in Arlington, Virginia. The fourth aeroplane, United Airlines Flight 93, which terrorists had bound for Washington D.C., however, crashed in a field near Shanksville, Pennsylvania. The crash occurred prematurely, as a result of heroic resistance and sacrifice on the part of the passengers against the hijackers on-board. Although never determined definitively, investigators concluded that it was likely that either the US Capitol Building or the White House was the intended fourth target. Nine-eleven is the deadliest terrorist attack in the US, till date, claiming the lives of 2996 people, including the 19 hijackers among the 265 passengers of the four flights, of which there were no survivors. A further 6000 people were injured; the vast majority of those killed or injured were civilians. The attacks, additionally, claimed the lives of numerous first responders and bystanders, while attempting to rescue any survivors at both the Pentagon and particularly at the World Trade Centre.

While the Nine-eleven attacks tragically claimed and impacted the lives of thousands, it additionally struck at the heart of several US institutions of national and symbolic importance. The attacks crippled Wall Street and disrupted a major point of presence (POP) for internet connectivity. The US markets remained closed until Wall Street reopened on September 17th 2001, marked by a sharp plunge in the stock market, causing a $1.4 trillion loss in market value. In its first week of trading following the attacks, the S&P 500 index fell more than 14%, while Gold and Crude Oil rallied. The industries most directly impacted were that of airlines, the flights of which were subsequently grounded by the Federal Aviation Administration (FAA). Insurers were also deeply affected, as a consequence of paying out billions of dollars in claims, including to victims and property owners. The economic fallout, thereof, falls within the realm of Black Swan events (see Black Swans, Chapter 2: Capital Evolution).

The World Trade Centre's North and South Towers, also known as the 'Twin Towers,' represented an iconic silhouette, recognised worldwide as a signature feature of the Manhattan skyline. The Twin Towers were a symbol of the role the US plays in global trade and commerce, which the Nine-eleven attacks razed to the ground. The site where the towers once stood, thereafter became known as 'Ground Zero.'

GROUND ZERO

The term 'Ground Zero' has two distinct meanings; the first describes the point on the earth's surface directly above or below an exploding nuclear bomb. The second describes a starting point or base for an activity. In terms of Nine-eleven, although a non-nuclear event, both meanings are applicable.

'Today, our fellow citizens, our way of life, our very freedom came under attack in a series of deliberate and deadly terrorist acts….

….Thousands of lives were suddenly ended by evil, despicable acts of terror. The pictures of airplanes flying into buildings, fires burning, huge -- huge structures collapsing have filled us with disbelief, terrible sadness, and a quiet, unyielding anger. These acts of mass murder were intended to frighten our nation into chaos and retreat. But they have failed. Our country is strong. A great people has been moved to defend a great nation. Terrorist attacks can shake the foundations of our biggest buildings, but they cannot touch the foundation of America. These acts shatter steel, but they cannot dent the steel of American resolve. America was targeted for attack because we're the brightest beacon for freedom and opportunity in the world. And no one will keep that light from shining….'[293]

- George W. Bush, President of the United States (2001 - 2009), September 11th 2001.

Following the Nine-eleven terrorist attacks, the US has wielded its hegemonic power and influence with previously unseen voracity, exploiting every instrument at its disposal to advance its foreign policy objectives. In doing so, the US has projected its vast military might across the globe into theatres, such as Afghanistan and Iraq in pursuit of those responsible for Nine-eleven. Furthermore, the US has exploited its dominance over the global monetary system to identify and extricate the sources of funding for terrorist organisations from around the world. Essentially, suffocating the fire by depriving it of oxygen.

Consequently, the US has exploited its control of the US dollar and its status to substantially increase its surveillance of global monetary flows and intercept, as well as curb financing towards rogue actors. In many instances, having endeavoured to achieve these objectives through imposing sanctions on its rivals. Under this system, if a business entity or country attempts to trade with a sanctioned entity in US dollars, the US has the power to sever its access to US currency and payment systems. Weaponising the dollar has consequently proven to be far more effective than any conventional ordnance (see Soft Power, Chapter 11: Hegemonic Dominance).

INTERMEDIATING CROSS-BORDER REMITTANCES

SWIFT

The Society for Worldwide Interbank Financial Telecommunication is known as SWIFT. SWIFT was established in 1973 and is a private institution headquartered in Belgium, which provides a secure global financial messaging system. Under Belgian law, SWIFT is considered to be a 'co-operative society' owned by its members which are financial institutions.

SWIFT is overseen by a committee of representatives from major central banks. These include the US Federal Reserve, The Bank of England, The European Central Bank, The National Bank of Belgium and the Bank of Japan.

It was conceived as a secure payment channel replacement for Telex (see Communication Technology, Chapter 2: Capital Evolution). Telex was the previous dominant technology mechanism to facilitate interbank payment instructions (messaging). Telex featured a free message format, however, was plagued by poor security and high latency. The system relied on the sending institution having to describe every transaction which were then interpreted by the recipient institution. This led to frequent human errors, friction and delays through the system's lack of standardisation. The SWIFT system by contrast, assigns a unique bank identifier code (BIC) (of between eight and eleven characters) to each financial institution. These are based on the ISO 9362 standard (see SWIFT ISO Standards below).

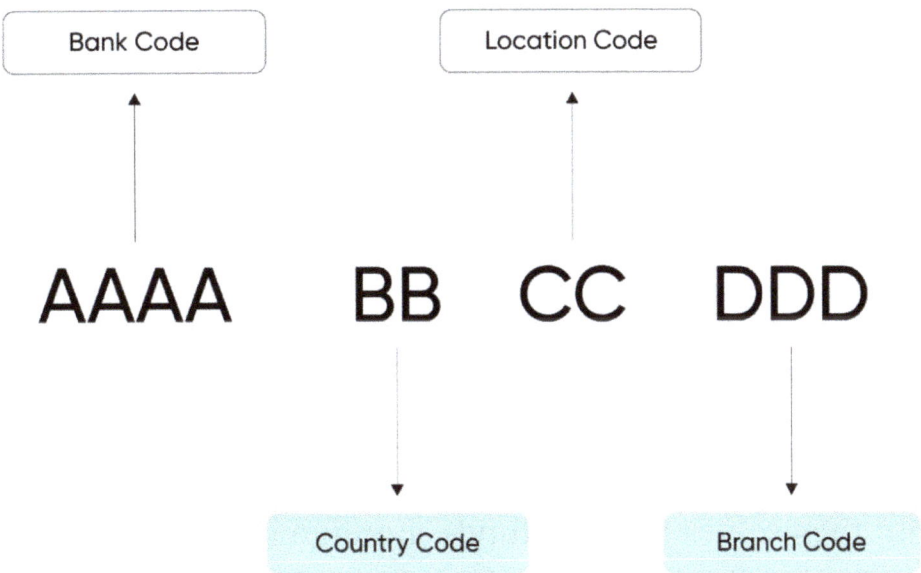

Fig 13.1 illustrates the format of a typical SWIFT BIC

- **AAAA** - represents the four-character code that identifies the bank or institution

- **BB** - represents the two-character ISO country code

- **CC** - represents the two-character location code, identifying the location within the country

Although these eight characters are consistent among all SWIFT BICs, some may feature a further three characters to identify the branch of the specific bank or institution (represented by **DDD** in Fig 13.1).

In order to initiate a cross-border payment transaction, the sender supplies their bank with the SWIFT BIC of the recipient's bank, and the accompanying account information of the recipient. The amount being remitted, the priority, as well as the currency being transferred all form part of the SWIFT message. The message establishes the 'commitment' (see below) and is formatted in a message scheme which eliminated the ambiguity experienced under the Telex system. The message functions as a clear instruction for the appropriate intermediaries (and correspondent banks) to route the payment to the recipient's account.

One of the principal tenets, under which SWIFT has historically grown and thrived, is its claim that it is a neutral entity. SWIFT serves in excess of 11000 financial institutions, spanning more than 200 countries and territories in transmitting and receiving, in excess of thirty-million secure messages per day.

These messages are predominantly international payment instructions, ordering the transfer of funds between global businesses and between domestic and foreign individuals, or combinations, thereof.

SWIFT do not themselves transfer funds. Foreign central banks and US-based correspondent banks' funds are transferred, via depository accounts held with the Fed. The SWIFT messaging is critical to establish the 'commitment' in order to initiate a cross-border payment transaction. Thereafter, intermediaries orchestrate the payment, via the appropriate channels. Dependent on priority, these may vary through the use of real-time gross settlement (RTGS), as well as clearing and settlement systems (CSMs) in multiple jurisdictions (see Chapter: 5 Payments). The Fed as a consequence of its monopoly over dollar-denominated international payments, is typically involved in the fulfilment of the majority of international transactions. SWIFT provides a secure and standardised means of communicating the "whom" and the "what," however, leaves the "how" to the individual actors within the transaction.

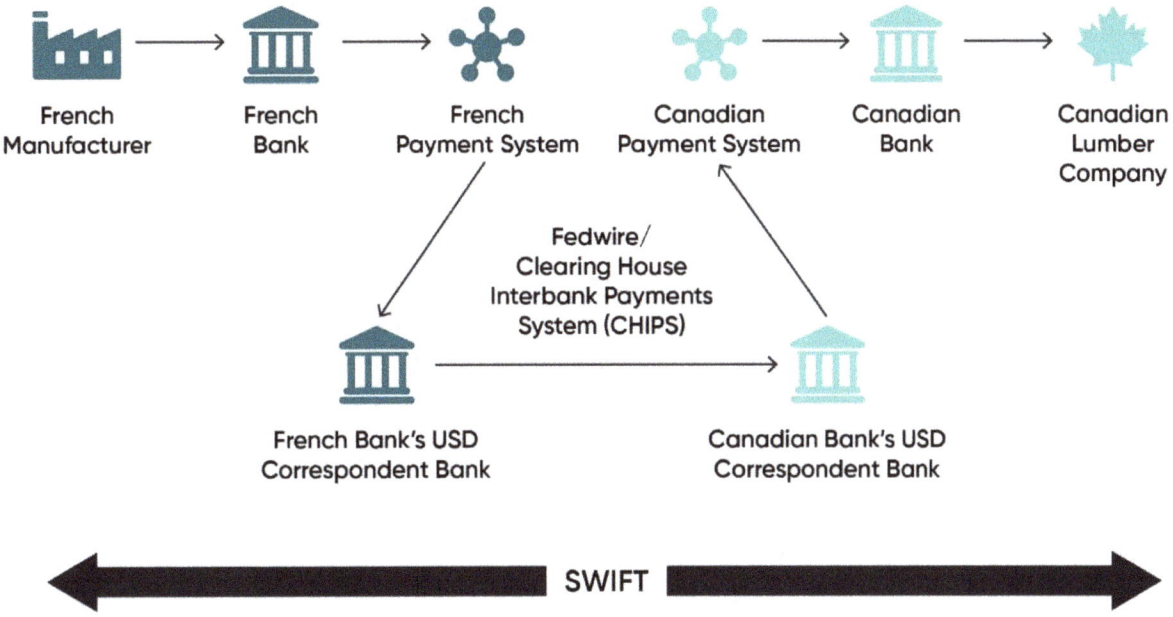

Fig 13.2 illustrates the role of SWIFT in Correspondent Banking as per the example described above

The necessity for demarcating (loose-coupling) of these capabilities (messaging, clearing and settlement) is further influenced by the varying levels of maturity in different monetary zones and banking jurisdictions. Each monetary zone will have its own RTGS and Net Settlement CSM infrastructure, with which the correspondent banks may have to intermediate (see Chapter 5: Payments). In addition, varying foreign exchange (capital account) controls and the liquidity posture in reserve currencies between countries may have a further influence in this regard.

This system and these practices have largely been perpetuated by analogous modernisation, as well as "organic" development. A position greatly amplified by fractured standardisation and poor co-operation between participating financial institutions. Friction has been further compounded by the reliance of the US, in acting as the intermediary and authority in these matters, where diplomatic relations between nations may be strained. This posture is particularly prevalent amongst US rivals.

SWIFT ISO STANDARDS

SWIFT is the registration authority for a number of ISO standards governing the syntax, scheme and encoding formats for financial messages (see Messaging, Chapter 5: Payments). Greater standardisation serves as the catalyst for accelerating the commoditisation of a technology capability (see Standardisation, Chapter 2: Capital Evolution) and enabling its interoperability and proliferation on a global scale (see Genesis of an Ecosystem, Chapter 3: Ecosystems).

SWIFT ISO Standards:

- **ISO 9362** - 1994 Banking Telecommunication Codes - BIC (Bank Identifier Codes)

- **ISO 10383** - 2003 Securities and related Financial Instruments - MIC (Market Identifier Codes)

- **ISO 13616** - 2003 IBAN Registry

- **ISO 15022** - 1999 Securities - Data Field Dictionary - Scheme for Messages (replacement of ISO 7775)

- **ISO 20022** - ISO 20022-1 2004 and ISO 20022-2 2007 Financial Services - Universal Financial Industry Message Scheme

ISO 20022

The significance of the development and adoption of the ISO 20022 standard cannot be overstated. A standard fully agreed upon internationally, for the development and implementation of messages (and a data model) for financial services. The entire financial services industry is expected to migrate to the use, thereof, in order to enable all financial counterparties to improve the consistency of industry communications and transactions. The finance sectors catered to under ISO 20022 are Interbank Payments, Securities, Corporate Treasury, Trade Services, Card Payments and Foreign Exchange. ISO 20022 represents a major catalyst in enabling inter-system integration, as well as an accelerant for the creation of alternative payment rails (see Standardisation, Chapter 2: Capital Evolution). Much like APIs (see API Economy, Chapter 3: Ecosystems), ISO 20022 is a major enabler for ecosystem expansion and competition across the financial sector, via continued FinTech development.

For Securities Funds, the previous message formats of MT 502, MT 509 and MT 515 are displaced, via ISO 20022 equivalent messages, thereby eliminating the necessity to maintain compliance with the ISO 15022 standard (see above). For Corporate Treasury, ISO 20022 provides a single global payment format which enables greater standardisation among Enterprise Resource Planning (ERP) systems (see Chapter 3: Ecosystems) and the creation of standardised consolidated payables files (CPFs) transmissible for bank processing. For Trade Services, SWIFT's Trade Service Utility (TSU) exploits ISO 20022's support for document matching in Purchase Orders (POs), Invoices and a variety of other relevant supply-chain data. ISO 20022 has enabled the creation of an open account trade settlement instrument known as Bank Payment Obligation (BPO). BPO offers buyers and suppliers a new method to secure and finance trade transactions. For Card Payments, ISO 20022 supports standardised messages between various actors within the payment card industry. These entities include merchants, Acquirers, Payment Networks and Issuers. The standardised messaging supports sales systems (POS), terminal management (PDQs), payment scheme clearing, as well as fee collection in the form of interchange and discount fees (see Chapter 5: Payments). For Foreign Exchange (Forex/FX), ISO 20022 will support FX messages for pre-trade, trade, post-trade, notification, clearing and settlement, as well as reporting and reconciliation.

ELEMENT HIERARCHY

ISO 20022 features notable improvements over MT messaging, such as the introduction of support for nested elements which facilitates the logical grouping of data.

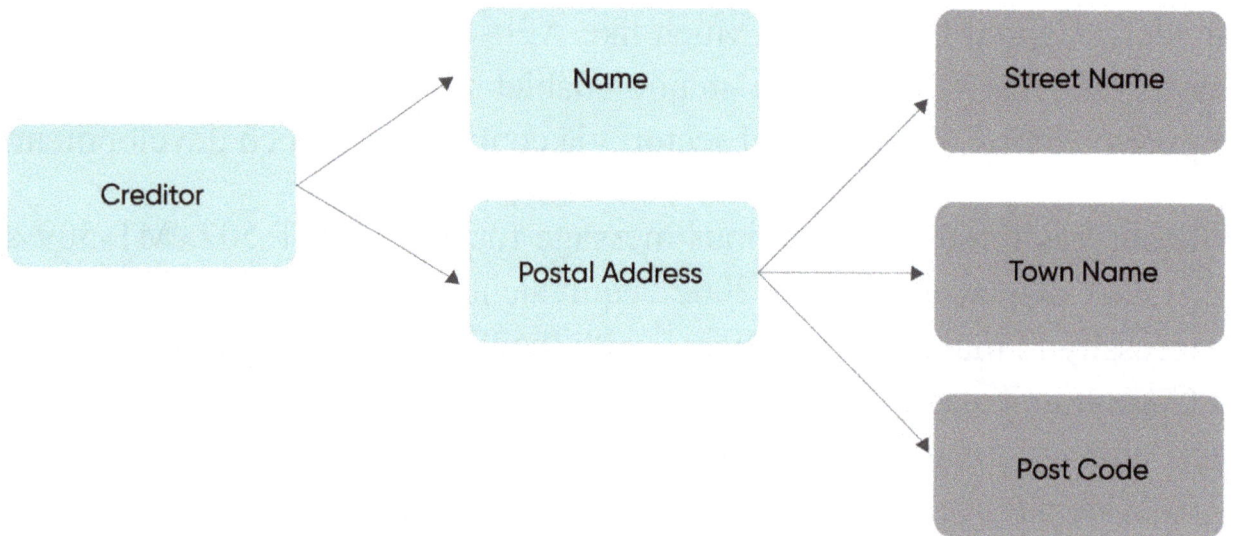

Fig 13.3 Example of the elemental hierarchy of a creditor in ISO 20022

DEDICATED ELEMENTS

The standard additionally features a number of dedicated elements such as:

End-to-end Identification	- fully identifies debtor and creditor in each transaction
Settlement Account	- eliminates the necessity for cross-field validation and includes granular sub-elements
Currency of account	- the specified currency, an example of a sub-element of the settlement account above
Service Level Code or **Proprietary**	- a dedicated element designed to capture specific service expectations such as priority

Charge Information - includes a sub-element to capture the Agent that is due transaction charges

Debtor Agent & Creditor Agent - mandatory roles which clearly identify the party servicing the customer

ENHANCED DATA MODEL

The data model of ISO 20022 features an enhanced and extensible use of financial language that accommodates local practices in a variety of jurisdictions. Examples include sub-elements which identify accounts, such as IBAN (see International Bank Account Numbers below). It additionally accommodates both 'Proprietary,' as well as ISO codes which may be defined externally to the transaction message. The data model furthermore accommodates the identification of agents and multiple parties, as well as granular postal addresses (Fig 13.3).

NEW ELEMENTS

The new elements include On Behalf Of (OBO) payments which use the **'Initiating Party'** field to capture the details of a party which initiates a credit transfer on behalf of a debtor. Other new elements include structured remittance information in order to provide rich invoice details to support reconciliation for a creditor. Furthermore, ISO 20022 includes dedicated instruction elements which may be used to assign instructions for specific parties. Examples include instructions for a 'Creditor Agent' or for the 'Next Agent' in a transaction.

CONTINUOUS LINKED SETTLEMENT SYSTEM

Apart from SWIFT, which facilitates the vast majority of financial messaging to establish the 'commitment,' prior to clearing and settlement in cross-border payments, via correspondent banking, the Continuous Linked Settlement System (CLS) functions as a cross-border payment messaging platform for settlement of foreign exchange trades. The system endeavours to eliminate settlement risks, through the implementation of a payment-versus-payment mechanism.

The payment-versus-payment mechanism is intended to eliminate the settlement risk evident when one party sells a currency, prior to receiving the currency purchased. The CLS system is managed by CLS Bank International, based in New York. The CLS system is solely dedicated to the settlement of foreign exchange trades.

TERRORIST FINANCE TRACKING PROGRAM

Confidence in SWIFT's neutrality has repeatedly been called into question. Following *Nine-eleven*, the US Treasury Department issued subpoenas to SWIFT seeking co-operation in identifying and sharing information on suspected terrorists and their networks. The US government had openly disclosed its intent to constrain its interest, solely to review information deemed relevant to specific terrorism investigations.

In 2006, it was alleged that the Central Intelligence Agency (CIA) and the US Treasury had gained direct unfettered access to SWIFT's database[294], leaving it within their sole discretion to determine what information was relevant to the Terrorist Finance Tracking Program (TFTP).[295]

By the close of 2009, SWIFT had transferred hosting of critical data sets from its US based server infrastructure to alternative systems in the European Union and Switzerland.[296] The systems migration was broadly interpreted as a means of restoring SWIFT's neutrality by escaping US jurisdiction.

An agreement, known as the TFTP Agreement,[297] which commenced on August 1st 2010, was negotiated between the US and the EU. The agreement governs the processing and transfer of specific data sets to the US Treasury Department from SWIFT. The United States maintains that the TFTP is *'rooted in sound legal authority.'*[298] In the US Treasury's view, it is in alignment with the International Emergency Economic Powers Act, 1977 and the United Nations Participation Act, 1945.[299]

In its final report, the Nine-eleven Commission's Public Discourse Project awarded the US government a '*high grade*,' for its efforts in combating terrorist financing. The report made particular reference to '*significant strides in using terrorism finance as an intelligence tool.*'[300]

The report refrained from explicitly crediting the United States' access to SWIFT's data sets for its progress in combating terrorism. However, it remains an inductively reasonable inference that access to this data and the analysis, thereof, has played a pivotal role in intelligence gathering and subsequent counter-terrorism successes.

In a comparable manner to which the US exploits its monopoly of access to transactional payments data gleaned, via the Fed, the US banking system and from SWIFT, via the inter US-EU TFTP Agreement, other countries may exploit transactional data harvested from state-sponsored payment systems (such as Digital Currency Electronic Payment, see Chapter 14: Tokenisation) for purposes other than those related exclusively to AML, Counter-terrorism Financing (CTF) and sanctions screening.

Such data is likely to offer advantages in expanding surveillance and advancing developments in Artificial Intelligence. In the custody of nations with neither mature nor established protections for individual privacy and those with questionable track records in human rights violations, such applications which may result from access to this data could be exploited to the detriment of those using these systems.

EXTRATERRITORIAL SANCTIONS

Sanctions are a foreign policy instrument designed to levy an economic penalty on countries or in some instances, on individuals. Typically, sanctions are imposed in response to either an act of aggression or conduct which falls short of the standards or laws of the international community. Consequently, sanctions function as a carrot-and-stick approach to apply pressure to the offending country (or party) to reverse its position. Sanctions essentially function as a means of dealing with political disputes non-militarily by means of affecting the sanctioned country (or entity) economically.

Unilateral sanctions are imposed by one nation state over another, whereas multilateral sanctions are imposed by multiple nation states working collaboratively. In most instances unilateral sanctions tend to be less effective than multilateral. However, unilateral sanctions imposed by a hegemonic power tends to realise a disproportionate economic impact.

Sanctions are intended to impose such economic penalties by preventing entities that are subject to a country's laws from engaging in business with a sanctioned entity. US secondary sanctions however, prohibit US companies and financial institutions from engaging in business with third-country companies that engage in business with sanctioned entities.[301]

This enables the United States to impose sanctions on entities that are not subject to US jurisdiction. This presents a choice to multi-national companies, in which they either elect to engage in business with sanctioned countries, or engage in business with the United States. Choosing the former has dire consequences, due to the US dollar's status as the principal global reserve currency. Since international transactions are predominantly conducted in US dollars and incidentally touch US soil through intermediaries, this ultimately exposes these entities to US sanctions through fleeting contact (see Dollar Jurisdiction above).[302]

The extraterritorial impact is amplified in its effect on SWIFT. In February 2012, the US Senate Banking Committee sanctioned SWIFT, applying pressure to sever Iran from the global financial system.[303] In March 2012, the EU joined the US in a consensus to impose sanctions on Iran.[304] The decision to impose sanctions on Iran came about as a result of intense international negotiations since 2002 surrounding Iran's Nuclear Programme.[305]

Since SWIFT is a Belgian entity and subject to the EU's jurisdiction, SWIFT capitulated *'under protest,'*[306] to isolating Iranian banks from its network, including Iran's central bank. Consequently, this action ultimately brought Iran to the negotiating table, which paved the way for the JCPOA (see below).

In order to limit the risks of the outbreak of a global or regional nuclear conflict, a number of geopolitical instruments have emerged. To provide context to the emergence of the JCPOA, an understanding of the Non-Proliferation Treaty is essential.

NON–PROLIFERATION TREATY

The Treaty on the Non-Proliferation of Nuclear Weapons or "NPT" was entered into and enforced from March 5th 1970 onwards.[307] The objective of the treaty is to prevent the spread of nuclear weapons and nuclear weapons technology. Additionally, the treaty seeks to promote the peaceful use of nuclear technology in energy generation, as well as to further the goal of unilateral nuclear disarmament.[308]

A testament to the NPT's significance is that apart from the five nuclear-weapon states who are party to it, there are a further 186 countries which have signed it. It should be noted that North Korea (a former signatory) has since withdrawn from the NPT since January, 2003.[309]

Nuclear-weapon states are defined as those which both built and tested a nuclear weapon, prior to January 1967. These are the United States, Russia (formerly the USSR), the United Kingdom, France and China.

There are a further four states which are either known or believed to be in possession of nuclear weapons. These states are India, Pakistan, North Korea and Israel. Apart from Israel, which is deliberately ambiguous as to whether or not it possesses nuclear weapons, these other states have openly declared their possession of these weapons and have tested them.

With a profound global consensus towards nuclear non-proliferation, there has been significant philosophical support gained towards eventually achieving the treaty's intended outcome. However, it has largely become incumbent upon the United States and its allies to lead and finance the efforts to ensure that global safety is achieved by preventing new nuclear-armed states from emerging.

The United States detonated two nuclear weapons over the Japanese cities of Hiroshima and Nagasaki on August 6th and 9th 1945, respectively. The two bombings killed between 129000 and 226000 people, most of whom were civilians, forcing an intervention by Japanese Emperor Hirohito to surrender to the US and its allies, effectively ending World War II. Thus far, these remain the only uses of nuclear weapons in an armed conflict. The NPT seeks to ensure this remains as such.

JOINT COMPREHENSIVE PLAN OF ACTION

The JCPOA (or the 'Iran Nuclear Deal' as it is often referred to), is an agreement entered into between Iran, Germany, the broader European Union and the permanent members of the UN Security Council. These members were the United States, France, Russia and China. The agreement was reached in Vienna, Austria in July 2015.[310]

The terms of the agreement were in aid of limiting Iran's nuclear capabilities for a fifteen-year-period, by eliminating its stockpile of Medium Enriched Uranium (MEU) completely. Furthermore, to reduce its stockpile of Low Enriched Uranium (LEU) by 98%.

Additionally, Iran would be expected to reduce the number of its centrifuges (used for Uranium enrichment) by 66% for the first thirteen-years of the agreement. For the full fifteen-year duration, Iran would be limited to enriching Uranium up to a maximum concentration of 3.67%, for which the first ten-years would be limited to a single facility using first generation centrifuges (which are less efficient). Iran also agreed to refrain from constructing any further 'heavy water' (deuterium oxide) production facilities for the same period.

ISOTOPES

Isotopes are atoms of the same element, however, are comprised of varying numbers of neutrons while retaining the identical numbers of protons and electrons. A feature of elements that vary by isotope, is that each variance will have a different mass.

URANIUM

Uranium, the heaviest naturally occurring element, is predominantly comprised of an isotope of 238 (U-238). Uranium will typically be comprised of a U-238 concentration of 99.27%, an isotope 235 (U-235) concentration of 0.711% with a minute proportion of isotope 234 (U-234).[311]

CRITICAL MASS

Although radioactive, U-238 is not as fissile, as upon absorption of a thermal neutron, the energy released by U-238 is insufficient to meet the *critical* level needed for weaponisation. In other words, regardless of the quantity of U-238 used, the material isn't capable in achieving the *critical mass* required for a cascade of nuclear fission chain reactions, which result in a nuclear explosion.

WEAPONISATION

Enriched Uranium is produced by feeding Uranium hexafluoride gas into centrifuges to separate out the most suitable isotope for nuclear fission, that of

U-235. The variance in mass of each isotope essentially makes separating the material possible using centrifugal force, created within the centrifuge. It is considered to be Low Enriched Uranium (LEU) at a level between 3% - 5% of U-235 and highly enriched, at levels of 20% or greater concentration. Highly Enriched Uranium (HEU) is predominantly used in research reactors and naval propulsion systems. However, Uranium is considered to be of a 'Weapons Grade,' when enriched to levels of 90% of U-235 or greater. Weapons Grade Uranium is capable of achieving *critical mass* within a range of approximately 47kg - 52kg (variably dependent on factors of weapon design and U-235 concentration).

BREAK-OUT PERIOD

The objective of the JCPOA is to maintain Iran's Uranium enrichment levels well below the 'Weapons Grade' threshold and limit its capabilities with which enriched material could be produced. Essentially limiting the quality and quantities of material required to rapidly produce a viable nuclear weapon, (known as the 'break-out period') although within tolerable levels for which non-military applications such as atomic energy initiatives could still be legitimately pursued.

TRUST BUT VERIFY

In order to monitor and verify Iran's compliance with the JCPOA, the International Atomic Energy Agency (IAEA), would have unfettered access to all Iranian nuclear facilities. IAEA inspectors would regularly and randomly inspect Iran's facilities to ensure compliance throughout the JCPOA's duration.

CARROT & STICK

In exchange for verifiably adhering to their commitments for the duration of the JCPOA agreement, Iran would receive relief from sanctions imposed by the US and European Union, as well as from nuclear-related sanctions imposed by the

United Nations Security Council. Such relief would include access to SWIFT and international correspondent banking.

DYSTOPIAN DIPLOMACY

NORTH KOREA

In March 2017, in compliance with United Nations sanctions, SWIFT severed North Korean banks from its system.[312] This followed four ballistic missile tests, a week prior and followed the assassination (using the nerve agent VX) of Kim Jong Nam, North Korean leader, Kim Jong Un's half-brother.[313]

This was in response to growing global concern over Pyongyang's development and testing of nuclear weapons and ballistic missile delivery systems.

SWIFT advocated that its decision to sever the North Korean banks was based on the premise that they were *'no longer compliant with SWIFT's membership criteria.'*[314]

IRAN

In May 2018, President Trump unilaterally withdrew the United States from the JCPOA.[315] In doing so, the United States re-imposed the pre-existing sanctions that were in force prior to the signing of the JCPOA. In addition, the US imposed a variety of new sanctions covering an estimated 700 individuals, entities and aircraft. Furthermore, an additional 300 targets and over 50 Iranian banks and their foreign subsidiaries were newly sanctioned.

In 2018, SWIFT (under threat of being sanctioned itself) complied with US sanctions, again severing Iran from the global financial messaging system. Although describing its actions as *'regrettable,'* SWIFT stated that its decision to capitulate had been *'taken in the interest of the stability and integrity of the wider global financial system.'*[316]

Following the implementation of the JCPOA, Britain and the EU had realised a lucrative trade surplus with Iran. With the sudden and unexpected US withdrawal from the JCPOA, free of an apparent good-faith basis for exiting the agreement, Britain and the EU remained incentivised and committed to create an alternative means to preserve the deal through continued trade. An innovative system would need to be devised, with which the non-US JCPOA signatories could continue to engage in business with Iran, while simultaneously avoiding any potential violation of US sanctions. The result was the development of INSTEX (see below).

INSTRUMENT IN SUPPORT OF TRADE EXCHANGES

In January 2019, the governments of Britain, Germany and France announced the creation of a new payments system, known as the Instrument in Support of Trade Exchanges (INSTEX).

INSTEX is a European Union controlled Special Purpose Vehicle (SPV), specifically designed to circumvent US Sanctions while simultaneously remaining compliant, therewith. INSTEX achieves this objective by facilitating businesses within the EU and Britain in continuing to trade with Iran, without violating US imposed sanctions by utilising an innovative extra-systemic mechanism.

As the hegemonic dominant country, the US is at the apex of the global financial system (see Chapter 12: Global Monetary System), and thus, imposing US sanctions, enforces US foreign policy on behalf of all nation states (as if it were a multilateral action). Following the United States withdrawal from the JCPOA in May 2018, and its reinstatement of sanctions against Iran, any new system that were to facilitate transactions across borders would be considered to be engaged in sanctioned conduct by the United States (see Extraterritorial Sanctions above).

INSTEX, therefore, could not be designed to simply act as a substitute for SWIFT. As established in the conventional anatomy of a transaction (see Anatomy of Payment Transactions, Chapter 5: Payments), messaging is decoupled from transacting. If INSTEX were simply a messaging substitute, the subsequent transaction performed by the participating actors (correspondent banks) would be in violation of US sanctions and vulnerable to punitive consequences imposed by the US.

In order to prevent exposing itself to circumstances in which it is in direct violation of sanctions, INSTEX implemented a netting (offsetting of obligations) paradigm. A conceptually identical instrument to clearing and settlement mechanisms (see Clearing, Chapter 5: Payments), although in the application, thereof, substitutes cross-border transactions with bartering.

By way of example, under this model, a European oil trader seeks to procure a volume of crude from an Iranian oil company. Simultaneously, an Iranian manufacturer seeks to procure a consignment of manufacturing equipment from a European machinery supplier.

In lieu of attracting two international transactions, the INSTEX system directs the two Iranian entities to transact with one another domestically, via Iran's Special Trade and Finance Instrument (STFI). STFI functions as a mirror-image system to INSTEX, via an Iranian SPV. The two European entities are also directed to transact with one another domestically. Consequently, no international financial transactions occur, and thus, allows all parties to remain compliant with US sanctions.

By extrapolating this paradigm at scale, and across multiple actors in both jurisdictions on a multilateral basis, international trade can be facilitated with a negligible net obligation to be settled. The settlement balance can be held in reserve for future transactions or settled in equivalent value commodities.

This mechanism effectively disintermediates SWIFT, the Fed, the United States and the US dollar from the messaging and the 'exchange of value' transaction.

As a by-product, the INSTEX system removes friction and avoids transaction charges that would otherwise be incurred by using the SWIFT system, and furthermore, eliminates charges incurred through the settlement of international payments, via correspondent banks, as well as any foreign exchange transfer premiums.

INSTEX is designed specifically to provide a mechanism to enable transactions with Iran's STFI system devoid of using SWIFT, correspondent banks and the US dollar without engaging in sanctioned conduct. INSTEX not only avoids violating US sanctions through monetary exchange, it additionally circumvents the EU's obligations under the 2010 TFTP agreement (see above) with the US, to share cross-border financial messaging data.

The first transaction via INSTEX was successfully conducted with Iran and confirmed by France, Germany and the UK in March 2020.[317]

Russia, a member of the UN Security Council and in its capacity as a co-signatory of the JCPOA, has persistently pursued being admitted access to the INSTEX system since its announcement. Russia has remained a vocal critic of US influence and control over the global financial system, particularly when exploited as leverage in enforcing US foreign policy.

SYSTEM FOR TRANSFER OF FINANCIAL MESSAGES

The System for Transfer of Financial Messages (SPFS) is a Russian developed equivalent to the SWIFT system, sponsored and funded by the Central Bank of Russia.

Russia embarked on the development of the system in 2014, after the US threatened to sever Russia from the SWIFT system in response to Russia annexing Crimea.

In December 2017, the first non-banking entity transaction was executed. By March 2018, over 400 institutions were connected to the SPFS network. As of 2019, Russia had reached SPFS integration agreements with the Eurasian Economic Union (EEU), as well as Turkey, India and Iran.

A stated intention by both Russia and China is to integrate SPFS with China's Cross-Border Inter-Bank Payments System (CIPS) (see below).[318]

MIR

Mir is Russia's national payment system adopted in May 2017. The system is operated by the Russian National Card Payment System, a wholly owned subsidiary of the Central Bank of Russia.

Due to sanctions against the Russian régime imposed in 2014, Russian banks were denied services from payment schemes, such as MasterCard and Visa.[319] Shortly thereafter, the Mir system was devised to prevent future disruption.[320]

CROSS–BORDER INTER–BANK PAYMENTS SYSTEM

The Cross-Border Inter-Bank Payments System (CIPS), is a Chinese sponsored initiative to mirror the functionality of SWIFT. CIPS, established in 2015, is occasionally referred to, as the 'China International Payments System.'

CIPS does not seek to facilitate funds transfers directly. Comparable to SWIFT, the system transmits payment instruction messages which are settled via correspondent accounts that institutions maintain with clearing banks. These institutions are either banks themselves or require their transactions to be settled, via banking counterparties (see Chapter 5: Payments).

CIPS provides controlled cross-border access to China's onshore RMB clearing system, CNAPS2 (see Chapter 5: Payments) for use in cross-border RMB payments, in order that offshore RMB settlements can access onshore liquidity directly.

As such CIPS will gradually replace the nominated clearing banks in various financial centres (examples of which are; the Bank of China in Hong Kong, the Industrial and Commercial Bank of China in Singapore and the China Construction Bank in London) with controlled access to CNAPS2. In the previous business model, the designated clearing banks provided controlled access to CNAPS2. CIPS is an important step in enabling RMB to become increasingly useable internationally and in eventually ascending to full convertibility (see SAFE, Chapter 16: The Rise of China).

CIPS maintains its standing as an interbank payments system which facilitates final settlement onshore. CIPS has eleven Chinese, and eight global direct access banks (see Direct & Indirect Participants, Chapter 5: Payments), plus hundreds of indirect access banks (see Correspondent Banking, Chapter 5: Payments).

As of 2016, CIPS could interact with SWIFT, allowing access to SWIFT's international member institutions.

CIPS uses the SWIFT industry standards (see SWIFT ISO Standards above) for financial messaging syntax and formatting. There is a common strategy amongst these SWIFT alternatives to align with these common standards (ISO 20022), which provide maximum flexibility and compatibility with each other as the underlying fabric of the global financial ecosystem evolves. ISO 20022 supports Chinese, as well as other extended character sets.

One notable and differentiated characteristic of CIPS is the focus purely on cross-border payments exclusively denominated in Renminbi (RMB). ISO2022 additionally supports the purpose of payment (POP) codes required by the People's Bank of China (PBOC) and which is supported by CIPS, to satisfy the legitimacy of transactions under China's capital account controlled currency régime (see SAFE, Chapter 16: The Rise of China). Over time, it is expected that CIPS will evolve to include capital-related transactions to enable foreign direct investment, as well as the trade of international RMB denominated securities (in support of China's burgeoning Bond Market).

This development sends a clear signal that the dominance of the US dollar in international trade is not absolute. The spheres of international clearing and cross-border payments are ripe for disruption and disintermediation. This is further reinforced by China's introduction of a peer-to-peer based Central Bank Digital Currency in 2020 (see Digital Currency Electronic Payment, Chapter 14: Tokenisation).

With growing alternatives such as CIPS and SPFS in the international arena, FinTech players are well positioned to capitalise on these contemporary frameworks. This is particularly attractive for markets eager to transact with China and Russia on an increasingly competitive basis, where direct engagement at a reduced premium may be construed as a competitive differentiator.

SINGLE EURO PAYMENTS AREA

The Single Euro Payments Area (SEPA) is a European Union driven initiative to deeply integrate and simplify Euro denominated payments within the bloc (see Chapter 5: Payments). SEPA members include European Union member states, members of the European Free Trade Association and a number of technical scheme members which are micro-states, such as the Vatican City and Monaco.

SEPA's aim is to defragment cross-border payments among members into a frictionless and standardised Euro based 'single payments' market, which emulates the 'single market' characteristics of the European Union itself.

Using SEPA, a European bank account holder can seamlessly transfer Euro denominated funds to any other European bank account holder, removing the necessity for holding multiple accounts across jurisdictions. Furthermore, this removes the necessity to rely on international payment messaging systems, such as SWIFT, as well as dollar-denominated correspondent banking, (for internal transactions) within the EMU.

Through the use of common standards such as ISO 20022, as well as standardised procedures and financial instruments, SEPA is able to target a significant reduction in the cost of moving capital among its Eurozone members regionally. SEPA is based on the interlinking cross-border payments model (see Interlinking, Chapter 5: Payments).

SEPA's legal foundation is established through the EU's Payments Services Directive (PSD). The European Commission and European Parliament enabled this regulation and its supporting legislation to promote the agenda of greater integration within the 'single market.'

This underscores the commitment to three key Pan-European payment mechanisms.

1. SEPA Cards Framework (SCF)

2. SEPA Credit Transfer (SCT)

3. SEPA Direct Debit (SDD)

The objective of SCF was to solicit commitment from Card Issuers, Acquirers and schemes to adopt general purpose EMV cards and drive interoperability, common technical standards and scheme licensing arrangements throughout the SEPA area. SCT facilitates the transfer of funds from one account to another (account-to-account or A2A), anywhere in the SEPA ecosystem and provided the transfer is initiated before the cut-off on a business day, funds will be cleared in the recipient's account the following business day. SCT uses the STEP2 PE-ACH CSM (see Clearing & Settlement Mechanisms, Chapter 5: Payments). Using the SCT Inst (SEPA SCT Instant Payment), an instant version of the mechanism (Real-Time Gross Settlement), funds are transferred as cleared effects within a ten-second-window, near instantly. SCT Inst uses the TARGET2 RTGS (see Real-Time Gross Settlement, Chapter 5: Payments).

SDD is divided into two categories to provide direct debit functionality. The first is known as Core SDD, a purely consumer-based service. All banks participating within the SEPA framework are compelled to offer their customers this facility.

The second is B2B SDD, intended for business customers. Unlike Core SDD, it requires a mandate to be submitted to the bank by the creditor and the debtor. Furthermore, it doesn't permit refund requests from debtors once their account has been debited.

In order to standardise the routing between bank accounts across the Eurozone, a common standard was required. This resulted in the creation of International Bank Account Numbers (IBAN).

INTERNATIONAL BANK ACCOUNT NUMBERS

An International Bank Account Number (IBAN) is an internationally agreed system of identifying bank accounts across national borders. IBAN is intended to facilitate the communication and processing of cross-border transactions, while reducing the risk for potential transcription errors. IBAN is based on the ISO 13616 standard, additionally intended to yield a standardised mechanism for participating financial institutions to achieve common routing and a frictionless consistent mechanism of delivering banking services across member countries. IBAN was originally adopted by the European Committee for Banking Standards (ECBS) before later being ratified as an international standard under ISO 13616 in 1997. The subsequent iteration of the standard was ratified in 2020 and indicates SWIFT as the registrar. IBAN in conjunction with SEPA relieves the necessity for an individual to hold accounts with multiple institutions within the European Union, where the standard was originally adopted. This was instrumental, given the volume of individuals who both reside or work in more than one country within the bloc. Since the freedom of movement is a key tenet upon which the EU is founded, members within the bloc were highly receptive to this principle. This is, additionally, true of businesses that may have a presence within multiple EU countries. By standardising on IBAN throughout the European Union and facilitated, via SEPA, banking as either an individual or as a business requires no more than a single bank account within the bloc. As of May 2020, seventy-seven countries had adopted the use of IBAN, having extended beyond Europe to include several countries within the Middle East and the Caribbean.

While the structure is consistent, the length of the IBAN may vary according to the account number format in the country in which the account is held. The maximum permissible length is thirty-four characters.

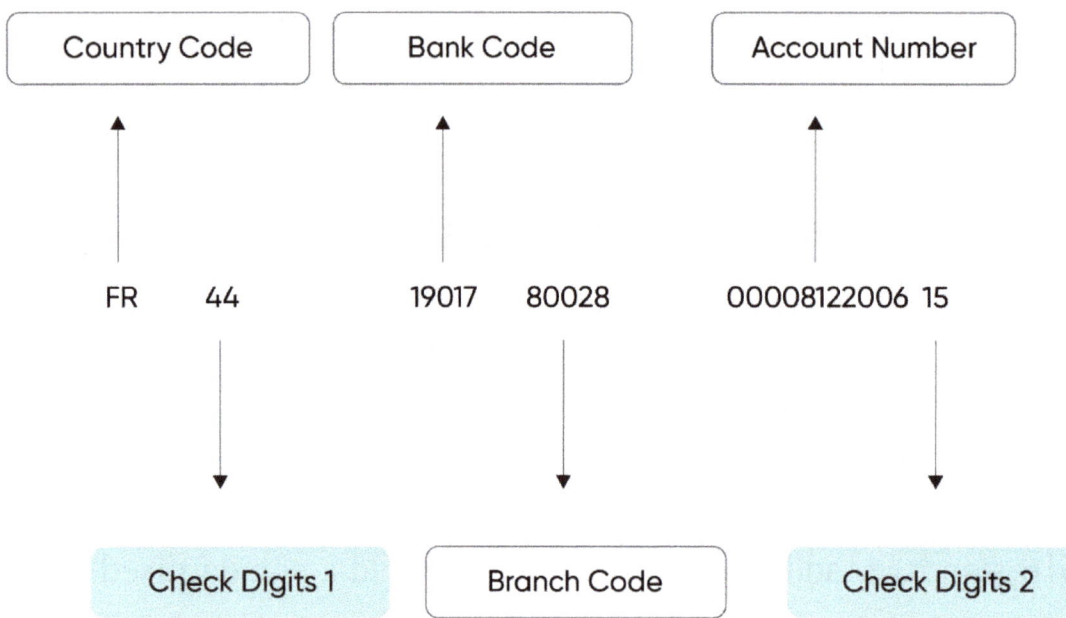

Fig 13.4 an example IBAN for a French Bank Account

By applying this level of standardisation, FinTechs may exploit the combination of IBAN and the SEPA framework to offer powerful propositions, particularly when combined with the Open Banking Framework, via PSD2 (see Open Banking, Chapter 4: Surfacing Utility).

As per Fig 13.4, the **country code** is the two-character ISO code for the country in which the bank account is held. The **check digits** are calculated from information contained within the remainder of the IBAN number and are used to validate the account and routing numbers. The **check digits** further enable an integrity check of the bank account number to confirm its provenance prior to submitting a transaction. The **bank code** identifies the institution with which the bank account is held. The **branch code** identifies the specific bank branch holding the account. This is comparable to a routing number, sort code or code guichet (a French Bank Code).

NEW CHANNELS

As is evident, the Uni-polar global monetary system is rapidly facing competition, via the emergence of state-sponsored alternatives. These initiatives are creating new pathways to facilitate international trade outside of the traditional financial plumbing governed by the United States. While FinTech has rapidly penetrated the private sector, the significant strides that state actors have made in modernising, as well as creating new international payments infrastructure, raises compelling questions as to whether FinTech is enabling a substantial reconfiguration of international capital flows and what the likely effects will be. In some instances, there is a clear political motive among US rivals to create a means of insulating themselves from US jurisdiction and extraterritorial sanctions. By linking SWIFT alternatives with one another, cross-border payments may be routed via intermediaries even when the originating or recipient nation state has been severed from SWIFT. Thus, undermining the effectiveness of exploiting extraterritorial sanctions in this manner. In others, a means of reducing the costs of settlement in international trade invoicing. In either case, FinTech is a key enabler in facilitating the creation of these nascent trade rails.

After decades of vocal contempt for US asymmetry and extraterritoriality (see Exorbitant Privilege, Extraterritorial Sanctions, Dollar Jurisdiction above), the realisation that the EU, Russia and China have actively put into effect a number of mechanisms to circumvent US dominance over the financial system, suggests that FinTech is well-placed to act as a catalyst in enabling a significant shift in the evolving geopolitical superstructure. Although these measures thus far, lack the *Creative Destruction* needed to represent a departure from the status quo of the financial system's asymmetry. While these mechanisms offer significant opportunities to reshape the capital flows worldwide, the FinTech sphere has cultivated technologies which may be of greater disruption, via tokenisation.

14

TOKENISATION

The concept of tokenisation is prolific throughout human history. At its core, tokenisation is the practice of creating a token, coupon or other artefact which represents some form of value.

In the pre-chartalism era, paper money represented a quantity of Gold or Silver (see Gold Standard, Chapter 9: Gold). In the post-metallism era (see Nixon Shock, Chapter 12: Global Monetary System), money is a token which represents a nominal share of a central bank's liabilities (see Quantitative Tightening, Chapter 8: Economic Cycles). All manner of financial assets is represented by a form of tokenisation. Examples include certificates for equities, treasuries, derivatives, fiduciary money and title deeds.

In a world increasingly dominated by technology, digital tokenisation should be expected to continue in the displacement of paper-based tokens across all asset classes. The advantages of reduced transactional friction and efficiencies gained through straight-through processing (see Straight-Through Processing, Chapter 4: Surfacing Utility) are compelling reasons to expect this trend to continue.

MONEY IS MEMORY

Transactional exchanges are recorded in ledgers. In 1996, Narayana Kocherlakota, former president of the Federal Reserve Bank of Minneapolis, authored a paper entitled (and in which he advocated that) 'Money is Memory.'[321] Essentially, among the salient arguments is the supposition that in substituting for a complex web of bilateral counterparty obligations, money is merely a surrogate for a publicly available and freely consumable mechanism for recording what is owed to whom. Thus, conjuring the notion that maintaining the integrity of records is of paramount importance. This has long been true of account-based money, whereby money is stored as electronic deposit entries in a digital ledger. The capability of recording and exchanging value digitally has historically been confined to centralised databases managed by, and visible only to a single entity such as a financial institution. When two such entities exchange value, via a transaction, each records a corresponding entry into their respective ledgers (see Interbank Payment Systems, Chapter 5: Payments). In such instances, neither party has visibility of the other's ledger, nor do any third-parties.

As a consequence of this relationship, a foundation of trust is required in that each counterparty has reflected an accurate representation of the aforementioned transaction. However, if both counterparties were able to transparently view each other's ledger as well as validate the transaction, the need for trust in the integrity, thereof, is eliminated. In other words, transparency diminishes the need for trust since transactions are visible and thus verifiable. Even though an institution may wish to promote transparency with regard to its ledger, the challenges imposed through decentralised control have long been an obstacle in achieving transparency among counterparties.

The systemic risks that surfaced through the inter-dependence of complex and over-leveraged malignant securities permeating the institutions of the global financial community may have been mitigated through a means of ledger transparency. The lack of transparency facilitated by shadow banking practices (see Shadow Banking, Chapter 10: Financialisation), prior to the GFC (see Coup de Grâce, Chapter 10: Financialisation), could, thus, have been significantly mitigated through the adoption of distributed ledger technologies.

DISTRIBUTED LEDGER TECHNOLOGY

Distributed ledger technology (DLT) is a digital system for recording the transaction of assets in which the transactions and their details are recorded in multiple places simultaneously. A full copy of the distributed ledger database is maintained across each of numerous individual computers known as 'nodes'. These nodes may be colocated, geographically dispersed or combinations thereof. Unlike conventional databases, there is no centralised administrator or authority. Each node communicates, via a peer-to-peer network, in order to maintain synchronicity of the ledger database, in which a majority of its members are needed to reach a consensus. The DLT thus maintains the state of the database across all nodes by means of a consensus protocol.

Thus, DLTs drastically reduce the necessity for intermediaries in transactions, thereby enabling peers (or counterparties) to transact directly. The first architecture to be deployed within the DLT spectrum was that of 'Blockchain.' A type of distributed (or shared), yet immutable digital ledger to which data is recorded sequentially and permanently in 'blocks.' The blocks house the records of transactions, facilitating the tracking of assets and the architecture of the technology is designed to cultivate and maintain trust. Or more accurately, eliminate the necessity for trust altogether.

BLOCKCHAIN

A blockchain is a chronologically sequenced chain of digital blocks, each of which contains data. The concept was originally pioneered by a group of digital researchers in 1991. The intent was to timestamp digital documents immutably to assure their unaltered authenticity at a particular point in time. Essentially a digital equivalent to notarising or certifying a document.

The technology largely remained dormant, with little to no adoption until 2009, which closely followed the release of a whitepaper published in October 2008 by Satoshi Nakamoto (a pseudonym for one or more anonymous individuals).

Subsequently, it was adapted to underpin the creation of the Bitcoin cryptocurrency.

Each block within the chain contains records of transactional data, usually represented in a Merkle Tree structure. Merkle Tree was pioneered and patented by Ralph Merkle in 1979.

The Merkle Tree data structure in each block contains a timestamp and a cryptographic hash of the previous block in the chain, creating a digital 'chain link' between blocks. The hash is the result of applying an algorithmic function to data, to assign it to a fixed-length string of numbers and letters, also known as an alphanumeric 'checksum.' The checksum acts as a digital fingerprint of the data, allowing it to be anchored as part of a sequence of blocks within the blockchain. A typical and commonly used algorithm for creating a checksum, is that of Message Digest 5 (MD5). MD5 creates a unique 32-bit alphanumeric signature from any form or quantity of data.

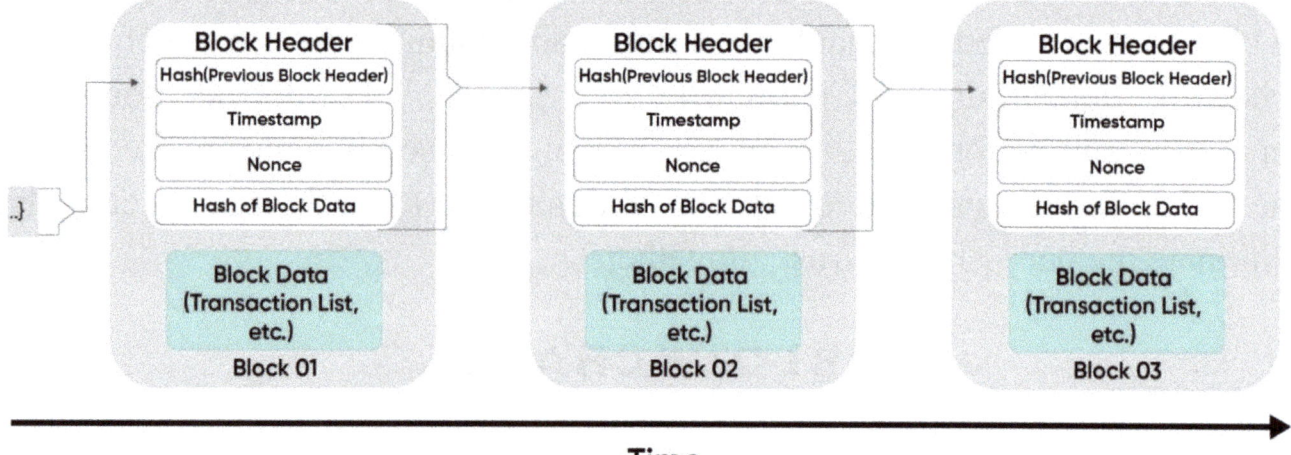

Fig 14.1 a typical Blockchain based on a Merkle Tree data structure such as that used by Bitcoin

Thus, as a chain grows the prospect of altering data in previously recorded blocks within the chain becomes less practical. A direct intervention in a previously recorded block to alter a record would alter the hash (checksum), therefore, it would immediately be known to all participants in the blockchain, resulting either in a fork (whereby a new branch of transactions in a separate chain is created in parallel to the original) or rejection. A hash is essentially the unique (alphanumeric, see MD5 above) signature created based on the specific data in each block. The algorithm used is implemented asymmetrically, whereby, the data may be used to derive a hash. However, the hash cannot be used to discern the original data. Such an algorithm would be symmetric. Therefore, the data hashed, cannot be reverse engineered. Once the data has been hashed and the hash is linked to the next block in the chain, the data (transaction records) therein is considered immutable. In order to ensure maliciously altered blocks are not cascaded throughout the chain, blockchains typically require a consensus verification of a block prior to a new block being appended. Common implementation examples include either a 'proof-of-work' or 'proof-of-stake' verification mechanism.

CONSENSUS & TRANSPARENCY

PROOF–OF–WORK

A proof-of-work verification ensures there is both a delay between updates to the chain and requires all members of the chain to verify the records. In order to add a malicious block, a single member node would have to be greater or equally powerful computationally, to greater than half of the entire network. To ensure that a modification attempt is not achievable without being noticed, the proof-of-work is verifiable by consensus of the blockchain members (an automated function performed by each 'node' computer), hence all members of the chain are stakeholders in assuring its validity.

MAJORITY & SYBIL ATTACKS

In a proof-of-work verification, greater than half of the chain membership nodes would have to be directed by a single entity, in order to successfully add a malicious block to the chain and achieve consensus. This is known as a 'Majority Attack.' In addition to majority attacks, another such attack is that of a 'Sybil Attack.' A Sybil Attack is named for the book titled 'Sybil' by Floreta Rheta Schreiber (1918 - 1988), published in 1973, the protagonist of which, is a woman suffering from dissociative identity disorder.[322] The paradigm describes an attack in which the reputation of a network service is subverted by creating a large number of pseudo-identities, which are exploited to gain a disproportionately large influence.

MINING

The process by which transactions are verified and new blocks are added to the chain, using a proof-of-work consensus model (or protocol) is known as 'mining.' Whereas in other consensus models, this is known as 'validation.' By way of example, Bitcoin 'mining' requires a contest among nodes to perform mathematical calculations to ascertain the value of a nonce (proof-of-work). The nonce has a predetermined value between 0 and 2^{31} (a 32-bit value). As a reward for correctly determining the nonce, the node which successfully does so, collects newly mined Bitcoins and exacts a transaction fee, while simultaneously adding the newly created corresponding block within the chain. Alternatively, in a proof-of-stake verification model, evident among a number of other varied crypto-currencies, a validator may exact a transaction fee (in the form of tokens), however, no newly created tokens (currency), via the validation process.

Every member (computer 'node') of the blockchain receives a full instance of the chain's data blocks on a peer-to-peer networking basis, via the internet. All the records in the blockchain, are digitally signed within each block in the chain and are, therefore, accepted as trustworthy and verifiably immutable. The nature of the blockchain architecture, promotes transparency of the records, as well as the chronology and credibility, thereof. In doing so, a decentralised network of trusted information through which multiple parties may transact is created. Each party is a stakeholder in assuring the integrity of the blockchain, which in turn instils confidence among its participants.

In instances where a fork has been created, a blockchain diverges into two potential branches (paths) forward from that point onwards. Each branch of the fork shares a common transaction history, prior to a new rule governing valid transactions being introduced and implemented. As different parties need to use common rules to maintain the history of the blockchain, users of the blockchain must support either one or the other. As a result of a rule fork, a blockchain can split creating a divergence into two separate paths from a specified block within the chain. This is akin to tree branches veering in different directions although sharing a common trunk. Without a manual intervention to accept a new rule, nodes will ignore the fork and remain members of the original chain.

Other common consensus and validation models are that of 'Proof-of-Space' and 'Proof-of-Stake.' Proof-of-Space consensus algorithms allow nodes in the blockchain network to decide 'mining rights' based on their contribution of available (hard drive) storage capacity. Storj, Chia, Burstcoin and SpaceMint are examples of crypto-currencies which use a Proof-of-Space consensus mechanism. Whereas, Proof-of-Stake consensus mechanisms determine the selection and weighting of validators in proportion to the quantity of their holdings in the associated crypto-currency. Essentially, the greater the holdings, therein, the greater the weighting in validating transactions.

BYZANTINE AGREEMENTS

These consensus and validation mechanisms (proof-of-work, stake and space) are the manifestations of 'Byzantine Agreements,' which require a set of parties in a distributed environment to agree on a value, even if some of the parties are corrupted; intentionally or otherwise. All in an attempt to achieve Byzantine Fault Tolerance. Byzantine Agreements derive their name from the 'Byzantine Generals' Problem,' first conceived in 1982 as an abstract concept as part of research conducted, by SRI International. This research was supported and sponsored by the National Aeronautics and Space Administration (NASA), the US Ballistic Missile Defense Systems Command and the US Army Research Office.[323]

The Byzantine Generals' Problem conceptually describes the logical dilemma that arises in communications, the validity, thereof, and the integrity to act on the information communicated. In a hypothetical scenario, a group of Byzantine

Generals and their respective armies surround an enemy town, although each army is in a different position along the perimeter. The dilemmas faced, include whether to attack the town or not; once a consensus is reached ensuring that it cannot be changed and finally to execute in a coordinated, synchronised fashion against the decision. Successfully navigating these dilemmas require integrity in communications conveying clear messages, a means with which to reach consensus in deciding to act upon the messages and a means through which to ensure that the decision is acted upon. All while ensuring fault tolerance for loss of potential communication, possible message corruption, lack of agreement, reneging or even intentional malice.

Hence, the term 'Byzantine Agreements,' has been co-opted to describe the consensus mechanisms developed to apply to DLTs in reaching consensus, validating the integrity, thereof, and assuring fault tolerance. Additional consensus mechanisms within this sphere should be expected to emerge over time, seeking greater efficiency, integrity, security and lower latency.

EFFICIENCY & PERFORMANCE

While Blockchain architecture enjoyed tremendous growth and success in underpinning crypto-currencies such as Bitcoin, the prospect of using the technology as a means of payment for goods and services at scale has been met with significant challenges. From a purely technological perspective, the process of achieving consensus across the entire network of the blockchain introduces significant latency in verifying payments.

Bitcoin as an example, limits the size of a single block within the blockchain to 1MB (One Megabyte). A single block can record approximately 500 transactions. Since proof-of-work mining is required prior to a new block being created, the average number of transactions which may be performed per second (tps) ranges between 3.3 - 7tps, with a theoretical maximum of 10tps. By contrast, card payment networks managed by schemes (payment networks), such as Visa and MasterCard (see Card Payments, Chapter 5: Payments), cater to demands measured in thousands of transactions per second for high volume events (HVEs), such as Christmas, Black Friday, Cyber Monday and Chinese Single's Day (11th November - 11/11).[324] With an ever-increasing bias towards high-speed digital payment channels, the viability of using Bitcoin and similar crypto-currencies underpinned by cumbersome implementations of Blockchain is less likely as a ubiquitous means of payment. In this regard, Bitcoin is particularly unpalatable since its transaction fees (exacted by miners) are substantial, regardless of the transaction value. By way of example, the prospect of paying a ~$100 transaction fee (variable based on prevailing Bitcoin price) regardless of the value of the purchase is unlikely to entice customers towards its use for routine low-value payments.

Proof-of-work for Bitcoin in particular requires more specialised and powerful computational power in the form of GPUs and ASIC processors dedicated to solving the nonce, in order to improve the odds of being rewarded for mining. The collective dedicated computational power and energy requirements for Bitcoin mining globally has been staggering. In less than a decade since Bitcoin's inception, annual mining for the crypto-currency has exceeded the energy consumption for entire countries over the same period.[325] This is due to all nodes on the blockchain simultaneously competing with one another to solve the complex puzzle to determine the nonce and reap the associated rewards (see above). Only one node will be successful in this endeavour for each block created, yet all nodes are consuming energy and computational processing power simultaneously. A model which is inefficient, expensive and arguably wasteful. The premise being a zero-trust model, whereby by design, each participant (node) must maintain a complete ledger instance of the blockchain. Furthermore, each participant must perform the identical computational activity as all other participants in order to prevent any one party becoming authoritative over the others. Such a model demands inefficiency in order to achieve such an outcome in such a manner.

While new computer central processing units (CPUs) emerge becoming increasingly efficient with each iteration (see Moore's Law, Chapter 2: Capital Evolution), as more miners join the blockchain at a greater cadence than CPUs advance, any efficiencies gained therefrom, are negated, via the collective parallel energy consumption of the blockchain participants. This phenomenon is thus manifesting in a dichotomy of *network effects*. The blockchain accrues greater integrity, resources, scalability and geographic resilience as new nodes join the network. Thus, it cultivates a positive effect in the form of greater resilience. By contrast, however, it creates a negative effect through the excessive consumption of energy and computational resources, which with each new participant therein, diminishes the network's efficiency (Fig 14.2).

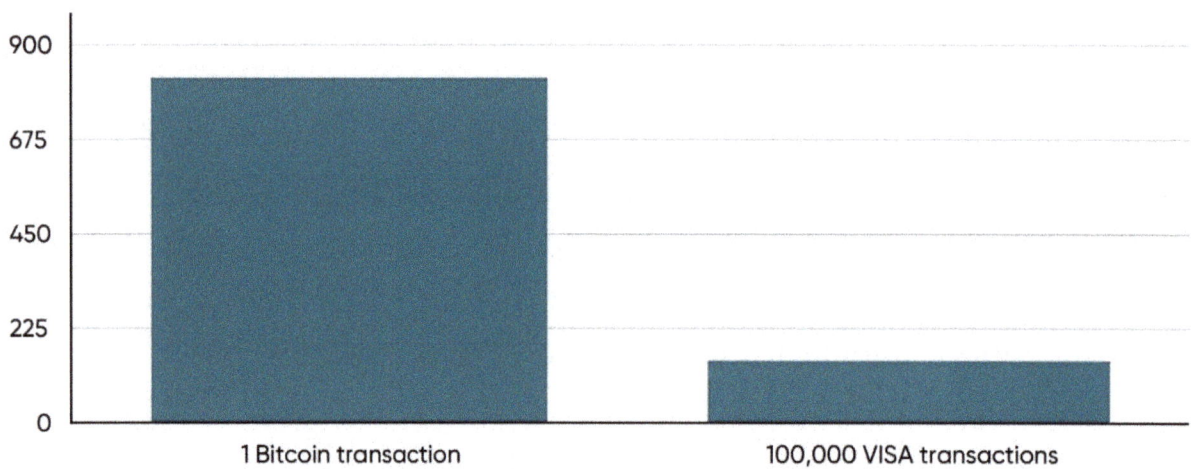

Fig 14.2 indicates the 2020 global energy footprint of one Bitcoin transaction vs. one-hundred-thousand VISA card transactions. (Source data: Statista, 2020)

Amidst growing pressure, to address the existential threats presented by climate change and the increasing cost inefficiency of Bitcoin transaction economics, an alternative architecture is required to combine the integrity of transactions with energy efficiency, cost effectiveness and low latency.

DIRECTED ACYCLIC GRAPH

One such alternative DLT architecture targeted at balancing the integrity of the ledger with accelerating the verification of records is that of Directed Acyclic Graph (DAG) technology. In mathematics, computer science and graph theory, a DAG is a directed graph with no directed cycles. In other words; a DAG consists of vertices and edges with each edge directed from one vertex to another. A vertex (or node) of a graph is one of the objects that are connected together. The connections between the vertices are known as edges (or arcs).

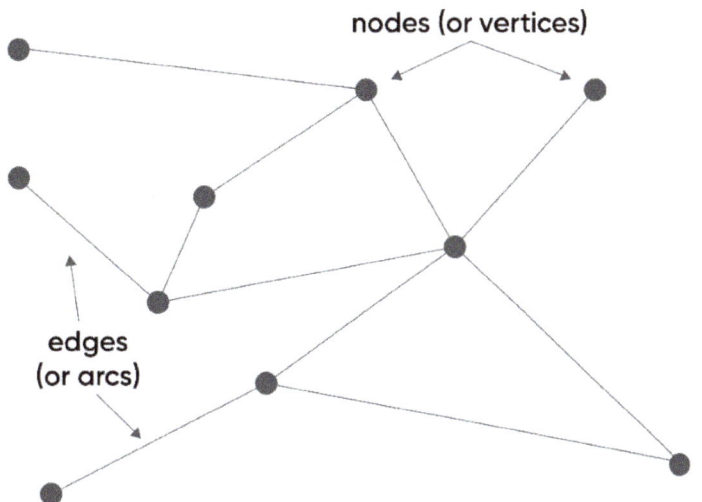

Fig 14.3 DAG with ten vertices (or nodes) and eleven edges (arcs).

In a DLT context, a DAG architecture requires a minority of nodes (at least two nodes), aside from the transaction originator, to verify transactions on the chain. The originator of a transaction upon transmission of value to a new node, initiates a verification with two nodes from which it has previously received independent transaction transmissions. Once the two nodes have verified the previous transactions, the new transaction can be initiated. If either of the two previous nodes fail to verify, the new transaction is not allowed to proceed. Since all nodes share a complete transaction history, via interactions with two or more nodes, the complete transaction record database is synchronised through the cascade of these interactions, via the network.

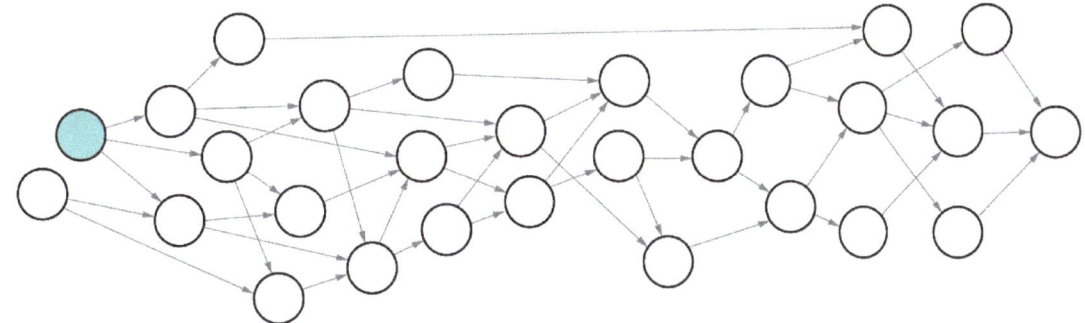

Fig 14.4 illustrates the verification interactions between nodes in a DAG DLT architecture.

The use of multiple verification nodes is essential to prevent a rogue actor from falsifying transaction records without being detected. Since all nodes within the chain require verification from two previous nodes, in each instance that a transaction is initiated, the necessary computational power and network resources to execute transactions is negligible, cost effective and achieves a low latency, while remaining trustworthy. The DAG architecture is asynchronous, computationally efficient and does not require intensive mining, thus, transactionally efficient and low cost. In a DAG architecture, only the genesis node, from which the chain originates, is exempt from rearward verification.

DAG-based protocols can accommodate transactions in the thousands per second and are built as novel structures that could enable and support highly scalable networks, applications and ecosystems. This is reflective of commoditisation, whereby an increased focus towards removing inefficiency and reducing cost is prevalent as an innovation becomes increasingly industrialised (see Co-Evolution, Chapter 2: Capital Evolution).

Consensus protocols in DAGs provide for an energy efficient block sequencing algorithm which eliminates the discarding of forked blocks. Hence, there is no wasted computational power or electricity in solving for a nonce, nor are there discarded blocks. This represents a significant departure from traditional blockchain technology and one of a number of viable alternatives being developed as an alternative to established financial technologies including blockchains.

TRANSACTIONS WITH TOKENS

Regardless of the DLT implementation, tokens are transferred between actors, via an address encoded with a public key, to which the recipient possesses a corresponding private key. The field governing private and public key pairs is that of Public Key Cryptography (PKC), a subset of asymmetric cryptography. PKC is built on the mathematical primitive of 'trapdoor functions,' whereby, a mathematical function may be applied to a value, in order to yield a result. The result, however, may not be easily reverse engineered to discern the value, to which the function was originally applied. However, with the trapdoor, the original value could easily be solved for. Prime factorisation is an example of a mathematical technique used to create a trapdoor function.

Trapdoor functions rose in prevalence within the field of cryptography, following the research and publications of asymmetric encryption techniques by prominent cryptographers, Ralph Merkle (see Merkle Tree above), Bailey Whitfield Diffie and Martin Hellman, in the 1970s. In 1976, Diffie and Hellman published a research paper covering what would subsequently become known as the 'Diffie-Hellman Key Exchange.' This breakthrough enabled a departure from pre-arranged code keys into a dynamically created, yet mathematically linked pair of keys, one public and one private. In the 1970s the majority of cryptographic research, particularly in the US, was classified and the field of cryptography was considered a national security matter. Cryptographic technologies and devices developed in this era were rated as munitions and were subjected to strict export controls.

Using PKC, data is encoded or encrypted with a public key, to which anyone has access, however, the aforementioned data may only be decoded or decrypted by the corresponding private key (the trapdoor), which is held exclusively by the recipient.

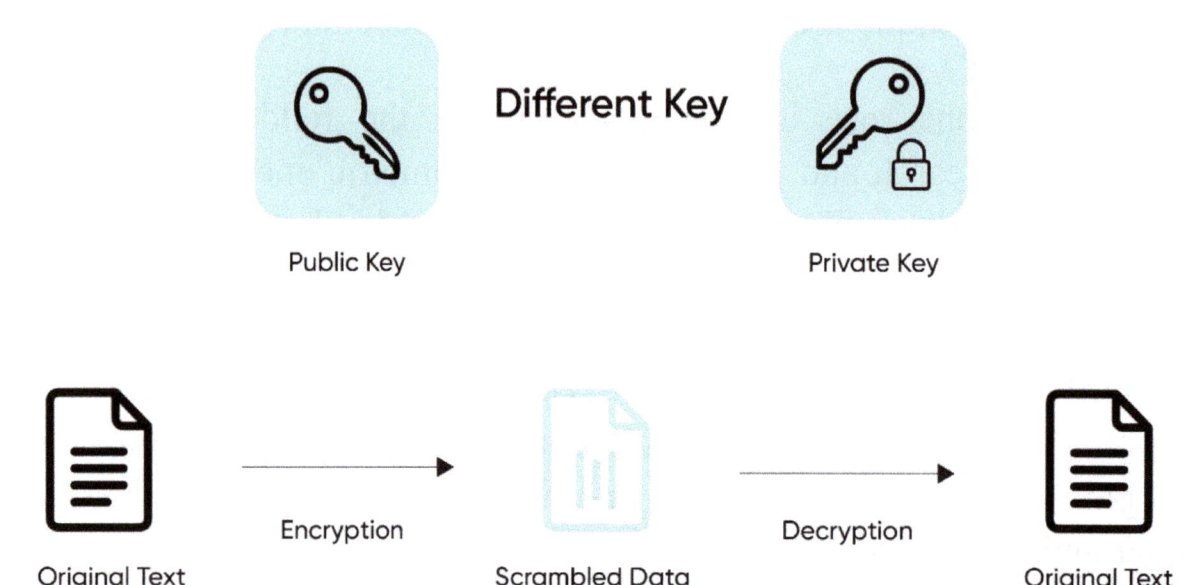

Fig 14.5 illustrates the asymmetric encryption of data using Public Key Cryptography (PKC).

PKC key pairs gained popularity in commercial use by encryption software companies, such as Pretty Good Privacy (PGP) in the late 1990s, which co-opted the technology to encrypt files and particularly emails. The software created a public key for the recipient and stored it on a public key server (PKS). The PKS indexed the public key to the recipient's email address and made it available to other PGP users online. The sender could send an email to the address associated with the recipient's public key or search for it if required (as if using a search engine or telephone directory), and encrypt the email therewith, prior to sending. To provide the recipient assurance that the encrypted email had genuinely been sent by the sender, the sender would sign the email with their private key. The PGP software would function as a plug-in to a user's email client and orchestrate the process of decryption using the recipient's locally stored private key, in order to facilitate a frictionless user-experience. Open-source versions, such as GPG (Gnu Privacy Guard, based on the OpenPGP standard RFC4880), gained popularity shortly thereafter, and leveraged the same private and public key pair model.

In a DLT context, tokens may be transmitted and recorded in the distributed ledger using an address encapsulating the recipient's public key, whereby the ledger replaces the role of the PKS as the database where the public key is stored. Numerous and differing public key addresses may be generated dynamically, from a single private key. The DLT maintains records received, as well as transmitted, assigned to the user's public key(s) (addresses). In order to access, sell or transfer tokens, the corresponding private key is required. This is a classic example of exaptation (see Prologue), whereby a number of existing technologies are co-opted for use in a novel manner. Much like the PGP plug-in model used to facilitate a frictionless and user-friendly experience, private keys may be managed, via a user's digital wallet. The digital wallet (see Digital Wallets, Chapter 5: Payments) orchestrates the signature of a transaction using the payer's private key and transmits the token to the payee's address (with the payee's public key embedded therein).

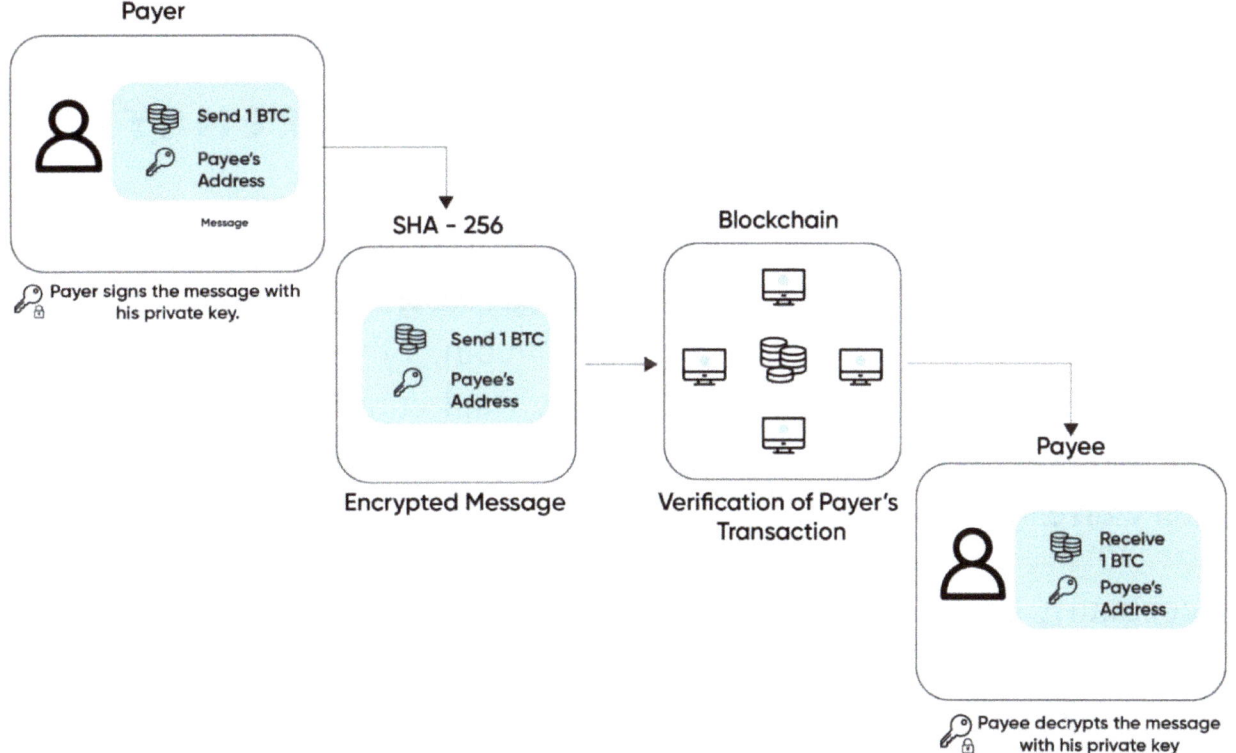

Fig 14.6 illustrates a P2P payment transaction between two actors using Bitcoin (BTC)

Digital wallets may either be resident within a smart device, computer and storage device or facilitated remotely, via an online service. For all intents and purposes, digital wallets emulate the storage of value in a physical wallet. If the private key is lost, the corresponding value is irretrievable. This is no different to misplacing a physical wallet or purse containing cash. Herein lies the critical distinction between digital currencies and most convertible virtual currencies, as well as tokens underpinned by DLTs.

Digital currency is a representation of physical currency (see Formats of Money, Chapter 6: Money) held in a bank account or available as credit, via a payment instrument such as cards, cheques (checks) or transferrable, via interbank transfer mechanisms. Such value is stored with an institution and in most advanced economies benefits from government protection or underwriting. Examples include the Financial Services Compensation Scheme (FSCS) in the United Kingdom and the Federal Deposit Insurance Corporation (FDIC) or National Credit Union Administration (NCUA) in the United States (see The Wall Street Crash of 1929, Chapter 10: Financialisation). Most convertible virtual currencies and digital tokens are unregulated and do not benefit from these consumer protection mechanisms.

CONVERTIBLE VIRTUAL CURRENCY

The term convertible virtual currency (CVC) is increasingly prevalent in regulations and legislation globally, used to describe tokenised currencies. CVCs include crypto-currencies such as Bitcoin, Ether (underpinned by the Ethereum blockchain), Litecoin and other virtual currencies. The category of CVCs additionally includes Stable-coins, Sovereign-coins and Central Bank Digital Currency (CBDC).

Conceptually, crypto-currencies are not pegged to an underlying asset. Much like fiat money, crypto-currencies are anchored by confidence (see Confidence, Chapter 6: Money), although, should such confidence be called into question, the currency would almost certainly be rendered worthless almost instantly. In May 2021, Bank of England governor Andrew Bailey conveyed a blunt message targeted at crypto-currency investors: *'Be prepared to lose all your money.'*[326]

'I'm afraid they don't have intrinsic value; now that doesn't mean to say that people don't put value on them because they can have extrinsic value. But they have no intrinsic value. So I'm going to say this very bluntly again, buy them only if you're prepared to lose all your money.' [327]

- Andrew Bailey, Governor of the Bank of England, May 6th 2021.

Fiat money derives public confidence through a government's assurance and a central bank's credibility that the fiat money is a *store of value* and a *medium of exchange*, redeemable for goods and services (see Functions of Money, Chapter 6: Money). In the pre-chartalism era, money was pegged to gold (see Gold Standard, Chapter 9: Gold). By contrast, crypto-currency derives confidence solely from faith that another party will exchange goods, services or money for it. The value of crypto-currencies tends to be highly subjective (see Subjective Value Theory, Chapter 2: Capital Evolution) and consequently volatile. In a number of instances, the volatility, thereof, is amplified purely reflexively and manipulated solely by supply and demand, in the absence of a tangible anchor.

BITCOIN

Returning to Bitcoin as an example, the algorithmic protocol governing the crypto-currency is predetermined to limit the maximum supply of Bitcoin that may be created to 21 million, estimated to occur by the year 2140. This assures scarcity of the tokens in that once 21 million have been mined, although transaction fees may continue to be collected, via mining, thereafter, no further Bitcoin can be created once this threshold has been reached. Bitcoin is essentially designed to prevent excessive inflation through creating a finite resource. By contrast, central banks are able to issue currency over which they are the monetary authority, in any volume at their discretion (discretionary monetary policy), thus, subject to inflationary pressures (see Monetary Policy, Chapter 8: Economic Cycles). Bitcoin by design, is engineered to increase in volume at a stable, predictable and periodically decreasing rate. This is broadly in alignment with Milton Friedman's k-percent rule (see Inflation, Chapter 8:

Economic Cycles), whereby, the money supply is increased by a central bank at a consistent rate each year regardless of the conditions exhibited by business cycles or debt cycles (see Credit & Debt, Chapter 8: Economic Cycles).[328] The volume of Bitcoin created per day, as well as the mining reward for solving the nonce, halves once 210000 blocks have been mined (approximately once every four-years). Economically, this relies on the assumption that the crypto-currency rises in value to offset the intrinsic cost of mining (see Intrinsic Value Theory, Chapter 2: Capital Evolution). Thus, Bitcoin's implementation of a fixed yet reducing 'acyclic monetary policy' fails to account for alignment in money supply growth to match that of the growth in annual GDP (see below).

The mathematically and definitively finite nature of the Bitcoin crypto-currency's expansion, disenfranchises its viability and prospects as a long-term alternative to traditional central bank issued currencies. If Bitcoin were, hypothetically, to be used as a traditional *medium of exchange* for everyday payments, payment transactions would be experienced in protracted, inconsistent and incoherent intervals, while the effects of its use would be increasingly deflationary.

Currencies to be viable, are required to be elastic in nature. This paradigm is further reinforced by the historical challenges experienced in maintaining the 'specie standard rule' under the variations of a Gold Standard (see Aftershock, Chapter 13: Global Trade Rails). A key lesson demonstrated through the contrast between Winston Churchill's *deflationary*, and Franklin D. Roosevelt's *inflationary* approaches in the wake of the Great War and the midst of the Great Depression, respectively. This illustrated that if a Gold Standard were to be maintained successfully, it was dependent on ensuring that it was calibrated at the optimal price and continually adjusted, thereafter (see Chapter 9: Gold). Hence, the elasticity to do so is critical. Elasticity is required to allow policy makers to govern inflation, ideally at a slow and stable rate (see The Taylor Rule, Chapter 8: Economic Cycles). The optimal rate of inflation, thereof, should preferably be in alignment with the rate of annual growth in global GDP (see Gold Reserves, Chapter 9: Gold). A metric which is typically supported by productivity, via population growth and employment. A currency which simply cannot increase in supply beyond an immutable level, isn't viable due to the expansion in credit required to support growth (see Monetarism, Chapter 8 Economic Cycles). Hence, the deflationary consequences (more people working for less currency), would limit credit expansion in the form of loans and consequently inhibit growth in GDP. Since gold volume grows through mining production at less than 2% per annum and global GDP grows at a rate of 3% - 4% per annum, the demise of the Gold Standard was inevitable. Thus, a similar fate should not be unexpected for Bitcoin as a *medium of exchange*.

'The volume of bank-money must be in due relation to the volume of output, the rate of earnings, the rate of profit, the velocities of different classes of deposits, and the requirements of the financial circulation.'[329]

- John Maynard Keynes, 1930.

The inelasticity further inhibits the ability to create a viable credit and debt infrastructure based on Bitcoin such as a bond market. The tolerance for borrowing 'money,' whereby, the unit of deferred payment (the principal) becomes more expensive (in the form of a negative yield bond) when the loan is repaid, isn't viable. In such circumstances, bonds of this nature would simply price themselves out of the market. Additionally, since governments are hindered in raising tax revenues in a deflationary economic climate (see Deflation, Chapter 8: Economic Cycles), the prospects for governmental support are bleak. The nature of these deflationary limitations in supply expansion, combined with the rising cost in energy consumption towards 'mining,' relegates the long-term prospects for Bitcoin to be no more than a speculative asset class.

However, with deference to Bank of England governor, Andrew Bailey's assertion that crypto-currencies lack intrinsic value (see above), this statement is technically inaccurate. Crypto-currencies such as Bitcoin, command an intrinsic value as a consequence of the capital required to purchase computational and hosting capacity, as well as the operational expenditure in electrical energy consumption required to power the mining process (see Intrinsic Value Theory, Chapter 2: Capital Evolution). In order to maintain viability as an asset class, Bitcoin relies on the spread in marginal yield between its *intrinsic value* (essential cost of production) and its *subjective value* (market price) to appreciate. Algorithmically, this relies on a perpetual cadence in trade being maintained between Bitcoin users, the tempo of which should naturally decelerate as a consequence of its deflationary characteristics. Thus, narrowing the spread, thereby disincentivising the proliferation of Bitcoin crypto miners.

Furthermore, as the energy consumption of crypto mining approaches levels which threaten the wholesale energy supply of nation states with advanced economies, governments therein, will likely introduce legislation to prohibit, restrict or regulate crypto mining. Efforts to reduce carbon footprints to net zero by 2050 in alignment with green energy initiatives and targets, such as those committed to under the Paris Agreement 2016, will likely gain the political consensus to pass such legislation (see Smart Cities, Chapter 15: Economy of Things). Enforcing compliance therewith, will likely be imposed, via regulations, on semiconductor manufacturers (particularly those that produce GPUs and ASICs). Measures of this nature will likely compel manufacturers to equip these chipsets with the capability to identify, whether the algorithms being processed match those of specific crypto-currencies. Should an offending algorithm be identified, countermeasures within the chipset would be required to either inhibit, or more likely prevent its use for 'mining,' thereof.

STABLE-COINS

Stable-coins by contrast are essentially crypto-currencies which are pegged to an underlying anchor, usually a fiat currency. In such a paradigm, harnessing the convertibility, security and exchangeability of crypto-currency underpinned by a Blockchain or broader DLT technology is desirable. These characteristics, coupled with the stability of being redeemable for a stable, yet liquid asset is intended to achieve greater viability as a means of payment. The greater the potential for volatility in the value of a virtual currency, the greater the perceived risk will be in its acceptance by a merchant or service provider for goods and services.

SOVEREIGN-COINS

Sovereign-coins differ from stable-coins in that a sovereign nation has elected to adopt and be accountable for the oversight of the stable-coin as part of its legal tender. A sovereign coin could either be a fiat currency equivalent, or a currency anchored by an underlying asset or commodity.

The Marshall Islands, which adopted the US dollar as its national currency elected to introduce a sovereign-coin known as Sovereign Digital Currency (SOV).[330] The SOV, a crypto-currency was adopted to initially complement USD with a longer term ambition to deprecate the use of physical USD in favour of a fully digital economy exclusively using the SOV. In this instance, the SOV acts as a surrogate for fiat currency. By contrast, the move closely followed Venezuela's introduction of the Petro crypto-currency, which is anchored by crude oil as the underpinning asset. The Petro is essentially a digital form of commodity money, although sovereign in nature (see Commodity Money, Chapter 6: Money).[331]

In the former, SOV unlike most crypto-currencies, is designed to mandate its holders to identify themselves in order to avoid the challenges associated with regulating an anonymous currency. Whereas in the latter, the Petro (PTR) exploits the natural anonymity of crypto-currencies similar to that of Bitcoin, Ether and others, which in turn enables circumvention of potential extraterritorial sanctions (see Chapter 13: Global Trade Rails) and exchange controls. Venezuela is intermittently subjected to sanctions and its fiat currency, the Bolivar regularly experiences volatility due to inflationary pressures and convertibility challenges. The combination of these factors, incentivised the country's promotion of an anonymous, freely transferable digital asset, which is commodity-based (see Commodity Money, Chapter 6: Money).

CVCs are technologically capable of a broad spectrum of implementations, which may be exploited by a variety of actors with varied agendas and priorities. The capabilities, thereof, provide the tooling for significant disruption and potential resistance to the established systems of financial institutions, central banks and governments.

CENTRAL BANK DIGITAL CURRENCY

The adoption, acceptance and proliferation of FinTech since the GFC has signalled a general systemic resistance and diminished confidence in both financial instruments and the institutions that manage them. It was out of this mistrust and loss of confidence that FinTech received its near instant acceptance and meteoric adoption. However, the trajectory, adoption and proliferation of CVCs since 2009 suggests that it represents resistance not only to financial institutions, however, to the financial system and monetary authorities that govern it. Such resistance, in response to moral hazard (see Moral Hazard, Chapter 10: Financialisation), represents not only a risk to banks, insurers and investment institutions, however, in addition to monetary and fiscal authorities, such as central banks and governments.

While deficit spending and expansion of the (M2) money supply have historically been severe in times of economic turmoil, the sheer volume of debt monetised through Quantitative Easing (QE) since the GFC has expanded the money supply and volume of debt to unprecedented levels (see Quantitative Easing, Chapter 8: Economic Cycles). The natural response is usually to convert money to inflation resistant (usually tangible) assets, such as commodities, real estate, fine art or other asset classes perceived to be either intrinsically or subjectively valuable (see Value, Chapter 2: Capital Evolution). In past depressions and recessions, a focus on balancing liquidity with returns has historically been applied. This has usually resulted in increased flows into hard assets such as gold and silver. The attraction, thereto, being seeking out a stable *store of value*, yet maintaining high liquidity through a *medium of exchange*, which is insulated against counterparty risk. Actors would, additionally, assign a proportion of their wealth into less liquid assets for greater returns. The modern trend, however, is augmenting toward opting out of the money supply in much the same manner, yet retaining the liquidity and convertibility of using CVCs in lieu of traditional stores of value or asset classes.

Central banks have recognised the existential threat CVCs pose as an alternative to not only conventional payment channels, however, to fiat currency as well as all associated controls. In 2018, a response compiled by the Bank of International Settlements (BIS) with contributions from a broad cross section of central banks, published a paper covering positioning regarding Central Bank Digital Currency (CBDC).[332] In October 2021, the British government (while holding presidency over the G7 countries) published the Public Policy Principles for Retail Central Bank Digital Currencies agreed among G7 countries.[333]

CVCs represent a disruptive influence brought about through *Creative Destruction*. However, central banks face tremendous *inertia barriers* in order to pivot towards preventing decentralised CVCs from disintermediating the monetary system over which they are the authorities (see Inertia, Chapter 2: Capital Evolution). To slow this effect, greater regulation of CVCs should be expected, however, the announcement of critical mass actors such as Facebook's Libra in 2019 and the Digital Yuan (e-CNY), known as Digital Currency Electronic Payment (DC/EP) by the People's Bank of China (PBOC), in 2020 had a stimulant effect on central banks and governments worldwide (see Red Queen Hypothesis, Chapter 2: Capital Evolution). China's DC/EP further threatening western power's dominance and altering a number of central banks' positions towards accelerating any plans to offer CBDCs, while simultaneously sponsoring greater regulatory scrutiny over CVCs (see Decelerating Effects, Chapter 2: Capital Evolution).

SYNTHETIC HEGEMONIC CURRENCY

In the private sector, Facebook's Libra; a blockchain based crypto-currency, was intended as a digital token or stable-coin anchored to a basket of fiat currencies and securities managed by the Libra Reserve. The Libra Reserve, managed by the Libra association and regulated by the Swiss Financial

Authorities, comprised Facebook, a subsidiary Calibra and a variety of other stakeholder organisations. The structure and gravity of the Libra proposition which would effectively be considered to be a Synthetic Hegemonic Currency (SHC), prompted immediate and significant resistance from, then US Treasury Secretary, Steven Mnuchin.

Mnuchin advised the media that the Libra crypto-currency posed a national security issue because of its potential to be used by '*money launderers and terrorist financiers.*' Mnuchin commented further about his concerns towards Libra's intended crypto-currency proposition by advocating that:

'Crypto-currencies have been exploited to support billions of dollars of illicit activity like cybercrime, tax evasion, extortion, ransomware, illicit drugs and human trafficking.' [334]

- *Steven Terner Mnuchin, US Treasury Secretary, 2017 - 2021.*

While Mnuchin's comments targeted specific negative vulnerabilities for which CVCs may be exploited, these characteristics are common to all CVCs as well as gold, silver, precious gems and cash (see Kimberly Process, Chapter 6: Money). Consequently, Mnuchin's statements were received with confusion, as the central issue was not whether crypto-currency was a *medium of exchange* exploited for illicit purposes, however, was how this specific crypto-currency (and its surrounding infrastructure) posed a material threat to the monopoly of control US Federal authorities (US Treasury and the Fed) maintain over the international monetary and financial system. Furthermore, this would undoubtedly be disruptive to the roles that international institutions (IMF, World Bank, WTO and BIS) maintain in support of trade stability and the global financial safety net (see Chapter 12: Global Monetary System).[335] [336]

This became evident, once the US senate convened hearings held in July 2019, where David Marcus, a Facebook executive and head of Calibra, was questioned perniciously as to whether Facebook should be trusted to manage people's money and to pioneer financial technologies as well as regulations that could drastically influence and potentially undermine global financial systems.[337]

There should be no doubt that a tech giant such as Facebook, endeavouring to commoditise central banking and to effectively privatise the global financial system by applying an ecosystem ILC/'Tower and Moat' strategy (see Innovate, Leverage & Commoditise, Chapter 3: Ecosystems), should be perceived as anything less than an unprecedented and substantial challenge to the establishment. If Facebook were to have succeeded in launching the Libra SHC and its surrounding proposition as originally intended, this would likely have represented the privatisation of the dominant currency paradigm (DCP) and the *Creative Destruction* of the financial system. Thus, a substantial proportion of the Federal Reserve System as well as the US governments' control over the financial system could easily have been usurped through disintermediation along with much of the commercial banking and financial services sector.

Furthermore, Facebook's Libra proposition (SHC) would have empowered Facebook to circumvent US foreign policy, set monetary policy and command an impenetrable hegemonic position in global liquidity and trade invoicing (see Dollar Hegemony, Chapter 13: Global Trade Rails). Such an outcome may have ultimately led to a collapse of the US dollar, and with it, a cascading collapse of global reserves held in dollar-denominated treasuries (~60% of global reserves, 2019/2020). The banks, bond markets and stock markets worldwide would have closely followed. Thereby, likely resulting in hyperinflation as central banks worldwide 'print money' to compensate. Thus, prompting a global deleveraging, as well as a liquidity crisis of incalculable detriment to the global economy (see Deleveraging, Chapter 8: Economic Cycles). In a best case, resulting in a protracted global inflationary depression; at worst, a third world war.

Following thorough, protracted as well as intense scrutiny and resistance from the US Senate and Treasury, Facebook capitulated. Subsequently, it announced the less ambitious Diem CVC, with the Libra SHC apparently lying dormant, at least in the interim. As noted by then member of the ECB's executive board,

Benoît Cœuré in September 2019, the associated *inertia barriers* in transitioning from one reserve currency to another may elapse over years, if not decades. This has been consistent with past hegemonic transitions and is attributed to a combination of the high costs associated with establishing new infrastructure to facilitate the use thereof as well as a variety of broader lock-in effects.[338] In other words, the *network effects* of reserve currencies have historically made them difficult to displace. However, Cœuré argued that the widespread adoption of a reserve currency is no longer an assurance of its persistence advantage over new currencies. He further argued that the friction and time required for such a shift is greatly reduced in an instance whereby the new *medium of exchange* is both enabled by digital technologies and introduced into an existing large-scale network of potential users. An example of which is a social networking platform, such as Facebook. Thus, an incumbent reserve currency may be vulnerable to disruption, via a rapidly expedited transition which has been initiated by a motivated party with the technology and resources to drive such an outcome. A similar argument was made by then Governor of the Bank of England, Mark Carney, in August 2019.

'Technology has the potential to disrupt the network externalities that prevent the incumbent global reserve currency from being displaced.'[339]

- *Mark Carney, Governor of the Bank of England (2013 - 2020), August 2019.*

While a macroeconomic and geopolitical threat of this nature and magnitude may have been contained and mitigated with a private sector organisation, it is significantly more challenging to do so on the global stage with the world's second largest economy.

DIGITAL CURRENCY ELECTRONIC PAYMENT

China's announcement of DC/EP in April 2020 with an intent to pilot the digital currency and payment system, represented a clear escalation of the threat CVCs pose to the global monetary system and central banks. Known to apply an ILC/'Tower and Moat' strategy at a nation-state level (see Innovate, Leverage

& Commoditise, Chapter 3: Ecosystems), China's leadership in digitising Renminbi is likely to aid in the internationalisation, thereof.

Internationalisation of Renminbi (Yuan) is essential to any plans China may pursue to achieve principal reserve currency status. Weak and strong signals to this effect have been evident in China's efforts to disintermediate the dollar through currency swap arrangements (see Swap Lines, Chapter 5: Payments), trade deals with rogue nation states and asserting its influence economically as well as fortifying its strength militarily. Digitisation of China's currency enhances opportunities for the use, thereof, in international settlements, by being both a currency (*medium of exchange*) and an easily exportable payments system. The consolidation of these functions improves the acceptance potential among international traders. As with the success of M-Pesa in Kenya (see Alternative Payment Methods, Chapter 5: Payments), the alternative payment method was quickly adopted domestically by surfacing the utility of payments in a frictionless and convenient manner outside the confines of the traditional banking and payments ecosystem. Thereafter, it was exported to, and adopted by other nations in Africa with similar limitations in payment and telecommunications infrastructure. By March 2020, M-Pesa dominated 98.8% of mobile payments[340] in Kenya with a significant growing market share in other countries to which it had been exported.

'History shows that the rise of a reserve currency is founded on its usefulness as a medium of exchange, by reducing the cost and increasing the convenience of international payments. The additional functions of money – as a unit of account and store of wealth – come later, and reinforce the payments motive.'[341]

- Mark Carney, Governor of the Bank of England (2013 - 2020), August 2019.

A similar argument could be made when considering the adoption and success of unregulated crypto-currencies. The frictionless use, thereof, and convenience in exchanging value across borders on a peer-to-peer basis, the utility of which is surfaced through digital wallets and smart device technologies, makes for a compelling and attractive proposition for its adoption. A collective proposition which reinforces the proliferation thereof, via *network effects*.

China's first-mover advantage is clear when examining the significance of a central bank backed digital currency and payment system as a key enabler to elevating the role China plays in international finance. This posture is further bolstered by declaring DC/EP (e-CNY) to be legal tender. Its status as legal tender compels people and businesses to accept it as a *medium of exchange*. Thereby, assuring its penetration throughout the economy is universal and its acceptance by both businesses and consumers is mandatory.

The principal reserve currency role is dominated by the US dollar (see Global Reserve Currency, Chapter 12: Global Monetary System), with international settlements in RMB representing approximately 2.5% of global trade invoicing prior to digitisation. A digital RMB version (e-CNY) with integral payment system (DC/EP), should be expected to boost this global market share over time. This is expected to elevate RMB's position as the fifth most active currency for global payments, by value.[342]

While China incrementally integrates itself into capital markets, it remains guarded in the extent to which it eases capital controls (see SAFE, Chapter 16: The Rise of China). DC/EP furnishes China with a vehicle through which to engage in debt financing both without engaging in securities issuance, while simultaneously maintaining stringent capital account controls. This is achieved by exporting its currency for external use between foreign actors as both a wholesale, as well as a retail digital asset without requiring a bond market to maintain liquidity. Thus, through surfacing its utility digitally, functions as an incentive to dissuade convertibility. In other words, since the currency is easy and convenient to use, it creates an incentive to hold it, rather than to convert it to other currencies.

Consider the implications if a CVC such as Bitcoin was stable, easy to earn, spend, trade and use for everyday purchases and expenses, seamlessly, cheaply, conveniently and was accepted as well as near instantly transferrable worldwide. This is the role that China has designed DC/EP to fulfil. Since countries exploit bond markets to supply and maintain liquidity through securities issuance, via open market operations respectively, China will likely benefit from several years of unchallenged dominance in CBDC issuance and proliferation. During which time, China is expected to promote its use broadly, in order to capitalise on global network effects. Should this strategy prove successful, elevating RMB's role towards a global *unit of account* is increasingly likely. In such circumstances, China's ability to influence commodity prices worldwide would be increasingly evident. A palatable prospect given China's role as the leading producer and exporter of consumer goods, and as a consequence, the world's largest consumer of raw materials and commodities. Presently, commodities and raw materials are priced in US dollars (see Dollar Hegemony, Chapter 13: Global Trade Rails). However, should this shift to pricing denominated in RMB occur, any incentive to intermediate trade invoicing via the US would likely dissipate. This is further reinforced by substantially higher costs associated in correspondent banking, via the US, as well as the associated regulatory implications (see Dollar Jurisdiction, Chapter 13: Global Trade Rails). A trend that has already gained momentum through China's swap agreements with Russia, both China's, as well as Russia's advancement in independent, yet compatible payment messaging systems (see China Inter-Bank Payment System, Chapter 13: Global Trade Rails) and its growing influence over the BRICS countries.

DATA PRIMACY

Under General Secretary Xi Jinping's leadership, the paradigm of social management in China has expanded to specifically include 'international social management.' The 'international' aspect has become particularly salient, since Hong Kong's new state law criminalises separatism, subversion, terrorism and collusion in and support for any such activities by anyone, regardless of where in the world they may be located. Thus, the implications of RMB's internationalisation with an accompanying digitally searchable repository of rich transaction data (see Terrorist Finance Tracking Program, Chapter 13: Global Trade Rails) makes for a compelling means of enforcing such laws beyond China's borders.[343] A precedent set by the United States in weaponising the US dollar, via extraterritorial sanctions (see Extraterritorial Sanctions, Chapter 13: Global Trade Rails).

Unlike crypto-currencies which are underpinned by a decentralised DLT implementation, the DC/EP is neither decentralised nor anonymous. The PBOC is able to create and introduce the currency into the money supply and thereafter track where and with whom it is spent, saved and invested in perpetuity. This is arguably one of the most powerful and intrusive data harvesting and surveillance tools ever conceived.[344] While useful information, such as monetary velocity (see Velocity, Chapter 8: Economic Cycles), is effortlessly discerned from tracking of this nature, the data collected may be abused to assert stringent controls or undue influence upon actors within, as well as outside the Chinese economy. The DC/EP by design, affords the PBOC unprecedented control over the currency issued and its payment system. Currency in issue, held by an individual, business entity or foreign government could conceivably be invalidated or frozen by the PBOC at the direction of the Chinese Communist Party (CCP) with a few keystrokes. A potentially devastatingly powerful system for asserting dominance, particularly once internationalised. While the PBOC may create a substantial repository of financial transaction data in order to legitimately supervise and police financial transactions, the design of DC/EP incorporates political-discipline-linked policy drivers which the CCP refers to as either 'social governance' or 'social management.' A PBOC official described 'anti-money laundering' as an *important means to prevent and defuse financial risks and consolidate social governance.*'[345] In other words, using DC/EP to enhance the party-state's control over its users (see Social Governance, Chapter 16: The Rise of China).

CENTRALISED VS. DECENTRALISED

In crypto-currencies the decentralised architecture of DLTs serves above all, two core purposes. Firstly, by being decentralised, neither the economics, nor supply, thereof, may be controlled by any one entity. Secondly, since the ledger is distributed among geographically dispersed nodes, the greater the number of nodes, the greater the resilience, thereof. This latter sentiment is synonymous with the Bitcoin motto, 'Vires in Numeris' ('Strength in Numbers', Latin). This however, does not insulate crypto-currencies from potentially large-scale attacks, which may be achieved by a rogue state actor capable of investing in sufficient computational capacity to perpetrate an effective majority or Sybil attack.

A CBDC however, although conceptually much like a sovereign-coin, is essentially a CVC issued and controlled directly by a central bank rather than a decentralised network of node participants. A CBDC to be viable, would need to surface the utility of a CVC, while remaining controllable by the issuing central bank in compliance with monetary policy and prevailing domestic legislation, as well as any agreed international treaties, accords and standards.

DATA–DRIVEN POLICY

Unlike Bitcoin and similar CVCs where monetary policy is embedded algorithmically into the currency and is immutable, central banks require the ability to adjust monetary policy dynamically in congruence with central bank governance (see Monetary Policy, Chapter 8: Economic Cycles). Policy decisions are based on economic conditions and policy objectives. CBDCs, therefore, are required to be issued and managed centrally to effect (discretionary) monetary policy.

Central banks rely significantly on economic indicators collected quarterly, to assess and adjust monetary policy. Data of this nature is collected from multiple sources including banks, clearing houses, stock exchanges, asset managers, regulators and consortiums. This methodology limits policy makers to adjusting policy on a periodic basis (see Chapter 7: Central Banks), leveraging historical data of the previous quarter and prior. A CBDC with tracking capabilities embedded, would allow policy makers access to real-time data which has the potential to radically alter the frequency with which policy adjustments are made. Real-time or higher frequency monetary policy adjustments could eventually be achieved through the use of AI (see Artificial Intelligence, Chapter 4: Surfacing Utility), whereby with sufficient access to real-time data sources including the money supply, central banks could potentially prevent or at least mitigate the damage caused by market anomalies usually identified in retrospect. By way of example, the ability to both accurately and expediently discern monetary velocity would have a profound impact on the effectiveness of monetary policy decisions (see Monetarist Theory, Chapter 8: Economic Cycles).

QUANTITY THEORY OF MONEY

Fisher's quantity theory of money, devised by Irving Fisher, advocated that:

'Other things remaining unchanged, as the quantity of money in circulation increases, the price level also increases in direct proportion and the value of money decreases and vice versa.'

- Irving Fisher, American Economist (1867 - 1947).

Fisher expressed his theory in terms of the equation:

$$PT = MV + M'V'$$

P = Price level

T = Volume of transactions in the economy

M = Total quantity of money (M2)

V = Velocity of circulation of M

M' = Total quantity of credit (credit money)

V' = Velocity of circulation of M'

Regarding the theory, Fisher's multiplication of M (money supply) and V (velocity) has attracted extensive criticism as M related to a point in time and V to a period of time. The former is a static concept whereas the latter is dynamic, therefore technically inconsistent to multiply two non-comparable factors. Additionally, Fisher incorrectly assumed that V was constant and independent of changes in M and M,' which weakened monetary policy making based on the adjacent monetarist theory, following a sharp fall in M1 velocity in 1982 (Fig 8.7). An outcome which prompted a loss of confidence in monetarism. In 1983, Macroeconomics expert, Robert J. Gordon dubbed the event:

'The velocity recession and the demise of monetarism'[346]

-*Robert J. Gordon, 1983.*

The renowned American economist and monetary history, as well as monetary theory expert, Milton Friedman (1912 - 2006), later argued in 1984 that a decline in velocity does not undermine Monetarism. Friedman advocated that the decline in velocity was a consequence of volatility through growth in the money supply in 1980 driven by changes in operating procedures by the Fed in October 1979.[347]

Despite numerous criticisms of Fisher's quantity theory of money by academics, there are notable examples where the theory's validity has been defended, citing substantial issuance of money having elevated prices. Notable examples include that of the hyperinflation in Germany (Weimar Republic 1921-1922) and in China 1947-1948.

Parallels may be drawn between the detrimental economic damage experienced in these past expansions of the money supply and the waves of QE following the GFC and stimulus during the COVID-19 pandemic.[348] Such parallels prompt concerns that uncontrolled expansion of the money supply would mirror the hyperinflation experienced in the past, stimulating demand for extra-systemic asset classes resistant to inflationary pressures. Much of this extra-systemic pressure flowed into crypto-currencies (predominantly Bitcoin) in 2020.

Within a CBDC, the ability to align M and V into comparable factors could be instrumental for the future of monetary policy making. Monetary velocity has been in steady decline since the mid-1990s (Fig 8.7).[349] The ability to monitor and analyse velocity in real-time may reveal insights into this phenomenon.

This is particularly pertinent in the United States economy where two thirds (66% - 70%) of GDP is traditionally supported by domestic consumption. Should velocity continue to decline, the US could face systemic contraction, and may eventually cede economic dominance to a rival superpower. China is the likely successor as the world's second largest economy. China has experienced an extraordinary and persistent economic growth trajectory since it acceded to the World Trade Organisation (WTO) in December, 2001.

CBDCs could afford innumerable benefits for consumers, economists as well as central bank monetary policy makers. However, there are legitimate concerns and significant opportunities for abuse by the authorities, via exploiting the associated learning effects (see Learning Effects, Chapter 3: Ecosystems). Introduction of CBDCs additionally represents potentially disruptive implications for both central banks and the financial sector.

By design, implementations of CBDC would almost certainly be required to accommodate Know Your Customer (KYC), Anti-money Laundering (AML) and Counter-terrorism Financing (CTF) tracking functionality to prevent or detect the currency's potential abuse by rogue actors. Such functionality calls into question the privacy implications and the level of anonymity the currency's users may reasonably expect in its use.

ABUSE

Private (or account-based) money managed on behalf of depositors ensures that KYC, AML and CTF obligations are met by banks and other regulated FIs. Whereas, crypto-currencies are typically free of such controls, and are thus, comparable to paper money in terms of anonymity. A CBDC would be expected to be comparable to account-based money in assuring the compliance functions performed through the banking system are adequately met without violating the holder's reasonable expectations surrounding privacy. Thus, establishing an equilibrium between compliance and anonymity will likely be among the greatest challenges for implementing CBDCs in western democracies.

Furthermore, a long-standing trend has emerged, whereby monetary and fiscal authorities have incrementally reduced the larger denominations of the currencies over which they maintain purview (see War on Cash, Chapter 6: Money). This trend has been reinforced through the proliferation of digitally enabled channels, such as payments cards, online transfers, alternative payment methods and CVCs (see Chapter 5: Payments). The risk CBDC poses to consumers is that of reducing the available denominations of physical cash, while the purchasing power of units of currency are simultaneously debased. The consequence of such factors erodes the shielding which consumers may use to guard themselves from undue surveillance and negative interest rates (see NiRP, Chapter 6: Money).

With the unprecedented levels of sovereign debt accumulated since the GFC through QE and the amplification thereof, via economic stimulus packages brought about by the COVID-19 pandemic, the pressure to apply negative interest rates is proportionately palpable.

The ability to apply negative interest rates directly to the money supply is a key incentive highlighted in the BIS CBDC positioning paper, published in 2018. It remains a common belief among policy makers that negative interest rates will stimulate monetary velocity. The principle being, there's an incentive to dispose of money, knowing that it effectively depreciates the longer it's held, therefore, a spending incentive.

A further assertion is the expectation of funding the creation as well as the maintenance of the infrastructure and technology needed to underpin the provision of a CBDC. This cost, thereof, would be defrayed by significantly reducing the physical elements of the M0 money supply. In other words; funding the CBDC is expected to be achieved by reducing the minting and maintenance of physical cash (base money) in circulation. This approach is further reinforced by the necessity to balance the volume of balance sheet liabilities held by the central banks, as well as the collective money supply.

A concern should be noted that in times of financial stress, central banks could experience flows into CBDC without the commensurate decline in physical cash. As a consequence, central banks would likely face challenges in broadening the assets held on their balance sheets to offset both physical cash and CBDC liabilities simultaneously. In the US, the Federal Reserve Act 1913 limits the Fed's options as to which asset classes may reside on its balance sheet. This limits the avenues which the Fed may pursue to monetise assets in such circumstances to counterbalance these collective liabilities. In such instances, the US Treasury may be compelled to issue bonds, creating an unnecessary fiscal deficit, purely to aid the Fed's balance sheet, thereby compounding the national debt without the corresponding necessity to do so. A move that could be interpreted and received very poorly on the international stage (see Triffin's Dilemma, Chapter 12: Global Monetary System). In such circumstances, flows into CBDC may additionally contribute towards destabilising commercial banks. Essentially facilitating a digital 'run on the banks,' whereby depositors seek to divest themselves of bank liabilities, in favour of a central bank issued currency (see Public vs. Private Money, Chapter 6: Money). Thereby, deepening the effects of a potential liquidity and/or solvency crisis.

DISRUPTION

Furthermore, the implications as to whether the introduction of CBDC may compete with or displace other interest-bearing instruments, such as treasuries and securities, by virtue of being a highly liquid interest-bearing asset, in itself are valid. Central banks would need to assess the implications on open market operations (see Open Market Operations, Chapter 8: Economic Cycles), banking intermediation and the impact on repo operations (see Chapter 5: Payments). It is almost inconceivable that central banks would forego the ability for a CBDC to be an interest-bearing instrument altogether. A decision of this nature, would impede the central bank's ability to impose a negative interest rate policy (see NiRP, Chapter 6: Money).

This thinking lends itself to the dilemma central banks face in assessing their role in the financial system. Central banks are at the apex of a hierarchical banking system and the Fed is at the apex among a hierarchy of central banks. Commercial banks hold accounts with the central bank and consumers, as well as businesses, hold accounts with commercial banks (see Chapter 5: Payments). Central Banks traditionally act as an intermediary between commercial banks, whereas commercial banks intermediate payments between depositors. Should consumers have direct access to a currency, which features an embedded peer-to-peer payment mechanism, managed directly by the central bank, commercial banks will likely find themselves disintermediated. Simultaneously, central banks may find themselves shouldering the overheads of dealing directly with consumer payments, potentially on a twenty-four-hour basis. Essentially, this will likely threaten the integrity of the multi-tier banking system.

Central banks are consequently faced with a decision as to whether to offer a CBDC as a wholesale digital asset issued to commercial banks, a generally available (retail) digital asset to the public, or both. Introduced as a wholesale digital asset may result in commercial banks being encouraged to issue digital assets of their own, comparable to fiduciary money (see Types of Money, Chapter 6: Money). Regardless, introduction of a CBDC carries with it, disruptive implications and consequences to the status quo. One such consequence is providing an adequate means for assuring the integrity and safety of payments between parties exchanging a CBDC. This would no doubt require a means of assuring that KYC and other obligations are met, while seamlessly facilitating the exchange, thereof (see Know Your Customer, Chapter 4: Surfacing Utility). Such obligations would traditionally be managed by commercial banks, which maintain accounts and records for each depositor. It is unlikely that central banks will wish to assume such obligations for each holder of a CBDC. While such challenges are numerous, they are not insurmountable. Unfortunately, the implications, thereof, are significantly disruptive. Overcoming these challenges will require executive leadership, political sponsorship and substantial investment in displacing the extensive framework of existing technologies and systems. An endeavour too challenging, to be addressed expediently. Hence, the US strategy is to bide its time in the short-term.

In January 2021, the Fed Chairman stated:

'We don't feel an urge or need to be first'

Referring to CBDCs. Powell further elaborated:

'Effectively, we already have a first-mover advantage because [the U.S. dollar is] the reserve currency.'

- *Jerome Powell, Federal Reserve Chairman (appointed February 2018).*

In indicating that it would likely be years rather than months before the US would introduce a CBDC, the extent to which the Fed investigated and invested in research and development, thereof, through Project Hamilton (named for US founding father Alexander Hamilton), suggests that the challenge lies with the potential disruption implications to the financial system, rather than that of technological difficulty. Project Hamilton is a joint research digital currency initiative (DCI) between the Boston Fed and the Massachusetts Institute of Technology (MIT). The objective of which is to explore how a dollar-based CBDC could be designed and implemented.[350]

FAST FOLLOWERS

In November 2020, former IMF Chair and Managing Director (2011 - 2019) and then President of the European Central Bank, Christine Lagarde, indicated that a digital Euro currency would likely emerge within a two-to-four-year window. Lagarde openly criticised unregulated crypto-currencies and like many of her peers, likely perceived the growth and adoption, thereof, as a systemic risk and threat to the financial system. Ironically, during her tenure at the IMF, Lagarde was a co-sponsor and major advocate for the digital initiative to transform Special Drawing Rights (SDRs) into an IMF issued CVC (see Special Drawing Rights, Chapter 12: Global Monetary System).

In such circumstances, an SDR would remain in its initially conceived role as a supplementary global reserve asset, issued exclusively by the IMF to nation states to assist in *balance of payments* relief as part of the global financial safety net (see Balance of Payments, Chapter 5: Payments). However, as a CVC, SDRs would be capable of evolving into a modern DLT-based supranational digital currency, available for intermediating settlements between countries on a routine basis. This would represent a departure from the SDR's traditional role, used exclusively under conditions of financial stress. Transforming SDRs into a CVC is fundamental to elevating its potential as a global *medium of exchange* among nation states. Digitisation, thereof, is key to a delicately conceived strategy spanning a decade long IMF initiative, intended to further fortify the global financial safety net through intermediating the deleveraging of sovereign debt burdens globally and ultimately assuming a principal reserve currency posture.[351]

This should illustrate the magnitude of potential disruption that Facebook's Libra proposition would likely have imposed on the financial system. Facebook intended to provide a CVC, payment infrastructure and commercial banking services to an instant market potential in excess of three-billion customers over which it commanded primacy over the customer relationship (~40% of global population, 2019). A captive market created within a single-platform proposition outside the confines of the financial system. In addition to exploiting Libra as a sensing engine, with which to mine data through which the corresponding *learning* and *network effects* would be unparalleled (see Runaway Leadership, Chapter 4: Surfacing Utility), Libra's currency component was designed and modelled on the SDR. As a Synthetic Hegemonic Currency available for general public consumption (retail digital asset), the proposition modelled in its image, could rival and undermine the SDR's efficacy as a global reserve asset available exclusively to nation states. Consequently, Libra's introduction may have disrupted the IMF's influence and role in global finance. Thereby, potentially disrupting or compromising the global financial safety net. An SHC, developed by a private enterprise with potential consequences to both global economic, as well as geopolitical stability. This illustrates the brazen decadence of 'Big Tech,' in which adopting a mantra of '*substituting the influencing of government with attempting to become government*' has become prevalent.

In the days prior to Powell's CBDC statement, Lagarde echoed criticism of crypto-currencies, Bitcoin in particular, and focused on unregulated CVC's exploitation in illicit activity. This statement followed a surge in Bitcoin demand, where the crypto-currency nearly doubled in price from previously recorded highs within a two month period prior. In the days that followed Powell's statement, the European Commission and European Central Bank released a joint statement that they were considering embarking on the creation of a digital Euro.

These statements and actions regarding CVCs from monetary authorities sent a clear message amidst the rhetoric, that the financial system itself is vulnerable to disruption and under siege, as a result of the slew of DLT technologies and unregulated crypto-currencies that continue to emerge. The parallels may be drawn between these statements and the atmosphere surrounding the possession of Gold in the United States in 1933, which immediately followed President Roosevelt's Executive Order 6102 (see The Great Depression, Chapter 9: Gold).

The executive order enforced surrender of privately held Gold bullion and outlawed private possession and ownership thereof, for over 40 years. Much like Gold, crypto-currencies are unregulated, anonymous and represent a palpable extra-systemic risk to the financial system. In a modern context, crypto-currency represents a greater threat by virtue of being dual-functional with an embedded digitally enabled cross-border payment system. Thereby, reinforcing its appeal as a *medium of exchange*. A system free of sanctions screening, anti-money laundering as well as foreign exchange (capital account) controls and counter-terrorism tracking. Although, unlike the forced surrender of gold in 1933, crypto-currency cannot be easily suppressed due to the ubiquity and freedoms the internet provides. As a consequence of its globally distributed nature, outlawing the use thereof in one jurisdiction isn't sufficient. A coordinated strategy would be required globally, to achieve meaningful control thereof.

The statements additionally indicated a lack of consensus and synchronicity among central banks in tackling the challenges. Three days prior to the European Commission and ECB's joint statement, Markus Ferber, a senior member of European Parliament while commenting on the necessity for a European 'masterplan' to attract and assist key financial services to the EU following the UK's Brexit departure, stated that:

'If the EU wants to compete with the greenback, it needs a financial system to match it.'

-Markus Ferber, European Parliament, January 18th 2021.

The statement strongly suggested that the European Union were not only discontent being the recipients of US foreign policy however, additionally set on challenging US dollar dominance and potentially US reserve currency dominance. The change in posture represented significant systemic resistance to US leadership and dollar hegemony (see Dollar Hegemony, Chapter 13: Global Trade Rails), over the global financial system. An escalation of this nature in European sentiment was to be expected, followed by the departure of the United Kingdom from the EU, representing the loss of a major financial centre compounded by absentee global leadership from the United States, over the course of US President Donald Trump's term (2017 - 2021), which drew to a close, two-days later.

The EU recognised these deficits as opportunities to forge a self-sufficient economic proposition to fill the power vacuum left by Brexit and diminished US influence on the global stage. In this instance, amplified by the US dollar's weakening through excessive securities issuance, via Quantitative Easing and poor economic performance, in the midst of the COVID-19 pandemic.

Powell's statement reinforced US complacency in addressing the obstacles associated with modernising the global financial system to accommodate the challenges presented by the digital age, confidently insulated against being disrupted by the dollar's reserve currency status. Compounded by China's aggressive stance toward internationalisation, left Europe at an inflection point, whereby inaction would leave Europe behind. Britain's voice, absent from the European table, post Brexit, nurtured such dissent and resistance. Britain, while a member of the EU, would be obligated to resist an independent European challenge to US dollar hegemony, remaining allied and aligned with US interests. A position further reinforced through holding the majority of reserves in US dollar denominated treasuries, with little in the way of hard assets, such as Gold inventory (see Gold Reserves, Chapter 9: Gold).

There should be little doubt that the European Union and China will exploit digital technologies including CBDCs to capitalise on opportunities to solicit a greater global market share of international trade invoicing, using Euro and RMB denominated instruments respectively. On June 1st 2021, the European Union announced plans to launch a bloc-wide digital wallet.[352] Such an initiative, is likely to lay the foundations for a Euro-based CBDC.

UNREGULATED PROLIFERATION

Securitisation describes the act of converting an asset, particularly a loan, into a tradable security for the purpose of raising capital. It may, additionally, be described as the process of transforming an illiquid asset, or group of assets into a security which may be traded. This process may be achieved through financial engineering (see Securities, Chapter 10: Financialisation).

While central banks, governments and the IMF pursue ambitions to create CBDCs and CVCs of their own, the open crypto-currency market has seen tremendous unconstrained growth and numerous new entrants. A plethora of open-source toolkits, blockchains and distributed ledger technologies continue to see substantial development and interest from institutional investors, private equity, investment banks and shadow banking organisations.

Monetary and fiscal authorities, as well as regulators, seem intent toward exploring the use of CBDCs to fill a vacuum of demand, exploited by unregulated crypto-currencies. This thinking is devoid of recognition that unregulated crypto-currencies have grown in popularity, due primarily to lack of regulation, as well as free of the controls and influence within the financial system.

The 'Howey Test' refers to a US Supreme Court precedent (SEC v W.J. Howey Co. 1946) in which a transaction either qualifies as an 'investment contract' or not. The former brings such transactions into the scope and purview of the Securities Act 1933 and the Securities Exchange Act 1934, whereas the latter does not. Crypto-currencies are perceived to fail the Howey Test as their value is not perceived to be generated on the efforts of others. Hence, they have remained out-of-scope thereof to date.

Additionally, crypto-currency due to its popularity and scarcity offered high yields in the form of capital gains, attracting greater interest from institutional investors. Such instruments are liquid, easily convertible and portable across borders.

Furthermore, a degree of credibility has been realised through the actions of a few notable industry and government actors. Tesla invested $1.5 Billion in Bitcoin, revealed in its December 31st 2020 SEC filing.[353] In February 2021, the automotive innovator, openly stipulated its intent to accept the crypto-currency as payment, (initially on a limited basis) in exchange for its products.[354] In May 2021 however, Tesla's CEO, Elon Musk announced that Tesla would no longer accept Bitcoin as payment, citing the unsustainable environmental impact through wasted energy consumption, which is required to mine and exchange the crypto-currency. In June 2021, El Salvador President Nayib Bukele announced his intention to advocate for Bitcoin to be formally adopted as legal tender within the country.[355]

Such yields and popularity of crypto, however, were the result of poor performance from conventional investment instruments, such as bonds and securities following the GFC 2007-2008, which saw interest rates plummet toward and nearing the zero bound for over a decade. Coupled with an unprecedented expansion of both the money supply and sovereign debt, systemically devaluing all conventional monetary instruments. Culpability for causing the GFC and protracted recession that followed is largely attributed to actors at every level of the financial sector, including monetary authorities, enabling moral hazard and exploiting financialisation (see Chapter 10: Financialisation). The rise of crypto-currencies is an unintended consequence, indigenous to altering or manipulating a complex adaptive system (see Prologue). The net result of which, is of the financial establishment's making.

In part, crypto-currency has been allowed to gain unfettered traction and sustain substantial growth, due to the financial sectors' perspective of what constitutes value within the spectrum of financial instruments. Gains realised through crypto-assets have largely been insulated against taxation as a by-product of its existence outside the purview of fiscal authorities. Crypto-currencies, free of regulation and traditional counterparties, neither pegged to a traditional value anchor nor guaranteed by a fiscal or monetary authority are conceptually worthless. Since perceived to be worthless in the traditional sense, neither the financial sector, nor the authorities, initially assessed these instruments to be a threat of consequence to the traditional monetary and payments system as well as its instruments. It is through this disdain and ambivalence that crypto-currency and its underpinning DLTs have been allowed to proliferate with negligible interference.

Despite expectations that unregulated crypto-currency would simply run its course and wither (see Hawthorne Effect, Chapter 2: Capital Evolution), the field has largely thrived and enjoyed the sanctuary of natural evolution, free of outside influence. Essentially akin to a wildlife reserve, with which mankind has not interfered. The net result thereof, represents a significant advancement in DLT technologies which has cultivated opportunities to create higher-order systems in parallel to CVCs. Such higher-order systems (see Higher-order Systems, Chapter 2: Capital Evolution) include applications which leverage blockchains and other DLTs to digitise and optimise business supply-chains and distribution channels.

SMART CONTRACTS

Smart contract functionality built upon DLTs has enabled further higher-order systems to emerge in the form of programmable money,[356] digital insurance and the creation of crypto-assets through securitisation. The principle is to enable DLTs to record the characteristics as well as events, actions and controls which are found in contracts. The technology may then be leveraged to automate outcomes based on the terms and conditions captured within the contract, eliminating the need for manual execution or arbitration thereof. Smart contracts were first conceived by American computer scientist and cryptographer Nicholas Szabo in an article published in Extropy (issue 16) in 1996. Szabo envisioned capturing contracts into programmed code that could be both *trust-less* and *self-enforcing*. Thereby, enhancing efficiency and removing ambiguity from contractual relationships.

The Ethereum blockchain implements a Turing-complete programming language (known as Solidity), which combined with a shared virtual machine (the Ethereum Virtual Machine or EVM), has manifested as an early standard for developing and deploying smart contracts. Solidity is object-orientated, featuring a strong procedural bias and its core components are implemented in the form of imperative instructions which define positive actions.

Conceptually, this capability has the potential to be highly-disruptive for all manners of business notwithstanding the impact to the legal system. The implications are immeasurable in the context of the insurance and finance sectors, whereby policies, mortgages, equities, securities and derivatives could be created between counterparties digitally. These are effortlessly recorded and maintained, via a digitally distributed ledger, whereby the terms are enforced automatically. A similar paradigm exists in the context of programmable money, whereby digital tokens may be transferred in a state of escrow and once settlement terms have been verified, the tokenised currency would be cleared and released to the recipient (see cross-chain swaps below). This is comparable to a prevalent concept in avoiding settlement risk in the exchange of securities, known in this arena as delivery versus payment (DvP).

DECENTRALISED AUTONOMOUS ORGANISATIONS

By aggregating multiple smart contracts, it is possible to devise applications with more advanced functionality. Examples of which include decentralised finance (DeFi) applications, such as lending platforms (such as MakerDAO) and liquidity pools (such as Uniswap and Aave). Furthermore, this may be exploited to underpin social media platforms (such as Akasha, Karma and Peepeth). In addition, smart contract aggregation may be co-opted to devise distributed governance systems for DLT-based assets. Early examples of which are referred to as, Decentralised Autonomous Organisations (DAOs). Examples include TheDAO, MolochDAO and DxDAO.

Coupled with a framework to govern the business logic and terms of financial instruments, which exploits the capabilities of AI to handle functions, such as assessing obligations and netting, traditional intermediaries, such as stock exchanges and clearing houses are likely to find themselves challenged by these developments. Such developments embody themes of first principles thinking, enabling *Creative Destruction* and *Componentisation*, further enabling *higher-order systems* (see Chapter 2: Capital Evolution). Such higher-order systems lend themselves to surfacing the utility of securitisation in a digital era, cultivating peer-to-peer cross-border payment systems and varied forms of tokenised value.

CRYPTO EXCHANGES

Crypto-currencies were initially brokered by crypto exchanges, such as Binance, Huobi, OKEx, BitMEX, Bybit, FTX and Deribit. As crypto securitisation becomes more pervasive, stock exchanges and regulated markets are expected to adapt to these changes in the interim, however, may ultimately be displaced by peer-to-peer virtual exchanges in the longer term.

INITIAL COIN OFFERING

The traditional mechanism for introducing a crypto-asset is via an Initial Coin Offering (ICO). It is a common misconception that an ICO is identical to raising capital through an Initial Public Offering (IPO) by listing a publicly traded company's shares on a stock exchange. In an IPO, an investor is acquiring an equity share in the listed entity which may, depending on the equity type, feature a particular set of entitlements. Examples may include voting rights and to dividends among others. In an ICO however, the investor is acquiring a speculative tokenised asset at an introductory price based on the potential described from a published whitepaper endorsed or sponsored by the individual or group launching an ICO. There is no guarantee of an entitlement to either voting rights or an equity share in the group, company or project which underpins the issued tokens.

It is reasonable to expect that exploiting smart contracts and DLTs to create securities and derivatives, such as options, futures, forwards and swaps, as well as equities, is a foreseeable outcome through further adoption of this technology in the future. In such circumstances, the exchange and clearing functions for financial securities and derivatives, performed by intermediaries such as brokers, stock exchanges and clearing houses, will likely be disrupted by virtual exchanges which broker ICOs and, thereafter, potentially rely on peer-to-peer exchanges of crypto-assets. An early indicator along these vectors is in evidence through the emergence of Initial Exchange Offerings (IEOs) and Initial DEX Offerings (IDOs). These entities broker ICOs to the market; IEOs do so via a centralised exchange, whereas an IDO is conducted algorithmically via a decentralised exchange (DEX).

The potential implications of applying the paradigm of peer-to-peer exchanges in crypto-assets to the existing trading and clearing functions of the financial ecosystem are of increasing intrigue among investors. These technologies and business models may concern authorities by enabling the circumvention of the financial controls and regulations within a jurisdiction through disintermediating the regulated parties within.

NEW INSTRUMENTATION

The potential and versatility of asset-securitisation, via peer-to-peer DLTs, is near limitless. It is conceivable that the ecosystem of securities and derivatives trading will evolve to enable digitally generated, peer-to-peer traded Asset Backed Securities (ABSs), Collateralised Debt Obligations (CDOs) and Credit Default Swaps (CDS) where transparency and risk is governed by AI, potentially assessing and surfacing a new means of identifying potential systemic risks. Such a paradigm would encourage financial innovation in a climate of transparency, promoting the creation of financial derivatives without the associated systemic risks of shadow banking and moral hazard which ultimately led to the GFC.

In this context, tokenisation could facilitate new forms of credit access, by offering peer-to-peer syndicated shares of digital title deeds. In such circumstances, a prospective homeowner engages a virtual exchange to 'crowd fund' the purchase of residential real estate (or another asset class) through an ICO, IEO or DAO, the shares of which are syndicated, via tradable crypto-tokens. The title deed, potentially an NFT (see below), may be syndicated via the associated share tokens and terms of settlement, which can be captured digitally, via the smart contract functionality, which are complementary to the DLT. The token holders may earn interest or dividends proportionate to a stake therein, which are tradable on a peer-to-peer basis, should liquidity be required. This is conceptually identical to the trade of Mortgage-Backed Securities (MBS) between financial institutions and the brokerage as well as syndication thereof amongst investors (see Chapter 10: Financialisation).

The revelation of prospects this presents, suggests that the established constructs of the financial system, may be advancing toward an overhaul in redesigning the architecture and roles of financial institutions at every level (see Economy of Platforms, Chapter 15: Economy of Things).

PEER-TO-PEER

In much the same manner that the frictionless, inexpensive and the near-instant nature of peer-to-peer (P2P) payments using crypto-currencies is disrupting and may disintermediate conventional payment models, such as correspondent banking, interlinking and single-platform mechanisms (see Chapter 5: Payments), the peer-to-peer model should be expected to have a similar impact on securities. Frameworks, such as the Digital Asset Markup Language (DAML), [357] provide the capabilities to build DLT native smart contract applications and tokens using fine-grained permissions, sophisticated data models and embedded business logic, which integrate with numerous blockchains and DLT implementations.

The P2P paradigm enables low-cost trade between actors, via digital wallets, the utility of which is surfaced, via smart devices. In much the same way payments have been disrupted by peer-to-peer trading in crypto-currency, a corresponding expectation in the creation and trade of securities, derivatives and equities should be expected to be challenged by the P2P model.

CROSS-CHAIN SWAPS

Circumstances may arise whereby actors may require a direct exchange of one crypto-currency for another, much akin to a conventional currency exchange for example from dollars to euros. In such circumstances, cross-chain swaps (also known as inter-chain exchanges or atomic cross-chain swaps), may be exploited as a mechanism to facilitate this type of 'currency exchange' that takes place between two different crypto-currencies that run on their own respective blockchains. This is a mechanism that allows users to exchange different crypto-currencies directly between two peers without being intermediated via an exchange.

In essence, what unfolds in a cross-chain swap, is crypto-currency is taken from the parties and deposited under a special schedule that guarantees that the operation can only be completed with the approval of both parties. In the event that either party acts maliciously, funds remain inaccessible in a state similar to that of escrow.[358] The mechanism is designed to mitigate counterparty risk on a peer-to-peer basis. In practice, cross-chain swaps may be exploited on a multilateral basis to ensure that so long as all parties conform to the protocol, then all parties are guaranteed that the exchanges will take place as intended. The clear advantage of this capability is in supporting the creation of new decentralised, secure, as well as private exchange mechanisms, to be created among crypto-currency users. This assists in generating greater dynamics in which crypto-currencies may be used by facilitating interoperability and exchangeability among crypto-currencies as new ICOs emerge.

The prospect, thereof, unlocks enormous potential for decentralised finance (DeFi) opportunities to be developed, all of which may be transacted on a P2P basis without the necessity for centralised intermediaries. Nonetheless, the BIS Innovation Hub's project Rosalind and SWIFT's initiative to make CBDCs interoperable and transferable across borders respectively, represent substantial efforts to prevent extra-systemic tokenisation ascending to dominance in these arenas.

NON-FUNGIBLE TOKENS

Another form of tokenisation, is that of Non-Fungible Tokens (NFTs). Unlike crypto-currencies in which one token commands the identical value as another (of the same type) and is hence fungible, NFTs are tokens which represent unique assets.[359] By way of example, one Bitcoin has the identical value as another Bitcoin. An NFT may however, either represent a unique asset such as the Title Deed for a specific real estate property or a unique digital asset, such as an original digital artwork. Much like crypto-currency, the immutable records of ownership are managed, recorded and transacted, via DLTs. In June 2021, Sotheby's agreed to auction the original source code developed by Sir Timothy Berners-Lee which effectively spawned the World Wide Web, as an NFT (see Communications Technology, Chapter 2: Capital Evolution).[360] In March 2021, a Joint Photographic Experts Group (JPEG) file entitled

'Everydays — The First 5000 Days' made by Michael Winkelman, a digital artist known as 'Beeple,' sold at an online auction orchestrated by the prominent auctioneers, Christie's for $69.3 million.[361] Conceptually, while a digital file may be duplicated in perpetuity, the verifiable recording of which instance of such a file is the original, via a DLT, whereby consensus as to its provenance is achieved, is what relegates all duplicates as either copies or derivatives, thereof. In essence it is the recognised consensus and verified authenticity of which instance is the original, combined with its auditable provenance, which gives the NFT its value.

This draws parallels with digital rights management (DRM), which is a systematic approach to copyright protection for digital media. Both the music and film industries faced unprecedented challenges in copyright infringement brought about by the emergence of digital encoding software in the 1990s. Waveform Audio File Formats (WAVs) and Moving Picture Experts Group (MPEG) layer 3 (known as MP3) files were effortlessly encoded from a compact disc (CD), and thereafter, duplicated and shared via the internet. DVD and Video were similarly exploited using software codecs to create MPEG layer 4 (MP4), as well as a variety of other digital formats. With the corresponding rise in free MP3 player applications and inexpensive portable MP3 player devices, these digital piracy practices substantially and materially affected the music and film industries. The introduction of DRM was instrumental in rehabilitating copyright protections particularly through the rise of Apple's iPod digital music players coupled with its iTunes software player and digital music store (see Smart Device Apps, Chapter 3: Ecosystems). Digital media purchased via Apple, and a number of others incorporated DRM functionality to prevent unrestricted duplication, which in turn, restored the protections previously realised, via physical media.

In much the same way DRM offers copyright protection and enforcement functionality to digital music and video, DLTs may offer the like to original digital artefacts. In instances where copyright and derivative works are legitimately contracted or licensed, the DLT and smart contract technology may be leveraged to facilitate, track and assure the compliance thereof.

EXPECTATIONS & CHALLENGES

Crypto-assets are thus likely to assume the role of Gold, bonds, treasuries and real estate in the world of digital natives. In the interim, actors searching for liquidity in the system without exchanging money for frozen, non-fungible assets and those divesting from holding cash in the light of diminished confidence in fiat currency as a *store of value,* as well as persistently poor interest rates and returns, are motivated to seek out alternatives.

CVCs and crypto-assets are proving to be a modern day reflection of society's dismay with monetary policy making and unconstrained deficit spending. A behaviour that draws parallels with the dollar confidence crisis, resulting in the creation of the 'Carter Bonds' of the late 1970s (see Dollar Confidence Crisis, Chapter 10: Financialisation). Digital instruments, such as CVCs, are far more adaptable and convertible than physical Gold or conventional investment vehicles. The appeal of near-instant tradability of CVCs and crypto-assets is a compelling differentiator in an economic climate as fragile as that left behind by the GFC and COVID-19 pandemic. Hence, CVCs and crypto-assets are drawing parallels to become attractive prospects as the money and securities of digital natives and the generations to come, respectively.

The scope of tokenisation through digital securitisation has the potential to permeate every level of Exter's inverse pyramid (see Exter's Pyramid, Chapter 9: Gold). The prospect of such a reality is particularly plausible, given the precedent set through Facebook's attempt at launching a Synthetic Hegemonic Currency (Libra).

The prospect of disintermediating the exchange of value, via P2P payments and securitisation, represents a daunting threat to the stability of the global financial system. The hierarchical banking model is significantly threatened by P2P payments enabled by CVCs, through diminishing aggregated capital raised by deposits from account holders (depositors). Without payments, traction to retain depositors is at significant risk. In the absence of capital raised from depositors, the means with which to offer credit facilities and profit therefrom, is increasingly challenging. In the card payments realm, however, the facility of dispute management remains a key capability, which P2P payments may find challenging to displace.

In the multi-party models which payment networks, such as Visa and Mastercard provide, the participating issuers act as guarantors for the quality of transactions. In doing so, consumers benefit from a vehicle through which to challenge a merchant should the goods purchased, fail to be delivered or arrive damaged. This remains an indispensable criterion in assuring the integrity in e-commerce transactions. Thus, until such time that P2P transactions include equivalent protections, the P2P model is unlikely to challenge the payment card industry's primacy. However, when considering that in order to surface the utility of an instant payment executed with a physical payment card instrument, this multi-party model requires numerous participants in order to realise the aforementioned outcome (Fig 5.8). Participants include Acquirers, Issuers, Payment Networks (Schemes), PayFacs (or PSPs), ISOs and gateways. Each participant exacts a transaction fee (collectively, in the form of interchange++) notwithstanding the fees exacted by banks, and net settlement CSMs. This paradigm is both costly and anachronistic.

Furthermore, for the banking sphere, the demand to access credit, could easily flow into digitally securitised instruments, such as crypto-assets, offering direct returns to investors against principal, yet remaining tradable at a low cost, in a near liquid state as a P2P transmissible security. Such outcomes will likely threaten institutional roles in maturity transformation (see Maturity Transformation, Chapter 10: Financialisation). In such circumstances, the value of brokering, intermediating, and clearing services provided by stock exchanges, clearing houses and investment banks, will likely face severe disruption.

Should the utility of making payments, accessing credit and dispute management be fully surfaced, free of intermediation, via either banks, card networks and particularly central banks, the safeguards and protections offered by these institutions and regulators over the financial system will likely deteriorate.

Furthermore, the ease in P2P transmissibility and the absence of controls evident in anonymous crypto-currencies, provides a vehicle through which extraterritorial sanctions and capital account controls may be circumvented. Crypto-currencies are, thus, drawing parallels to mechanisms, such as SPFS, CIPS, SEPA and INSTEX. Essentially, these instruments are further representative of a growing systemic resistance towards the world order and by extension, the United States' hegemonic posture.

The P2P model combined with DLTs, open-source and standardisation are symptomatic of commoditisation and the Apex predator hypothesis (see Chapter 4: Surfacing Utility). In this sphere, *Creative Destruction* through a *first principles* approach, is facilitating an *exaptation* of technologies to unfold. This *exaptation* is instrumentally being co-opted to displace the previous orthodoxy in favour of a new nimble and 'energy efficient' challenger.

Central banks, governments and regulators are, therefore, faced with an unenviable challenge to embrace technological and financial innovation, tempered with the appropriate controls to ensure stability and accountability within the financial system remains intact. This challenge is particularly critical given the protracted period of financial stress experienced since the GFC and the amplification, thereof, as a result of the COVID-19 pandemic.

While Blockchain, DAG and broader DLT technologies will continue to develop towards balancing a trustworthy *store of value* and a viable *medium of exchange* through greater focus on transactional speed, integrity and efficiency, the digitally-enabled decentralised paradigm these technologies facilitate, will continue to promote the creation of new digital channels while permeating and disrupting analogue business models and vertically-integrated value, as well as supply chains. Effectively, enabling the creation of new value propositions, via the 'Economy of Things.'

15

ECONOMY OF THINGS

BEHAVIOURAL SURPLUS

In the wake of the 'Dot Com' crash (see Dot Com, Chapter 10: Financialisation), Google pioneered the first steps towards creating what has become known as 'Surveillance Capitalism.'

The crash in technology stocks had severely damaged investor sentiment towards technology companies. Under the threat of a retreat among Google's investors, the then search-engine company was able to placate its backers. Google did so by enticing its investors with the prospect that the search-engine company was able to harness its extensive searchable agglomeration of data, via 'data mining', to discern valuable patterns in consumer behaviour. This 'behavioural surplus' could be exploited to provide greater certainty to Google's advertising customers, in that their advertising investments would result in greater and measurably improved sales conversions.

DIGITAL EXHAUST

A behavioural surplus is by its nature representative of data which exceeds that which is required for traditional service improvement (such as traditional customer satisfaction feedback). The surplus (rich data signals, also known as 'digital exhaust') is harvested, and thereafter, harnessed without the user's knowledge, conscious disclosure or consent and is exploited to benefit business customers through providing insights. Monetising the successful exploitation, thereof, creates what is known as a 'surveillance dividend.' The surveillance dividend represents the measurable yield achieved through exploiting the insights determined, via inadvertently disclosed user data, in order to realise a profit that would otherwise not be achievable. In 2011, the US supermarket chain Target began marketing baby products to a man whose daughter was pregnant. Curiously, the man wasn't aware his daughter was expecting. Target had analysed the purchasing habits of the man's daughter and discerned to a high level of probability that she was newly pregnant.[362] A key factor in this determination was a switch the man's daughter had recently made to an array of less fragrant bathroom products. Since pregnancy may elicit greater sensitivity to aroma, this factor played a substantive role in discerning Target's insight, via the analysis of her purchase history.

AFFECTIVE COMPUTING

Examples of 'digital exhaust' include facial micro expressions, genomic, gender and age characteristics which are harvested from the images containing faces and self-portraits (more commonly known as 'selfies') uploaded and shared via social media. Computational analysis via AI algorithms may also be exploited to discern ethnicity, the interests, and even the emotional state of those depicted therein.[363] This form of analysis falls within the sphere of Affective Computing. Affective Computing is an interdisciplinary field of computer science, psychology and cognitive science aimed toward the development of algorithms and devices, which can interpret and simulate human affects.[364]

SURVEILLANCE DIVIDEND

Other forms of digital exhaust include clues as to an individual's likely education level by analysing their use of colloquialisms, spelling, vocabulary and grammar in posts, via online forums or search engine queries. All such data insights are representative of a surplus to what was required to provide the service through which the data was harvested. Aside from deterministic insights, patterns of behaviour may be modelled and trained stochastically across a variety of clustered data sets of people with certain characteristics. The models are 'trained' (term of art for 'refined') by observing how these people may behave over a period of time. Inserting a person's data within an arc which has been formulated through such models enables tremendous accuracy in predicting their likely preferences, behaviour, as well as their probable responses to certain stimuli. A simplistic example could be through analysis, determining that a social media user prefers to dine out once a week on a Friday evening, discerned through analysing location 'check-in,' geolocation tags from uploaded images and posting tags. Through analysing the embedded details, the approximate area, cuisine genre and likely value of a potential sales opportunity could be predicted and sold to restaurants which meet the criteria in the catchment area. Through a directed advert (or discount coupon) at precisely the right moment and time, the probability of a successful sales conversion rises substantially.

Monetising the digital exhaust (behavioural surplus), while incorporating Affective Computing, to create a 'surveillance dividend' is achieved through the use of Data Science and Artificial Intelligence (see Harnessing & Monetising Data, Chapter 4: Surfacing Utility). Through analysing millions (if not billions) of images, posts and other behavioural data (e.g. via Cookies), Surveillance Capitalists are able to exploit such data in a shift from observation to actuation.

The extent to which Surveillance Capitalists are able to actuate using *prescriptive analytics* and *behavioural surplus* data was revealed in published scholarly articles, detailing Facebook's massive-scale contagion experiments.

'We show, via a massive (N = 689,003) experiment on Facebook, that emotional states can be transferred to others, via emotional contagion, leading people to experience the same emotions without their awareness. We provide experimental evidence that emotional contagion occurs without direct interaction between people (exposure to a friend expressing an emotion is sufficient), and in the complete absence of nonverbal cues.'[365]

-Adam D.I. Kramer (Core Data Science Team, Facebook Inc.), Jamie E. Guillory and Jeffrey T. Hancock (Cornell University, Ithaca, USA) - (Experimental evidence of massive-scale emotional contagion through social networks, published June 2014).

And reinforced by:

'We argue a main but underappreciated reason why the Facebook emotional contagion experiment is ethically problematic is that it co-opted user data in a way that violated identity-based norms and exploited the vulnerability of those disclosing on social media who are unable to control how personal information is presented in this technologically mediated environment.'[366]

- Evan Selinger (Department of Philosophy, Rochester Institute of Technology, USA) and Woodrow Hartzog (Cumberland School of Law, Samford University, USA) (Facebook's emotional contagion study and the ethical problem of co-opted identity in mediated environments where users lack control, published May 2015)

The articles reveal a consensus on two important findings discerned from the Facebook contagion experiments.

1. Realisation that users can be manipulated through an online medium to a tremendous and effective extent.

2. The methods used to manipulate users can be exploited without the user's awareness.

It may be argued that these capabilities have a long-standing pedigree through media, such as movies, books, articles and music, being exploited to elicit emotional responses. However, the ability for the advertising industry to market a good or service by manipulating a potential customer in a manner specific to them at precisely the optimal moment of vulnerability, in order to realise a sales conversion, is what differentiates this level of 'instrumentarian' power.

Furthermore, the collective realisation of the transition from observation to actuation surfaces the notion that not only may a potential customer be manipulated into a purchase transaction, but this may be achieved, via clandestine means. In other words, subliminal cues may be embedded in webpages to influence the real-world emotional states of human consumers. This forms the basis for what has become known as 'Surveillance Capitalism.'

SURVEILLANCE CAPITALISM

'If something is free, you're the product.'[367] - *Richard Serra, 1973.*

The 21st century is shaping up to what many believe will likely become known as the 'Digital Century.' An era anticipated to be defined by the accelerated growth in technological consumption and digital advancements experienced since the 1990s.

In November 2004, Google acquired Keyhole Inc.; a little-known 3D mapping start-up. Keyhole led by John Hinkey and funded by the CIA, via In-Q-Tel, evolved within Google into Google Earth.[368] The advancements made in geospatial visualisation services facilitated by Google Earth, enabled the creation of the smart phone augmented reality (AR) and location-based game, 'Pokémon Go.' Pokémon Go was released in 2016 and published by Niantic in collaboration with Nintendo.[369] Niantic was a spin-off company, divested out of Google in October 2015.[370] Approximately half-a-billion smart phone users downloaded the game in its first year of release.

Once registered, a player creates and customises an avatar, which is displayed on a map based on the player's geographical location. Features on the map include 'PokéStops' and 'Pokémon Gyms.' The PokéStops use items known as 'Lure Modules.' In gameplay, the Lure Modules are used to manifest wild and occasionally rare Pokémon characters to which players are attracted.

It has long been possible for tech giants such as Google and Facebook to capitalise on the surveillance dividend by predicting and influencing computing and mobile click-through rates in the virtual world (via websites and apps) and selling such influence to business advertising customers. Pokémon Go, however, revealed the ability to actuate and derive a surveillance dividend by influencing behaviour in the real-world.

Businesses such as Starbucks and McDonalds were among those which were sold the 'Lure Modules.' As a *quid pro quo*, the game would drive footfall using rewards (in the form of PokéStops), thereby luring and guiding customers towards these businesses during gameplay. Increased footfall had thereby been purposely engineered in much the same way as click-through rates, in order to create sales opportunities for these businesses. All the while, the players remained unaware as to what had transpired. This falls within the sphere of 'economies of action' whereby a technology company is effectively exploiting economies of scale and scope (via data agglomeration) in order to remote control and engineer behaviour to facilitate a business end. The participants, however, are both unaware and misled by playing a game, in order to engage in a fun and recreational activity. The entertainment value facilitates this shadow practice in order to prevent the participants from asking questions which may challenge this business model. This represents the transcendence from click-through actuation to real-world actuation, via surveillance capitalism. It additionally places emphasis on the second key finding revealed from the Facebook massive-contagion experiments (see above), in which influence was achieved without the user's knowledge. This is viewed as the key factor in achieving a successful outcome. This is the position advocated by esteemed Harvard University professor, Shoshana Zuboff, in her book, 'The Age of Surveillance Capitalism,' published in 2019.[371] Furthermore, the rise in exploiting gamification techniques in software services (inclusive of FinTech propositions) using contemporary frameworks such as 'Octalysis,' are further indications as to the extent to which surveillance capitalism is capable of influencing users for business outcomes. Octalysis was developed by actionable gamification and behavioural design expert, Yu-kai Chou, detailed in his book, 'Actionable Gamification,' published in 2015. Simplistic examples of gamification techniques incorporated into websites and apps (apart from Pokémon Go) include eBay's 'bidding system' and the 'Like' feature, among social networking platforms designed to elicit what is known as the 'Aura Effect.'

ZUBOFF'S FAUSTIAN BARGAIN

Following the release of the iPhone in 2007 (see Chapter 3: Ecosystems), and the subsequent proliferation of smart devices, Zuboff advocates that these devices became the perfect platforms for developing and releasing apps that offer a *quid pro quo* of contextual personalised services (see Chapter 4: Surfacing Utility) in exchange for digital surplus data. Zuboff describes this *quid pro quo* as, a form of *'Faustian Bargain,'* whereby the consumer sacrifices their privacy in exchange for personalised digital services and convenience. However, a *'Faustian Bargain'* implies a level of transparency in which the parties are aware of the ultimate outcome. Surveillance Capitalism offers no such transparency. The user is unaware that his preferences and *modis operandi* are being exploited for other parties' financial gain. In March 2021, research conducted by Douglas Leith at Trinity College, Ireland, revealed that Google collected up to twenty times as much data from Android devices as Apple did from its iOS devices.[372]

'When idle, Android sends roughly 1MB of data to Google every 12 hours, compared with iOS sending Apple about 52KB over the same period. In the US alone, Android collectively gathers about 1.3TB of data every 12 hours. During the same period, iOS collects about 5.8GB.'

- Douglas Leith, Trinity College, Ireland, 2021.

Regardless, the inference is that tech companies exploit these platforms to harvest rich data sources, which in turn, may be exploited to cultivate valuable insights which may be monetised. Essentially, commodifying their customers' data as if it were a raw material with which to create goods and services (see Commodification, Chapter 2: Capital Evolution). This practice should be expected to amplify exponentially through immersive platforms and sensor data gleaned, via the 'Internet of Things.'

INTERNET OF THINGS

The Internet of Things (IoT) is the term used to describe the concept of connecting smart devices, sensors and embedded systems, via the internet. The value of IoT is surfaced through connecting various devices for the purpose of collecting data, monitoring, processing, analysis, as well as the control, thereof.

The core concept of IoT originated as early as 1982, when a modified Coca-Cola Vending Machine at Carnegie Mellon University, Pittsburgh, Pennsylvania, USA became the first ARPANET (see Chapter 2: Capital Evolution) connected appliance.[373] The vending machine was capable of remotely transmitting, whether it was low on inventory, as well as whether its existing inventory was cold or not. The term 'Internet of Things' was originally coined by Kevin Ashton in 1999.[374] In 1994 however, the concept was described by Reza Raji in an article entitled 'Smart networks for control' in an IEEE Spectrum publication.[375]

IoT is a higher-order system of the internet and the slew of advancements made in short-range wireless communication technologies, such as Bluetooth Mesh Networking, Wi-Fi, NFC (see Chapter 5: Payments) and related technologies. IoT may additionally exploit wired communications over Local Area Networks (LANs), as well as satellite-centric communications, such as Very Small Aperture Terminal (VSAT). However, the proliferation of IoT at scale has largely been constrained historically by the limited address space of IPv4 (see Chapter 2: Capital Evolution) and the limitations of short-range low-density communications technologies. IPv4 allows for 4.3 billion publicly addressable devices in total. From 2019 to 2025, the number of IoT devices globally is expected to rise from 7.5 billion to 25 billion.[376] Hence, IoT is expected to leverage Internet Protocol version 6 (IPv6) in the longer-term to cater to the scalability requirements for growth in the number of internet-connected devices.

QUIC

It has long been recognised that TCP/IP, originally installed in the ARPANET in 1983 (see Chapter 2: Capital Evolution), may no longer be the appropriate protocol to meet the demands of the modern internet. In May 2021, the Internet Engineering Task Force (IETF) published the standard for a new encrypted transport layer protocol, known as the Quick Universal Datagram Protocol Internet Connections (QUIC).

The nascent protocol addresses numerous limitations in terms of latency and security that TCP has been expected to cater to as the demands imposed upon the internet have evolved. The QUIC protocol is designed to shoulder the demands of the modern internet, particularly given the rise of apps, meta-apps, streaming and the necessity to seamlessly switch between Wi-Fi and cellular networks, particularly with the proliferation of mobile smart devices and the Internet of Things.[377] QUIC surfaces the best qualities of TCP connections and Transport Layer Security (TLS) encryption, capable of making HTTP traffic (see Chapter 3: Ecosystems) faster, as well as more secure, efficient, reliable and resilient.[378] From a scalability perspective QUIC is compatible with being underpinned by either IPv4 or IPv6 alike (see above). QUIC was initially devised as an experimental protocol by Google. However, after five-years of maturation in collaboration with industry stakeholders, such as Fastly and Mozilla (among others), the release of the IETF RFC9000 standard signals that the protocol is ready for broader adoption.

This represents a departure from previous approaches to overcome the limitations of TCP/IP, whereby the underlying layers of communication technologies were incrementally refined to improve the performance of a protocol, dating back to the inception of the internet itself. Transitions included analogous modernisation of ethernet, coaxial to copper cabling (cat 5/cat 6) to fibre optics and the introduction of course-wavelength, as well as dense-wavelength division multiplexing and eventually the introduction of optical amplifiers (Semiconductor; Erbium-doped and Raman). This is all in an attempt to optimise and effectively compensate for the limitations of TCP.

However, in an increasingly decentralised topology brought about by the proliferation of internet-connected devices (IoT), the introduction of QUIC is an instrumental enabler. IoT devices are nimble, compact and light-weight yet expected to collect, process and transmit data expediently and efficiently, thus, requiring data transport protocols which reflect these characteristics and requirements.

DOMOTICS

The field of Domotics, being a portmanteau of 'domus' ('home', Latin) and 'robotics,' deals with the technology and automation capabilities required in order to create a 'Smart Home.' In the 1970s, X10 was conceived and developed, being the first home automation network technology. The X10 protocol facilitated the communication between electronic devices, primarily using power line wiring for signalling and control. Via X10, signalling is achieved through 'brief' radio frequency bursts, which represent digital information.

The modern smart home, however, is equipped with Wi-Fi and connected to the internet, via broadband. In such circumstances, the scope for domotics has broadened extensively. Modern domotics is able to leverage wirelessly connected devices (typically via Wi-Fi) including security systems, such as cameras and passive motion sensors, as well as safety devices such as smoke detectors, air quality sensors and door chimes. Collectively, this creates the fabric for a deeply connected and automated home environment.

The addition of network connected control systems to manage thermostats, electrical sockets and lighting dimmer switches has been particularly helpful in facilitating home automation capabilities for assisted living and remote home management. Domotics has additionally made inroads into spheres, such as heating, ventilation and air conditioning (HVAC), whereby not only may these systems be controlled remotely, they may also be optimised and controlled cohesively via artificial intelligence to yield a specific outcome in sustaining environmental conditions within a home or other structure.

Furthermore, smart kitchens featuring internet connected washing and drying machines, dishwashers, as well as refrigerators have become prevalent, whereby, a refrigerator may sense and monitor its contents and automatically order food items as and when inventory diminishes below a particular threshold. The prospect this has introduced in creating new business models for commerce and FinTech is significant and surfaces the notion of IoT centric, as well as inter-device commerce. It additionally enables nascent business models, such as pay-per-use appliances, whereby the use of home appliances may be charged dynamically as a utility (see Commoditisation, Chapter 2: Capital Evolution). Examples include washing machines which charge per wash cycle.

In order to enable such business models, devices connected from within the home to external web services and APIs are able to feed data into centralised cloud systems (see Chapter 3: Ecosystems), which may report usage as well as facilitate control, via smart device apps, as well as web-portals. In addition, the telemetry collected may be exploited to effect centralised billing for services provided, via the homeowner's (or tenant's) payment instrument, method or gateway (see Chapter 5: Payments). Telemetry data is highly desirable to Surveillance Capitalists, keen to exploit the dimensions that new forms of digital exhaust will yield from observing people and actuating accordingly. The addition of virtual assistant capable devices within the Apple HomeKit, Amazon Alexa and Google Assistant ecosystems, such as the Apple HomePod and Amazon Echo product lines amplifies the effects, thereof dramatically. While virtual assistant devices are instrumental in surfacing the utility of home automation through voice control (see Natural Language Processing, Chapter

4: Surfacing Utility) over the lighting, appliances and entertainment systems within the home, these devices are capable of eavesdropping on every conversation and capturing every ambient sound within range. Since NLP processing and responses are discerned centrally, these devices transmit such data to centralised systems. Thereafter, the data may be exploited as the Surveillance Capitalists see fit. While this may be expected from devices which are inherently designed to capture audio, the revelation that other smart devices may be fitted with microphones prompted a backlash in the United States. Google's NEST line of smart home products is a prominent example of such, whereby numerous devices were revealed to be equipped with embedded microphones. In response, US Vice President (then California Senator) Kamala Harris commented:

'Americans shouldn't have to fear that the products in their home could be spying on them.'[379]

- Kamala Harris, US Senator California, 2019.

5G RADIO AREA NETWORKS

Fifth generation (5G) wireless is largely perceived as an increment to the 4G/Long-Term Evolution (LTE) mobile technology standard, based on the IEEE 802.11ac wireless networking standard. The 5G smart phone race gained pace in 2019 with companies such as Huawei and Samsung taking the lead.

The 3rd Generation Partnership Project (3GPP) is the global industry organisation engaged in developing the technical specifications for 5G. 3GPP identifies present and future use cases for cellular technology and defines the technical features needed to bring such use cases to fruition. 3GPP, is furthermore, engaged in ensuring that such standards and specifications enable interoperability on a global scale. In June 2019 '5G Release 15,' which defined much of the basic operation of 5G was completed. The release defined the 5G New Radio (NR) and the 5G system (also known as 5G core network), along with enablers for IoT use cases.

Such enablers include massive machine-type communications (mMTC), Vehicle-to-everything communications (V2x), Mobile Communications System for Railways (FRMCS), Mission Critical (MC) interworking with legacy systems and API exposure (see Chapter 3: Ecosystems) for third-party access to 5G services.

3GPP, in response to the standards and use cases identified by the International Telecommunication Union - Telecommunications (ITU-T) embarked on responding through its 'Study on New Services and Markets Technology Enablers (or SMARTER) Project.' The SMARTER Project, in addition to a category known as 'fixed broadband' identified a number of high-level use cases, for which 5G would be expected to cater. The use cases distilled into the necessity to develop mMTC (see above), Enhanced Mobile Broadband (eMBB) and Ultra-Reliable Low Latency Communications (URLLC).

mMTC is designed to cater to very large-scale machine-to-machine interactions including battery operated devices within the IoT ecosystem. Devices which require low-latency and highly reliable connectivity in short bursts in order to remain energy efficient require this capability. Examples of use cases include, lighting and road sign control, smart waste management, asset tracking, as well as environmental monitoring (temperature and humidity sensors). A major limitation of previous cellular technologies has been the device density within a cellular coverage area. With mMTC, 5G is able to serve approximately one-million-devices per square kilometre. mMTC combined with IPv6 is expected to act as a catalyst, thereby enabling an explosion in the number of IoT devices deployed.

eMBB is intended to address the growing demands for cellular data consumption by human beings. eMBB enables 8K video streaming, Augmented Reality (see above) and Virtual Reality (AR/VR) demands, which are anticipated to be required through the greater consumption and interaction, via visual media. Consumers are expected to adopt interfacing with the internet, via meta-apps (also known as super apps). Meta-apps are highly contextualised and experiential applications which are immersive in nature exploiting AR and VR (see above), as well as Mixed Reality (MR) technologies (see Metaverse below). eMBB is expected to enable higher-order systems in the immersive technology sphere to emerge, such as AR capable smart glasses[380] and vehicles equipped with AR windscreens and windows.[381] In a comparable manner to which the smart phone displaced the personal computer as the most popular consumer internet interface, these technologies (immersive wearables) may incrementally replace the smart phone as the primary interface in engaging digital services. The visual medium provides new opportunities to surface the utility of digital services including digital commerce. A new generation of FinTech is expected to emerge to capitalise on engaging commerce and the shopping experience within a transcendent juxtaposition of the physical and digital worlds. In such circumstances, visual and verbal cues enabled by Augmented Reality and Natural Language Processing (see Chapter 4: Surfacing Utility) enable an entirely new sphere of payment instruments, payment methods and technologies to emerge. Examples of which may include biometric as well as instrument-less payments.

URLLC is designed to offer high-accuracy positioning (less than two meters), ultra-high reliability (99.999%, equivalent to five minutes of service loss per annum), remain highly available even while mobile, all the while delivering ultra-low latency (sub-millisecond). These characteristics represent the truly revolutionary differentiators of 5G over previous cellular generations. URLLC is expected to enable higher-order systems within the spheres of industrial automation, remote healthcare and robotics, as well as intelligent transportation systems, such as autonomous vehicles (self-driving cars).

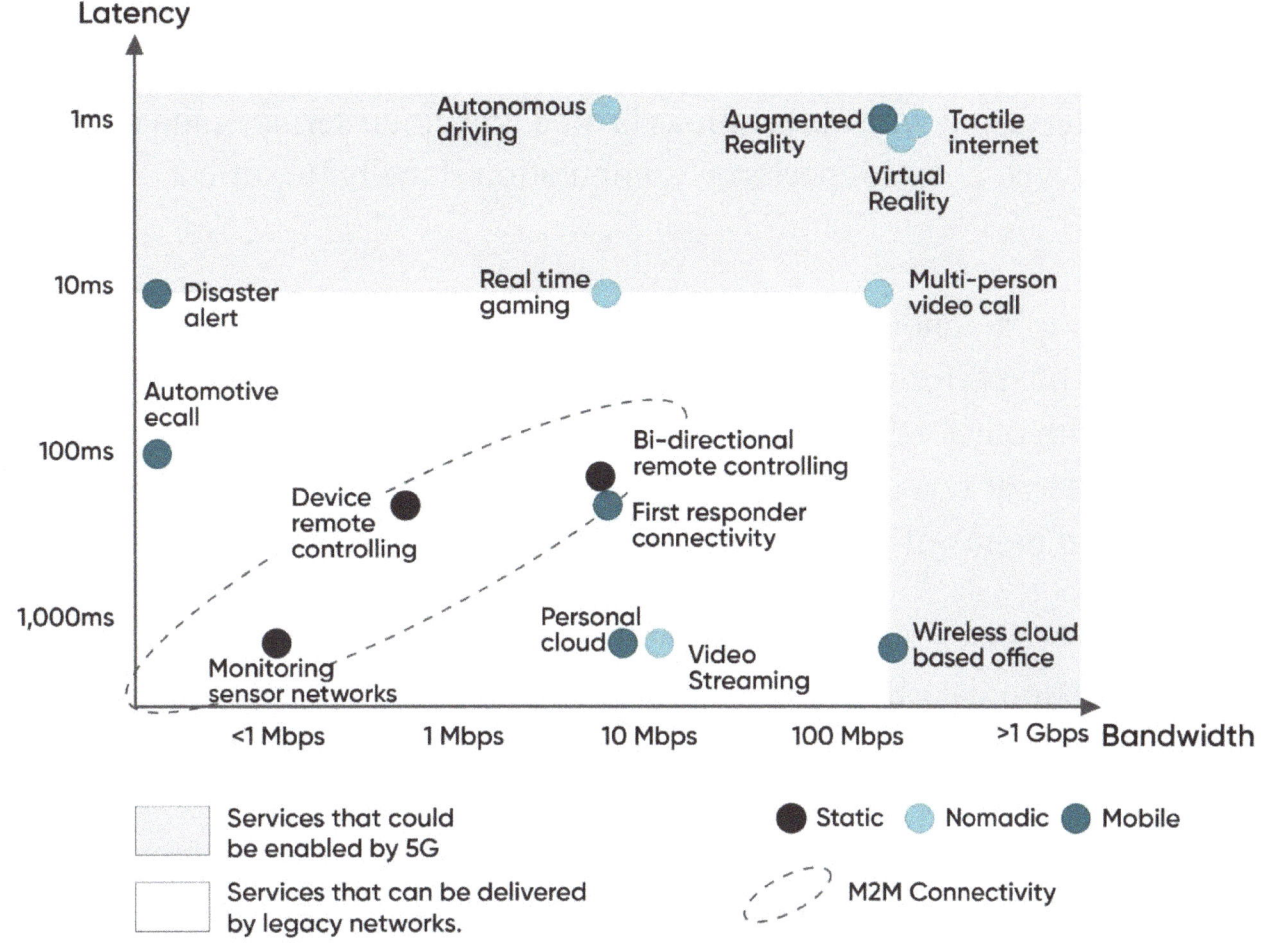

Fig 15.1 relationship between bandwidth and latency enabling/constraining technology advancements

Forecasts predict that by 2024, there are likely to be 1.9 billion 5G subscriptions worldwide.[382] By 2025, approximately half of overall mobile connections are projected to be 5G enabled in developed Asia and North America.[383]

MOBILE EDGE COMPUTING

Multi-access edge computing (MEC) (also known as Mobile Edge Computing) is a European Telecommunications Standards Institute (ETSI) network architecture concept. The principle is centred on exploiting the tremendous processing and computational power provided by smart phones and modern embedded devices at the edge of the network. With greater consolidation of services within the cloud (see Chapter 3: Ecosystems), the trend towards improving the user experience at the edge gave rise to Content Delivery Networks (CDNs), such as Fastly (see QUIC above) and Akamai. However, in an IoT-centric world with greater sophistication expected in real-time communications and fault tolerance, powerful devices are expected to be capable of interfacing with applications hosted, via cloud services and corporate data centres, yet able to perform computation locally to effect expedient outcomes.

In the context of autonomous vehicles, much of the processing of data inputs is expected to be performed within the vehicle itself, while simultaneously interacting with other vehicles over low latency 5G (and incremental) networks, as well as external services such as Global Positioning Systems (GPS), traffic data feeds and points of interest (POI).

Autonomous vehicles as an example will rely on inputs from sensors, cameras, GPS and location data from other vehicles and potential hazards, all managed by a localised artificial intelligence (AI) capability embedded within the vehicle. AI in this context facilitates the functions of 'Computer Vision' (an interdisciplinary scientific field concerned with enabling computers to interpret/understand images and video) and brings 'Edge Intelligence' to fruition. Vehicles would be expected to continue to operate safely, even when communication with the internet is unavailable, hence, reliance on centralised computation would not be viable. Advancements in Machine Learning, such as Tiny ML are enablers for proliferating AI at the edge.[384] Edge Intelligence is additionally necessary to accommodate the real-world application of what AI has 'learned' and to share this, via centralised data-rich environments within the cloud, while bringing this intelligence to the edge environment for other vehicles and embedded systems. This is vital in order to facilitate the graphics and visually enriched applications (meta-apps), which are expected to dominate the user interfaces of the 5G and IoT world.

TOUCHLESS EXPERIENTIAL ENVIRONMENT

The impact of the COVID-19 pandemic, drove the necessity to reduce physical contact with people and things. The conditions prompted greater adoption of digital commerce and contactless payments (see Chapter 5: Payments). The pandemic additionally accelerated the co-opting of technologies such as AI (powered by Edge Intelligence and Cloud Computing) as well as IoT to create an environment, in which a new technological shroud could be forged. A shroud in service of augmenting the physical world in which economic activity takes place. Such are the building blocks of smart cities.

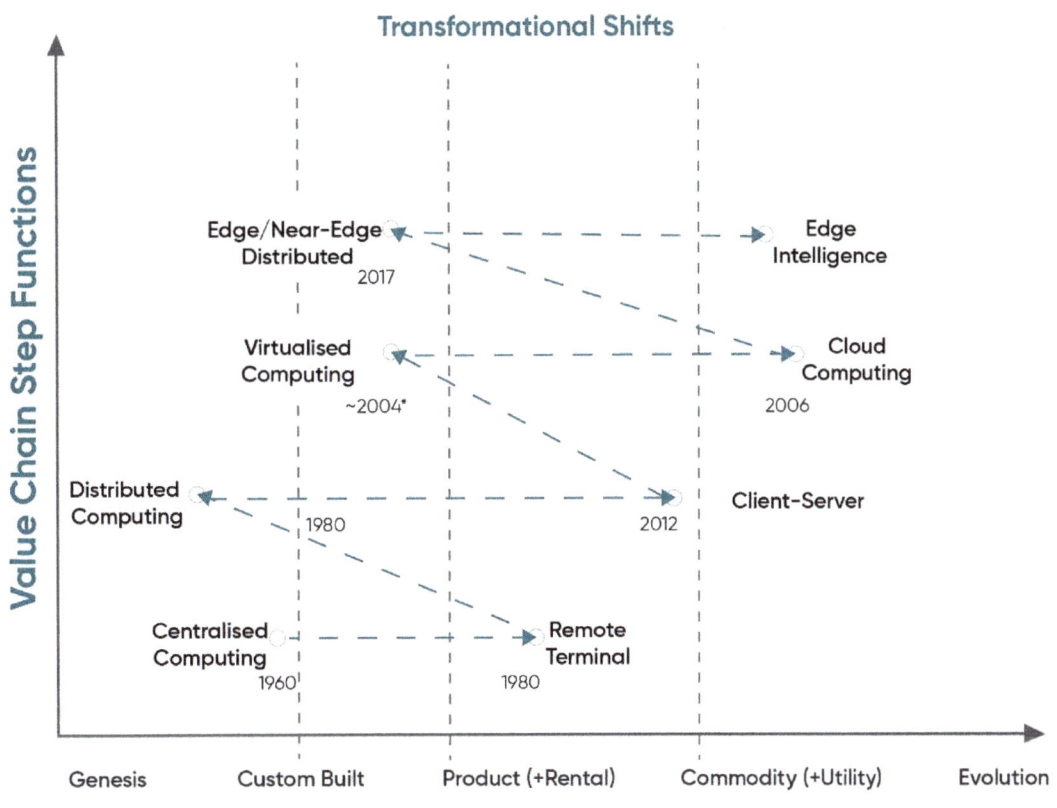

Fig 15.2 Wardley Map illustrating the evolution towards Edge-Intelligence

SMART CITIES

The long-heralded rise of 'Smart Cities' has been expected to bring with it, a data-centric set of solutions to tackle a quandary of urban related challenges. Compounded by growing pressure to address climate change and to usher in greater sustainability measures, governments are expected to sponsor and prioritise investment in infrastructure development. Both Monetary and Fiscal policy (see Chapter 8: Economic Cycles) of this nature, is anticipated to be set in aid of meeting objectives to reduce carbon footprints and promote sustainability.[385] With cities in particular, consuming over two-thirds of the world's energy, there is mounting pressure to transition to lower-carbon and renewable energy systems.[386]

Commercial buildings alone account for approximately 20% of energy consumption in the US, an estimated 30% of which is wasted.[387] In considering that all urban commercial buildings are required to be carbon net-zero by 2050 in alignment with the objectives of the Paris Climate Agreement signed in 2016 (also known as the Paris Climate Accords),[388] decarbonising cities is likely to prove to be among the most cost-effective means through which governments tackle global climate change objectives. In the European Union, European Directive 2010/31/EU Energy Performance of Buildings, requires EU member states to ensure that the energy efficiency of buildings is enforced throughout the bloc. Hence, the demand for sustainable buildings (smart buildings) is compounding. In addition, several international standards have emerged to evaluate and grade building designs in order to promote environmentally sustainable structures. Standards, such as Leadership in Energy and Environmental Design (LEED), originated in the US and was developed by the Green Building Council. A broadly equivalent standard to that of LEED is the British developed Building Research Establishment Environment Assessment Method (BREEAM). In Japan, the Comprehensive Assessment System for Built Environment Efficiency (CASBEE) is another such standard.

To this end, smart building management systems, dynamic energy metering and management, smart water and waste management, as well as public transport and optimal traffic shaping, will all form parts of the scope into which technology will play a central role in sculpting the smart cities of the digital century. The focus of these advancements will likely be centred on optimising energy consumption and resources, while reducing the carbon-footprint of intra-urban travel and transportation.

The private sector in its ability to capitalise on the associated surveillance dividends, as well as public sector investments, such as the Green New Deal[389] and the European Green Deal,[390] will likely share in the wave of investment to modernise the urban landscape. This should distil into the development of a series of higher-order systems underpinned by enabling technologies, such as the Cloud, and AI, as well as IoT, 5G, and intelligent edge computing (see above).

In this context, it is foreseeable that autonomous vehicles will likely be governed, or at least influenced in part by a fabric of services in order to navigate the roads of urban centres. Centralised services which orchestrate and prioritise traffic flows in order to optimise traffic and to balance safety, convenience, air quality, noise pollution, as well as energy consumption, are likely to feature prominently within the typical smart city domain.

The objective of a smart city is to create an optimal balance between civil operations, the efficient use of resources, while promoting economic growth and prosperity, as well as a high quality of life for its residents. The success, thereof, will likely pivot on the outcomes achieved through the effective exploitation of smart technologies, optimal processes and the overarching management thereof, in contrast to the volume or sophistication of technology deployed therein. An example of this may be illustrated through making use of connected transport systems in conjunction with demand profiling. This would ensure the optimal use of natural resources, while improving air quality and reducing the carbon footprint of intracity travel. This may be achieved through exploiting smart technologies gathering data from smart devices and sensors, via low latency communications infrastructure, such as 5G where computer-based simulations and predictive analytics may be used to optimise transport systems. Smart technologies may be deployed to actively monitor roads, railways and subways, which can anticipate and thereby mitigate potential disruptions. Such capabilities additionally enhance safety by identifying opportunities to engage in preventive maintenance. Public safety is a high priority in any community. Thus, safe, clean and efficient cities, enabled via smart technologies, with access to high quality education and public services, will act as a magnet for new residents and businesses, thereby promoting economic growth and greater societal harmony.

Another characteristic of smart cities to be anticipated is the level of real-time surveillance required in order to manage and optimise traffic flows and footfall within the urban centres. Closed Circuit Television Cameras (CCTV) have featured prominently in developed urban centres for some time. In 2020 - 2021, the estimated number of CCTV cameras in London reached ~691,000.[391] Londoners should be expected to be surveilled by approximately ~300 cameras on any given day spent outside of their homes. The technology has historically been expensive to procure, monitor and maintain. However, with the commoditisation of wireless internet-enabled cameras, as well as 5G, the proliferation of real-time surveillance augmented with AI powered facial and object recognition, as well as tracking, should be expected to increase considerably.

While smart cities represent significant opportunities for a more sustainable future there are disadvantages that need to be considered. Namely, the real and perceived impact on personal privacy and anonymity. A surveillance economy relies on technologies which observe behaviour and the capture thereof in the form of data, which may be processed centrally in order to analyse this data for use in optimisation. However, this lends itself to potential abuse in which it may be exploited to compromise individual autonomy and manipulate public opinion. Furthermore, by relying to a greater extent on computing and network technologies to deeply connect the systems within a smart city, some of which may be deemed critical infrastructure, resilience and cybersecurity become of greater concern. With vulnerability to systems through stability and potential threats of hacking by unauthorised parties, public trust in cybersecurity will need to be cultivated and maintained.

Conceptually, the acceptance of the smart city paradigm will likely permeate throughout the world. However, it should be expected to vary significantly by country and in certain countries may vary greatly within. Examples to this effect is that of China, whereby the CCP's centralised leadership and governance maintains firm governmental control over its citizens and infrastructure. China is very forward looking in terms of its investment in technology and aspires towards a global leadership position in this sphere and among others (see Made in China 2025, Chapter 16: The Rise of China). China has substantial interest in developing smart cities both for its own consumption, as well as for export, thereof to external markets. The United States, by contrast, is highly developed technologically and has tremendous capabilities vested in educational institutions and private enterprises. However, culturally and legally, the US places a substantial premium on individual autonomy and privacy, in addition to being politically divided in a number of key areas. Thus, while smart cities will emerge in the US, these will likely manifest through collaborations between private enterprise and local governments, in lieu of a nationally-driven federal level strategy. It should be expected that countries worldwide will likely settle their positions regarding smart cities between the parentheses of these two extremes.

Aside from the implications for enhancing the capabilities of law enforcement and emergency first responders, the IoT spectrum, smart city fabric, combined with immersive technology offers a slew of capabilities to create the technological shroud (Touchless Experiential Environment) to offer entirely nascent business models and enable new economic practices to emerge. An early subset example of such is that of 'Amazon Go.'

Amazon Go is a subsidiary of the tech giant Amazon, established in January 2018.[392] Within its first three-years of trading, it opened twenty-nine convenience stores spanning the US and the UK (branded as 'Amazon Fresh' in the latter). By co-opting sensors, cameras and through the use of AI, the stores achieve a frictionless, light-touch shopping experience. Customers use their Amazon credentials and smart phones with an app generated QR code (see Chapter 5: Payments) upon entry to the store, after which they are surveilled by cameras and their Amazon account charges their registered payment instrument upon exit with the goods selected. The experience is free of human interaction, and bypasses the necessity for any form of formal checkout. To the shopper it remains a matter of ingress by identifying yourself, select the goods and egress.

The AI and IoT capabilities involved include that of computer vision (achieved through the use of Convolutional Neural Networks), Deep Learning (see

Artificial Intelligence, Chapter 4: Surfacing Utility) and sensor fusion. Combined with QR codes, geofencing (a virtual perimeter for a real-world geographic area) and FinTech, in the form of Amazon Pay, the Amazon Go stores manifest an exemplary example of surfacing the utility of the shopping experience. This is collectively achieved through the application of first principles thinking (see Chapter 4: Surfacing Utility) and by co-opting IoT technologies (cameras and sensors) to facilitate a frictionless, consistent, seamless and experiential economic interaction. In June 2021, Grabandgo, a checkout-free tech company secured $39m in series B funding to implement its computer vision and AI-centric shopping and payments technology into several grocery chains.[393] This signals the commoditisation of the checkout-free experiential business model and the emergence of 'instrument-less' payments as a growing business paradigm, facilitated by interdisciplinary technological fusion towards the creation of the 'Economy of Things.'[394]

M2M COMMERCE

The prospects of a digital-first and increasingly connected economy combined with the proliferation of IoT, creates the climate and associated platforms for economic activity to transcend from human induced commerce to that of a hybrid model, where both humans and devices (things) engage in economic discourse. A non-human example of which is that of a self-driving vehicle owned by an individual, who while not using it, syndicates the vehicle for use by a ride-sharing platform. In such a scenario, the vehicle may be directed to pick-up, transport and drop-off passengers, much like any taxi or ride-sharing service. In such instances, the vehicle would require the necessary technology to seamlessly accept payments (via an embedded POS device), as well as be capable of being tracked and retrieved should any malfunction arise. In addition, the vehicle will likely need the ability to make payments unsupervised.[395] Such a situation may arise should the vehicle require refuelling while unattended. In all likelihood, the ability to refuel autonomously will prompt development of automated and robotic refuelling capabilities at refuelling stations and vehicle charging stations. Such propositions (such as

Scott Automation's Robofuel) already exist, using vision sensing and detection systems to guide robotic refuelling nozzles to optimally orientate and dock with a truck's fuel tank.[396] In such instances, the vehicle will require the ability to function as a payment instrument in order to pay for fuel or an electrical recharge autonomously, while unattended. Over time this may be extended to servicing and repairs, in which the vehicle engages in robotic decision-making through price discovery. Essentially, this creates circumstances in which a vehicle may be required to maintain agency over its own commercial viability.

Integrating POS and payment instrument functionality into vehicles, robots, drones and other devices may be a challenging endeavour to sustain due to the rigorous security capabilities required to sustain secure payments. Examples include, the Apple Secure Enclave subsystem designed to keep sensitive data secure regardless of whether the smart phone's application processor kernel is compromised.[397] This is an essential capability to ensure smart phones remain PCI-DSS compliant for NFC transactions (see Contactless Payments, Chapter 5: Payments). This technology benefits from being updated frequently as new capabilities are released with each smart phone generation, typically every one to two years. However, since vehicles are high-value assets which may be depreciated over and kept for many years, the integrated payments technology would quickly become outdated and thus rendered defunct. Regardless, the opportunities that machine-to-machine (M2M) commerce represent will likely drive research and development in resolving this challenge. A potential solution may be to emulate the 'Amazon Go' business model (see above), by billing a vehicle on an observation basis (using CCTV and Computer Vision) with a preregistered payment instrument tied to its registration and license plate. Fraud may be prevented by combining observation with a vehicle's unique NFC or RFID tag, which is scanned at the point-of-sale.

Other examples of M2M commerce includes that of devices within the IoT spectrum being exploited to generate consumable resources, which may be monetised. In such instances, the opportunity exists to co-opt distributed ledger technologies to create tokens of value associated with the resources being produced. Such tokens may subsequently be traded as asset-backed securities or convertible virtual currency underpinned by the commodity value of the resource being generated (see Chapter 14: Tokenisation). Such propositions already exist in the form of instances, such as SolarCoin.[398] SolarCoin is a crypto-currency based on a token issued to claimants per megawatt hour of electricity yielded, via solar energy production. In this instance, solar energy is produced and consumed, via an electrical grid and the monetisation, thereof, is globally portable as a commodity based crypto-asset. With greater seamless integration and automation of IoT devices, business models, whereby, devices offer services to be consumed, via other devices may become increasingly prevalent. Distributed ledger technologies, CVCs, and CBDCs are likely to play an instrumental role in facilitating the exchange of value between IoT devices on a peer-to-peer basis. DLTs are additionally capable of recording all manner of transactions and may be used to record other forms of data. Essentially functioning as a distributed database.

The higher-order systems that may emerge through the combination of IoT, AI and DLTs where *sensing, thinking and remembering* respectively represent opportunities to create a daunting plethora of possible outcomes in a digital era receptive to connected services and digital commerce.

The prospect of an economy in which both people and (smart) 'things' engage in economic discourse (hybrid economy) represents fertile territory for further innovation in inter-device payments, via M2M commerce. However, additionally represents major opportunities, as well as challenges for the insurance industry. Hence, InsureTech should be expected to be an area in which bridging the divide will feature extensively.

INSURETECH

Since 2010, InsureTech has introduced rapid pricing and quotation solutions, as well as advanced the field of analytical underwriting. The term underwriting originated from the practice of having each risk-taker write their name beneath the total amount of risk they were accepting in exchange for a specified premium (fee).

The insurance 'stack' is, and historically has been comprised of three core layers. Brokers, Primary Carriers and Reinsurers. Brokers sell insurance policies to the end-consumer. Primary Carriers underwrite the policies sold through the brokers, and hence, carry a significant proportion of the risks associated. Consequently, Primary Carriers are subject to substantial overheads. Overheads typically include the costs associated with policy management, claims processing functions, employing actuarial teams, contact (call) centres and complying with licensing and regulatory compliance régimes. In addition, primary carriers will incur costs through managing the investment of premium income.

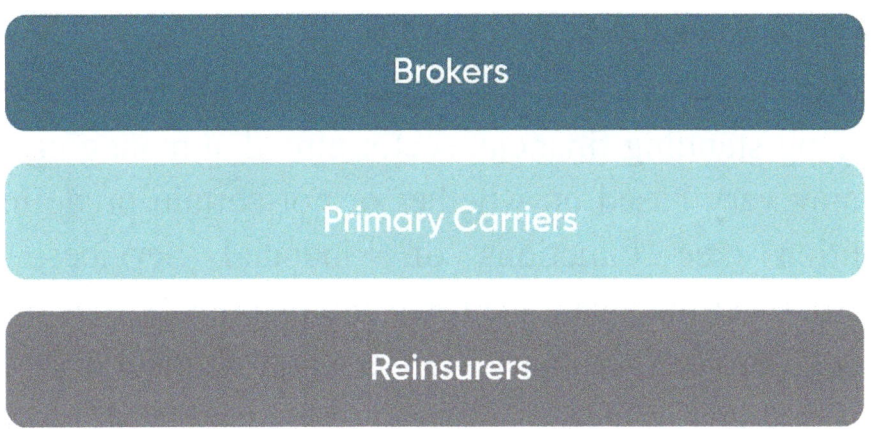

Fig 15.3 the original three-tier insurance 'stack.'

Reinsurers are positioned at the base of the insurance stack and act as a 'spillway' for primary carriers by insuring their risks against excessive losses. Reinsurance is essentially insurance for insurers. This is accomplished by purchasing insurance from another insurance company to insulate itself from the risk of a major claims event. With reinsurance, the insurer is able to cede (by passing part or all of) its own insurance liabilities to another (typically larger) insurance company. In circumstances whereby an insurer cedes its risk to a reinsurer, this is typically detailed in a report known as a 'bordereau.' The bordereau typically details the assets being underwritten as well as any claims which may have been paid. The reinsurer relies upon the bordereau in order to quantify its potential liabilities against its expected premiums. Reinsurance ceding allows an insurer to remain solvent in the event of a major claim, in addition to helping keep premiums competitive for its customers. This is known as *Treaty Reinsurance,* whereby the reinsurer accepts all the risks associated with certain policies. However, *Facultative Reinsurance* occurs in circumstances where the reinsurer performs its own underwriting for some or all of the policies intended to be reinsured. Since *Facultative Reinsurance* is generally the simplest means through which an insurer may obtain reinsurance protection and additionally conducive to customisation for specific risks and circumstances, the InsureTech sphere is undoubtedly primed to exploit data gleaned, via IoT, and processed via AI, in order to benefit from the granularity in quantifying risk. This is expected to drive greater weighting towards *Facultative Reinsurance* within the sector.

MANAGING GENERAL AGENTS

Insurance is a long-standing financial sector aimed at managing the *entropy of value*, which may vary based on whether or not certain predefined risks may come to fruition (see Functions of Financial Services, Chapter 10: Financialisation). Over the years, the roles and responsibilities of the insurance sector's tranches (Brokers, Primary Carriers and Reinsurers, Fig 15.3) have become intertwined and numerous overlaps have occurred. More recently, an additional layer has emerged in the form of Managing General Agents (MGAs). Also known as Managing General Underwriters (MGUs), an MGA finds its niche between Brokers and Primary Carriers, adopting a number of the functions of each. In the insurance sphere's periphery, a number of delegated authority entities and Third-party Administrators (TPAs) have existed for some time. Examples include Delegated Claims Administrators (DCAs), as well as 'Coverholders.' MGAs fall within the latter.

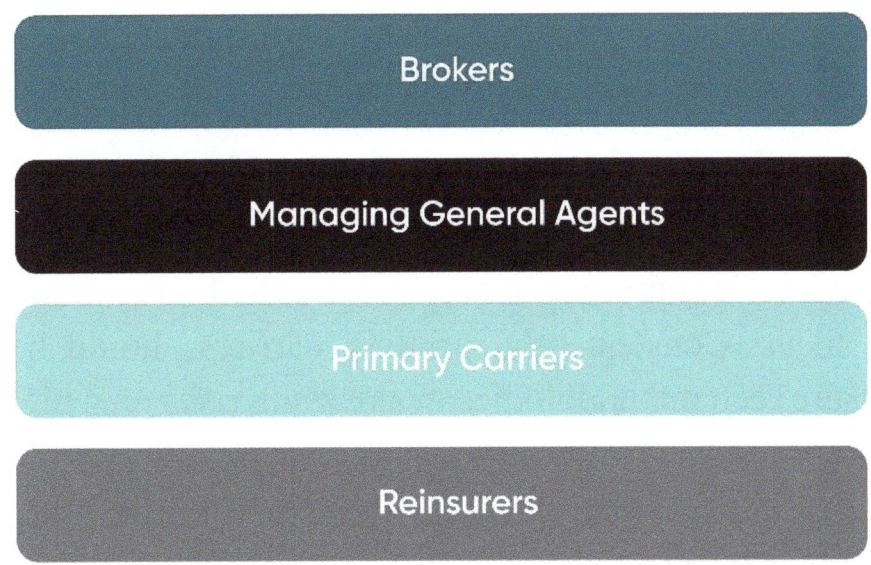

Fig 15.4 the insurance stack featuring Managing General Agents

MGAs are comparable to brokers that essentially borrow underwriting authority from 'Fronting Carriers' (a specific type of Primary Carrier, also known as a 'Front'). Historically, MGAs were focused on the underwriting of niche risks. However, MGAs have subsequently evolved into the incubation platforms for InsureTechs to build full-stack insurance carriers.

By exploiting the MGA model, InsureTechs are able to offload their risk to Primary Carriers or engage directly with Reinsurers. The MGA model, thus, enables nimble InsureTechs to build products and underwrite policies without the necessity to carry the risks on their own balance sheet.

The insurance sector has faced significant challenges to remain profitable. The Gross Written Premium (GWP) is the sum of direct and assumed premiums (revenue) before deducting reinsurance. The rising costs measured as a percentage of GWP have plagued the sector as inefficiencies have accrued through poor digital modernisation and degrading legacy systems (see Standardisation, Chapter 2: Capital Evolution). In order to assess profitability, insurers use the combined ratio formula. The combined ratio is equal to the sum of losses and expenses incurred, divided by the earned premium (GWP). The combined ratio is typically represented as a percentage, whereby a ratio below one-hundred-percent is indicative that the insurer is realising an underwriting profit. A ratio above one-hundred-percent however, indicates that the insurer is paying more money out in claims than it is receiving in premiums. Thus, many insurers rely on scale and risk diversity in order to remain profitable.

For Primary Carriers, scale has long been an advantage. However, to achieve scale and to manage complex, diverse pools of risk amid ever-intensifying and unfavourable market conditions, insurers have had to commit tremendous resources and focus. Consequently, primary carriers should be expected to adopt MGA InsureTech methodologies in assessing risks on a higher frequency or even a real-time basis.

Such an approach is largely at odds with the norms of the insurance industry, which often requires a long-term view, considering long-tail risks. This is due to insurers underwriting policies that may last a lifetime (e.g. life insurance) or insurance, which may incur a long-tail liability; essentially, liability for claims that do not proceed to final settlement until a length of time beyond the policy year. High incurred, but not reported (IBNR) claims, contribute to this 'tail' effect, since these losses are usually not settled until several years after the expiration of the policy in question. Thus, the need to build and maintain historic knowledge and project results far into the future.

A shift towards technology enabled data primacy is, thus, expected to offer the greatest opportunities to the insurance sector, thereby creating a data-driven disruption in order to better service both mature, as well as emerging digital channels. The latter in particular being those created, via the Internet of Things, as well as AI, and their corresponding trophic cascade (of higher-order systems) including autonomous vehicles, robots, drones and smart infrastructure. These technologies combined with a data-driven mind-set facilitate the means with which to embrace nascent business models, such as behavioural underwriting.

BEHAVIOURAL UNDERWRITING

As with the example of Pokémon Go (see above), whereby 'Lure Modules' sold to businesses were able to drive footfall towards these businesses through urban centres, these economies of action demonstrated the ability to engineer behaviour to facilitate a business end. Building on this paradigm, the ability of InsureTechs to capitalise on behavioural underwriting is expected to grow exponentially through harnessing the data collected, via the Internet of Things.

An example would include, uploading the GPS journey data from a vehicle's infotainment system to discern the motorist's compliance with traffic laws, speed limits and capabilities, as well as skills as a driver. Analysis of this nature may be exploited to influence the motorist's insurance premiums for both vehicle cover, as well as potentially for life cover. Since behaviour could influence premiums, this will likely reflexively influence behaviour.

This builds on the prevalence of dynamic pricing models (such as surge pricing), whereby premiums may increasingly fluctuate dynamically as greater sources of real-time data and AI are exploited to assess and calculate risk factors. Thereby, reinforcing this business model through exploiting information asymmetry (see Information Asymmetry, Chapter 10: Financialisation).

On September 22nd 2021, Tesla CEO Elon Musk announced that Tesla owners in Texas, USA would be able to purchase vehicle insurance from Tesla from October 2021 onwards.[399] Tesla is expected to expand its offering into New York State in 2022. Tesla initially launched its insurance proposition exclusively in California in late 2019. However, the move to expand into other states signals a degree of confidence that pursuit of its insurance portfolio is on sound-footing. The basis for which is predicated on Tesla's ability to monitor its vehicles, via sensor fusion and AI to the extent where underwriting risks that would, in normal circumstances, be left to chance and statistics, may be mitigated through monitoring its vehicles and drivers in real time. Hence, by exploiting its vast data sources gleaned, via the Internet of Things and its analytical capabilities, the company is in a superior position to offer increasingly competitive insurance products and services. These represent opportunities for Tesla and other nimble InsureTechs to exploit practices such as adverse selection over digital channels, via parametric insurance (see Adverse Selection, Chapter 10: Financialisation).

PARAMETRIC INSURANCE

Additionally known as index-based insurance, parametric insurance represents a departure from conventional underwriting in which claims are paid out, based on predefined trigger events which must meet specified thresholds in a policy. Unlike conventional indemnity-based insurance, in which the insuree (or insured) is reimbursed for losses incurred for the total loss of value as a consequence of an event, such as a fire, flood or accident, the parametric policy insurer needs to verify that the trigger event metrics equalled or exceeded the pre-agreed levels specified within the policy.

The principal advantage for the insuree in parametric insurance, is the speed with which claims may be assessed and settled. However, the disadvantage lies with often not being compensated sufficiently to reflect the level of loss incurred by the event. The latter is a consequence of the loss assessment being executed against the measures of the trigger event(s). A characteristic that insurance carriers find attractive by reducing the exposure of potential claims against the combined ratio (see above). By way of an example, if a homeowner were to insure their home against storm damage, a policy may be engineered to pay out a higher claims ratio should the storm's epicentre be within a specific radius, while outside of this metric a claim will pay out substantially less. In circumstances such as this, the losses could potentially be equal or greater to a property, which met the lower threshold than the property which met that of the higher. Although, the higher threshold will attract a greater claim value than the lower. Thus, parametric insurance may not be the appropriate cover in all circumstances. However, the prospect of underwriting and managing claims based on a data-driven paradigm, whereby sensor data gleaned, via IoT, facilitates the insurer in assessing claims against the varied trigger events underwritten within the policy. Examples of which may include; the wind speed of the storm measured at the property location, combined with the level of rainfall which may have contributed to greater damage. Exploiting greater sensor fusion capabilities combined with AI offers insurers the potential to tailor such instruments with tremendous granularity in assessing claims and underwriting risks. Additionally, the digitally friendly nature of this business model, combined with enabling technologies has the potential to create insurance propositions, which are priced (rated), underwritten and claimed against entirely digitally. By co-opting smart contract functionality in distributed ledger technologies, the policy itself may be executed as a smart contract, with programmable trigger events and thresholds, whereby claims are assessed, via sensor data, in an end-to-end automated and digital mechanism. This is conceptually similar to the creation of derivatives and programmable money, via smart contracts (see Smart Contracts, Chapter 14: Tokenisation).

AGGREGATORS

Aggregators are conceptually businesses that collect data in the form of requirements and customer information, via a web site (or API), package, as well as format the data and transmit it to Primary Carriers, Brokers and MGAs for quotations. Once the quotations have been formulated, Aggregators collate the responses and render such in an *aggregated* consumable price comparison format for potential customers, via a web site (as well as via an API). Aggregators benefit from this business model by exacting a referral fee from carriers, brokers and agents which participate in their platforms. In turn, insurers which participate in the aggregator's platform are able to broaden their capture rate of the potential market.[400]

In a comparable manner to which the insurance industry's participant structure has evolved through interleaving business model transformation, the componentisation of the industry (Fig 15.4), the expertise and specialist capabilities, thereof, become conducive to sharing their services, via an economy of platform capabilities.

ECONOMY OF PLATFORMS

The principal purpose of the field of Enterprise Architecture is to organise and harness people, processes and technology in an efficient manner within an organisation to best serve the business in achieving its intended outcomes.

Enterprise Architects tend to examine the various capabilities within an enterprise in order to identify opportunities to remove duplication, reduce waste, enable scalability, enhance security, as well as improve resilience in an effort to fortify common capabilities which may be leveraged across broader areas within the enterprise. An example of which may be initiating a migration of disparate customer relationship management (CRM) systems across various global regions into a single robust and standardised CRM, which is capable of serving the needs of all regions and lines of business cohesively. Such an endeavour drives greater efficiency through standardisation, cost effectiveness through collective bargaining (demand aggregation) and creates a common component platform from which data primacy may be cultivated and exploited to create new revenue streams.

In applying this lens from a first principles perspective to the financial services sector, the proliferation of FinTech start-ups, has introduced numerous market actors competing to occupy a niche previously held by an entrenched minority of large incumbents. Ultimately, this distils into a saturated market of competitors. Consequently, this creates a high supply in contrast to customer demand, thus, resulting in an expansion in consumer choice. High supply and low demand abrades margins, placing downward pricing pressure for equivalent services within the market.

In such circumstances, it is to be expected that both FinTechs and incumbents will attempt to differentiate themselves through harnessing the areas in which they may either cultivate new specialist expertise, or already possess superior capabilities. A positive reinforcement effect will likely be realised as these entities begin to concentrate their focus in a specific area of specialty across the value chain. Consequently, actors will likely divest themselves of services/capabilities in areas within which their value propositions are weaker. Thereby, effectively rebalancing the market supply in contrast to demand. This draws parallels to the CRM example within an enterprise (see above), whereby too many instances competing to offer comparable services are ultimately consolidated into a single service, which can cater to the business imperatives required by the organisation.

This shift is being driven by technological commoditisation of nascent and sophisticated higher-order systems which may be exploited to surface utility while creating increasingly contextual, immersive and experiential products and services. A posture which is accelerated through industry standardisation, such as that of ISO 20022, combined with componentisation effects enabled by Microservices, Serverless Computing and the API economy. Ultimately, catalysed by an emulsion of regulatory forces, such as that of Open Banking initiatives, as well as receptive state sponsorships to stimulate FinTech innovation as evidenced by the UK's Financial Conduct Authority (FCA) Sandbox launched in 2016, as well as the Kalifa Review of UK FinTech, published in February 2021.[401] The review, which was commissioned by H.M. Treasury (UK) in 2020, was led by former Worldpay Chairman Ron Kalifa OBE. Worldpay at the point of its multi-billion-dollar IPO in 2015 was broadly recognised as the UK's most successful FinTech company. The Kalifa Review identifies the clusters within the UK which are conducive to cultivating FinTech centres of excellence, as well as identifies areas in which government investment and support should be directed to enable and reinforce the success, therein. An example of which was a recommendation to broaden access to the FCA Sandbox on a rolling basis, in lieu of specific time-limited windows based on a cohort approach. Since August 2021, the FCA Sandbox has been deemed to be 'always open.' Thus, allowing firms to access the Sandbox testing services at the appropriate point in their development lifecycle. This is expected to maximise the benefits of live market testing for progressing their innovative models. The Sandbox provides a 'safe envelope' for firms to test novel and innovative FinTech propositions in a controlled environment, without risking exposure to the financial ecosystem.

It remains inevitable, however, that market saturation will occur, prompting a consolidation of competitors in niche areas. Thus, it is reasonable to forecast that the landscape will evolve into a marketplace of platforms, in lieu of full stack competitors.

INTER-INSTITUTIONAL NETWORK INFRASTRUCTURE

Within the sphere of banking and insurance, the ability for banks and insurers to directly interact with one another is critical to reducing friction and improving transparency in transacting with one another. Distributed Ledger Technologies are ideally placed to provide the secure infrastructure to facilitate underwriting transactions between reinsurers and primary carriers, as well as MGAs. Comparably, DLTs may be exploited to facilitate record-keeping for investments, loans and payments between banking institutions. Thereby, displacing the necessity to maintain complex correspondent banking relationships and the use of payment messaging networks, such as that of SWIFT, as well as CSMs. Should central banks embrace DLTs through addressing the issuance of CBDCs, it is likely that the necessity to maintain RTGS systems would likely dissipate over the longer-term.

It is unlikely that numerous competitive DLTs for the purpose of inter-institutional transactions will endure in the longer-term. However, in the short-term it is likely to observe numerous competitors attempting to dominate this sphere. By way of example, RippleNet provides a decentralised DLT network for the real-time settlement of international payments. In addition, RippleNet's On-Demand Liquidity (ODL) proposition exploits Ripple's XRP crypto-currency to intermediate cross-border payments while maintaining higher liquidity by displacing the necessity for pre-funding. This is achieved due to the exchange being managed, via XRP, in lieu of conventional correspondent banking.

Other notable examples include that of J.P. Morgan's Inter-bank Information Network (IIN), which was later rebranded to 'Liink.' The DLT network is focused towards enhancing information sharing across compliance queries, validating account information and executing payments. In June 2021, Broadridge brought its DLT-based REPO platform online. Average volumes in the week since its launch were $31 billion daily.[402] DLT-based trade finance networks, such as Contour, Vakt and Aroko, are further examples of endeavours to exploit DLT technologies for inter-institutional transactions.

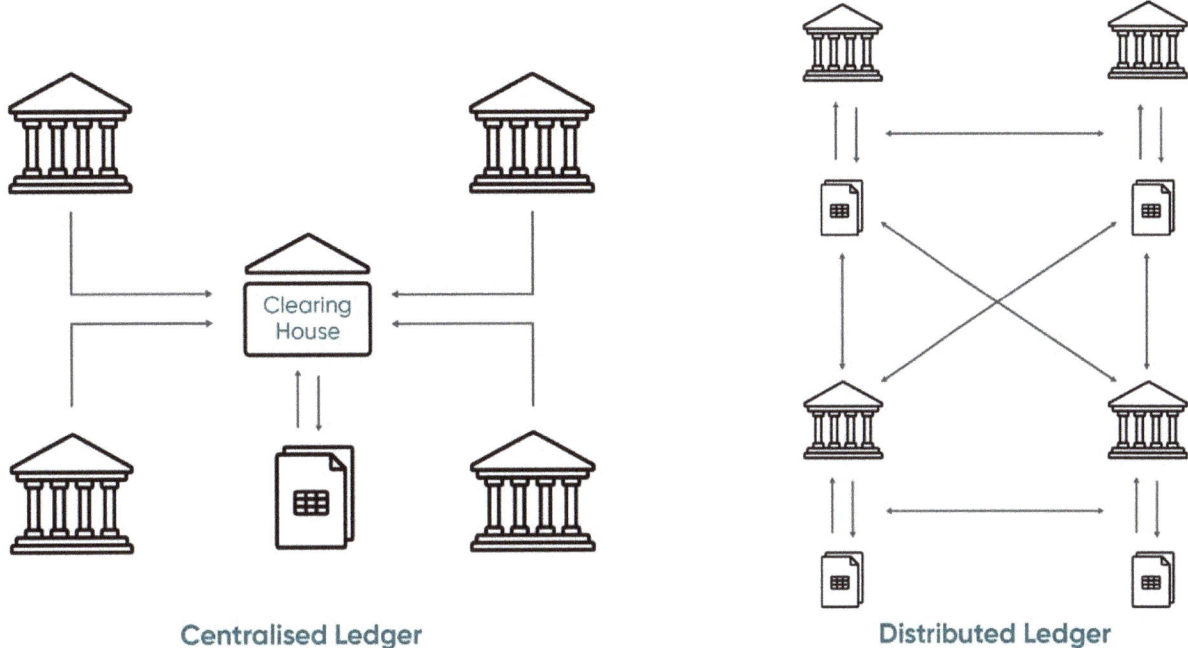

Fig 15.5 Centralised vs. Decentralised 'Permissioned' DLT banking architecture

A distributed ledger architecture offers opportunities to central banks and regulators to be members of a 'permissioned' ledger in order to maintain a real-time view of the banking institutions, over which they maintain a purview. Access of this nature instils confidence in these institutions as transparency is maintained with monetary authorities and real-time risks, as well as liquidity postures are clearly visible and understood.

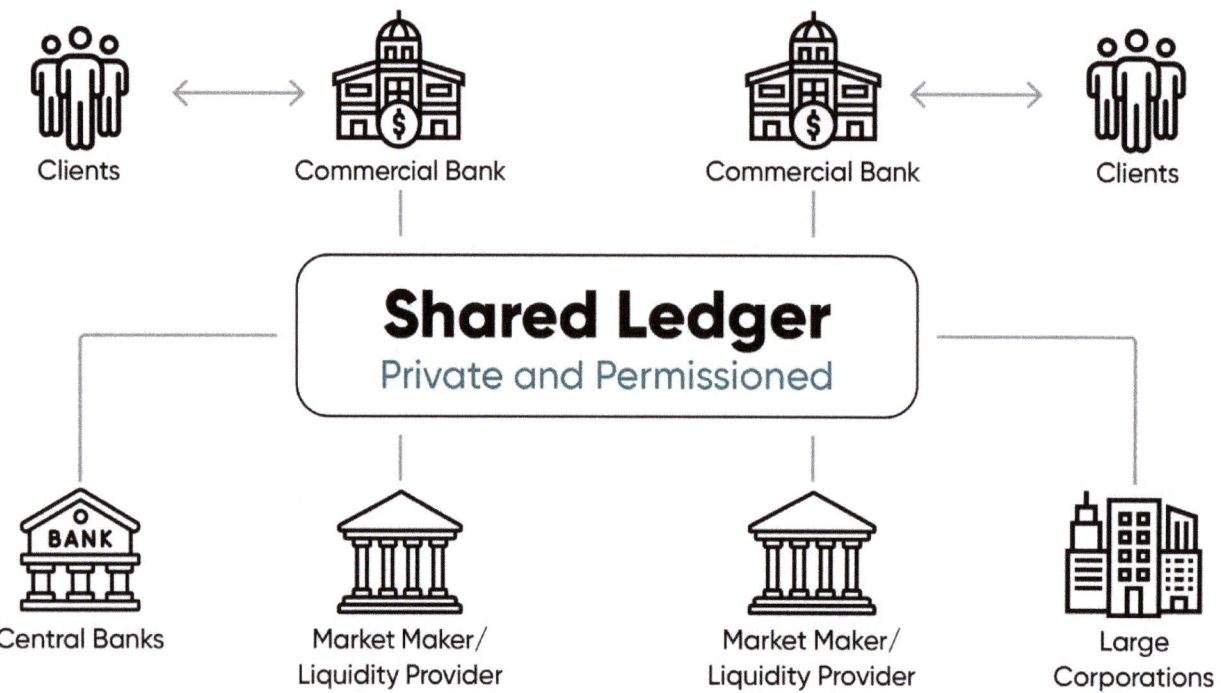

Fig 15.6 Decentralised private or permissioned distributed and shared ledger

Since member institutions are able to transact with one another on a real-time, frictionless and consistent basis within the network, transaction costs will likely be reduced. Erroneous or failed transactions should ultimately be eliminated, promoting reliability and convenience for businesses and consumers.

BANKING INFRASTRUCTURE

In addition to payments, banking technology infrastructure enables core banking functions, such as managing accounts, posting deposits, updating the general ledger and intra-day ledger balancing. Historically, core banking systems have been provided by a minority of dominant technology companies. Common banking systems include; FIServ's DNA, Oracle's FlexCube and Edgeverve's Finacle. These products, among others, combined with custom-developed applications and workflows comprise the typical 'systems of record' that underpin banks' technology-enabled capabilities.

With the introduction of modular banking propositions, pioneered by companies such as TrueLayer, Plaid and Tink, the prospect of introducing a modular ecology into the banking sphere is increasingly likely. These companies specialise in enabling banks to offer their services, via externally consumable APIs. Consequently, exploiting such an approach enables banks to offer their platform services (including Open Banking) to external FinTechs and partners, via the API economy. Thus, in all likelihood, banks will incrementally evolve into back-end platforms to facilitate the evolving demands of decentralised finance (DeFi) and digital channels. By way of example, Alibaba provides financial infrastructure to banks in several countries outside of China. Ant Financial provides its AlphaRisk service to financial services firms in order to improve their credit scoring capabilities. It additionally offers its Caifuhao platform to asset-management firms to derive insights about their customers. In 2018, British challenger bank Starling Bank, launched its internal platform as a Banking-as-a-Service proposition available to FinTech companies and banks. The platform was exploited by notable FinTechs, such as CurrencyCloud, Raisin and Moneybox in the UK. It is expected to be approved for use in the EU in the latter 2022 timeframe. In the US, with Open Banking having not been embraced in line with the UK and the EU, as well as e-money licensing being regulated on a state-by-state basis, the environment has been more conducive to cultivating Banking-as-a-Service platforms to enable FinTech. Such Banking-as-a-Service platforms include companies such as Green Dot, Synapse and Finix.

The trend towards cultivating banking platforms represents the componentisation of the traditional banking portfolio. A similar pattern was evident in the payment card industry through the emergence of payment gateways, ISOs and PayFacs (see Card Payments, Chapter 5: Payments). This trend should be expected to manifest in the insurance sphere over time, as evidenced through the emergence of MGAs and Aggregators (see InsureTech above). This promotes the broader integration of best-in-class products and services being aggregated and tailored to suit the consumer, via FIs, which maintain customer relationship primacy. However, behind the customer-facing façade there exists a variety of specialised product or service platforms each specialised in a specific aspect of delivering the outcomes for the customer.

Banks in particular are likely to be best-placed to provide differentiated services, such as maturity transformation, via their Banking-as-a-Service platforms (see Maturity Transformation, Chapter 10: Financialisation), whereas FinTechs which consume the platform are more likely to intermediate payments and act as demand aggregators for services, which are fronted through customer relationship primacy, and subsequently fulfilled via the API economy. These platform services are likely to be varied and specialised in areas such as insurance, investment portfolio management, pensions, short and long-term credit facilities and B2B remittance among others.

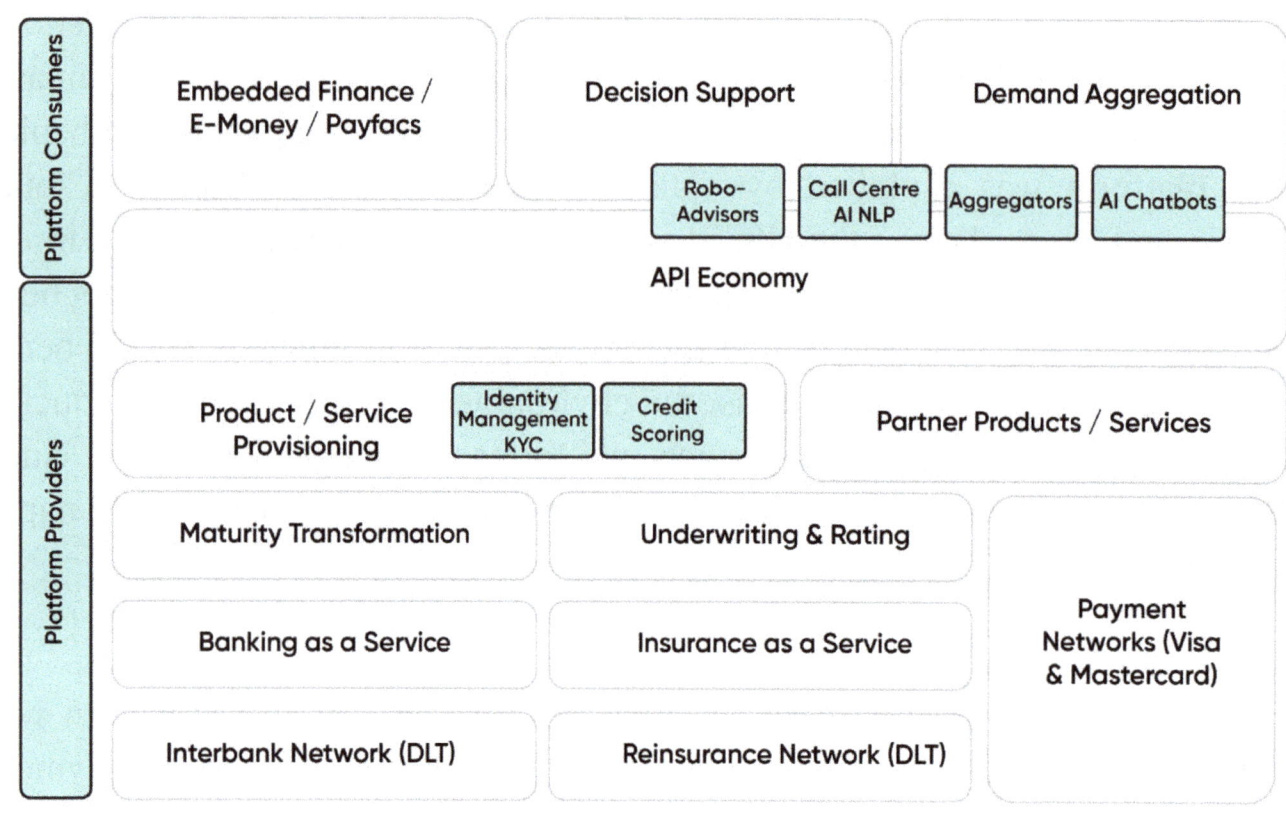

Fig 15.7 Economy of Platforms

As greater componentisation occurs within the financial services sphere (see Componentisation, Chapter 2: Capital Evolution), the viability of embedding financial services capabilities directly into the business value chain becomes both possible, as well as increasingly palatable. Thus, embedded finance is anticipated to represent an exciting opportunity for businesses capable of capitalising on the open nature of the economy of platforms.

EMBEDDED FINANCE

The future of financial services is expected to be greatly influenced by the emergence and proliferation of embedded finance. Finance will come to resemble other industries of the internet era, anticipated to be more interconnected and increasingly versatile, as well as customisable. This should be enabled and powered by component services that can be inserted into individual businesses in different sectors. Consequently, this further alters the manner in which financial services will be exposed to the end consumer.

Conceptually, embedded finance enables any business to assume the role of a FinTech entity, a position made possible through the industrialisation of FinTech as it becomes increasingly commoditised (see Commoditisation, Chapter 2: Capital Evolution). Thus, as FinTech descends within the value chain and becomes increasingly componentised, as well as standardised, this facilitates the emergence of new higher-order systems (see Higher-order Systems, Chapter 2: Capital Evolution). In a comparable manner to which Serverless Computing enabled standardised components, which could be exploited in the development of (low-code) Microservices, so FinTech has assumed the role of enabling embedded finance, via platforms and APIs (see Chapter 3: Ecosystems).

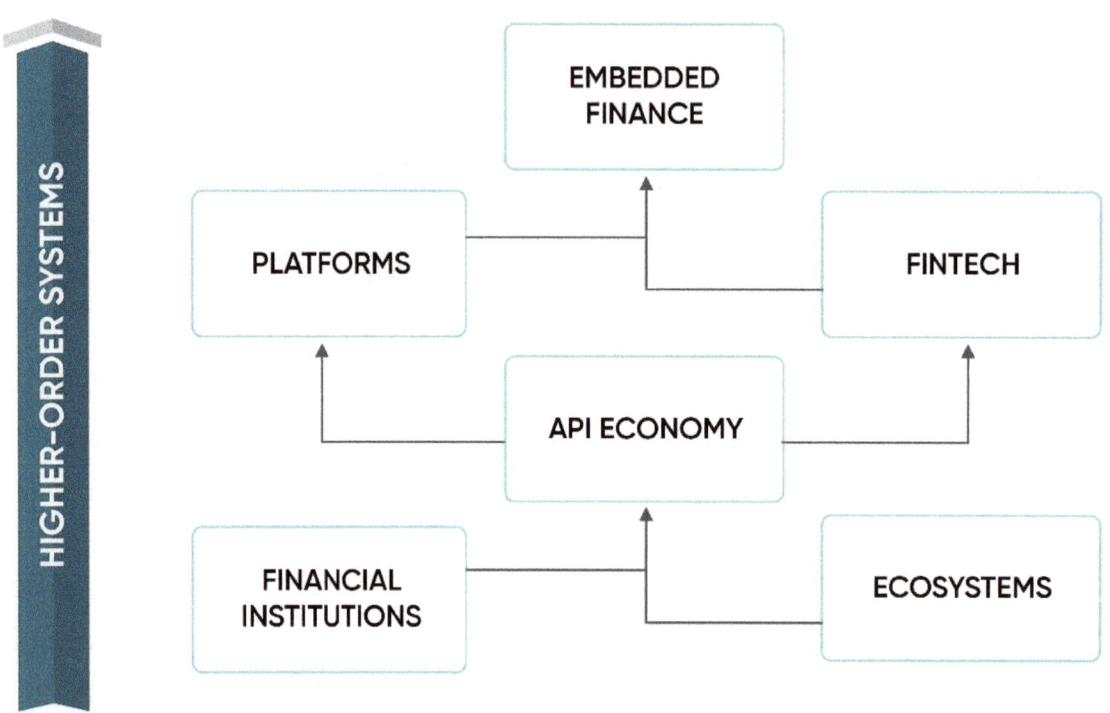

Fig 15.8 Higher-order systems enabling 'Embedded Finance'

Consequently, a non-banking or non-finance company is, therefore, capable of disintermediating traditional FIs from transactions, and thereby asserting greater control over its end-to-end customer experience. The prevailing economic conditions furthermore creates incentives for non-financial firms to exploit embedded finance in order to stage a deeper incursion into the financial services value chain. An example includes the convenience of payments being processed directly by the merchant, which offers opportunities to create value-added capabilities in providing its goods and services. Simultaneously, the merchant is able to harvest greater margins which would otherwise be realised by the financial sector. However, it additionally enables opportunities which may be exploited to create new revenue streams and new channels. Tailored customer targeting strategies may be pursued in these circumstances in which instalment options, loyalty benefits and broader customer acquisition approaches may be leveraged.

By disintermediating PayFacs, Payment Networks, and traditional banks, the cost of customer acquisition may be lowered. While new revenue streams may be created through providing credit facilities, e-money and benefitting from seigniorage. As the barriers to entry are abraded in tandem with the transformation of traditional FIs into platform services, via the API economy, the opportunities for embedded finance to enter the mainstream grow exponentially. Private-label cards (PLCs) to offer prepaid facilities, as well as traditional payment cards, credit facilities, and tailored insurance propositions form part of this spectrum.

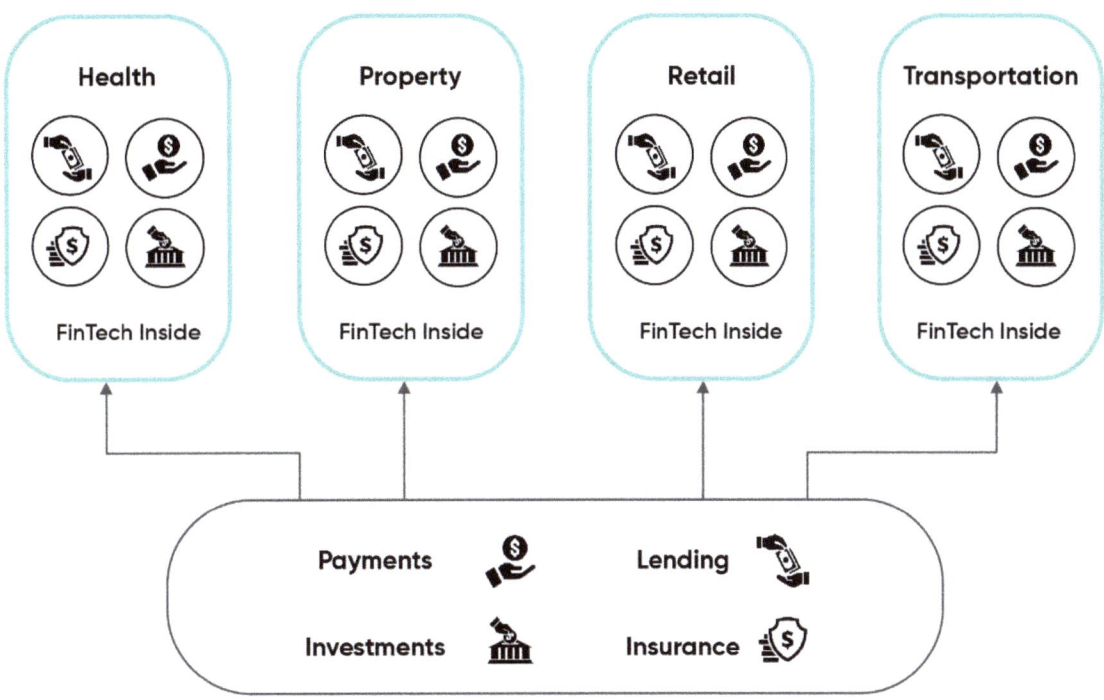

Fig 15.9 'early adopter' industry sectors exploiting embedded finance

The shift in employment behaviours and the prevailing economic conditions with the rise of the gig economy and zero-hour contracts, saturates the market with subprime customers, which ordinarily would be perceived to be less creditworthy. This creates a market of underbanked potential customers who would greatly benefit from facilities offered by embedded finance companies, free from the constraints of traditional prudentially regulated entities. The success of Buy Now, Pay Later (BNPL) FinTechs, such as Klarna and ClearPay, demonstrated the market potential for short-term credit facilities elevating conversion rates amongst mid-tier and subprime consumers.

The low relative costs of API-based coordination with other companies reinforces incentives for greater collaboration and integration (see API Economy, Chapter 3: Ecosystems). Thus, collaborators may invest in specific capabilities within the value chain, while simultaneously participating in larger business ecosystems that broaden opportunities to diversify channels and to explore new business models, via *network effects*.

Examples of such may manifest in use cases, whereby embedded finance may be surfaced through flexible finance options at the point of sale, payments directly embedded into a ride sharing or taxi app, on-demand car insurance when hiring a vehicle, as well as travel insurance when booking a flight. Other examples could include mortgage deals offered within a home buying app. The potential number of permutations is limitless.

Embedded finance, will in addition to the B2C market, likely stimulate innovation within the business-to-business (B2B) sphere through disintermediating traditional FIs and FinTechs by optimising supply chains and potentially creating sector specific net settlement systems in a comparable manner to the banking sector (see Clearing & Settlement Mechanisms, Chapter 5: Payments). Furthermore, inter-company credit facilities, tokenisation, smart contracts and underwriting will likely permeate through common industry segments (see Chapter 14: Tokenisation). This trend is a natural function of elementary decomposition, which manifests in componentisation and abstraction, via commoditisation fuelled by competition (see Chapter 2: Capital Evolution). However, this is driven within the envelope of an overarching series of cyclic macroeconomic forces towards greater financialisation (see Arsonists & Firefighters, Chapter 10: Financialisation).

Embedded finance represents a form of *Creative Destruction* which will likely pivot on the credibility of non-financial firms seeking to capitalise on the opportunities embedded finance will yield. As history has unfolded, financial institutions, products and services evolved thereby creating banks, insurers, payment networks, asset managers and others. The form in which these entities manifested were a reflection of the business models and technologies that were prevalent at the time. As FinTech becomes increasingly industrialised, a co-evolution of practice is to be anticipated (see Co-evolution, Chapter 2: Capital Evolution). Ultimately, the banking, insurance and investment banking business models, among others in the financial sphere, should be expected to undergo a metamorphosis. This may conceivably influence the nature of maturity transformation and underwriting practices, thereby altering the business models of financial institutions. Thus, reinforcing financial institutions evolving into service providers, via the economy of platforms.

The technological and institutional disruptive influences brought about through the creation of the Internet and its higher-order systems, such as the Cloud and FinTech, has created the tools and capabilities to question how and where the core functions of financial services are delivered (see Functions of Financial Services, Chapter 10: Financialisation). Based on a first principles perspective, the nature of financial services should be expected to be highly differential from its predecessors (see First Principles, Chapter 4: Surfacing Utility). Hence, new disruptors will undoubtedly emerge unimpeded by inertia barriers, and will likely offer the greatest innovation potential in this sphere. Such has been the trend with the emergence of Cloud Computing and FinTech. Thus, this should be expected to be prevalent in the embedded finance era.

As the maturity of ecosystems has and the emergence of platforms is disrupting many of the long-held assumptions and conventional wisdom surrounding the finance sector, the prospect of embedding finance strategically, offers both smaller businesses as well as regional competitors the ability to capture opportunities previously dominated by larger incumbents. However, larger incumbents may not be able to shield their market share from 'digital first' embedded finance companies successfully. Hence, disintermediating them, and thereby eroding their dominant position (see Apex Predator Hypothesis, Chapter 4: Surfacing Utility). An example includes that of Shopify, which enabled merchants to accept payments from payment networks, such as Visa and MasterCard, without being intermediated, via a payments gateway or an Acquirer (see Platform Payment Processing, Chapter 5: Payments). Others include Uber, Bolt and Lyft, which exploit embedded payment services in order to create a seamless and streamlined experience for their customers.

However, if larger incumbents can leverage their influence to design and deliver more comprehensive offerings, make advantageous acquisitions, as well as forge mutually beneficial partnerships, they may prevent consumers from diversifying towards smaller competitors and their offerings. Tech giants, such as Amazon and Apple, have established partnerships with Goldman Sachs, which leverage its platforms in order to embed financial capabilities (see Runaway Leadership, Chapter 4: Surfacing Utility).

The automotive industry in particular represents a significant opportunity, whereby the transition from internal combustion engines to battery-powered electric motors coupled with mechanical automotive engineering being increasingly displaced by electrical systems and computerised controls has been prevalent. With the increased embedding of computer-controlled and sensor-infused systems within vehicles and, thus, accessible via the Internet of Things, the prospect of diversifying revenue streams and capturing a share of new markets is at the forefront of the automotive industry's agenda (see Surveillance Capitalism and Behavioural Underwriting above).

The sector is primed to capitalise on its vast potential to exploit data generated by its products and customers, as well as to harness the opportunities embedded finance may offer. This paradigm builds on an existing practice within this sector whereby, vehicle manufacturers partnered with finance companies to create branded propositions. Essentially, offering both the vehicle, as well as the associated finance as a combined proposition of the brand. Embedded finance offers such brands the opportunity to deeply integrate and modernise these partnerships, as well as drive greater penetration of financial services among its customer base over which it commands relationship primacy.

While the automotive industry is uniquely placed to be a major beneficiary in the embedded finance, as well as immersive technology spheres, tech giants, such as Facebook, have far greater ambitions. Ambitions which extend towards capitalising on a visual and experiential medium, such as the Metaverse.

METAVERSE

On October 28th 2021, then Facebook CEO, Mark Zuckerberg, announced the rebranding of Facebook to Meta.[403] As the new parent company for Facebook's brands, Meta ('Beyond,' Greek) signalled the intent to reflect the diverse nature of the social networking company's aspirations in creating a variety of virtual, augmented and mixed reality frameworks. The framework and its platforms are intended to cultivate a rich, socially interactive environment, which may transcend from the two-dimensional internet into an immersive three-dimensional experience.

The 'Metaverse' borrows its conceptual ideology from the 'Multiverse Theory,' of which there have existed numerous hypotheses over the centuries. One of the earliest stems from ancient Greece, in which it was proposed that infinite parallel worlds existed as a consequence of atomic collisions.[404] The common thread to the various iterations and variations of multiverse theory is in that each posits that a number of alternate or parallel realities (or universes) co-exist with one another that transcend space, time, matter and energy.

The term 'Metaverse' is also synonymous with the science fiction novel 'Snow Crash,' by Neal Stephenson, originally published in 1992, where the term was first used. In Stephenson's Metaverse, users gain access to it through personal terminals that project a high-quality virtual reality display onto goggles which they wear. In Stephenson's novel, characters that participate in the Metaverse, are rendered as virtual avatars.[405]

In practice, the Metaverse is conceptually a transcendence of the internet, in which a combination of augmented, virtual and mixed reality technologies are exploited to create a virtually rendered shared space where people, bots and things may interact. Essentially, an internet in which people are within, in lieu of an internet which is interacted with from the outside. Thus, a truly immersive construct which manifests in a digitally interactive world.

A critical aspect of assuring the success of such an endeavour will hinge on the co-operation of many businesses, standards bodies and consumers. Thus, it is unlikely to be the platform of a solitary ecosystem originator (see Chapter 3: Ecosystems) which retains exclusive dominance, thereof. Tech giants, such as Facebook (now Meta), Apple, Microsoft and Google, have invested billions of dollars in developing immersive technology capabilities both in the software, as well as in the hardware spheres. However, in order to truly achieve a globally immersive Metaverse, the compatibility and integration across the platforms of each framework will drive the necessity to interact seamlessly. Initially, it should be anticipated that each of these major competitors will attempt to gain a leadership position in this sphere (see Red Queen Hypothesis, Chapter 2: Capital Evolution) and engage in ILC/'Tower & Moat' strategies (see Innovate, Leverage & Commoditise, Chapter 3: Ecosystems). However, as the commoditisation of this technology cultivates 'componentisation effects,' fuelled by standardisation, open-source as well as *network* and *learning effects*, the barriers to entry will be lowered. Simultaneously, *laissez-faire* market forces will drive greater competition, and thus, greater interoperability (see Chapter 2: Capital Evolution).

The Metaverse offers the prospect for surfacing utility in an entirely experiential, contextual and immersive form. The gaming industry has provided significant insights into how this paradigm may manifest itself through the success of games such as Pokémon Go, Fortnite and Roblox.

While computerised gaming has a long-standing pedigree in creating imaginative and highly-immersive constructs in which participants engage in interactive environments and gameplay, the potential for this technology to be truly disruptive became apparent in April 2020. As the world's economies shut down with the rising penetration of the COVID-19 pandemic, Fortnite creators, Epic games, co-opted the technology to create a virtual concert dubbed 'Astronomical.' This was created as a virtual amusement park in which participants could attend the concert featuring American rapper, Travis Scott. Scott appeared as an avatar and performed for the participants. The first virtual concert was attended by 27.7 million (of which 12.3 million were concurrent)

Fortnite players. In total, the concerts were attended by 45.8 million Fortnite players.[406] The in-game concert dwarfed the previous record from Epic's Marshmello in-game concert in which 10.7 million players attended in 2019.[407] While many believe this is reminiscent of a combination of factors, such as the lockdown measures in response to the pandemic accompanied by interest in a novelty (see Hawthorne Effect, Chapter 2: Capital Evolution), the prospects for business, diplomacy, healthcare, education and the financial sector are far too significant to ignore.

The implications for business interactions whereby, symposiums and conferences could be held virtually with participants from around the world all in attendance virtually is daunting. The economics of event coordination, venue management, business travel, accommodation and subsistence would rapidly be displaced by the productivity and savings gained through virtual eventing. This extends into collaboration, whereby remote workers may interact with one another. Engineering teams may design, as well as simulate concepts and prototypes in a virtually rendered environment. This may be further reinforced through additive manufacturing (3D Printing) whereby, what is designed in the Metaverse may be 'printed' physically thereafter. All from the comfort of the collaborators' homes.

The impact on e-commerce is substantial. The retail experience may be completely transformed by virtually synthesising garments and goods on a life like 'carbon-copy' avatar and selected for purchase in the Metaverse for real world delivery. An entirely new market for avatars may also be created, whereby fashion designed exclusively for use in the Metaverse may be procured as NFTs (see Non-Fungible Tokens, Chapter 14: Tokenisation). This surfaces the concept of commerce in the Metaverse, which is an ideal environment in which to transact in both NFTs, as well as CVCs. CVCs may be purchased in the real world and exploited for transactions in the Metaverse for Meta-goods and Meta-services (see Convertible Virtual Currency, Chapter 14: Tokenisation). The Metaverse represents a form of *creative destruction,* in which an entirely nascent virtual economy may be created, which ultimately co-exists with that of the real world. In a number of instances however, it will transcend it.

IMMERSIVE COMMERCE

The Metaverse is an ambitious aspiration, which is envisioned to be a game-changer amongst tech giants for the future of entertainment, business, education, retail and numerous other industries. An environment, which represents near limitless potential for surveillance capitalism. The fields of spatial computing, Artificial Intelligence, data science, edge intelligence, graphics processing, virtual, augmented and mixed reality, as well as 5G among others are required to create the higher-order system that the Metaverse represents.

Collectively, this forms part of a long-term vision of realising the 'Tactile Internet.' An internet in which people are immersed and able to see, as well as touch virtual objects. Smart eye-wear, as well as vehicles, the windows and windscreens, of which are capable of rendering augmented reality applications, are likely to become the most broadly consumed medium for human-internet interaction.

While the Metaverse may well enable people from around the world to engage in various activities, thereby assisting in pushing beyond the boundaries of our social group potential (see Dunbar's Number, Chapter 4: Surfacing Utility), it is our deeply entrenched need for tangible, physical social interaction which will ultimately prevail.

Thus, since both smart phones and wearable smart-eye glasses capable of augmented reality rendering will undoubtedly prevail as the dominant platforms within the smart technology sphere, the nature of visualisation of data and commerce are likely to pivot towards a visual engagement interface to which people speak (see Natural Language Processing, Chapter 4: Surfacing Utility) in order take action as well as touch virtually – all as an overlay to the real world. Conceptually, this aspiration is known as the 'Tactile Internet.'

Visual AI will undoubtedly play a pivotal role, while 5G and its successive technologies will be required to ensure seamless transmission and delivery of content to these interfaces. Capabilities such as visual discovery and voice discovery, will rely on deep tagging (known as 'searchandising') in order to assist consumers in finding the goods and services they desire, via this immersive dimension. Personalisation will feature prominently, whereby digital exhaust, such as real-time behavioural data, is exploited to cultivate direct personalised consumer insights as to preferences, location and potential constraints (see Surveillance Capitalism above). All the while, being exploited to surface utility in an intimately personalised and experiential form. The economy of things facilitating observation, analysis and actuation combined with the financial platforms, therein, will facilitate the underpinning interfaces to enable embedded finance to transform e-commerce into an immersive and experiential reality.

16

THE RISE OF CHINA

'Let China sleep, for when she wakes, she will shake the world.' - Napoleon Bonaparte.

Prior to 1979, under Chairman Mao Zedong's leadership, China maintained a centrally planned and governed economy. A substantial proportion of China's economic output was directed and controlled by the state, which set production targets, imposed rigorous pricing controls, and governed the allocation of resources throughout the economy.

During the 1950s, China's individual household farms were collectively organised into large aggregated communes.

In order to promote rapid industrialisation, the Chinese government invested heavily in physical and human capital during the 1960s and 1970s. Consequently, by 1978 almost seventy-five percent of China's industrial production was produced by state-owned enterprises (SOEs), governed by centrally set output targets. In this era, private enterprises and foreign firms were precluded from participating, effectively, leaving China's economy largely isolated and extremely unsophisticated. This served an agenda of the Chinese government to make China's economy relatively self-sufficient, although the lack of technology and expertise imposed limitations on production capabilities, as well as product complexity. Foreign trade was generally limited to sourcing goods and raw materials that could not be obtained domestically. Thus, virtually every mechanised product had to be imported.

This included machinery, transportation equipment, power generation equipment, as well as tools. Policies of this nature were highly disruptive and had a distorting effect on the Chinese economy. The economy was predominantly agriculturally based, and dependent on beasts of burden and human labour. With paltry wages, it was cheaper to leverage scores of labourers to dig a hole over several days, in lieu of using an excavator which could accomplish the same task in a few hours. As a consequence, conventional *laissez-faire* mechanisms to efficiently allocate resources in alignment with market demands were obscured by the government's centralised targets and policy constraints. Thus, conventional incentives for firms and workers to drive greater productivity and efficiency were essentially compromised. This additionally had a detrimental effect on the quality of output. Living standards were poor, labour costs were low and skills were in short supply. Furthermore, output targets were set based solely on volume, in lieu of both volume and quality. Output quality was further handicapped by poor technology in addition to a deficit in expertise and training.

Following the death of Chairman Mao Zedong in 1976 and the end of the Cultural Revolution (1966 - 1976), in 1978, the Chinese government embarked on reforming its isolationist economic policies by incrementally opening trade and investment with western economies. In 1979, the government initiated pricing reforms and ownership incentives, which enabled farmers to sell a portion of their crops on the free market. In practice, collective farms were assigned strict quotas against which they were expected to deliver. However, in instances where production output exceeded the quotas, the excess could be sold and the proceeds could be used to improve conditions on the collective farms.

SPECIAL ECONOMIC ZONES

As part of its reforms, the Chinese government established four coastal special economic zones (SEZs) for the purpose of attracting foreign investment, technology transfer, boosting exports, and importing high technology products.

Technology transfer into China boosted the 'know how' of Chinese personnel, thereby enhancing the collective capabilities of domestic enterprises. Thus, paving the way for the export of Chinese products into world markets.

The cities of Shenzhen, Zhuhai, Shantou and Xiamen (Amoy) became the epicentres of these SEZs. A fifth SEZ was established when the island province of Hainin was included in 1985. Further reforms followed thereafter, in a series of stages intended to incrementally decentralise economic policy-making in a number of sectors, predominantly centred on trade. Consequently, economic control was devolved to provincial authorities which enabled businesses to compete within the auspices of free market principles, in lieu of centralised state governance. Within the SEZs, businesses were incentivised to attract foreign direct investment with tax and trade duty relief, while individual citizens were encouraged to embrace entrepreneurship. In parallel, state price controls were gradually eliminated on a broad range of products. With diminishing trade barriers and greater inflows of foreign direct investment, greater competition was promoted as a result of China's trade liberalisation. This forms the basis for China's economic strategy in experimenting with economic policies to assess which are producing favourable outcomes versus those which do not. Thereafter, such policies could be replicated in other parts of China, thereby emulating only those policies which are suitable and successful within the economy. This approach reflects what China's *de facto* leader during this period, Deng Xiaoping (1904 - 1997) referred to as:

'Crossing the river, by touching the stones.'

- *Deng Xiaoping, Chairman of the Central Advisory Commission (1982 - 1987).*

In practice, however, economic growth within the SEZs and along the Eastern Seaboard in general, far outpaced the rate of growth outside of the SEZs. Consequently, the anticipated spill over effects ultimately weren't realised and substantial economic divisions remain in evidence.

WORLD TRADE ORGANISATION

In 2001, China acceded to the World Trade Organisation (WTO), at which juncture it had committed to embracing the WTO's open market-orientated approach, and to embed these free market principles into its trading system and institutions. Consequently, the international community and the WTO expected China to continue on a path of economic reform and embrace a transformation into a market-orientated economy, as well as trade régime.

Although China failed to internalise the norms and practices of competition-based trade and investment, it exploited the benefits of WTO membership to rapidly become the world's largest exporter. Its vast human capital and enormous industrial capacity allowed China to expand its global market share expeditiously through distorting global prices, via its government's state-led, mercantilist approach to trade and investment. This provided an unfair advantage to Chinese businesses through a non-market economic structure where labour costs are controlled and state-owned enterprises benefit from domestic protection and foreign capital. This was, furthermore, reinforced by a long-standing practice of exchange rate manipulation of China's currency. A policy, which enables China to remain artificially competitive among global export markets. Collectively, these factors have cultivated a radical disruption to its economic posture within the global hierarchy, facilitated by its approach to production and competition, which enabled China to rapidly transition from a Low-income, to a Middle-income economy (see Pre-Hegemony, Chapter 11: Hegemonic Dominance).

China's promotion of domestic entrepreneurship and its success in global exports began to rapidly distort the composition of its middle class (see The Middle Class, Chapter 8: Economic Cycles), whereby demographic data indicates that in the year 2000 approximately 3.1% of its population (~39.1 million) were considered to be among its middle class. By 2018, this figure grew to 50.8% (~707 million).[408] The definition of the 'middle class' tends to vary by country. However, in general, it relates to purchasing power in lieu of dollar denominated spending ability.

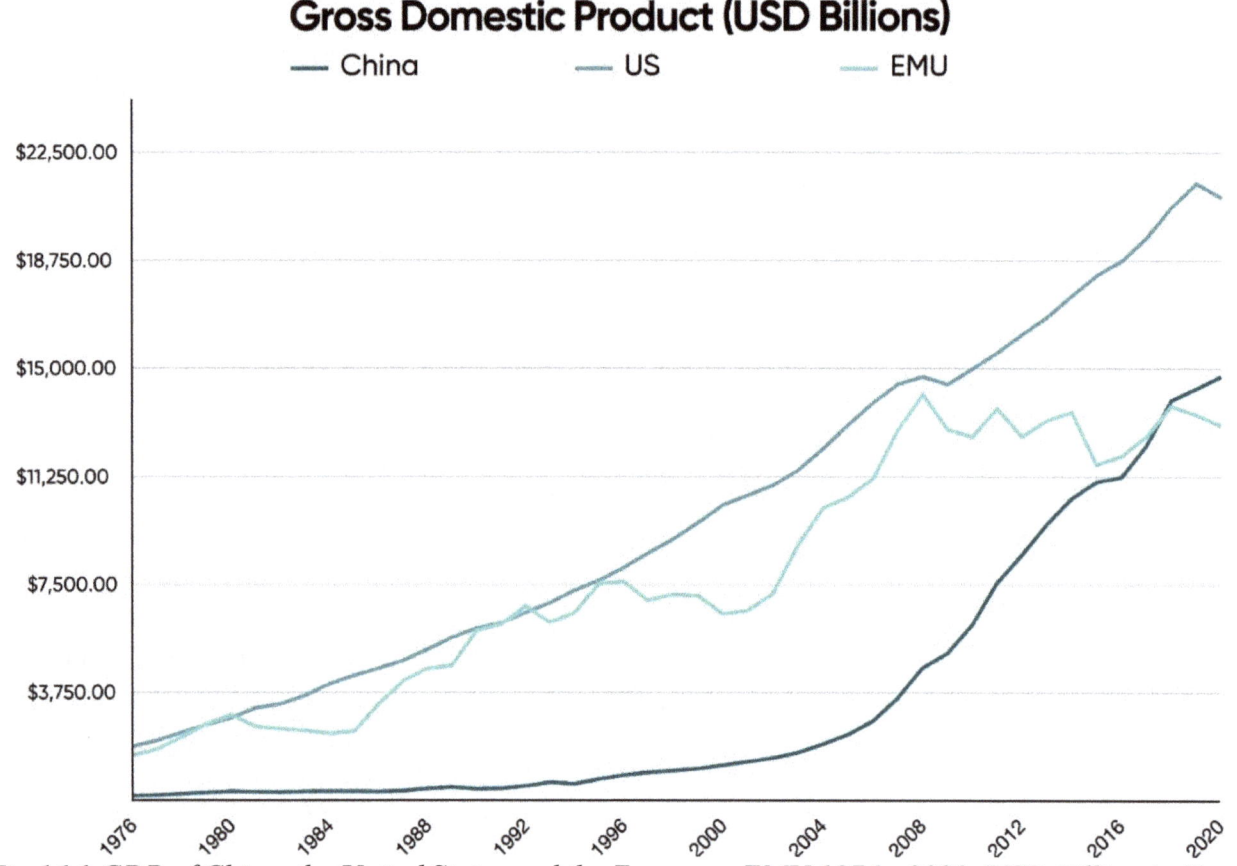

Fig 16.1 GDP of China, the United States and the European EMU 1976 - 2020 (USD Billions). (Source data: World Bank, 2021)

The rise in wealth among China's population complemented its growth in GDP (Fig 16.1), for which China's banking sector were no longer suitable to cater.

STATE–DOMINATED BANKING SECTOR

Historically, China's banking system has been dominated by either state-owned, or state-controlled banks. Typically, the management, thereof, has fallen to appointees drawn from the ranks of the CCP's cadre system. Consequently, this has enabled the government to exert its influence over banking practices, as well as lending decisions.[409] A posture which tends to benefit state-owned enterprises in the form of preferential credit treatment by government banks, while private businesses and individuals are often required to pay higher interest rates or obtain credit elsewhere. State-owned enterprises accounted for an estimated $1.4 trillion dollars borrowed domestically in 2009, representing approximately 85% of all bank loans in China.[410]

FINANCIAL INCLUSION

FinTech in China saw meteoric adoption from 2008 - 2013, initially as a means of accelerating financial inclusion for China's underbanked and unbanked population. With China's economy opening to external markets, the state-dominated banking sector (see above) had evolved to reflect the needs of China's large state-owned enterprises. This created a vacuum to fulfil the financial needs for China's burgeoning SME and consumer market, as well as its growing middle class. In 1978, when economic reform was initiated (see above) the proportion of China's citizens living on $2 (or less) per day, reflective of the international poverty line of $1.90 per day (World Bank, 2011 PPP) represented ninety-percent of its population. In 2015, this proportion had declined to 0.7% of its population (~9.9 million, 2015).[411]

Falling income inequality in China's SEZs is additionally evident, via the World Bank's Gini Index, indicating a fall of 2.9% over the period 2008 - 2015.[412] However, the average income per capita in the SEZs is far greater when compared to the average income outside of the SEZs. This is a consequence of limited spill over from the SEZs into the broader Chinese economy.

Regardless, economic growth has consequently resulted in shared (albeit not equal) prosperity (Fig 16.1). Furthermore, in examining the rise in the 'standard of living' from 1996 - 2018, China had accomplished in 22 years what took the current hegemon, the United States 90 years, and the previous hegemon, the United Kingdom 120 years to achieve. Over the period 2007 - 2018, China's average monthly wages rose by 263%.[413] Sustaining wage growth at this level indefinitely is highly unlikely, although should this trend continue, Chinese goods will eventually price themselves out of the market. In such circumstances, China's economy will experience stagnation (see The Middle-income Trap below). Nonetheless, the substantial increase in wages exposed a significant vacuum in consumer and SME financial services.

PEER–TO–PEER LENDING

With banking facilities largely tailored to the needs of large state-owned enterprises, SMEs in addition to China's everyday consumers lacked access to credit facilities. This accounted for the early success of P2P lending FinTechs, which accounted for almost four-thousand (~3844, Fig 16.2) start-ups emerging by the close of 2015 (see Accessing Credit, Chapter 4: Surfacing Utility).

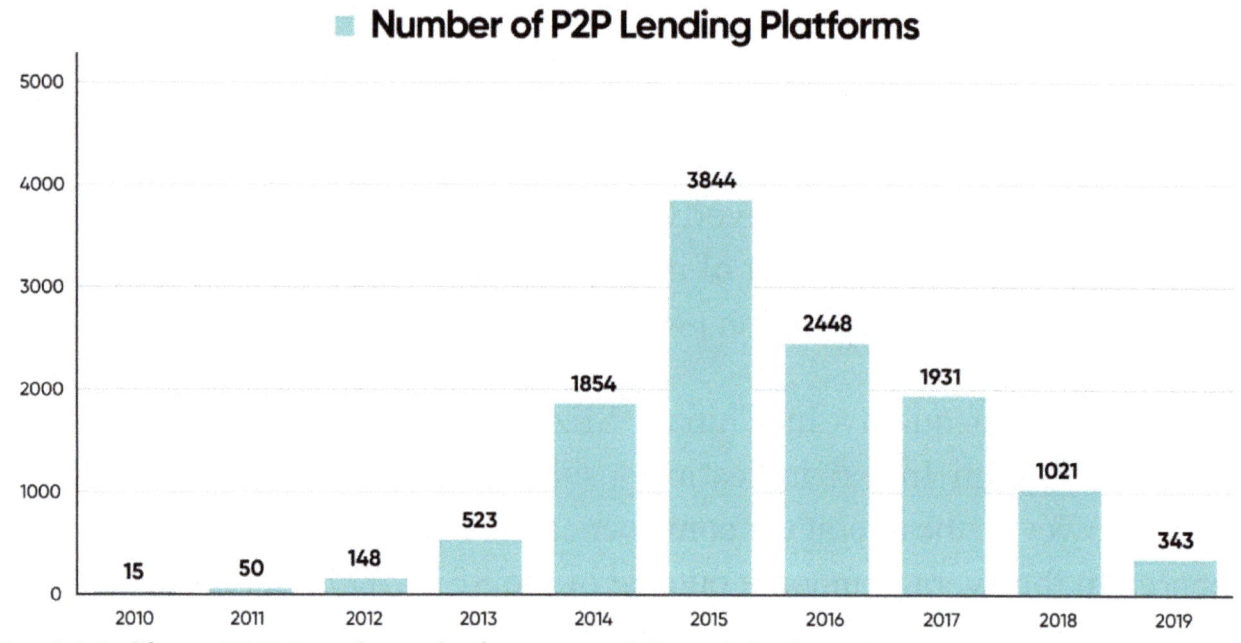

Fig 16.2 China P2P Lending platforms growth and decline (2010 - 2019). (Source data: Statista, 2020)

The P2P Lending sector represented a palatable proposition to all parties as investors and lenders were attracted to the competitive returns potential of these platforms combined with benefits such as 'cash back' for credit-based purchases. Borrowers were attracted by these platforms' cost effective pricing, flexible repayment channels, as well as financing discounts.

However, with the challenges associated with delegated monitoring, evident amidst rising default rates and fraud, greater regulation was imposed (see

Delegated Monitoring, Chapter 4: Surfacing Utility). Consequently, P2P lending dwindled, with a minority of FinTechs in this sphere evolving into formalised lenders, while the remainder disappeared (Fig 16.2). P2P Lending was perceived to be an extension of China's shadow banking sector (see Shadow Banking, Chapter 10: Financialisation) and was, thus, an area over which China's regulators sought to exert greater control (see Algorithmic Governance below).

CONSUMER PAYMENTS & CREDIT

Unlike western advanced economies, credit card issuance in China was exceptionally low. A natural consequence of limited banking services for consumers and SMEs. This was further reinforced by a long-standing cultural reluctance amongst Chinese people to take on debt. While credit cards are perceived in the western world as an instrument of convenience in order to make payments, in China they were perceived as a means of accessing credit in order to facilitate borrowing. This nuance assists in accounting for the success of the Octopus card in Hong Kong. An e-money payment instrument designed purely for convenience with no credit component (see Digital Wallets, Chapter 5: Payments). Thus, the poor penetration of conventional payment instruments and insufficient infrastructure, combined with a deficit in customer data with which to assess creditworthiness created a substantial opportunity for the FinTech sector. FinTechs exploited China's rapid smart phone penetration, as well as technologies, such as cloud computing, big data and artificial intelligence to offer digital payment technologies, as well as alternative credit scoring methodology (see Social Credit System below). Furthermore, with rising incomes, the lack of wealth management and investment channels with which everyday citizens could invest and save, exposed further gaps in the financial sector.

CHINESE TECH GIANTS

Tech companies were at the forefront to capture the opportunities this presented. Ant Group (formerly Ant Financial, an affiliate of the Alibaba Group) was established in 2014, and Tencent Holdings established in 1998, invested in cultivating alternative financial services in the FinTech sphere. The growth and success of e-commerce penetration from 2010 onwards provided a natural runway for FinTech to capitalise on the success, thereof. With greater commerce conducted, via digital channels, the opportunity to create digital financial technologies to support the growth thereof, was a natural evolution. Two digital payment propositions, Alipay and WeChat Pay rapidly dominated this market. Combined, these propositions commanded a 92% market share of China's digital payments sphere by 2019 (Alipay 54% and WeChat Pay 38%; Q4 2018).

Fig 16.3 China's Online Payments (2011 - 2017) denominated in RMB. (Source data: Statista, 2020)

This has been reinforced by China's ascent into an online shopping behemoth. A large population with booming access to digital technology has reciprocally boosted sales, via digital channels, which have risen at a prodigious rate. China's business to consumer (B2C) e-commerce market grew by almost a third in 2017 alone. As a consequence thereof, the country's online shopping market was worth $1.2 trillion by 2019.[414] Online sales have since risen, albeit disproportionately boosted by the impact of the COVID-19 pandemic. This represented a compound annual growth rate of 9.2% to 2021.

Tech giants have largely grown through creating reciprocal e-commerce and FinTech single-platform model propositions where the incentive to use the platform is realised through surfacing its utility for making frictionless online and offline payments, via digital wallets. The former has been achieved through e-commerce channels and the latter through QR code enabled apps (see Quick Response Codes, Chapter 5: Payments) exploited by bricks-and-mortar merchants. Digital wallets have the added advantage of either biometric or password authentication. Thus, a superior proposition to credit cards or physical e-money instruments, such as the Octopus card. In order to reinforce this model, digital wallets may be used by consumers at no charge, either for payments or for the funding, thereof. However, withdrawal from these digital wallets into the commercial banking system attracts a cost penalty in the form of a withdrawal fee (see Digital Wallets, Chapter 5: Payments). Thereby, creating an incentive to store funds in an e-money form within the Tech giants' platforms indefinitely (see E-Money, Chapter 6: Money).

China's FinTech Giants

FinTech Sectors	Ant Financial	Tencent	Ping An	JD.com
Payments	Alipay	Tencent Pay	E-wallet	JD Pay
Wealth Management	Yu'e Bao	Li Cai Tong	LU.com	JD Finance; JD Expert
Financing	Ant Check Later	Weilidai	Ping An Orange	JD Finance
Insurance	Zhong An Insurance	WeSure; Zhong An Insurance	Ping An Insurance; Zhong An Insurance	
Banking	MYbank	WeBank	Ping An Orange	
Credit Scoring	Zhima Credit	Tencent Credit	LU.com	JD Credit

Fig 16.4 China's Tech Giants dominating the FinTech sector, 2021

Furthermore, digital wallets need not be used as credit instruments, and thus reconcile with the Chinese psyche in avoiding the necessity to incur debt through the use, thereof. However, should credit be required, the digital wallet may be used to facilitate this. Essentially, this enables the tech giants to act as 'banks' for depositors, and in addition to offering payment channels, intermediate, as well as offer credit facilities, wealth management, as well as insurance services to a captive consumer base (Fig 16.4). In 2018, the overwhelming majority of payments by value had consequently been dominated by the tech giants' digital wallet (single-platform) propositions (Fig 16.5). As a result thereof, in just ten-years over the period 2008 - 2018, China's major urban centres had transformed from a predominantly underbanked cash-based emerging economy into a highly sophisticated and buoyant 'near cashless' society enabled by FinTech.

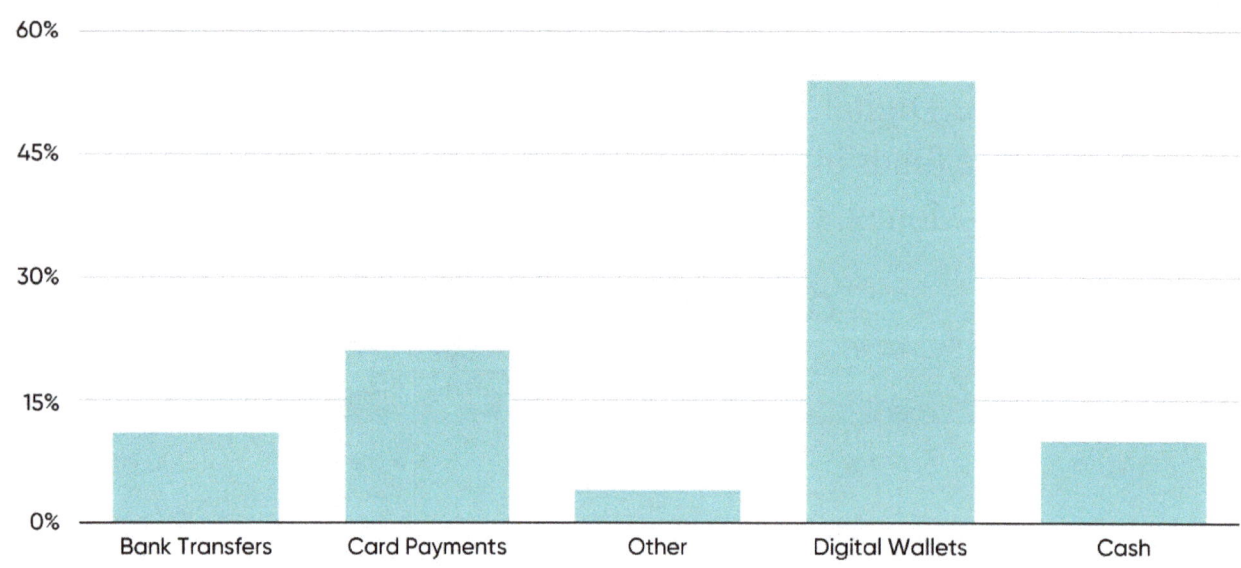

Fig 16.5 China's Payment Methods by value (percentage). (Source data: Edgar, Dunn & Company, 2018)

Through substantial penetration within financial services, combined with the proliferation of sales channels and social media within these tech giants' ecosystems, a wealth of diverse data sets has been amassed. This agglomeration has enabled these behemoths to exploit big data analytics and artificial intelligence to boost customer acquisition, as well as retention, via *learning* and *network effects*. Artificial intelligence has enabled these platforms to provide intelligent customer service features, deploy intelligent marketing methods while additionally conducting investment research in a dynamic and data-driven envelope. A testament to the scalability thereof, is in the shift from passively waiting to assist a customer, to a model where an AI agent is actively serving the customer proactively and is available on demand to service customers twenty-four-hours per day. By contrast, mature incumbent banks in western advanced economies have persistently struggled to maintain appropriate capacity with contact centres and human agents.

Furthermore, China's Tech Giants have employed strategies which are congruent with surveillance capitalism techniques and methods pioneered by tech giants outside of Asia (see Surveillance Capitalism, Chapter 15: Economy of Things). These strategies, embrace analogues to ILC/'Tower & Moat,' as well as self-reinforcing 'Runaway Leadership' tactics through the acquisition and mining of data. By co-opting these *instrumentarian* capabilities and methods, the Chinese tech giants, have displaced the lack of a mature consumer credit scoring system (such as FICO scoring) by exploiting vast unconventional data dimensions, such as those gleaned from social media, to weigh into a new form of AI-driven credit scoring (Fig 16.4). Through the use of affective computing, an applicant's creditworthiness may be assessed using computer vision to analyse micro expressions, voice stress levels and other indicators in response to questions to determine truthfulness in a credit interview (see Affective Computing, Chapter 15: Economy of Things). Thus, providing an enviable advantage through information asymmetry (see Information Asymmetry, Chapter 10: Financialisation).

A further testament to China's ability to safeguard its economy from external actors attempting to assume a leadership position is evident in China's e-commerce, social media and FinTech tech giants being exclusively of domestic origin. Whereas, US tech giants, such as Amazon, Google and Facebook, have successfully penetrated and realised a dominant position in markets worldwide, in China these behemoths are minor players. China is, thus, not beholden to US innovation in the tech sector, essentially it is free to make advances, while shielding itself from both US financial, as well as technology externalities.

COVID-19 PANDEMIC

The application rates of Chinese FinTech consumers across both small and medium-sized enterprises are considered to be among the highest adoption levels in the world. The former being 87% and the latter being 61%, respectively.[415] Economic activities such as payments, wealth management, lending and insurance were, thus, effectively immune to the impact of the COVID-19 outbreak. This was largely due to the widespread penetration of digital channels, e-commerce and FinTech amongst China's consumers and businesses. While some commercial banking branches were closed during the pandemic for fear of contact infection, online businesses continued to operate, which kept China's extensive FinTech enabled financial services industry running without interruption. By July 2020, online payment users in China had exceeded 800 million (~57% of China's population and greater than twice the population of the United States).

In October 2020, the World Bank published a report on financial management departments in 114 countries and regions, which indicated that in the wake of the COVID-19 outbreak, 72% of the institutions that contributed to the report had either initiated, or were preparing to launch digital infrastructure. It was broadly recognised that there was an urgent need for global financial institutions to develop, reinforce and support the implementation of digital infrastructure. From the financial sector's perspective, the optimal, most advanced and most practical technology must be exploited to renovate areas including payments, credit enquiry, lending, securities and insurance. Technologies such as blockchain, multiparty computing and federated learning were highlighted among the innovations to be applied to the financial sector. However, as the world becomes increasingly digitally-orientated, the issue of data privacy becomes more challenging and requires further scrutiny.

FINTECH REGULATION

EMBRYONIC PHASE

Over the period 2008 – 2013, FinTech in China experienced an embryonic phase, which was largely chaotic and unstructured. This was fuelled by economic growth as well as e-commerce penetration and enabled by the emergence of cloud computing, which made FinTech businesses leaner and nimbler in being more easily adaptable to differential business conditions. In addition, cloud computing enabled these start-ups to exploit third-party technology to experiment with innovation (see P2P Lending above), as well as rapidly scale their capacity as they gained traction. Thereby, collectively reducing their start-up costs for conventional in-house technology investments.

DIVERSIFICATION PHASE

Over the period 2013 - 2016, China's FinTech sector entered a phase of diversification, whereby with the commensurate rise in nascent financial channels, there was a simultaneous failure among others, predominantly P2P Lenders (Fig 16.2). The diversification phase experienced increased regulation over the sector.

LEGITIMISATION PHASE

Since 2017, China's FinTech sector has entered a legitimisation phase as greater regulation, structure and financialisation maturity has been increasingly evident. Greater regulation initially disrupted the sector as FinTechs were challenged to adhere to new forms of compliance obligations, which had been absent prior. In China, regulation is not perceived to be opposed to innovation, but rather as complementary and mutually reinforcing. China's regulatory approach is both inclusive and explorative in the application of FinTech. Following the success realised through the introduction of regulatory sandboxes, which were created in the UK and Singapore (see Economy of

Platforms, Chapter 15: Economy of Things), the People's Bank of China (PBOC) established tools to regulate FinTech innovation. Regulatory sandboxes were subsequently piloted in Beijing, Shanghai, Shenzhen, Xiong'an, Hangzhou and Guangzhou. The PBOC additionally announced the establishment of the Fintech Committee and the development plan, for which it is intended to be responsible. This plan identifies the guiding ideology, basic principles, objectives and the key tasks for the committee over the coming years. One encouraging sign is that some key areas have introduced incentive policies in their own jurisdictions, including the Guangdong–Hong Kong–Macao Greater Bay Area (or more broadly known as the 'Pearl River Delta').

Furthermore, China has developed certification systems for financial planners, investors and FinTech talent, and bolstered its efforts to deploy specific certification systems in numerous other fields. In addition, China has taken the education of FinTech very seriously. More than twenty higher learning institutions across the country have since begun to offer undergraduate degrees in FinTech, or with FinTech inclusive curricula.

Hence, China has recognised the necessity to establish a diversified governance mechanism in order to best exploit the use of FinTech and develop it with a view to both upgrading, as well as enabling synergies with its legacy financial sector (see State-Dominated Banking Sector above). Historically, the traditional governance mechanism has been segmented by institution or by process. As the sector continues to evolve through the application of technology, a series of transformations is expected to occur (see Economy of Platforms, Chapter 15: Economy of Things). China's supervisory bodies must, thus, keep pace with the times, and establish a multi-level FinTech governance system, which includes legal constraints, administrative supervision, industrial self-discipline and the promotion of institutional integrity.[416] This has, and will continue to, enable FinTechs to mature and become increasingly legitimised within the structure of China's increasingly financialised economy.

TECHNOLOGY INFLUENCES

As China's regulatory posture with regard to finance has historically been less mature, this has enabled FinTech to rapidly advance largely unhindered, offering tremendous insight as to how FinTech will likely disrupt existing paradigms in advanced economies (see Decelerating Effects, Chapter 2: Capital Evolution). In June 2018, Ant Group's Alipay launched a new service which executed the world's first cross-border remittance underpinned with a Blockchain (see Inter-institutional Network Infrastructure, Chapter 15: Economy of Things). In April 2018, one Shanghai-based branch of the China Construction Bank was hailed as the world's first unmanned bank branch, where customers are served by, and interact exclusively with robots.

Cloud Computing, Big Data, Artificial Intelligence, Blockchain and 5G have all featured prevalently in enabling China's FinTech growth in exaptive propositions and platforms. China's two dominant payment platforms, Alipay and WeChat Pay, have rapidly installed AI-powered facial recognition payment systems in China's largest cities, thereby making 'instrument-less' payments a commonplace practice, therein (see Smart Cities, Chapter 15: Economy of Things). In a comparable manner to which China's economic reforms prompted *trade liberalisation*, the rapid proliferation of FinTech and its mutually reinforcing effects on *financialisation* in China has catalysed a trend towards *financial liberalisation*. The CCP has not been ignorant to the roles that these technologies, as well as FinTech itself, is capable of playing in China's longer term ambitions. Nor is the CCP ignorant to the threat this poses to its party-state control over its citizens. One measure it has taken in response, is that of embracing 'Authoritarian Capitalism.'

AUTHORITARIAN CAPITALISM

In 1993, the Chinese objective of transforming into a 'socialist market economy' was declared by the Chinese government. At its core, this was an experimental approach to reform in order to harness the economic efficiencies associated with domestic competition while applying caution towards the associated destabilising effects, thereof. The state-owned, as well as state-controlled, banking sector (see above) acted as a counterweight to the associated risks as a consequence of its centralised state-controlled structure.

An unintended consequence of China's *financial liberalisation* through the rapid proliferation of FinTech (see Financial Inclusion above) has manifested through the implicit transfer of power over domestic financial capital to both individual, as well as corporate actors, beyond the party-state control of the Chinese government. This, in turn, is perceived to be a material threat to the stability of CCP rule over the longer-term. Essentially, as China evolves into a market-orientated economy comparable to that of western industrialised nations, the associated social changes associated with capitalist democracies is expected to incrementally challenge the CCP's party-state control over its citizens.

The rise of China's buoyant and sophisticated FinTech sector, thus, represents a paradoxical challenge for China's government. Whereby, increasing financial efficiency supports growth in domestic consumption and broadens China's financial base and its importance as a legitimacy-enhancing vehicle within the global market for manufacturing and trade. However, it has deeply integrated FinTech ecosystems and the transformative effect this has taken on its socio-political methods of control over its citizens through the practices of constraining capital, become increasingly counterintuitive in a climate of technological innovation and *financial liberalisation* which FinTech cultivates.

At a micro-cultural level, financial inclusion and *financialisation* tends to reshape the way people perceive their lives and their surroundings. Thus, promoting ideologies of individual responsibility, autonomy and self-determination. Essentially, promoting calculative practices of personal management and individual freedom. Collectively, this is synonymous with concepts of neoliberalism and democracy. All of which, challenges the CCP's authoritarian control over Chinese society.

Furthermore, since 1978, the CCP has endeavoured to maintain the status quo over its citizens' residual trust in the government's guarantee of social and economic progress in an era of profound social, technological and economic transformation. This has proven increasingly challenging amidst the rising complexity associated with transformation towards an increasingly market-orientated economy, in conjunction with an increasingly financially liberated society. Thus, giving rise to a climate conducive to realising a deficit in trust, manifesting across a broad spectrum of social challenges, such as consumer protection and environmental regulation, as well as tackling endemic deficits, such as corruption and fraud. In recognition thereof, the CCP has engaged in activities to upgrade its governance both ideologically and technically, as a means with which the CCP may increase its capacity and viability in maintaining its authority over its citizens.

ALGORITHMIC GOVERNANCE

The CCP's response to these challenges has become increasingly apparent as it attempts to reconcile the characteristics of a capitalist market economy with the strictures of an authoritarian political régime. Central to this paradigm of governance is a long-standing form of complex systems-thinking traceable to the 1970s, which advocates for technology being exploited as a vehicle through which Leninist social management may be achieved. The constituent elements thereof, are evaluated in the context of their potential utility, which may be surfaced in order to achieve social harmony and economic advancement. The net result of which manifests in a form of 'cyber-Leninism' which in 21st century China has been visible through the CCP's approach to exploiting technology to restructure the Party's governing framework.

The rise of digital credit scoring pioneered by China's FinTech tech giants has been influenced by these political traits, which creates a foundation for an evolving society moving towards authoritarian capitalism. In this context, China's government seeks to incorporate its Neo-statist logic, in which it can maintain control over financial market modernisation while tempering the authority vested in corporate, as well as SME actors. Thus, when examining digital credit scoring through the lens of political and social governance its utility as a form of *instrumentarian power* to assert dominance and control over China's citizens greatly overshadows its importance through the economic dimensions of financial inclusion and *financial liberalisation*. It additionally underscores the role that FinTech capabilities are being co-opted to facilitate in the rise of China's surveillance state. An example of which is evident through the implicit surveillance mechanisms that data-driven AI credit scoring, and by extension FinTech and financialisation, thus, implicitly weaves more deeply into the fabric of China's society (see Surveillance Capitalism, Chapter 15: Economy of Things)[417].

Digitally-enabled financial inclusion facilitated by FinTech has thus created a potential rapid diffusion mechanism in order to harvest and assimilate personal economic and behavioural data (digital exhaust), the latter of which would represent a surplus that is otherwise not required for the making of financial decisions, however, which can be exploited to influence wider social attitudes and incentives in service of the state's control over its citizens.

This has been evident in the close co-operation and industry-government coordination in the development of credit databases and data-processing techniques (through exploiting AI), which has blurred the lines between 'public' and 'private' in harnessing the financial system as a political, as well as economic tool.

One of the principal objectives of the 2015 *Guiding Proposal* was to effect a consolidation of the FinTech sector, particularly that of the P2P lending industry (see Peer-to-Peer Lending above), while both broadening and deepening the financial services offered by larger businesses. This consolidation additionally took on greater political significance, as a minority of tech giants could be regulated more effectively than thousands of small entities, while through these larger entities the government could foster political support and reciprocally reinforce their governance position. Whilst regulatory arbitrage beyond the state-owned banks in a financially repressed and conservative regulatory environment had been one of the initial catalysts for the emergence of FinTech, industry consolidation was viewed as a vehicle for both, reducing financial risk, and increasing monitoring capacity.

SOCIAL CREDIT SYSTEM

In March 2016, the National Internet Finance Association (NIFA) was established in Shanghai under the firm stewardship of both former PBOC officials, as well as the purview of the PBOC. Collectively, this highlighted the Chinese government's commitment to exercise control over the evolution of China's credit scoring infrastructure. In September 2016, NIFA launched the Credit Information Sharing Platform (CISP) in conjunction with the PBOC. CISP was seen as a key enabler in overcoming the challenges associated with credit scoring in the absence of traditional credit assessment capabilities. Its emergence further reinforcing the trend towards cultivating the Economy of Platforms (see Economy of Platforms, Chapter 15: Economy of Things). At its launch, CISP included seventeen NIFA members inclusive of Ant Financial and JD Finance (see Chinese Tech Giants above), which truly graduated Chinese credit scoring into the algorithmic era. The mutual interests between the FinTech giants and government were apparent in the former PBOC Deputy Governor, then NIFA president's launch statement.

'The credit information recorded through the platform can not only improve the internet finance industry credit system, but also complement with the existing data in the national financial credit information database and other industry credit databases, further consolidating the social credit system's information foundation.'

- *Li Dongrong, President, National Internet Finance Association, September 2016.*

Further national policy support for the social credit system became evident when one of China's leading trading hubs, the city of Yiwu, was designated as one of twelve 'demonstration cities' for the integration of social credit scoring by the National Development and Reform Commission. NIFA actively engaged in the development of strategies to integrate social credit scoring, via the CISP platform, into both national and local government systems for the management of the city across the spheres of finance, foreign trade, as well as market supervisory functions. For the CCP, CISP has represented a vehicle through which to achieve its ambitions of party-state control over its citizens, via actionable information asymmetry (see Information Asymmetry, Chapter 10: Financialisation).

Subsequently, key members of NIFA have been vocal about the 'close working relationship' between regulators and industry players, particularly those with vast quantities of customer data and credit scoring capabilities (see Chinese Tech Giants above).

SOCIAL GOVERNANCE

Practical applications of China's social credit system as a means to exert its social governance agenda have been evident in cities, such as Schenzen. Whereby, on public transportation such as buses, a commuter with an average social credit score attracts a standard bus fare. Whereas, a commuter with a good social credit score pays a discounted fare. While a commuter with an inferior score, pays substantially more. A further example is evident in the 'public shaming' of jay walkers in the city, whose images are displayed on large integrated television screens embedded within bus stops and pedestrian crossings peppered around the city. The offenders are identified by AI-enabled CCTV monitoring through the city's 'Smart Eyes' system (see Smart Cities, Chapter 15: Economy of Things). Offenders are, furthermore, automatically penalised by an automated reduction in their social credit score. These are emblematic examples of 'behavioural engineering' for the purpose of sustaining order, via social governance. A demonstration of China's exploitation of the *instrumentarian power* it has harnessed in the form of *economies of action* enabled by *economies of scope* and *scale* in data gleaned, via surveillance and FinTech credit scoring. Thus, cultivating an exaptation in the form of algorithmic governance, via FinTech innovation (see Surveillance Capitalism, Chapter 15: Economy of Things).

SAFE

The State Administration for Foreign Exchange (SAFE), headquartered in Beijing was established in 1978. SAFE is tasked with governing China's capital account posture (see Balance of Payments, Chapter 5: Payments), via foreign exchange market activities, and managing China's foreign exchange reserves.

While monitoring China's *balance of payments* position is among SAFE's principal responsibilities, SAFE is additionally responsible for setting China's exchange rate policy and managing the convertibility of RMB. By extension, SAFE manages China's foreign exchange reserves and its gold reserves. Furthermore, SAFE is charged with regulating crypto-currency.

China has a long-standing history of maintaining tight control over its capital account. Its policy régime under which its state-controlled banking sector (see State-Dominated Banking Sector above) were required to extend funds to SOEs at favourable terms, in lieu of private enterprises (including SMEs), despite their lower productivity reinforced a climate of financial repression. However, since China's domestic economic and financial boom, as well as its rapid drive towards financial inclusion enabled by FinTech (see Financial Inclusion above), combined with its SOE's declining share of GDP, pressure to gradually engage in liberalisation of its capital account has been mounting.

Historically, domestic households have been restricted from investing abroad, while foreign investors have been restricted from accessing Chinese financial markets. The majority of China's capital flow restrictions are quantity-based. A posture which is expected to gradually change over time (see Tectonic Shift, Chapter 17: Odyssey). However, in 2019, an examination of a disparity in China's *balance of payments* position suggests that enforcement of capital account restrictions and the private sector's efforts to circumvent, such restrictions has resulted in a *de facto* capital account régime which varies from the official quantity-based restrictions.

Among the vehicles exploited to circumvent China's capital account restrictions, has been the use of crypto-currencies, such as Bitcoin, which are both extra-systemic and portable across borders (see Chapter 14: Tokenisation). In September 2017, China's Bitcoin Exchanges were directed to suspend their services following instruction from the Chinese government (at the behest of SAFE).[418] This included the trading of crypto-currencies, as well as simultaneously prohibiting the issue of new ICOs. Additionally, this represented a pivotal milestone in China's transition towards the *legitimisation phase* of its FinTech sector (see FinTech Regulation above). In January 2018, a leaked memo from the 'Leading Group of Internet Financial Risks Remediation' indicated that Bitcoin miners should make an '*orderly exit*' from China having consumed extensive resources and stoked speculation among convertible virtual currencies. This highlighted an extension of China's policy towards eliminating participation in extra-systemic mechanisms, with which circumventing capital account controls may be achieved.[419]

As with comparable examples of financially repressed societies, mechanisms that emerge with which to circumvent such controls are exploited as a valve to relieve the pressure thereof. This is synonymous with systemic resistance which is cultivated as a natural consequence of overly constraining an ordered system (see Prologue). Capital account controls have enabled China to accrue a substantial war chest of foreign exchange reserves through its extensive trade surplus, via both SOEs, and its private sector. The adjudication, thereof, via its authoritarian capitalism, has ostensibly aided it in cultivating a means with which to invest in overcoming the 'Middle-income Trap.'

THE MIDDLE–INCOME TRAP

The impact and significance of FinTech in the wealth management, financing and investment spheres should not be underestimated. Economic reforms in China catalysed a 'componentisation effect,' thereby initiating a decentralisation of economic production, which led to substantial growth in both household, as well as corporate savings. Consequently, gross savings as a share of China's GDP is the highest among major economies. Thus, domestic savings has enabled China to support a high level of investment. However, since China's gross domestic savings levels far exceed its domestic investment levels, combined with its capital account controls (see SAFE above) has enabled China to transform from a debtor, into a creditor nation. In other words, evolving into a net global lender (see Debt Trap Diplomacy below).

Productivity gains, whereby increases in efficiency have been realised, are another major factor in China's rapid economic growth. Improvements in productivity were largely the result of resource reallocation towards more productive pursuits, particularly in sectors that were formerly tightly controlled by the central government. Such sectors included agriculture, trade, and services. By way of example, agricultural reforms boosted production, thereby freeing human capital to pursue employment in the growing and more productive manufacturing sector. China's decentralisation of its economy, additionally led to the rise of non-state enterprises (such as SMEs), which were more market-orientated, as well as more efficient. These businesses pursued more productive activities than the centrally controlled SOEs.

In addition, a greater proportion of the economy (predominantly that of the export sector) was exposed to competitive forces. Local and provincial governments were allowed to establish and operate various enterprises without interference from the government. Combined with foreign direct investment, this infused China with a slew of new technologies and a simultaneous co-evolution of practices that amplified efficiency (see Co-evolution, Chapter 2: Capital Evolution).

TECHNOLOGICAL ADVANCEMENT & INNOVATION

As China's technological sophistication has developed and begun to converge with that of advanced economies (predominantly, through its adoption of foreign developed technology, see IDAR below), its level of productivity gains, and thus, real GDP growth, is expected to slow substantially. China is aware of this challenge, and is thus, expected to evolve into a major innovation centre for new technology, while simultaneously implementing a series of new comprehensive economic reforms.

In a comparable manner to which China has experienced rapid economic development and growth, a number of other developing economies (predominantly those within Asia and Latin America) experienced substantial growth in the 1960s as well as the 1970s. These nation states did so to a large extent by implementing comparable policies to that of China, in order to boost exports while promoting, as well as protecting certain sectors or segments of their economies. However, at a particular juncture along these growth vectors, these economies experienced stagnation. In economics, this phenomenon is known as the 'Middle-income Trap.'

Essentially, a number of developing economies which the World Bank classifies as 'Low-Income,' based on a per capita gross national income (GNI) methodology, had successfully transitioned toward the 'Middle-income' band. However, since these nation states were unable to sustain the necessary levels of productivity gains to achieve a further transition into 'High-income' economies, they remained trapped at the 'Middle-income' level. This was in part, due to their inability to address structural inefficiencies in their economies, although it is the inability to innovate and prevail against inertia barriers, embrace *creative destruction,* as well as ascend within the value chain that renders many such nations states incapable of escaping the middle-income trap.

Examples in Latin America include nation states, such as Argentina, Brazil, Mexico, Colombia and Peru. Each of these economies industrialised and thereafter, lost competitiveness with inferior economies on manufactured exports, however, were incapable of adapting in order to compete with high-income economies in high-value innovation. Consequently, they have remained trapped at the middle-income level for prolonged periods of time. Based on World Bank data, of over one-hundred-countries classed as middle-income in 1960, only thirteen had successfully transitioned to the high-income band forty-eight-years later. Large middle-income nation states today have, thus, been trapped in this band for over six decades. By contrast, the earlier industrialisers such as the United Kingdom, France, Germany and the United States required no more than forty-two-years to transition from the middle-income to the high-income bands.[420]

The challenges associated with escaping the middle-income trap have been investigated and debated among economists and social scientists for some time. The consensus as to how to transition to the high-income band advocates the pursuit of savings and investment strategies, investing in infrastructure improvement, education and most critically, investing in innovation through research and development (R&D).

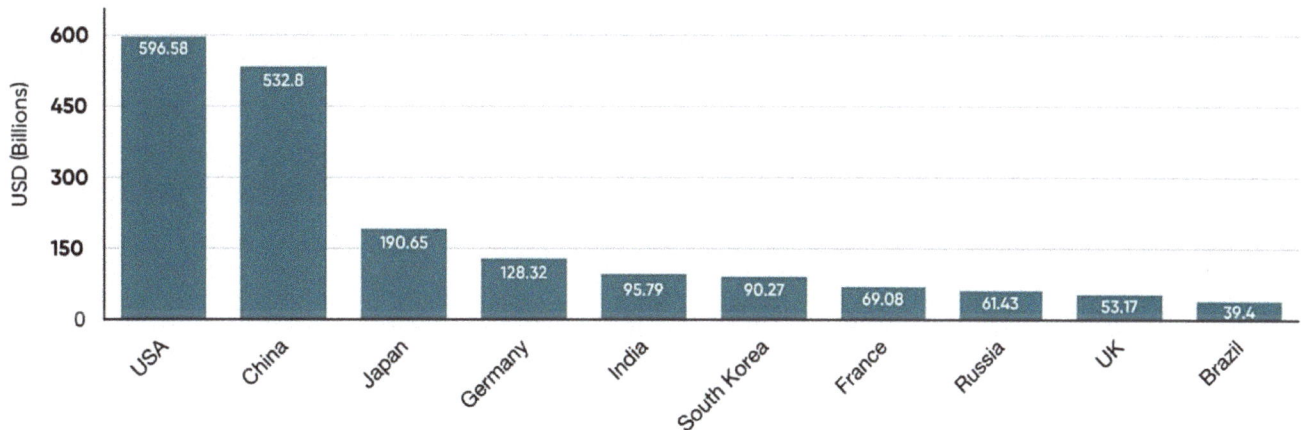

Fig 16.6 Top 10 national Research and Development (R&D) expenditures worldwide in 2020 (USD Billions). (Source data: Statista, 2020)

Since 2008, China's FinTech sector has meaningfully catalysed its domestic economic sophistication and enabled the country to embrace *financialisation*, while simultaneously experiencing growth and sophistication in *industrialisation*. Its vast population and high adoption rate of digital technology and the associated data generated therefrom, has enabled the country to make substantial advances in technologies, such as Big Data, Artificial Intelligence, 5G communications, as well as a slew of *higher-order systems,* built upon these foundations (see Higher-order Systems, Chapter 2: Capital Evolution).

MADE IN CHINA 2025

In 2015, China's government announced its 'Made in China 2025' initiative (MIC 2025).[421] A plan intended to upgrade and modernise its manufacturing in ten key sectors through extensive government support. The objective in this regard, is to elevate China into a major player (if not the leader) in these spheres globally. The 2015 'Made in China 2025' document identified the sectors as follows:

1. Aerospace & Aviation Equipment
2. Electrical Equipment
3. Advanced Railway Equipment
4. Agricultural Equipment & Machinery
5. Maritime Engineering (including technologically advanced maritime vessels)
6. New Materials
7. Sustainable/Renewable Energy & (Electric) Vehicles
8. Biopharmaceuticals & Medical Technologies (including medical devices)
9. Next Generation Information Technology
10. High-end Numerical Control Machinery and Robotics

The spheres of Information Technology and Robotics include, Artificial Intelligence, Internet of Things (IoT) technologies inclusive of smart appliances, Drones, Semiconductors and 5G technologies, as well as infrastructure (see Chapter 15: Economy of Things). All of which are perceived as enablers to achieve substantial productivity gains for all ten MIC 2025 sectors. Leadership in Artificial Intelligence development has, thus, become of paramount strategic importance in enabling the greatest advances across this spectrum. MIC 2025, thus, highlights China's forward looking promotion of *interdisciplinary*, as well as *first principles thinking* (see First Principles, Chapter 4: Surfacing Utility). Furthermore, China's investments in Research and Development (R&D) in 2020, was second only to that of the United States (Fig 16.6).

China's objectives are to achieve an average annual GDP growth rate of 4.8% from 2020 - 2035 and 3.4% from 2030 - 2050. It seeks to achieve a per capita GDP of $20,000 by 2025. This essentially would enable China to transition from a Middle-income, to a High-income country. By 2035, China seeks to achieve a target of $45,000 (35% of US levels), and $120,000 by 2050 (approximately half of US levels). [422]

CHINA STANDARDS 2035

China has developed an ambitious plan to assume a leadership role in global standards for a series of next generation technologies – a move that could have enormous implications for technology industries worldwide.

The China Standards 2035 plan lays out a blueprint for China's government and a number of leading technology companies to set global standards for technologies, such as 5G, the Internet of Things (IoT), and Artificial Intelligence, among others. The China Standards 2035 plan is intended to reciprocally reinforce China's other industrial policies, namely the controversial Made in China 2025 policy (see above). An essential means of enabling China to become global leaders in high-tech innovation (see Sensing Engines, Chapter 3: Ecosystems).

The plan is the culmination of a two-year research project that was initiated in early 2018, and was led by the General Administration of Quality Supervision, Inspection and Quarantine (AQSIQ) and implemented by the Chinese Academy of Engineering.

It is clear that this initiative puts forward ambitious plans for China to reshape the global technology industry. Due to its importance to China's leadership, whether or not businesses directly operate in China, the implications thereof for every business that makes use of technology worldwide are substantial (see

Genesis of an Ecosystem, Chapter 3: Ecosystems). Global leadership in technology standardisation among 'key stone' technologies (such as AI, IoT and 5G) places China in a position to cultivate self-reinforcing *learning* and *network effects,* on an unparalleled scale (see Runaway Leadership, Chapter 4: Surfacing Utility). A move which enables China to become the greatest beneficiary from innovations (in the form of higher-order systems), regardless of where in the world these may originate (see Innovate, Leverage & Commoditise, Chapter 3: Ecosystems). In addition, it would enable China to a large extent to exert control over the rate of commoditisation of a specific, as well as a variety of next generation technologies for its own industrial and commercial benefit (see Standardisation, Chapter 2: Capital Evolution).

INTERNET PLUS

The extent to which China would be able to manipulate the rate of commoditisation of higher-order systems as a consequence of its 'China Standards 2035 Plan' (see above), is complementary to China's Internet Plus initiative.

In the field of industrial development, the US put forward a concept known as the 'Industrial Internet.' In congruence with this line of thinking, Germany had proposed a comparable concept known as 'Industry 4.0.' At its core, this is conceptually based on the principle of exploiting the internet as a platform which may be co-opted to disrupt traditional industries, in lieu of purely exploiting the internet as a communication medium. FinTech and a slew of higher-order systems has ostensibly facilitated the disruption of the traditional financial services sector bringing about with it the *creative destruction* of its traditional business models. Hence, the exploitation, thereof, by co-opting the internet and its higher-order systems enabled, via IoT and AI, are key capabilities which may bring about a comparable *creative destruction* within the traditional industrial sectors.

Furthermore, each of these industries which are disrupted through this evolution will enter its own commoditisation lifecycle (see Commoditisation, Chapter 2:

Capital Evolution). The ambitions of China's Internet Plus initiative are to both disrupt these industries with the use of the internet ecosystem, as well as to rapidly industrialise these innovations in order to derive the greatest efficiency and profitability, therefrom, beyond the reach of the competitive capabilities among globally industrialised nations. Internet Plus, is thus, a major enabler in realising China's MIC 2025 ambitions, thereby creating a series of metaphorical 'Towers,' while its 'China Standards 2035' (see above) initiative fortifies its leadership role in these spheres. Thereby, creating an impenetrable metaphorical 'Moat' (see Tower & Moat, Chapter 3: Ecosystems).

Examples include '*Internet+Finance = FinTech,*' as well as
'*Internet+Agriculture = AgriTech.*'

In addition, China's Internet Plus ambitions include medical systems, the manufacturing industry, as well as government. Aside from the Chinese government's objective of evolving China into a '*powerful industrial country,*' the 'Internet Plus' strategy will, most critically, produce new economic forms and cultivate a suitable environment to promote innovation and entrepreneurship. Moreover, according to the official statement, the plan exerts a profound influence on adapting to an information (or data-driven) economy, '*rebuilding innovation systems, intriguing creativity, cultivating emerging industry and devising, as wells refining a public service pattern.*' The vehicle through which this vision may be realised will be enabled by the emerging *economy of platforms* and is ultimately anticipated to distil into the *economy of things* (see Chapter 15: Economy of Things). Hence, evolving into the bedrock enablers for Smart Cities and global industrial leadership, while simultaneously commanding the highest value dividends at every level of the industrial, as well as service value chains.

The associated data generated therefrom, should enable China to maintain a leadership position in Artificial Intelligence development, thereby benefitting from surveillance dividends and self-reinforcing *learning* and *network effects* (see Runaway Leadership, Chapter 4: Surfacing Utility).

IDAR

Introduce, Digest, Absorb and Re-Innovate (IDAR) is an approach implemented by China's government since 2006. The approach seeks to achieve substantial advancement across all sectors of the Chinese economy through siphoning the innovations and technologies from external sources (particularly Western powers), through technology transfer. This is seen as an interim measure until such time as China is capable of cultivating and producing its own innovations and technologies through domestic research and development. Indigenous capabilities in these areas is an essential stepping stone towards realising a dominant global position and IDAR has functioned as a means of bridging the gap towards this end.

Exploiting an ILC/'Tower & Moat' strategy, as well as harvesting data, via telecommunications technologies such as 5G, are powerful tools to passively absorb intellectual property, trade secrets and intercept data about people and systems. These surveillance capabilities may be utilised in advancements, such as Artificial Intelligence and broader cutting-edge technologies and methods. Access to information may also be leveraged politically and used to subvert challenges to Chinese Communist Party ideals and philosophy. Digital payments systems and digital money are further capabilities which may be exploited to siphon data and assert economic dominance through the control and flow of capital. A precedent set by the United States (see Terrorist Financing Tracking Program; Extraterritorial Sanctions, Chapter 13: Global Trade Rails). The greater the sophistication and convenience of the FinTech led capability, the easier it is to export to other nations and to exploit in order to assert control (see Digital Currency Electronic Payment, Chapter 14: Tokenisation).

ONE BELT, ONE ROAD

THE SILK ROAD

The Silk Road was formed during the westward expansion of China's Han Dynasty (206 B.C. - 220 A.D.), which forged a series of trade networks throughout what at present are the Central Asian nation states of Afghanistan, Kazakhstan, Kyrgyzstan, Tajikistan, Turkmenistan, and Uzbekistan, as well as both modern-day India and Pakistan. Collectively, the Silk Road trade routes extended in excess of four-thousand miles from China to the footsteps of Europe.

The Silk Road cultivated one of the earliest known waves of globalisation, which connected both eastern and western markets. Thereby, facilitating the sharing and spreading of goods, ideas and culture across Europe, the Middle East and China. While Chinese goods such as silks, spices and jade moved west, ivory, glass and precious metals, such as gold and silver moved east. During the course of this period, the Chinese innovation of paper money featured prevalently as a *medium of exchange* in order to facilitate trade over greater distances (see Paper Money, Chapter 6: Money). Use of the Silk Road was extensive under the leadership of the Roman and Byzantine Empires, as well as China's Tang Dynasty (617 - 907 CE) thereafter. However, with the conflicts brought about by the crusades and the advances by the Mongols in Central Asia, the use thereof as a trade route diminished.

In contemporary terms, this has contributed to the economic isolation of several Central Asian nation states which were once buoyant with commerce brought about by the Silk Road. By way of example, in recent years, intra-regional trade of Central Asian countries has only accounted for ~6.2% of all cross-border trade invoicing in the region.

THE BELT & ROAD INITIATIVE

During two official visits, the first to Kazakhstan and the second to Indonesia in 2013, Chinese General Secretary Xi Jinping announced an initiative which was two-pronged. The first was an overland Silk Road Economic Belt. The second was a Maritime Silk Road. Collectively, these were initially known as the 'One Belt, One Road' initiative. However, thereafter it has become known as the Belt and Road Initiative (BRI).

The BRI lays out a vision for creating a vast network of railways, energy pipelines, bridges, highways, seaports and streamlined border crossings, which would extend both westward through the mountainous former Soviet republics and southward, to Pakistan, India, and the remainder of Southeast Asia. In addition to physical infrastructure, China shared plans to build fifty special economic zones, modelled after the Shenzhen SEZ (see Special Economic Zones above), which China created in 1980, during its economic reforms under then leader Deng Xiaoping.

The BRI would undoubtedly provide a major boost for both China's economy, as well as its soft power image (see Soft Power, Chapter 11: Hegemonic Dominance). China additionally intends to stimulate economic development in poorer regions of its country. With interest rates persistently near the zero bound since the GFC (see Quantitative Easing, Chapter 8: Economic Cycles), the BRI creates a vehicle through which to achieve these objectives, while providing a means with which China may gain a better return on its surplus foreign exchange reserves (see Debt Trap Diplomacy below). Furthermore, the BRI will create new overseas business opportunities for Chinese businesses and simultaneously engage new markets for industries which either currently, or in the future will accrue surplus capacity. The BRI, is thus, a critical means of deploying surplus capacity to assist China in escaping the Middle-income trap (see The Middle-income Trap above).

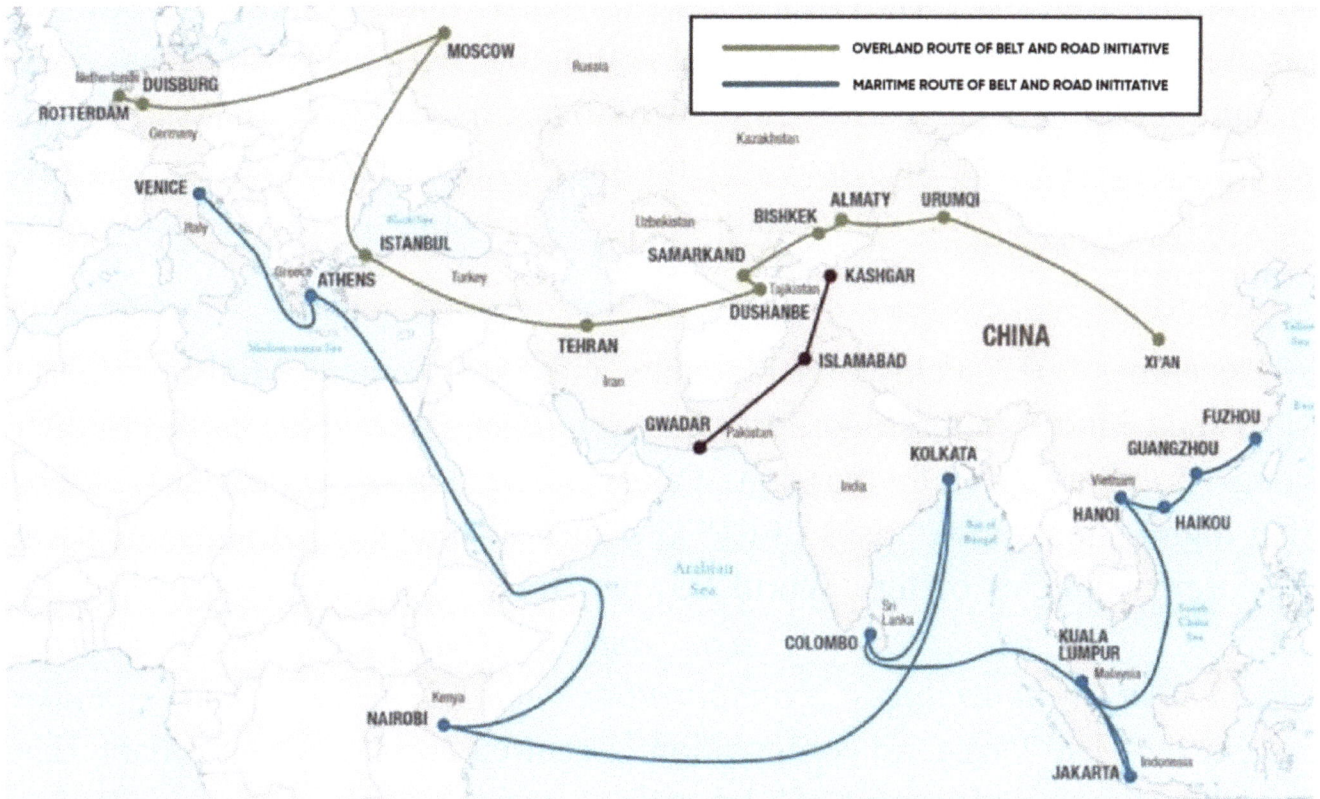

Fig 16.7 China's Belt & Road Initiative.(Source: SmartPort, March 2018)[423]

An economic network and infrastructure of this magnitude would undoubtedly aid in the *internationalisation* of RMB (Chinese Yuan), via *network effects* and thus:

'Break the bottleneck in Asian connectivity.'

- Xi Jinping, General Secretary, Chinese Communist Party, 2013.

CHINA–PAKISTAN ECONOMIC CORRIDOR

In 2013, the China-Pakistan Economic Corridor (CPEC) was initiated. CPEC represented the lynchpin project of the Belt and Road Initiative, comprising a collection of infrastructure projects which collectively attracted an approximate cost of $62 billion as of 2020. CPEC's infrastructure projects include the construction of high-speed railways, highways, energy-generation projects and major upgrades to the Gwadar Port Complex, inclusive of the creation of a 2300 acre free trade area in proximity to the port, which functions as a Special Economic Zone (SEZ). The Gwadar Port serves as a major hub linking the land-based belt with its Maritime Silk Road within the BRI. A critical access point to support bidirectional maritime shipment to and from both West Asia, as well as Africa. Thus, a critical gateway through which China may import raw materials and crude oil, while additionally distributing goods to its overseas export markets.

In December 2017, Pakistan's Planning and Development Minister, Ahsan Iqbal and Chinese Ambassador, Yao Jing, jointly announced the launch of their Long-Term Plan (LTP) for the China-Pakistan Economic Corridor (CPEC). The plan highlighted various risks to CPEC's success inclusive of adjustments in the foreign policies of the 'World Powers' towards Central Asia. The LTP defines CPEC as *'a growth axis and a development belt featuring complementary advantages, collaboration, mutual benefits and common prosperity.'* The long-term co-operation is centred around 'seven pillars' that furnish every possible aspect of bilateral economic and financial co-operation.

The corridor's core and radiation zones establish the geospatial superstructure of *'one belt, three axes and several passages.'* The LTP advocates that *'The CPEC will greatly speed up the industrialisation and urbanisation process in Pakistan and help it grow into a highly inclusive, globally competitive and prosperous country capable of providing high-quality life to its citizens.'*

With regards to the *internationalisation* of China's currency (see The Belt & Road Initiative above), one of the most salient features of the LTP, is the equal treatment in status of the Chinese RMB with that of the US dollar.

This represented a substantial departure from Pakistan's foreign exchange régime, which prior to the LTP's announcement, exclusively permitted only dollar-denominated transactions for international trade (see Dollar Hegemony, Chapter 13: Global Trade Rails). The LTP stipulates that Pakistan will promote and explore RMB denominated offshore financial business within the Gwadar Free Zone, one of the fifty intended BRI SEZs (see above). Furthermore, monetary co-operation inclusive of enhancing as well as broadening the use of bilateral currency swap agreements between China and Pakistan is outlined therein (see Swap Lines, Chapter 5: Payments). This will encourage clearing and settlement for financial institutions from either country through China's state-sponsored FinTech initiatives, predominantly the Cross-Border Inter-Bank Payment System (see Cross-Border Inter-Bank Payment System, Chapter 13: Global Trade Rails), in order to bilaterally promote the free flow of capital neither using the dollar, nor intermediating transfers via the Fed (see De-dollarisation; Tectonic Shift, Chapter 17: Odyssey).

DEBT TRAP DIPLOMACY

While BRI projects additionally offer the promise of boosting the domestic economies of countries in which China is investing in infrastructure, unlike the World Bank's investments or grants from other countries (see World Bank, Chapter 12: Global Monetary System), BRI projects are funded by low-interest loans for which China is the creditor (see The Belt & Road Initiative above). The BRI could, thus, pose substantial financial risks, should borrowing countries become incapable of servicing these debts. In October 2017, then US Secretary of State, Rex Tillerson commented on the BRI:

'We have watched the activities and actions of others in the region, in particular China, and the financing mechanisms it brings to many of these countries which result in saddling them with enormous levels of debt. They don't often create the jobs, which infrastructure projects should be tremendous job creators in these economies, but too often, foreign workers are brought in to execute these infrastructure projects. Financing is structured in a way that makes it very difficult for them to obtain future financing, and oftentimes has very subtle triggers in the financing that results in financing default and the conversion of debt to equity.'

- Rex Tillerson, US Secretary of State (2017 - 2018), October 2017.

Tillerson's statement with regards to converting 'debt' to 'equity' is in reference to the phenomenon known as 'Debt Trap Diplomacy,' whereby China furnishes BRI participant countries with loans to build infrastructure, subsequently importing its own labour force (surplus capacity) to complete the project and, thus, starves the participant nation from the economic benefits, thereof. The participant country, which is thereafter incapable of servicing the loan, is leveraged by China to surrender either the infrastructure itself, or a national asset of vital strategic importance to longer term Chinese objectives. A prominent example is that of Sri Lanka's Hambanthota deep water seaport (and 15000 acres of land surrounding it), which since 2017 is under lease to China Merchant Port Holdings for 99 years. The port gives China control of territory in close proximity to India and a strategic foothold along a critical commercial and military waterway.

Announced in 2013, the BRI represented a lifeline to many low-income and some middle-income countries which had been detrimentally impacted by the globally protracted recession (known as The Great Recession) in the wake of the GFC (see Coup de Grâce, Chapter 10: Financialisation). By contrast, China has persistently run a substantial trade surplus with the US, as well as with the EU and the UK, placing it in a strong position to use its extensive war chest of foreign exchange reserves accrued therefrom, to exploit its economically vulnerable neighbours.

China has, thus, become the world's largest creditor to low-income countries. The Institute of International Finance's (IIF) data shows that China's outstanding debt claims worldwide have soared from $875 billion in 2004, to over $5.5 trillion in 2019.[424] Thus, enabling China to commercially indoctrinate vital trading hubs and strategic assets within the BRI ecosystem.

STRING OF PEARLS THEORY

The 'String of Pearls' hypothesis is a geo-economic strategy which originated from a US defence contractor, Booz Allen Hamilton, in his paper 'Energy Futures in Asia,' published in 2004. Hamilton's paper highlighted that China's investments in seaports in key strategic locations within the Indian Ocean may be leveraged to create a network of naval bases stretching from southern China to Pakistan.

In 2008, China's anti-piracy operation in the Gulf of Aden, representing its first out-of-area Naval operation resurfaced the 'String of Pearls' hypothesis as China's officials debated the merits of establishing overseas military bases to provide shore-based logistics support to enable comparable operations in the future. The operation had revealed the challenges in supporting the logistics of delivering fuel and food to forces thousands of miles away from its coastal waters. China's Colonel Dai Xu was the most cited Chinese military officer who had publicly advocated for the creation of a network of naval bases in the wake of China's first anti-piracy operation. The sentiment was additionally echoed by China's academic community.

'China should not rule out an overseas supply base since its interests lie beyond its borders and the ability to protect them has become an imminent necessity.'

- Jin Canrong, Professor of international relations, Renmin University.

China's export-led economy is dependent on international trade, which is predominantly conducted by sea. Furthermore, a crucial aspect of its vast manufacturing capabilities is its dependence on Coal which historically has accounted for the bulk of its energy supply. In addition China remains dependent on the import of crude oil, which remains an indispensable resource in energy generation, manufacturing and transportation. China's oil supply is imported almost exclusively by sea. In September 2013, China overtook the US as the world's largest net importer of crude. Historically, approximately eighty-percent of China's oil imports have traversed the Indian Ocean, via the Malacca Strait, into the South China Sea. Since China possesses no large-scale substitutes for transport fuel affecting cars, trucks, ships, aircraft and its train network, its economy is vulnerable to disruptions in its oil supply.

THE MALACCA DILEMMA

In this context, a reasonable concern that a blockade (or the threat, thereof) by a foreign power in the Malacca Strait may have devastating consequences for China's economy. This is among a number of security threats that China will have considered in its BRI strategy. Extricating itself from the risks associated with the 'Malacca Dilemma' represents a substantial motivation to establish an overseas naval presence as well as land-based transport links as an alternative supply line for the country (see The Belt & Road Initiative above). Collectively, this gives greater credence to the 'String of Pearls' hypothesis as a lens through which to better interpret China's BRI and its use of 'Debt-Trap Diplomacy.'

India in particular has vocally advocated that the Chinese BRI initiative is a bid to incrementally dominate Asia, via the 'String of Pearls' strategy. India has warned that China's use of 'Debt-Trap Diplomacy,' whereby China creates unsustainable debt burdens for its Indian Ocean neighbours is a vehicle through which to gain control of regional choke points (pearls). This unsettled posture is exacerbated by China's decades-long embrace of Pakistan, India's long-standing rival (see China-Pakistan Economic Corridor above).

In isolation, this may be perceived as a premature conclusion to have drawn on the part of India. However, when considering the 'String of Pearls' hypothesis through the lens of China's state-sponsored FinTech initiatives, the concept bears greater consideration.

CHINA'S FINTECH PEARLS

China's ambitions with regards to the creation of a CBDC, CIPS and Clearing Banks should not be underestimated by the international community. While China does not appear to be openly seeking to displace the US dollar-based systems, or replace the US dollar as the principal global reserve currency, it is in China's interests to be capable of leveraging an international payment process that is US dollar independent (see Chapter 13: Global Trade Rails). The geopolitical implications of Chinese dominated payment systems and the *internationalisation* of RMB are an increasingly critical issue. It may be prudent to examine these as potential 'pearls' which incrementally erode the United States' influence in Asia.

Independently, the anticipated effects of a Chinese CBDC, Clearing Banks and CIPS which provides messaging, clearing, and settlement for international RMB transactions on global trade invoicing should be negligible. However, collectively, the long-term implications of an aggregate of these 'pearls' cannot be overstated.

The growing maturity of Chinese FinTech platforms and propositions such as Alipay and WeChat Pay in particular, enable direct payment intermediation between China's domestic consumers. Collectively, a CBDC, Clearing Banks, CIPS, and China's internal digital channels ecosystem create a compelling set of digital propositions that facilitate expedient and efficient payments, integrated InsureTech and substantial wealth management portfolios such as that of 'Yu'e Bao' both within China and to other nation states that elect to join the systems and utilise Chinese denominated currency instruments. Either via SEZs created within the BRI, or in order to engage in frictionless trade with China.

This rapidly evolving modern payments and monetary ecosystem, as it is increasingly developed and matured, can easily be integrated to incorporate other countries, via the API economy and thus cultivate greater internationalisation, via *network effects*. Weak signals to this effect are evident through Alipay and WeChat Pay having made significant inroads in Southeast Asia. Given trade and investment with China, Southeast Asian central banks have found it advantageous to join Chinese systems to promote greater efficiency in financial transactions. Thus, building upon the foundations of China's partnerships and currency swap agreements with Russia, Pakistan and Iran (see Tectonic Shift, Chapter 17: Odyssey).

China's imperial-style expansion through the Belt and Road Initiative will benefit China greatly if countries upon which the BRI depends, benefit from Chinese loans and seek to modernise their financial infrastructure, based on Chinese developed payment systems and FinTech platforms.

Between the years 2016 - 2019, RMB denominated payments increased in excess of 120% in Africa, further signalling the effectiveness of China's incentives to integrate a digital channels ecosystem with BRI countries. Once fully integrated, the Chinese system would allow for cross-border remittances between institutions and individuals free of reliance upon correspondent banking and US dollars. While China may not openly be seeking to take on the responsibility of leading the international monetary and financial system in the short-term, these collective capabilities offer a substantial strategic advantage for the country to galvanise an independent multinational economic system free of external accountability.

In a comparable manner to which the US has been able to assert foreign policy through extraterritorial sanctions, thereby exploiting its dominance over the financial system, China's proliferation of its own payment systems and currency swap agreements provides a degree of inoculation against US foreign policy. Simultaneously, however, China's loans to other nations draws parallels with Britain's foreign investment practices during its hegemonic reign. This additionally enables China to cultivate the means with which to assert its own foreign policy on other nations as its soft power posture proffers. Thus, a significant and essential stepping stone in creating *new configurations of power* and paving the pathway to hegemonic dominance in the longer-term (see Chapter 11: Hegemonic Dominance).

In other words, *'Crossing the river, by touching the stones.'*

17

ODYSSEY

The status quo of Fibonacci style debt cycles in ever increasing amplitude and frequency is daunting. The sheer magnitude of international debt, is beyond comprehension. This should give us all pause.

We live in an age of paradox. Rapid advances in technology and an explosion in credit continues to drive soaring share prices, however, measured productivity has declined substantially since the GFC, while for the majority of the US workforce, real income has stagnated since the mid-1990s.

Financialisation promotes speculation and the creation of wealth in response to the deflationary forces which result from technological advancement and commoditisation. This creates dangerous concentrations of wealth that leave societies increasingly divided. The expansion of credit which results from speculation and reinforces the inflationary effects needed to counter deflation distils into greater accretion of debt burdens, thus, promoting instability. Eventually, debt burdens become unserviceable, resulting in a systemic collapse as the system attempts to either correct, or reset itself through a deleveraging. The deleveraging broadens the divide between the wealthy and the working class while the middle class suffers attrition through soaring defaults. As credit evaporates, recessions or depressions ensue. This exacerbates the effects of social inequality and may even provoke social unrest. Disenfranchised and divided, society becomes polarised and vulnerable to the influence of extreme populist and nationalist agendas. Such manoeuvring is usually harnessed to garner support for extreme social change through adversarial political manipulation. Simultaneously, with a limping economy lacking liquidity, credit and spending, further deflation is experienced.

Governments are left with few options in such circumstances. In order to rehabilitate the economy, liquidity is injected, via deficit spending, and 'printing' money. This subsequently promotes further financialisation and greater reliance on credit to boost growth in order to stave off deflation. Thus, this is a cyclic phenomenon.

The net effect thereof, is the refinancing of past debt burdens in greater magnitudes with each iteration. Consequently, this requires greater expansions of credit to create diminishing returns in economic growth. Ultimately, a negative-sum game.

The more returns continue to diminish, the greater the incentives compound for non-financial businesses to combat deflation by investing in intangible financialised instrumentation. Such endeavours include automation, technological advancement and financial innovation. Thus, greater investment in technological advancement and financial incentives result in a confluence of market forces. This is a trend which has fuelled investment in FinTech.

GENERAL-PURPOSE TECHNOLOGY

A technology that emerges which has the ability to transform an economy or alter societies through its impact thereon is known as a General-purpose Technology (GPT).

GPTs meet three critical criteria.

1. Pervasive (Ubiquity vs. Certainty)

2. Subject to improvement over time (Componentisation, Standardisation & Commoditisation)

3. Enables further innovation (Higher-order Systems)

Historically, GPTs have included technological innovations such as the wheel, the steam engine and electricity (see Chapter 2: Capital Evolution). In contemporary terms, GPTs include computers, the internet and artificial intelligence. In their notable book, 'Economic Transformations: General Purpose Technologies and Long-Term Economic Growth,' published in 2005, economists Richard Lipsey, Kenneth Carlaw and Clifford Bekhar stipulated that GPTs represent singular, recognisable generic technologies which when initially introduced, are subject to a great deal of improvement. However, as these technologies improve, they become broadly used and indelibly transformative over the economy and society. Thus, highlighting a principal characteristic thereof, in which GPTs may be exploited for a variety of different uses and therefore prompt, as well as enable innumerable spill over effects.[425]

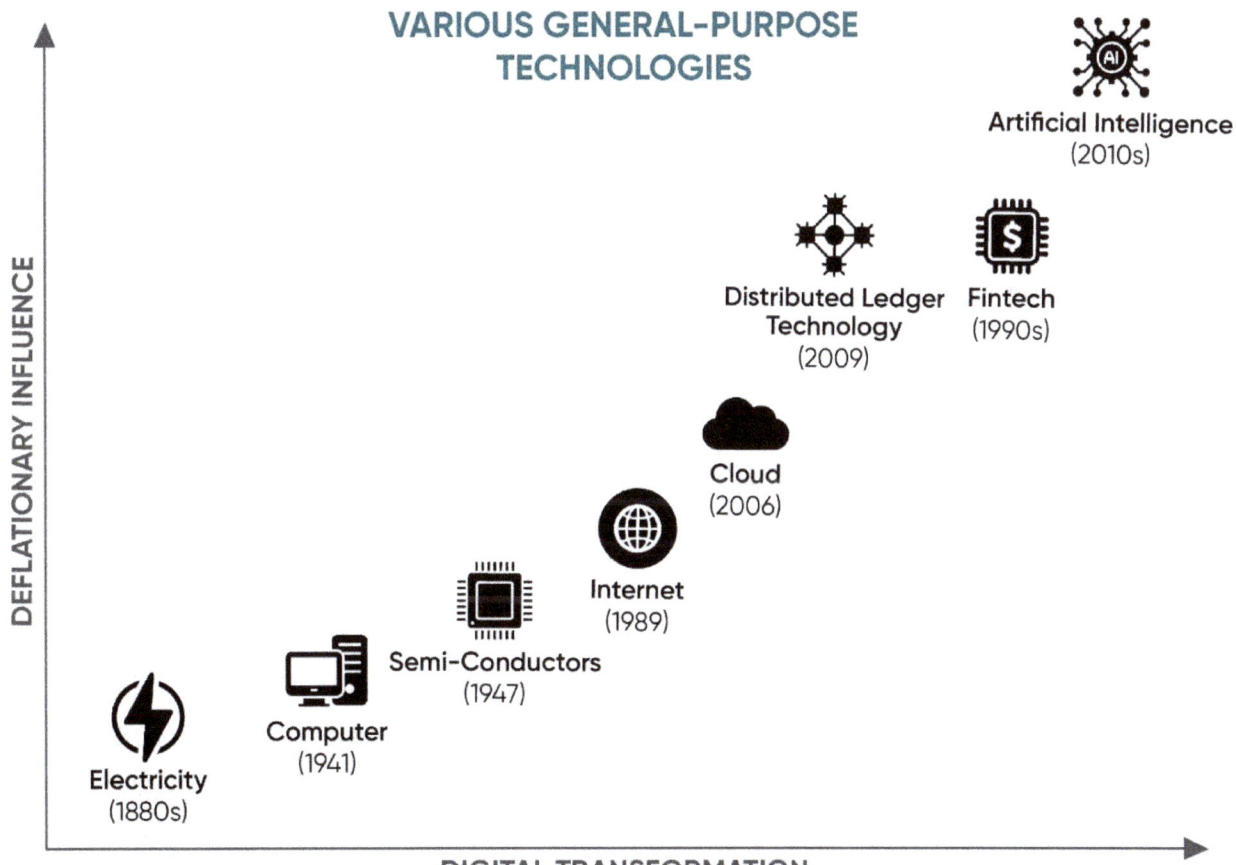

Fig 17.1 Instrumental General-purpose Technologies in Digital Transformation

Essentially, GPTs are instrumental in enabling *creative destruction* (see Creative Destruction, Chapter 2: Capital Evolution).

Leadership in GPTs represents an opportunity to establish an indirect commanding position over every downstream industry, which is affected by these technologies (via Tower & Moat Strategy & Information Asymmetry). This is facilitated via the asymmetrical relationship between the principal and every cascading participant in the ecosystem. Thus, leadership in GPTs additionally enables biases to be embedded within. This enables GPTs such as AI to become the harbingers of 'Authoritarian Capitalism,' should it be exported to external markets.

As FinTech becomes increasingly industrialised through the *economy of platforms*, embedded finance capabilities and machine-to-machine commerce, via the *economy of things,* will likely enable a future where FinTech may become broadly recognised amidst the ranks of GPTs. In a comparable manner to which electricity and computing have been commoditised (see Chapter 2: Capital Evolution), it is probable that FinTech and the enablers thereof, such as Distributed Ledger Technologies (Fig 17.1) will be formally recognised and exploited as such.

THE FUTURE IS DEFLATIONARY

Inflation erodes purchasing power requiring greater volumes of money and credit, whereas efficiencies derived through technology such as speed, automation, energy and waste reduction, as well as convenience are increasingly deflationary.[426]

In considering the inflationary forces of our present economic system, natural resources which supply our energy reserves are increasingly constrained. As the global money supply is inflated, the relative price of supply-constrained resources increase. As vital resources such as crude oil and coal rise in price, the spill over effects on the global economy become increasingly inflationary. These increases cascade through global supply chains and is ultimately reflected in the *consumer*, as well as *retail price indices*.

In order to remain competitive and promote velocity, businesses respond by cutting costs wherever possible. An increasingly attractive vehicle for doing so is in the greater exploitation of digital channel development in order to substitute for legacy business models. Examples of this include, developing an app to sell goods online, in lieu of maintaining a bricks-and-mortar store or embracing targeted advertising, via social media channels, in lieu of print media or televised marketing. These examples demonstrate an attempt to reduce costs in order to combat inflationary forces. The key to achieving such in these approaches is dependent on establishing primacy over customer relationships and exploiting the data generated therefrom.

Over the longer term, energy generation is expected to pivot towards renewable and sustainable sources such as wind, tidal, solar and eventually nuclear fusion. In the interim however, technology which enables efficient consumption of non-renewable sources is critical to our long-term survival. In response to this, there has been a rapid shift from internal combustion engines to electric vehicles with widespread government support in many advanced economies in the late 2010s and early 2020s.

As with conventional monetary policy and economic frameworks, businesses primarily run on information asymmetry (see Information Asymmetry, Chapter 10: Financialisation). The digital revolution and the necessity to prevail against inflation reinforces this trend. Thus, with the explosion in data generated, via e-commerce, social media, cloud computing, and indeed FinTech amongst others, the rise of data-driven technology companies and platforms has grown exponentially. The rise in data commodification through surveillance capitalism has set the world on an unprecedented economic trajectory. As the Internet of Things, Artificial Intelligence and Distributed Ledger Technologies become increasingly sophisticated, as well as pervasive, the resulting *economy of things* will undoubtedly drive greater economic outputs with fewer economic inputs. The "things" in this context are economic inputs as resources are invested in their development. These follow the natural pattern of commoditisation. Through competition and proliferation, the standard of living is improved, while the associated costs, thereof, face downward pricing pressure (see

Commoditisation, Chapter 2: Capital Evolution). Thus, increasingly deflationary. Therefore, it should be reasonable to conclude that much of technology's deflationary impact lies ahead of us, rather than behind us.

Consider waste disposal and sanitation services in a smart city environment, in contrast to that of an urban centre, in which municipal workers and vehicles are employed to perform these functions. In the former, autonomous electric vehicles and AI-driven robotics may efficiently perform these functions at peak performance perpetually, as well as at times convenient to prevent congestion for the city's inhabitants and commuters. In addition, this can be achieved without the necessity to eat or sleep. In such circumstances, the displacement of human labour costs, in the form of potential disputes, medical benefits and absences due to illness or vacations among other inefficiencies are abraded. The reduced labour is offset to some extent by the labour necessary to produce the vehicles, machinery and infrastructure to facilitate this system. Moreover, service, maintenance and security would be necessary to keep the process functional. The additional labour may well be at a higher cost, thus, further offsetting the deflationary effect.

This draws parallels with human-driven markets, which are often limited by resources and divergences caused by constraints that may be otherwise overcome through exploiting the appropriate technology. Over time however, commoditisation driven by competition results in the proliferation of the technology and through syndicating the costs thereof, thus, reinforces the deflationary effect.

AI AGENCY

Applying this paradigm by allowing AI agents to engage in trade and value exchanges would require a framework capable of facilitating discourse by replicating the characteristics of traditional markets although differ by virtue of existing within a digital sphere. In the short-term, algorithmic action is likely to continue in supplementing human decision-making. However, at some future juncture investors will likely have to decide whether or not to relinquish decision-making power to algorithmic protocols. Consequently, the rules-based order underpinned by the rule of law may be applied, although functioning as algorithmic constraints within a realm designed and purposely built to be far more effective, as well as "smarter" and leaner from its inception. In addition, it remains arguable as to whether markets can function effectively in an exclusively algorithmically-governed arena. By way of example, for each transaction in equities trading there is a buyer and a seller each of whom has a different viewpoint on the value and the future value of the stock. If all investors were to use the identical algorithms and data, trade would likely cease. If the algorithms differ however, whereby each is customised to each investor, this becomes an aid to the investor who is making a decision by proxy. Alternatively, identical algorithms and data may produce differing results as a consequence of *fuzzy logic*, whereby results may be influenced by the random nature thereof.

Consequently, measures would be required to limit the potential impact of AI agency. The enabling technologies required to cultivate such a framework exist in the form of APIs, common standards (ISO 20022), Distributed Ledger Technologies, the Internet of Things and Artificial Intelligence. Collectively, these form the essential components which may be co-opted to cultivate an ecosystem governed by a framework which enables AI agents to search, engage in price discovery and trade with one another algorithmically. Such an ecosystem would likely function as a series of higher-order systems, featuring service directories, transaction repositories, statistical references and archival collateral. Essentially, a perpetually growing record of immutable economic activity, referenced canonically, while engaged in trade and commerce. Conceptually, this is synonymous with the notion that 'Money is memory,' as advocated by leading monetary theorist, Narayana Kocherlakota (see Money is Memory, Chapter 14: Tokenisation).[427]

Akin to conventional economies, a digital economy would progressively accrue value as the transaction volumes aggregated and the complexity thereof amplified. Through a digital fabric, competing services may be price discovered, replicating the insurance industry's aggregator business model (see

Aggregators, Chapter 15: Economy of Things). Individuals may participate by co-opting instrumentation, such as digital wallets using the prevailing smart-tech (phones; immersive wearables; ingestibles and implants). Via 5G and its successors, smart sensors, AI-driven edge intelligence and robotics all the while collecting data, collectively facilitate interaction, response and participation with human actors within a hybrid economy. In this instance, the rules of such a system, would likely be enforced, via smart contracts, and trust, therein, would be fostered through decentralised adjudication by co-opting DLTs. Should economic activity persist on this basis, data and transactions would be recorded chronologically within, thus providing the allegorical record to become progressively smarter, more efficient and increasingly useful intuitively, interactively and iteratively. Consider examples which exist within primary foreign exchange (FX) venues, whereby market-makers are already able to access real-time prices at millisecond-denominated intervals. Project Rio, an application developed by the BIS Innovation Hub, enables its entire market order book to be monitored at one-hundred-millisecond intervals.[428]

Should an autonomous AI agent require information regarding a specific product, commodity or service in a specific region, a discovery process may utilise the computational resources of the network to investigate and discern the appropriate vendor and price to fulfil the requirement. In an ideal scenario, each data provider, sensor and service provider within the ecosystem should be able to hierarchically disseminate and defray its costs, via the requestor's inquiry. In doing so, thereby creating economies of scale, while discovery results are recorded. This should enable subsequent requests to benefit from the historical record, driving greater efficiencies in resource expenditure and improved price performance. This is conceptually comparable to the process by which Machine Learning algorithms behave, via surveillance capitalism.

In an IoT and 5G enabled economy, both the volume of, as well as the velocity at which data is generated and transmitted is expected to be unprecedented. In such circumstances, data which is generated will rapidly become outdated prior to it being adequately harnessed by people who could potentially benefit from it. It is, thus, essential to cultivate the capability to collect, process and store data in a manner in which the value thereof may be monetised as broadly as possible within a short feedback loop. It is unlikely such a feat would ever be possible without the use of powerful computational capacity and analytics capabilities. However, the full value potential would additionally be exceedingly difficult to achieve in isolation. Hence, the necessity for an ecosystem centric capability in which AI agents may share data, insights and interact seamlessly.

In such circumstances, maintaining exclusive human agency over economic activity would be tenuous. The velocity at which transactions occur and the limitations in sustaining meaningful human interactions, creates an imbalance in the nature of discourse therewith (see Dunbar's Number, Chapter 4: Surfacing Utility). By contrast, surrendering agency to an AI is likely to leave people uncomfortable, unless the rules of the system are strictly governed by human actors. China's model for authoritarian capitalism and algorithmic governance could evolve into such under the direction of the CCP (see Authoritarian Capitalism, Chapter 16: The Rise of China). This is of particular pertinence, should China assume either a greater, or a leadership role in global economic and monetary affairs. This is a posture reliant on uninhibited access to data.

In practice, we as human beings surrender agency to others whenever we travel by air, train or sea. However, in doing so, there is an expectation of mutual peril in which we take comfort that those in charge, do so in both our best interests and theirs. Furthermore, trust in travel is incrementally established over time in observing the statistics surrounding accidents. Should a disastrous incident occur, trust therein will likely evaporate. In the wake of *nine-eleven*, tall building projects and air travel stagnated for years until trust was incrementally rebuilt (see Nine-eleven, Chapter 13: Global Trade Rails). Thus, incrementally cultivating trust in algorithmic protocols and AI agents will likely follow a similar pattern, whereby confidence, therein, is slow to build and will rapidly diminish should a failure materialise (see Confidence, Chapter 6: Money). This will undoubtedly manifest, even if such is the result of a minor glitch surfacing which is expediently identified and remediated, thereafter. However, trust therein will likely suffer irreparable reputational damage should such adverse effects be a consequence of Moral Hazard (see Moral Hazard, Chapter 10: Financialisation).

DATA SOVEREIGNTY & PRIVACY

Never before has the issue of data sovereignty and individual privacy been as greatly challenged by advances in technology than that of the IoT and post-5G era. In a 4G and pre-IoT world, individuals may elect to refrain from embracing digital services and smart devices. Big Tech grew large through *runaway leadership,* via *information asymmetry*, cultivating an environment in which it could harness *learning effects,* and thus, foster *network effects* and eventually make them largely self-reinforcing. *Learning effects* are of value to consumers, whereas *network effects* are of greater value to businesses. Tech giants benefitted through establishing primacy over the customer relationship and cultivating *network effects,* as a result of value gained through *learning effects* derived, therefrom.

Tech giants, such as Amazon, Google and Facebook, dominated the tech sphere and grew into behemoths predominantly through commodifying and exploiting their customers' data. This data was gleaned through the consumption of services on a voluntary basis. However, in an IoT and post-5G era where sensor technologies are constantly observing human interactions and behaviour, opting out is no longer an option. In this 'Orwellian' world, state actors, such as China, are eager to magnify the data absorption surface area in order to achieve a globally dominant position in GPTs, Artificial Intelligence and FinTech in particular. This approach exploits *instrumentarian* capabilities in order to achieve an economically superior position and, furthermore, use such to export its model for authoritarianism and social governance. While apparently successful, thus far within the strictures of an authoritarian régime, the acceptance of such power would be challenging to achieve in democratically run societies. Such approaches lack consideration for potential harm to the individual or the cost to the human aspect thereof. Thus, economic development on a global scale requires an accommodation in the overall approach.

Shielding or potentially eliminating an individual's exposure to such capabilities through reducing their digital footprint or through withdrawing from the digital realm, could be achieved by divesting oneself of smart devices, as well as either unsubscribing from, or electing not to register with digital service providers. Purchasing goods, as well as services and conducting banking, may all have been achieved face-to-face in the physical world. In the extreme, it may even be conceivably possible, although onerous, to conduct all of an individual's economic interactions and meet their obligations exclusively in cash.

However, by 2030 most of the workforce and a majority of economically active consumers are expected to be comprised of both digital natives, as well as highly digitally literate individuals. It should be expected that this is likely to be accompanied by a commensurate decline in the availability of cash in favour of digital alternatives, such as CBDCs (see War on Cash, Chapter 6: Money). This suggests that consumer appetites for automation and convenience are likely to vastly outweigh society's concerns surrounding individual privacy and anonymity (see Zuboff's Faustian Bargain, Chapter 15: Economy of Things). Hence, it is unlikely that an IoT, post-5G and increasingly immersive world will experience the level of resistance to privacy intrusion, via surveillance capitalism that society is increasingly expected to exhibit, as awareness thereof increases.

In addition, there are further factors to consider. In advanced economies, and the US, in particular, companies which engage in practices that ultimately result in circumstances from which either their customers or bystanders eventually suffer damages will usually be held accountable. In many instances, such business entities may face litigation in the wake of poor, unethical, or illegal business practice. Litigation may ensue on either an individual or class action basis for compensation or restitution. Enumerable precedents exist in which businesses have demonstrated reasonable measures including those limited by technology in order to argue that they are not culpable. Strategies of this nature have proven effective in a number of instances in order to avoid compensatory or punitive damages being awarded to plaintiffs.

In an advanced state of technological development, whereby AI-centric technologies, such as computer vision and decision engines, being fed data from IoT sensors and cameras, may be able to interpret and anticipate an incident and thus intercede in order to mitigate the danger in certain circumstances, it raises the question as to whether jurists would reasonably accept similar arguments in the future. In practice, verdicts may sway either way due to opposing experts disagreeing on what constitutes 'state of the art' technology. This is particularly salient, should one company possess a technology which is as yet unavailable to the general market. However, longer term, by applying a *first principles* approach to safety, using current and future technologies, the argument for an individual's privacy over society's collective wellbeing may be challenging to sustain. For the United States, however, cases are decided on an individual basis by juries. The fear of unpredictability of juries, thus, tends to sway companies towards embracing more conservative approaches. Consequently, this may have a decelerating effect on such an outcome coming to fruition in the short-to-medium term (see Decelerating Effects, Chapter 2: Capital Evolution).

ASYMMETRIC MONETARY SYSTEM

With the rise in globalisation, developments within the international arena have a greater impact worldwide. Such developments may manifest diplomatically, politically and economically. This has amplified the effects of the inherent flaws evident in the international monetary and financial system.

The demise of metallism in the 1970s brought about by the Nixon Shock, the failure of the Smithsonian Agreement and the collapse of the Bretton Woods system, resulted in a reliance on floating-exchange-rates to act as 'shock absorbers' for inflation-output volatility worldwide (see Depression, Chapter 8: Economic Cycles). The effectiveness, thereof, has been in persistent decline and deteriorated ostensibly since the GFC. This has challenged the canonical view of maintaining an asymmetric monetary system based on the dominant currency paradigm (DCP). This is a fundamental consequence of a growing and destabilising asymmetry becoming increasingly evident as a result, thereof.

GROSS DOMESTIC PRODUCT

In western advanced economies, particularly those typically considered to be high-income countries, GDP is reliant to a greater extent on domestic consumption, whereas in low-income countries, GDP is driven predominantly by net exports. This is illustrated by the formula for GDP:

$$Y = C + I + X + G$$

Y = Gross Domestic Product

C = Consumption

I = Private Investment

X = Net Exports

G = Government Spending

In high-income countries exports tend to be more expensive. A consequence of higher wages resulting is less competitive exports, whereas in low-income countries wages are competitive, thus, making exports attractive to external consumers.

Since domestic incomes are low and net exports are high, fiscal spending ("G") need not run a substantial deficit in order to keep the private sector in surplus (see Sectoral Balances below).

BOTTOMLESS PIT

August 15th 2021, marked the semi-centennial anniversary of the 'Nixon Shock.' A fifty-year experiment into the purely chartalism era of fiat money.

The absence of a tangible reserve asset pegged to currency for over half a century, has enabled the Federal Reserve to 'print' unconstrained volumes of dollars to supply every central bank in the world with the reserve currency. The volumes required to settle the *balance of payments* in international transactions has only grown with increased global trade.

The dominant currency paradigm (DCP) compels the incumbent hegemon (the United States) to run larger and larger trade deficits with other nations in order to supply them with liquidity (see Triffin's Dilemma, Chapter 12: Global Monetary System). This action, therefore, amplifies the decimation of blue-collar industries which seem to be convenient and expendable casualties. The sustained, yet gradual erosion, of US manufacturing, where outsourcing this portion of the economy and offshoring to other countries has functioned as an expedient instrument of exploiting a convenient solution to supply other nation states with dollars. It remains ambiguous as to whether this has been a deliberate strategy on the part of the US Government, or a consequence of corporate greed and financialisation, enabled by liberal trade policies. It may well be a combination of both, however, the end result is the same.

The net effect of these circumstances, has exacerbated US social and income inequality, whereby as their share of GDP has historically remained fairly consistent and stable in these sectors, the associated domestic employment levels within these industries has plummeted. This correlates with a shift from primary manufacturing towards prioritising high technology development. Domestic employees who have remained in these industries however, have experienced stagnation in wage growth (see Social Inequality below). Consequently, domestic industrial capabilities have suffered and compelled the United States to drive greater resources towards high-value endeavours.

This remains a complex issue, as at the national level, the loss of manufacturing jobs has been replaced by the increase in service-related employment. The unemployment rate, once the effects of the GFC had dissipated (ten-years-later), has remained fairly stable (~4%) in the US (ignoring perturbations due to the COVID-19 pandemic).[429] The US has experienced skill shortages at every level, as this is effectively near full employment (see Dual Mandate, Chapter 7: Central Banks). However, with diminished domestic production capacity, the United States' role as a net importer is reinforced and thus relies on domestic consumption ("C") and deficit spending ("G") in order to support GDP ("Y"). In order to sustain growth in domestic consumption, greater access to inexpensive credit is required to drive inflation (see Credit & Debt, Chapter 8: Economic Cycles).

SOCIAL INEQUALITY

Although employment levels remain consistently high, income and social inequality has distilled into a catalyst for the rise of extremist behaviour, which nurtures populism, nativism, tribalism and protectionism. This pattern usually results in the election of charismatic leaders who espouse divisive rhetoric to an increasingly receptive population of marginalised and desperate communities. These leaders, blinded by either extreme nationalist or socialist ideologies, raise tensions with other nations through trade wars, imposing exorbitant tariffs as they attempt to pander to their electorate support base. These attempts to create and safeguard employment in domestic industries previously outsourced results in inferior economic performance through uncompetitive market pricing. Ultimately, this leads to greater hardship for these industries through politically guided sponsorship or regulations biased towards domestic employment. These measures create a climate which is prejudicial towards exports and invites domestic competition from imported equivalents. In such circumstances, industries which find business conditions to be unfavourable may elect to divest themselves of domestic production in favour of external markets. This leads to greater shifts in skills competencies, industry capabilities and employment volatility accompanied by greater income inequality and furthermore may under extreme conditions provoke social unrest.

"PRINTING" MONEY

In order to provide access to inexpensive credit, the central banks within advanced economies, (the Fed in particular) increase the money supply by lowering interest rates and "printing" money, via monetary policy. The effects, thereof, are intended to be inflationary. The objective of which aside from driving GDP growth among others, is to act as a counterweight to deflationary forces in the economy. However, while much of the focus of technology's increasingly pervasive role in transforming society is discussed, analysed and examined, very little consideration is given to its deflationary consequences (see The Future is Deflationary above).

Through the evolution of capital, via innovations transforming into marketable goods, services and utilities, with each iteration of the commoditisation process, the intrinsic value thereof declines. Through competition, downward pressure on its subjective value is imposed, the effect of which is deflationary. Historically, this effect is gradual, however, with the vastly accelerated cadence of technological commoditisation and its increased penetration worldwide, the corresponding deflationary effects are increasingly apparent (see Chapter 2: Capital Evolution).

The monetarist theory ($MV = PQ$) illustrates the manner in which velocity is critical to promote growth in an economy. As the utility of everyday services is incrementally surfaced through technology, traditional non-digital entities are disintermediated. The intermediaries are actors who contribute to velocity, and through their displacement, velocity suffers.

While a decline in monetary velocity is not exclusively the result of technological advancement, the rise in technological modernisation since the mid-1990s certainly reinforces the pattern, thus, reinforcing a deflationary effect.

Examples include the deflationary effect that FinTech has brought about by reducing the cost of day-to-day banking activities. Prior to the smart phone and cloud era, managing direct debits, cross-border remittance and numerous banking activities would have to be conducted in-person in a bank branch or via an authenticated telephone call. Travel to, and from a bank, as well as the time expended to queue and to perform the tasks collectively represented expense and time commitments which may, today, be achieved at the customer's convenience from any location at any time. The relative costs of which are negligible by contrast to the previous practices. Thus, as technology becomes increasingly sophisticated, as well as pervasive, the marginal costs accrued in achieving the identical outcome tend to reduce, hence the impact is deflationary. A comparable argument could be made for the deflationary consequences of e-commerce as a contrast to bricks-and-mortar shopping. A vastly superior experience in terms of relative cost and time expenditure.

Historically, similar effects were evident through electrification which revolutionised production and lowered the essential (intrinsic) cost of producing goods. Comparable effects were evident through the invention of the internal combustion engine, which radically altered the cost and efficiency of transportation and logistics. All brought about by *creative destruction* and each rendering a corresponding deflationary effect.

In his book, 'The Price of Tomorrow: Why Deflation is Key to an Abundant Future,' published in 2020, Jeff Booth stated:

'Our economic systems were not built for a world driven by technology where prices keep falling. They were built for a pre-technology era when labour and capital were inextricably linked, an era that counted on growth and inflation, an era where we made money from scarcity and inefficiency. That era is over. But we keep on pretending that those economic systems still work.'[430]

- Jeff Booth, The Price of Tomorrow, 2020.

The lack of price stability of the US dollar, since the Bretton Woods system ceased, amplifies this effect whereby, as the dollar's value is diluted, so the demand increases. Dilution and demand has resulted in an explosion of credit in order to service the diminishing returns of traditional investment ("I"). Thus, speculation with credit has fuelled the seigniorage of financial institutions and amplified financialisation, thereby driving the necessary inflation required to promote economic growth and to aid in taxation. Consequently, this cultivates an economic conundrum in which perpetually creating greater volumes of debt is persistently required in order to combat deflation.

The practice of attempting to outrun deflation is known as reflation. However, without a means of stimulating velocity, reflation may be achieved exclusively through creating greater volumes of debt (see Chapter 8: Economic Cycles). This tactic tends to mask the symptoms of slowing growth through the expansion of credit in lieu of addressing the underlying cause. This is akin to managing the symptoms without attempting to cure the disease.

Since the demise of metallism, without a Gold Standard (or an equivalent supply-constrained reserve asset) to anchor and limit the expansion of credit, the artificial constructs of fiat money has seen no ceiling in expansion and effectively in the first one-hundred-years since the establishment of the Fed, 1913 - 2013, revealed a decline in the dollar's purchasing power by ~95%.

However, over the same period the standard of living has markedly improved. As new innovations have been commoditised, competition and mass production, thereof has imposed a deflationary effect. Illustrating this phenomenon is demonstrable when considering that a radio may have cost the retail consumer ~$200 in 1920, yet by 1930 only ~$35 and by 2020 ~$5. However, with the rate of technological commoditisation rapidly increasing, the rate of deflation requires greater and greater reflation in order to counter the effects thereof.

BLOOD IN THE WATER

By contrast to blue-collar industries and catalysed by a period of deregulation from the early 1980s to the mid-2000s, the financial services sector experienced exponential growth in its share of GDP. Employment and wages in the sector further fuelled income inequality from the opposing end of the spectrum.

While short and long-term debt cycles are inevitable in capitalist economic systems, the unconstrained expansion of credit by policy makers, political leaders and the inherent weakness of the chartalism paradigm, ensures that the magnitude of recessions and depressions are increasingly severe.

The remedies applied when these 'bubbles burst' and 'black swans' are born, are dovish interest rate policies and the monetisation of debt through quantitative easing, thereby risking hyperinflation. These policy influences have a temporary reassuring effect, however, fail to rehabilitate the economy. Thus, ensuring that a subsequent crisis, is increasingly severe, through the compounding effects of perpetually mounting and increasingly unserviceable debt burdens. In other words, comparable to a *Zeno's Dichotomy Paradox* (Fig 2.1), in deleveraging today, debt is not settled. It is simply refinanced in order to be dealt with in the future. Through central banks operating in this manner, time is essentially purchased, yet never paid for.

Since there is no limit to the quantity of fiat money that can be "printed," this behaviour may be perpetuated time and time again. While less immediately apparent to a reserve currency, no currency is immune to the ultimate effects thereof. With each iteration, confidence therein is diluted. However, with the immediate crisis averted, there remains little in the way of an incentive to unwind the debt burdens once these have been refinanced. Discipline is not something that the financial services community would welcome, particularly having reaped the benefits of free-reign for over half-a-century.

With each cyclic iteration, the resulting political tension geometrically amplifies the effects of Triffin's Dilemma, whereby domestic priorities and foreign policy obligations are at irreconcilable loggerheads.

The combination of these factors distils into circumstances in which developments within the US economy create significant spill over effects onto both the trade performance and the financial conditions of all other countries, even those with relatively limited direct exposure to the US economy. In an increasingly globalised economy, this paradigm is anachronistic and increasingly unsustainable.

DOMINANT CURRENCY PARADIGM

As a consequence of the dollar's dominance in global trade, developments in the US economy (discretionary monetary policy; economic performance; rising debt-to-GDP), particularly those which may affect the dollar's exchange-rate, tend to have a cascading (or spill-over) effect on the rest of the world (asymmetric relationship). This reflects a departure in macroeconomics from an open economic model in which export pricing is set in the producer's currency, in favour of the dominant currency paradigm (DCP). Under the DCP, export pricing is set in a 'vehicle currency' (principal global reserve currency).[431]

The widespread use of the US dollar in global trade invoicing and its prominence in global banking as well as finance are mutually reinforcing. With large volumes of trade being invoiced and paid for in dollars, holding dollar-denominated assets (treasuries) has commensurately risen. Increased demand for dollar assets reflexively diminishes their returns, which creates an incentive for businesses to borrow in dollars. The dollar's liquidity and perceived safety properties further encourage this practice. Consequently, businesses with dollar-denominated liabilities have an incentive to invoice in dollars to assist in reducing the currency misalignment between their revenues and liabilities (hence, global unit of account and standard of deferred payment). Greater dollar issuance by non-financial businesses and growing dollar funding for local banks corners central banks into accumulating substantial dollar reserves.

The net effect of these practices eventually amplifies the real burden of debt borrowed in dollars, while simultaneously reducing the value of collateral (assets) denominated therein. Ultimately, this posture distils into tighter credit conditions, which negatively impacts stronger businesses, however, results in weaker businesses defaulting. The latter of which is particularly prevalent in emerging market economies and even more likely to manifest under conditions of either domestic or global financial stress. This is a predicament experienced when floating-exchange-rates prevalent since the demise of the Bretton Woods System, adjust (as a result of dollar volatility), in an attempt to 'absorb the shock' of US domestic conditions and monetary policy. This position was advocated by then Governor of the Bank of England, Mark Carney in August 2019 in highlighting the growing asymmetry which is evidently destabilising the International Monetary and Financial System. [432]

In extreme instances such as depressions, countries outside of the United States which carry domestic debt denominated in US dollars endure the effects thereof as inflationary which subsequently limits policy makers' capabilities in response (see Depression; Unconventional Methods, Chapter 8: Economic Cycles). This constitutes a set of circumstances which creates incentives for developing and emerging market economies to trade and accrue debt in domestic currencies in lieu of US dollars. This, in essence, returns to the paradigm in broad alignment with an open economic model and thereby resisting the dominant currency paradigm. In practice, this presents a number of challenges given that major infrastructure projects such as dams, airports and power stations may require billions of dollars in financing. Raising substantial sums of capital for such endeavours would barely move the US market, given the dollar's standing and liquidity properties. However, raising large sums of capital in alternate currencies would likely provoke substantial volatility in global markets.

Although identified by Belgian-American economist Robert Triffin, more than fifteen-years after John Maynard Keynes's death, the effects of Triffin's Dilemma had been anticipated by Keynes. Hence, Keynes had advocated for the creation of 'Bancor' at the Bretton Woods conference in 1944.

Keynes had intended the imbalances of monetary asymmetry to be shouldered by Bancor as a supranational global reserve currency under the stewardship of an International Clearing Union (see Special Drawing Rights, Chapter 12: Global Monetary System). This would ensure that the imbalances incurred, could be shared among multiple nation states in lieu of a single hegemon. Keynes anticipated that an independent monetary authority was needed, to act as an 'Apex predator' to an ecosystem of central banks around the globe.

In the wake of the GFC, in his speech, entitled 'Reform the International Monetary System,' delivered on March 29th 2009, then governor of the People's Bank of China, Zhou Xiaochuan advocated for strengthening global currency controls under the stewardship of the IMF. Zhou Xiaochuan, openly and explicitly, named the dollar's reserve currency status as a contributing factor to the global savings and investment imbalances that had paved the way for the crisis. The governor's remarks are illustrated by the 'Global Savings Glut Hypothesis,' which draws correlations between Triffin's Dilemma and the excessive deficits the United States has to maintain in order to supply dollars to the world (see Twin Deficits below). He suggested that restoring confidence and preventing further imbalances could be achieved by incrementally deprecating the use of the US dollar as the global *medium of exchange*, in favour of SDRs issued by the IMF.

SECTORAL BALANCES

In macroeconomics, an examination of 'Sectoral Balances' illustrates the challenge presented by Triffin's Dilemma within the DCP, whereby the sum of all assets and liabilities, as well as all surpluses and deficits, must net zero.[433]

For every lender there must be an equivalent borrower, for every credit there must be a debit.

By examining the elements of GDP (see Gross Domestic Product above), the following formula (known as the 'magic equation') aids in illustrating this:

$(I - S) + (G - T) + (X - M) = 0$

I = Private Investment

S = Savings

G	=	Government Spending
T	=	Taxation
X	=	Exports
M	=	Imports

Which distils into 'Private Investment' less 'Savings' being the surplus or deficit of the private sector. 'Government Spending less Taxation' being the surplus or deficit of the Government. Finally, 'Exports less Imports' being the Foreign Surplus/Deficit. These sectoral constructs, when added, must net zero to balance. Thus, distilling into:

Private Domestic Sector + Government Surplus/Deficit + Foreign Surplus/Deficit = Zero

TWIN DEFICITS

Most countries, in order to run a private sector surplus are able to offset government deficit spending by running a trade surplus in order to net zero (see Gross Domestic Product above). The United States, however, is compelled to run a trade deficit with all other countries collectively, in order to supply dollar liquidity as reserve currency. As a result, in order to fulfil this obligation and to maintain its reserve currency status, the US must run larger public sector deficits in order to enable the private sector to run a surplus. If the US government run a surplus, the shortfall must be reconciled by the private and foreign sectors. Such circumstances, manifest in the form of domestic or global recessions respectively.

The US government as a consequence, tends to run larger and larger deficits by "printing" greater volumes of dollars to keep the private sector and foreign sector in surplus. The foreign sector surplus provides the world's dollar requirements, which in turn makes the US a net importer. The private sector surplus supports high incomes, which in turn supports domestic consumption. In order to net zero, this compels the government to run twin deficits (foreign

& domestic) by 'printing' money and spending it. The excessive printing of dollars places greater downward pressure on the dollar, undermining the value of reserves held by foreign governments (see Dominant Currency Paradigm above). Diminished confidence in the dollar is further reinforced when the associated debt monetised in order to "print money" reaches levels which are perceived to be too great to ever be repaid.

Thus, Zhou Xiaochuan further argued that the breakdown of the original Bretton Woods system was largely the result of refusing to adopt Keynes's Bancor concept. In addition, American economist James Bradford DeLong vocally asserted that on every point where Keynes was overruled by his American counterparts during the Bretton Woods negotiations, ultimately events have subsequently proven him to be correct.[434]

While Keynes was undoubtedly correct and Triffin as well as others have made comparable assertions, it is wise to consider this through a lens synonymous with the political climate of the era. These issues were highly political in Keynes's time and arguably even more political today.

NEW CHALLENGER

Since October 1st 2016, the Chinese Yuan (Renminbi) has been included in the basket of currencies which underpin the IMF's SDRs (see SDR Basket, Chapter 12: Global Monetary System). The IMF's recognition of China's rapidly growing economic power, has unequivocally enabled China to assert its influence over global monetary affairs and to play a substantial role in the global financial ecosystem. However, the decision to include a national currency in the SDR basket of a country which actively maintains capital account controls (see SAFE, Chapter 16: The Rise of China) in addition to persistently engaging in exchange-rate manipulation remains a concerning, and questionable judgement call on the part of the IMF. China's state-sponsored FinTech initiatives such as CIPS, the establishment of globally dispersed Renminbi clearing houses and its introduction of a CBDC have established the foundations for internationalisation of the Yuan. In conjunction with the IMF's decision to include the Yuan in the SDR basket, this may be construed as a weak signal that the internationalisation of the Yuan will be accompanied by allowing the currency to float, and to be exchanged freely. Collectively, these are strong signals that Chinese independence of dollar hegemony and immunisation against potential US extraterritorial sanctions are fundamental to its continued growth trajectory. The adoption of the Yuan as a reserve currency by Zimbabwe, is another clear, albeit a weak signal along these vectors.

In practice however, China's growth since acceding to the WTO has remained dependent on its ability to produce competitively-priced exports. Should its currency be allowed to float prematurely, RMB would likely appreciate to levels which price China's exports out of the market globally. Thus, it remains critical that China transition into a high-value innovation centre prior to easing capital account and exchange rate controls.

The *Exorbitant Privilege* of holding the principal reserve currency status has enabled the United States to assert its soft power influence and project its military, economic and monetary dominance around the globe. Consider the advantage of launching a military campaign into an overseas theatre and paying for any supplies that might be required locally in a currency which you are able to "print." By contrast, any other nation which attempts a similar action, is incapable of achieving parity, as payment is limited by its holdings of reserves denominated in the dominant nation's currency.

China, a large beneficiary of running a substantial trade surplus with the United States has experienced unprecedented growth in a relatively short period of time (see Chapter 16: The Rise of China). In an interview with former Czech president Václav Havel, Harvard Scholar Graham Allison, paraphrased the president's remarks as:

'The rise of China has happened so quickly that we have not yet had time to be astonished.'[435]

- Václav Havel, President of the Czech Republic (1993 - 2003).

China has emerged as a nimble and rapidly growing adversary to challenge the dominance of the United States as a global superpower.

China's desire for custodianship of principal reserve currency status is increasingly evident. Such status would enable China in accelerating the expansion of its 'empire' through the Belt and Road Initiative (BRI). The BRI is a multi-trillion-dollar project to rebuild the old 'Silk Road' trade route (see The Silk Road, Chapter 16: The Rise of China). Although modernised and far more elaborate and prolific in nature, the BRI comprises a land-based economic belt of several corridors stretching across Asia to Europe. In addition, it includes a number of sea lanes and Chinese controlled seaports strategically placed in surrounding coastal countries, stretching from the South China Sea throughout Malaysia, and from Pakistan through the Malacca Straight, as well as key ports in Africa. This is nothing short of the most ambitious imperial expansion strategy since the Macedonian conquests of Alexander the Great, although, arguably comparable to the 'building of roads' used to expand, fortify and control the Roman Empire (see The Belt & Road Initiative, Chapter 16: The Rise of China).

POLITICAL INERTIA

The sheer cost of this project and the projected length of time to realise its fruition brings into acute focus the nature of China's ambitions and surfaces significant flaws in Western societies' ability to compete therewith over the longer term. The nature of short-term executive leadership, which is limited to a maximum of two, four-year-terms in the United States assures that forming and fulfilling truly long-term strategies to assert US dominance and maintaining the continuity thereof, is beyond challenging. This is further inhibited by a pluralistic balance of power being distributed across three branches of government and a dual-party system, which in recent years has become increasingly polarised ideologically. A natural consequence of greater social inequality and divisive political agendas.

Both, China and Russia, have removed these barriers in recent years, assuring that their respective political leaders are able to serve for life. China's single party system further reinforces this structure of harnessing common values toward unwavering goals and ideology. The ability to both plan and execute long-term strategies, in contrast to Western rivals, is an immeasurably powerful advantage.

Dollar hegemony continues to impede China's ability to expand at a pace of its choosing. The reliance on US dollars to settle payments for BRI contractors and globally sourced commodities, as well as raw materials is a significant impediment. The internationalisation of Renminbi and a potential pivot to Renminbi as the principal global reserve currency in particular, would remove this hinderance.

Such an ambition is all but essentially dependent upon a dominant leadership position in FinTech and general-purpose technologies (GPTs), such as Artificial Intelligence, in order to secure China's role as the world's principal innovation centre. Since GPTs are capable of cascading through, and disrupting every downstream industry, leadership therein, would provide the epistemic advantage required to gain global consensus towards China's eligibility as a viable hegemonic successor.

It remains challenging to argue that centrally-controlled governments, such as those of China and Russia, are anything but highly effective. This is evident in their ability to carry out significant feats decisively and over remarkably short periods of time. However, in the contest for ideas, democracies remain the dominant incubators for innovation and the harbingers of creativity. The concepts of free thinking, as well as free enterprise, in addition to the mobility of resources, as well as capital remain indispensable characteristics of the western socio-economic model, which much of the world has embraced. Both, China and Russia, have not bought into this model. Furthermore, convincing the world that their model is superior will be a challenging endeavour. From China's perspective, its *instrumentarian* capabilities such as *social governance* and *authoritarian capitalism* may be viewed as the vehicles with which to nurture acceptance of this model, as it proliferates among nation states within its orbit, via the Belt & Road Initiative.

However, in order to ascend into a true innovation centre capable of rivalling that of the US, requires a freedom of thinking, debate and expression. This is absent from the Chinese model, where the important decisions are taken by a minority of powerful government leaders. Notwithstanding the extent to which these ideologies are polarised and thereby potentially inconceivable in reconciling the possibility that the western world may succumb to embracing the strictures of an authoritarian model in the future, it would be wise to remain cognisant as to the extent to which surveillance capitalism has realised success in the private sector. In western societies, this has largely been achieved, via clandestine means, and through pernicious influence. Thus, dismissing the risks of such *instrumentarian* capabilities being exploited to influence and engineer behaviour, and by extension usurp democracy, may be premature.

STATECRAFT

China has both geopolitical, as well as geo-economic, motivations which underpin its ambitious BRI strategy. General Secretary Xi Jinping is arguably the world's most competent and powerful leader among today's statesmen. His vision for a more assertive China has been broadly promoted amidst a backdrop of stagnating US domestic growth and trade friction, experienced during the Trump administration (2017 - 2021). These factors have contributed to China's accelerated exploration of new markets, signalling a recognition that sustaining long-term trade with the US is not an absolute.

The BRI combined with MIC 2025, the China Standards 2035 initiatives, as well as China's exploitation of ILC/'Tower & Moat' Strategies, via Internet Plus, in the absorption of foreign intellectual property and innovations, via IDAR, as well as 5G, represents a level of statecraft which far surpasses that of western powers. China seeks to take a leadership position in general-purpose technologies (GPTs) in addition to exploiting GPTs to escape the 'Middle-income trap.'

Akin to the manner in which tech giants grow their ecosystems through App Stores, Sandboxes and platform APIs, IDAR and 5G act as the sensing engines for new innovations (see Sensing Engines, Chapter 3: Ecosystems). CIPS and DC/EP (e-CNY), additionally fall within this category (see Chapter 14: Tokenisation). The China Standards 2035 initiative acts as a vehicle through which to establish an 'ecosystem originator' status by establishing a leadership position in key global standards through which it may define the control points for the downstream ecosystems which grow therefrom (see Genesis of an Ecosystem, Chapter 3: Ecosystems). Internet Plus, MIC 2025 and the BRI are vehicles through which to scale the downstream ecosystems, as well as market the goods and services which are derived therefrom. Furthermore, for China the BRI in particular represents a counterweight to the United States' 'Pivot to Asia' strategy, as well as a vehicle through which China may cultivate new markets while boosting China's domestic incomes and consumption.

China's BRI is additionally critical to promote economic development in its western province of Xinjiang, as well as securing its long-term energy supplies from Central Asia, as well as the Middle East. This is particularly critical to overcome China's vulnerability to energy supply disruptions, via the Malacca Strait (see The Malacca Dilemma, Chapter 16: The Rise of China).

Furthermore, the BRI is critical to China's strategy to restructure its economy in order to efficiently deploy surplus capacity, a factor which may prevent China from transitioning beyond the middle-income band (see The Middle-income Trap, Chapter 16: The Rise of China). Key to realising such an outcome is through the achievement of productivity gains, via innovations fuelling automation, technology and finance (AI, FinTech and Financialisation) which are increasingly necessary to offset overcapacity in order to sustain a GDP surplus in the economy. A posture which places the west in a precarious position with regards to data privacy, whereby protecting anonymity and personal freedoms inhibits the ability to make greater advances in AI development. AI advancement remains critically dependent on access to greater volumes of highly correlated and enriched data. China's ideology which places value on the collective at the expense of the individual, enables it to harvest and mine data free of these hindrances. Thus, in the contest for a globally dominant position in AI development, western powers are likely relegated to assume a secondary role.

DE–DOLLARISATION

The impact of enforcing foreign policy, via extraterritorial sanctions, in addition to subjecting other nation states to US externalities, lends itself to creating a climate conducive to fostering systemic resistance (see Chapter 11: Hegemonic Dominance). This sentiment proliferates among global actors which refuse to fall victim to the economic damage that ensues from defying the US. This has led to the creation of alternative international payment rails (see Chapter 13: Global Trade Rails), which represent one of a number of strong signals that the asymmetrical relationship the US maintains with the rest of the world has been leveraged beyond a tolerable threshold.

In addition, much of this behaviour is politically motivated, emanating from long-standing ideological rivalries and power-struggles amidst a backdrop of economic volatility and trade friction. This has been persistently exploited, opportunistically, in an attempt to dethrone the United States' role as a source of moral conscience and a global law enforcer. There should also be no doubt that China's ambitions extend towards assuming a greater role in global affairs.

Given China's role as the world's largest industrial manufacturer since 2011, and its corresponding market demand for ~53% of global commodities supply annually (2011 - 2019 Avg.), the attraction to displace the dollar as the global unit of account is of increasing priority. Purchasing raw materials denominated in RMB, and selling finished goods denominated in dollars, being the ideal interim objective.

In alignment with these vectors, comparable to an overly-constrained system either ordered or complex, systemic resistance is evident through the development of alternative systems (CIPS, SPFS, INSTEX & SEPA) which have emerged (see Chapter 13: Global Trade Rails). While such behaviour is to be expected from rivals, it is the emergence of alternatives developed by allies, which is the most compelling indicator that the established orthodoxy is experiencing a substantial metamorphosis (see Apex Predator Hypothesis, Chapter 4: Surfacing Utility). A metamorphosis forged within a chrysalis enabled by state-sponsored FinTech initiatives and innovations accelerated, via the exploitation of greater standardisation, such as ISO 20022.

While the emergence of alternative payment rails appear to be centred exclusively surrounding the means of exchanging value, via payment infrastructure on the globe, the development, thereof, as mechanisms to exchange value outside of US dollar-denominated reserves is of greater significance. This pattern of behaviour suggests a resistance to dollar hegemony in conducting the world's business. Thus, creating an immunisation against the cascading (spill over) effects of US domestic conditions and policies, translating into global volatility (see Dominant Currency Paradigm above). A consequence of this erodes the extent to which the US is able to run current account deficits. This, in turn, places greater pressure on the domestic US economy to make up the shortfall or face a contraction in GDP (see Sectoral Balances above). In addition, the US would likely experience unprecedented inflation as a consequence of no longer being able to export such, via dollar-denominated securities issuance. A contraction in GDP coupled with ballooning inflation, would further reinforce diminished confidence in the dollar as demonstrable through past precedents (see Guns & Butter; Dollar Confidence Crisis, Chapter 10: Financialisation).

DEATH BY A THOUSAND CUTS

Resistance to the use of dollars is likely to permeate among nation states wishing to circumvent US controlled payment rails, as well as those which may have either lost or believe confidence in the dollar itself is in decline. The latter being brought about by mounting sovereign debt burdens accrued since the GFC and amplified by the COVID-19 pandemic. A posture which cultivates the necessity to seek out an alternative *medium of exchange*, global *unit of account* and in particular, a robust *store of value*.

In 2009, then-Russian President, Dmitry Medvedev, called for a supranational currency to displace the US dollar as the principal global reserve currency, at the G8 summit in L'Aquila, Italy. Medvedev presented the sample prototypes of a 'unity in diversity' coin minted in Belgium to the G8 leaders at the summit.[436]

In 2010, a report compiled and released by the United Nations Conference on Trade and Development, called for abandoning the US dollar as the principal global reserve currency.

'The dollar has proved not to be a stable store of value, which is a requisite for a stable reserve currency'[437]

- *U.N. World Economic and Social Survey, 2010.*

In July 2014, China, in conjunction with Brazil, Russia, India and South Africa, announced the formation of a $100 billion 'New Development Bank,' to be headquartered in Shanghai. In 2015, the Brazil, Russia, India, China and South Africa (BRICS) New Development Bank, proposed disbursements in national currencies. In April 2020, at the annual board of governors meeting of BRICS finance ministers, the bank's president, K.V. Kamath, conveyed that in 2019, a quarter of the $15 billion of financial aid was denominated in local currencies. Kamath exclaimed that the BRICS had no intention of destabilising the dollar however,

'fifty-percent (of projects) should be local currency financed.'

- *Kundapur Vaman Kamath, President, BRICS New Development Bank, 2020.*

This highlights the sway in international sentiment that emerging market economies have adopted in the evolving geopolitical landscape. The BRICS countries have expressed a commitment to trading in national currencies. While the magnitudes, thereof, may be modest in value, the challenge to the status quo is of significance. Extra-systemic finance arrangements of this nature while representative of relatively unsubstantial capital sums, will undoubtedly create the platform upon which others may be attracted away from dollar-denominated finance infrastructure and institutions.

In anticipation of dollar volatility and an alternative global reserve currency potentially emerging, a number of nations states have embarked on a strategy to fortify their reserves by increasing holdings in gold (see Gold Reserves, Chapter 9: Gold). A behaviour no different to that of any actor divesting itself of an asset class in which confidence is diminished, or amidst a climate of uncertainty (see Exorbitant Privilege, Chapter 13: Global Trade Rails).

This is evident through Turkey rapidly acquiring gold in 2017, and continuing on an ambitious bullion acquisition trajectory throughout 2018.[438] In his speech at the opening ceremony of the Global Entrepreneurship Congress, held in Istanbul on April 16th 2018, Turkish President, Recep Tayyip Erdoğan, suggested that international loans should be made in (or based on) gold, in lieu of US dollars. A position he claimed, he'd proposed at an earlier G20 summit.[439]

Russia's acquisition of gold, exceeding a notable threshold of two-thousand metric tonnes in reserve holdings, and a simultaneous reduction of its reserves held in US treasuries to a record low in 2018,[440] represents a compelling signal that Russia (a close ally of China) may view any future *balance of payments* to be settled either in gold, or potentially in an alternative currency or instrument outside of those denominated in US dollars.

For a number of years, China has been Iran's largest customer for oil exports.[441] With Iran severed from the SWIFT system, an alternative payment channel and *medium of exchange* is required to enable continued trade. Gold bullion has functioned as a convenient medium for facilitating transactions of this nature, prior to CIPS becoming an operational alternative. Unlike the US dollar and the SWIFT system, the US and other western countries have neither control over, nor visibility of gold traded between nations. Although under the terms of its Articles of Agreement, gold holdings and transactions are required to be reported to the IMF by member nations.

Gold is tangible, free of digital interference and largely untraceable. It cannot be hacked, 'frozen' or interfered with electronically. Gold offers a degree of anonymity which mitigates repercussions, via 'sanctionable' conduct. Gold, additionally, provides shielding from the deflationary and inflationary effects of market conditions, as well as monetary and fiscal policy influences, making it an attractive *medium of exchange* for international settlements. These practices are consistent with the historical precedent observed under the *price-specie flow mechanism* (see Chapter 9: Gold). The mechanism, described the practice used to periodically settle the *balance of payments* in gold bullion between nation states. Since the US dollar became a proxy for gold under the Bretton Woods System and the British Pound (and other major currencies) a proxy for gold under the Gold Standard prior, it thus, stands to reason that in order to circumvent the dollar, a return to direct gold transactions between dissenting nations would serve as a logical extra-systemic practice, at least in the interim.

Although a practice of this nature may be construed as a means of mere circumvention, it may additionally represent weak signals synonymous with 'the crisis sub-phase' of hegemonic transition. This is evident in the characteristics of inter-state rivalries and the emergence of new configurations of power (see Hegemonic Decline, Chapter 11: Hegemonic Dominance).

The combination of diminishing reserves held in dollar-denominated treasuries and significant increases in reserves held, as well as transactions settled in gold bullion, is an unequivocal challenge to the US dollar's status as the principal global reserve currency. These behaviours are clearly the result of growing concern that the United States' influence over the global monetary system as a means of enforcing foreign policy (see Extraterritorial Sanctions, Chapter 13: Global Trade Rails) is not a tolerable position for China, Russia and a number of dissenting nations. It additionally echoes the behaviours of France, the Netherlands and other nation states in the 1960s and early 1970s, redeeming bullion for dollars (gold demonetisation) in the face of the United States' excessive debt financing practices under the Bretton Woods System (see Exorbitant Privilege, Chapter 13: Global Trade Rails).

SWAP AGREEMENTS

In 2014, China and Russia signed a three-year currency swap agreement worth 150 billion Yuan (approx. $24.5 billion). The bilateral agreement was renewed for a further three-years in 2017 and again in 2020. The swap agreement enables either country to access the other's currency directly, without the necessity to intermediate transactions, via the US dollar (see Swap Lines, Chapter 5: Payments).[442] Russia's strategic relations with China deepened after the 2014 partnership and energy centred agreements were signed. Unilateral US extraterritorial sanctions impeded Russian companies, such as Rusal Aluminium, from accessing the dollar-based financial system in 2017, and subsequently Rosneft Oil in 2020. Since then, the US has imposed over thirty active financial (and trade) sanctions that sever access to the Fed. Each have severely targeted and destabilised weaker economies, such as those of Iran, Iraq and Venezuela.

Russia has continually advocated for currency swap agreements to be drawn with various trading partners. The Eurasian Economic Union (EEU) with Armenia, Belarus, Kazakhstan, Kyrgyzstan in particular. The EEU has a projected population of approximately 183 million and a GDP of approximately $5 trillion, seventy-percent of which is denominated in Russian Rubles and local currencies. Several Central and West Asian countries have expressed an interest in joining this union. Vietnam engaged in a bilateral trade agreement with the EEU, which subsequently realised savings in exchanges and charges as a result of disintermediating the US dollar.

'It is convenient for trades involving imports of bulk commodity goods such as crude oil, energy and military equipment from Russia. As some of those goods are subject to US unilateral sanctions, it can be a way for Chinese enterprises to avoid secondary sanctions'

- *Jiang Yi, Deputy Director of Russian Studies, Chinese Academy of Social Sciences, 2020.*

'As cooperation between China and Russia continues to strengthen, the trend will become more prominent, shedding the dominance of the US dollar in international trade settlements'

- *Song Kui, President of the Contemporary China-Russia Regional Economy Research Institute, Northeast China's Heilongjiang Province, 2020.*

India engaged in a currency swap agreement with the United Arab Emirates, as well as a $75 billion currency swap with Japan. Furthermore, India agreed a $400 million currency swap agreement with a number of South Asian countries. India has since published mediated rates of exchange for Turkish and Korean currencies. Turkey embarked in trading in national currencies with both China and Russia. Russia has, additionally, proposed pursuing trade denominated in Euros, directly with the EU.

The consequences of US extraterritorial sanctions, monetary policy asymmetry and exchange rate pass-through, via the DCP, has manifested in numerous affected countries having established ties with China and Russia for trade and economic sustainability. Russia engaged in the sale of Venezuelan crude oil. China procured Iranian crude initially with gold and since integrating Iran with CIPS, has purchased crude with RMB denominated payments. An arrangement initiated, via the Iran-China silk route agreements (see Belt & Road Initiative, Chapter 16: The Rise of China). China has since become Iran's largest trading partner. Iran has, furthermore, diversified trade with Afghanistan and traded oil with India, settling payment for crude in gold bullion.

These measures represent a move to inoculate nation states against US influence and monitoring via the global monetary system. Furthermore, this facilitates a systemic circumvention in order to shield against the dollar being weaponised as a means of enforcing extraterritorial sanctions. However, this additionally enables state actors to assume greater control over their domestic monetary policy, rather than reflexively adjusting policy and exchange rates to insulate US externalities via economic asymmetry. Additionally, the measures represent a mitigation against a potential loss of confidence in the dollar's perceived standing as a store of long-term value. The latter being a consequential loss of confidence, which is symptomatic of the multi-trillion-dollar expansion of the US dollar money supply since the GFC. A posture further reinforced by the unprecedented levels in the US debt-to-GDP ratio. The ratio climbed from 106% in March 2020 to an unprecedented level of 138% by the close of June 2020. The latter being a consequence of lockdown measures in response to the COVID-19 pandemic which laid siege to the global economy.

THE PRECIPICE

In October 2020, IMF Managing Director, Kristalina Georgieva, called for an intervention in what she described as '*A New Bretton Woods Moment.*'[443] This coincided with the US national debt having reached a new all-time high of ~$27 trillion. A level greater than half of annual global economic output (average global GDP annually).

'Today we face a new Bretton Woods moment. A pandemic that has already cost more than a million lives. An economic calamity that will make the world economy 4.4% smaller this year and strip an estimated $11 trillion of output by next year. And untold human desperation in the face of huge disruption and rising poverty for the first time in decades. Once again, we face two massive tasks: to fight the crisis today— and build a better tomorrow.'

- Kristalina Georgieva, IMF Managing Director, October 2020.

These factors have incentivised and prompted other countries to engineer circumvention mechanisms to disintermediate the US dollar and the influence of the United States from global trade. The IMF's call, stemming from a desire to fortify the global financial safety net and broker a more pluralistic balance through global macro-prudential co-operation. Essentially, a departure from financial system asymmetry which has been prevalent historically amongst monetary hegemonies (Triffin's Dilemma). Such mechanisms present tremendous opportunities for FinTech to enable and capitalise on the fluid geo-economic climate and evolving geopolitical landscape. This is, additionally, commensurate with a growing appetite for frictionless cross-border payment mechanisms and indeed, even the currency being transacted seeking out greater stability as a long-term store of value.

In the 1970s, in the wake of the Nixon Shock and the demise of the Bretton Woods system, the world capitulated in accepting the demise of metallism in the face of the United States' uni-polar monetary system and uncontested hegemonic power. In such circumstances, the international monetary and financial system continued through maintaining the *pretence* that nothing had essentially changed (see Nixon Shock, Chapter 12: Global Monetary System). In so doing however, the continued practices surrounding excessive debt financing via twin deficits exacerbated by the GFC and the COVID-19 pandemic has pushed this paradigm beyond retrievable limits. Compounded by the accelerating cadence of technological advancement and deflationary digital proliferation, these limits are being further stretched beyond any form of tolerance. As the parenthesis surrounding these opposing inflationary and deflationary forces broadens, there should be little doubt that eventually the system must succumb. Consider a balloon which is inflated continually, until it eventually bursts.

Since such an outcome is all but a certainty, unlike in the 1970s, the growing economic strength of non-US actors and the availability of commoditised technology capabilities, offers the means with which to create a viable alternative to the US-led financial system. Thus, prompting a 'tectonic shift.'

TECTONIC SHIFT

Central banks around the globe generally hold sixty-percent of reserves in US dollars and twenty-five to thirty-percent of foreign currency reserves in Euros. Reserves are typically held in US dollar-denominated Treasury Securities and Euro-denominated Securities respectively.[444] In order to meaningfully displace the dollar as the principal global reserve currency, an alternative bond market featuring the infrastructure and the instruments to support primary liquidity, dealers, auctions, settlement and payment, as well as repo would be required. Such an infrastructure, of sufficient maturity to displace that of the Fed and Wall Street, apart from that of the United Kingdom, doesn't yet exist to a comparable maturity in China or other countries in its immediate orbit. With Europe's loss of Britain's financial infrastructure following Brexit, the European Union is expected to embark on a number of initiatives to create an alternative bond market capable of rivalling that of the United States. It is increasingly probable that China will endeavour to follow suit, as evidenced through China's CIPS system being designed to enable international trade in RMB denominated securities. China's monetary internationalisation is further reinforced by RMB's addition to the IMF's SDR basket and its release of DC/EP Central Bank Digital Currency (e-CNY), with accompanying payment system in 2020 (see Chapter 14: Tokenisation).[445]

Most crucially, China's rapid and substantial acquisition of gold coupled with the aforementioned instrumentation and initiatives illustrates a compelling agglomeration of the necessary infrastructure to fortify its ability to take a leadership role in the global economy and the financial system in the longer-term.

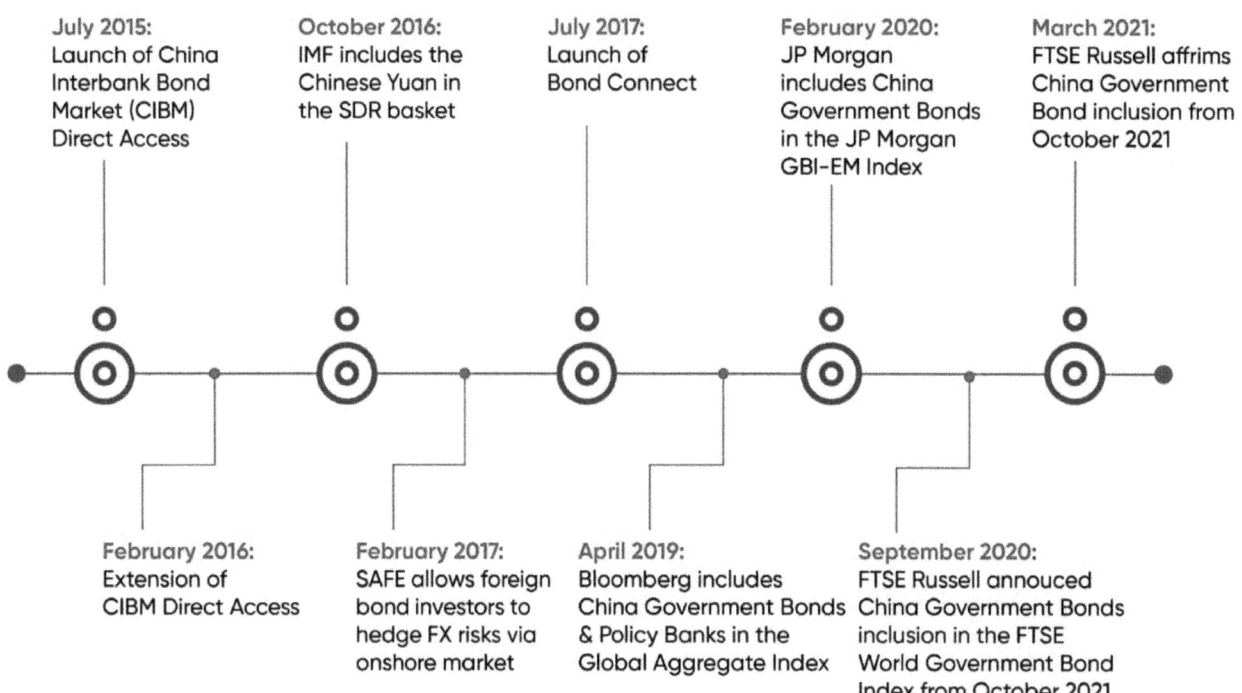

Fig 17.2 China's integration progress into global capital markets

Disentangling even a fraction of global commerce from the US, would be a major undertaking and since the GFC, there have only been a few alternative instruments and agreements which have emerged. However, standardisation, via ISO 20022 and the emergence of FinTech, has enabled a rapid development of alternative mechanisms, each capable of being seamlessly integrated with one another in a relatively short period of time. Historically it is the *medium of exchange* that has played a greater role in influencing the direction of travel in driving adoption, whereas the *unit of account* and *store of value* has followed (see Paper Money, Chapter 6: Money).[446]

In March 2020, a conference of finance ministers of the Shanghai Cooperation Organisation, which included China, Russia, several Central Asian states, as well as India and Pakistan agreed to finalising a roadmap to conduct bilateral trade, investment, mutual settlements and issue bonds in national currencies in an effort to displace the use of US dollars.[447]

UNRESTRICTED WARFARE

'Unrestricted Warfare,' is the title of a book published in February 1999, by the People's Liberation Army (PLA) Literature and Arts Publishing House in Beijing. It was authored by two former PLA Colonels, Qiao Liang and Wang Xiangsui.

'The first rule of unrestricted warfare is that there are no rules, with nothing forbidden.'

- *Qiao Liang, interview with Zhongguo Quingian Bao, June 1999.*

The implications of this line of thinking among senior Chinese military officers suggests the tone for the broader model of China's engagement with other nation states. Essentially, that all engagement is adversarial and that there are no boundaries to the nature and methods of 'warfare' which may be pursued.

This paradigm is synonymous with the rise in state-sponsored cyber warfare, which has become prevalent in recent years. Such attacks, have exploited vulnerabilities in computerised control systems, critical infrastructure, as well as exploiting surveillance capitalism techniques to engage in disinformation campaigns, as well as meddle in elections.

'Liberal democracies across the globe are under attack. They are being attacked not by traditional weapons of war but by disinformation—intentionally false or misleading information designed to deceive targeted audiences.'[448]

However, *unrestricted warfare* may additionally include economic warfare, whereby, deliberate action may be pursued in order to destabilise an adversary through economic manipulation. In their book, 'War by Other Means: Geo-economics and Statecraft,' published in 2016, Blackwill and Harris define geo-economics as:

'The use of economic instruments to promote and defend national interests, and to produce beneficial geopolitical results; and the effects of other nations' economic actions on a country's geopolitical goals.'[449]

-Robert D. Blackwill & Jennifer M. Harris (Definition of Geo-economics)

When applied in combination with Tzu's principles outlined in his book, 'The Art of War' (see Competition, Chapter 2: Capital Evolution), the overlay provides a lens through which to interpret events which have unfolded in both the geo-economic, as well as geopolitical landscapes.

Tzu's principles are instrumental in establishing both situational, as well as self-awareness. Thus, providing a framework through which to strategically leverage one's own strengths while simultaneously exploiting an adversary's weaknesses.

'To subjugate the enemy's army without doing battle is the highest of excellence.'[450]

- Sun Tzu

In the context of the China-US relationship, personal freedoms which western democracies hold dear, such as individual privacy, autonomy and self-determination, may be exploited as weapons with which to undermine the United States. By contrast, China's ability to 'read the terrain' and take decisive action in achieving its objectives as part of a broader series of milestones within a long-term strategy is immeasurably powerful.

These factors should be considered in the context of the 'String of Pearls Theory,' whereby incrementally fortifying China's economic and strategic influence through alliances and its exploitation of 'Debt-trap Diplomacy' are compounding. Furthermore, China's growing technological sophistication and its rapid modernisation, as well as expansion of its military assets and capabilities are strong signals which reinforce these vectors.

Examples include, China's rapid development of hypersonic missiles, the expansion of its nuclear arsenal, and its advancements in both amphibious, as well as long-range naval warfare capabilities. Development of these capabilities are clear signals that China foresees a potential conflict with extra-regional opponents. Furthermore, the rapid development of these capabilities is a testament to the extent and speed at which China has assimilated advanced technology through technology transfer from western powers. A plethora of interdisciplinary expertise and ingenuity is required in order to successfully produce a viable hypersonic missile, an area of weapons development in which China has assumed a global leadership posture. Among these disciplines is the ingenuity to create entirely new materials. This is a stated objective of China's MIC 2025 initiative (see Made in China 2025, Chapter 16: The Rise of China). New materials are a critical factor, as air friction at hypersonic velocities exceeds the melting temperatures of conventional materials, such as traditional aircraft grade alloys.

Much of this military modernisation is tailored to face an adversary which relies on naval aviation capabilities, such as those provided by aircraft carriers. A long-standing advantage held by the United States and the United Kingdom in their ability to project a substantial and effective force into theatres across the globe with super carriers. While a few other nation states possess aircraft carriers, only the US, UK and China possess more than one operational vessel. China is acutely aware that achieving parity is insufficient, achieving a superior position is required in order to assure deterrence. Thus, its development of effective anti-carrier weaponry through its Anti-ship Ballistic Missile (ASBM) programme is a clear indication as to which adversaries it may expect to face in the future.[451]

China has invested in developing a variety of aircraft carriers (including the Type-003 which is designed to rival the US Ford class and the UK Queen Elizabeth class super carriers). Apart from these carriers' substantial scale and capabilities, each uses an Electromagnetic Aircraft Launch System (EMALS). This represents the latest technological advancement in the rapid launch of fighters.[452] In addition, China has built fighter interceptor aircraft (such as the J20), which are modelled closely on the US F-35 family of fighters.[453]

Furthermore, as GPTs, such as AI, become more deeply embedded within consumer goods and the industrial supply chain, a comparable shift will proliferate through the weapons industry and the military forces which use them. Evidence to this effect has already been noted through militarised Unmanned Aerial Vehicle (UAV) technologies (known as Drones). Examples of which include, the MQ-9 Reaper (also known as the Predator B), a weaponised autonomous hunter-killer UAV designed for high-altitude reconnaissance and long-endurance surgical strike missions.

Throughout military history, there are numerous instances whereby a single weapons system became the emblematic differentiator of an entire age of warfare. This conjures parallels with the advent of the longbow used by the English archers at Agincourt in the Middle Ages, or the heavily armoured tanks that epitomised the ground-based engagements of World War II. This corresponded with what has been called 'the Uni-polar moment' (epistemic inequality), synonymous with the end of the Cold War, when the US stood alone and unchallenged as the dominant global superpower.

AI enabled warfare may consequently represent as substantial an existential threat, as both thermal nuclear war as well as the climate crisis. A critical aspect of such, is the shorter feedback loops in decision making (see AI Agency above). Either surrendering exclusive human agency over warfare, or abstracting such from human decision-making will undoubtedly yield unintended consequences, for which future generations may never forgive this one.

In his book, 'Stealth War: How China Took Over While America's Elite Slept,' published in 2019, China expert and retired US Air Force Brigadier General Robert Spalding, revealed the shocking success China has realised through infiltrating American institutions, siphoning proprietary technologies and in compromising US national security interests.

As China's strength has proffered, the US posture has stagnated. A position which invites both nation states into potentially falling victim to the 'Thucydides' Trap.'

THUCYDIDES' TRAP

In the notable book, 'Destined for War: Can America and China Escape Thucydides' Trap?' by Graham Allison, published in 2017, Allison's analysis of great power rivalries spanning five-hundred-years, explores the risks of China's economic ascent, imperial growth strategy and military sophistication as a growing threat to US dominance. A model, which historically, more often than not, leads to a contest for supremacy, via an armed conflict (see Hegemonic War, Chapter 11: Hegemonic Dominance).

This phenomenon has become known as the 'Thucydides' Trap' in reference to Thucydides' 'History of the Peloponnesian War' which describes the events and causes of the hegemonic conflict between Athens and Sparta. This conflict, which resulted in the destruction of classical Greece and its city-state system represents a pattern which is repeated time and time again. Allison, (a long-term mentee of former US Secretary of State and National Security Advisor, Henry Kissinger,) provides a sobering analysis which explores the parallels between past rivalries and conflicts, in contrast to the China-US relationship.

Unlike in past circumstances, there is a substantial interdependence between the US and China economically. Consequently, there remains a mutual incentive to avoid relations between these trading partners being allowed to deteriorate towards potentially falling victim to the 'Thucydides' Trap.'[454] This has been referred to as 'Mutually Assured Financial Destruction,' in reference to the Cold War era doctrine of *Mutually Assured Destruction*.[455] However, China's dependence on US markets may diminish, as its market share diversifies and grows through broader global penetration, via its BRI, and through assuming a leadership position in GPTs (see Statecraft above). Furthermore, as China's actions taken towards insulating itself against US externalities gain critical mass, its incentive to avoid potential friction and to refrain from actively engaging in adversarial behaviour may decline (see De-dollarisation above).

In such circumstances, as parity between the US and China draws economically and militarily imminent, so the risk that friction between these powers may distil into a climate which invites a contest for superiority, will likely escalate. Thus, it remains a risk that a hegemonic conflict between these world powers may eventually unfold. The key to preventing such an outcome will likely pivot on tackling the fundamental factors, which creates the climate in which volatility invites conflict.

LOOKING AHEAD

'The United States finds itself in a paradoxical situation. By any standard of national capacity, we are in a position to achieve our objectives and to shape international affairs. Yet, as we look around the world, we encounter upheaval and conflict. The United States has not faced a more diverse and complex array of crises since the end of the Second World War.'[456]

- Henry Kissinger, 2015.

The common characteristic at the core of the world's economic and monetary systems, which reinforces the pattern of disproportionate capital concentrations, economic cycles, and ultimately results in hegemonic conflicts is *asymmetry*. This is evident in *information asymmetry*, the *dominant currency paradigm* and *central banking*. These may be broadly interpreted as artefacts of *Gresham's Law*, the residue of which has manifested through the contemporary paradigms of *chartalism* and *quantitative destruction*. In other words, *bad money has driven out good money*, essentially constituting an artefact of form over substance. Furthermore, these instruments and the 'bad money' which they have espoused, serve to exacerbate, and perpetuate the factors which result from cyclic phenomena that either exclusively foster or aid in cultivating social inequality and amplify potential frictions. Unchecked, the resulting disequilibrium may induce global tensions to escalate. Perhaps ultimately erupting into an armed conflict.

In the longer term, a means of preventing future imbalances is required. The necessity to do so is evident in the proliferation and widespread adoption of extra-systemic remittance systems, and flows into asset classes such as gold, silver, convertible virtual currencies as well as crypto-assets. With debt levels having reached an unprecedented magnitude and conventional monetary policy no longer being capable of regulating inflation, alternatives will need to be explored in order to deleverage the global debt posture. Thus, in the short-to-medium term, restoring confidence in the present system is an imperative. One such vehicle to do so, may be through negotiation to restructure or forgive global debt, via a 'Debt Jubilee.'

DEBT JUBILEE

With the overwhelming majority of nation states carrying substantial debt burdens, a debt jubilee may be held in which all nation states participate to either restructure or forgive each other's debt. Conceptually, a debt jubilee is comparable to debt restructuring orchestrated by domestic authorities in the wake of a deleveraging event, albeit on a global scale (see Unconventional Methods, Chapter 8: Economic Cycles). Such an endeavour requires the co-operation of all nation states, as global debt relationships are systemic and interdependent obligations may be highly complex in nature. Due to the asymmetry of relationships between high-income countries and low-to-middle-income countries, forgiving debt may be highly inflationary for some and deflationary for others. This will likely have the most material effect on nation states, such as the US and China. The US, in particular, has exported the majority of its inflation through treasury issuance since the Bretton Woods System came into effect. US Treasury secretary, John Connally's, dictum of *'the dollar is our currency, but it is your problem'* was a response to European finance ministers raising concerns over the impact of the US exporting its inflation, via treasury issuance (see Connally's Dictum, Chapter 12: Global Monetary System). The US objective will be to maintain its external debt levels, via treasury issuance, while simultaneously reducing (or eliminating) its domestic holdings, thereof.

The necessary co-operation required to successfully hold a global debt jubilee would be unprecedented. In all likelihood, such a conference would have to be brokered, via the United Nations and the IMF, while requiring the participation of nation states with which the United States has either frictional or tenuous diplomatic relationships. Examples of these include nation states, such as Iran and North Korea. Furthermore, as a major rival with a very strong balance sheet (19% debt-to-GDP, 2020), Russia, is unlikely to be forgiving towards other nations in such circumstances. In addition, China has benefitted greatly from its practices surrounding 'Debt-trap Diplomacy' in furthering its imperial-style expansion and foreign policy objectives (see Debt-trap Diplomacy, Chapter 16: The Rise of China). This represents a soft power capability it is unlikely to surrender willingly. Political agendas and vested forms of prejudice will almost certainly scuttle any chance of agreement. Thus, the prospects for holding a global debt jubilee, whereby participants are prepared to negotiate in good faith although possible, are unlikely to be anything more than disingenuous.

NEGATIVE–INTEREST RATES

In December 2021, it was revealed that the German government had collected revenues of 5.855 billion euros in federal government securities issuance at a negative interest rate (-0.56%) in 2021.[457]

Negative-interest Rate Policies (NiRP) are attractive for governments and central banks as the debt carried on their balance sheets will incrementally erode as a consequence thereof. However, for businesses, the financial sector and the general population, negative interest rates erodes their savings and liquidity (see NiRP, Chapter 6: Money). For the banking industry in particular, it fundamentally undermines the banking business model (see Banking Business Model, Chapter 5: Payments) and compromises the value of maturity transformation (see Maturity Transformation, Chapter 10: Financialisation). Furthermore, it is expected to drive depositors, investors and savers towards cash, e-money instruments and extra-systemic convertible virtual currencies. A set of circumstances which may in itself destabilise the financial system by driving investment towards jurisdictions, which offer returns while divesting from jurisdictions which don't. In addition, once a major financial centre embraces NiRP, belief therein, will likely suffer an enduring crisis of confidence as a consequence of setting such a precedent.

While negative interest rates have been experimented with and implemented in some jurisdictions, the effects thereof are unlikely to yield a meaningful recovery from accrued debt burdens. Although, investors and depositors are willing to pay a nominal fee for the administration of their accounts, substantial resistance will be evident as a consequence of an 'implicit tax' being imposed through negative interest rates. An alternative that may be considered could be a return to a form of Gold Standard.

MONETARY EDIFICE

RETURN TO A GOLD STANDARD

John Maynard Keynes is often misquoted as indicting Gold as *'a barbarous relic.'* His actual contention at the time was *'In truth, the gold standard is already a barbarous relic.'*[458] This was his view quoted from his book, 'A Tract on Monetary Reform,' published in 1924. Keynes's contention in this regard was in reference to the Gold Exchange Standard of the mid-1920s to the early 1930s, which during the intra-war period had fallen short of the stability and security offered by the Classical Gold Standard, prior to the Great War (see Gold Standard, Chapter 9: Gold).

It should be noted that although Keynes wavered in his support for a *specie standard* during the intra-war period, he actively supported the Gold Standard in 1914, and again at Bretton Woods in 1944. Keynes remained among the most assertive advocates toward Britain remaining on the Gold Standard in 1914. He recognised that while other nations were moving off the Gold Standard, Britain would be reliant on a favourable credit posture in order to borrow money to both fund its war efforts, as well as to rebuild, thereafter.

His advocacy 'paid dividends' through American loans brokered, via J.P. Morgan & Co., which were instrumental in supplementing purchases made with gold that enabled Britain to fight and with the assistance of its allies, ultimately prevail. By contrast, Germany received no loans during the war. The US ultimately joined the war and supported Britain in securing its victory for ideological and moral reasons. However, it was the confidence in Britain through remaining on the Gold Standard that had established the superior credit posture with which to offer greater financial support.

In 1944 at the Bretton Woods conference, Keynes, representing Britain, had advocated for a return to the Gold Standard. He was ultimately overruled by then Under Secretary of the US Treasury, Harry Dexter White. White effectively sabotaged Keynes's strategy as a means of irrevocably destroying any potential restoration of the British Empire. It was later revealed that White was a soviet spy, acting as an agent for then Soviet Union Premier, Joseph Stalin (1878 - 1953). Notwithstanding White's actions which were largely successful, Britain was exhausted and bankrupted by the Great War, the Great Depression and World War II. The Bretton Woods Conference represented a transition of hegemonic power from Britain to the United States, rendering any potential restoration of Britain's prior standing beyond reach. In the 1950s, what remained of the 'British Empire' fundamentally crumbled.

The reintroduction of a Gold Standard to the financial system would be comparable to introducing an Apex predator into an ecosystem, which has spawned a massive and ravenous financial population. Financial sector incumbents will resist and dismiss the notion of returning to a Gold Standard which would effectively halt the overflowing liquidity and render unconstrained business behaviours extinct. Furthermore, the reintroduction of a Gold Standard would significantly limit the ability of governments to engage in unconstrained deficit spending, while central banks would lose the ability to perpetuate discretionary monetary policy making.

A mixture of strong and weak signals in the global financial ecosystem are effective barometers in reinforcing that many governments and central banks around the world foresee the demise of the US dollar reserve currency status on the horizon. A natural preventive measure to mitigate the uncertainty thereof, is through the fortification of reserves, via the acquisition of gold. Should a transition of hegemonic power occur, nation states with strong economic infrastructure and performance capabilities, vast natural resources and the most substantial holdings in Gold Reserves will undoubtedly command the greatest influence at a future Bretton Woods style conference. It is unlikely that dollar-denominated fiat reserves will retain their former credibility and be counted as a tangible measure of reserve assets in such circumstances (see Chapter 11: Hegemonic Dominance).

Annual withdrawals from the Shanghai Gold Exchange of less than ~120 metric tonnes in 2008 (GFC), a decade later exceeded ~15500 metric tonnes per annum and rising. During this period, Russia increased its Gold Reserves by 400%. Equally compelling, if not more significant, is over the same period Russia systematically divested its reserves of US treasuries, effectively reducing its holdings of dollar-denominated reserves to near zero. Simultaneously, China reduced its holdings of US treasuries by ~$1.3 trillion (see Death By A Thousand Cuts above).

In practice, the prospect of a return to a Gold Standard is unlikely. While there are sufficient Gold Reserves to underpin every global asset class, the price per troy ounce to do so would be exorbitant. Gold priced at a higher level would be inflationary, while priced at a lower level would be deflationary (see Gold Standard; The Great War; The Great Depression, Chapter 9: Gold). An initial calibration to underpin either the global M2, or more likely, the M1 money supply would likely yield the desired outcome (constraining debt levels and restoring confidence in the existing money supply), however, as business conditions demanded increased liquidity and credit, the effects of a Gold Standard would constrain growth. In the short-term, such conditions would undoubtedly promote greater output volumes in the gold mining industry worldwide, fuelled by higher margins. Undoubtedly, this will be accompanied by the exploitation of ore deposits previously considered to be economically or politically unpalatable. Notwithstanding a surge in output volumes however, the same vulnerabilities which have been evident historically under *specie standard* variations will ultimately manifest themselves. Examples of these included, the periodic hoarding of bullion and disruptions in the supply thereof (see Deflation, Chapter 8: Economic Cycles). As such, constant recalibration would be required, which would undermine the efficacy of a stable monetary anchor.

A Gold Standard with a stable gold price could be achieved in the short-term, as central banks conduct open market operations through "printing" money and using these newly created funds to purchase gold, in lieu of purchasing bonds. In order to calibrate the price of gold to suitably underpin the money supply, a holder of substantial bullion reserves (such as the Fed) could establish the appropriate price level by offering bullion for sale at a specified price, while simultaneously offering to purchase bullion at a lower price level. By doing so, the variance between these price points establishes a spread. Thus, the mean of the spread would essentially calibrate the spot price which has been artificially engineered to underpin its liabilities. This approach creates an incentive for selling bullion to the central bank, while simultaneously dissuading potential buyers. The net result of this will undoubtedly flood the central bank with bullion. By way of example, consider a bullion investor who purchased one Troy ounce of gold for two-thousand dollars or less being offered upward of fifty-thousand dollars or more to sell.

However, once private sector bullion holdings are exhausted (~150000 tonnes worldwide), the rate at which new metal enters the market (~1.6%) would unlikely sustain the rate of economic growth (~3.5%), and thus, its lack of 'elasticity' would prompt economic conditions to become increasingly deflationary. Furthermore, much of the criticism surrounding crypto-currency, Bitcoin, in particular, is centred on the wasteful computational capacity and energy consumption required for the 'mining,' thereof. When contrasted with the energy, labour and risks associated with the end-to-end process of physically mining and refining gold in order for bars of bullion to reside unseen in the vaults of central banks, it begs the question as to which paradigm is more or less sensible. In practice, neither paradigm is likely to be sustainable nor endure over the longer term.

'Advocates of the ancient standard do not observe how remote it now is from the spirit and the requirements of the age.'[459]

- *John Maynard Keynes, 1924.*

SUPRANATIONAL CURRENCY

As was advocated for by then PBOC governor Zhou Xiaochuan, Special Drawing Rights issued by the IMF could be exploited to function as the exclusive supranational reserve currency (see above). Essentially, in alignment with Keynes's 'Bancor' concept (see Special Drawing Rights, Chapter 12: Global Monetary System). This could, thereby, displace the dollar's role as the principal global reserve currency and by extension, instigate a departure from the current *dominant currency paradigm* and *US asymmetry*.

The manner in which the Fed and other central banks monetised the debt, in the wake of the GFC, inflated central banks' balance sheets with 'toxic' illiquid assets. Since the GFC, limited quantitative tightening and subsequent stimulus, via quantitative easing, has further inflated these debt burdens, leaving the integrity of central banks' balance sheets in a compromised position (see Quantitative Destruction, Chapter 8: Economic Cycles).

The IMF could conceivably issue SDRs to central banks in order to purchase their 'assets,' and thereby absorb the sovereign debt burdens in the form of assets collectively held on its own balance sheet. Such an outcome would be favourable among central banks, particularly the Fed, by essentially providing the equivalent relief central banks provided to the commercial banking sector. This would effectively deleverage the world's central banks (Fig 17.3).

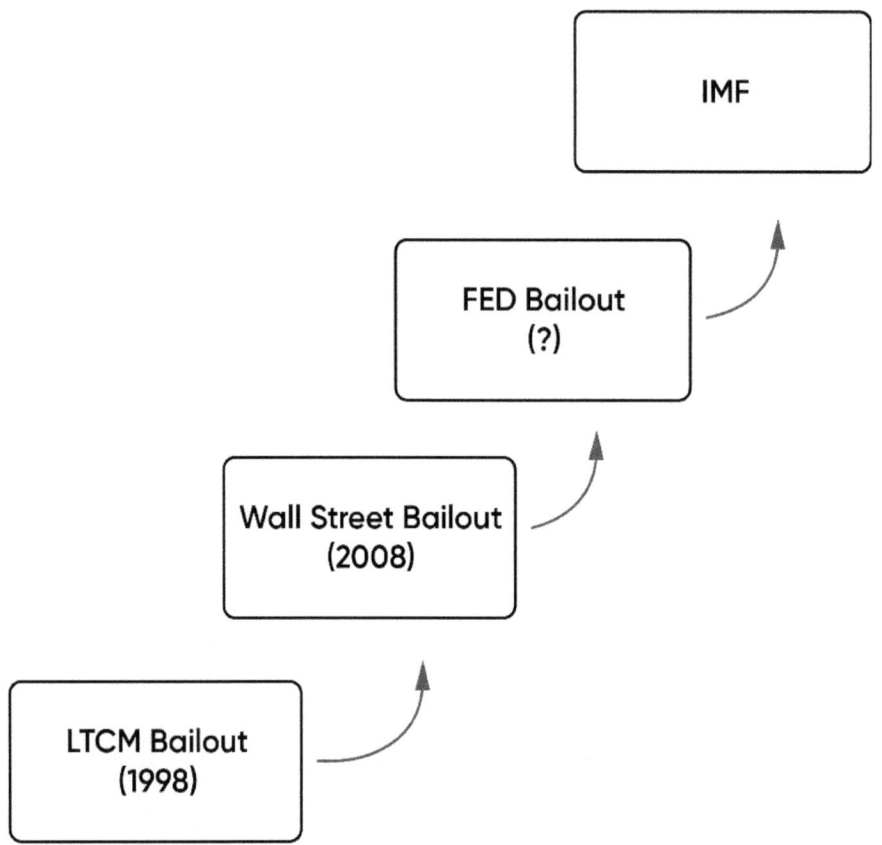

Fig 17.3 Hierarchical Bailouts - debt accrued by the Fed

Such a manoeuvre would be welcomed by the IMF as an opportunity to assume a substantially more influential role in global monetary affairs. This would reinforce a more routine use of SDRs (via network effects) as a supranational currency, in lieu of the infrequent issue thereof, evident since 1970. Over the period 1970 - 2021, 660.6 billion SDRs have been issued collectively across five (one special and four general) allocations (see SDR Allocations, Chapter 12: Global Monetary System).

In such circumstances, SDRs would be allocated and traded among central banks as a tokenised virtual currency on a 'permissioned' distributed ledger. This would effectively constitute a central bank digital currency (CBDC), exclusively for use by central banks (see Fast Followers, Chapter 14: Tokenisation).

Absorption of the Fed's (and other central banks') debt by the IMF, would essentially constitute a 'back door' debt jubilee (see Debt Jubilee above). In terms of the articles of agreement, an 85% majority vote among IMF member nation states would be required to either ratify, or abstain from objecting to such a decision.

Since the United States is the sole nation state which commands over 15% of the voting rights, the US may unilaterally veto any decision requiring the 85% threshold to be met (see International Monetary Fund, Chapter 12: Global Monetary System). However, the BRICS countries (Brazil, Russia, India, China and South Africa) with the aid of another member, such as Venezuela (BRICS+V), could collectively command greater than 15% of the voting rights by consortium. Thus, with China's growing influence over the BRICS and its broader soft power influence over BRI countries, via 'Debt-trap Diplomacy,' extra-systemic trade rails and currency swap agreements (see Swap Agreements above), a *quid pro quo* for abstaining from an objection to deleverage the Fed's balance sheet is expected.

Based on the PBOC's remarks (see Dominant Currency Paradigm above), the price thereof, is the surrender of the United States' principal reserve currency status in favour of SDRs. In such circumstances, China would have achieved a substantial elevation in its currency's internationalisation. A consequence of the RMB being the third-highest proportion of the SDR basket (see SDR Basket, Chapter 12: Global Monetary System). Over time, China's economic growth trajectory, if persistent, should enable an incremental ascent to the highest allocation within the basket. Thus, achieving a 'bloodless transition' towards principal reserve currency status. Surrender of the dollar's status would bring about an end to US monetary hegemony and the United States' 'Exorbitant Privilege' (see Exorbitant Privilege, Chapter 13: Global Trade Rails). A price which the United States can neither afford, and would likely never agree to voluntarily.

Should such an outcome be realised, the mass divestment of US Treasuries worldwide would result in the United States experiencing unprecedented hyperinflation as its internal market floods with the world's dollar money supply. Essentially, reversing the impetus of Connally's dictum (see Debt

Jubilee above). In other words, 'the dollar is your currency, and nobody else's problem.'

DECENTRALISED FINANCE

Decentralised Finance (DeFi) is a prevalent theme within the FinTech sphere, whereby exploring a pluralistic distribution of economic control is envisioned as a vehicle with which to re-orientate the financial system and the economy. Philosophically and ideologically, this line of thinking is comparable to remediating capitalism's short-comings by embracing socialism. In practice, however, either ideology is inherently flawed, predominantly since human actors are both imperfect and often abuse the system's vulnerabilities.

In order to create a sustainable replacement suitable to the needs of the digital century, a first principles rethink is required, backed by international co-operation on an unprecedented scale. The world is facing imminent existential threats, such as the climate crisis, social inequality, a dangerously over-leveraged financial system and an increasingly deflationary economy. Tolerance for the level of governmental inertia is wearing thin. Every business and entity requires a rules-based order within which they can operate effectively. This is both prevalent in *laissez-faire* (free markets/market determined) nation states that feature minimal government intervention, as well as those where governments monopolise entire sectors and heavily regulate competitive conditions.

The rules-based order (rule of law) is an essential foundation regardless of the *medium of exchange* in order to ensure a frictionless flow of capital for goods, services and financial assets. This foundation provides the framework for ensuring economic discourse is equitable and capable of adjudicating, as well as settling potential disputes that may arise. Without these, there could be no trust and, thus, no confidence.

In the light of economic swings that result as a consequence of 'booms and busts' (debt cycles) in the world economy which often distil into currency wars, trade wars and even kinetic wars, perhaps the rationale for eliminating the emotive factors would better serve society in the digital century.[460] The prospects of a machine-driven economy would likely see markets behave very differently. Although financial markets have experienced anomalies such as 'flash crashes' due to bots and algorithmic trading agents reacting disproportionately to market indicators, other areas, such as commodities and equities, have achieved relative price stability and efficiency as a result of intelligent agents substituting for humans on the trading floors of major stock exchanges.

A supranational currency either similar to, or the SDR itself, could viably act as a synthetic hegemonic currency for *balance of payments* intermediation between nation states. An internationally equitable rules-based order may underpin such an artefact, whereby monetary policy applied thereto is algorithmically governed. Factors such as, inflation-output volatility and exchange-rate pass through, may require creative solutions to ensure stability. However, indefinitely sustaining an asymmetric monetary system, seems anachronistic given the present-day technological capabilities at governments' and central banks' disposal.

FINAL THOUGHTS

There are no easy options that lie ahead. A return to a Gold Standard would eventually have significant global deflationary consequences and executed without careful consideration will likely trigger a depression of unprecedented magnitude. In doing so, however, the restoration of this 'Apex predator' would bring order and stability to a crumbling financial ecosystem, albeit for an interim period.

The alternative is to successfully negotiate a global debt jubilee, which may have equally, if not more severe global economic implications. Such an event would represent an unprecedented level of diplomatic co-operation between every nation state on the planet.

Failing a debt jubilee, a potential shift towards the use of a supranational currency, such as the SDR (or an equivalent), may be pursued.

Ultimately, a more sustainable system should be embraced, free of the inherent flaws evident as a consequence of an asymmetric monetary system. The FinTech incursion into the financial system has, in many instances, begun to reshape financial institutions (including central banks) and even disrupted money itself. This has the effect of irrevocably altering the geo-economic and geopolitical landscapes. Conventional methods of asserting foreign policy for some nation states have been rendered less effective as a consequence, thereof. For others, it has created a new vehicle through which growth and prosperity may be achieved. As these shifts progress, much of the world's conventional wisdom will continue to be challenged, a climate which lends itself to unpredictability and uncertainty amidst increasing volatility. However, there should be little doubt that FinTech will continue to play an instrumental role in reshaping our world as the digital century unfolds.

A cautious optimism should be maintained that a peaceful resolution can be achieved. However, it would be wise to remain conscious that the monetary hegemony of the United States cannot indefinitely sustain the status quo. Should these aforementioned alternatives fail, history teaches us that monetary hegemony passes custodianship from one nation state to another. Such an event is typically preceded by a significant military altercation with severe human casualties, economic hardship and catastrophic infrastructure damage.

In practical terms, such an altercation would be between the superpowers, the old Apex predator struggling to remain dominant, with the new 'energy efficient' and adaptive challenger seeking to occupy the vacuum left behind by his predecessor. In an age where these competitors are nuclear superpowers with extraordinary military might, an equitable and peaceful resolution should be pursued.

The only questions that remain are as to what the vehicle will be, and when.

'It is not the strongest of the species that survive, not the most intelligent, but the one most responsive of change.'[461]

- Charles Darwin (paraphrased from On The Origin of Species, 1861).

GLOSSARY OF TERMS

1	FinTech	Financial Technology
7	EMH	Efficient-market Hypothesis
16	GFC	Global Financial Crisis of 2007-2008
19	E-Money	Electronic Money
20	EMI	Electronic Money Institution
22	EU	European Union
22	PSD2	Second Payment Services Directive
23	FCA	Financial Conduct Authority
24	FSCS	Financial Services Compensation Scheme
31	ROIC	Return on Invested Capital
35	R&D	Research & Development
35	M&A	Mergers and Acquisitions
41	LTV	Labour Theory of Value
46	HRM	Human Resources Management
55	ENIAC	Electronic Numerical Integrator and Computer
55	LEO	Lyons Electronic Office
57	CEO	Chief Executive Officer
57	ARPANET	Advanced Research Projects Agency Network

57	ARPA	Advanced Research Projects Agency
57	TCP/IP	Transmission Control Protocol/Internet Protocol
58	IPv4	Internet Protocol version 4
58	DARPA	Defense Advanced Research Projects Agency
58	WWW	World Wide Web
58	HTTP	HyperText Transfer Protocol
64	GWP	Gross Written Premiums
65	ISO	The International Organisation for Standardisation
67	IEEE	Institute of Electrical and Electronic Engineers
67	IETF	Internet Engineering Task Force
67	ANSI	American National Standards Institute
67	NIST	National Institute of Standards and Technology
67	ISA	International Society of Automation
67	BSI	British Standards Institution
67	CEN	European Committee for Standardization
67	ASME	American Society of Mechanical Engineers
67	ASTM	American Society for Testing and Materials
67	SAE	Society of Automotive Engineers
67	CSA	Canadian Standards Association
67	API	Application Programming Interface

68	OAI	OpenAPI Initiative
68	ODI	Open Data Institute
68	W3C	World Wide Web Consortium
70	ITIL	Information Technology Information Library
71	XP	Extreme Programming
71	COTS	Commodity off-the-shelf
71	SAFe	Scaled Agile Framework
72	SLA	Service Level Agreement
72	KPI	Key Performance Indicator
73	SI	Systems Integrator
74	FIST	Fast, Inexpensive, Simple & Tiny
74	NASA	National Aeronautic and Space Administration
74	DevOps	Development and Operations
74	FBC	Faster, Better and Cheaper
75	ERMA	Electronic Recording Machine, Accounting
88	FI	Financial Institution
89	EDSAC	Electronic Delay Storage Automatic Calculator
89	NT	New Technology
90	MCSE	Microsoft Certified Systems Engineer
90	RAM	Random Access Memory
90	DMZ	Demilitarised Zone

92	BSD	Berkley Software Distribution
92	CPU	Central Processing Unit
92	CRM	Customer Relationship Management
93	SaaS	Software-as-a-Service
94	SOA	Service Orientated Architecture
94	B2B	Business-to-Business
95	CRUD	Create, Read, Update and Delete
96	REST	Representational State Transfer
97	SOAP	Simple Object Access Protocol
97	CORBA	Common Object Request Broker Architecture
99	HTML	HyperText Markup Language
99	XML	Extensible Markup Language
99	JSON	JavaScript Object Notation
103	PaaS	Platform-as-a-Service
103	S3	Simple Storage Service
103	EC2	Elastic Compute Cloud
103	IaaS	Infrastructure-as-a-Service
103	AWS	Amazon Web Services
104	GUI	Graphical User Interface
104	NIC	Network Interface Card
104	SRI	Stanford Research Institute

105	MttR	Mean-time-to-Recovery
106	MttD	Mean-time-to-Delivery
106	TOGAF	The Open Group Architecture Framework
109	CI/CD	Continuous Integration/Continuous Delivery
111	NoOps	No Operations (Just Development)
111	Ops	Operations
115	TCO	Total Cost of Ownership
117	OS	Operating System
117	PDA	Personal Digital Assistant
117	GPRS	General Packet Radio Service
118	SDK	Software Development Kit
119	Y2K	Year Two Thousand
122	ILC	Innovate, Leverage and Commoditise
132	ATM	Automated Teller Machine
134	CSRS	Consumer Subscription Retail Services
135	VCR	Video Cassette Recorder
135	DVD	Digital Versatile Disc
135	P2P	Peer-to-Peer
136	MFI	Microfinance Institution
143	DDTC	Data-driven Technology Company
144	STP	Straight-through Processing

145	KYC	Know Your Customer
147	KYD	Know Your Data
147	GDPR	General Data Protection Regulation
150	ETL	Extract Transform Load
150	BLOB	Binary Large Object
151	DW	Data Warehouse
151	ELT	Extract Load Transform
152	ECM	Enterprise Content Management
152	ERP	Enterprise Resource Planning
156	GPS	Global Positioning System
157	AI	Artificial Intelligence
160	SME	Subject Matter Expert
163	ASI	Artificial Super Intelligence
163	AGI	Artificial General Intelligence
163	ANI	Artificial Narrow Intelligence
167	GPU	Graphics Processing Unit
167	ASIC	Application-specific Integrated Circuit
171	ANN	Artificial Neural Network
172	CNN	Convolutional Neural Network
172	BM	Boltzmann Machine
172	MCMC	Markov-Chain Monte Carlo

172	RNN	Recurrent Neural Network
172	NLP	Natural Language Processing
172	NLUI	Natural Language User Interface
174	MPT	Modern Portfolio Theory
176	IFWG	Intergovernmental FinTech Working Group
182	FLoC	Federated Learning of Cohorts
182	IDFA	Identifier for Advertising
182	AAID	Android Advertising Identifier
189	PPP	Paycheck Protection Programme
191	IMF	International Monetary Fund
194	CSM	Clearing and Settlement Mechanism
194	MT	Message Type
194	BIS	Bank of International Settlements
196	RTGS	Real Time Gross Settlement
197	CHAPS	Clearing House Automated Payment System
197	CNAPS	China National Advanced Payment System
197	HPVS	High Value Payment System
197	TARGET2	Trans-European Automated Real-time Gross Settlement Express Transfer System
198	CHIPS	Clearing House Interbank Payment System
198	ACH	Automated Clearing House

198	NACHA	National Clearing House Association
198	OFDI	Originating Financial Depository Institution
198	RFDI	Recipient Financial Depository Institution
199	BACS	Bankers' Automated Clearing System
199	PE-ACH	Pan-European Automated Clearing House
199	BEPS	Bulk Electronic Payment System
199	LIBOR	London Interbank Offered Rate
199	SEPA	Single Euro Payments Area
201	IRS	Inland Revenue Service
204	USD	United States Dollar
208	DTCC	Depository Trust and Clearing Corporation
208	FIMA	Foreign and International Monetary Authority
211	POS	Point-of-Sale
211	PAN	Primary Account Number
211	EMV	Europay, Mastercard & Visa
211	CVC	Card Verification Code
211	CVV	Card Verification Value
211	CVV2	Card Verification Value version 2
212	CIA	Central Intelligence Agency
212	BIN	Bank Identification Number
212	PED	Pin Entry Device

212	NFC	Near-Field Communications
213	PCI	Payment Card Industry
214	PDQ	Process Data Quickly
214	EFTPOS	Electronic Funds Transfer Point of Sale
214	PIN	Personal Identification Number
214	2FA	Two-factor Authentication
214	APACS	Association for Payment Clearing Services
220	AML	Anti-Money Laundering
220	MID	Merchant Identifier
220	TID	Terminal Identifier
221	SMB/SME	Small-Medium Business/Enterprise
223	PCI-DSS	Payment Card Industry Data Security Standard
224	APM	Alternative Payment Method
225	SMS	Short Messaging Service
226	EMD	Electronic Money Directive
226	EMR	Electronic Money Regulations
226	PSR	Payment Service Regulations
226	PSP	Payment Service Provider
226	PayFac	Payment Facilitator
229	HKD	Hong Kong Dollar
230	TFL	Transport For London

230	WMATA	Washington Metropolitan Area Transit Authority
230	WHO	World Health Organisation
231	QR	Quick Response
233	HCE	Host Card Emulation
234	ECML	Electronic Commerce Modelling Language
234	SPC	Secure Payment Confirmation
235	VAT	Value Added Tax
235	SDLT	Stamp Duty Land Tax
236	BNPL	Buy Now, Pay Later
238	HVE	High Volume Event
239	TPS	Transactions Per Second
239	CDN	Content Delivery Network
242	GDP	Gross Domestic Product
250	ICO	Initial Coin Offering
254	NAV	Net Asset Value
259	NiRP	Negative-interest Rate Policy
264	VOC	Vereenigde Oost-Indische Compagnie
265	EEA	Exchange Equalisation Account
270	FOMC	Federal Open Markets Committee
273	ECB	European Central Bank
273	ESCB	European System of Central Banks

273	EMU	Economic and Monetary Union
273	NCB	National Central Bank
277	HPM	High Powered Money
278	OMO	Open Market Operation
285	PPP	Purchasing Power Parity
298	CGT	Capital Gains Tax
300	QE	Quantitative Easing
301	QT	Quantitative Tightening
303	MMT	Modern Monetary Theory
304	ZiRP	Zero-interest Rate Policy
308	SAS	Special Air Service
308	SBS	Special Boat Service
319	LBMA	London Bullion Market Association
326	GST	General Sales Tax
338	CD	Certificate of Deposit
346	DJIA	Dow Jones Industrial Average
347	FDIC	Federal Deposit Insurance Corporation
352	SPV	Special Purpose Vehicle
352	SPE	Special Purpose Entity
352	SEV	Special Economic Vehicle
353	SOX	Sarbanes–Oxley Act 2002

353	LTCM	Long Term Capital Management L.P.
354	AIG	American Insurance Group
355	NASDAQ	Nation Association of Securities Dealers Automated Quotations
356	ABS	Asset-Backed Security
356	MBS	Mortgage-Backed Security
358	OTC	Over-The-Counter
359	CDO	Collateralised Debt Obligation
359	BTO	Bespoke Tranche Opportunity
360	CDS	Credit Default Swap
361	IG	Investment Grade
366	Libor-OIS	Libor-Over Night Index Swap
367	FSOC	Financial Stability Oversight Council
367	OLA	Orderly Liquidation Authority
368	SEC	Securities and Exchange Commission
368	OCR	Office of Credit Ratings
375	NATO	North Atlantic Treaty Organisation
375	UN	United Nations
391	IMFS	International Monetary and Financial System
394	ITO	International Trade Organisation
394	WTO	World Trade Organisation

394	IBRD	International Bank for Reconstruction and Development
395	SDR	Special Drawing Right
397	RMB	Renminbi
402	USSR	The Soviet Union/Union of Soviet Socialist Republics
402	MAD	Mutually Assured Destruction
406	DCP	Dominant Currency Paradigm
406	EME	Emerging Market Economy
411	G10	Group of Ten
414	POP	Point of Presence
414	FAA	Federal Aviation Administration
416	SWIFT	Society for Worldwide Interbank Financial Telecommunication
417	BIC	Bank Identifier Code
420	MIC	Market Identifier Code
421	CPF	Consolidated Payables File
421	TSU	Trade Service Utility
421	PO	Purchase Order
421	Forex/FX	Foreign Exchange
423	IBAN	International Bank Account Number
423	OBO	On Behalf Of

424	CLS	Continuous Linked Settlement
424	TFTP	Terrorist Finance Tracking Program
425	CTF	Counter-Terrorism Finance
427	NPT	Treaty on the Non-Proliferation of Nuclear Weapons
427	JCPOA	Joint Comprehensive Plan of Action
428	MEU	Medium Enriched Uranium
428	LEU	Low Enriched Uranium
429	U-234	Uranium Isotope 234
429	U-235	Uranium Isotope 235
429	U-238	Uranium Isotope 238
430	HEU	Highly Enriched Uranium
430	IAEA	International Atomic Energy Agency
432	INSTEX	Instrument in Support of Trade Exchanges
433	STFI	Special Trade and Finance Instrument
434	SPFS	System for Transfer of Financial Messages
435	EEU	Eurasian Economic Union
435	CIPS	Cross-Border Inter-Bank Payments System
436	POP	Purpose of Payment
436	PBOC	People's Bank of China
438	SCF	SEPA Cards Framework

438	SCT	SEPA Credit Transfer
438	SDD	SEPA Direct Debit
439	ECBS	European Committee for Banking Standards
445	DLT	Distributed Ledger Technology
446	MD5	Message Digest 5
452	DAG	Directed Acyclic Graph
454	PKC	Public Key Cryptography
456	PGP	Pretty Good Privacy
456	PKS	Public Key Server
456	GPG	Gnu Privacy Guard
458	NCUA	National Credit Union Administration
458	CVC	Convertible Virtual Currency
458	CBDC	Central Bank Digital Currency
463	SOV	Sovereign Digital Currency
463	PTR	Petro
465	e-CNY	Digital Yuan
465	DC/EP	Digital Currency Electronic Payment
466	SHC	Synthetic Hegemonic Currency
471	BRICS	Brazil, Russia, India, China and South Africa
472	CCP	Chinese Communist Party

480	DCI	Digital Currency Initiative
480	MIT	Massachusetts Institute of Technology
487	EVM	Ethereum Virtual Machine
487	DvP	Delivery vs Payment
488	DAO	Decentralised Autonomous Organisation
488	DeFi	Decentralised Finance
489	IEO	Initial Exchange Offering
489	DEX	Decentrialised Exchange
489	IDO	Initial DEX Offering
490	NFT	Non-Fungible Token
491	DAML	Digital Asset Markup Language
493	DRM	Digital Rights Management
493	WAV	Waveform Audio File Format
493	MPEG	Moving Picture Experts Group
493	MP3	MPEG Layer 3
493	CD	Compact Disc
493	MP4	MPEG Layer 4
501	AR	Augmented Reality
504	IoT	Internet of Things
504	LAN	Local Area Network
504	VSAT	Very Small Aperture Terminal

505	IPv6	Internet Protocol version 6
505	QUIC	Quick Universal Datagram Protocol Internet Connections
505	TLS	Transport Layer Security
507	HVAC	Heating, Ventilation and Air-conditioning
508	5G	Fifth Generation
508	LTE	Long Term Evolution
508	3GPP	3rd Generation Partnership Project
508	NR	New Radio
509	MMTC	Massive Machine-type Communications
509	V2x	Vehicle to Everything Communication
509	FRMCS	Mobile Communication System for Railways
509	MC	Mission Critical
509	ITU-T	International Telecommunication Union-Telecommunications
509	SMARTER	Study on New Services and Markets Technology Enablers Project
509	eMBB	Enhanced Mobile Broadband
509	URLLC	Ultra-Reliable Low Latency Communications
509	VR	Virtual Reality
510	MR	Mixed Reality
514	LEED	Leadership in Energy and Environmental Design

514	BREEAM	Building Research Establishment Environment Assessment Method
514	CASBEE	Comprehensive Assessment System for Built Environment Efficiency
516	CCTV	Closed Circuit Television
519	RFID	Radio-frequency Identification
519	M2M	Machine-to-Machine
522	MGA	Managing General Agent
522	MGU	Managing General Underwriter
522	TPA	Third-party Administrator
522	DCA	Delegated Claims Administrator
524	IBNR	Incurred, but not Reported
530	ODL	On-Demand Liquidity
530	IIN	Inter-bank Information Network
537	PLC	Private-Label Cards
546	SOE	State-owned Enterprise
547	SEZ	Special Economic Zone
557	FICO	Fair, Isaac and Company
565	NIFA	National Internet Finance Association
565	CISP	Credit Information Sharing Platform
567	SAFE	State Administration for Foreign Exchange

569	IDAR	Introduce, Digest, Absorb, and Re-Innovate
570	GNI	Gross National Income
572	MIC 2025	Made in China 2025
573	AQSIQ	General Administration of Quality Supervision, Inspection and Quarantine
578	BRI	Belt & Road Initiative
579	CPEC	China-Pakistan Economic Corridor
580	LTP	Long Term Plan
582	IIF	Institute of International Finance
588	GPT	General-Purpose Technology
629	ASBM	Anti-ship Ballistic Missile
629	EMALS	Electro-magnetic Aircraft Launch Systems
630	UAV	Unmanned Aerial Vehicle

REFERENCES

[1] Snowden D, "Lecture: Complex Adaptive Systems, Domain Driven Design Europe", *Amsterdam*, 30 January - 2 February 2018

[2] Snowden D, "Lecture: Complex Adaptive Systems, Domain Driven Design Europe", *Amsterdam*, 30 January - 2 February 2018

[3] Prigogine I, *"The End of Certainty: Time, Chaos, and the New Laws of Nature,"* pp. 166, 1996

[4] Snowden D, "Lecture: Complex Adaptive Systems, Domain Driven Design Europe", *Amsterdam*, 30 January - 2 February 2018

[5] Williams G. M., "Cry Wolf: Things That Make You Go Hmmm.. ", October 2018

[6] Report to the Council of The European Monetary Institute on Prepaid Cards by the Working Group on EU Payment Systems, May 1994

[7] Treanor J, "Misconduct 'has cost UK's banks £53bn over 15 years'", *the Guardian*, 2016

[8] Detrixhe J, "China No Longer Runs the World's Largest Money Market Fund", *Quartz*, 2020

[9] Roe P, "Ensure Your Customers Understand How Their Money Is Protected," *Financial Conduct Authority*, 2021

[10] TZU S, "The Only Award-Winning English Translation" of Sun Tzu's *the Art of War*, July 2, 2014

[11] Schumpeter J. A, Capitalism, Socialism and Democracy, pp. 82-83, 1942

[12] Schumpeter J. A, Capitalism, Socialism and Democracy, pp. 82-83, 1942

[13] Salaman G. and Storey J, "Managers' theories about the process of innovation*"*, Article in *the Journal of Management Studies*, March 2002

[14] Conway M, *"How Do Committees Invent?"*, 1968

[15] Simon. H. A, "The Architecture of Complexity," *Proceedings of the American Philosophical Society*, Vol. 106, No. 6, pp. 467-482, December 12, 1962

[16] Simon H. A, "The Architecture of Complexity," *Proceedings of the American Philosophical Society*, Vol. 106, No. 6, pp. 467-482, December 12, 1962,

[17] Martin D, "Leigh Van Valen, Evolution Revolutionary, Dies At 76", *Nytimes.com*, 2010

[18] Prof. Van Valen L, "A new evolutionary law," *Evolutionary Theory Journal*, 1973

[19] "Labor Theory Of Value – Definition," *Britannica*, 2021
https://www.britannica.com/topic/labor-theory-of-value

[20] Arnaert B, "In Defense of Extreme Subjectivism: The case for a paradoxical foundation of Austrian Economics," July 2019

[21] Menger C. and the "Incomplete Revolution of Subjectivism" by Lachman, L. M, *Atlantic Economic Journal* pp. 57-59 6(3), 1978

[22] Wardley S, in "devising the Wardley Mapping Technique at Fotango Ltd," London, 2005

[23] Wardley S. and Duncan J., "Underpinning Theory in the development of Wardley Mapping," 2005

[24] Freiberger P, "ENIAC | History, Computer, Stands For, Machine, & Facts", *Encyclopedia Britannica*, 2021

[25] Jevons W. S, "The Coal Question; An Inquiry Concerning the Progress of the Nation, and the Probable Exhaustion of Our Coal-Mines," 1865

[26] Peace, War & Wonder features extensively in the work of Simon Wardley and is demonstrable in the *Wardley Mapping Technique*

[27] Wardley S, "The Best Summary Post That You've Done' … On Mapping." *Blog.gardeviance.org*, 2014

[28] Wardley S, "Ubiquity vs. Certainty", *Development of Wardley Mapping*, 2005

[29] Clark G, "Innovation Diffusion: Contemporary Geographic Approaches," 1984

[30] Parkhill D. F, *The Challenge of the Computer Utility*, 1966

[31] Collingwood R. G, "Economics as a Philisophical Science," *The International Journal of Ethics,* pp 177, 162-185, 36(2), 1926

[32] Ward D, "F.I.R.E.: How Fast, Inexpensive, Restrained and Elegant Methods Ignite Innovation," *HarperBusiness*, 2014

[33] Prof. Van Valen L, "A new evolutionary law," *Evolutionary Theory Journal*, 1973

[34] Collingwood R. G, "Economics as a Philisophical Science," *The International Journal of Ethics* 36(2): 162-185, pp 177, 1926

[35] Christensen C. M, "Competence-Induced Failure," *The Innovator's Dilemma: When New Technologies Cause Great Firms to Fail - Harvard Business School,* 1997

[36] Lundstrom J, *Biodiversity in young versus old forest*, 2008

[37] Perrings Charles C., K. G. Mäler, C. Folke, C. S. Holling, and B.-O. Jansson, editors, "Biodiversity in the functioning ecostems: an ecological synthesis – Biodiversity loss, Economic and Ecological Issues," *Cambridge University Press, Cambridge*, pp. 44-83, 1995

[38] Watts S, "REST Vs CRUD: Explaining REST & CRUD Operations", *BMC Blogs*, 2018

[39] Forrest B, "Zimki, Hosted Javascript Environment - O'reilly Radar", *Radar.oreilly.com*, 2006

[40] Mell P. and Grance T, "The NIST Definition of Cloud Computing", *National Institute of Standards and Technology, Special Publication 800-145*, 2011

[41] Simon Wardley (a friend and former colleague of the author, at Fotango) known for creating "Wardley Maps" and his pioneering work in Commoditisation

[42] Robson D, "How to Avoid the 'Competency Trap'", *BBC Worklife,* June 2020

[43] Mawston N. and Joy B, "Global Mobile Phone Shipments Top 1 Billion Units in 2006", *Global mobile phone shipments top 1 billion units in 2006,* January 2007

[44] University TO, "Design Essentials: Small Objects of Desire - for Ipod/Iphone on Apple Podcasts", *Apple Podcasts,* August 21, 2014

[45] Dell Technologies, "Data Domain Cloud Tier : Integrating Data Domain with Amazon AWS S3", *Data Domain Cloud tier: integrating data domain with amazon aws S3 | Dell US*, 2021

[46] Ari Levy L. K, "The Five Biggest Tech Companies Now Make up 17.5% of the S&P 500 - Here's How to Protect Yourself", *CNBC,* January 28, 2020

[47] Admin, "Everything You Need to Know about China's 'Internet plus' Future", *China Telecom Americas,* March 15, 2021

[48] Bartz D, "Breaking up Big Tech in Focus as New U.S. Antitrust Bills Introduced", *Reuters,* June 11, 2021

[49] "US Tech Giants Accused of 'Monopoly Power'", *BBC News,* October 6, 2020

[50] Godwin C, "US Lawmakers Introduce Bills Targeting Big Tech", *BBC News,* June 12, 2021

[51] "Text - H.R.3816 - 117th Congress: American Choice and ..." 2021-2022

https://www.congress.gov/bill/117th-congress/house-bill/3816/text

[52] "H.R.3826 - 117th Congress: Platform Competition and ..." (2021-2022)

https://www.congress.gov/bill/117th-congress/house-bill/3826/text

[53] "H.R.3825 - Ending Platform Monopolies Act - Congress.gov"

https://www.congress.gov/bill/117th-congress/house-bill/3825

[54] "H.R.3849 - 117th Congress (2021-2022): Access Act of 2021"

https://www.congress.gov/bill/117th-congress/house-bill/3849

[55] "Text - S.228 - 117th Congress (2021-2022): Merger Filing Fee ..."

https://www.congress.gov/bill/117th-congress/senate-bill/228/text

[56] "Statement: The Party Is Over, Big Tech", *Public Citizen,* June 2021

[57] Christensen C. M, "The Innovator's Dilemma: When New Technologies Cause Great Firms to Fail", *The Innovator's Dilemma: When New Technologies Cause Great Firms to Fail - Harvard Business School,* 1997

[58] Moore G, *Crossing the Chasm,* 1991

[59] Darwin C. R, "Darwin C. R, On the Origin of Species by Means of Natural Selection, 1861", *Darwin online,* 2008

[60] Rogers E, *Diffusion of Innovations,* 1962

[61] Clark G, "Innovation Diffusion: Contemporary Geographic Approaches," *researched at Lancaster University in England, 1984*

[62] "Open Authentication Standards More Secure than Passwords", *FIDO,* 2020

[63] "Financial Innovation in China: Alibaba's Leftover Treasure - 余额宝", *Channels,* August 30, 2017

[64] Turing A. M, Computing Machinery and Intelligence, *Mind 49* pp. 433 - 460, 1950

[65] Bayes T. and Price R., "An Essay towards Solving a Problem" in the *Doctrine of Chances,* 1763

[66] Rumelhart D., Hinton G. and Williams R, "Learning representations by back-propagating errors", *Nature* pp. 323, 533–536, 1986

[67] PYMNTS.com, "Google Abandons Plans for User Bank Accounts", *Google Abandons Plans for User Bank Accounts | PYMNTS.com,* 2021

[68] "Banking as a Service - October 2020", *Payments News & Mobile Payments Trends, Consumer Payments News, Financial Technology News,* October 1, 2020

[69] "III. Central Banks and Payments in the Digital Era", *The Bank for International Settlements,* June 24, 2020

[70] "Secure Payment Confirmation", *W3C,* 2021

[71] "Banking Cost Analysis," *Ark Research,* 2018

[72] Wood C. "Goodbye Banks", crypto.com, 2018

[73] Lang H. and Pedersen B, "Fed Proposes Criteria for FINTECHS Seeking Central Bank Services", *American Banker,* June 1, 2021

[74] "Worldwide Currency Usage and Trends", *Swift,* 2020

[75] "Currency Composition of Official Foreign Exchange Reserve", *IMF Data*

[76] Egan M, "Russia Dumped 84% of Its American Debt. What That Means", *CNNMoney,* July 30, 2018

[77] Yeung K, "China Dumps More US Treasuries, as Holdings Hit 3.5 Year Low", *South China Morning Post,* November 20, 2020

[78] Thomas K, "Is the US Dollar's Role as the World's Reserve Currency under Threat?", *International Banker,* September 30, 2020

[79] Krugman, P. "The international role of the dollar: theory and prospect", *Exchange Rate Theory and Practice, National Bureau of Economic Research, University of Chicago Press,* pp. 261-278, 1984

[80] Dreier D, "Commercial Register", *Explained* - https://www.moneyland.ch/en/commercial-register-definition

[81] "Early English white banknotes" - *pam West British bank notes* - http://www.britishnotes.co.uk/news_and_info/picture_library/englishpictures/whitenotes/early.php

[82] "Rare Coins and Valuable Notes", *The Sun* - https://www.thesun.co.uk/topic/rare-coins-valuable-notes/

[83] Jevons W. S, *Money and the Mechanism of Exchange*, p. 81, 1896

[84] Coindoc C. D, "U.S. Silver Coins: When They Ended and What They're Worth", *CoinSite*, February 11, 2020

[85] Tamari B. "Gresham's Law," *Economics Quarterly*, p. 115, 1982, - Translated by Etta L, 2011

[86] Whipps H, "The Profound History of Coins", *LiveScience,* November 16, 2007

[87] Benson C. C, *Global Payments: And the FinTech Innovations changing the Industry (First Edition)*, p. 13, 2020

[88] Abel J, "Digital Printers Let Counterfeiters Operate with Ease", *ConsumerAffairs,* 2014

[89] Jx, "Why Large Denomination Notes Poses a High Money Laundering Risk", *AML* April 21, 2018

[90] "The Kimberley Process (KP)", *KimberleyProcess* - https://www.kimberleyprocess.com

[91] Hummel J. R, "Abolishing Cash", *Milken Institute Review,* April 26, 2019

[92] "Introduction of Quantitative and Qualitative Monetary Easing with a Negative Interest Rate," *Bank of Japan*, 2016 - https://www.boj.or.jp/en/announcements/release_2016/k160129a.pdf

[93] Sanglap R, "Bank of Tokyo-Mitsubishi to Quit as Government Bond Dealer", *S&P Global,* July 13, 2016

[94] "Going Negative: The ECB's Experience", *European Central Bank,* August 26, 2020

[95] Arteta C. and others, "Negative Interest Rate Policies: Sources and Implications", *SSRN,* August 16, 2016

[96] Smith K. A, "Negative Interest Rates Explained: How Could They Affect You?", *Forbes,* May 26, 2020

[97] Brett D, "Will You 'Pay to Save'? What Negative Interest Rates Mean for Investors", *Schroders.com*, December 18, 2019

[98] Burden L., Brush S. and Metcalf T, "U.K. Banks Prepared for Negative Rates in Case Recovery Crumbles", *Bloomberg.com*, July 26, 2021

[99] "The Seven Denominations", *The Seven Denominations | U.S. Currency Education Program*

[100] Nguyen J, "Why Do We No Longer Use $1,000 Bills?", *Marketplace*, December 23, 2015

[101] Rowlatt J, "Why India Wiped out 86% of Its Cash Overnight", *BBC News*, November 14, 2016

[102] European Central Bank, "Banknotes", *European Central Bank*, February 18, 2021

[103] K. B, "India Tops the List of Countries That Are for Cashless Economy - 79% Indians in Favour", *TechRadar*, March 9, 2021

[104] "Evolving Payments Landscape in Africa Threatens Traditional Bank" - https://www.theasianbanker.com/updates-and-articles/evolving-payments-landscape-in-africa-threatens-traditional-bank-account-service

[105] Fox News and The Associated Press, "Canada Cuts Costs by Eliminating Penny, While Us Still Clings to Iconic Coin", *Fox News* February 2, 2015 - https://www.foxnews.com/politics/canada-cuts-costs-by-eliminating-penny-while-us-still-clings-to-iconic-coin

[106] "Australia to Be a Cashless Society by 2022", *Australian FinTech*, February 3, 2021 - https://australianfintech.com.au/australia-to-be-a-cashless-society-by-2022/

[107] Fourtane S, "Sweden: World's First Cashless Society", *Interesting Engineering*, December 24, 2020

[108] Gruin J, "Financializing authoritarian capitalism: Chinese fintech and the institutional foundations of algorithmic governance", *University of Amsterdam*, 2019

[109] *Age UK* - https://www.ageuk.org.uk/

[110] Peachey K, "Cash Access as Vital as Running Water, Says Age UK", *BBC News*, June 25, 2021

[111] "The Impact of Digital Natives on the Future of Business", *Digital Marketing Resource Center,* March 24, 2015

[112] Taylor T, "The Punch Bowl Speech: William McChesney Martin", *The Punch Bowl Speech: William McChesney Martin,* January 1, 1970

[113] Nicols G, "English Government Borrowing, 1660-1688", *Journal of British Studies* v.10 (2): pp. 83–104

[114] Rossith, "Britain in the Wars with France – 1793 – 1815", *Historia Nerdicus,* February 1, 2013

[115] *Bank of England* - https://www.bankofengland.co.uk/about/history

[116] Kynaston D, "Till Time's Last Sand: A History of the Bank of England 1694-2013", *Bank of England Archives,* 2013

[117] Amadeo K, "US Secretary of the Treasury: Function, BIOS, Role", *The Balance* - https://www.thebalancemoney.com/united-states-secretary-of-the-treasury-3306167

[118] Sherman N, "The Panics of the Fed", *BBC News,* December 1, 2017

[119] Warburg P. M, | Federal Reserve History - https://www.federalreservehistory.org/people/paul-m-warburg

[120] Warburg P. M, "The Defects and Needs of Our Banking System", *New York Times: Annual Financial Review* p. 14-15, 38-39, January 6, 1907

[121] *Board of governors of the Federal Reserve System* - https://www.federalreserve.gov

[122] "The Twelve Federal Reserve Districts", *Board of governors of the Federal Reserve System,* April 24, 2017 - https://www.federalreserve.gov/aboutthefed/federal-reserve-system.htm

[123] Steelman A, "The Federal Reserve's "Dual Mandate": The Evolution of an Idea, Economic Brief" No. 11-12, *Federal Reserve Bank of Richmond,* December, 2011

[124] Zagreb, "Croatia's Right-Wing Eurosceptics Seek Referendum on Euro Adoption", *Apple News,* April, 2021 -https://apple.news/ANCem0TKEQ8GMkGh6Waa7qg

[125] Kenton W, "Maastricht Treaty Definition", *Investopedia,* September 30, 2021

[126] Johnston M, "Understanding the Downfall of Greece's Economy", *Investopedia,* July 2, 2021

[127] Friedman M. and Schwartz A, "A Monetary History of the United States 1867-1960", 1963 - https://www.jstor.org/stable/j.ctt7s1vp

[128] Kenton W, "Monetarist Theory Definition", *Investopedia,* May 19, 2021

[129] Barro R. and Grilli V, *European Microeconomics,* Ch. 8, p. 139, 1994

[130] Staff USIC, "Inflation Calculator: Find US Dollar's Value from 1913-2022", *US Inflation Calculator,* October 13, 2021

[131] Fisher I, *The Purchasing Power of Money, its Determination, Relation to Credit, Interest and Crises,* pp. 103-104, 1911

[132] Friedman M, "Inflation and Unemployment", *Nobel Memorial Lecture, The University of Chicago, Illinois, USA*, December 13, 1976

[133] Dalio R, *Principles for Navigating Big Debt Crises*, 2018

[134] Dalio R, *A Template for Understanding Big Debt Crises*, 2018

[135] Fisher I, *The Debt-Deflation Theory of Great Depression,* pp. 337 – 357, 1933

[136] "Germany and the Depression, 1929-1933", *BBC News* - https://www.bbc.co.uk/bitesize/guides/zcwxrdm/revision/3

[137] Kelton S, *The Deficit Myth: Modern Monetary Theory and the Birth of the People's Economy*, June 2020

[138] "Section 3: Consumption and the Keynesian Multiplier", *Inflate Your Mind* - https://inflateyourmind.com/macroeconomics/unit-5/section-3-consumption-and-the-keynesian-multiplier/

[139] James G. Rickards Interview discussing debt-to-GDP and the New Great Depression, 2020

[140] Rickards J. G, "Lecture: Where Are We now? Inflation, Deflation & Debt in the International Monetary System", *Charles Koch Institute,* September 10, 2013 – https://www.youtube.com/watch?app=desktop&v=ehlo89mzHJk

[141] Franzese I, "What States Have Accepted Gold & Silver as Legal Tender?", *Irene Franzese,* May 10, 2020

[142] Frost N. and Guilford G, "The Quiet Campaign to Reinstate the Gold Standard Is Getting Louder", *Quartz,* July 3, 2019

[143] Banerji R, "Gold Standard: Could It Return in the US?", *BBC News,* August 30, 2012

[144] McNab A, "Bravo Two Zero", *Bantam Press,* pp.198-199, 1993

[145] Blair T, "Because You Never Know When 20 Gold Sovereigns Might", *Army Rumour Service,* December 7, 2007

[146] "Hallmarking Convention" - https://hallmarkingconvention.org/en/home

[147] "Gold Processing", *Encyclopædia Britannica* - https://www.britannica.com/technology/gold-processing/Refining#ref81544

[148] "Gold Bars Marking: Mandatory Marking on Precious Metals", *Automator,* February 21, 2021 -https://www.automator.com/en/gold-ingots-marking-adding-value-to-precious-metals/

[149] Haddock D. J, "Spotlight on a visit to the Rand Refinery", *Journal of the South African Institute of Mining and Metallurgy,* 1988

[150] "The Independent Precious Metals Authority", *LBMA* - https://www.lbma.org.uk

[151] *Wikimedia Commons,* April 26, 2021 - https://commons.wikimedia.org/wiki/Main_Page

[152] "Central Bank Gold Agreements", *World Gold Council* - https://www.gold.org/official-institutions/central-bank-gold-agreement

[153] London Good Delivery – Gold and Silver", *LBMA* - https://www.lbma.org.uk

[154] "Gold Processing", *Encyclopædia Britannica* - https://www.britannica.com/technology/gold-processing/Refining#ref81544

[155] "A History of the World: Gold Coin of Croesus", *BBC.co.uk*, 2010 - https://www.bbc.co.uk/ahistoryoftheworld/objects/7cEz771FSeOLptGIElaquAt

[156] Elwell C, "Brief History of the Gold Standard in the United States", *Congressional Research Service,* 2011

[157] Knapp G. F, *The State Theory of Money 4th Edition,* translated to English, 1924

[158] Hume D, *On the Balance of Trade,* 1752

[159] Crabbe L, *The International Gold Standard and U.S. Monetary Policy from World War I to the New Deal,* pp. 425, 1989

[160] Crabbe L, *The International Gold Standard and U.S. Monetary Policy from World War 1 to the New Deal,* pp. 425, 1989

[161] "FDR Takes United States off Gold Standard", *History.com,* November 24, 2009 - https://www.history.com/this-day-in-history/fdr-takes-united-states-off-gold-standard

[162] Keynes J. M, *The Economic Consequences of Mr. Churchill*, pp. 10-13, 1925

[163] "Economic Slump", *The National Archives*, November 28, 2008 - https://www.nationalarchives.gov.uk/cabinetpapers/themes/economic-slump.htm

[164] Bordo M. D. and Schwartz A, *The Specie Standard as a Contingent Rule: Some Evidence for Core and Peripheral Countries,* 1990

[165] Manchester W, *The Last Lion: Winston Spencer Churchill Visions of Glory 1874 - 1932,* 1983

[166] "Buy Gold & Silver Bullion Online: Free Shipping", *JM Bullion,* March 24, 2021

[167] "Hoarding of Gold", *New York Times* pp. 16, 1993 - https://www.nytimes.com/1974/08/15/archives/bill-signed-to-allow-owning-gold-in-us-gold-ownership-in-u-s.html

[168] *GovTrack* - https://www.govtrack.us/congress/bills/93/s2665/text

[169] Uslaw.link - https://uslaw.link/citation/us-law/public/93/373

[170] "Welfare Statism", *Merriam-Webster* - https://www.merriam-webster.com/dictionary/welfare

[171] Dr. Greenspan A, *Gold and Economic Freedom,* 1966

[172] "New York Fed Gold Vaults", *BullionStar Singapore* - https://www.bullionstar.com/gold-university/new-york-fed-gold-vaults#en-1713-11

[173] "Gold", *Bank of England* - https://www.bankofengland.co.uk/gold

[174] "Bank of England Gold Vaults", *BullionStar Singapore* - https://www.bullionstar.com/gold-university/bank-england-gold-vaults

[175] "Bank of England Gold Vaults", *BullionStar Singapore* https://www.bullionstar.com/gold-university/bank-england-gold-vaults

[176] Manly R, "The IMF's Gold Depositories – Part 1, The Legal Background", *BullionStar Singapore* - https://www.bullionstar.com/blogs/ronan-manly/imfs-four-gold-depositories/

[177] Butler J. and Downs B, "A Banker for all Seasons: the Life and Times of John Exter", *Champion of Sound Money,* 2013

[178] Embedded Finance: The Future of the Economy, *Anthemis,* November 2019

[179] Foroohar R, Makers and Takers: "How Wall Street Destroyed Main Street," 2016

[180] Philippon T., Why has the US Financial Sector grown so much? The Role of Corporate Finance, Working Paper 13405, *National Bureau of Economic Research,* 2008 - http://www.nber.org/papers/w13405

[181] Research by Taylor A. M., Schularick M. and Jorda O, "Makers and Takers: How Wall Street Destroyed Main Street by Rana Foroohar, Introduction," p.7; "The Great Mortgaging, *VOX, Center for Economic Policy Research,*" October 12th, 2014; published in *Macrofinancial History and the new Business Cycle Facts,* 2016

[182] Rigden P, discussing Modern Global Finance at the Johannesburg Stock Exchange, *Diagonal Street,* 1994

[183] Wright C. and Fayle C. E, *A History of Lloyd's - From the founding of Lloyd's Coffee-house to the Present day,* 1928

[184] "Silver and Gold Summit", *Cambridge House International,* November 2017

[185] "Bierman H, "The 1929 Stock Market Crash", *EHnet* - https://eh.net/encyclopedia/the-1929-stock-market-crash/

[186] Papadimitriou D, *Stability in the Financial System,* p. 66, 1996

[187] Bierman H, "The 1929 Stock Market Crash", *EHnet* - https://eh.net/encyclopedia/the-1929-stock-market-crash/

[188] Williams J. C, "The Risk of Deflation", *The Federal Reserve Bank of San Francisco,* March 27, 2009

[189] "DJIA Daily Performance History", *S&P Dow Jones Indices* - https://www.spglobal.com/spdji/en/indices/equity/dow-jones-industrial-average/#overview

[190] The policy of leaving things to take their own course, without interfering; In economics, the abstention by governments from interfering in the workings of the free market.

[191] Smith A, *An inquiry into the Nature and Causes of the Wealth of Nations,* 1776

[192] Johnson L. B, "January 4, 1965: State of the Union", *Miller Center* - https://millercenter.org/the-presidency/presidential-speeches/january-4-1965-state-union

[193] Bryan M, "The Great Inflation", *Federal Reserve History* - https://www.federalreservehistory.org/essays/great-inflation

[194] Butler J. and Downs B, *The Life and Times of John Exter A Banker for All Seasons*, pp. 2, July 2013

[195] Elwell C. K, "Brief History of the Gold Standard in the United States", *Congressional Research Service*, 2011

[196] Pierce L. J, "Interest Rates and their Prospect in the Recovery", *Staff Board of Governors, Federal Reserve*, 1975

[197] "OPEC USD Prices per Barrel", 2021 - https://www.statista.com/statistics/262858/change-in-opec-crude-oil-prices-since-1960/

[198] "Dow Jones - DJIA - 100 Year Historical Chart", *MacroTrends* - https://www.macrotrends.net/1319/dow-jones-100-year-historical-chart

[199] US Bureau of Labor Statistics, USA, 1970-1980 – https://www.bls.gov/ - https://www.thebalancemoney.com/unemployment-rate-by-year-3305506

[200] Duggan W., "This Day in Market History: Paul Volcker Take Over As Fed Chair", *Yahoo Finance*, August 6, 2018 - https://finance.yahoo.com/news/day-market-history-paul-volcker-165748192.html

[201] Rickards, J. G., Currency Wars: The Making of the Next Global Crisis, pp. 124, 2011

[202] Crawford C, "The Repeal of the Glass-Steagall Act and the Current Financial Crisis", *Journal of Business and Economic Research* January, 2011

[203] Philippon T., Why has the US Financial Sector grown so much? The Role of Corporate Finance, Working Paper 13405, *National Bureau of Economic Research*, 2008 - http://www.nber.org/papers/w13405

[204] Enron named as "America's Most Innovative Company", *Fortune Magazine*, 1995- 2001

[205] Mark-to-market or fair value accounting refers to accounting for the fair value of an asset or liability based on the current market price.

[206] The term "counterparty" rose in prevalence following the Basel I Accord of 1988

[207] Nigam R, "Enron Scandal", *WallStreetMojo,* June 2, 2021

[208] "DJIA Daily Performance", *S&P Dow Jones Indices* - https://www.spglobal.com

[209] "Enron Files for Bankruptcy", *History.com,* November 24, 2009 - https://www.history.com/this-day-in-history/enron-files-for-bankruptcy

[210] Lowenstein R, *When Genius Failed: The Rise and Fall of Long Term Capital Management,* 2000

[211] "Remarks by Chairman Alan Greenspan", *FRB: Speech, Greenspan* - https://www.federalreserve.gov/boarddocs/speeches/1996/19961205.htm

[212] Shiller R, "Irrational Exuberance" preface xii, *Princeton University,* 2000

[213] "Maturity Transformation", *MoneyWeek,* May 20, 2018

[214] Kay J, "Other People's Money: The Financialization of the Economy", *Maastricht University,* April 11, 2016

[215] "Central Bank of Ireland", *Explainers | Central Bank of Ireland* - https://www.centralbank.ie/consumer-hub/explainers/what-is-shadow-banking

[216] Thiemann M, *The Growth of Shadow Banking: A Comparative Institutional Analysis,* 2018

[217] O'Connell D, "The Collapse of Northern Rock: Ten Years On", *BBC News,* September 11, 2017

[218] Keely B. and Love P, "From Crisis to Recovery", *OECD Insights,* 2010

[219] Aisen A. and Franken M, *IMF Working Paper: Bank Credit During the 2008 Financial Crisis: A Cross-Country Comparison,* 2010

[220] "The Dodd-Frank Wall Street Reform and Consumer Protection Act: Background and Summary", *Congressional Research Service,* pp. 2; pp. 6, 2017

[221] "About the Office of Credit Ratings", *The Securities and Exchange Commission,* July 2012

[222] "Dodd-Frank Act", Securities and Exchange Commission, Section 922 pp. 2, 6 & 8, *Whistleblower Protection,* 2011

[223] Remarks by President Trump at the signing of S. 2155, Economic Growth, Regulatory Relief, and Consumer Protection Act 2018 at the White House – https://www.govinfo.gov/content/pkg/DCPD-201800367/pdf/DCPD-201800367.pdf

[224] Former Treasury Secretary Larry Summers; Jamie Dimon -(CEO) J.P. Morgan Chase & Co.

[225] "Participation in Online IPO", *Freedom24* - https://en.freedom24.com/ipo/stripe-ipo

[226] Doyle M, *Liberalism and World Politics*, 1986 – Ferguson N, *Empire: How Britian Made The Modern World*, 2004

[227] Gilpin R, *War and Change in World Politics*, 1981

[228] Strange S, *States and Markets*, p. 558, 1994

[229] Wallerstein I, "The Itinerary of World-Systems Analysis; or How to Resist Becoming a Theory"; *Three Hegemonies in P.K. O'Brien & A. Clesse*, pp. 357 – 362, 2002

[230] Keynes J. M, *A Treatise on Money*, Volume 2, p. 307, 1930

[231] Milner H. V, *Resisting Protectionism: Global Industries and the Politics of International Trade*, p. 3, 1988

[232] Russo J, *Planting an Empire: The Early Chesapeake in British North America*, p. 15, 2012

[233] Chase-Dunn C and Hall T. D, *The Historical Evolution of World Systems*, 1994

[234] Gilpin R, *U.S. Power and the Multinational Corporation*, p. 80, 1975

[235] Allison G, *Destined for War: Can America and China Escape Thucydides*, 2017

[236] "Thirty Years' War Ends", *History.com*, August 21, 2018 - https://www.history.com/this-day-in-history/thirty-years-war-ends

[237] "Nation-States and Sovereignty", *Introduction to Nation-States* - https://courses.lumenlearning.com/boundless-worldhistory/chapter/nation-states-and-sovereignty/

[238] Harreld D. J, "The Dutch Economy in the Golden Age (16th – 17th Centuries)", *EHnet* - https://eh.net/encyclopedia/the-dutch-economy-in-the-golden-age-16th-17th-centuries/

[239] Chase-Dunn C and Hall T. D, *The Historical Evolution of World Systems*, 1994

[240] Polanyi K, *Trade and Market in the Early Empires*, p. 5, 1957

[241] Parchami A, *Hegemonic Peace and Empire: The Pax Romana, Britannica and Americana*, p. 94, 2009

[242] Wallerstein I, *Three Hegemonies*, p. 358, 2002

[243] Arrighi G. & Silver B. J, *Chaos and Governance in the Modern World System*, 1999

[244] Rigden P, *Global Financial Analysis*, June 1995

[245] Schwartz A, *The Operation of the Specie Standard: Evidence for Core and Peripheral Countries, 1880 – 1990*, 1996

[246] Walter A, *World Power and World Money: The Role Hegemony and International Monetary Order*, p. 88, 1991

[247] Keynes J. M, *A Treatise on Money*, Vol. 2 pp. 306-307, 1930

[248] Edelstein M, "Foreign Investment, Accumulation and Empire" 1860–1914 In R. Floud & P. Johnson (Eds.) pp. 190-226, *The Cambridge Economic History of Modern Britain*, 2004

[249] Keynes J. M, *A Treatise on Money*, Vol. 2 p. 212, 1930

[250] Panel remarks by Benoît Cœuré, Member of the Executive Board of the ECB, at the Banque centrale du Luxembourg-Toulouse School of Economics conference on "The Future of the International Monetary System", 17 September 2019

[251] H. Cleveland, *The International Monetary System in the Interwar Period*, p. 17, 1976

[252] Eichengreen B, "Conducting the International Orchestra: Bank of England leadership under the Classical Gold Standard," *Journal of International Money and Finance*, p. 6, 1985

[253] Gilpin R, *The Political Economy of International Relations*, p. 126, 1987

[254] Polanyi K, *The Great Transformation*, p. 24, 1944

[255] Milner H. V, *Resisting Protectionism: Global Industries and the Politics of International Trade*, p. 3, 1988/1989

[256] Shannon T. R, *An Introduction to World-System Perspective*, pp. 121-122, 1989

[257] Kindleberger C, *The World in Depression*, p. 28, 1929 - 1939, 1973.

[258] Fox William T. R, *The Superpowers: The United States, Britain and the Soviet Union - Their Responsibility for Peace*, 1944

[259] Hull C, *The Memoirs of Cordell Hull*, pg. 81, January 1948

[260] Conway E, *The Summit: The Biggest Battle of the Second World War - Fought Behind Closed Doors*, p. 123, 2014

[261] IMF Articles of Agreement 2020 - Article III, Section 3(c) p. 4 – www.imf.org/external/pubs/ft/aa/ - www.imf.org/external/pubs/ft/aa/pdf/aa.pdf

[262] Ocampo J. A, *Finance & Development - Point of View: The SDR's Time Has Come*, p. 62, 2019

[263] "Press Release: IMF Executive Board Completes the 2015 Review of SDR Valuation", *IMF*, December 1, 2015 - https://www.imf.org/en/News/Articles/2015/09/14/01/49/pr15543

[264] IMF Press Release No. 21/235, August 2, 2021 – www.imf.org/en/News/Articles/2021/07/30/pr21235-imf-governors-approve-a-historic-us-650-billion-sdr-allocation-of-special-drawing-rights

[265] Eichengreen B. J. & Flandreau M, *The Federal Reserve, the Bank of England and the Rise of the Dollar as an International Currency, 1914 - 1939* p. 1., Published 2010

[266] Bryan M, "The Great Inflation", *Federal Reserve History,* November 22, 2013

[267] US Revenue Act 1964, also known as the Tax Reduction Act, proposed by J.F. Kennedy and signed into law by L.B. Johnson 1964

[268] Odell J. S, "U.S. International Monetary Policy," *Princeton University Press*, p. 218, 1982

[269] Col. Parrington A. J, *Mutually Assured Destruction, USAF*, 1997

[270] James H. and James M, "The Origins of the Cold War: Some New Documents," *The Historical Journal* 37(3), p. 617, 1994

[271] CFI Team, "Fiat Money", *Corporate Finance Institute* January 26, 2021

[272] Jevons W. S, *Money and the Mechanism of Exchange*, p. 81, 1875

[273] James H, *International Cooperation since Bretton Woods*, p. 203, 1996

[274] Bank for International Settlements (2019), Triennial central bank survey. Foreign exchange turnover in April 2019, 16 September Gopinath, G., 2015, "The international price system", *Working Paper Series*, No 21646, *National Bureau of Economic Research*

[275] Carney M, Bank of England Governor Speech - *Delivered at Jackson Hole Symposium*, 2019

[276] Radcliffe B, "A Primer on Reserve Currencies", *Investopedia* May 19, 2021

[277] Smart C, "The Future of the Dollar-and Its Role in Financial Diplomacy", *Carnegie Endowment for International Peace,* December 16, 2018

[278] Bernanke B. S, "The Dollar's International Role: An 'Exorbitant Privilege'?", *Brookings,* July 29, 2016

[279] Volcker P. & Gyohten T, *Changing Fortunes: The World's Money and the threat to American Leadership,* p. 42, 1992

[280] Eichengreen B. J, *Exorbitant Privilege: The Rise and Fall of the Dollar and the Future on the International Monetary System,* 2011

[281] Keynes J. M, *A Treatise on Money,* Vol. 1 pp. 216-217, 1930

[282] "January 4, 1965: State of the Union", *Miller Center* Archive - https://millercenter.org/the-presidency/presidential-speeches/january-4-1965-state-union

[283] Ash A, "A Crisis to Shatter the World", *BullionVault,* October 11, 2007

[284] Bordo M, Monnet E and Naef A, "The Gold Pool (1961-1968) And The Fall Of The Bretton Woods System. Lessons For Central Bank Cooperation", *Working Paper 24016,* November 2017

[285] "BBC on This Day | 19 | 1967: Wilson Defends 'Pound in Your Pocket'", *BBC News,* November 19, 1967 - http://news.bbc.co.uk/onthisday/hi/dates/stories/november/19/newsid_3208000/3208396.stm

[286] Deb H. C, "London Gold Market (Closing)", *London Gold Market (Closing),* March 14, 1968 - https://api.parliament.uk/historic-hansard/commons/1968/mar/14/london-gold-market-closing

[287] US Congress - Public Law 90-269 March 18, 1968 – House of Representatives no. 14743 – https://www.govinfo.gov/content/pkg/STATUTE-82/pdf/STATUTE-82-Pg50.pdf#page=1

[288] "Memorandum of Discussion - Federal Reserve", March 14, 1968 - https://www.federalreserve.gov/monetarypolicy/files/fomcmod19680314.pdf

[289] Elwell C. K, "Brief History of the Gold Standard in the United States" - *Congressional Research Service,* June 2011

[290] Meier G. M, "The 'Jamaica Agreement," International Monetary Reform, and the Developing Countries", *Stanford Graduate School of Business,* January 1, 1976

[291] A. J, & Bordo M. D, "The Specie Standard As A Contingent Rule: Some Evidence For Core And Peripheral Countries", 1880 – 1990

[292] "Dollar Devalued 10 per Cent; Japan Decides to Float Yen: News: The Harvard Crimson", *News | The Harvard Crimson,* February 13, 1973 - https://www.thecrimson.com/article/1973/2/13/dollar-devalued-10-per-cent-japan/

[293] "9/11 Address to the Nation - American Rhetoric" - https://www.americanrhetoric.com/speeches/gwbush911addresstothenation.htm

[294] Lichtblau E. and Risen J, "Bank Data Is Sifted by U.S. in Secret to Block Terror", *The New York Times,* June 23, 2006

[295] "Terrorist Finance Tracking Program (TFTP)", *U.S. Department of the Treasury* March 4, 2021 - https://home.treasury.gov/policy-issues/terrorism-and-illicit-finance/terrorist-finance-tracking-program-tftp

[296] Distributed Architecture, *SWIFT*, June 2008 - https://www.swift.com/swift-resource/8201/download

[297] "Terrorist Finance Tracking Program (TFTP)", *U.S. Department of the Treasury,* March 4, 2021 https://www.treasury.gov/resource-center/terrorist-illicit-finance/Terrorist-Finance-Tracking/Documents/TFTP%20Fact%20Sheet%20revised%20-%20(2-15-11)%20(2).pdf

[298] TFTP Fact Sheet, August 2nd 2010 - "Terrorist Finance Tracking Program (TFTP)", *U.S. Department of the Treasury,* March 4, 2021

[299] US Treasury – TFTP – home.treasury.gov/policy-issues/terrorism-and-illicit-finance/terrorist-finance-tracking-program-tftp

[300] "WorldCat.org" (*OCLC WorldCat.org* 2005)

[301] Huawei's Chief Financial Officer Meng Wanzhou was charged with bank fraud. According to the Justice Department, Meng lied to a US bank about Huawei's business with Iran, putting the bank at risk of violating US law.

[302] Zable S, "Instex: A Blow to U.S. Sanctions?", *Lawfare,* March 6, 2019

[303] Younglai R. and Rampton R, "U.S. Pushes EU, Swift to Eject Iran Banks", *Reuters,* February 16, 2012

[304] Gladstone R and Castle S, "Global Network Expels as Many as 30 of Iran's Banks in Move to Isolate Its Economy", *The New York Times,* March 15, 2012

[305] Fact Sheet, *Iran Nuclear Overview,* June 25, 2020 – https://www.nti.org/analysis/articles/iran-nuclear/

[306] Bale S, "Swift Instructed to Disconnect Sanctioned Iranian Banks Following EU Council Decision: Swift - the Global Provider of Secure Financial Messaging Services", *SWIFT,* March 15, 2012

[307] "Treaty on the Non-Proliferation of Nuclear Weapons (NPT) – UNODA", *United Nations* - https://www.un.org/disarmament/wmd/nuclear/npt/

[308] "Treaty on the Non-Proliferation of Nuclear Weapons (NPT) – UNODA", *United Nations* - https://www.un.org/disarmament/wmd/nuclear/npt/

[309] Democratic People's Republic of Korea: Accession to Treaty on the Non-Proliferation of Nuclear Weapons (NPT) United Nations Office for Disarmament Affairs, 2003

[310] "Joint Comprehensive Plan of Action Vienna, 14 July 2015 Preface", July 14, 2015 - - https://www.europarl.europa.eu/cmsdata/122460/full-text-of-the-iran-nuclear-deal.pdf

[311] "Nuclear Fuel Facts: Uranium", *Energy.gov* - https://www.energy.gov/ne/nuclear-fuel-facts-uranium

[312] Bergin T, "Swift Messaging System Cuts off Remaining North Korean Banks", *Reuters,* March 16, 2017 - https://www.reuters.com/article/us-northkorea-banks/swift-messaging-system-cuts-off-remaining-north-korean-banks-idINKBN16N2SZ

[313] Dowd V, "Assassins: How CCTV Gave Kim Jong-Nam Murder Documentary Added Intrigue", *BBC News,* February 8, 2021 https://www.bbc.co.uk/news/entertainment-arts-55940440

[314] Bergin T, "Swift Messaging System Cuts off Remaining North Korean Banks", *Reuters,* March 16, 2017 - https://www.reuters.com/article/us-northkorea-banks/swift-messaging-system-cuts-off-remaining-north-korean-banks-idINKBN16N2SZ

[315] Landler M, "Trump Abandons Iran Nuclear Deal He Long Scorned", *The New York Times,* May 8, 2018

[316] Reuters Staff, "Swift Says Suspending Some Iranian Banks' Access to Messaging System", *Reuters,* November 5, 2018 - https://www.reuters.com/article/us-usa-iran-sanctions-swift-idUSKCN1NA1PN

[317] Brzozowski A, "EU's INSTEX Mechanism Facilitates First Transaction with Pandemic-Hit Iran", *www.euractiv.com,* April 1, 2020

[318] Russia Briefing, "Russian & Chinese Alternatives for Swift Global Banking Network Coming Online", *Russia Briefing News,* June 17, 2019

[319] "Visa and MasterCard Block Russian Bank Customers", *BBC News,* March 21, 2014 - https://www.bbc.co.uk/news/business-26678145

[320] Voronova T and Tétrault-Farber G, "Mir Card Payment System Looks beyond Russia", *Reuters,* April 19, 2019 - https://www.reuters.com/article/us-russia-cards-idUSKCN1RV0KZ

[321] Kocherlakota N. R, Money is Memory, Research Department Staff Report 218, Federal Reserve Bank of Minneapolis (October 1996). Money Is Memory, *Journal of Economic Theory,* volume 81, issue 2, pp. 232 – 251, August 1998

[322] Schreiber F. R, *Sybil,* 1973

[323] Lamport L., Shostak R., and Pease M, The Byzantine Generals Problem - *ACM Transactions on Programming Languages and Systems*, Vol. 4, No.3, p. 382-40, July 1982

[324] "Small Business Retail", *Visa* - https://usa.visa.com/run-your-business/small-business-tools/retail.html

[325] "Comparisons", *CCAF.io* - https://ccaf.io/cbeci/index/comparisons

[326] Williams-Grut O, "Bank of England's Bailey on crypto: 'Be prepared to lose all your money'," *Yahoo Finance UK,* May 6, 2021

[327] Williams-Grut O, "Bank of England's Bailey on crypto: 'Be prepared to lose all your money'," *Yahoo Finance UK,* May 6, 2021

[328] Friedman M. and Schwartz A, *A Monetary History of the United States, 1867 – 1960,* 1960

[329] Keynes J. M, *A Treatise on Money* Vol. 1, 1930

[330] "Sov", *SOV* - https://sov.foundation/

[331] Aitken R, "Does Venezuela's Oil-Backed 'Petro' Have the Power to Showcase National Cryptocurrencies?", *Forbes,* June 2, 2018

[332] Committee on Payments and Markets Infrastructure - Markets Committee - *Central Bank Digital Currencies published by the Bank of International Settlements,* March 2018

[333] Treasury HM, "G7 Public Policy Principles for Retail Central Bank Digital Currencies and G7 Finance Ministers and Central Bank Governors' Statement on Central Bank Digital Currencies and Digital Payments", *GOV.UK,* October 14, 2021- https://www.gov.uk/government/publications/g7-public-policy-principles-for-retail-central-bank-digital-currencies-and-g7-finance-ministers-and-central-bank-governors-statement-on-central-ban

[334] Helms K, "Treasury Secretary Mnuchin Gives Testimony on Cryptocurrency, New Regulations Rolling out Soon", *Bitcoin News | Bitcoin.com,* February 13, 2020

[335] Helms K, "Trump Views Crypto a Threat, Proposes Countermeasures in New Budget", *Bitcoin News | Bitcoin.com,* February 11, 2020

[336] Sinclair N, "Mnuchin: We Are Looking 'Very Carefully' at Bitcoin", *Yahoo! Finance,* November 7, 2017

[337] Testimony before the US Senate Committee on Banking, Housing and Urban Affairs, Testimony of David Marcus, Head of Calibra, July 16, 2019 – https://www.banking.senate.gov/imo/media/doc/Marcus%20Testimony%207-16-19.pdf

[338] Panel remarks by Benoît Cœuré, Member of the Executive Board of the ECB, at the Banque centrale du Luxembourg-Toulouse School of Economics conference on "The Future of the International Monetary System", September 17, 2019

[339] Carney M, Governor of the Bank of England delivering a speech at the Jackson Hole Symposium, 23 August, 2019

[340] Sector Statistics Report , Communications Authority of Kenya, March 2020

[341] Carney M, Governor of the Bank of England delivering a speech at the Jackson Hole Symposium, 2019

[342] SWIFT RMB Tracker, March 2021 – https://www.swift.com/our-solutions/compliance-and-shared-services/business-intelligence/renminbi/rmb-tracker

[343] Thomas E and others, "The Flipside of China's Central Bank Digital Currency - ASPI", *Australian Strategic Policy Institute,* October 14, 2020

[344] Hoffman S, Australian Strategic Policy Institute, *Report Part Title: DC/EP and Surveillance,* 2020

[345] Quoted regarding AML work, the PBOC's Changchun Branch, Jinlin Province Financial Supervision Administration, 29 April 2019

[346] Gordon R. J, "The 1981-1982 velocity decline: a structural shift in income," *Proceedings, Federal Reserve Bank of San Francisco,* issue Dec, pp. 67-107, 1983

[347] Hall, Thomas E., and Nicholas R. Noble. "Velocity and the Variability of Money Growth: Evidence from Granger-Causality Tests: Note." *Journal of Money, Credit and Banking*, vol. 19, no. 1, *Wiley, Ohio State University Press*, pp. 112–116, 1987 - https://doi.org/10.2307/1992250.

[348] Federal Reserve Bank of St. Louis M2 Monetary Base - https://fred.stlouisfed.org/graph/?id=BOGMBASE

[349] Federal Reserve Bank of St. Louis M2 Velocity - https://fred.stlouisfed.org/series/M2V

[350] Federal Reserve Bank of Boston, "Project Hamilton Phase 1 Executive Summary", *Federal Reserve Bank of Boston,* February 3, 2022

[351] Ocampo J. A, "The Future of the IMF's Special Drawing Right (SDR) – IMF F&D", *IMF,* December 2019

[352] PYMNTS.com, "European Union Advances Plans for Digital Wallet", *European Union Advances Plans For Digital Wallet | PYMNTS.com,* June 1, 2021

[353] "United States Securities And Exchange Commission", *Inline XBRL Viewer,* December 31, 2020 - https://www.sec.gov/ix?doc=/Archives/edgar/data/1318605/000156459021004599/tsla-10k_20201231.htm

[354] Kovach S, "Tesla Buys $1.5 Billion in Bitcoin, Plans to Accept It as Payment", *CNBC.com,* February 8, 2021

[355] "Bitcoin: El Salvador Plans to Make Cryptocurrency Legal Tender", *BBC News,* June 6, 2021

[356] PYMNTS.com, "Allaire on Roadmap for Digital Dollar Stablecoins", *Allaire On Roadmap For Digital Dollar Stablecoins | PYMNTS.com,* September 11, 2020

[357] "DAML: Open Source Smart Contract and DLT Programming Language", *Daml.com | open source Smart Contract and DLT Programming Language*

[358] Herlihy M, "Atomic Cross-Chain Swaps" Computer Science Department, Brown University, Rhode Island,– *arXiv Vanity,* May 18, 2018

[359] Brown A, "What Is an NFT-and Should You Buy One?", *Forbes,* February 26, 2021

[360] Cellan-Jones R, "Web Founder Berners-Lee to Auction Source Code as NFT", *BBC News,* June 15, 2021

[361] Reyburn S, "JPG File Sells for $69 Million, as 'NFT Mania' Gathers Pace", *The New York Times,* March 11, 2021

[362] Hill K, "How Target Figured out a Teen Girl Was Pregnant before Her Father Did", *Forbes,* February 16, 2012

[363] Wakefield J, "AI Emotion-Detection Software Tested on Uyghurs", *BBC News,* May 25, 2021

[364] Clayton J, "Apple Criticised for System That Detects Child Abuse", *BBC News,* August 7, 2021

[365] Kramer A. D. I, Guillory J. E. and Hancock J. T, "Experimental Evidence of Massive-Scale Emotional Contagion ... - PNAS", June 2, 2014

- https://www.pnas.org/content/111/24/8788

[366] Selinger E. and Hartzog W, "Facebook's Emotional Contagion Study and the Ethical Problem of Co-Opted Identity in Mediated Environments Where Users Lack Control", May 13, 2015

[367] Roy S, "Facebook: If Something Is Free, 'You' Are the Product", *TechHQ,* November 3, 2021

[368] Kaesler S, Lorenz J-T and Schollmeier F, "Friends or Foes: The Rise of European Aggregators and Their Impact on Traditional Insurers", *McKinsey & Company,* December 10, 2018

[369] Webster A, "Pokémon Go's Wild First Year: A Timeline", *The Verge,* July 6, 2017

[370] Takahashi D, "Ingress Maker Niantic Spins off from Google and Raises up to $30m from Pokémon and Nintendo", *VentureBeat* October 15, 2015

[371] Zuboff S, *The Age of Surveillance Capitalism: The Fight for a Human Future at the New Frontier of Power,* 2019

[372] Espósito F, "Research Shows Google Collects 20x More Data from Android than Apple Collects from IOS [u]", *9to5Mac,* March 30, 2021)

[373] "The 'Only' Coke Machine on the Internet", *CMU School of Computer Science -* https://www.cs.cmu.edu/~coke/history_long.txt

[374] Ashton K, "That 'Internet of Things' Thing", *RFID JOURNAL,* June 22, 2009

[375] Raji, R. S. "Smart networks for control". *IEEE Spectrum.* 31 (6): pp. 49–55, 1994

[376] Ericsson Mobility Report, Cisco, ReThink, 2019-2022 - https://www.ericsson.com/en/reports-and-papers/mobility-report?gclid=Cj0KCQiA-JacBhC0ARIsAIxybyM1oK_lbep5Tmlg7SAZKRk_rKt4QwWfQIrZvQ3GvM6tPFxwnvKNLc8aAtfIEALw_wcB&gclsrc=aw.ds

[377] Iyengar J. and Thomson M, "RFC 9000", *RFC 9000: QUIC: A UDP-Based Multiplexed and Secure Transport,* May 2021 - https://www.rfc-editor.org/rfc/rfc9000.html

[378] Lang F, "It Might Be Time to Switch over to a Faster, More Resilient Internet Protocol", *Time to Switch Over to a More Resilient Internet Protocol | IE,* May 31, 2021

[379] Taylor V, "Google Confirms Which Nest Products Have Microphones", *AfroTech,* February 27, 2019

[380] "Snapchat Spectacles Ar: Augmented Reality on Your Face", *BBC News,* May 21, 2021

[381] "Apple Invents an Augmented Reality Windshield That Will Even Support Facetime Calls between Different Vehicles", *Patently Apple* - https://www.patentlyapple.com/patently-apple/2018/08/apple-invents-an-augmented-reality-windshield-that-will-even-support-facetime-calls-between-different-vehicles.html

[382] "Global 5G Subscription Forecast 2019-2026", *Statista.com,* August 25, 2021

[383] "Forecast 5G Adoption by Region 2025", *Statista.com,* August 11, 2021

[384] Stewart M, *Tiny Machine Learning: The next Ai Revolution,* October 2, 2020 - https://towardsdatascience.com/tiny-machine-learning-the-next-ai-revolution-495c26463868

[385] Bahnsen DL, "Against a Social-Justice Fed", *National Review,* June 10, 2021

[386] UN Commission on Science and Technology for Development, 2016 - https://unctad.org/meeting/commission-science-and-technology-development-nineteenth-session

[387] US Environmental Protection Agency; Coalition for Urban Transitions, *WorldGBC,* 2020

[388] "Paris Agreement", *Climate Action* - https://ec.europa.eu/clima/policies/international/negotiations/paris_en

[389] Friedman L, "What Is the Green New Deal? A Climate Proposal, Explained", *The New York Times,* February 21, 2019

[390] "A European Green Deal", *European Commission - European Commission,* May 2019

[391] Ratcliffe J, "How Many CCTV Cameras Are There in London? (Update for 2020/21)", *CCTV.co.uk,* November 18, 2020

[392] Johnston C, "Amazon Opens a Supermarket with No Checkouts", *BBC News,* January 22, 2018

[393] PYMNTS.com, "Grabango Gets $39m to Install Checkout-Free Tech", *Grabango Gets $39M To Install Checkout-Free Tech | PYMNTS.com,* June 8, 2021

[394] The term 'Economy of Things' was first used by the author in a research paper entitled – Future IoT: An Archetypal Model for Commerce amongst Machines, by Bradley J. Rigden, published for Atos International, April, 2014

[395] Prototyped at Worldpay by Bradley J. Rigden and Kevin Gordon in 2018

[396] "Robofuel", *Scott* - https://www.scottautomation.com/products/robofuel/

[397] "Secure Enclave", *Apple Support* - https://support.apple.com/en-gb/guide/security/sec59b0b31ff/web

[398] "Solarcoin", *SolarCoin Claims Portal* - solarcoin.org

[399] FOX Business, "Elon Musk Hopes To Roll Out Tesla Insurance Worldwide, Beginning With Texas Next Month" *InsurtechInsights.com,* 2019

[400] Levine Y, "Google's Earth: How the Tech Giant Is Helping the State Spy on Us", *The Guardian,* December 20, 2018

[401] HM Treasury, "The Kalifa Review of UK Fintech", *GOV.UK,* April 16, 2021

[402] Ledger Insights, "Broadridge's DLT Repo Platform Goes into Production", *Ledger Insights - blockchain for enterprise,* June 14, 2021

[403] Thomas D, "Facebook Changes Its Name to Meta in Major Rebrand", *BBC News,* October 28, 2021

[404] Sedacca M, "The Multiverse Is an Ancient Idea", *Nautilus,* January 30, 2017

[405] Stephenson N, *Snow Crash,* June 1992

[406] Goslin A, "Fortnite's Travis Scott Event Drew over 27 Million Players", *Polygon.com,* April 24, 2020

[407] Frushtick R, "Watch the Full Marshmello Fortnite Concert Here", *Polygon.com,* February 2, 2019

[408] "How Well-off Is China's Middle Class?", *ChinaPower Project, Chinapower.csis.org,* September 30, 2021

[409] "China's Political System", *Mercator Institute for China Studies, Merics,* p. 213, December 8, 2016

[410] State Capitalism's Global Reach "New Masters of the Universe - How State Enterprise is Spreading", *The Economist,* January 21, 2012

[411] World Bank; National Statistical Offices for national poverty rates, March 2019 - https://www.worldbank.org/en/topic/poverty

[412] World Bank Gini Index 2007 – 2016 - https://data.worldbank.org/indicator/SI.POV.GINI

[413] "2018 Business Climate Survey", *AmCham China, amchamChina.org,* January, 2017

[414] J.P. Morgan, 2019 Payment Trends - Global Insights Report - https://www.jpmorgan.com/merchant-services/insights/reports/united-kingdom

[415] Hatch M and others, "Eight Ways Fintech Adoption Remains on the Rise", *Ernst & Young, ey.com,* August 31, 2020

[416] Li Dongrong 22 Jun 2021, Dongrong L, "The Irreversible Rise of Fintech in China", *CentralBanking.com,* June 22, 2021

[417] Gruin J, "Financializing authoritarian capitalism: Chinese fintech and the institutional foundations of algorithmic governance", *University of Amsterdam,* 2019

[418] Russell J, "The First of China's Top Bitcoin Exchanges Has Announced It Will Suspend Trading", *TechCrunch,* September 14, 2017

[419] Hsu S, "China's Shutdown of Bitcoin Miners Isn't Just about Electricity", *Forbes,* January 16, 2018

[420] Taylor M. M, "The Politics of Latin America's Middle Income Trap", *Blog, Council on Foreign Relations,* May 16, 2017

[421] Xinhuanet, "China to Invest Big in 'Made in China 2025' Strategy", *Xinhua,* May 19, 2015

[422] Morrison W. M, "China's Economic Rise: History, Trends, Challenges, and Implications for the United States", *EveryCRSReport.com,* June 25, 2019

[423] Winsen Jvan, "New Silk Road Calls for Rotterdam to Take on a Directing Role", *SmartPort,* March 8, 2018

[424] AEI China Global Investment Tracker, Institute of International Finance, 2020 - https://www.aei.org/china-global-investment-tracker/

[425] Lipsey R. G, Carlaw K. I. and Bekhar C. T, *Economic Transformations: General Purpose Technologies and Long-Term Economic Growth,* pp 131 – 218, 2005

[426] Goldfarb, Avi & Tucker C, "Digital Economics", *Journal of Economic Literature,* 57 (1): pp. 3-43, March 1, 2019

[427] Kocherlakota N. R, "Money Is Memory", *Journal of Economic Theory,* volume 81, issue 2 pp. 232 – 251, 1998

[428] "Bank for International Settlements", press release, 22 January 2021; and A Carstens, "Central bank innovation – from Switzerland to the world", *speech at the founding ceremony of the BIS Innovation Hub Swiss Centre, Zurich,* 8 October 2019

[429] Unemployment Rate and Recessions since 1948, *National Bureau of Economic Research,* December 2021

[430] Booth J, "The Price of Tomorrow: Why Deflation Is the Key to an Abundant Future" p. 15, *Amazon,* 2020 - https://www.amazon.com/Price-Tomorrow-Deflation-Abundant-Future/dp/1999257405

[431] Gopinath G, Casas, C., Diez, F., Gourinchas, P.O., Plagborg-Moller, M, "The International Price System" - *NBER Working Paper 21646 Dominant Currency Paradigm, American Economic Review* 110 (2020) pp. 677 – 719, *NBER,* October 19, 2015

[432] Carney M, "Mark Carney: The Growing Challenges for Monetary Policy in the Current International Monetary and Financial System", *The Bank for International Settlements,* August 27, 2019

[433] Gordon R. J, *Macroeconomics* (12th Edition), p. 34, 2013

[434] Delong B, Review of Robert Skidelsky, 'John Maynard Keynes: Fighting for Britain'" 1937-1946, *DeLong,* 2000

[435] Roggeveen S. and others, "China, America and the Thucydides Trap: An Interview with Graham Allison", *lowyinstitute.org,* August 23, 2017

[436] Voltaire Network, "Medvedev Shows off Sample Coin of New 'World Currency' at G-8", *Voltaire Network,* July 11, 2009

[437] Charbonneau L, "Scrap Dollar as Sole Reserve Currency: U.N. Report", *Reuters.com,* June 29, 2010

[438] Novem, "Why Is Turkey Currently Buying Lots of Gold?", *Medium.com,* November 14, 2019

[439] "Int'l Loans 'Should Be Based on Gold, Not Dollars': Erdoğan - Latest News", *Hürriyet Daily News,* April 16, 2018

[440] "Dollar Detox: Russia's Gold Reserves near 2000 Tons to Set Historic Benchmark", *RT International,* July 25, 2018

[441] Albert E, "China Is Buying Record Amounts of Iranian Oil", *The Diplomat,* March 10, 2021

[442] Times G, "2020 Election Reflects Rapid Us Political Decay and Decline", *Global Times,* 2020

[443] Georgieva K, "A New Bretton Woods Moment", *IMF.org,* October 15, 2020

[444] Ito H, and McCauley R. N, "The Currency Composition of Foreign Exchange Reserves", *The Bank for International Settlements,* December 13, 2019

[445] https://home.kpmg/cn/en/home/insights/2017/01/going-global-chinas-currency.html

[446] Gopinath G. and Stein J. C, How global currencies work – Past, present and future "Banking, Trade, and the Making of a Dominant Currency" *NBER Working Paper,* No. 24485, *NBER.org,* April 9, 2018

[447] Chenoy A, "Bypassing the Dollar: The Rise of Alternate Currency Systems", *TheWire.in*

[448] Bergmann M. and Kenney C, "War by Other Means: Russian Active Measures and the Weaponization of Information", *Washington, DC: Center for American Progress,* June 2017

[449] Blackwill R. D. and Harris J. M, *War by Other Means: Geoeconomics and Statecraft,* p. 20, 2016

[450] TZU S, Paraphrased translation from *The Art of War,* July 2, 2014

[451] Sutton H. I, "China's Aircraft Carrier Killers, and Who Else Has Them", *Naval News,* November 18, 2021

[452] Sutton H. I, "China's New Super Carrier: How It Compares to the US Navy's Ford Class", *Naval News,* July 2, 2021

[453] *Military Watch Magazine,* December 16, 2021 - https://militarywatchmagazine.com/article/chengdu-J20-mass-production

[454] Katz R, "Mutual Assured Production: Why Trade Will Limit Conflict between China and Japan", *Foreign Affairs 92,* no. 4: pp. 18–21, July/August 2013

[455] Bremmer I. and Gordon D, "Where Commerce and Politics Collide", *The New York Times,* October 7, 2012

[456] Testimony of Henry Kissinger, Global Challenges and U.S. National Security Strategy, Hearing Before the Senate Comm. on Armed Services, 114th Congress, 29th January 2015 - https://www.armed-services.senate.gov/hearings/18-01-25-global-challenges-and-us-national-security-strategy

[457] Wagner R, "German Government Makes Billions from Debt Thanks to Negative Rates", *Reuters.com,* December 22, 2021

[458] Keynes J. M, "A Tract on Monetary Reform," *MacMillan & Co.,* p. 172, 1924

[459] Keynes J. M, "A Tract on Monetary Reform," *MacMillan & Co.,* p. 173, 1924

[460] Rickards, J. G, *Currency Wars: The Making of the Next Global Crisis,* 2011

[461] Darwin C, "On the Origin of the Species by Means of Natural Selection", *Darwin online,* published 1861

ACKNOWLEDGEMENTS

It would be remiss of me to convey that writing this book has been anything less than one of the most daunting and challenging endeavours of my career. However, notwithstanding the obstacles involved, it will arguably be remembered chiefly among my most rewarding experiences.

This is largely due to the relentless encouragement and support I have received from a few key people, to whom I'm deeply grateful.

First and foremost, I should like to extend my gratitude to Louis Bialy, whose expertise, insights and wealth of experience were invaluable in helping me sculpt, refine and balance the majority of this content. Lou's steadfast attention to detail and his support were furthermore indispensable in areas which included among others, global standardisation, Artificial Intelligence, the mining industry, geopolitics and a number of historically salient areas.

Secondly, I should like to thank Vishwanath Callikan for his encouragement, support and numerous comments, particularly in areas such as Crypto-assets, Blockchain and with a variety of infographics.

Thirdly, I extend my thanks to Timothy Reynolds for his invaluable input which assisted me in refining the nuances surrounding 'Payments.' Tim's decades of experience in this arena have fortified his pedigree in the payments industry and established his stature as an almanac for which a number of subtle details in this book would not have been surfaced otherwise.

Furthermore, I'm particularly grateful to several inspiring leaders, mentors, educators and colleagues with whom I have had the privilege of working with, and/or learning from. Namely, Simon Wardley, James Duncan, Artur Bergman, Attilla Szenvedi, Alastair Turner, Gilad Shafir, Paul Brown, Nimisha Patel, Tim Reynolds, Nick Telford-Reed, David Walker and Ron Kalifa OBE.

In addition, I should like to acknowledge the love, dedication and encouragement I received from my parents; Paul & Barbara Rigden, for which I am eternally grateful.

I should like to thank the team at Woodbridge Publishers; Ida and Daniel in particular, for their expertise, professionalism and support in bringing this book to fruition.

Finally, and most importantly, I should like to thank my wife, Kiera. Without her love, support, understanding and unwavering patience, I could not have succeeded in writing this book.

ABOUT THE AUTHOR

Brad Rigden is a technologist and executive whose colourful career has placed him at the heart of several game-changing industry trends.

Rigden emigrated to the United Kingdom in 2003, after having read law, economics and computer science in South Africa. He joined London-based Canon Europe subsidiary, Fotango, in November 2003, where among his exploits, he and now Fastly founder and Chairman, Artur Bergman, co-developed 'Borg.'

Borg was an expert system delivered as the dynamically-scaling computing platform which underpinned Fotango's Zimki proposition. Zimki was one of two pioneering public cloud computing platforms which debuted in March 2006. Zimki and Amazon's S3 proposition, essentially kickstarted the cloud computing era.

Rigden joined Siemens in 2006 and continued in the 'utility computing' sphere by designing and managing the utility storage portfolio for Siemens Business Services (later Siemens IT Solutions & Services). This portfolio underpinned the data storage and business continuity requirements for several major British public sector organisations. Noteworthy clients included National Savings & Investments, the National Assembly for Wales, the Vehicle and Operator Services Agency, and the British Broadcasting Corporation. These services were furthermore instrumental in supporting the BBC's transition towards digital media management, digital broadcasting, and content delivery via the internet. Following the acquisition of Siemens IT Solutions & Services by Atos Origin, Rigden supported the further development and refinement of the 'Atosphere' Cloud Computing proposition and the then newly formed Atos International's 'Canopy' spin off. Canopy was underpinned by a strategic partnership with VCE. The latter being a consortium formed by VMWare, Cisco and EMC.

In 2014, Rigden joined Worldpay, a leader in the global payments sector and among the United Kingdom's most successful FinTech companies. As a Lead Enterprise Architect, Rigden supported the payments innovator through its post-divestment separation from the Royal Bank of Scotland, numerous acquisitions, regional and global expansions, and its highly successful multi-billion-dollar IPO.

Following Worldpay's merger with Vantiv, Rigden joined Royal Sun Alliance, one of the United Kingdom's oldest and largest insurance carriers as its Chief Technology Officer. There, he championed several transformative and digital initiatives.

Since departing Royal Sun Alliance, Rigden has consulted for several venture capital and private equity concerns, particularly centred on investments in start-ups and scale-ups in the FinTech sphere. These span several domains which include PaymentTech, Open Banking, InsureTech, DeFi, crypto-assets, and embedded finance.

Over the years, Rigden has contributed towards and championed several initiatives which have influenced industry standards, inventions, and patents. He remains an innovation thought leader, an open-source advocate, and has exploited Artificial Intelligence, as well as Distributed Ledger Technology among several nascent technologies in numerous digital transformations. He lives with his wife, Kiera, in the United Kingdom.

Milton Keynes UK
Ingram Content Group UK Ltd.
UKHW051342220923
429196UK00011B/413